Thomson Reuters™

Congratulations!

Your purchase of this book includes student token access to the ProView® eBook version too.

To access your eBook visit the web address below or scan the QR code and enter your unique token number concealed in the box below:

token.proview.thomsonreuters.com

AF622463

Your unique token number

Follow the instructions on the page to enter your unique token number and you will then be asked to log in with your username and password. If you do not have an existing account, then you will be prompted to create one using your email address.

The token can be redeemed only once.

For more information about using ProView® visit:

www.sweetandmaxwell.co.uk/proview/default.aspx

If you have any questions, please contact our Customer Support team on 0345 850 9355.

Important Note: Please retain this information. The unique token is your proof of purchase and is required in order for you to redeem the ProView® eBook version. Returns will not be accepted on books where the scratch foil is not intact.

WILLS, ADMINISTRATION AND TAXATION LAW AND PRACTICE

WILLS, ADMINISTRATION AND TAXATION LAW AND PRACTICE

FOURTEENTH EDITION

PROFESSOR L.C. KING, LL.B. (BRISTOL), DIP. CRIM. (CANTAB.)
Solicitor (hons); Professional Development Consultant, University of Law

Sweet & Maxwell

Thomson Reuters™

Published in 2024 by Thomson Reuters,
trading as Sweet & Maxwell.
Thomson Reuters is registered in England & Wales, Company No.1679046.
Registered Office and address for service:
5 Canada Square, Canary Wharf, London, E14 5AQ.
For further information on our products and services, visit
http://www.sweetandmaxwell.co.uk.

Computerset by Sweet & Maxwell.
Printed and bound by CPI Group (UK) Ltd, Croydon, CR0 4YY.
A CIP catalogue record for this book is available from the British Library.

ISBN (print): 978-0-414-12004-4

ISBN (ProView e-book): 978-0-414-12008-2

ISBN (3P ebook): 978-0-414-12007-5

First Edition 1983
Second Edition 1986
Third Edition 1988
Fourth Edition 1990
Fifth Edition 1992
Sixth Edition 1994
Reprinted 1994
Seventh Edition 1997
Eighth Edition 2003
Ninth Edition 2008
Tenth Edition 2011
Eleventh Edition 2014
Twelfth Edition 2017
Thirteenth Edition 2020
Fourteenth Edition 2024

ACKNOWLEDGMENTS

The publishers and authors wish to thank the following sources:

Crown copyright material reproduced under the terms of the Open Government Licence v3.0
The Incorporated Council of Law Reporting for England and Wales
The Law Society *www.lawsociety.org.uk* ©The Law Society
LexisNexis, *Butterworths Wills, Probate and Administration Service*
Parliamentary information licensed under the Open Parliament Licence v3.0
Solicitors Regulation Authority *www.sra.org.uk*

While every care has been taken to establish and acknowledge copyright, and contact the copyright owners, the publishers tender their apologies for any accidental infringement. They would be pleased to come to a suitable arrangement with the rightful owners in each case.

PREFACE TO THE FOURTEENTH EDITION

This book was originally written for students. However, many practitioners have found it to be a useful first source of reference. This edition has been written with that in mind and deals with practical matters such as the way in which the General Data Protection Regulation affects private client practitioners and the requirements of the Trust Register.

This edition was prepared over the summer of 2024 and so straddled the General Election but went to press before the first Budget of the new Labour Government. There is much speculation as to changes to rates (and possibly even structure) of the capital taxes. The law is stated as at 10 September 2024 but I am very aware that future changes to the tax rules in this area are extremely likely.

I would like to thank the production team at Thomson Reuters who coped magnificently as always with constant changes.

Lesley King

TABLE OF CONTENTS

TABLE OF CASES

TABLE OF STATUTES

TABLE OF STATUTORY INSTRUMENTS

Chapter One

INTRODUCTION: WHAT TO DO AFTER DEATH

When a person dies there are a number of practical steps which must be taken. For example, the death must be registered, the funeral arranged and the property of the deceased must be made safe. These matters are usually dealt with by members of the deceased's family or by friends. **1-001**

The question then arises "Who is to be entitled to the deceased's assets?" It is at this point that a solicitor is most likely to be consulted. It is often assumed that the disposition of property depends entirely on whether or not a deceased made a valid will, but in fact the disposition of many substantial assets is not affected by the presence or absence of a will. For example, if a deceased owned a house as a beneficial joint tenant with another person then that property will pass automatically to the survivor as a result of the right of survivorship; if the deceased had taken out insurance policies for the benefit of other people the proceeds of such policies will frequently be paid directly to those people; if the terms of the deceased's employment provide for payment of a lump sum on death it is common for the trustees of the scheme to be given a discretion to pay the lump sum to the person or persons they consider appropriate (the employee is entitled to inform the trustees of his or her wishes as to the destination of the lump sum but the trustees have an overriding discretion). These matters are discussed in Ch.21.

The disposition of other assets does, however, depend on whether or not there is a valid will. If there is no valid will then the disposition of property will be determined by the intestacy rules (explained further in Ch.3). If there is a will it is necessary to discover whether or not it is valid. This requires a consideration of whether or not the testator had sufficient mental capacity at the time the will was made and whether the appropriate formalities were complied with (see Ch.2). It is quite possible for a will to dispose successfully of some but not all of the deceased's assets. This may be because the will does not deal with all of the deceased's property or because some of the gifts fail (see Chs 16 and 17). In such cases the disposition of the property is governed partly by the will and partly by the intestacy rules.

It may be difficult to discover whether or not a will exists. If one cannot be found amongst the deceased's papers it is advisable to contact any solicitors consulted by the deceased to discover whether or not a will was deposited with them and to contact the deceased's bank to discover whether or not the deceased had a safe deposit box which might contain it. There is a procedure whereby wills can be deposited during a person's lifetime at the Principal Registry of the Family Division, but this is little used. However, it would obviously be worth contacting the Registry if a will is proving difficult to find (there are similar provisions for Scotland and Northern Ireland). There are also commercial organisations, such as Certainty, which provide a will registration and search service.

It is necessary for someone to undertake the task of finding the will and checking whether or not it is valid. It is also necessary for someone to collect in the assets of the deceased, pay the debts and other liabilities of the deceased and then transfer the remaining assets to the persons entitled. In order to collect in the assets a person dealing with the estate will often have to *prove* that they have the authority to deal with the deceased's assets. This is done by producing a grant of representation obtained from HM Courts and Tribunal Service by the person(s) entitled to administer the estate.

Similarly there may be problems when it comes to transferring property of the deceased to the persons entitled. In the case of chattels it will often be sufficient to hand them to the person entitled. Other assets (for example, land) are held in the name of the deceased and must somehow be transferred into the name of the new owner if the new owner is to be able to deal with them. A grant of representation enables the person named in the grant to act on behalf of the estate of the deceased person to transfer property into the name of the new owner.

If the deceased appointed someone in the will to administer their estate, that person is described as an executor and obtains a grant of representation, called a grant of probate, which merely *confirms* that person's authority to act in connection with the estate. If no executor was appointed or if the appointed executor is not willing or able to act there is a set order for determining who is entitled to act; such a person is described as an administrator and must obtain a grant of letters of administration which *confers* authority to act. Executors and administrators can both be referred to as "the personal representatives" of the deceased.

It will often be necessary to obtain a grant of representation in connection with the administration before assets can be collected in or transferred to -beneficiaries. The procedure is explained in Ch.10.

Acting as executor or administrator is a time-consuming task. It is also one that carries with it duties and obligations and if those duties are not properly carried out then there may be personal liability (this is discussed further in Ch.11). Readers may wonder why anyone is ever willing to act as a personal representative. There are a variety of reasons. Professionals will be willing to act as executors provided the will authorises them to charge for their services; beneficiaries will usually be willing to act since until someone accepts office it may be impossible to distribute the assets; friends or relatives of the deceased appointed as executors may be willing to accept office as a mark of their respect for the deceased and as a way of helping the bereaved.

Chapter Two

IS THERE A VALID WILL?

1 Formalities Required by Wills Act 1837

Introduction to formalities

The formalities required for a valid will are set out in s.9 of the Wills Act 1837, as substituted by s.17 of the Administration of Justice Act 1982. A will which fails to comply with these formalities is invalid and cannot be admitted to probate. **2-001**

The substituted s.9 provides that:

> "No will shall be valid unless—
>
> (a) it is in writing, and signed by the testator, or by some other person in his presence and by his direction; and
> (b) it appears that the testator intended by his signature to give effect to the will; and
> (c) the signature is made or acknowledged by the testator in the presence of two or more witnesses present at the same time; and
> (d) each witness either—
>   (i) attests and signs the will; or
>   (ii) acknowledges his signature,
>
> in the presence of the testator (but not necessarily in the presence of any other witness), but no form of attestation shall be necessary."

Different formalities are required in the case of a statutory will for someone who lacks the mental capacity to make a will for themselves (see para.2-030 and following) and a privileged testator may make a valid will informally (see paras 2-013–2-014).

"In writing"

A will must be "in writing". The writing may be the handwriting of the testator, or any other person, it may be word processed or by any form of printing, or (presumably) produced by a photographic process. The writing may be in ink, pencil or produced by any other means which make it visible. However, using a combination of ink and pencil writing raises a rebuttable presumption that the parts in pencil are deliberative only and they may be excluded from probate in the absence of evidence that the testator intended them to be final. **2-002**

A will may be made on any material and may be written in any language (or even in code, provided that evidence is available from which the code may be deciphered).

The signature

Signature of the testator

2-003 Any mark made by the testator is a valid signature provided the testator intended it to be their signature. Testators should be encouraged to sign with their usual signatures so as to avoid any doubt as to the validity of the signature.

The following have been held to be signatures:

(a) a mark made by a rubber stamp with the testator's name on it (*In the Goods of Jenkins* (1863));
(b) the thumb print of an illiterate (*In the Estate of Finn* 105 L.J.P 36); and
(c) a set of initials (*In the Goods of Savoy* (1851)).

The signature need not consist of a name at all. Thus in *In the Estate of Cook* (1960) a document ending with the words "your loving mother" was admitted to probate on the basis that the testatrix in writing them had intended to refer back to her name which appeared earlier in the document.

The mark relied on as a signature must be complete in the sense that the testator completed as much as they *intended* to be their signature. For example, in *Re Colling* (1972) the testator started to sign his name in the presence of two witnesses one of whom left before he had finished writing. The will was held not to be properly executed since the signature was not completed in the presence of two witnesses. In *In the Goods of Chalcraft* (1948) the testatrix started to sign her name and wrote "E. Chal" before she became too weak to continue. This was held to be a valid signature on the basis that she had decided to end the signature at that point and so the signature was complete.

Signature by another person

2-004 The signature of someone on behalf of the testator is valid provided it is made "in his presence and by his direction". The testator must be present both mentally and physically when the signature is made (see para.2-005, for the meaning of "presence"). The Court of Appeal held in *Barrett v Bem* (2012) that a "direction" requires some positive and discernible communication (although it can be non-verbal) by the testator that he wishes the will to be signed on his behalf by the third party. Passive acquiescence is not sufficient.

The person signing at the testator's direction may be any person including one of the witnesses or even beneficiaries although, as was said in *Barrett v Bem*, signature by a beneficiary is not desirable and will raise questions as to the testator's knowledge and approval of the will (see para.2-032 and following below). The person signing may sign either with their own name or with the testator's name (it is best for the person signing to sign their own name and write that they are signing on behalf of the testator, in their presence and by their direction).

The testator intended by their signature to give effect to their will

2-005 The original s.9 required that the signature should be "at the foot or end" of the will. This led to a number of cases where probate was refused because the position of the signature did not comply exactly with this description. The Wills Act Amendment Act 1852 was then passed to extend the meaning of "foot or end". However, the excessively complicated wording of that Act forced the courts to make some very narrow distinctions. The substituted s.9 now no longer requires that the signature should be at the foot or end of the will. It is sufficient that "it appears that the testator intended by his signature to give effect to the will".

The exact scope of this requirement is a matter for the court. In *Wood v Smith* (1991) the court accepted that the signature could be at the top. In the same case the court also held that a signature at the top was valid even though written before the rest of the will. However this is only the case if the signature and writing of the will were "all part of one transaction". A signature in the margin of a will would probably satisfy the requirement and so probably would a signature on a separate page attached to the beginning or end of the will. A handwritten will which happened to include the testator's name (for example by starting with words such as "This is the will of me John Smith ...") might be refused probate on the basis that the words were not intended as a validating *signature* at all but merely as a description of the testator.

The practice (resulting from the wording of the Wills Act Amendment Act 1852) of admitting part of a document to probate but of refusing to admit the parts which appear physically after the signature in certain circumstances, would seem no longer to be possible. This is because the substituted section contemplates that the signature validates all or none of the will.

A signature on an envelope containing an otherwise unsigned will is valid if it was intended to give effect to the will. However, if the signature was written for some other reason (for example, to *identify* the will) the will is not validly signed.

In *Marley v Rawlings* (2012) a husband and wife by mistake each signed the will intended for the other. The Court of Appeal held that the husband's will was not valid as he had not intended his signature to give effect to the will which he signed. The Supreme Court disagreed. Mr Rawlings had clearly signed the document in front of him, and had done so with the intention of it being his last will and testament. Thus, whatever other problems the document might have, it was unambiguously intended to be a formal will, and it was signed by Mr Rawlings in the presence of two witnesses on the basis that it was indeed his will. Accordingly, s.9(a) was satisfied. There was no doubt that it was Mr Rawlings's intention at the time he signed the document that it should have effect as his will and, hence, s.9(b) was also satisfied.

The document could, therefore, be admitted to probate, after which its other problems could be addressed. See paras 2-034–2-037, for a discussion of the remedy of rectification.

Signature made or acknowledged in the presence of at least two witnesses

The substituted s.9 (like its predecessor) requires that the testator's signature is **2-006**
"made or acknowledged by the testator in the presence of two or more witnesses present at the same time". A signature is made in the presence of witnesses if they see the testator in the act of signing. The witnesses are not required to look at the signature itself nor need they know that the document is a will. It is not necessary to prove that the witnesses actually saw the act of signing; it is sufficient to show they were in such a position that they *could* have seen.

An acknowledgement of signature can be made by words or by conduct. There is an acknowledgement if the testator, or someone else in their presence, asks the witnesses to sign a document and they see their signature on it. The witnesses need not know that the document is a will. However, they must see the signature or at least have an opportunity of doing so. If the *signature* is covered up there is, therefore, no valid acknowledgement (however, the fact that the rest of the will is covered up does not prevent the acknowledgement being valid). The acknowledgement must be made to two or more witnesses present *at the same time*. A will is not, therefore, valid if an acknowledgement is made by the testator to each witness in the absence of the other.

In *Lim v Thompson* (2009) the court held that a will had not been duly executed as it was a photocopy which had been signed by the testator prior to copying but signed by the witnesses after copying. A photocopy of a will with a photocopied signature of the testator is not a document which was signed by the testator at all.

The order of events is crucial. The Court of Appeal made this point in *Re Sangha (Deceased)* (2023). Nugee LJ said that it was essential for due execution that the testator signs or acknowledges while all three individuals are together and that the witnesses *subsequently* sign or acknowledge.

Witnesses

Attestation

2-007 The substituted s.9 requires that each witness must attest and sign the will or acknowledge their signature in the presence of the testator. They must do so *after* the testator has signed or acknowledged. It is not essential that they should sign in each other's presence although, as we have already seen, they must both be present when the testator signs or acknowledges their signature. In *Re Sangha, deceased* [2023] EWCA Civ 660 the Court of Appeal considered that the following was not sufficient:

- T signs in presence of W1.
- W1 signs in T's presence.
- W2 enters.
- T acknowledges his earlier signature in the joint presence of W1 and W2.
- W2 signs. In order for the will to be validly executed, W1 would have to acknowledge the earlier signature after T's acknowledgement. However, the acknowledgement can be inferred from conduct.

Couser v Couser (1996) provides useful guidance on the meaning of "presence" and "acknowledgment". The testator and first witness had both signed the will before the second witness arrived. The testator informally acknowledged his signature by asking the second witness to sign. The first witness had got up to make coffee and was some distance away although in the same room. She gave no formal acknowledgment of her signature but, throughout the period in which the second witness was signing, kept up a discussion with the testator as to whether or not his will would be valid. The judge held that the second witness had signed in the presence of the first witness because the second witness was clearly in such a position that she could have seen. He also held that her continued discussion of the will amounted to an acknowledgment of her own signature. Thus, the two witnesses had signed or acknowledged after the testator had acknowledged his signature in the presence of both the witnesses. *Couser v Couser* had considered the earlier case of *Casson v Dade* (1781) 1 Bro. C.C. 99, a case which attracted a great deal of attention during the self-isolating required by the coronavirus pandemic. In *Casson v Dade* a testatrix who suffered from asthma was overcome by the heat in her attorney's office while executing her will, so retired to her carriage to sign it, accompanied by her witnesses. After having seen the execution, the witnesses returned to the office to attest it. The carriage was accidentally moved to a position where, it was sworn, it was possible for the testatrix to see into the office. The will was regarded as witnessed in the presence of the testatrix. The decision suggested that a self-isolating testator could sign the will on one side of a window with the witnesses outside, put the will outside the front door and have it witnessed on the other side of the window. In *Baker v Hewston* (2023) a will was held to be valid in unusual circumstances. The testator stayed in his car parked on the driveway in front of his house, the two witnesses saw him sign the will through the window. The testator then passed the will to them through the window and they each witnessed. This was an ingenious arrangement which predated the amendment to the Wills Act permitting "remote attestation" as to which see below.

The signatures of the witnesses must "attest" the will, that is the signature must be placed on the will with the intention of validating the testator's signature and not, for example, for the purpose of merely identifying the will. The signatures may appear anywhere on the will and need not be next to or after the testator's signature. A witness is not required to know that a testator who had already signed a will had to acknowledge their signature. It is enough that the witness intended to and did sign the will as a witness and, before doing so, saw and heard the words and deeds which constituted the deceased's acknowledgment of their earlier signature. This was the position in *Kayll v Rawlinson* (2010) where the testator signed in the presence of one witness who also signed; when the second witness arrived the testator said "John has signed it, I have signed it, will you sign it?" The will was held to be properly attested.

The testator must be mentally and physically present when the witnesses sign. A testator is not mentally present if, for example, he lapses into a coma before the witnesses have finished signing. The testator need not have actually seen the witnesses sign: he is regarded as physically present if he could have seen them had he chosen to look. Thus, in *Casson v Dade* (1781) the testatrix signed in her solicitor's office in the presence of two witnesses and then retired to her carriage, which was waiting in the street outside. There was no evidence that she saw the witnesses sign but, if she had turned her head, she could have seen them through the windows of the carriage and the office. The will was admitted to probate.

Capacity of witnesses

No particular rules are laid down as to who may act as a witness. The sole test is whether the witnesses were capable of attesting at the time when they signed. A minor may therefore witness a will although very young children may not since they would not be capable of understanding the significance of what they were doing. A blind person cannot act as a witness since they cannot have the opportunity to see the signature; similarly, a person who is very drunk or of unsound mind would be incapable of attesting. **2-008**

In choosing witnesses a testator should bear in mind that the witnesses may be required to give evidence as to due execution. The persons chosen should therefore not be very old or likely to be hard to trace. A beneficiary of the will or a beneficiary's spouse should not be chosen since, although their signature is perfectly valid, they will usually lose their legacy if they witness (Wills Act 1837 s.15, see Ch.16). A charging clause is no longer a legacy for these purposes (see Trustee Act 2000 s.18) and so a person benefiting from such a clause can safely witness the will containing it.

Attestation clauses

2-009 An attestation clause recites that the proper formalities have been complied with. A simple clause might read "Signed by the said [Testator] in our joint presence and then by us in his presence" and would be written next to the testator's signature and immediately above the witnesses' signatures. The value of such a clause is that it raises a presumption of due execution. The presumption is a strong one and in several recent cases the Court of Appeal has stated that the testator and witnesses must be taken to have done what the attestation clause declares they have done unless there is clear evidence to prove that this is not the case.

In *Re Sherrington* (2005) the Court of Appeal allowed the defendant's appeal against the first instance decision that a will was invalid because, inter alia, the witnesses had not been aware that they were being asked to witness a signature. The witnesses claimed that they thought they were signing their names on some sheets of paper. However, their evidence was confused and conflicting. The Court of Appeal said that in the absence of the strongest evidence, the intention of the witness to attest is inferred from the presence of the testator's signature on the will, the attestation clause and the signature of the witness. The Court of Appeal took the same approach in *Channon v Perkins* (2005) where the witnesses initially said that they could not recollect having witnessed the will and, by the time they appeared in court were adamant that they had not signed it, although their signatures appeared beside the attestation clause. The beneficiaries of the will sought to rely on the presumption of due execution. The Court of Appeal repeated that the strongest evidence is required to challenge a will which appears from its face to have been properly executed. Neuberger LJ (as he then was) said that there were two reasons for this requirement: a practical reason which is that

> "oral testimony as to the way in which a document was executed many years ago is not likely to be inherently particularly reliable on, one suspects, most occasions"

and a principled reason which is that setting aside a will, properly executed on its face, representing the apparent wishes of the testator, on the basis of extraneous evidence, means that the court "is thereby declining to implement the wishes of the testator following his death".

The question then arises of what constitutes the "strongest evidence" for the purposes of this kind of case remains to be explored. Arden LJ suggested in *Channon v Perkins* (at [45]) that there is a sliding scale according to which-evidence will constitute the strongest evidence in one case but not in another. What constitutes the "strongest evidence" in any particular case will depend on the totality of the relevant facts of that case, and the court's evaluation of the probabilities. The court must look at all the circumstances of the case relevant to attestation. The more probable it is, from those circumstances, that the will was properly attested, the greater will be the burden on those seeking to displace the presumption as to due execution to which the execution of the will and the attestation clause give rise. If the evidence of due attestation is weak, then the burden of displacing the presumption as to due execution may be more easily discharged. She said that simple lack of recollection was insufficient but:

> "evidence from both witnesses that they were nowhere near the place of execution stated in the attestation clause on the particular date would be likely to carry more weight".

In *Kayll v Rawlinson* (2010) Richards J said (unsurprisingly) that where it was common ground that an attestation clause did not reflect what had actually happened (stating that the testator had *signed* in the presence of both witnesses when the most that had happened was that he had acknowledged) that some evidence of due execution by later acknowledgment, in the presence of both witnesses, was required.

If there is no attestation clause the registrar, before admitting the will to probate, must require an affidavit of due execution or witness statement from a witness or, if this is not convenient, from any other person who was present at execution. If such an affidavit or witness statement cannot be obtained, other evidence (such as an affidavit or witness statement to show that the signature on the will is in the handwriting of the deceased) will be required. A will may be accepted for proof without evidence if it is clear that the distribution of the estate is not thereby affected. In other cases where there is no evidence the court may apply the maxim *omnia praesumuntur rite ac solemniter esse acta* and admit the will to probate if it appears to have been signed and witnessed but this will usually require a hearing before a judge and will, therefore, lead to delay and added expense. Affidavits or witness statements of due execution are dealt with in r.12 of the Non-Contentious Probate Rules 1987.

Where the will has been signed by another person at the direction of the testator, or where the testator is blind or illiterate, special forms of attestation clauses are desirable. The clause should make it clear that the testator had knowledge of the contents of the will at the time of execution.

A will does not have to be dated, although it is desirable that it should be to avoid uncertainty as to which of several testamentary documents is the last will. In *Corbett v Newey* (1996), a will was held to be invalid where the testatrix had handed her executed will to her solicitors with a blank next to the date. Her intention was that the will was not to come into effect until certain lifetime gifts had been completed. She wanted her solicitors to date the will when the gifts were complete. However, the court held that the will was invalid because it had not been intended to have immediate effect. It is not possible to execute a will conditionally.

Arrangements for execution

In an increasingly litigious climate it is important for those preparing wills to take care over the arrangements for execution. In *Esterhuizen v Allied Dunbar* (1998), a will drafting company was held liable in negligence to a disappointed beneficiary where a will was invalid as a result of having been witnessed by only one person. Longmore J said: **2-010**

> "It is in my judgement not enough just to leave written instructions with the testator. In ordinary circumstances just to leave written instructions and to do no more will not only be contrary to good practice but also in my view negligent."

For their own protection, will drafters should have in writing an offer in the following terms:

- The client can visit the will drafter's office for execution.
- If the client prefers, the will drafter will visit the client's house with a member of staff.
- If the client prefers, the client can make their own arrangements.

In *Gray v Richards Butler (Supervision of Execution of a Will)* (2000) a will was invalid because the two witnesses had not been present at the time that the testator signed or acknowledged the will. The case was decided before *Esterhuizen* but was not reported until a later date. Lloyd J took a different approach to Longmore J in *Esterhuizen* and found that the solicitor had not been negligent in failing to offer to supervise the execution of the will. He commented that the solicitor's written instructions were "most comprehensive" and that his conduct did not fall short of that required of the "reasonably competent solicitor". It was in his opinion necessary "to bear in mind the very clear terms of the attestation provision of the will".

There was a clear assumption in *Gray* that a solicitor has a duty to examine a will returned post-execution. On the particular facts the court accepted that there was nothing about the will which should have aroused the solicitor's-suspicion. It follows though that a solicitor who fails to offer to inspect a will may well be negligent if the will turns out to be wrongly executed. In *Humblestone v Martin Tolhurst Partnership* (2004) the court said that a firm which accepts a will for storage has a duty to inspect it, whether or not it is asked to do so.

When a professional is asked to prepare a will for a client it is best, in order to avoid problems, to adopt the following procedure wherever possible:

(a) The will is prepared by the will drafter from the client's instructions and explained to them.
(b) The client attends at the will drafter's office and, in the presence of two witnesses, places their signature at the end of the will next to a suitable attestation clause.
    (i) The witnesses must not be beneficiaries or spouses or civil partners of beneficiaries.
    (ii) Even if the will drafter is not a witness, they should be present to ensure that the correct procedure is adopted.
(c) The witnesses sign in the presence of the testator (as required by law) and of each other (not required, but useful so that either witness can give evidence as to the other's signature if necessary).
(d) For the avoidance of doubt as to what has been attested and to prevent accidental loss of parts of the will, it is sensible to fasten all the pages together securely. A number of cases have held that, where a will is written on more than one piece of paper, there must be physical contact between the pages at the time of attestation if the will is to be valid, but it is doubtful whether this rule survives the enactment of the substituted s.9. Some practitioners ask the testator and witnesses to initial every page to avoid allegations of later insertions. This can be burdensome for elderly or frail clients.
(e) It is good office practice to keep an attendance note explaining what was done and referring to the addresses of the witnesses so that they can be contacted if necessary to prove due execution.
(f) A copy of the will should be kept and the will drafter should insert on it the names of the testator and witnesses and date of execution. (Such a copy may be admissible to probate if the original is lost, see paras 2-042 and 10-004.)

If the client wishes to execute the will at home, the will drafter should offer to supervise execution and have a written record that the offer was made and rejected. The solicitor can make a separate charge for the supervision provided this was made clear in the terms of engagement. The will must be accompanied by very clear instructions. In particular the client should be warned not to allow anyone who is or whose spouse or civil partner is a beneficiary to witness, should be told where to sign, should be told to sign their usual signature in ink and should be told to sign in the presence of the witnesses and before they sign. There should also be an offer to inspect the will after execution.

If a will is to be executed in hospital the will drafter should bear in mind that many hospitals prohibit medical staff witnessing wills. If this rule applies it is safer to take witnesses to the hospital than to rely on finding witnesses there (other patients are not suitable since there may be doubt about their capacity and they are likely to be hard to trace if needed to give evidence).

If there is any possibility that the capacity of the testator to make a will may be challenged at a later date it is advisable to try to get a doctor to witness the will and/or to make a written statement as to the testator's mental state on the relevant day (see para.2-029).

Covid and remote witnessing

Problems caused by Covid

The requirement that the will must be signed in the presence of two witnesses present at the same time caused concern at the beginning of the Covid-19 pandemic as to how testators would be able to comply with the s.9 requirements. Fortunately, "presence" has been given a generous interpretation as we saw in *Casson v Dade* (1781) discussed above at para.2-007 which is generally accepted as authority that what is required for "presence" is a line of sight. **2-011**

However, the existence of a line of sight is not enough; it is also necessary that there is consciousness of what is going on. Justice Gorell Barnes said in *Brown v Skirrow* (1902):

> "You cannot be a witness to an act that you are unconscious of; otherwise the thing might be done in a ball-room 100 feet long and with a number of people in the intervening space. In my view, at the end of the transaction, the witness should be able to say with truth, 'I know that this testator or testatrix has signed this document'." (see p.5)

During the period of social isolation required by the Covid pandemic, most practitioners became adept at ways of procuring "safe" execution. For example, witnesses stood outside a window or on the outside of an open door. Some testators have executed wills in parks sitting on adjacent benches, or inside a car with the witnesses signing on a bonnet.

However, there was argument as to whether or not "presence" could include virtual presence via a video link. The Law Society of Scotland suggested that it could, but the Law Society of England and Wales said that it could not and most professional bodies agreed. There was pressure for legislation to clarify the position. On 25 July 2020 the Ministry of Justice announced that there would be legislation to allow remote witnessing for a limited period.

Temporary legislation

The Wills Act 1837 (Electronic Communications) (Amendment) (Coronavirus) Order 2020 (SI 2020/952) came into force on 28 September 2020. Article 2 amended the Wills Act 1837 as follows: **2-012**

The existing s.9 became s.9(1), and a new s.9(2) provided as follows:

> "For the purposes of paragraphs (c) and (d) of subsection (1), in relation to wills made on or after 31 January 2020 and on or before 31 January 2022, 'presence' includes presence by means of videoconference or other visual transmission."

The change was extended to wills made on or before 31 January 2024 by the Wills Act 1837 (Electronic Communications) (Amendment) Order 2022 (SI 2022/18). That period has now expired. Wills executed within the period covered by the provisions remain valid.

Note that s.9(1)(a) is not amended, so if a will is signed on behalf of a testator, it must be in the actual presence of the testator. Remote presence is not enough.

Article 3 provides that the Order does not allow a remotely witnessed will to be proved if a grant of probate has been issued before 28 September 2020. The position in relation to other types of grant is unclear.

The procedure for remote witnessing was not straightforward. The "Guidance on making wills using video-conferencing", which the government published on 25 July 2020 made the following points:

- Witnessing pre-recorded videos is not permitted—the witnesses must see the will being signed in real-time.
- The witnesses and testator can all be at different locations, on a three-way link, or two can be physically together with one at a remote location.
- The testator must physically sign the will (or acknowledge an earlier physical signature). Electronic signatures are not permitted. The testator will date the will with the date of signature.
- The will must then be taken or posted to the witnesses.
- The witnesses must physically sign the will in the virtual presence of the testator, and, if possible, in the virtual or physical presence of each other.
- The witnesses will sign with the date on which they are signing, which may be different from the date on which the testator signed and the date on which the other witness signs. The execution process is not complete until everyone has signed.

The will is not valid until both witnesses have signed. If the testator dies before all signatures have been added, the will cannot take effect.

Privileged wills

The form of the will

2-013 Wills Act 1837 s.11 allows a testator who has privileged status to make a will informally. The will can be made in any form including a mere oral statement. Such a will can be referred to as a nuncupative will or oral will. The only requirement is that the statement made should show an intention to dispose of property in the event of death even if the person making it does not know that they are making a will. Such a will is valid even if made by a minor, provided the minor has privileged status.

Privileged status

2-014 The right to make a privileged will extends to any soldier on actual military service or mariner or seaman being at sea.

"Soldier" includes a member of the RAF and naval or marine personnel serving on land. The exact extent of "actual military service" is open to some doubt. Broadly speaking the term may be said to include activities closely connected with warfare, whether or not war has been declared and whether or not the testator has actually arrived at the scene of the fighting. In *Re Jones* (1976) a soldier serving in

Northern Ireland at a time of widespread terrorist activity was held to have privileged status. Similarly, the term "being at sea" cannot be defined precisely. A seaman on leave who is not in receipt of instructions to join any particular ship is not "at sea": *Re Rapley (Deceased)* (1983). However, a mariner is treated as being at sea for this purpose when he is still on land but under orders to join his ship.

It is the circumstances in which the will was made which are relevant in deciding whether a person had privileged status, not the circumstances in which death occurred. See, for example, *Re Servoz-Gavin (Deceased)* (2009) where a ship's radio officer made oral statements to his cousin about what he wanted to happen to his property after his death while under orders to join his ship. He died many years later in a nursing home and his statement was accepted as a valid privileged will.

Incorporation of documents

Requirements for incorporation

Although a properly drawn will should be contained in one document, if possible, an unexecuted document can be incorporated into a will by referring to it in the will. The document is then admitted to probate as part of the will. **2-015**

An unexecuted document is incorporated if:

(a) it is in existence at the time of execution of the will (or of a codicil republishing the will);
(b) it is *referred to* in the will as being in existence at the time of execution; and
(c) it is clearly identified in the will.

Document in existence

Whether a document is in existence at the time of execution is a question of fact. **2-016**
The person who seeks to have it admitted to probate must prove its existence at that time.

Referred to as in existence

The document must be referred to in the will as in existence at the time of **2-017**
execution. Thus a will which says "I leave £100 to each of the persons named in the list *now* to be found in my desk" satisfies this condition (and the list will be validly incorporated provided it can be shown that it was in fact in existence when the will or confirming codicil was executed). A will which says "I leave £100 to each of the persons named in a list which *I will write* before my death" does not satisfy this condition. Even if the list was made before execution, it will not be admitted to probate as the will refers to its coming into existence at a later date. There are some marginal cases where the wording of the will does not make it clear whether or not the document exists at the time of execution. In such cases the court will refuse to incorporate the unexecuted document. For example, in *University College of North Wales v Taylor* (1908) probate was refused where the will referred to "any memorandum amongst my papers".

If the will is republished by a codicil, an unexecuted document will be incorporated if it is in existence at the time of execution of the codicil *and is referred to as being in existence* in either the will (which is republished and so speaks from the date of the codicil) or the codicil. *In the Goods of Smart* (1902) demonstrates that this is so, but on the facts of that case probate of the unexecuted document was refused because the will referred to its coming into existence in the future.

The document must be identified

2-018 The unexecuted document is only incorporated if it is identified by the will. The identification must be sufficient to indicate, without ambiguity, what document is referred to.

Practical considerations

2-019 Incorporation of documents by reference should be avoided unless absolutely necessary, both because of the danger of drafting the will in a way which does not properly incorporate them and because of the danger that the document referred to might be lost before the testator dies.

A properly drafted will should make clear whether or not a document referred to is being incorporated. If it does not, HM Courts and Tribunal Service is likely to require any such document to be produced and may call for evidence in the form of an affidavit or witness statement as to whether or not the document is incorporated. See para.10-056.

Once a document has been incorporated into a will it is treated as an ordinary part of the will and must be submitted with the rest of the will. Wills are a matter of public record so that the whole of the will, including the unexecuted document incorporated by reference, is available to the public. There is no point, therefore, in putting sensitive information into a document to be incorporated into the will, with the intention of keeping that information secret.

Pilot trusts

2-020 It is often convenient to leave property on trusts already created during the deceased's lifetime (pilot trusts). This is often done when a trust for a disabled beneficiary is required. Once the trust is established any family members who wish to do so can leave property to the trust by will. When drafting such gifts it is important to comply with the above requirements. The trust must be already in existence and referred to as such in the will.

The document referred to becomes testamentary and must be construed with the will. Therefore anything in the document which would be invalid in the will is inoperative.

In *Re Jones* (1942) a testator left a legacy to trustees appointed under a declaration of trust for the benefit of [X] made at the same date as the Will or "any substitution therefore or modification thereof or addition thereto which I may hereinafter execute". The gift failed on the basis that the testator was trying to reserve power to alter the gift in the will by a later unexecuted document. In *Re Edwards' Will Trusts* (1948) a testator left the residue of his estate upon the trusts and subject to the powers and provisions of a lifetime settlement "so far as such trusts and provisions are subsisting and capable of taking effect". The settlement provided that the trust funds were to be held for the benefit of the settlor's wife and children subject to a power for him to appoint the property as he saw fit. He made an appointment after the date of the will. The Court of Appeal held that the gift to the settlement was effective but on the original terms unaffected by the subsequent appointment.

2. Capacity

Age

Persons under the age of 18 cannot make a valid will (Wills Act 1837 s.7 as amended by the Family Law Reform Act 1969 s.3(1)(a)) unless they have privileged status (see para.2-013 and Wills Act 1837 s.11). Nor can the Court of Protection make a statutory will for a minor who lacks testamentary capacity (see para.2-030). **2-021**

On the death of a minor (other than one who has made a privileged will) their estate will be administered under the intestacy rules.

Persons aged 16 and over can, however, make a valid statutory nomination of certain assets provided the nomination is in writing and witnessed by at least one person. For a fuller discussion of nominations see Ch.21.

Testamentary capacity

The common law test

The test of testamentary capacity has traditionally been that set out in *Banks v Goodfellow* (1870) according to which a testator only has testamentary capacity if they have "a sound and disposing mind and memory". This requires the-testator to be capable of understanding: **2-022**

(a) *The nature of the act and its effects.* It is not necessary for the testator to understand the precise legal machinery involved in the will so long as they understand its broad effects.
(b) *The extent of the property of which he is disposing.* The testator is not expected to be able to produce a detailed list of every item of-property owned. It is sufficient if they have a broad recollection of its extent.
(c) *The claims to which he ought to give effect.* This means that the testator must be able to bring to mind the persons who are "fitting objects of the testator's bounty" (per Sir J Hannen in *Boughton v Knight* (1873)). It does not of course mean that having done so he must dispose of his property to those people. It is sufficient that he is capable of considering them. In *Battan Singh v Amirchand* (1948) a testator who was very ill in the last stages of consumption left his property to certain creditors stating that he had no living relatives. In fact he had three nephews of whom, the evidence showed, he was very fond. The court said that he clearly lacked testamentary capacity having forgotten the moral claims of his nephews.

In addition

> "no disorder of the mind shall poison his affections, pervert his sense of right, or prevent the exercise of his natural faculties—that no insane delusion shall influence his will in disposing of his property and bring about a disposal of it which, if the mind had been sound, would not have been made."

See para.2-028 for a fuller discussion of this element.

In *Key v Key* (2010) Briggs J accepted that the symptomatic effects of bereavement are capable of being almost identical to that associated with severe depression and can, therefore, mean that someone suffers a temporary loss of capacity. He accepted that it was not possible to point to any "conspicuous inability of the deceased to satisfy one of the distinct limbs of the *Banks v Goodfellow* test". However, taking the evidence as a whole, it was clear that the testator in question was simply unable during the week following his wife's death to exercise the decision-making powers required of a testator—or, at least, those propounding the will had not proved that he was. He admitted that that this was "a slight development of the *Banks v Goodfellow* test, taking into account decision-making powers rather than just comprehension", but considered that advances in the understanding of the mind and, in particular affective disorders justified it.

The Mental Capacity Act test

2-023 The Mental Capacity Act 2005 (MCA) introduced statutory provisions relating to capacity to make decisions. Section 1 provides that for the purposes of the Act a person is:

(a) to be assumed to have capacity until the contrary is established on the balance of probabilities;
(b) not to be treated as unable to make a decision unless all practicable steps to help them to do so have been taken without success; and
(c) not to be treated as unable to make a decision simply because they make an unwise one.

Section 2 provides that a person lacks capacity in relation to a matter if at the material time they are unable to make a decision for themselves in relation to the matter because of an impairment of or a disturbance in the functioning of the mind or brain. It does not matter whether the disturbance is permanent or temporary.

Section 3 provides that a person is unable to make a decision for themselves if unable to:

(a) understand the information relevant to the decision;
(b) retain the information relevant to the decision;
(c) use or weigh that information as part of the process of making the decision; or
(d) communicate the decision (whether by talking, using sign language or any other means).

The fact that a person is only able to retain information relevant to the decision for a short time does not prevent them being regarded as able to make the decision.

The information relevant to making a decision includes information about the reasonably foreseeable consequences of:

(a) deciding one way or another; or
(b) failing to make the decision.

Which test?

2-024 The MCA deals with decisions taken on behalf of a person by the Court of Protection and, therefore, is not directly relevant to the test of capacity which continues to be governed by the common law test. This has been confirmed in *Kicks v Leigh* (2014), *Walker v Badmin* (2014), *James v James* (2018), *Clitheroe v Bond* (2021) and *Baker v Hewston* (2023). However, the Act will undoubtedly influence the approach of the judiciary to questions of capacity. The Code of Practice which accompanies the MCA says at para.4-033:

"The Act's new definition of capacity is in line with the existing common law tests, and the Act does not replace them. When cases come before the court on the above issues, judges can adopt the new definition if they think it is appropriate. The Act will apply to all other cases relating to financial, healthcare or welfare decisions."

Munby J clarified the meaning of *"if they think it is appropriate"* in *Local Authority X v MM* (2007). While judges sitting in the Court of Protection and exercising the statutory jurisdiction under the MCA are obviously bound to apply the statutory principles contained in that Act, judges sitting elsewhere and deciding cases for which there is an existing test can adopt the formulation from the MCA but only if it corresponds to the existing common law test, having regard to the existing principles of the common law.

The MCA test does not correspond to the common law test. In *Walker v Badmin* (2014) Nicholas Strauss QC sitting as a Deputy Judge identified three points of difference:

(1) The effect of s.1(2) of the MCA is that the burden of proof of capacity remains always on the person alleging lack of capacity whereas at common law once a doubt has been raised the burden is on the person propounding the will to prove capacity: see below.

(2) Section 3 of the MCA requires the person making the decision to be able to understand all the information relevant to the making of a decision. This, at least arguably, may in some cases require more of the testator than the common law test, which merely requires the testator to be able to understand the three elements set out in the test (effect, extent of property and claims to be considered).

(3) The effect of s.3 would render a will invalid if the testator was unable to understand, use or weigh information as to the reasonably foreseeable consequences of the choices open to him. This probably requires more of a testator than the common law test. For example in *Simon v Byford* (2013) the Court of Appeal said that it was not necessary for the testatrix to understand the significance to others of the division of shares in the family company which she owned. In her final will she left them equally between her four children whereas in an earlier will she had left a controlling interest in the company to the one son who ran the company.

However, in *Baker v Hewston* (2023) HH Judge Tindal suggested that the differences between the statutory and common law tests were over-stated in *Walker v Badmin*:

(1) At common law there is an initial presumption of capacity where the will is duly executed and appears rational on its face. In such case the evidential burden then shifts to the objector to raise a real doubt about capacity in which case the evidential burden shifts back to the propounder to establish capacity. The difference between the common law and the Act as to the burden of proof would be unlikely to make any difference in practice in most cases, as there is usually a considerable body of evidence available to the court, which will enable it to decide the issue. It is unsatisfactory, and rarely appropriate, to decide the issue by reference to the burden of proof.

(2) The statutory test does not require an individual to understand "all" relevant information law test. Capacity is issue specific and therefore what is relevant will vary. It would be appropriate to regard the relevant information under s.3 as corresponding to that under the common law test.

(3) The statutory test requires the ability to weigh "reasonably foreseeable

consequences". Again, capacity is issue specific and in the context of a will which is a unilateral act, it is arguable that s.3 does not require understanding of the consequences for others.

The time at which testamentary capacity is to be judged

2-025 Capacity is time specific. The question is "has this person got the capacity to make this particular decision at this particular time?" Thus, in relation to testamentary capacity: the testator normally has to have capacity to make a will at the time the will is signed and witnessed.

However, the rule in *Parker v Felgate* provides a limited exception to the time specific element. Under the rule a will may be valid even though the testator has lost testamentary capacity by the time the will was executed provided:

(a) the testator had testamentary capacity at the time he gave a solicitor instructions to prepare a will;
(b) the will was prepared in accordance with those instructions; and
(c) at the time the will was executed the testator remembered having given instructions for a will to be prepared and believed that the will had been prepared in accordance with those instructions. It was immaterial that the testator did not remember precisely what the instructions were or could not understand the will if it were read to him.

This principle was extended to a will prepared by a solicitor on the basis of his client's own draft (*In the Estate of Wallace, Solicitor of the Duchy of Cornwall v Batten* (1952)). However, because of the possibility of abuse, this principle is applied with caution, if at all, where instructions were relayed to a solicitor through an intermediary (*Battan Singh v Amirchand*). *Clancy v Clancy* (2003) is a modern example of the rule in application.

The rule was approved by the Court of Appeal in *Perrins v Holland* (2010), an unusual case where the interval between giving instructions and executing the will was 15 months. The rule was extended to lifetime documents in *Singellos v Singellos* (2010).

Capacity does not have to be perfect

2-026 It is important to remember that the only issue is whether or not the testator has sufficient mental capacity to make a will. It is perfectly possible for a person to be incapable of managing their own property and affairs on a day-to-day basis and yet be capable of making a valid will.

Ewing v Bennet (2001), *Barrett v Kaspryyk* (2000) and *Simon v Byford* (2013) all make the point that a testator need not have unclouded mental faculties.

A lower level of capacity will be sufficient where the property and family circumstances are simple than when they are complex (see *James v James* (2019)).

The burden of proof

2-027 The person putting forward a will has to prove that the will is valid. This includes showing that the testator has capacity. At common law if the will is rational on its face and the testator is normally capable there is a presumption of mental capacity. However, where there is evidence casting doubt on the testator's capacity, the presumption is rebutted and the person alleging that the will is valid must prove that the testator fulfilled the *Banks v Goodfellow* test.

As Briggs J put it in *Key v Key* (2010):

"(i) While the burden starts with the propounder of a will to establish capacity, where the will is duly executed and appears rational on its face, then the court will presume capacity.
(ii) In such a case the evidential burden then shifts to the objector to raise a real doubt about capacity.
(iii) If a real doubt is raised, the evidential burden shifts back to the propounder to establish capacity nonetheless."

Vaughan v Vaughan (2002) is a good illustration of the principle. The testatrix was aged 82 and in poor health having had several strokes. Behrens J found that there was grave suspicion of incapacity. He accepted that there was some evidence on both sides. However, it *was for the person putting forward the will to prove capacity* and he had not done so. The effect of the burden of proof was that a person who alleges that a will was made in a lucid interval has to prove it (see *Brown v Deacy* (2002)). The burden of proof at common law differs from that which applies under the MCA. Section 1(2) of the Act specifically provides that for the purposes of the Act a person must be assumed to have capacity unless it is established that they lack capacity. However, this does not affect the common law test.

Wherever possible objective medical evidence should be obtained. It is dangerous to rely on the opinions of friends or family who may be partial but also may be genuinely unaware of deterioration in the mental abilities of someone they have known well for many years. In an unreported case, *In the Estate of Ellen Wilkes (Deceased)* (2000), a consultant physician specialising in the care of the elderly gave expert evidence. He warned against the acceptance at face value of statements, whether by medical practitioners or others, indicating that the testatrix was mentally well at the relevant times, without some form of objective diagnostic analysis. In the absence of such a test, comments about the testatrix's apparent mental ability are purely subjective. In the consultant's opinion they should be viewed with caution since a person may appear to have intact mental functions despite severe deficits in reality. It is common to encounter elderly people who seem quite well, but do badly in simple objective tests. In the case of a Mini Mental State Examination, he would expect at least 25 out of 30 points for a person with capacity to make a will, but it would be perfectly possible to have a good interaction with a person who only scored 10 points.

However, the Mini Mental State Examination is, itself, not entirely suitable for determining testamentary capacity as it is largely concerned with short-term memory. In *Charles v Fraser* (2010) a consultant psychiatrist found that an elderly woman had testamentary capacity on the basis of such an examination where she had, in fact, forgotten the existence of her many relatives.

Professionals often feel embarrassed about raising the issue of mental capacity with clients, but it is always necessary to consider the question. It can be approached on the basis of avoiding any possibility of an unnecessary challenge at a later date.

Insane delusions

An insane delusion is a belief in the existence of something in which no rational person could believe and which could not be eradicated from the testator's mind by reasoned argument (*Dew v Clark and Clark* (1826)). In *Clitheroe v Bond* (2021) **2-028**

Falk J held that it was not necessary to show that an attempt had been made to disabuse the deceased of their belief. That is one way of demonstrating that the belief is delusional—and indeed the obvious way in many cases—but there are other ways. Another way, would be if it could be shown that the belief was formed and maintained in the face of clear evidence to the contrary of which the individual was plainly aware, such that there is no sensible basis on which to conclude that the individual was simply mistaken or had forgotten the true position, as opposed to being delusional. A further alternative would be to demonstrate that the individual had no basis on which they could rationally have formed and maintained the mistaken belief. The key question in each case is whether the relevant irrational belief is fixed.

A person suffering from a delusion can make a valid will provided the delusion is on a subject in no way connected with the will (for example, a belief that the testator is pursued by evil spirits). However, if the delusion affects the testator's judgment, either generally or on one point which affects the dispositions made, the testator does not have testamentary capacity. If the delusion affects the whole will (as in *Dew v Clark and Clark* where the testator had an irrational dislike of his daughter as a result of which he left her nothing in his will) probate will be refused to the whole will. If the delusion affects only part of the will then only that part will be excluded from probate (as in *In the Estate of Bohrmann* (1938) where one clause of a codicil was omitted from probate).

In *Sharp v Adams* (2006) the Court of Appeal considered the will of a deceased father who had inexplicably left everything to his employees to the exclusion of his two daughters. He was suffering from advanced multiple sclerosis and on a drugs regime which was likely to impair the functioning of his brain. The Court of Appeal held that, while the first three elements of the *Banks v Goodfellow* test were satisfied, a fourth (no poisoning of the affections) was not. The trial judge was correct in saying that the justice or otherwise of the testator excluding his daughters from benefit must, as a matter of common sense, have a bearing on the decision, so long as inquiry is directed to the testator's soundness of mind and not to general questions of perceived morality. Leaving the residuary estate to the employees was understandable. Leaving nothing at all to his daughters was not.

In *Kostic v Chaplin* (2007) the testator was suffering from severe delusions believing that there was an international conspiracy of dark forces against him. The conspiracy included his family, friends and professional advisers. He left his substantial estate to the Conservative Party. The court held that his natural affection for his family had been poisoned by his disorder of mind. His delusions had brought about a disposal of property which would not have been made had he been of sound mind.

Practical precautions

2-029 A solicitor who has any doubts as to the capacity of a client proposing to make a will or any suspicion that lack of capacity may later be alleged should try to avoid future problems by following the so-called "Golden Rule", set out in full in Ch.13, and obtaining medical advice. It is desirable that a medical practitioner examine the testator preferably at the time the will is signed since the severity of certain mental conditions, for example, senility, vary markedly over relatively short periods of time. A full and careful attendance note setting out the details of execution should be made by the will drafter. If possible, the note should be made contemporaneously.

The so-called "Golden Rule" suggests that in addition to trying to obtain medical approval the rule requires solicitors to:

(a) discuss any earlier will with the client (and the reasons for changing it); and
(b) take the instructions in the absence of anyone who may stand to benefit or who may have influence over the testator.

This is sensible advice. Earlier wills may indicate a settled pattern of giving; if the latest will diverges markedly from that pattern, the will drafter will be alerted to the need to explore the reasons for the change. Discussion may then reveal that the client has forgotten particular family members or is confused about the extent of assets.

It is not always possible to interview clients alone as they will sometimes insist that a companion remains with them. However, the Court of Appeal commented in *Hawes v Burgess* (2013) on the difficulty of assessing capacity with someone else present particularly if the third party answered questions on the testator's behalf. Practitioners who allow a third party to remain should be aware that this may make the will vulnerable to attack after death and make sure that they have a clear attendance note establishing that it was the client's wish that the third party remained.

Note, however, that the Golden Rule deals only with the way in which will drafters should conduct themselves as a matter of good practice. It does not suggest that a will is invalid merely because the steps laid down have not been followed. See *Allen v Emery* (2005). Where no medical evidence is obtained the lack of a contemporaneous medical opinion will make it harder for those propounding the will to discharge the burden of proof.

Statutory wills

Section 16(1) and (2) of the MCA allows the court to make decisions on behalf of a person who lacks capacity to make that decision. Section 18(1)(i) states that the court's powers extend to the execution of a will. Schedule 2(2) provides that the will may make any provision (whether by disposing of property or exercising a power or otherwise) which the person lacking capacity could have made, if capable, except that it cannot dispose of immoveable property situated outside England and Wales. **2-030**

A statutory will must:

(a) state that it is signed by the person for whom it is made (the "testator") acting by the authorised person;
(b) be signed by the authorised person with the name of the testator and their own name, in the presence of two or more witnesses present at the same time;
(c) be attested and subscribed by those witnesses in the presence of the authorised person; and
(d) be sealed with the official seal of the court.

Before the enactment of the MCA the court tried to make the will which the person lacking capacity would have made if acting reasonably and on competent legal advice had they enjoyed a brief lucid interval. In other words it was a case of substituted judgement.

The position is quite different since the Act came into force. The court must act in the best interests of the person lacking capacity. Section 1(5) provides that:

"An act done, or decision made, under this Act for or on behalf of a person who lacks capacity must be done, or made, in his best interests."

Section 4 expands on the concept of "best interests" and provides that the person making the decision must consider all the relevant circumstances. In particular s.4(6) provides that:

He must consider, so far as is reasonably ascertainable:

(a) the person's past and present wishes and feelings (and, in particular, any relevant written statement made by him when he had capacity),
(b) the beliefs and values that would be likely to influence his decision if he had capacity, and
(c) the other factors that he would be likely to consider if he were able to do so.

When making a statutory will it is not immediately apparent how the Court of Protection is to determine the testator's "best interests" since the testator will be dead by the time the will comes into effect. A number of cases have grappled with this issue.

In *NT v FS* (2013) Behrens J reviewed the decisions on statutory wills since the MCA came into force and produced a summary of how to make a decision that is in the testator's best interests.

(1) The MCA marks a radical change in the treatment of persons lacking capacity. The overarching principle is that any decision made on behalf of P must be in P's best interests. This is not the same as inquiring what P would have decided if he or she had had capacity. It is not a test of substituted judgment but requires the court to apply an objective test of what would be in P's best interests.
(2) The court must follow the structured decision-making process laid down by the MCA. Thus the court must consider all relevant circumstances and in particular must consider and take into account the matters set out in s.4 (such as the testator's past and present wishes and feelings, the views of anyone caring for the testator).
(3) The court must then make a value judgment giving effect to the paramount statutory instruction that the decision must be made in the best interests of the person who lacks capacity.
(4) The MCA contains no hierarchy between the various factors which have to be borne in mind. The weight to be attached to different factors will inevitably differ depending on the individual circumstances of the particular case. There may however in a particular case be one or more features which, in a particular case, are of "magnetic importance" in influencing or even determining the outcome.
(5) When evaluating all the factors to determine the best interests (the balance sheet approach), the views and wishes of the person who lacks capacity in regard to decisions made on his behalf are to carry great weight. However, there is no presumption in favour of implementing those wishes. The weight to be attached to those wishes and feelings will always be case-specific and fact-specific. In some cases, in some situations, they may carry much, even, on occasions, preponderant, weight. In other cases, in other situations, and

even where the circumstances may have some superficial similarity, they may carry very little weight.

Behrens J then acknowledged that while two cases (*Re P* (2009) and *Re M, ITW v Z* (2009)) had held that it was in a person's best interests to be remembered with affection by their family for "*having done the right thing*" in his will, other judges had not agreed. Morgan J in *Re G(TJ)* (2011) had pointed out that it was the court that was acting not the testator. Furthermore, in so far as there is a dispute between family members, the unsuccessful members are not likely to think that he had done the right thing. Behrens J did not find the "right thing" test a helpful consideration on the facts of the case. However in *Jones v Parkin* (2014) Judge Hodge QC said that in his judgment "the right thing" was to be judged from the perspective of the well-informed and disinterested, objective bystander not from that of relatives or friends competing for a share of the incapacitous person's testamentary bounty. Further, he considered that the concept of being remembered "as having done the right thing" still had relevance even if the right thing had to be done by the court on behalf of the testator.

Re Peter Jones (2014) is a helpful case in which the court made the following points:

(1) Each case turns on its own facts and a factor which is of magnetic importance in one case may be relatively insignificant in another superficially similar case. For many but not all people it is in their best interests that they be remembered with affection by their family as having done the right thing by their will. This is something which the judge is entitled to take into account.
(2) However, where a person with capacity has recently made a will excluding a potential beneficiary and/or has expressed views that he disliked them and did not want them to share in his estate, and then loses capacity, a third-party decision-maker cannot "correct" those wishes by substituting his own or society's view as to what should rightfully have been done. To do so would run counter to testamentary freedom and the wishes, feelings, beliefs and values provisions of the MCA, and lead to inconsistent and arbitrary outcomes. The onset of mental incapacity is not an opportunity for moral correction.
(3) The court can authorise a statutory will that makes good the patient's omissions but must not seek to correct his considered acts and decisions.

The Court of Protection will not normally make a statutory will on the basis of allegations that the existing will is invalid because this would be to become embroiled in family disputes and trespass on the jurisdiction of the probate court. However, in *Re D, VAC v JAD* (2010) Hogg J accepted that the overarching consideration was a judicial evaluation of what is in the protected person's "*best interests*". Given the very strong doubts that had been raised as to the validity of the previous wills, he was willing to order the execution of a statutory will rather than leaving the testatrix's estate to be eroded by the costs of litigation after her death and her memory to be tainted by the bitterness of a contested probate dispute between her children.

Procedure for a statutory will

Practice Direction F which supplements Pt 9 of the Court of Protection Rules sets out the procedure for an application for a statutory will. A draft will must be ap- **2-031** proved by the Court of Protection. Notice of the application must be served on everyone affected by the proposed will. Once the court has approved the terms of the will, the applicant then executes the will on behalf of the person lacking capacity and must return the original and two copies to the court for sealing. The court returns the original and one copy to the applicant. In *Re Hughes (Deceased) Times,* January 8, 1999 it was accepted that the sealing can take place after the death of the patient. The sealing merely confirms that the statutory will, as executed, conforms to its authorisation. It is not analogous to the signing of the will by a mentally capable testator.

A statutory will cannot be made for a minor. Where a minor receives a large damages award legal advisers should consider what will happen to the funds if the minor dies intestate. It is preferable that such sums should be settled on the minor for life rather than held for the minor absolutely. *Bouette v Rose* (2000) is an example of the unsatisfactory operation of the intestacy rules. The property passed equally to the child's mother who had cared for her throughout her life and to the child's father who had had no contact with her. Fortunately, the mother's application under the Inheritance (Provision for Family and Dependants) Act 1975 as a person maintained by the deceased was successful.

Where a minor with significant assets owned absolutely is terminally ill, the correct procedure is to apply to the Court of Protection for a settlement of the property under MCA ss.16 and 18. *LCN v CJF* (2019) is a good example of such an application.

A statutory will cannot deal with land in another jurisdiction. See Mental Capacity Act 2005 Sch.2, para.4(4).

3. Knowledge and Approval

Presumption

2-032 A testator must know and approve the contents of the will (except in the case of a statutory will). If a testator signs a will having no knowledge of the contents, the will is invalid. The time at which knowledge and approval is required is normally the time of execution of the will. However, in cases where the rule in *Parker v Felgate* applies (see para.2-025), it is sufficient if the court is-satisfied that the will put forward embodies the instructions given by the testator and intended by him to be carried out (*Perrins v Holland* (2010)).

The burden of proof of knowledge and approval lies on the person propounding the will; however, there is normally a rebuttable presumption that a testator who executes a will (particularly if they have read the will or have had the will read over to them) does so with knowledge and approval of the contents.

This presumption does not arise in the following cases:

(a) *In the case of a blind or illiterate testator or where another person signs on behalf of the testator.* In such cases the registrar will require evidence that the testator had actual knowledge of the contents. It is advisable in such a case for the attestation clause to include a statement that the will was read over to and approved by the testator. If it does not, evidence will be required from the witnesses or from some other person present.

(b) *Where there are suspicious circumstances.* If there is evidence of suspicious circumstances, the will is not admitted to probate unless the propounder can prove that the testator did know and approve the contents.

The most obvious example of a suspicious circumstance is where the will is prepared by a major beneficiary or close relative of a major beneficiary. In *Wintle v Nye* (1959) the House of Lords (per Viscount Simmonds) expressed the view that:

> "It is not the law that in no circumstances can a solicitor or other person who has prepared a will for a testator take a benefit under it. But that fact creates a suspicion that must be removed by the person propounding the will. In all cases the court must be vigilant and jealous. The degree of suspicion will vary with the circumstances of the case. It may be slight and easily dispelled. It may, on the other hand, be so grave that it can hardly be removed."

In *Wintle v Nye* it was held that the gift to the draftsman was not admissible to probate for want of knowledge and approval but that the rest of the will could stand.

Solicitors are subject to special rules of professional conduct in relation to receiving legacies from clients; these are dealt with in para.2-038.

Judges used to apply a two-stage approach the issue of knowledge and approval (see, for example, *Barry v Butlin* (1836) and *Tyrrell v Painton* (1894):

(1) Are the facts sufficient facts to rebut the presumption of knowledge and approval and "excite the suspicion of the court"?
(2) Has the person seeking to prove the will managed to allay those suspicions?

However in *Gill v Woodall* (2010) Neuberger LJ said at [22] that where a judge had heard evidence of fact and expert opinion over a period of many days

> "the value of such a two-stage approach to deciding the issue of the testatrix's knowledge and approval appears to me to be questionable".

In his view, the approach which it would, at least generally, be better to adopt was that summarised by Sachs J in *Re Crerar (unreported)* but followed by Latey J in *Re Morris, decd* (1971) at p.78, namely that the court should

> "consider all the relevant evidence available and then, drawing such inferences as it can from the totality of that material, it has to come to a conclusion whether or not those propounding the will have discharged the burden of establishing that the testatrix knew and approved the contents of the document which is put forward as a valid testamentary disposition. The fact that the testatrix read the document, and the fact that she executed it, must be given the full weight apposite in the circumstances, but in law those facts are not conclusive, nor do they raise a presumption of law."

Similarly, in *Hawes v Burgess* (2013) Mummery LJ said that the relevant questions to ask were:

(a) Do the circumstances of the will arouse the suspicions of the court as to whether its contents represent the wishes and intentions of the deceased as known to and approved by her?; and
(b) Has scrutiny of those circumstances by the court dispelled those suspicions?

There have been a number of cases where the Court of Appeal has emphasised that in the case of simple wills where the testator has had an opportunity to see the will the presumption of knowledge and approval will operate.

In *Fuller v Strum* (2001) the Court of Appeal considered a will prepared by a major beneficiary. It stated the general principle that the court's suspicion ought generally to be excited where a party prepares a will under which they take a benefit. The court will not pronounce in favour of that will unless the suspicion is removed. Prima facie, if the person with the burden of proof gives no evidence, the issue will be decided against them. However, *additional evidence is not always required where a beneficiary prepares a will.* The preparation of the will is merely a suspicious circumstance of more or less weight depending upon the circumstances.

The circumstances of a particular case may raise such grave suspicion that it can hardly be removed. *Fuller v Strum* (2002) was not such a case. The will was short and simple and the testator had had an opportunity to read it.

The Court of Appeal expressly approved the approach of Lloyd J in *Hart v Dabbs* (2001), describing it as "properly objective". The major beneficiary had been instrumental in the preparation of the will. He was arrested on suspicion of murdering the testator but later released for lack of evidence. The will was held valid on the basis that it was a short, simple document and there was no reason to doubt the testator's knowledge and approval: "so long as he read the document he would have had no difficulty taking in its provisions even if someone else prepared it".

In *Re Sherrington* (2005) the trial judge had found that the circumstances were such as to excite the suspicion of the court. The Court of Appeal, while agreeing that there were some surprising features (such as the exclusion of the testator's children from benefit), found that the circumstances were not sufficient to excite suspicion. The Court of Appeal attached particular weight to the fact that the will was short and simple and the deceased had had ample opportunity to read it.

The effect of these cases seems to be to make it harder to sustain a claim of want of knowledge and approval in a case where the will is simple and the testator has had an opportunity to read it.

However, where the testator has not had such an opportunity (see *Franks v Sinclair* (2006)) or intermediaries are involved (*Sifri v Clough & Willis* (2007)) a claim of lack of knowledge and approval is more likely to succeed.

In *Franks v Sinclair* the solicitor who had prepared a rather complicated will read it over to the elderly testatrix. He did not explain the meaning of the various clauses and did not leave a copy of the will with the testatrix. The court held that reading a will over to a client might be sufficient when the terms are straightforward, as in *Fuller v Strum* (2002) and *Hart v Dabbs* (2001), but not where clauses are complicated. Such wills require explanation. The Court of Appeal took a similar approach in *Gill v RSPCA* (2010) where it found that probably the will had been read over to the client without explanation. The client suffered from extreme agoraphobia and anxiety disorder and would have been in such a state of panic in the solicitor's office that she would have been unable to take in the terms of her will, if simply read over to her. The solicitor sent a draft of the testatrix's will to her house but he also sent a draft of her husband's will and the Court of Appeal determined that, since both drafts were probably sent in one envelope, there was no certainty that the testatrix had ever seen her will. The will was held to be invalid for lack of knowledge and approval.

Mistake

2-033 A mistake may mean that the testator had no knowledge or approval of the will as a whole (for example, where they execute the wrong will) or of only part of the will (as in *Wintle v Nye*). If a testator includes words in their will having intended to write other words, the words mistakenly included will be omitted from probate; similarly if a testator includes words in their will but does not know or approve them then those words will be omitted from probate. An example of the latter type of mistake occurred in *Re Phelan* (1972). The testator bought three printed will forms and, thinking that every holding of shares had to be dealt with in a separate will, executed three wills in favour of X, each will disposing of a separate shareholding. Each will was executed on the same day and each contained a printed revocation clause. Stirling J held that as the words of revocation were clearly included in the wills by inadvertence and misunderstanding they could be omitted from probate.

It used to be said that the probate court will not interfere where a testator deliberately selects certain words and includes them in the will even if it is clearly shown that the testator was mistaken as to their legal effect. Thus in *Collins v Elstone* (1893) a testatrix deliberately included a revocation clause under the misapprehension that it would revoke only a small part of her earlier will. The court held that the revocation clause could not be omitted from the will. The rule is the same where a draftsman prepares a will on behalf of a testator and deliberately selects words being mistaken as to their legal effect; those words will be admitted to probate (*Re Horrocks* (1939)). The probate court has always had power to omit words from probate.

However, in *Marley v Rawlings* (2014) the Supreme Court made it clear that the modern approach to the interpretation of wills should mirror the more flexible modern approach to the interpretation of lifetime documents as set out in a number of House of Lords decisions, starting with *Prenn v Simmonds* (1971) and culminating in *Rainy Sky SA v Kookmin Bank* (2011). Lord Neuberger summarised this (at [19]) as follows:

> "When interpreting a contract, the court is concerned to find the intention of the party or parties, and it does this by identifying the meaning of the relevant words, (a) in the light of (i) the natural and ordinary meaning of those words, (ii) the overall purpose of the document, (iii) any other provisions of the document, (iv) the facts known or assumed by the parties at the time that the document was executed, and (v) common sense, but (b) ignoring subjective evidence of any party's intentions."

He said (at [20]) that the approach to interpreting wills should be the same:

> "Whether the document in question is a commercial contract or a will, the aim is to identify the intention of the party or parties to the document by interpreting the words used in their documentary, factual and commercial context."

Earlier case law is therefore likely to be ignored in favour of the more flexible approach indicated by the Supreme Court. In a number of cases decided since the Supreme Court decision (*Brooke v Purton* (2014); *Burnard v Burnard* (2014); *Re Freud (Deceased)* (2014); *Reading v Reading* (2015); *Royal Society v Robinson* (2015)) first instance judges have felt able to interpret wills in a way which gave effect to the clear intention of the testator without needing to consider the statutory remedy of rectification dealt with below.

Rectification of will

Introduction

Prior to the Administration of Justice Act 1982 the court did not have any power to insert words even where it was obvious that words had been omitted accidentally. **2-034**
However, s.20 of that Act alters this rule to a limited extent. It provides that if a court is satisfied that a will is so expressed that it fails to carry out the testator's intentions in consequence of:

(a) a clerical error; or
(b) a failure to understand his instructions,

it may order that the will be rectified so as to carry out their intentions.

If, therefore, a typing error is made in a will the probate court can order that words included by mistake be omitted and that words omitted by mistake be inserted. Similarly if a solicitor misunderstands their instructions the court can order that the mistake be rectified.

Meaning of clerical error

2-035 In *Wordingham v Royal Exchange Trust Co* (1991) the draftsman omitted a clause containing a power of appointment which should have been included in the will. This was held to be a clerical error and so rectification was ordered. However, if the testator or draftsman is mistaken as to the legal effect of words deliberately selected for inclusion in or exclusion from the will, the court cannot interfere. *Bush v Jouliac* (2006) is a nice illustration of the difference between the two. A solicitor drafted a will leaving the testatrix's estate equally between her son and daughter. He had a clear instruction that, should the son predecease his mother, his share was not to pass to his daughter. The solicitor did not include words to exclude Wills Act 1837 s.33 (which gives children of a deceased child the right to the share their parent would have taken). The court held that, had the solicitor been ignorant of the section, rectification would not have been possible. However, the solicitor said in evidence:

> "I can confirm that my error in drafting was not a failure to appreciate section 33 of the Wills Act needed to be expressly excluded, but rather an inadvertent clerical error in failing to insert the necessary words."

Rectification was, therefore, allowed. For further recent examples see *Joshi v Mahida* (2013) where a solicitor's error in the wording of a legacy was held to be clerical and therefore rectifiable and conversely *Kell v Jones* (2013) where the draftsman had deliberately selected the words used in the will after careful thought with the result that rectification was not possible.

In *Marley v Rawlings* (2014) Lord Neuberger reviewed the first instance decisions on the meaning of "clerical error" and concluded that the expression should not be construed restrictively. He said at [75]:

> "I accept that the expression 'clerical error' can have a narrow meaning, which would be limited to mistakes involved in copying or writing out a-document, and would not include a mistake of the type that occurred in this case. However, the expression is not one with a precise or well-established, let alone a technical, meaning. The expression also can carry a wider meaning, namely a mistake arising out of office work of a relatively routine nature, such as preparing, filing, sending, organising the execution of, a document (save, possibly, to the extent that the activity involves some special expertise). Those are activities which are properly be described as 'clerical', and a mistake in connection with those activities, such as wrongly filing a document or putting the wrong document in an envelope, can properly be called 'a clerical error'."

For recent successful applications for rectification on the basis of clerical error see *Kelly v Brennan* (2020) and *Bracey v Curley* (2022). In neither case was rectification actually required as the court was willing to admit extrinsic evidence to establish the intended meaning. However, the claimant had applied for rectification in the alternative and the court therefore expressed a view on its availability.

In *Reading v Reading* (2015) Asplin J said that, had rectification been required, she would have refused to grant it on the basis that the will drafter's error was not in her opinion a "clerical" error. He had overlooked the fact that his firm's precedent for a nil rate band discretionary trust used the term "issue" in the class of beneficiaries and therefore excluded the testator's stepchildren (contrary to the instructions given). In her opinion this was an error which related to the professional judgment and expertise of the solicitor who drafted the will. In *Bracey v Curley* (2022) Philip Mott QC sitting as a Deputy High Court Judge doubted the correctness of this view. However, the circumstances of the two cases were different so he was not forced to depart from that decision, or to decline to follow it, in order to conclude that rectification would be available here. *Reading v Reading* involved a positive choice of a word which had an established legal meaning, whereas *Bracey v Curley* involved the omission of words intended to make clear what conditions applied to a disposition.

Failure to understand testator's instructions

There are fewer cases decided on this point. A recent example is *Royal Society v Robinson* (2015) where the solicitors preparing the will did not appear to understand that the bulk of the testator's assets were outside the UK and included a statement that the will was limited to UK assets. **2-036**

Does the will have to be a valid will?

In *Marley v Rawlings* (2012) the Court of Appeal refused rectification where a husband and wife had signed each other's will. It took the view that the error made the will invalid because it was not properly executed in accordance with Wills Act 1837 s.9(a) and (b) and that rectification was available only where there was a valid will to rectify. **2-037**

However, on appeal the Supreme Court did allow rectification (*Marley v Rawlings* (2014)). Lord Neuberger, who delivered the judgment of the court, was persuaded that the requirements of s.9 of the Wills Act were satisfied. Mr Rawlings had signed the document in the presence of two witnesses and did so with the intention of it being his last will and testament. Accordingly, Lord Neuberger accepted that s.9(a) was satisfied. There was no doubt that it was Mr Rawlings's intention at the time he signed the will that it should have effect and so s.9(b) was also satisfied. It was true that the will did not make sense, at least if taken at face value, but that could be dealt with at a later stage.

Lord Neuberger was prepared to go further than this saying at [60]:

> "it does not appear to me that a document has to satisfy the formal requirements of section 9, or of having the testator's knowledge and approval, before it can be treated as a 'will' which is capable of being rectified pursuant to section 20."

However, this was obiter.

The remedy is discretionary: see *Grattan v McNaughton* (2001). The evidence of error or misunderstanding must be clear. As Chadwick J (as he then was) said in *Re Segelman* (1996),

> "the probability that a will which a testator has executed in circumstances of some formality reflects his intentions is usually of such weight that convincing evidence to the contrary is necessary".

Cases in which the court held that there was such convincing evidence include *Price v Craig* (2006), *Hobart v Hobart* (2006) and *Clarke v Brothwood* (2006). In *Bell v Georgiou* (2002) the evidence was not convincing and the court dismissed the application as being based on mere speculation as to the testator's intention.

After the expiry of six months from the date of the grant of representation an application for rectification cannot be made except with leave from the court. It is possible to make applications out of time and *Chittock v Stevens* (2000) decided that such applications will be governed by the same guiding principles as applications under the Inheritance (Provision for Family and Dependants) Act 1975 s.4. Personal representatives who distribute after that date will not be liable on the ground that they should have taken into account the possibility of an out-of-time application being made.

An application for rectification may be made to a registrar unless a probate action has been commenced.

The application must be supported by a witness statement setting out the grounds of the application together with such evidence as can be adduced as to the testator's intentions and as to whichever of the following matters are in issue:

(a) the respects in which the testator's intentions were not understood; or
(b) the nature of any alleged clerical error.

Unless otherwise directed, notice of the application shall be given to every person having an interest under the will whose interest might be prejudiced by the rectification applied for and any comments in writing by any such person shall be exhibited to the affidavit or witness statement in support of the application (Non-Contentious Probate Rules 1987 r.55).

A disappointed beneficiary may sometimes have a choice of remedy available; typically the beneficiary may have a possible negligence action against the solicitor who drafted the will as well as a possible action for rectification. In *Walker v Medlicott* (1999) the Court of Appeal stated that, where possible, a claimant must mitigate their damage by bringing proceedings for rectification of the will first. Only if that remedy is unavailable or unlikely to be successful should the claimant consider the negligence action. *Horsfall v Haywards* (2000) was an example of a case where rectification would not have been appropriate. The proceeds of sale of the estate assets had been transmitted to Canada and it appeared very unlikely that the beneficiaries would be able to recover them even if the rectification application was successful.

Special rules relating to those regulated by the Solicitors Regulation Authority (SRA)

2-038 Those regulated by the SRA are subject to special rules of conduct set out in the SRA Standards and Regulations 2019 replacing the SRA Code of Conduct 2011.

The SRA Standards and Regulations 2019, unlike the Code of Conduct makes no specific references to legacies to those preparing wills. However, the obligatory Principles which underpin the Standards require those regulated to act with honesty and integrity (principles 4 and 5) and in the best interests of the client (principle 7).

The SRA issued the following Ethics Guidance for Private Client practitioners entitled "Drafting and preparation of wills" on 6 May 2014 (updated 25 November 2019). The guidance is not mandatory and is issued to help those regulated by the SRA understand their obligations and how to comply with them. However, the SRA may have regard to it when exercising its regulatory functions.

> "*Gifts to you or someone in your business*
>
> If you draft a will where the client wishes to make a gift of significant value to you or a member of your family, or an employee of your business or their family, you should satisfy yourself that the client has first taken independent legal advice with regard to making the gift.
>
> This includes situations where the intended gift is of significant value in relation to the size of the client's overall estate, but also where the gift is of significant value in itself. Paragraph 6.1 of each of the Codes requires you not to act if there is an own interest conflict or a significant risk of an own-interest conflict. In a situation like this, you will usually need to cease acting if the client does not agree to taking independent legal advice.
>
> There may be some exceptions where you can continue to draft the will even if the client has not received independent legal advice for example, if you draft wills for your parents and the surviving parent wishes to leave the residuary estate to you and your siblings in equal shares.
>
> However, whether it is appropriate to do so will depend upon the specific circumstances of each situation, and in each case you should consider whether your ability to advise, and be seen to advise, impartially is undermined by any financial interest or personal relationship which you have."

The Law Society has a helpful Practice Note, "*Preparing a will when your client is leaving a gift for you, your family or colleagues*" (22 May 2023).

It suggests that a member of the firm who is asked to draft a will making such a gift should consult the firm's compliance officer for legal practice (COLP) the senior responsible officer (SRO) if the firm is a member of the Wills and Inheritance Quality Scheme (WIQS) or a senior experienced practice member. The person consulted must consider potential conflicts of interest and the best interests of the client. The Note continues:

"The COLP, SRO or a senior experienced practice member should consider whether in the circumstances you should not act, unless the client:

- obtains independent legal advice from someone completely unconnected with your firm, and
- provides written confirmation that they have obtained such advice

However, in some circumstances it may be sufficient for the client to confirm in writing that they do not wish to obtain independent legal advice. This will avoid clients incurring the costs of two professional advisors in situations where it is not warranted."

In relation to what is a significant gift it says:

"You should carefully consider any gift to determine whether it may be considered significant in the particular circumstances. You can assume that the following gifts would be considered significant:

- anything worth more than one per cent of the client's current estimated net estate;
- anything that might become more valuable at some point in the future, especially after the death of the client; and,
- anything that provides a benefit to an individual which is more valuable than their relationship to the deceased reasonably justifies.

You should exercise great care if the proposed gift in question is a specific item or items with an uncertain value, like a painting or piece of furniture. If you are in doubt, ask your COLP, SRO or a senior experienced practice member."

4. Force, Fear, Fraud or Undue Influence

Introduction

2-039 If a will is made as a result of force, fear, fraud or undue influence it will not be regarded as the act of the testator and will be refused probate. A person who alleges that a will was made as a result of one of these factors must *prove* it. There are no presumptions to assist in discharging the burden of proof.

Force or fear

2-040 There is little authority on this but, obviously, if it can be shown that a testator made a will only because they were being injured or threatened with injury the will cannot be admitted to probate.

Fraud and undue influence

2-041 Fraud is different from undue influence. In relation to the setting aside of a will it is usually referred to as "fraudulent calumny". The basic idea is that if A poisons the testator's mind against B, who would otherwise be a natural beneficiary of the testator's bounty, by casting dishonest aspersions on his character, then the will is liable to be set aside. The relevant legal principles were summarised by Lewison J in *Re Edwards* (2007) and applied in *Nesbitt v Nicholson* (2013):

- The person alleged to have made the false aspersions must have made them knowing them to be false or not caring whether they are true or false.
- If a person believes that he is telling the truth about a person then even if what he tells the testator is objectively untrue, the will is not liable to be set aside on that ground alone.
- The question is not whether the court considers the disposition of the estate to be fair but whether he acted as a free agent.
- The burden of proof is on those attacking the will.

Although the claim succeeded in *Re Edwards*, accusations of fraudulent calumny often fail because it is impossible to prove that the person knew the accusations to be false. See, for example, *Kunicki v Hayward* (2016) where Mr Recorder Klein, sitting as a Deputy Judge, found that, if the claimant's sister had made statements alleging that he was not to be trusted, the claimant had failed to establish that she did not have an honest belief as to the truth of the representation.

Mr Recorder Klein although clearly considering that he should apply the principles in *Re Edwards* appeared to add the following two requirements:

(i) that the will was made only because of the fraudulent calumny; and
(ii) the false aspersion was made for the purpose of inducing the deceased to alter his testamentary dispositions.

In *Christodoulides v Marcou* (2017), decided shortly after *Kunucki*, there was an appeal from the finding of fraudulent calumny on the basis that the Recorder had found the allegation to be proved without addressing these two additional factors. Morgan J rejected the appeal:

- The first additional requirement was wrong. The use of the word "*only*" should not be understood as requiring a finding that there must have been no other reason operating in conjunction with the effect of the fraud for the testator to change his or her intentions.

- In relation to the second requirement, there were dicta in two House of Lords decisions *Allen v McPherson* (1847) and *Boyse v Rossborough* (1856) which suggested that a challenge to a will based on fraudulent calumny requires the challenger to show that the false representations were made for the purpose of causing the testator to alter his testamentary intentions. However, this point was not taken at the trial and could not be taken for the first time on appeal or witness statement.

Morgan J left open for argument in a later case whether when considering a challenge to a will based on fraudulent calumny, the court should require the challenger to show that the fraud was practised for the specific purpose of inducing the testator to change his testamentary intentions.

A different type of fraud would be obtaining a gift from a testator as a result of pretending to be lawfully married to him. As Lord Langdale said in *Giles v Giles* (1836) it is clear that

> "a legacy given to a person in a character which the legatee does not fill, and by the fraudulent assumption of which character the testator has been deceived, will not take effect".

See also, *In the Estate of Posner* (1953).

Undue influence is something which overpowers the volition of the testator without convincing the judgment; a testator may be persuaded but not coerced. It is often difficult to draw the line between zealous persuasion and undue influence; so long as the testator retained real freedom of choice a court will not interfere but if it can be shown that the testator merely surrendered to intolerable pressure this will amount to undue influence. The court will more readily find undue influence where a testator was weak (whether mentally or physically).

In the case of lifetime gifts there is a presumption of undue influence where a donee stands in a fiduciary relationship to a donor, for example, father and child, doctor and patient, solicitor and client, but there is no such presumption in the case of testamentary gifts. This is because many of the relationships which give rise to the presumption in relation to lifetime gifts are precisely the relationships which would lead a testator to want to make a gift by will. Thus, if there is no positive evidence of undue influence there is no question of refusing probate (*Parfitt v Lawless* (1872)). *Re Good, Carapeto v Good* (2002) is an example of the difficulty of proving undue influence. The court accepted that the circumstances gave rise to a legitimate suspicion of coercion. However, the judge felt that there was insufficient evidence to satisfy him that there had been coercion as opposed to legitimate persuasion. For examples of legitimate persuasion see *Hubbard v Scott* (2011) *and Brennan v Prior* (2013).

In *Barclays Bank v Etridge* (2001) Lord Nicholls, albeit in a different context (the correct procedure to be followed by banks where one party to a marriage is offering the matrimonial home as security for a loan to that party), considered the obligations of solicitors in cases where there may be undue influence. He said that a solicitor has to ensure that the client receives a clear explanation of the nature and consequences of the act in the absence of the person seeking to benefit. It is not necessary for the solicitor to approve of the transaction. However, in a case "where it is glaringly obvious that the wife is being grievously wronged ... the solicitor should decline to act further".

Killick v Pountney (2000) is an example of a successful allegation of undue influence. The court emphasised the importance of taking instructions from the client in the absence of any person who might benefit from the will or exert influence on the client. Undue influence was also successfully pleaded in *Re Edwards* (2007) where there was clear evidence that the deceased's son had poisoned the deceased's mind against the beneficiaries of the original will by making untruthful accusations against them, causing the deceased to change her will in his favour. For further examples of cases where the evidence justified a finding of undue influence see *Pearce v Beverley* (2013); *Schrader v Schrader* (2013) and *Schomberg v Taylor* (2013).

The action which the court will take if fraud or undue influence is proved depends on the effect that the fraud or undue influence produced. If it resulted in the entire will being made in a particular way the entire will is refused probate; if it resulted in a legacy being given to a beneficiary that legacy will fail (*Giles v Giles* (1836); *Kennell v Abbott* (1799)). If a testator was prevented from revoking a will in favour of X and making one in favour of Y the court may allow Y to claim that the property should be held by X on trust for him (*Betts v Doughty* (1879)).

5. Lost Wills

2-042 If a will has been lost or accidentally destroyed it is possible to obtain probate of a copy or reconstruction provided an order is first obtained. If, however, a will which was known to have been in the testator's possession cannot be found after his death there is a presumption that it was destroyed by the testator with the intention of revoking it (*Eckersley v Platt* (1866)). This presumption will have to be rebutted if an order for the proof of a copy or reconstruction is to be obtained.

The strength of the presumption will vary depending on the circumstances of the case. In *Rowe v Clarke* (2005) the court held that "the strength of the presumption in any given case depends on the character of the custody which the testator had over the will". In this case the testator had kept his papers in some disorder and had not attempted to keep the original will secure so the presumption was very weak. There was sufficient evidence to rebut the presumption. Importantly the court also held that the presumption can apply where there is no evidence that the will was not in existence at the date of death. The person claiming revocation does not have to prove non-existence of the will. The presumption was also rebutted in *Nichols v Hudson* (2006) and *Wren v Wren* (2006).

The procedure for obtaining an order is set out in the Non-Contentious Probate Rules 1987 r.54. The same procedure is used where probate of an oral will is sought. The order can be made by a district judge or registrar, but they can require that the matter be referred to a judge of the Family Division. The application must be supported by a witness statement setting out the grounds of the application and by such evidence on affidavit as the applicant can adduce as to:

(a) the will's existence after the death of the testator or, where there is no such evidence, the facts on which the applicant relies to rebut the presumption that the will has been revoked by destruction;
(b) the contents of that will (in respect of an oral will); and
(c) the accuracy of that reconstruction (in respect of a reconstruction of a will).

The district judge or registrar may require additional evidence in the circumstances of a particular case as to due execution of the will or as to the accuracy of the copy will and may direct that notice be given to persons who would be prejudiced by the application. See further para.10-004.

6. Codicils

Definition

A testamentary instrument which is executed in the same way as a will and which supplements the terms of an existing will (either by adding to it, by amending it or by revoking it in part) is usually referred to as a codicil. A codicil must comply with the same requirements as a will if it is to be admitted to probate. **2-043**

Republication

The execution of a codicil to a will "republishes" the will provided there is some indication of an intention to republish. Any reference to the earlier will in the codicil is sufficient to amount to an indication of an intention to republish. When a will is republished it takes effect as if executed at the date of the codicil but with the incorporation of any changes made by the codicil. **2-044**

Republication may affect the construction of a will both in respect of persons and property. In *Re Hardyman, Teesdale v McClintock* (1925) a will made in 1898 gave a legacy to the "wife of my cousin". The wife died with the result that the gift to her lapsed. The testatrix later executed a codicil to her will (which did not refer specifically to the legacy). This republished the will at the date of the codicil. Since the cousin had no wife living at that date the gift in the will took effect as a gift to the first person the cousin married after the date of the codicil.

In *Re Reeves, Reeves v Pawson* (1928) the testator gave his daughter "my present lease" in certain named property. At the time the will was executed the testator owned a short lease of the property. He later took a longer lease of the same property and then executed a codicil which referred to the will. The daughter was held entitled to the new (long) lease which the deceased owned at the date of the codicil.

If a will is altered before its republication and the alteration is not executed then the republication has the effect of validating the alteration. However, there is a presumption that unexecuted alterations were made after the execution of the codicil so that evidence will be required to rebut the presumption.

The republication of a will by a codicil executed by independent witnesses has the effect of saving a gift to a witness of the original will (who would otherwise be deprived of the gift under Wills Act 1837 s.15). This remains so even if the beneficiary witnesses a later codicil.

Revival

A *revoked* will can be revived by re-execution of the will or by execution of a codicil to the will showing an intention to revive. A mere reference to the earlier instrument is not sufficient to revive it; there must be words which make it clear that the effect of that document is being confirmed. A will cannot be revived unless it is still in existence. The effect of revival is the same as republication. **2-045**

The revocation of a will by a codicil is not sufficient to revive an earlier revoked will. Once revoked a will stays revoked unless there is a formal act of revival. For example, a testator makes a will in 1980 and then makes a will in 1981 which revokes the 1980 will. The testator then executes a codicil which revokes the 1981 will. The 1980 will is not thereby revived. The codicil is the only document admissible to probate.

Revocation

2-046 A codicil may expressly revoke an earlier will or codicil in whole or in part. If no express revocation clause is included it will impliedly revoke an earlier instrument to the extent that it is inconsistent with it. Revocation is dealt with in the next section.

7. REVOCATION

Introduction

2-047 The various ways in which wills can be revoked are dealt with in paras 2-049–2-060.

Mutual wills

2-048 A will is always revocable during the lifetime of the testator (unless the testator loses testamentary capacity). A will cannot be made irrevocable. If a testator contracts not to revoke he is still free to do so. However, in that case revocation would be a breach of contract and the testator's estate would be liable to pay damages.

Equity may intervene under the doctrine of mutual wills to impose a trust on a testator's property. This occurs where two or more people make wills in agreed terms and agree that neither will revoke without the consent of the other. The agreement does not have to be included in the will; it can be oral or in writing, incorporated into the will or proved by clear and satisfactory extraneous evidence on the basis of probabilities: *Re Goodchild* and *Re Cleaver (Deceased)* (1981). See also *Fry v Martin Densham-Smith* (2010) where the Court of Appeal accepted the trial judge's inference from the surrounding circumstances that an agreement existed.

If the first to die carries out their part of the agreement, equity will regard it as unconscionable for the survivor to deviate from the agreed terms and will, therefore, impose a trust on the property of the survivor that is subject to the agreement. The survivor remains free to revoke their will but, because of the existence of the trust in favour of the deceased's estate, the new dispositions of the property will be ineffective. The personal representative will take the property subject to a trust in favour of the agreed beneficiaries. Ideally, solicitors should enquire as to the existence of an agreement to leave property in a particular way when taking instructions to change a will and when taking-instructions to act in an administration.

In *Thomas and Agnes Carvel Foundation v Carvel* (2007) the Carvel Foundation was the beneficiary of a mutual will agreement between Thomas and Agnes Carvel. Thomas died first and when Agnes died the Foundation was unhappy with the actions of her executor. The Foundation was unable to remove the executor under s.50 of the Administration of Justice Act 1985 because only a beneficiary of the will can make such an application and the Foundation was a beneficiary of the trust imposed by equity, not a beneficiary of Agnes' will. However, the survivor of two persons who make mutual wills is a trustee and the trust binds those who claim under him. Accordingly, Agnes' executor was a trustee. The Foundation was, therefore, able to apply under s.1 of the Judicial Trustees Act 1896 to remove the unsatisfactory executor/trustee.

The trust "floats" during the lifetime of the survivor and crystallises only on the survivor's death. This means that the survivor is free to deal with the property during their lifetime, which raises some concern as to what happens if the survivor gives away or dissipates the joint assets. In *Re Cleaver* (1981), Nourse J quoted with approval from the judgment of Dixon J in *Birmingham v Renfrew* (1937) in which he said:

> "No doubt gifts and settlements, inter vivos, if calculated to defeat the-intention of the compact, could not be made by the survivor and his right of disposition, *inter vivos* is, therefore not unqualified."

The doctrine of mutual wills applies only where the first party to die does so having carried out the terms of the agreement. In *Re Hobley (Deceased)* (1997) the first party to die had executed a codicil revoking one of the gifts in his will. The court said that it could not attempt to assess the importance of the deviation from the original agreement. An apparently minor alteration by one testator might have sentimental importance to the other. The doctrine of mutual wills required any alteration to have been agreed by both parties. Consequently, the second spouse was not bound by the agreement.

The case of *Re Dale* (1994) confirms that it is not necessary that the testators agree to leave property to *each other*. Equity will intervene to impose a trust on the property of the survivor where the agreement is that each testator shall leave property to a third party, for example, their children.

In *Goodchild v Goodchild* (1996) the Court of Appeal confirmed the first instance decision that in order for wills to be mutual there must be clear evidence of mutual intention not to revoke unilaterally. In *Goodchild*, the evidence was insufficient. However, the court found that the testator's belief that her husband would give effect to what she thought were their mutual intentions, established a moral obligation binding on him. The obligation justified a claim by the adult son under the family provision legislation (see para.20-042).

Lack of evidence of agreement that the wills were not to be revoked unilaterally also caused a claim for mutual wills to fail in *Birch v Curtis* (2002). It is clearly good practice to include a recital of the agreement where it is intended that the doctrine is to apply. In *Charles v Fraser* (2010) the judge was critical of a solicitor who had not recorded the mutual wills agreement.

However, where wills are *not* intended to be mutual it is helpful to include a statement that the parties are free to revoke. It may avoid the waste of costs that arises when unnecessary challenges are made to a will. It would have been particularly useful in *Birch v Curtis* where the court accepted that there was an agreement as to how the surviving husband was to leave his property but no evidence as to whether there was a further agreement not to revoke.

Healey v Brown (2002) demonstrates the significance of the Law of Property (Miscellaneous Provisions) Act 1989 s.2 in relation to mutual will agreements. The section provides that an agreement to dispose of land or an interest in land is unenforceable unless in writing and signed by both parties. In *Healey v Brown* husband and wife had made wills which appeared to be mutual and which agreed that the survivor was to leave the matrimonial home (held as beneficial joint tenants) to the wife's niece. After his wife's death the husband transferred the house into the joint names of himself and his son from an earlier marriage. It was held that because the agreement between the spouses related to land and was not signed and in writing, the doctrine of mutual wills, which requires a legally binding contract, could not apply. The court held that equity can intervene to impose a constructive trust where, as here, it is unconscionable to provide no remedy. However, a constructive trust of this type is limited to the property received from the promisor and cannot affect property already held by the promisee (see *Re Goodchild* (1996)). The only way in which property already held can be impressed with a constructive trust is where the original owner has consented (as is the case with mutual wills). In this case, therefore, the son held the property half for himself absolutely and half for the niece.

In *Olins v Walters* (2007), however, Norris J held that s.2 is only relevant where the agreement is *expressed* to relate to land. In *Olins* the deceased's will simply asked her executors to convert her estate (which included land) and then disposed of the proceeds. In these circumstances the lack of a signed document was not fatal.

In *Legg v Burton* (2017) Paul Matthews J said (at [23]) that to make the success of a claim for mutual wills depend on whether a gift of land in a will is drafted as a gift of a particular interest in land or as a gift of residue happening to contain land seemed to him "rather capricious, even unprincipled". The form of the gift should not defeat its substance. He suggested the necessary equitable obligation to bind the conscience of the testator might arise from a proprietary estoppel rather than from a contract.

Revocation by marriage or formation of a civil partnership

Introduction

2-049 Section 18 of the Wills Act 1837 (as substituted by the Administration of Justice Act 1982) provides that the marriage of the testator automatically revokes any will made before marriage. Section 18B has exactly the same effect in relation to the formation of a civil partnership. There are, however, three exceptions to this rule:

(1) Sections 18(3) and 18B(3)

2-050 Where it appears from a will that at the time it was made the testator was expecting to be married to or to form a civil partnership with a particular person and that they intended that the will should not be revoked by the marriage or formation of the civil partnership, the will shall not be revoked by the marriage or formation of the civil partnership.

These subsections save a will from being revoked provided that two conditions are satisfied:

(a) The testator must have been expecting to be married to or form a civil partnership with a *particular* person at the time of execution. A will made by a testator who expected to marry someone soon after making the will but who had not decided whom to marry would, therefore, be revoked by the subsequent marriage of the testator. It is not, however, required that the testator should be engaged to marry at the time when the will is made.

It must "appear from the will" that the testator is expecting to marry or form a civil partnership with a particular person so that an express statement to that effect should be included. It is probable that in the absence of such a statement a reference to "my fiancée" or "my future civil partner" in the will would satisfy this requirement.

In *Court v Despallieres* (2009) it was held that a will was revoked by the subsequent formation of a civil partnership despite including a statement that the will was not to be revoked by "subsequent marriage, Civil Union Partnership nor adoption". The statement did not satisfy the requirements of s.18B since it was merely a general statement that the will was intended to survive marriage, civil partnership or adoption and it did not show that the deceased expected to form a civil partnership, let alone with a particular person.

(b) It must also "appear from the will" that the testator intended that the will should not be revoked by the marriage or formation of the civil-partnership. There is no guidance in the Act as to how such an intention is to be shown. It is possible that if the will gives substantially all of the testator's estate to the expected spouse or civil partner this condition might be satisfied. However, it is preferable to include an express statement as to the testator's intention in a professionally drawn will. A suitable clause would be:

> "I declare that I make this will expecting to [be married to] [form a civil partnership with][insert name of expected spouse or civil partner] and that I intend that this will shall not be revoked by my [marriage to][civil partnership with] the said [name of expected spouse or civil partner spouse]."

Where such a statement is included, it is helpful to add a declaration that the will is not conditional on the marriage or formation of a civil partnership taking place. This would be the case in any event as wills are never conditional unless there is an express statement to that effect. But including the statement will head off any argument.

Marriage to or civil partnership with any person other than the person indicated in the will revokes the will.

(2) Sections 18(4) and 18B(4)–(6)

Where it appears from a will that at the time it was made the testator was expecting to be married to or to form a civil partnership with a particular person and that they intended that *a disposition in the will* should not be revoked by the marriage or formation of the civil partnership: **2-051**

(a) that disposition shall take effect notwithstanding the marriage or civil partnership

(b) any other disposition in the will shall take effect also, unless it appears from the will that the testator intended the disposition to be revoked by the marriage or civil partnership.

In a professionally drawn will the testator's intention should be made clear by the use of a suitable declaration. For example, the testator may wish to give £10,000 to X notwithstanding the formation of a civil partnership. A suitable declaration would be:

> "I give £10,000 to X and declare that this gift is to take effect notwithstanding the formation of my civil partnership with Y."

If the testator wishes any other dispositions to be revoked by the marriage or civil partnership it must "appear from the will" that this is their intention (ss.18(4)(b) and

18B(6)). If the testator includes a declaration that one disposition is not to be revoked by a marriage or formation of a civil partnership and does not make any such declaration in relation to other dispositions, there will be uncertainty as to whether those other dispositions *are* to be revoked by the marriage or formation of the civil partnership. An express declaration to that effect should be included in the will for the sake of clarity. For example:

> "I declare that all the gifts contained in this will other than the gift to X are to be revoked by the celebration of my forthcoming marriage with Y."

An appointment of executors is not a "disposition" nor are administrative provisions (such as an extension to the statutory power of insurance). Such clauses will, therefore, be revoked by marriage or the formation of a civil partnership even though the dispositive parts of the will are saved from revocation in whole or in part by s.18(4) or s.18B(4)–(6). However, if the entire will is saved from revocation by s.18(3) or s.18B(3) it is clear that the non-dispositive clauses remain effective.

(3) Sections 18(2) and 18B(2)

2-052 The exercise of a power of appointment by will remains effective notwithstanding a subsequent marriage or the formation of a civil partnership. In this case the appointment is saved from revocation whether or not the will is expressed to be made in expectation of the marriage or formation of the civil partnership and whether or not the testator was expecting to marry or form a civil partnership when the will was made. The exercise of a power of appointment is not, however, saved from revocation by s.18(2) or s.18B(2) where the property appointed would pass to the personal representatives of the testator in default of appointment.

Marriage (Same Sex Couples) Act 2013

2-053 This Act allows the marriage of same sex couples. The bulk of the Act came into force on 13 March 2014. From that date all references to marriage, married couples, etc. in existing legislation for England and Wales are amended to include marriage of a same sex couple. References in private legal instruments such as wills and settlements will be construed as including marriage of a same sex couple if the instrument is made after the Act comes into force unless the context provides otherwise.

Section 9(1) provides that existing civil partners may convert their civil partnership into a marriage. There was some uncertainty as to whether such a marriage would revoke existing wills. A subsequent amendment was made to s.18 to provide that the changing of a civil partnership into a same sex marriage does not revoke an existing will or codicil.

Section 2(1) of the Civil Partnerships, Marriages and Deaths (Registration etc) Act 2019 authorised the Secretary of State to make regulations to amend the Civil Partnership Act 2004, so that opposite sex couples are eligible to form civil partnerships in England and Wales (provided that they would be eligible to do so apart from the question of sex). The Civil Partnership (Opposite-sex Couples) Regulations 2019 came into force on 2 December 2019 allowing opposite sex civil partnerships to take place. Part 8 of the Regulations limits the Marriage (Same Sex Couples) Act 2013 to maintain the current position on conversion rights, so that only same sex civil partners can convert their civil partnerships to marriage for the time being. Paragraph 91 of '*Implementing Opposite-Sex Civil Partnerships: Next Steps*' (the government guidance published with the Regulations in July 2019) states:

> "This approach avoids making short-term changes ahead of the outcome of the public consultation on the future of conversion rights conducted earlier this year... Further regulations on conversion rights may follow next year, depending on the outcome of the consultation."

Divorce or dissolution of a civil partnership

Section 18A of the Wills Act 1837 provides that if a marriage is dissolved or annulled by the decree of a court, the former spouse is to be treated for the purposes of any appointment as an executor as having died on the date of the divorce or annulment. If the spouse was appointed as sole executor, the deceased will, therefore, die without an executor requiring an application for letters of administration with the will annexed to be made. However, if any person has been appointed co-executor with the former spouse, that person will remain entitled to take a grant of probate. **2-054**

Section 18A also provides that on dissolution or annulment of a marriage any devise or bequest to the former spouse shall pass as if the former spouse had died on the date of the dissolution or annulment. If the will contains no substitutional gift the property given to the former spouse will, therefore, fall into residue or if itself a gift of residue will pass on intestacy.

Section 18C makes the same provisions in relation to the dissolution or annulment of a civil partnership.

The provisions of ss.18A and 18C are subject to any contrary intention expressed in the will and the failure of gifts to the former spouse or civil partner is expressly stated to be without prejudice to any claim under the Inheritance (Provision for Family and Dependants) Act 1975 (as to which see Ch.20).

It should be noted that ss.18A and 18C apply only to dissolution or annulment decreed by a court. A separation does not, therefore, in any way change the effect of the will of a person who has a spouse or civil partner. A person contemplating separation should always consider making a new will. Furthermore, even when a dissolution or annulment is decreed the only effect is to cause gifts to the former spouse or civil partner to lapse; the will should therefore be reviewed at such time to ensure that it disposes of the property as the testator wishes in view of the changed circumstances.

Re Sinclair (Deceased), Lloyds Bank v Imperial Cancer Research Fund (1985) revealed a problem with s.18A as originally drafted. It provided that in the event of a divorce or annulment, any gift to the spouse would "lapse".

A testator had left property to his wife provided she survived by one month with a substitutional gift to the Cancer Research Fund if she did not so survive. The testator and his wife divorced and the gift to her, therefore, "lapsed". The testator then died and his former wife survived by more than one month. Clearly the wife could not take the gift but the question arose as to whether the substitutional gift to the Fund took effect or whether there was an intestacy. The Court of Appeal held that the word lapse meant no more than "fail" so that a divorced beneficiary was not deemed to have died before the testator. The-substitutional gift to the Fund, therefore, could not take effect. The residuary gift having failed, the property therefore passed under the intestacy rules to the testator's brother. The decision in *Re Sinclair* led to the amendment of will precedents so that substitutional gifts were expressed to take effect "[I]f the gift to my said spouse shall fail *for any reason* ..." to allow the conditional gift to take effect.

The Law Reform (Succession) Act 1995 removed the problem that had been revealed by *Re Sinclair*. The Act amended s.18A of the Wills Act so that where a marriage has been dissolved or annulled the former spouse shall be treated as having died on the date of the annulment or dissolution. The new provisions dealing with civil partnership are also worded in this way. This means that a substitutional gift drafted to take effect "if my spouse predeceases or fails to survive me by [a specified period]" can now take effect where the marriage is dissolved. It is, therefore, unnecessary to include the words "or if this gift fails for any other reason" to cover the possibility of the marriage ending in termination.

Similar substitutional problems continued to exist where a gift in a will failed as a result of the forfeiture rules. The Court of Appeal decisions in *Re Jones (Deceased)* (1997) and *Re DWS* (2001) illustrated this. However, the Estates of Deceased Persons (Forfeiture Rule and Law of Succession) Act 2011 deals with this and similar problems to some extent: see Ch.16.

Destruction

Introduction

2-055 A will may be revoked by "burning, tearing or otherwise destroying the same by the testator or by some person in his presence and by his direction with the intention of revoking the same" (Wills Act 1837 s.20). Both an act of destruction and an intention to revoke are required for this type of revocation. Neither alone is sufficient.

"Burning, tearing or otherwise destroying"

2-056 A physical act of destruction is required; simply crossing out the wording of the will or the signature of the testator or writing words such as "cancelled" or "revoked" across the will is insufficient to revoke. For example, in *Cheese v Lovejoy* (1877) the testator wrote "all these are cancelled" on the will and crossed out part of it. He then threw the will away, but it was found by a servant who preserved it. The will was produced after the testator's death and was held to be valid. Although the testator had intended to revoke the will, he had done nothing which could be regarded as "burning, tearing or otherwise destroying" it. Whether destruction has occurred is a question of degree. For example in *In the Estate of Adams (Deceased)* (1990) parts of the will had been heavily scored through with a ball-point pen. This was held to amount to destruction of those parts. The amount of interference with the will was far greater than mere crossing out.

If the testator destroys part of a will this may amount to revocation of the will as a whole if the part destroyed is sufficiently substantial or important (for example, the attestation clause). However, destruction of part may be treated as revocation of only part where the part destroyed is less important. Thus, in *Re Everest* (1975) the testator cut off the part of the will containing trusts of residue. It was held that the rest of the will remained valid. In *Hobbs v Knight* (1838) the testator cut out his signature from the will. This was held to be a revocation of the whole will. In deciding how far the revocation extends the court will hear evidence of the testator's intention. In the absence of such evidence the court will decide on the basis of the state of the will after the destruction. A testator wishing to revoke a will by destruction should ensure that the will is totally destroyed. However, since doubts may arise after death as to the testator's true intention at the time of destruction it is usually preferable to effect the revocation by means of a further testamentary instrument.

Revocation by destruction is only effective if the testator has completed the intended act of destruction. This is illustrated by the curious case of *Doe d. Perkes v Perkes* (1820) where the testator tore a will into four pieces in the presence of a beneficiary with whom he was angry. He was then restrained from further destruction by a third party and, when his anger had subsided, was heard to say "[I]t is a good job it is no worse"; from this the court inferred that the testator had intended more tearing so the act of destruction was incomplete and the will still valid.

If the destruction is carried out by some person other than the testator, it is only effective if done in the testator's presence and by his direction. A destruction in the absence of the testator or without his direction cannot be ratified by the testator; a further testamentary instrument would be required to revoke the destroyed will.

Intention

The testator must *intend* to revoke the will at the time of the destruction. Accidental destruction does not, therefore, revoke a will nor does destruction by a testator who thinks the will is invalid (since then their intention is merely to destroy an apparently useless piece of paper). **2-057**

If a will known to have been in the testator's possession is not found after their death it is presumed that they destroyed it with intention to revoke it. Similarly if a will is known to have been in the testator's possession and is found torn or otherwise destroyed at their death there is a presumption that the-testator destroyed it with the intention of revoking it. Either of these presumptions may be rebutted (for example, by evidence that the testator kept his papers with such lack of security that the most likely explanation is that the will was lost: see *Rowe v Clarke* and para.2-042).

If a will is destroyed but not revoked (because of lack of intention to revoke or because the destruction was done in the absence of the testator) it remains valid. Probate may be obtained of a copy or reconstruction if the terms can be proved with sufficient certainty (see paras 2-042 and 10-004).

Conditional revocation

Where a will is destroyed with an intention to revoke, the revocation may be intended to be absolute (and therefore immediately effective) or conditional (and therefore only effective if the condition is satisfied). Extrinsic evidence is admissible to prove whether the revocation was conditional. **2-058**

A common reason for revoking a will is that the testator wishes to make a new will disposing of their property in a different way. A testator who has left his estate to X and now wishes to leave it to Y may revoke his existing will before making a new one. If this is done primarily to exclude X from benefit, the court will infer that the revocation of the original will was absolute. If on the other hand it can be shown that the testator wanted to benefit Y but would have preferred X to take rather than those entitled on intestacy, the court will infer that the revocation was conditional on the execution of a valid will leaving the property to Y so that X will take unless a new will has been made. This is often referred to as "the doctrine of dependent relative revocation" since the revocation is dependent on the making of the new will. However, there must be some evidence that the testator's intention to revoke was conditional. For example, in *Re Jones* (1976) the testatrix made a will leaving a smallholding to certain beneficiaries. She later told her bank manager that she wished to leave the smallholding to her nephew because of the beneficiaries' attitude to her and because they had acquired their own property. The testatrix died soon after this conversation and the will was found mutilated after her death (the signatures and the gift of the smallholding having been cut out). The court held that the will was not saved from revocation since the testatrix's intention was to revoke whether or not she was able to make a new will.

The fact that a new will is intended is only one of many things which may lead to the inference that revocation was conditional. For example, in *In the Estate of Southerden* (1925) the testator made a will in favour of his wife. He thought that his wife would take all his property on intestacy and so destroyed the will by burning it. Because of the size of the estate the wife was entitled to only part of the testator's property on intestacy; the court held that the-intention to revoke by destruction was conditional on the wife taking the whole estate. It therefore remained valid as the condition was not satisfied.

In *Re Finnemore (Deceased)* (1991) the deceased made three wills. Each made a gift to C and each contained a revocation clause. C's husband witnessed the second and third wills. On the face of it this meant that C could not take because of the Wills Act 1837 s.15 (see paras 16-038–16-044). However, the court held that the revocation clauses in the second and third wills were conditional on the validity of the gifts contained in them. The clauses were, therefore, ineffective to revoke the gift in the first will to C. They were, however, effective to revoke the rest of the first and second wills.

A testamentary instrument

2-059 A will may be revoked in whole or in part by a later will or codicil or by "some writing declaring an intention to revoke the same and executed in the manner in which a will is ... executed" (Wills Act 1837 s.20).

The clearest way in which a later will may revoke an earlier one is where it contains an express revocation clause. Such a clause should always be included in a new will which deals with the whole of the testator's property. A common form of wording is "I hereby revoke all former wills and testamentary dispositions heretofore made by me". If a codicil is drawn up, great care should be taken with the wording of any revocation clause to ensure that it revokes only those parts of the earlier will which the testator intends to revoke or replace.

Similarly, a revocation clause must be carefully drawn where a client has made a will to deal with foreign property. The revocation clause should either except from revocation the will dealing with the foreign property or be limited to revoking wills dealing with property in a particular jurisdiction, for example England and Wales. Care needs to be taken when limiting a will to a particular jurisdiction. In *The Royal Society v Robinson* (2015) the will was limited to "the United Kingdom" but the testator's major assets were in the Channel Islands and the Isle of Man which are not part of the United Kingdom. The same mistake was made in *Partinngton v Rossiter* (2021). For the problems that can result from unclear drafting, see, for example, *Re Estate of Sangha, deceased* (2023). The deceased had made a will in India in 2007 dealing with both his English and Indian assets. He then made another will in India in 2016 which disposed only of his Indian assets. This contained a clause stating:

> *"This is my last and final WILL and all such previous documents stand cancelled."*

A Deputy Master held that the words could not be clearer and the whole of the 2007 will was revoked.

On appeal a Deputy Judge held that only the parts of the will dealing with the Indian assets was revoked. It was a question of construction, and specifically the word "such" did it mean:

- "all wills stand cancelled", or
- "all will dealing with my Indian property stand cancelled"?

He said that he did not find it easy to say which was the correct interpretation but he found assistance in two material facts:

(1) If the deceased had intended to revoke the will dealing with his English property he would have mentioned the fact or at least alluded to it, and some significance must be attached to his decision not to do so.
(2) There was a plausible alternative explanation for the wording, namely that it was intended to refer to a 2003 will which also related exclusively to the deceased's Indian property.

The Court of Appeal restored the decision of the Deputy Master.

In deciding which will or wills are valid and effective and should be admitted to probate, the court is sitting as a court of probate. As such it is always open to the court to consider the intention of the testator and for this purpose to consider evidence outside the confines of the will in question. It follows that even where a will contains a general revocation clause, there can in any particular case be evidence which establishes that this was not the testator's intention.

However, it is also well established that if a will, duly executed, does contain a general revocation clause, that is in itself powerful evidence that this was the testator's intention and that a "heavy burden" lies on those seeking to establish otherwise.

The Court of Appeal agreed that the clause was a general revocation clause. The natural meaning of the provision that "all such previous documents stand cancelled" is that "such" refers to all previous wills. If the court is to reach some other conclusion it needs some basis in the evidence to do so and, in this case, there was none.

Even without express words of revocation a will or codicil revokes an earlier will or codicil to the extent that it is inconsistent with it.

Example 1

Tamzin makes a will which leaves "everything to Alfred". She then makes a will which leaves "my house to Ben". The will in favour of Alfred remains valid and passes everything except the house.

The doctrine of conditional revocation may apply to save a will (or part of it) from revocation by a later will or codicil. This applies where the revocation (express or implied) in the later instrument is conditional on the effectiveness of that instrument (see, for example, *Re Finnemore (Deceased)* (1991) (see para.2-058)). If the later will starts with a revocation clause but then disposes of the property in a way which is ineffective (for example, because of ambiguity as to the identity of the beneficiary) the court may construe the revocation clause as conditional so that it will not be admitted to probate.

Revocation by privileged testator

A testator who enjoys privileged status (see para.2-014 above) may revoke a will informally whether the will was made informally or not. A testator who makes a **2-060** privileged will while a minor may revoke it while still a minor even if they have lost the privileged status before revoking (Family Law Reform Act 1969 s.3). However, it seems that the revocation cannot then be made by an informal document but only by destruction (if there is a written will capable of -destruction) or by a formal, attested document.

Alterations and obliterations

2-061 Section 21 of the Wills Act 1837 provides that:

> "No obliteration, interlineation or other alteration made in any will after the execution thereof shall be valid ... except so far as the words or effect of the will before such alteration shall not be apparent, unless the alteration shall be executed in like manner as hereinbefore is required for the execution of a will ...".

An alteration made before execution with the knowledge and approval of the testator is valid. However, an alteration in a will is presumed to have been made after execution except that an alteration which completes a blank space in the will is presumed to have been made before execution. Either of these presumptions may be rebutted by internal evidence from the will itself or by extrinsic evidence (for example, a statement from the draftsman or a witness). Once an alteration is shown to have been made before execution it is admissible to probate as part of the will.

An alteration made after execution of the will which is itself signed by the testator and by at least two witnesses is admitted to probate as it complies with the formalities required by the Wills Act 1837. It follows that an alteration which is witnessed is not valid unless the alteration (or the will as altered) is signed by the testator (see *Re White (Deceased)* (1990)). For the avoidance of doubt any alteration to a will, even if made before execution, should be attested. It is sufficient if the testator and witnesses of the will put their initials in the margin next to the alteration.

A slightly different problem arises where words are crossed out or otherwise made more difficult to read without the alteration being attested. If the original wording is "apparent" it is admitted to probate, the crossing out being ignored. Wording is regarded as apparent if it can be read by ordinary means such as close inspection through a magnifying glass or by holding the document up to the light.

Where the original wording is not apparent because it has been scratched out, covered over or otherwise obliterated, it is excluded from probate if the obliteration was made by the testator with an intention to revoke. The effect of obliterating words in this way is that they are revoked.

If the obliteration was made by someone other than the testator or by the testator but without intention to revoke, extrinsic evidence (such as evidence from drafts or copies, infra-red photographs or removal of paper stuck over the words) is permitted to prove the original wording.

Where the testator made the obliteration with a conditional intention to revoke, the court will allow the original wording to be proved by extrinsic evidence and admitted to probate if the condition has not been satisfied. The most likely example of such a conditional intention is that the original wording should only be revoked if substituted wording is admissible to probate. For example, if the will originally says "I give to X the sum of £1,000", the testator obliterates "£1,000" and writes "£1,500" instead—clearly the court can infer that X is to get £1,000 if the substitution of £1,500 is not effective. If the substitution is ineffective because it has not been executed, the court will admit extrinsic evidence to prove the original wording. This is really another example of conditional revocation and the same considerations apply as in the case of conditional destruction (see para.2-059).

Chapter Three

INTESTACY

1. Introduction

There are many advantages to be gained by making a will but the majority of people die without having made one, either out of ignorance of the courses of action open to them, or reluctance to contemplate their own deaths, or from a mistaken belief that, for them, a will is pointless. The devolution of certain assets is fixed irrespective of whether there is a will. Thus, property held as joint tenants passes by the right of survivorship and nominated property passes to the nominee (see Ch.21). **3-001**

The problem where there is no will is to determine who is to share in the other assets of the deceased's estate. The answer is to be found in Pt IV of the Administration of Estates Act 1925, as amended, which lays down who is entitled to an intestate's residuary estate (that is, the deceased's assets after the payment of debts and expenses). The Act specifies the entitlements of the deceased's immediate family; the provisions were based on "the average will" filed with the Probate Registry in the years before 1925, although they have been amended since.

The Inheritance and Trustees' Powers Act 2014 made significant changes to Pt IV of the Administration of Estates Act 1925 for deaths on or after 1 October 2014. This chapter does not consider the earlier rules.

While the intestacy rules ensure that the "next-of-kin" share in the estate, the proportions are arbitrary and therefore often unsuitable; inevitably they give no rights to cohabitants, friends or charities who might have benefited had the deceased made a will.

If cohabitants, relatives or dependants feel that the intestacy rules do not make adequate financial provision for them, they may be able to bring a claim under the Inheritance (Provisions for Family and Dependants) Act 1975 s.1(1) which provides that the court is not bound to assume that the intestacy rules make reasonable provision for the next-of-kin—see Ch.20.

Where property passes as bona vacantia, it may be possible for a deserving claimant to obtain a payment from the Crown, Duchy of Lancaster or Duke of Cornwall. See para.3-023.

2. Total or Partial Intestacy

For the intestacy rules to apply, the deceased must have died either totally or partially intestate. **3-002**

The deceased dies totally intestate if he or she has either made no will at all, has made an invalid will, has revoked any wills that he or she has made or has made a will which does not effectively dispose of any property.

The deceased dies partially intestate if he or she has left a valid will which disposes of only part of his or her estate. This can happen in two ways:

(a) the deceased may have made a valid will which fails to dispose of the whole estate (for example, because it contains no residuary gift). An example of such a will is one leaving money in a building society account to X but not dealing with the rest of the estate; or
(b) the deceased may have made a valid will which dealt with the whole of his or her estate, but the residuary gift may fail in whole or in part (for example, because a residuary beneficiary predeceases the testator and the will does not contain a substitutional gift).

In general the same rules apply whether the deceased died totally or partially intestate. Where there are differences these will be indicated later.

3. UNDISPOSED OF PROPERTY IS HELD ON A STATUTORY TRUST

The general rule

3-003 The Administration of Estates Act 1925 s.33(1) as amended by the Trusts of Land and Appointment of Trustees Act 1996 provides:

> "on the death of a person intestate as to any real or personal estate, such estate shall be held on trust by his personal representatives with the power to sell it."

Section 33(2) provides that:

> "The personal representatives shall pay out of:
>
> (a) the ready money of the deceased (so far as not disposed of by his will, if any); and
> (b) any net money arising from disposing of any other part of his estate (after payment of costs),
>
> all ... funeral, testamentary and administration expenses, debts and other liabilities ... and out of the residue of the said money the personal --representatives shall set aside a fund sufficient to provide for any pecuniary legacies bequeathed by the will (if any) of the deceased."

Partial intestacy

3-004 The statutory trust imposed by s.33 applies to a partial intestacy as well as to a total intestacy. The provisions of the will take precedence over the intestacy rules. Thus, if the undisposed property was left on an *express* trust (for example, T leaves "residue on trust to A and B in equal shares" and A predeceases T), the express trust prevails over the statutory trust. This may appear to be a minor point but will be important if the *terms* of the express trust differ from s.33 (for example, by directing payment of inheritance tax attributable to lifetime gifts made by the deceased).

4. ORDER OF ENTITLEMENT UNDER THE INTESTACY RULES

Order of entitlement under the Administration of Estates Act 1925

3-005 Before considering the detailed rules relating to the entitlements of the beneficiaries it is useful to set out the basic structure of the Administration of Estates Act provisions. First, where there is a surviving spouse or civil partner he or she takes everything unless the intestate also left issue (that is children, grandchildren and remoter lineal descendants one or more of whom satisfy the requirements of the statutory trusts (see para.3-015).

If the intestate left no surviving spouse or civil partner, the estate is distributed as follows:

(a) to issue on the statutory trusts; but, if none, then to
(b) parents absolutely (and equally if both are alive); but, if none, then to
(c) brothers and sisters of the whole blood (i.e. the children of the same parents as the deceased) on the statutory trusts; but, if none, then to
(d) brothers and sisters of the half blood (i.e. those who share one parent with the deceased) on the statutory trusts; but, if none, then to
(e) grandparents absolutely and equally if more than one; but, if none, then to
(f) uncles and aunts of the whole blood (i.e. brothers and sisters of the whole blood of one of the parents of the deceased) on the statutory trusts; but, if none, then to
(g) uncles and aunts of the half blood (i.e. those with one parent in common with one of the parents of the deceased) on the statutory trusts; but, if none, then to
(h) the Crown, Duchy of Lancaster or the Duke of Cornwall as bona vacantia.

Each category must be considered in the order listed above and only if there is *no one* in a particular category is it necessary to consider the next category. Furthermore, since a blood relationship, an adoptive relationship or a relationship under the Human Fertilisation and Embryology Act 2008 is vital under the intestacy rules, the *spouse or civil partner* of a person within one of these categories has no right to share in the estate.

Human Fertilisation and Embryology Act 2008

This Act makes significant changes to the legal definition of the term "parent" with important implications for the application of the above rules in several types of case. **3-006**

(1) Under s.33, where a woman has carried a child as a result of the placing in her of an embryo or of sperm and eggs she, and she alone, is treated as the mother of that child unless the child is subsequently adopted or another person obtains a parental order (as to which see below). Under s.33 the husband of the mother is treated as the child's father unless it is shown that he did not consent to the procedure. Similarly where a woman is artificially inseminated with donor sperm, her husband is the father of the child unless it is shown that he did not consent (s.35).
(2) Where a woman is not married or where her husband is shown not to have consented, another man may, in certain cases, be treated as the father of the child. The main requirements are that the procedures involved are conducted in the UK by persons licensed to provide them and both parties have given written notices of consent to the man being treated as the father which have not subsequently been withdrawn (ss.36–38).
(3) Where a woman is a party to a civil partnership and bears a child as a result of the placing in her of an embryo or of sperm and eggs or as a result of artificial insemination, her civil partner is treated as the other parent of the child unless she is shown not to have consented to the procedure (s.42).

(4) Under ss.43–45 another woman may be treated as the second parent subject to the same conditions, mutatis mutandis, as apply to a man under ss.36–38.

Under s.48 a person treated as the mother, father or parent of the child under these provisions is treated as the mother, father or parent *for all purposes* and "reference to any relationship between two people in any enactment, deed or other instrument or document (whenever passed or made) are to be read accordingly". As far as intestacy is concerned this means that the effect of parenthood under the act stretches beyond the child and its parents. For example, a child who is treated as a child of the mother's civil partner will also be treated as the brother or sister of the half blood of the civil partner's other children and the grandchild of the civil partner's parents.

The Act also provides for parenthood in cases of surrogacy (ss.54–56). This requires an application to the court for a "parental order" within six months of the birth. The child has to have been carried by a woman who is not one of the applicants. The embryo must have been created with the gametes of at least one of the applicants, the applicants must be a married couple, civil partners or living as partners in "an enduring family relationship", they must be both over 18 and at least one of them must be domiciled in the UK, Channel Islands or Isle of Man. The child must be living with the applicants. The woman who bore the child and any other parent of the child (under this Act or otherwise) must consent. The surrogate mother must not have received payment other than for reasonable expenses. Once the order is made the child is effectively treated as adopted by the couple in whose favour the order is made.

5. THE RIGHTS OF SURVIVING SPOUSES AND CIVIL PARTNERS

The spouse's entitlement

Introduction

3-007 The Law Reform (Succession) Act 1995 s.1 introduces a statutory survivorship period for spouses of intestates dying on or after 1 January 1996. The same period applies to civil partners. In order to take an interest on intestacy a spouse or civil partner must survive the intestate for 28 days before taking an interest. As a result of the Marriage (Same Sex Couples) Act 2013, spouse includes a same sex spouse.

For the purposes of the intestacy rules, a divorced spouse has no rights in the deceased's estate and for deaths occurring on or after 1 January 1970, neither has a *judicially* separated spouse, since they are treated as already being dead provided the separation is still continuing (Matrimonial Causes Act 1973 s.18(2)). This is not the case, however, if there is a magistrates' court separation order in effect (see s.18(3)) although no such separation order may be made after the Domestic Proceedings and Magistrates' Courts Act 1978. A civil partner has no inheritance rights after dissolution of the civil partnership nor after a separation order has been made (see Civil Partnership Act 2004 s.57).

When clients consult a solicitor with a view to obtaining a divorce, judicial separation, dissolution of a civil partnership or separation order, the solicitor should ask the clients whether or not they have made wills. If they have not, the solicitor should advise them to make wills since property will pass under the intestacy rules to the spouse or civil partner if the client dies before the final order (the decree absolute in the case of a divorce and the final order in the case of dissolution of a civil partnership). If the clients have existing wills, they should review them in the light of the changed circumstances.

In the case of polygamous marriages *Official Solicitor to the Senior Courts v Yemoh* (2010) decided there can be more than one spouse for the purpose of intestacy rules. The deceased had left eight wives and the court held that together they constituted the surviving "spouse". The statutory legacy would, therefore, be divided amongst the various widows.

The extent of spouse's entitlement to the deceased's undisposed of "residuary estate" depends on whether any issue survived the intestate.

Spouse or civil partner without issue of the intestate If the intestate left a surviving spouse or civil partner but no issue, the personal representatives hold *the whole of the estate* on trust for sale for the spouse or civil partner *absolutely*. No other relatives have any rights to share in the estate. This is not the case, however, for deaths before 1 October 2014 where a surviving spouse might have to share the estate with parents or siblings of the deceased, depending on its value. **3-008**

Spouse or civil partner with issue of the intestate The estate of an intestate who leaves a surviving spouse or civil partner and issue is divided between the spouse or civil partner and the issue. For deaths occurring on or after 1 October 2014, the spouse or civil partner receives: **3-009**

(a) The deceased's "personal chattels" absolutely. "Personal chattels" are defined in Administration of Estates Act 1925 s.55(1)(x) as amended by the Inheritance and Trustees' Powers Act 2014 They are:

> "tangible movable property, other than any such property which—
> - consists of money or securities for money, or
> - was used at the death of the intestate solely or mainly for business purposes, or
> - was held at the death of the intestate solely as an investment".

The effect of the second exception is that items used on some occasions for business purposes can still be personal chattels. For example a car or computer may be used for a mixture of personal and business purposes but provided the usage is *mainly* personal, the item is a personal chattel.

The third exception is intended as a narrow exception for property held solely as an investment which had no personal use at the date of the deceased's death so would not include property which had some personal use but which the deceased also hoped might maintain or increase its value. Gold jewellery would normally be a personal chattel even if bought with a view to its likely future increase in value. Gold bars would not.

The change to the definition has some implications for those drafting wills.

Many wills refer to the s.55(1)(x) definition when making gifts of personal chattels. Section 3(2) of the Inheritance and Trustees' Powers Act 2014 provides that, where a will or codicil, executed before 1 October 2014, contains a reference to personal chattels defined (in whatever form of words) by reference to s.55(1)(x) of the Administration of Estates Act 1925, subject to contrary intention, it will be read as referring to the old definition of personal chattels irrespective of the date of death. **3-010**

The old definition is:

> "carriages, horses, stable furniture and effects (not used for business purposes), motor cars and accessories (not used for business purposes), garden effects, domestic animals, plate, plated articles, linen, china, glass, books, pictures, prints, furniture, jewellery, articles of household or personal use or ornament, musical and scientific instruments and apparatus, wines, liquors and consumable stores, but do not include any chattels used at the death of the intestate for business purposes nor money or securities for money".

(b) A "statutory legacy" payable free of tax and costs, together with interest from death until payment at the Bank of England rate that had effect at the end of the day on which the intestate died. The statutory legacy is

- £322,000 for deaths occurring on or after 26 July 2023.
- £270,000 for deaths occurring before 26 July 2023 and on or after 6 February 2020.
- £250,000 for deaths occurring before 6 February 2020 and on or after 1 October 2014.

In the case of deaths occurring prior to 1 October 2014 different rules apply. A full list of historic values is available in HMRCs' IHT Manual at IHTM12122.

The costs and interest come from the residue of the estate.

The Inheritance and Trustees' Powers Act 2014 inserts a new Sch.1A into the Administration of Estates Act 1925 which requires the Lord Chancellor to reset the statutory legacy every five years. Unless the Lord Chancellor otherwise determines, the statutory legacy will be -"index-linked" by reference to the consumer prices index. The first such order was required to be made within five years of 1 October 2014. In fact the first order (the Administration of Estates Act 1925 (Fixed Net Sum) Order 2020 (SI 2020/33)) was laid before parliament on 14 January 2020). Subsequent orders must be made within five years of the previous order.

The Lord Chancellor is required to make an order increasing the amount of the statutory legacy between five-year review dates if the consumer prices index in any month reaches a figure which is more than 15 per cent above its base amount. The rate of increase will be at the discretion of the Lord Chancellor. When this mechanism is triggered, the five-year period will be reset to commence from the date of such an order. An inflation order was made on 5 July 2023, the Administration of Estates Act 1925 (Fixed Net Sum) Order 2023 (SI 2023/758) was passed, increasing the statutory legacy by almost 20 per cent to £322,000.

(c) If there is anything left in the estate after (a) and (b), the spouse or civil partner receives half of the residue absolutely.

The other half of the residue goes to the issue on the statutory trusts. The statutory trusts are defined at para.3-015.

The special rules applying to spouses and civil partners

Acquiring the matrimonial home

3-011 If the intestate and the surviving spouse or civil partner were joint beneficial tenants of the dwelling house in which the surviving spouse was resident at the deceased's death, the property will pass by survivorship to the surviving spouse or civil partner. If, however, the intestate was the sole owner or held a share as a tenant-in-common, the house or the interest as tenant-in-common in the house will be part of the undisposed-of property. The surviving spouse or civil partner may wish to acquire the house. This can be achieved in a number of ways.

The Second Schedule to the Intestates' Estates Act 1952 (the 1952 Act) gives a surviving spouse or civil partner the right to *require* the personal representatives to appropriate "any dwelling house in which the surviving spouse was resident at the time of the intestate's death" in total or partial satisfaction of an absolute and/or capitalised interest in the estate.

If the dwelling house is worth more than the absolute entitlement of the spouse or civil partner, the personal representative can still be required to appropriate the dwelling house but the spouse or civil partner must then pay "equality money" from his or her own resources to make up the difference (Sch.2 para.5(2)). The house is valued at the value at the date of appropriation, not death (*Re Collins* (1975)). If it is a time of rising property values, it is important to advise a client to make such an election quickly.

The surviving spouse or civil partner must exercise the right within 12 months of the grant of representation (although the court has power to extend the time limit) by notice in writing to the personal representatives.

The surviving spouse or civil partner will frequently be a personal representative of the deceased. If the spouse is one of two or more personal representatives then notice must be given to the other(s). The schedule does not mention the giving of notice where the spouse is the sole personal representative.

A personal representative is in a fiduciary position as regards the estate and, like a trustee, must not profit from that fiduciary position. The schedule provides that where the spouse is one of two or more personal representatives the rule that a trustee should not purchase trust property is not to prevent the purchase of a dwelling house from the estate. The schedule says nothing of the position where a spouse is a sole personal representative. A spouse who is a sole personal representative and who wishes to exercise the right to take a dwelling house ought to do one of the following:

(a) secure the appointment of a second personal representative;
(b) obtain the consent of the other beneficiaries (but this is only appropriate if they are of full age and capacity); or
(c) obtain the consent of the court.

The need for such steps is confirmed by the case of *Kane v Radley-Kane* (1998). The case concerned an appropriation by a surviving spouse of shares under Administration of Estates Act 1925 s.41 rather than an election to take a dwelling house. However, the court referred to the right of election under the 1952 Act. It emphasised the fact that the right only exists where the spouse is one of two or more personal representatives and that a sole personal representative would have to take additional steps.

During the 12-month period the personal representatives need to obtain the written consent of the surviving spouse or civil partner if they wish to dispose of the house, unless they have to sell it to raise money for the administration when there is no other asset available.

When a surviving spouse or civil partner chooses to exercise this right, it does not matter whether the deceased held the freehold or merely a leasehold interest in the house (except where the lease has less than two years to run). However, in four circumstances set out in Sch.2 paras 2 and 4(2) to the 1952 Act, the consent of the court is required before the spouse or civil partner can exercise the right. Such consent is required if the house:

(a) forms part of a building, the whole of which is comprised in the residuary estate;
(b) is held with agricultural land similarly comprised;
(c) as to the whole or part was used as a hotel or lodging house at the death of the intestate; or
(d) as to part was used for non-domestic purposes at the death of the intestate (which would be the case if, for example, part of the house was used as a shop).

In these circumstances, the court must be satisfied that the exercise of the right will not diminish the value of the other residuary assets nor make them more difficult to sell.

If a surviving spouse or civil partner wishes to avoid an application to the court or if the right of election is unavailable for any other reason (for example, expiry of the 12-month time limit) or if the spouse wants to take other assets it is possible to make use of the ordinary power of appropriation contained in s.41 of the Administration of Estates Act 1925. This power allows personal representatives to appropriate assets in or towards satisfaction of pecuniary legacies or entitlement under the intestacy rules provided the legatee or next-of-kin consents and provided no specific legatees are prejudiced. The power is freely available and the court's consent is not normally required. However, the spouse or civil partner has no right to insist on such an appropriation and so must seek the agreement of the personal representatives.

As with the right of election under the 1952 Act a spouse who is a sole -personal representative must take care not to breach the rule against self-dealing. In *Radley-Kane* (1998) the second wife of the intestate acted as the sole administrator, despite the fact that there were children of the intestate, on the basis that the value of the estate was below the limit of her statutory legacy. She appropriated to herself shares in a private company which had been valued for probate purposes at £50,000. Two years after the death she sold the shares for over £1.1 million. The court held that the appropriation of assets in satisfaction of a pecuniary legacy due to a personal representative was in clear contravention of the self-dealing rule. The administrator should either have obtained the consent of the beneficiaries or sought directions from the court. The court did, however, accept that an appropriation without consent would be permitted if the assets were equivalent to cash (for example, government stock or quoted shares).

Redemption of a pre-1 October 2014 life interest

3-012 Where an intestate died before 1 October 2014 and was survived by a spouse or civil partner and issue, the spouse or civil partner was entitled to a life interest in one-half of the residue of the estate instead of an absolute interest.

Section 47A of the Administration of Estates Act 1925 allowed the spouse or civil partner to elect to convert the life interest into a capital sum. The election had to be made within 12 months of the grant of representation (although the court had a discretion to extend it) in writing to the personal representatives (s.47A(6)). If the sole personal representative was the surviving spouse or civil partner, the election was made to the Senior Registrar of the Family Division of the High Court. The formula for determining the capital value of the interest is laid down in statutory instruments, the latest of which is the Intestate Succession (Interest and Capitalisation) (Amendment) Order 2008 (SI 2008/3162).

Abolition of hotchpot

The Law Reform (Succession) Act 1995 s.1(2) abolished the requirement under the Administration of Estates Act 1925 s.49(1)(aa) that surviving spouses bring benefits received by will into account against entitlement on intestacy. Thus, there is no longer any hotchpot requirement for surviving spouses (or civil -partners). This applies in respect of deaths on or after 1 January 1996. **3-013**

6. THE RIGHTS OF ISSUE

General

As we saw in para.3-005, after the surviving spouse or civil partner, the issue are the next category of next-of-kin who share in the deceased's estate. The issue take their share of the estate on the statutory trusts. If a spouse or civil partner survives, the issue take one half of the residuary estate after the statutory legacy has been deducted. **3-014**

If there is no surviving spouse or civil partner then the issue take the whole residuary estate.

The statutory trusts

The "statutory trusts" are set out in the Administration of Estates Act 1925 s.47. Under this section the property is held equally for the children of the intestate who are either alive or *en ventre sa mere* at the date of the intestate's death. The children who satisfy this requirement have a mere contingent interest unless and until they reach 18 or marry or form a civil partnership under that age. **3-015**

If a child dies under 18 and without marrying or forming a civil partnership, the property is dealt with as if that child had never existed.

From 27 February 2023 the Marriage and Civil Partnership (Minimum Age) Act 2022 raised the legal age of marriage and civil partnership in England and Wales to 18 years. The laws on marriage and civil partnerships in Scotland and Northern Ireland are devolved so are unaffected by this change and it continues to be possible to marry or form a civil partnership there from 16.

So far, we have only referred to "children" since it is children who are the primary beneficiaries under this heading. However, if a child predeceases the intestate and that child leaves issue at the date of death, those grandchildren or their issue take *per stirpes* the share which their parent would have taken provided those issue reach 18 or marry or form a civil partnership under that age. No child can take whose parent is living (subject to s.46A of the Administration of Estates Act 1925, discussed below).

Example 1

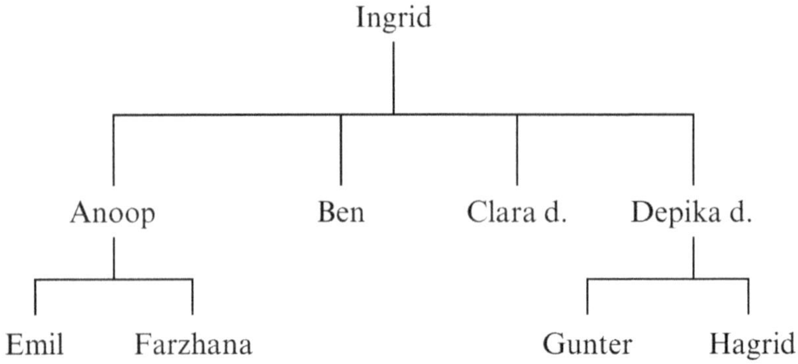

Clara and Depika predeceased Ingrid who died intestate. Anoop, Ben and all the grandchildren are over 18. The estate will be divided into three parts. Anoop and Ben each have vested interests in one-third of the estate. Clara has predeceased the intestate without leaving issue and has no entitlement. Depika has predeceased the intestate but has left issue. Depika's issue divide her one-third share equally between them so that Gunter and Hagrid take one-sixth of the estate each. If Gunter or Hagrid had also predeceased Ingrid but were survived by children, the children would share the property that would have passed to their parent provided they, themselves, satisfy the statutory trusts.

Example 2

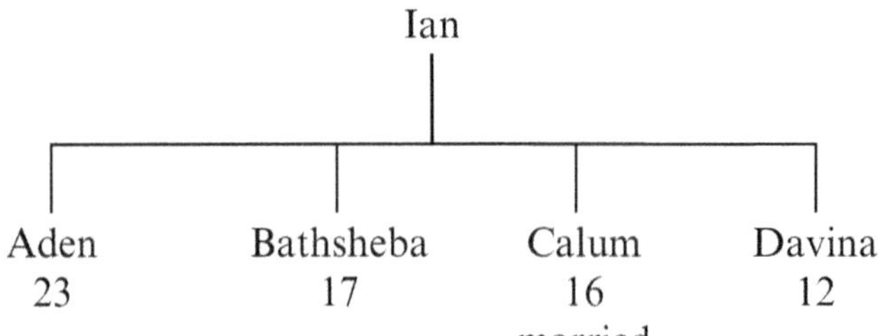

Ian died intestate; all the children survived Ian. Aden and Calum have vested interests immediately on the death of the intestate. If they die before receiving their share of the deceased's property, their share will pass to their estates. Bathsheba and Davina have only contingent interests and, therefore, if either dies without attaining the age of 18 or marrying or forming a civil partnership, her share of the estate will be divided amongst Ian's other children.

Example 3

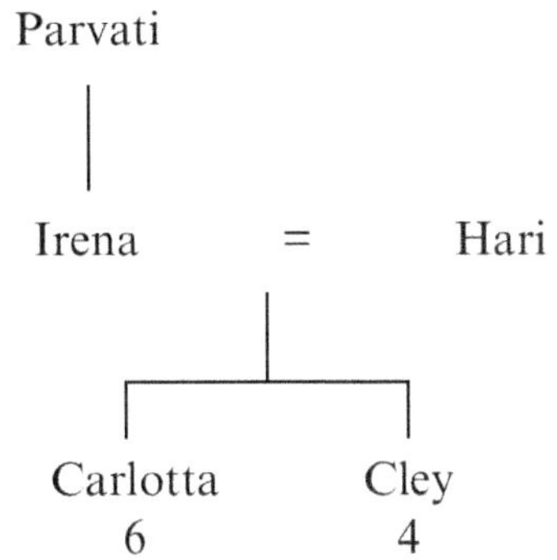

Irena dies intestate in January 2024, survived by her husband Hari, her two children and her mother, Parvati.

Hari, therefore, receives the personal chattels, the £322,000 statutory legacy (plus interest) and one-half of the residue absolutely. The other half of the residue is held on the statutory trusts for the two children. If either dies before reaching the age of 18 or marrying or forming a civil partnership, the property will be held for the other on the statutory trusts. If both die unmarried and before reaching 18, the estate is dealt with as if they had never existed. Hari will be entitled to the half of the residue which had been held on the statutory trusts for the issue.

If Hari dies before the two children, his estate will benefit. This is because the property is distributed as it would have been at the date of Irena's death had neither Carlotta nor Cley existed. Note that Irena's mother, Parvati, has no entitlement.

The rule that no one can take under the statutory trusts whose parent is living has been modified by the new s.46A of the Administration of Estates Act 1925 which was inserted by the Estates of Deceased Persons (Forfeiture Rule and Law of Succession) Act 2011 with effect from 1 February 2012. It provides that a person who disclaims an interest in the estate of an intestate or forfeits it by killing the intestate is to be treated as having predeceased the intestate. The result is that issue can be substituted under the statutory trusts. For disclaimer and forfeiture see paras 16-014 and 16-045.

Before 1 February 2012 there was a problem if a beneficiary with a contingent interest under the statutory trusts died without reaching the age of 18 and without marrying or forming a civil partnership, but with a child. The statutory substitution was only possible where a member of the class predeceased the intestate not where they survived but failed to attain a vested interest.

Section 3 of the Estates of Deceased Persons (Forfeiture Rule and Law of Succession) Act 2011 amends the Administration of Estates Act 1925. The amendment provides that a beneficiary who dies on or after 1 February 2012 with issue but without having reached 18 and without having married or formed a civil partnership will be treated as having died immediately before the intestate. Hence a substitution will be possible.

Example 4

Iolanthe dies intestate with a daughter Diana who is 16 and a single mother of Grace, aged 1. If Diana dies before her 18th birthday without marrying or forming a civil partnership, Grace will be substituted for Diana.

Slightly oddly s.47(1) is not amended and this refers to the substitution of issue "living at the death of the intestate". It would, therefore, appear that a grandchild of the intestate born after the death of the intestate could not be substituted.

In Example 4 therefore if, on Iolanthe's death, Diana was 12 but gave birth to Grace when she was 16 and then died without attaining a vested interest, Grace would not be substituted.

Hotchpot: Abolition of hotchpot

3-016 The Law Reform (Succession) Act 1995 s.1(2) abolishes the requirement under the Administration of Estates Act 1925 ss.47(1)(iii) and 49(1)(a) that children and issue bring lifetime advances and benefits received by will into account against entitlement on intestacy. Thus, there is no longer any hotchpot requirement for children or issue. This applies in respect of deaths on or after 1 January 1996.

Adopted, legitimate and illegitimate children

Adopted children

3-017 For the purposes of entitlement under an intestacy arising on or after 1 January 1976, an adopted child is treated as the legitimate child of its adoptive parent or parents and of no one else. (This rule applies if the adoption order was made by a court in the UK, the Isle of Man or the Channel Islands. The same rule applies to certain foreign adoptions.) The child is thus debarred from claiming on the intestacy of its natural parents and is treated as a child of the adopting parents. Such a child may therefore be entitled to take on the intestacy of adoptive grandparents and brothers and sisters. Conversely, inheritance rights as a member of the "birth" family will normally be lost.

Adoption and Children Act 2002 s.69 provides that this rule does not prejudice an interest vested in possession in the adopted person before the adoption or an interest expectant (whether immediately or not) upon such an interest. This did not assist a child with a contingent interest under the statutory trusts arising on intestacy. The problem was recognised in *S v T* (2006), shortly before a five-year-old boy was adopted. The court agreed to use its powers under the Variation of Trusts Act 1958 to vary the terms of the statutory trusts to preserve the boy's rights to his intestate father's estate. For adoptions occurring on or after 1 October 2014 the Inheritance and Trustees' Powers Act amends s.69 to preserve

> "any contingent interest (other than a contingent interest in remainder) which the adopted person has immediately before the adoption in the estate of a deceased parent, whether testate or intestate".

The provision is limited to rights to a parent's estate and will not preserve the child's contingent interest in the estate of other members of the birth family.

Legitimated children

3-018 Sections 5(1)–(4) and 10(1) of the Legitimacy Act 1976 provide that a legitimated child is entitled to share on a deceased's intestacy as if it had been born legitimate.

Children whose parents were not married at the time of their birth

3-019 In the case of deaths occurring before the coming into force of the Family Law Reform Act 1987 (the 1987 Act), an illegitimate relationship was not recognised for the purposes of distribution of property on intestacy subject to two limited exceptions.

In respect of deaths occurring after 4 April 1988, the distribution of assets on intestacy (and otherwise) is to be determined without regard to whether or not the parents of a particular person were married to each other.

Protection of personal representatives

Section 20 of the 1987 Act removes the protection which existed under the old law for personal representatives who distributed property in ignorance of the existence of illegitimate claimants. Prima facie, it appears, therefore, that personal representatives should undertake investigations to discover whether or not there are hitherto unknown relatives of the deceased alive whose parents were not married. Presumably, however, the protection against claimants of the estate available generally to personal representatives under the Trustee Act 1925 s.27 and the *Benjamin Order* procedure (see para.14-009) extends to cover the claims of persons whose parents were not married. Moreover, s.18(2) of the 1987 Act makes special provision for the administration of an intestate's estate. It provides that where the parents of a child who dies intestate were not married to each other at the time of that child's birth there is a presumption that the child has not been survived by "his father or by any person related to him only through his father". Thus, personal representatives will be able, in the absence of evidence to the contrary, to distribute on the basis that no such persons are alive. **3-020**

Section 43 of the Human Fertilisation and Embryology Act 2008 (see 3-006 above) allows a child to have a second female parent. The s.18(2) presumption also applies to second female parents (see the Family Law Reform Act 1987 s.18(2A)).

The Children Act 1989 has been amended to provide automatic parental responsibility for an unmarried father or second female parent provided they are named on the birth certificate. They did not previously have parental responsibility. For deaths on or after 1 October 2014 the Inheritance and Trustees' Powers Act 2014 disapplies the s.18(2) presumption where the father or other female parent is registered as the child's parent.

Example 5

(1) X, whose parents have not married, dies intestate without a spouse, civil partner or issue. He is known to be survived by his mother, but nothing is known of his father or of his father's relatives. X's mother will take the whole estate since the personal representatives are entitled to presume that the father and the father's relatives have predeceased X.

(2) As above, X, whose parents did not marry, has died intestate without a spouse, civil partner or issue. His mother is dead and the only relative on his mother's side still living is her brother of the whole blood (X's maternal uncle). Nothing is known of X's father or of any of the father's relatives except that the father's brother of the whole blood is known to be alive (X's paternal uncle). X's estate will be divided between the two uncles. X's personal representatives are entitled to presume that the father and father's relatives other than the brother have predeceased X.

(3) Had X's father (or second female parent) been registered as a parent, the presumption would not apply.

Human Fertilisation and Embryology Act 2008

3-021 As we have already seen (para.3-006) a child may be treated as the child of one or both parents as a result of the provisions of this act.

7. THE RIGHTS OF OTHERS

3-022 It should be noted that the other relatives who take on the statutory trusts (that is brothers and sisters of the whole and half blood and uncles and aunts of the whole or half blood) must fulfil the same requirements as issue; that is, they must be living at the intestate's death and reach 18 or marry earlier. A person who predeceases the intestate can be replaced *per stirpes* by their own issue provided they reach the age of 18 marry or enter a civil partnership earlier.

8. BONA VACANTIA

3-023 In the case of property passing as bona vacantia s.46(1)(vi) of the Administration of Estates Act 1925 gives the Crown a discretion to make provision for dependants of the intestate whether they are related to the deceased or not. Similarly the Crown may provide for "other persons for whom the intestate might reasonably have been expected to make provision".

If the intestate died resident within the Duchy of Lancaster or in Cornwall, the Duchy or the Duke of Cornwall respectively take the assets as bona vacantia subject to the same discretions.

When deciding whether to make a discretionary grant, and deciding upon its value, the Treasury Solicitor is likely to consider the factors which the court must consider when exercising its jurisdiction under the Inheritance (Provision for Family and Dependants) Act 1975 (the 1975 Act).

Potential applicants for a discretionary payment do not have to be eligible to make a claim under the 1975 Act.

There may be circumstances where it is advantageous to claim under bona vacantia rather than under the 1975 Act. For example, cohabitants who claim reasonable financial provision under the 1975 Act can only receive what is reasonable for their maintenance. There is no such restriction on claims under the bona vacantia jurisdiction.

That said, it is rare for estates to be genuinely bona vacantia. Genealogists are so skilled that they will normally be able to trace next of kin.

CHAPTER FOUR

INHERITANCE TAX

1. INTRODUCTION

Definitions

Inheritance tax is, prima facie, payable where there is a *chargeable transfer*. A chargeable transfer is defined as "*any transfer of value* which is made to an individual but is not ... an exempt transfer" (Inheritance Tax Act 1984 (IHTA 1984) s.2(1)). A transfer of value is defined in IHTA 1984 s.3(1) as **4-001**

> "a *disposition* made by a person ... as a result of which the value of his estate immediately after the transfer is less than it would be but for the disposition ...".

The amount by which the value of the transferor's estate is less as a result of the disposition is the *value transferred* on which inheritance tax is prima facie payable.

Lifetime transfers of value occur as a result of gifts of property or sales at an undervalue. Section 4 of the IHTA 1984 provides that a deceased person is to be treated as if they had made a transfer of value immediately before their death the value of which is equal to the value of their whole estate immediately before death.

The "estate" is the aggregate of all the property to which a deceased person was beneficially entitled immediately before death (IHTA 1984 s.5) apart from certain types of interest in possession (IHTA 1984 s.5(1)(a)(ii)) and excluded property (IHTA 1984 s.5(1)(b)). In fact the charge on death is the most important type of charge as lifetime transfers are normally exempt or potentially exempt (in the latter case they become exempt if the donor survives seven years) unless they are to settlements, in which case they are normally immediately chargeable.

The structure of inheritance tax is rather complicated as the outline above will show. This is largely because the tax is a modification of capital transfer tax. Capital transfer tax was a tax on both lifetime and death transfers (with far less extensive exemptions than apply to inheritance tax). The Act which is now called the IHTA 1984 was formerly the Capital Transfer Tax Act 1984. That Act in its unamended form continues to apply to certain transactions entered into before 18 March 1986. References in documents (for example, wills) made before that date to capital transfer tax are taken as references to inheritance tax.

Occasions of charge to inheritance tax

There are three categories of transfer which can give rise to inheritance tax (exemptions or reliefs may be available to extinguish or reduce a charge—these are dealt with later). **4-002**

(a) *A transfer on death.* Such a transfer is taxed at the full rates of tax.

(b) *A potentially exempt transfer.* This is defined in IHTA 1984 s.3A as a lifetime transfer of value made on or after 18 March 1986 by an individual, which would otherwise be chargeable, whereby property becomes comprised in the estate of another individual to the extent that it constitutes a gift:
   (i) to another individual;
   (ii) into a disabled trust;
   (iii) made before 22 March 2006 into an accumulation and maintenance trust or a trust with a qualifying interest in possession; or
   (iv) made on or after 22 March 2006 into a trust for a bereaved minor or young person on the coming to an end of an immediate post-death interest.

   The most common example of a potentially exempt transfer is an outright gift to an individual. However, a potentially exempt transfer can arise when the transferor omits to exercise a right (such as by failing to sue on a debt).

   The taxation of settlements and trusts is dealt with in Ch.7 but, as we will see there, before 22 March 2006 a transfer of value by an individual into a settlement with an interest in possession was a potentially exempt transfer.

   A potentially exempt transfer becomes fully exempt if the transferor survives seven years after the transfer. If they die within seven years the transfer becomes chargeable at the rates in force at the date of death (see para.4-014 for the calculation of tax and the reduction where the transferor survives more than three years).

(c) *A chargeable transfer* made before death. This type of transfer is immediately taxable but at only half the rates which apply on death. If the transferor dies within seven years, the transferee becomes taxable at the full rates in force at the date of the death with a credit for tax already paid.

   As a result of changes introduced by the Finance Act 2006 most lifetime transfers made to settlements on or after 22 March 2006 are chargeable. The only exceptions are a transfer to a trust for a disabled beneficiary or a transfer to a trust for a bereaved minor or young person following the lifetime termination of an immediate post-death interest (see Ch.7). Lifetime transfers made before 22 March 2006 to settlements were chargeable only if they were to a settlement without a qualifying interest in possession which did not qualify as an accumulation and maintenance settlement (see Ch.7).

   In addition to transfers to settlements, lifetime chargeable transfers can arise in relation to events occurring within settlements without a qualifying interest in possession; for example, anniversary charges and exit charges (see Ch.7).

2. THE ESTATE ON DEATH

What is included?

4-003 Section 5 of the IHTA 1984 provides that a person's estate is the aggregate of all the property to which they are beneficially entitled at the moment before death other than excluded property and certain interests in possession (see IHTA 1984 s.5(1)(a)(ii)). A person who has a general power which enables them, or would if they had the necessary capacity enable them, to dispose of any property as they think fit shall be treated as beneficially entitled to that property. This provision has enabled HMRC to include in a death estate the whole of a bank account which was held in joint names but which, in reality, was operated for the benefit of only the deceased. See *Sillars v IRC* (2004); *Perry v CIR* (2005); *O'Neill v IRC* (1998). The provision was used in *Kempe v CIR* (2004) to include the proceeds of a life policy which the policy holder had designated in favour of family members. The terms of the designation were unusual in that the policy holder had the right to change the designation at any time.

The estate at death also includes property subject to a *donatio mortis causa* (a gift made before death in anticipation of death and conditional upon it occurring). Although delivery of the asset or the means of obtaining it will have been made, the property given will still be treated as part of the deceased's estate for inheritance tax purposes.

Beneficial entitlement does not include property held in a fiduciary capacity. In *Anand v IRC* (1997) bank accounts held in the name of the deceased were held not to be part of the estate because they represented "family money" held by him in a fiduciary capacity as "treasurer" for the family as a whole.

The deceased's beneficial interest in property passing by survivorship is part of the estate because the deceased was entitled to it immediately *before* the death.

The estate will include the value of the property held in a settlement in which the deceased had an interest in possession if:

(a) the interest was in existence on 22 March 2006; or
(b) the interest is:
    (i) an immediate post-death interest;
    (ii) a transitional serial interest; or
    (iii) a disabled person's interest.

As a result of s.5(1B) (inserted by the Finance Act 2010 to prevent tax avoidance), the estate will include interests in possession to which a person becomes entitled on or after 9 December 2009 where the original transfer was not a transfer of value because it fell within IHTA 1984 s.10 (no gratuitous intent). Settled property is discussed in Ch.7.

Excluded property

Excluded property does not form part of the owner's estate on death for inherit- **4-004**
ance tax purposes so that, in effect, it is exempt from tax (s.6(1)). As far as lifetime transfers are concerned the position is slightly more complicated. A lifetime transfer of excluded property is not a chargeable or potentially exempt transfer unless the transfer causes a reduction in value of non-excluded property in which case there is, to the extent of that reduction, a chargeable or potentially exempt transfer as the case may be.

There are three main categories of excluded property:

(a) Reversionary interests in settled property unless, as provided in IHTA 1984 s.48:
    (i) acquired for money or money's worth;
    (ii) vested in the settlor or settlor's spouse; or
    (iii) expectant on a lease for life at a nominal rent;
(b) Most types of property situated outside the UK and owned by a person domiciled outside the UK and some types of property situated in the UK but owned by a person not domiciled in the UK (IHTA 1984 s.6); but see the rules on deemed domicile at para.4-005 and-following below; and

(c) Settled property situate outside the UK provided the settlor was domiciled outside the UK when the settlement was made.

Section 6(1B) and 6(1BA) of IHTA 1984 provide for deaths on or after 3 December 2014 that a decoration or other award awarded:

- for valour or gallant conduct;
- for or in connection with, a person being, or having been, a member of the armed forces of any country or territory, or an emergency responder within the meaning of IHTA 1984 s.153A (emergency service personnel etc. see para.4-059);
- for, or in connection with, public service or achievement in public life;

is excluded property provided it has never been the subject of a disposition for a consideration in money or money's worth.

Finance Act 2019 inserted a new Sch.A1 into IHTA 1984 designed to bring into charge UK residential property owned through overseas companies or partnerships. It provides that an interest in a close company or partnership is not excluded property if the value of the interest is directly attributable to a UK residential property interest. An interest in a close company or partnership is disregarded if the value of the interest is less than five per cent of the total value of all the interests in the close company.

Loans are not excluded property if and to the extent that money or money's worth made available under the loan is used to finance, directly or indirectly, the acquisition by an individual, a partnership or the trustees of a settlement of a UK residential property interest.

References to a loan in the schedule include an acknowledgment of debt by a person or any other arrangement under which a debt arises; and in such a case references to money or money's worth made available under the loan are to the amount of the debt.

Deemed domicile

Why have deemed domicile rules?

4-005 A person can retain their domicile of origin despite residing in another country for many years. (See para.20-002 and following for a fuller discussion of changing domicile.)

The UK has had deemed domicile rules for many years. Initially deemed domicile rules applied for inheritance tax only, but Finance (No.2) Act 2017 extended them to capital gains tax and income tax as well as toughening the rules.

Note that following the announcement in the Budget of Spring 2024 that the government would bring to an end the non-dom' tax regime, there will be a consultation to move from a domicile-based system for UK inheritance tax (IHT) to a residency based one with effect from 6 April 2025.

The rules before 2017

4-006 IHTA 1984 s.267 provided that a person was deemed domiciled in the UK once they had been resident for not less than 17 out of the last 20 tax years. This was often less than 17 full calendar years of residence. For example, if a person arrives in the UK part-way through a tax year, but spends sufficient time here to become resident, the period for deemed domicile will start from the previous April, being the start of the tax year in which the client became tax resident.

If a person who had acquired deemed domicile under the 17/20 rule ceased UK residence for at least four complete tax years, they lost their deemed domicile status from the start of the fourth year of non-residence. This was because if they remained non-resident in the fourth year, they would no longer have been UK resident for 17 of the previous 20.

Changes introduced by Finance (No.2) Act 2017

New deemed domicile rules were introduced which apply as from 6 April 2017. **4-007**

They apply for income and capital gains tax purposes, not just inheritance tax, although there are some differences to reflect the fact that a charge to inheritance tax is a much more serious thing for an individual than a charge to income tax or capital gains tax.

There are two new rules.

Rule 1: the 15 of previous 20 rule. For income tax and capital gains tax purposes a person is deemed domiciled if resident in the UK for at least 15 of the 20 tax years immediately preceding the relevant tax year.

For inheritance tax purposes an individual is deemed domiciled if resident in the UK:

(a) for at least 15 of the 20 tax years immediately preceding the relevant tax year, and
(b) for at least one of the four tax years ending with the relevant tax year.

The effect of (b) is to replicate the previous position on losing domicile under the 17 out of 20 rule. A deemed UK domicile will cease for inheritance tax purposes after four tax years of non-residence.

Note, however, that if the individual returns to the UK within six tax years, they will immediately become deemed domiciled for inheritance tax because they will fulfil the 15 out of 20 test.

Rule 2: the "formerly domiciled resident" rule. This change is designed to deal with the situation (regarded as abusive) of a person who was born in the UK and whose domicile of origin was in the UK and who works abroad, acquires a domicile of choice in the new jurisdiction and then returns to the UK claiming to still be domiciled in the new jurisdiction. Rather inelegantly, such persons are referred to in the legislation as-"formerly domiciled residents" (FDR).

As an example of the mischief at which this second new rule is aimed consider the following example:

Example 1

Jasper was born in the UK and whose domicile of origin was in the UK. He worked in Hong Kong and diligently acquiring a domicile of choice there. On returning to the UK he claims to retain his Hong Kong domicile of choice and was therefore entitled to be taxed only on income and gains remitted here.

An individual is now deemed domiciled for income tax and capital gains tax if:

(a) the individual was born in the UK,
(b) the individual's domicile of origin was in the UK, and
(c) the individual is UK resident for the relevant tax year.

FDRs are treated as UK domiciled for income tax and capital gains tax purposes where they are UK resident for the tax year in which the relevant time falls (Income Tax Act 2007 s.835BA(2) and (3)).

Therefore, from 6 April 2017, a FDR will acquire a deemed UK domicile for income tax and capital gains tax purposes as soon as they become UK resident (that is, from the start of the first tax year in which they assume or resume UK residence).

Example 2

Rufus was born in the UK in 1975 with a UK domicile of origin. He acquires a domicile of choice in Monaco in 2010 but becomes resident in the UK on 1 January 2024 (he retains his domicile of choice in Monaco). He is deemed domiciled in the UK for 2024/25. It does not matter how many years Rufus spent abroad nor his reasons for resuming UK residence. He loses FDR status for income tax and capital gains tax purposes in the first year when he becomes non-resident.

For inheritance tax there is an additional requirement:

(d) the individual is resident in the UK for at least one of the two tax years immediately preceding the relevant tax year.

The relaxation for inheritance tax reflects the fact that acquiring domicile for inheritance tax purposes has such serious tax consequences: worldwide assets become subject to inheritance tax.

Example 3

If Rufus in the previous example dies on 5 April 2024 he would not be deemed domiciled for inheritance tax. If he dies on or after 6 April 2024 (still UK resident) then he is deemed UK domiciled so that his worldwide estate is subject to inheritance tax, including property in trusts set up when he was not UK domiciled.

Changes for 2025 onwards

4-008 In the June 2024 Budget, the then Chancellor of the Exchequer, Jeremy Hunt, announced changes to the "non-dom" remittance basis of taxation for foreign income and gains. The Labour Party, then in opposition, had been advocating such changes.

Treasury proposals in the June 2024 Budget were as follows:

- From 6 April 2025, new arrivers to the UK, or individuals returning to the UK after at least 10 years overseas, could elect not to be taxed on their foreign income or gains during the first four years of UK tax residence (the FIG regime). They would also be able to bring such funds into the UK without further tax (albeit that bringing the funds into the UK could expose them to inheritance tax as they would then become UK situated assets).
- Current remittance basis users who had been in the UK for fewer than four tax years on 6 April 2024 would be eligible for the FIG regime for the remainder of their first four years of UK tax residence.
- Individuals who had already been resident in the UK for four tax years on 6 April 2025 would not be eligible for the FIG regime and would be subject to UK taxation on their worldwide income and gains.
- Generous transitional arrangements would apply to those moving from the remittance basis.

As explained at 4-008 above, a consultation on the IHT treatment of "non-doms" was announced.

The general election intervened. A Labour government was elected. Labour had broadly supported the Spring Budget changes. On 29 July 2024, they released a policy document confirming they will abolish the tax regime for non-doms and replace it with a new residence-based regime from 6 April 2025. The proposals mirror those announced by the Conservative Government, but transitional relief will be less generous than that originally proposed.

There will be a rebasing of foreign capital assets for certain individuals with the rebasing date expected to be announced at the Autumn Budget (30 October 2024). Business Investment Relief will continue to be available.

A Temporary Repatriation Facility for FIG that arose to former remittance basis users before 6 April 2025 will be introduced, albeit the rate of tax and the length of time are not confirmed. The government say that they wish to make the Repatriation Facility as attractive as possible and details on whether it may also extend to stockpiled income and gains in offshore structures will be confirmed at the Autumn Budget.

There will now be no formal consultation on the proposals to bring in a residence-based test for inheritance tax (IHT). Instead, the government will review stakeholder feedback and carry out further engagement over the summer.

The new rules will apply to IHT on chargeable events occurring on or after 6 April 2025 and the test for whether overseas assets are within the scope of IHT will be whether a person has been UK resident for 10 tax years prior to the year of the chargeable event. Once you meet this 10-year test, you stay within the UK IHT net for the next 10 years whether resident in the UK or not. Consequently, individuals would need to be non-UK tax resident for at least 10 years after leaving the UK to be outside of IHT.

Deaths occurring before 6 April 2025 will be subject to the current rules.

In addition, the use of Excluded Property Trusts to exempt overseas assets from IHT will end. More details on these rules, together with potential transitional arrangements is expected to be published at the Autumn Budget.

Deductible Liabilities

Liabilities are taken into account in valuing a transferor's estate to the extent that they were incurred for consideration in money or money's worth or imposed by law (IHTA 1984 s.5) and provided there is no right to reimbursement (IHTA 1984 s.162(1)). **4-009**

In the case of death, the value of the estate for tax purposes is the net amount after deducting debts (and other liabilities incurred for consideration) and liabilities imposed by law (such as a liability to pay damages in tort). Certain liabilities are non-deductible (see paras 4-010–4-011).

Reasonable funeral expenses can be deducted (IHTA 1984 s.172) including a reasonable sum for mourning for family and servants. The cost of a gravestone or tombstone is also deductible. Paragraph IHTM10373 of HMRCs' *IHT Manual* states that in deciding what is reasonable HMRC should take account of the deceased's background and profession and may

> "distinguish between a gravestone and a memorial, which could be a plaque inside a church or a memorial monument. This is because a memorial is not strictly allowable as a reasonable funeral expense".

Paragraph 10371 states that deductions claimed should be accepted without enquiry unless the expenses seem to be: "wholly unreasonable or large in relation to the estate as a whole, or inconsistent with information on the file."

A mortgage or other liability which is an incumbrance on particular property is normally taken as reducing the value of that property (rather than the estate generally) so far as that is possible (but see para.4-011 for special rules applying where liabilities are incurred to finance the purchase of relievable property). This rule is unimportant where the whole net value of the estate is taxable anyway, but it is significant where exemptions, such as the spouse exemption (see para.4-049 and following), are available.

For example, an estate consists of a house worth £100,000 and £100,000 of investments. The house is subject to a mortgage of £10,000. The value of the estate on death is, therefore, £190,000 for tax purposes. If the house is given to the spouse of the deceased and the investments to the children an asset worth £90,000 will pass to the spouse and will be exempt (since the mortgage reduces the value of the property given to the spouse). The remaining £100,000 will be regarded as passing to non-exempt beneficiaries and, therefore, chargeable to inheritance tax. If the mortgage could reduce the inheritance tax value of the investments, a house worth £100,000 would have passed to the spouse (and been exempt) leaving £90,000 to be regarded as passing to the non-exempt beneficiaries (and chargeable to inheritance tax).

The rule is also significant where the estate includes property eligible for 100 per cent business or agricultural property relief. For example, an estate consists of property worth £100,000 eligible for 100 per cent business property relief and quoted shares worth £100,000. There is a liability of £100,000. If the liability is charged on the property eligible for relief, it will reduce the value of that property leaving the £100,000 of quoted shares chargeable to tax. If the liability is charged on the quoted shares, none of the estate will be chargeable to tax. However, the rules have been changed for debts incurred on or after 6 April 2013. See 4-020 below.

Unrelieved debts of an insolvent deceased are not deductible from the value of settled property in which the deceased had an interest in possession at the date of death: see *St Barbe Green v IRC* (2005). The same principle applies where property is treated as part of the estate under the reservation of benefit rules.

The fact that a guarantee in support of a business has been charged over a particular asset does not mean that the asset is a business asset: see *IRC v Mallender* (2001).

Incidental costs of transferring assets are ignored in calculating the value transferred unless they are incurred by the transferee in which case they reduce the value transferred. This rule has no application to transfers on death because the transfer on death (which takes place for tax purposes the moment before death) is an automatic transfer on which no incidental costs can arise.

Where an estate includes property situated outside the UK, an allowance is made against that property for any expense incurred in administering or realising the property which is shown to be attributable to the situation of the property. The allowance cannot exceed five per cent of the value of the property.

A liability to pay an insurance company a sum from the death estate in return for a payment from the company is not deductible unless the policy proceeds form part of the death estate.

Non-deductible debts: Finance Act 1986, s.103

4-010 Section 103 of the Finance Act 1986 provides that a liability consisting of a debt incurred by the deceased or an incumbrance created by them shall not be deductible to the extent that the consideration given for the debt consists of "property derived from the deceased".

Example 4

Mother gives money to son who lends it back to her. On mother's death the debt owed to the son is not deductible.

The so-called "loan" or nil-rate band debt arrangement involves a surviving spouse or civil partner incurring a liability to a nil rate band discretionary trust created by the first spouse or civil partner to die. The survivor enjoys the combined assets of the couple but the debt reduces the value of their estate on death. This arrangement was very popular before the introduction of the transferable nil-rate band as a way of allowing the first spouse to die to make use of their nil-rate band while allowing the surviving spouse to have the benefit of the couple's combined assets. It is also a useful way of reducing the value of the survivor's estate for the purposes of the residence nil rate band taper threshold (as to which see 4-019 below).

Section 103 could cause problems in relation to such schemes.

First, let us look at an example showing the circumstances in which the debt arrangement might be used.

Example 5

The first spouse to die (H) gives a nil-rate band legacy to a discretionary trust for the benefit of his wife (W) and children and the residue of the estate to W. The estate is £425,000 of which the matrimonial home is £325,000. Instead of the executors using liquid funds to pay the legacy, they transfer all the assets to W and either:

(1) accept an IOU from W which they then give to the trustees of the nil-rate band settlement; or
(2) transfer the assets to W subject to a charge for the amount due to the trust.

W has the use of all the assets and when she dies there is a liability which reduces the value of her estate. HMRC accept that the arrangement works when "properly drafted".

The will must give the trustees power to accept the debt in lieu of cash and should relieve them from liability if there are insufficient funds to pay off the debt when W dies.

Now let us look at the circumstances in which s.103 might present a problem.

Example 6

The facts are as above but some time before H's death W gave H a substantial gift as part of an equalisation of estates exercise. If W incurs a debt in connection with H's estate, HMRC will argue that s.103 makes the debt non-deductible. HMRC was successful with this argument in the case of *PRs of Phizackerley v HMCR* (2007).

If a couple want to use the debt arrangement and s.103 may be a problem because one spouse has made gifts to the other, a solution is for the first to die to leave the residue to the survivor for life so that it is the trustees of the settlement who incur the debt, not the spouse.

Another possibility is for the executors to charge the assets transferred to W with the debt so that W does not "incur" the debt. The debt must be a non-recourse debt meaning that the trustees have no right to recover the debt from the surviving spouse. The trustees must only be able to recover from the proceeds of sale of the charged property. This was the most common route as it avoids liability to stamp duty land tax. However, s.103 problems can still arise if the house is sold and the trustees then advance funds to W for the purchase of a replacement property in return for an IOU. In such a case, provided the trustees have power to do so, they should use the funds available from the repayment of the charge to buy an interest in the replacement property with the surviving spouse.

Stamp duty land tax is payable if an interest in land is acquired for consideration. It is normally not an issue on death because beneficiaries do not provide consideration. However, stamp duty land tax will become payable if, for example, a surviving spouse gives an IOU to the trustees of a nil-rate band discretionary trust in return for which the spouse takes an interest in land. HMRC accepts that there is no liability if the interest in land is transferred subject to a non-recourse charge (see SDLTM04045). A non-recourse charge is one where the transferee of land incurs no personal liability for the debt charged on the land. The trustees cannot recover from the transferee, only from the proceeds of sale of the land.

Since the introduction of the transferable nil-rate band, debt arrangements are used much less frequently as the first spouse (or civil partner) to die can leave everything to the survivor and transfer the unused nil-rate band to the survivor. However, there has been a slight increase in their use following the introduction of the residence nil-rate band. The residence nil-rate band starts to be withdrawn once an estate exceeds the taper threshold of £2 million (see 4-019 below). Using a debt/charge arrangement helps reduce the value of the survivor's estate.

Non-deuctible debts: Finance Acts 2013 and 2014

4-011 Finance Act 2013 introduced three new sections, ss.162A–162C, into IHTA 1984. These sections limit the deductibility of certain debts to prevent the loss of tax. A similar provision dealing with liabilities incurred to fund foreign currency bank accounts was introduced by the Finance Act 2014.

(a) New s.162A: liabilities attributable to financing excluded property

Section 162A provides that a liability which is attributable to financing (directly or indirectly) the acquisition of any excluded property, or the maintenance or enhancement, of the value of any such property is not normally deductible.

Example 7

Alain, a non-UK domiciliary, raises a loan on his Mayfair home to purchase non-UK situs investments. (The non-UK property is excluded property.)

The liability charged against the UK property will be ignored in calculating the inheritance tax liability of Alain.

There are three statutory exceptions to this general rule. These are where the excluded property:

- has been sold (for full consideration) and the proceeds are chargeable assets in the deceased's estate (s.162A(2));
- is no longer excluded property (s.162A(3)); or
- has fallen in value (s.162A(4)), subject to conditions set out in s.7.

The section applies in relation to transfers of value made, or treated as made, on or after 17 July 2013 irrespective of when the liability was incurred (FA 2013, Sch.36, para.5).

(b) New s.162B: liabilities attributable to financing certain relievable property

Relievable property is property which attracts business, agricultural property relief and woodlands relief. See para.4-063 and following for details of these reliefs

Section 162B provides that a liability which is attributable, in whole or in part, to financing (directly or indirectly) the acquisition, maintenance or enhancement of relievable property must reduce the value attributable to the relievable property before it can reduce the value of any other property.

Before the introduction of the section a commonly used planning technique was for elderly taxpayers to raise a mortgage on (say) their main residence using the monies to purchase property qualifying for 100 per cent business property relief (after the expiry of the required two-year ownership period). The debt charged on the residence would have reduced the inheritance tax value of the residence (see para.4-011) resulting in a tax saving on the taxpayer's death. Now it will reduce the value of the relievable property.

Example 8

Habibah borrows £450,000, which she charges on her house, and uses the funds to acquire Alternative Investment Market (AIM) shares. At the date of Habibah's death the AIM shares are worth £575,000 and qualify for business relief. The rest of her estate is worth £1.5 million.

At the date of her death the liability is taken to reduce the value of the AIM shares that can qualify for business relief from £575,000 to £125,000. Business relief applies to the £125,000.

The total estate, including the AIM shares is £2,075,000 (£1.5 million plus £575,000). This is reduced by business relief of £125,000 and the liability of £450,000. The value of the chargeable estate is £1.5 million.

The section applies in relation to to deaths and other transfers of value made, or treated as made, on or after 17 July 2013 but only to liabilities incurred on or after 6 April 2013: see Finance Act 2013, s.176, Sch.36, para.5(2), (3). For this purposes, where a liability is incurred under an agreement, if the agreement was varied so that the liability could be incurred under it, the liability is to be treated as having been incurred on the date of the variation and, in any other case, the liability is to be treated as having been incurred on the date the agreement was made (FA 2013 Sch.36 para.5(2), (3)).

(c) New s.175A: liabilities only deductible if discharged after death or real commercial reason for not discharging

Section 175A provides that a liability is deductible if:

(1) it is actually discharged on or after death out of the estate and is not otherwise prevented under any other provision of the Act from being taken into account; or
(2) if it is not so discharged, it may only be taken into account to the extent that:
    (a) there is a real commercial reason for the liability or the part not being discharged;

(b) securing a tax advantage is not the main purpose, or one of the main purposes, of leaving the liability or part undischarged; and
(c) the liability or the part is not otherwise prevented, under any provision of this Act, from being taken into account.

"Tax" includes income tax and capital gains tax (s.175A(6)).

Section 175A(3) provides that there is a real commercial reason for a liability, or part of a liability, not being discharged where it is shown that:

(a) the liability is to a person dealing at arm's length; or
(b) if the liability were to a person dealing at arm's length, that person would not require the liability to be discharged.

Example 9

Adrian makes a loan of £25,000 to his father, which is secured on his parent's house. A normal rate of interest is charged, but they agree to allow the interest to be added to the capital sum owing. The liability is not to be repaid until after the death of both parents, so when Adrian's father dies two years later the loan is not repaid.

Since the loan was not due to be repaid until the death of the survivor, an arm's length creditor would not have any cause to seek repayment, so the liability may be allowed as a deduction against the estate.

However in other cases the non-payment may be designed to secure a tax advantage in which case it will not be deductible.

Example 10

Harvey dies leaving a legacy equal to the nil-rate band (NRB) to a discretionary trust with the residue of the estate passing to his wife, Wendy. The trustees of the NRB trust exercise their powers and pass the whole of Harvey's estate to Wendy in return for her agreement to repay an amount equal to the NRB (£325,000). Interest is chargeable on the debt at 3 per cent per annum, compounded annually.

On Wendy's death four years later, interest has increased the liability from £325,000 to £365,790.

Provided the whole £365,790 is repaid out of Wendy's estate, the full sum can be deducted from her estate.

The interest received by the NRB trustees will be income of the trust and will, therefore, attract the trust rate of income tax (see para.7-060 and following). The trust rate of income tax on non-dividend income is 45 per cent for tax year 2020/21, so the income tax liability for the trust will outweigh the benefit of the inheritance deduction in Wendy's estate. If the beneficiaries of the two estates are the same, Harvey's trustees may decide to forego the interest.

If Wendy's executors repay only £325,000, that sum can be deducted from her estate for inheritance tax purposes. There is unlikely to be any commercial purpose to the interest not being repaid as, had the creditor been at arm's length, they would have wanted the interest repaid as well. As a result, the £40,790 of the liability that is not repaid from the estate will not be allowed as a deduction against the estate—but equally, the trustees will have no income tax liability.

Where a liability is not deductible under s.175A, it is not taken into account when determining the extent of the inheritance tax exemption for transfers to spouses and civil partners. The exemption, therefore, applies to the full value of the property that the spouse or civil partner receives (IHTA 1984 s.175A(4)).

Example 11

James makes a loan of £25,000 to his father, secured on his parent's £500,000 house. The loan is interest-free and repayable on demand. On the father's death, the loan is not repaid as the son is content for it to remain outstanding until his mother's death. The property passes to his mother under his father's will.

An arm's length creditor would not leave the loan outstanding so the liability cannot be deductible from the value of the father's estate so the chargeable value of the house is, therefore, £500,000 rather than £475,000. But the liability is also not taken into account when considering the spouse exemption. So even though the spouse actually receives the £500,000 subject to the £25,000 liability, the spouse exemption applies to the full £500,000 value of the property.

Because a deceased's personal representatives need a grant of representation before they can access funds held in the deceased's name, they will not normally have paid debts of the deceased at the time they are calculating the value of the estate for tax purposes. However, HMRC have said (*IHT Manual* para.IHTM28031) that the starting assumption is that all arm's length liabilities will be repaid. HMRC will make no enquiries to establish that liabilities which are clearly commercial and at arm's length have been repaid. Examples of such liabilities are:

- utility bills;
- credit card bills;
- council tax;
- payments due to HMRC;
- outstanding care fees;
- professional fees (to the date of death);
- overpaid pension;
- payments for goods and services.

If an arm's length liability for which a deduction is included is not actually repaid, the inheritance tax account would then be incorrect and the taxpayer would have to inform HMRC about the adjustment to be made.

Section 175A applies in relation to transfers of value made, or treated as made, on or after 17 July 2013 to all liabilities whenever incurred.

(d) New s.162AA: liabilities attributable to financing non-residents' foreign currency accounts

This provision is similar to s.162A. IHTA 1984 s.157 provides that the value of the estate of a person who is neither domiciled nor resident in the UK immediately before his death does not include the balance of any foreign currency account. Section 162AA provides that a liability which is attributable, in whole or in part, to financing (directly or indirectly) the balance on such an account is not deductible except in so far as the liability exceeds the balance, provided the excess does not arise for either of the following reasons:

(a) arrangements the main purpose (or one of the main purposes) of which is to secure a tax advantage; or
(b) an increase in the amount of the liability (whether due to the accrual of interest or otherwise).

The section applies in relation to transfers of value made, or treated as made, on or after 17 July 2014 irrespective of when the liability was incurred.

3. THE CALCULATION OF TAX

Two rates of tax

4-012 In respect of transfers made before 15 March 1988 the rates of tax were "progressive", that is to say, the rate of tax increased as the total of taxable gifts made by the transferor increased. However, in respect of transfers made on or after that date there are only two rates of tax. There is a nil-rate band and, once that has been exhausted, tax is charged on further transfers at the rate of 40 per cent. The nil-rate band was increased to £325,000 in 2009/2010 and is frozen at that figure until the end of 2027/28.

A reduced rate of tax

4-013 A reduced rate of inheritance tax (36 per cent) was introduced in Finance Act 2012 for those who leave a proportion of their estate to charity. See para.4-108 and following.

Cumulation

4-014 In order to establish whether or not the nil-rate band has been exhausted in respect of a particular chargeable transfer, it is necessary to take into account all previous chargeable transfers made by the transferor within the seven years before the present transfer (IHTA 1984 s.7(1)). This is called the principle of cumulation. The present transfer is added to all the previous transfers in the last seven years and the tax is then calculated as if the present transfer were the highest part of a single transfer equal to all the transfers (including the present one) made within the last seven years. It is therefore taxed at 40 per cent to the extent that it exceeds the nil-rate band.

The full rate of 40 per cent applies where the transfer is made on death or was made before death but death follows within *three* years. If the transfer is a chargeable transfer made before death the tax charged at the time of the transfer is at half the full rates in force at the date of death (IHTA 1984 s.7(2)) unless the rates have increased in which case the rates at the time of the transfer are used (IHTA 1984 Sch.2). If the transfer is a potentially exempt transfer or a chargeable transfer and death occurs within seven years (but not less than three years) of the transfer, the tax is charged on the value of the transfer (at the date it was made) at the following percentage of the full rates in force at the time of death unless the rates have increased in which case the rates at the time of the transfer are used (IHTA 1984 Sch.2):

(a) where the transfer is made more than three years but not more than four years before the death, 80 per cent;
(b) where the transfer is made more than four years but not more than five years before the death, 60 per cent;
(c) where the transfer is made more than five but not more than six years before the death, 40 per cent;
(d) where the transfer is made more than six but not more than seven years before the death, 20 per cent. (IHTA 1984 s.7(4)).

In the case of a *chargeable* transfer made before death the reduction in the rates mentioned above will be available only to the extent that it does not reduce the amount of tax due on that transfer below the amount originally paid on the lifetime transfer. Thus, no refund of tax is allowed.

Example 12

(1) On 1 October 2024 Ann makes a potentially exempt transfer to Ben, her nephew, of £455,000. A has made no previous chargeable transfers and no exemptions or reliefs are available. The potentially exempt transfer is treated initially as one which will prove to be exempt. No inheritance tax is payable at the time of the transfer. (For the purposes of this illustration and the following ones in this section exemptions and reliefs are ignored.)

If Ann dies within three years of the transfer, the potentially exempt transfer becomes chargeable and tax will become payable at the full rates in force at the date of death. Thus, assuming that the 2024/25 rates are still in force at the time of the transferor's death, the first £325,000 will be taxed at nil per cent and the remaining £130,000 will be taxed at 40 per cent; a total of £52,000 will be payable.

If Ann dies more than three years after but within seven years of the transfer, the potentially exempt transfer becomes chargeable but at only a percentage of the full rate in force at the date of the death. Thus, assuming that the 2024/25 rates are still in force at the time of the transferor's death and Ann's death was within four years of the transfer, tax will be charged at 80 per cent of the full rate, that is:

$$80\% \times £52{,}000 = £41{,}600$$

(2) On 1 October 2025 Sammi makes a chargeable transfer to a settlement of £455,000. Sammi has made no other chargeable transfers and no exemptions or reliefs are available. As explained in the previous example, tax calculated at the full rate on such a transfer would be £52,000. Since this is a lifetime transfer tax is payable at half that rate so £26,000 will be payable.

(3) Having made the chargeable transfer of £455,000 referred to in the previous example, Sammi dies three years and six months later when the table of rates provides for (say) £355,000 to be taxed at a nil-rate and the balance at 40 per cent. The recalculation of tax on the transfer will give a tax figure of:

			Rate		Amount
£		£	%		£
0	–	355,000	0	=	Nil
355,000	–	455,000	40	=	40,000
					40,000

Only 80 per cent of that tax figure of £40,000 is payable since death occurred more than three years after the transfer. Thus,

Tax payable on death 80 per cent × £40,000 = £32,000

Credit must be given for any tax already paid. Thus,

	£
Tax payable on death	32,000
Less: Lifetime tax paid	(26,000)
Extra tax now payable	6,000

If the table of rates on Sammi's death provides for (say) £385,000 to be taxed at a nil-rate and the balance at 40 per cent the recalculation would give a tax figure of:

		Rate		Amount
£	£	%		£
0	– 385,000	0	=	Nil
385,000	– 455,000	40	=	28,000
				28,000

Only 80 per cent of that tax figure of £28,000 is payable since death occurred more than three years after the transfer. Thus,

Tax payable on death 80 per cent x £28,000 = £22,400

At the time the lifetime transfer was made £26,000 was paid in tax. No more tax is due but no reclaim is permitted so there will simply be no extra tax payable on death.

As we explained briefly above, when deciding which rates of tax are to be charged on a particular chargeable transfer it is necessary to take into account all previous chargeable transfers made within seven years before the present transfer. An illustration may be helpful. For the purposes of this illustration exemptions and reliefs have been ignored.

Example 13

Alan is single and has made no previous chargeable transfers. He makes the following lifetime transfers:

20 May 2017	£100,000 to Leo
20 May 2018	£425,000 to a discretionary trust
20 May 2023	£130,000 to Leah
20 Dec 2024	Alan dies, owning £360,000 of assets

Since the 2017 transfer is potentially exempt, it is assumed that it will prove to be an exempt transfer until either seven years expire or the transferor dies within that period. Therefore, no tax is payable in 2017 and the transfer is not cumulated with the chargeable transfer to the discretionary trust made in 2018. On 20 May 2024, the 2017 transfer actually becomes exempt.

The transfer to the discretionary trust in 2018 is a chargeable transfer made before death and as such is taxed at half the full rates of tax. Tax will be calculated as follows:

			Rate		Amount
£		£	%		£
0	–	325,000	0	=	Nil
325,000	–	425,000	20	=	20,000

Therefore £20,000 will be payable in 2018.

The 2023 transfer is potentially exempt and so, as with the 2017 transfer, no tax is paid at the time of the transfer.

On A's death in 2024, tax on the 2018 transfer will be recalculated at the full rates in force in tax year 2024/25. Since death has occurred more than six years after the transfer, only 20 per cent of the full tax is payable. If this is less than the £20,000 already paid, then no refund is available.

As a result of A's death within seven years of the 2023 transfer, it becomes chargeable. In fact death has occurred within three years of the transfer and so tax will be calculated at the full rates in force in tax year 2024/25. As £425,000 of chargeable transfers have already been made the rates appropriate to a transfer from £425,000–£555,000 will be used. Finally, the tax due on the transfer on death will be calculated at the full rates for tax year 2024/25. As £555,000 of chargeable transfers have already been made in the seven years before death, the rates appropriate to a transfer from £555,000 to £915,000 will be used.

Transfer of unused nil-rate band between spouses

Where spouses or civil partners die on or after 9 October 2007 their personal representatives can claim an increase in their nil-rate band for the purposes of the charge to tax on death if their spouses or civil partners died before them with a proportion of their nil-rate band unused. The nil-rate band of the survivor is increased by the proportion that was unused on the first death. Finance Act 2008 inserted ss.8A–8C into IHTA 1984 to make the necessary amendments. However, the change took effect as from 9 October 2007. **4-015**

The unused proportion of the nil-rate band is normally claimed by the personal representatives who must do so within two years of the end of the month of death or such longer period as HMRC allow (s.8B(1)(a)).

It is irrelevant when the first spouse or civil partner died, whether or not they had any assets at the time of the death and where they were domiciled. What matters is the proportion of the nil-rate band unused. The nil-rate band of the survivor is increased on death by that proportion.

Example 14

Faheem died in 2002/2003 when the nil-rate band was £250,000. He used only half of it. His wife, Jumilla, died some years later when the nil-rate band is £350,000. Jumilla's personal representatives can claim an additional 50 per cent of the £350,000 nil-rate band in force on her death so Jumilla's nil-rate band will be 150 per cent of £350,000. If Jumilla made no lifetime chargeable transfers, there will be a nil-rate band of £525,000 available to her death estate.

The unused proportion of the nil-rate band of the first spouse to die can only be transferred on death. It is not available against the tax payable during the deceased's lifeime on immediately chargeable lifetime transfers. However, it is set against any additional inheritance tax which becomes payable as a result of death so will cover additional tax payable on lifetime transfers.

Example 15

Assume that Jumilla in the previous example had made a lifetime chargeable transfer to a discretionary trust on 4 April 2024 of £625,000 and died on 9 June 2029 (when the nil-rate band was £350,000) with a death estate of £525,000, the position would be as follows.

On 4 April 2024 she has only her own nil-rate band available so the first £325,000 of the lifetime transfer is taxed at 0 per cent and the remaining £300,000 at 20 per cent giving an immediate tax liability of £60,000.

When Jumilla dies in 2029 the tax on the lifetime chargeable transfer will have to be recalculated at the full death rates.

Her personal representatives will be able to claim the unused 50 per cent of her husband's nil-rate band. As the nil-rate band at the date of her death is £350,000, this increases Jumilla's nil rate band by £175,000 to £525,000.

Her enhanced nil-rate band is set against the lifetime transfer and is exhausted.

On these figures there is no benefit to Jumilla's personal representatives in claiming the transferable nil-rate band because it will be used entirely on the lifetime transfer and none will be available to the death estate.

Section 8B(1)(b) provides that if no claim is made by the personal representatives within two years following the end of the month of death, any other person liable for tax chargeable as a result of the death can make a claim. The requirement to wait two years seems pointless and it is thought that HMRC would allow a claim from a lifetime transferee provided the personal representatives confirm that they will not be making a claim.

It is possible to take portions of unused nil-rate band from any number of previous spouses or civil partners. However, s.8A(6) restricts the additional nil-rate band that can be inherited so no death estate can benefit by more than the value of one additional nil-rate band.

There is an important planning point here. If a widow and widower marry each other having inherited a full nil-rate band from their respective deceased spouses, neither can inherit any further nil-rate band from the other. To avoid wasting their inherited nil-rate bands they should consider creating nil-rate band discretionary trusts in their wills for the benefit of their surviving spouse and issue. Each can transfer assets up to a double nil-rate band without a payment of inheritance tax. (Note, however that the trust will have only a single nil-rate band available so there will be ongoing anniversary and exit charges calculated on the excess: see Ch.7 for the taxation of settlements).

It does not matter how many years previously the first spouse or civil partner died so long as there was unused nil-rate band at that date. The nil-rate band thresholds for inheritance tax, capital transfer tax and estate duty are available on the gov.uk website. In the case of estate duty there was no spouse exemption for most of the life of the tax, so the nil-rate band of the first to die may have been exhausted even though the whole estate was left to the surviving spouse.

It does not matter how much or how little the first spouse to die owned. For example, if Simone dies in 1990 without any assets and her husband, Harold, dies in June 2024, Harold's nil-rate band will be increased by an additional 100 per cent of £325,000 transferred from Joan.

It is also irrelevant that the first spouse or civil partner died domiciled outside England and Wales. For example, Harry marries Susan, who is domiciled and resident in Australia. He moves to Australia. Susan dies in 2020 leaving everything to Harry. Harry moves back to England in 2021 and dies in 2024 domiciled in England and Wales. Harry's personal representatives can claim Susan's unused nil-rate band.

HMRC will require documentation to show that there was a spouse/civil partner and that there was unused nil-rate band so personal representatives should obtain certificates of death and marriage together with a copy of any will, inheritance tax account, valuations of assets and details of matters such as lifetime gifts and property assigned by survivorship which reduce the nil-rate band available. HMRC recognises that it may not be possible to obtain all the relevant information where the first spouse died many years ago but clearly, in the case of deaths occurring on or after 9 October 2007, it will be important to preserve all relevant information.

Section 8C makes provision for the position where tax deferred on the first death (for example, in relation to heritage property or woodlands) becomes payable.

The residence nil-rate band

When is residence nil rate band available?

The Finance (No.2) Act 2015 inserts new ss.8D–8M into IHTA 1984 to introduce an additional nil-rate band (RNRB) available for deaths on or after 6 April 2017 when a residence, or interest in a residence, is "closely" inherited, that is by lineal descendants. **4-016**

Finance Act 2016 inserted further provisions to allow estates to claim a downsizing allowance where the deceased disposed of a residence completely or moved to a cheaper property on or after 8 July 2015. While any reduction in the burden of inheritance tax is welcome, the legislation has been heavily criticised for its complexity and hidden traps.

Residence or interest in a residence

Section 8H(2) defines a residence as an interest in a dwelling house which has been the person's residence at any time during the period of ownership. Section 8H(5) provides that a dwelling includes "any land occupied and enjoyed with it as its garden or grounds" other than woodland subject to a deferral election. **4-017**

There is no requirement that the dwelling has to be the deceased's main residence or a UK property. A holiday home can qualify so long as it has been used as a residence. The capital gains tax cases on what constitutes a residence will be relevant. Temporary "camping out" in a property is not enough to make it a residence: see *Goodwin v Curtis* (1998). In *Dutton-Forshaw v RCC* (2015) the court reviewed the case law and said that the question of what constitutes a residence is one of fact. Permanence and continuity of occupation are important factors, but the degree required will vary depending on the circumstances. Clearly a property which was never a residence of the deceased, such as a buy-to-let property, will not qualify. However the property does not have to have been a residence throughout the period of ownership. It is sufficient that it was a residence at some point.

The RNRB could be available on a dwelling which had been:

(1) bought as an investment and rented commercially until the deceased moved into it shortly before death and used it as his residence; or
(2) the deceased's residence for a time but which was let out commercially from the date the deceased had to go into care.

Closely

The residence must be "closely" inherited. "Closely", as defined in s.8K, means that it must pass to: **4-018**

- a lineal descendant of the deceased;
- a spouse/civil partner of a lineal descendant; or
- a surviving spouse/civil partner of a lineal descendant who predeceased the deceased provided the surviving spouse/civil partner has not remarried).

Section 8K extends the normal meaning of "child" for this purpose. A child includes a step-child, a foster child, a child who is subject to a special-guardianship order and a child of the deceased who has been adopted by a third party.

A step-child is a child of a person's spouse or civil partner; the child of a cohabitee is not a step-child. A child who was at any time a step-child of the deceased remains a step-child after the marriage or civil partnership has ended in divorce or dissolution. Similarly foster children and children subject to a special guardianship order remain children of the foster parent or special guardian even though the arrangement has terminated.

Inherited

4-019 "Inherited" is defined in s.8J as a disposition effected by will, the intestacy rules or otherwise. Events occurring after death, such as a sale of the property, are irrelevant so the relief is not lost if a residence is sold during the administration. An appropriation of a residence by the personal representatives to satisfy a pecuniary legacy is not a disposition effected *by* the will or intestacy rules with the result that the relief is not be available.

A post-death variation complying with the requirements of IHTA 1984 s.142 is treated as the deceased's disposition for all inheritance tax purposes (see Ch.19). Hence, a variation which passes a residential interest to lineal descendants will attract the RNRB (other requirements being satisfied).

Property left to certain types of settlement will be treated as "inherited" under s.8J(4). The settled property must be held for the lineal descendant (B) on trusts which create:

- an immediate post-death interest for B;
- a disabled person's trust interest for B; or
- a bereaved minor or bereaved young person interest.

These three types of trusts are discussed in Ch.7. It is worth noting here, however, that very few settlements qualify. Leaving property on discretionary or contingent trusts is not treated as "inheriting" even if all the beneficiaries are lineal descendants. Under a typical grandparental settlement, "to such of my grandchildren as reach 21" the beneficiaries are not treated as "inheriting" because the settlement is a relevant property trust.

Where the RNRB is not available because the settlement is the wrong type it will often be possible for the trustees to obtain the RNRB by making an appointment within two years of death which is read back into the will for inheritance tax purposes under IHTA 1984 s.144 (see Ch.19).

Example 16

T leaves her estate (which includes a residence) on trust for such of her grandchildren as are living at the date of her death and reach the age of 21. When she dies, the grandchildren are all minors. The trust is a relevant property trust and, as things stand, the RNRB is not available to the estate. However, the trustees will usually have express powers to appoint capital and, in any event, will have the statutory power to advance capital under Trustee Act 1925 s.32. They can use their powers to appoint the residence to the grandchildren absolutely (in which case it will be held on a bare trust for them) or on immediate post-death interest trusts. Provided the appointment is done within two years of the death, it will be read back into the will under IHTA 1984 s.144 and the estate will benefit from the RNRB.

How much is the RNRB?

The maximum value of the RNRB was £100,000 in 2017/2018, rising by £25,000 each tax year until it reached £175,000 in 2020/2021. It is frozen until the end of 2027/28 but thereafter will increase in line with Consumer Prices Index. **4-020**

An estate will not necessarily benefit from a full RNRB. The RNRB is capped at the value of the deceased's interest in one residential property. Debts charged on a property are deducted so only the net value is relevant. The value is also reduced by any available agricultural or business property relief.

Where an estate includes more than one residence or interest in a residence, the personal representatives must nominate which one is to qualify (s.8H(4)). If the deceased had two residential properties, one worth more than the residence nil rate band and one worth less, then the personal representatives are likely to choose the more valuable. If both properties are worth less than the residence nil-rate band, the claim is limited to one so some of the RNRB will be wasted.

The taper threshold

When the net value of an estate is more than the taper threshold, s.8D provides that the RNRB (made up of the deceased's own allowance plus anything transferred from a predeceased spouse or civil partner—see para.4-015) is withdrawn by £1 for every £2 that the value of the estate exceeds the taper threshold. The adjusted amount (which may be nothing) is called the "adjusted allowance". The taper threshold is £2 million until the end of 2027/28 and will then be increased by reference to the Consumer Prices Index. In 2020/21 when the RNRB is £175,000 a person dying with an estate of £2,350,000 will lose the whole of it. **4-021**

Note that the threshold looks only at the value of the "estate". Estate is defined in IHTA 1984 s.5 as everything in the beneficial ownership of the deceased immediately before death (other than excluded property) and after deducting liabilities. Exemptions and reliefs are not deducted; it is the pre-exemption or relief value which matters. Note however, that the estate is valued *immediately* before death so lifetime gifts completed before death enable taxpayers to reduce their estates to below the level of the taper threshold.

Example 17

A wealthy individual leaves his entire estate worth £5 million to his children. £4 million of the estate attracts 100 per cent business property relief but the relief does not reduce his estate which exceeds the taper threshold to such an extent that no RNRB would be available.

However, if on his death bed he gives away £4 million, his death estate is reduced to £1 million and a full RNRB becomes available.

Transferred RNRB

Section 8F provides that any unused RNRB can be transferred to a surviving spouse or civil partner (provided the survivor dies on or after 6 April 2017). It does not matter when the first of the couple died, even if the death occurred before the RNRB was available. The personal representatives of the survivor must make a claim to transfer the RNRB (s.8L). There is no transfer between cohabitees. **4-022**

As with the ordinary nil rate band, it is the unused percentage of the RNRB that is transferred to the survivor not the amount of the RNRB at the date of the first death.

Example 18

Sarah dies in June 2017 when the RNRB is £100,000. She leaves-everything to her husband, Harry. Harry dies in March 2021 when the RNRB is £175,000. Harry's residence nil-rate band will be increased by an additional £175,000

As with the transfer of the ordinary nil-rate band a person can inherit percentages of unused RNRB from more than one dead spouse or civil partner but no one can inherit more than 100 per cent (s.8G).

Where the first spouse or civil partner died before 6 April 2017 their estate cannot have benefited from the RNRB as it was not available. That means that 100 per cent of the RNRB will be available for transfer unless the value of their estate exceeded £2 million and the RNRB is tapered away. For the purposes of taper, persons dying before 6 April 2017 are deemed to have had a RNRB of £100,000.

Example 19

Colin dies in 2001 with an estate of £2.1 million, all of which he leaves to his civil partner, Peter. Colin's deemed RNRB of £100,000 will be tapered by 50 per cent. If Peter dies in 2024/25 when the RNRB is £175,000, his RNRB will be increased by 50 per cent of £175,000. However, if Peter's estate exceeds £2 million, his increased RNRB will be subject to taper.

Deceased dying with an interest in a trust

4-023 Section 8J(5) provides that a residence that was held in trust for the deceased will qualify for RNRB if:

- the deceased had either an immediate post-death interest, a qualifying interest in possession or a disabled person's interest (for types of settlement see para.7-010); and
- on their death a lineal descendant of the deceased beneficiary becomes beneficially entitled to the property.

Example 20

Wanda leaves her estate, which includes a residence, to her husband, Hector, for life (this is an immediate post-death interest) and following his death to their daughter absolutely. Hector's estate can benefit from the RNRB.

But, if following Hector's death, trusts arise, whether discretionary or giving a contingent interest for the daughter, no RNRB is available because the daughter is not beneficially entitled within the meaning of s.8J.

In such a case the trustees should use any powers of appointment they have available under the terms of the trust to modify the terms of the trust during Hector's life to create an absolute entitlement for the daughter on his death.

Lifetime transfers

4-024 The RNRB is available on the death estate not to lifetime transfers so, for example, if a father gives his residence to his son in 2014 and dies in 2017, the transfer is chargeable to inheritance tax but no RNRB is available to Dad's estate.

There are, however, two cases where an estate may benefit from RNRB even though a residence has been given away.

(1) Where the gift is made on or after 8 July 2015, and the downsizing provisions apply. For downsizing, see para.4-025 and following.
(2) Where the reservation of benefit rules apply to a gift of a residence to a lineal descendant. Gifts with a reservation are discussed at para.4-031 but the effect of the rules is that where a person makes a gift, but continues to derive a benefit from the gifted property, the property continues to be treated as part of their estate for inheritance tax purposes. In the case of a reservation of benefit the RNRB is available only if the lineal descendant is: "the person to whom the disposal was made" (s.8J). This produces some inconsistent results.

Example 21

A father gives his residence to his son in 2014 and moves in with his son in 2020. This creates a reservation of benefit. He dies in May 2024, still living in the property with his son. The RNRB is available because the disposal was made to a lineal descendant.

However, if the father settles the residence on himself for life, remainder to his son absolutely, although there is a reservation of benefit, the RNRB is not available because the disposal was not to a lineal descendant. (No downsizing allowance is available because IHTA 1984 s.8H(4D) provides that a transfer which creates a reservation of benefit is not a disposal for this purpose, although the termination of the reservation of benefit is).

The downsizing legislation

The government recognised at an early stage that if taxpayers had to own a residence at the date of death in order to benefit from the RNRB, this would result in elderly people clinging onto properties when they ought to be selling them and moving into smaller accommodation or into care. It undertook to introduce a mechanism to allow taxpayers to benefit from the RNRB despite having disposed of a residence completely or moving to cheaper accommodation. This was done in Finance Act 2016 which inserts new ss.8FA–8FE and 8HA into IHTA 1984, applying where a person disposes of a residential property on or after 8 July 2015 either completely or by moving to a less valuable property. **4-025**

The chargeable transfer on death must exceed the value of any residence owned at the date of death and there must be assets which are closely inherited.

The downsizing addition is capped at the value of the assets which is closely inherited. The legislation is impenetrable in detail but reasonably straightforward in outline.

It is necessary to calculate the "lost relievable amount" by expressing the value of the "former residential interest" as a percentage of the "former allowance", taking 100 per cent if it would otherwise be higher.

There are five steps to work out the amount of additional threshold that's been lost:

- *Step 1.* Work out the additional threshold that would have been available when the disposal of the former home took place. This figure is made up of the maximum additional threshold due at the date of disposal (or £100,000 if the disposal occurred before 6 April 2017) plus any transferred additional threshold which is available at the date of death.
- *Step 2.* Divide the value of the former home at the date of disposal by the figure in step 1 and multiply the result by 100 to get a percentage. If the

value of the former home is greater than the figure in step 1 the percentage will be limited to 100 per cent. If the value of the home disposed of is less than the figure in step 1, the percentage will be between 0 per cent and 100 per cent.

- *Step 3.* If there is a home in the estate on death, divide the value of the home on death by the additional threshold that would be available at the date of death (including any transferred additional threshold). Multiply the result by 100 to get a percentage (again this percentage is limited to 100 per cent). If there is no home in the estate at death this percentage will be 0 per cent.
- *Step 4.* Deduct the percentage in step 3 from the percentage in step 2.
- *Step 5.* Multiply the additional threshold that would be available at the date of death by the figure from step 4. This gives the amount of the lost additional threshold.

Example 22

Dan, who is divorced, sells a property for £250,000 in 2020 and moves into residential accommodation. The downsizing addition is calculated as follows:

The value of the former residence exceeded the RNRB available at the date of sale (£175,000). It is 142 per cent of the RNRB. Dan is therefore treated as having a downsizing addition 100 per cent of the available RNRB on death.

If he dies in 2020/21 this allowance will be £175,000 but it will be limited to the value of assets which are closely inherited.

The calculation is more complicated when there is transferred RNRB available. The following example is taken from para.6066 of HMRC's *IHT Manual.*

Example 23

Sam's husband left his estate to her on his death in July 2017. She sold her home for £104,000 in July 2019 and moved into residential care. She died in December 2020 with an estate worth £800,000, and left half to her daughter and the other half to a friend.

The RNRB in July 2019 is £150,000. The RNRB in December 2020 is £175,000

Sam's husband had not used any RNRB so there was a brought-forward allowance of £150,000 (100 per cent of the RNRB) available to Sam at the date of disposal in July 2019. There is a brought-forward allowance of £175,000 on Sam's death.

Step 1

Sam's former allowance equals the RNRB at the date of disposal (£150,000), plus the brought-forward allowance at disposal (£150,000), plus the difference between the brought-forward allowance at death and at disposal (£175,000 – £150,000 = £25,000). Sam's former allowance is therefore £325,000 (£150,000 + £150,000 + £25,000).

Step 2

The value of the sold property was £104,000. Sam's former allowance is £325,000. Expressed as a percentage £104,000 ÷ £325,000 = 32 per cent.

Step 3

Sam's RNRB on death is £350,000. This is multiplied by the percentage in step 2 to give a lost relievable amount of £350,000 x 32 per cent = £112,000.

The actual amount of the downsizing addition is the lower of the lost relievable amount (£112,000) and the value of other assets which are left to direct descendants. As £400,000 of other assets are left to Sam's daughter, a downsizing addition of £112,000 is due.

Downsizing and residences held in trust

There was a problem where a married couple (or civil partners) jointly disposed of a residence. If the first to die did not make use of the downsizing allowance (because, for example, they leave everything to the survivor), the survivor got little benefit from the transferred downsizing allowance. Due to a quirk in the drafting, the problem did not arise if the couple have moved to a cheaper property. **4-026**

However, the Finance Act 2019 removed this problem for deaths on or after 29 October 2018 by amending s.8FA.

When the original draft downsizing provisions were published in December 2015, there were oddities in the way they worked in relation to the disposal of a property held in a trust in which the deceased had a qualifying interest in possession such as an immediate post-death interest.

Significant amendments were made to the downsizing provisions (see s.8H(4A)–(4F) and s.8HA) in relation to settlements which include a residence or interest in a residence in which a beneficiary has a qualifying interest in possession.

As a result:

(1) Where trustees dispose of the residence or interest in a residence and the beneficiary continues to have a qualifying interest in the settlement, the beneficiary will be treated as having disposed of the residence.
(2) Where trustees terminate the beneficiary's interest or the beneficiary disposes of his interest during his lifetime, the beneficiary will be treated as having disposed of the residence.
(3) Where a person has two or more interests in a residence (such as a half share owned outright and an interest in possession in half) and both interests are disposed of on the same day, they will be added together for the purposes of the downsizing allowance. This will not be the case if they are disposed of on different days.

A further amendment provides that a gift of a residence which creates a reservation of benefit is not a disposal for the purposes of the downsizing allowance. However, if the reservation ceases (for example because the donor moves out of the property), there is a disposal for downsizing purposes at that point.

Grossing-up

The basic principles

Where inheritance tax is paid by the donor (as it may be in the case of a chargeable transfer made before death), the loss to the donor resulting from the transfer is the value of the gift *plus* the inheritance tax on it. It is on this gross figure that inheritance tax is payable. In such a case the value of the *net* gift is known but in order to calculate the gross loss to the estate it is necessary to "gross-up" the net gift. Inheritance tax is then calculated on the *gross* loss to the donor. In order to gross up a net figure, use the formula: **4-027**

Net amount x 100/100 – tax

Example 24

Andrew has made chargeable transfers which have exhausted his nil-rate band. He now makes a chargeable transfer to a discretionary trust of £10,000 and agrees to pay the inheritance tax attributable to the transfer.

The tax payable is calculated by "grossing-up" the gift of £10,000 that is by treating the £10,000 as a net amount the tax on which has been notionally deducted. The whole transfer falls within the 40 per cent tax band but, as it is a transfer made *before* death, tax will be charged at one-half the full rate, that is at 20 per cent. Thus, it can be seen that the gift is 80 per cent of the gross amount transferred.

The gross figure can, therefore, be found by multiplying the net amount by 100 and dividing it by 80.

Net × 100/80 = gross

i.e. £10,000 = 100/80 = £12,500

The difference between the gross and net amounts is the amount of the tax, i.e. £12,500 - £10,000 = £2,500.

Where inheritance tax is paid by the donee the gross loss to the donor is known and no grossing-up calculation is necessary.

Example 25

Alan has made chargeable transfers which have exhausted his nil-rate band. He now makes a chargeable transfer to a discretionary trust of £10,000; the donee is to pay the inheritance tax attributable to the transfer.

The gross loss to the donor is £10,000. The transfer falls within the 40 per cent band but, as it is a transfer made before death, the tax will be charged at one-half the full rate, that is at 20 per cent. The inheritance tax is, therefore:

£10,000 × 20% = £2,000

Notice that in the first example the donee receives £10,000 and the donor loses £12,500 whereas in the second example the donee receives £8,000 and the donor loses £10,000. In the case of lifetime transfers it is, therefore, important for donors to consider carefully the amount they can afford to transfer and the amount they wish the donee to receive. Where the gift consists of an asset rather than cash, the problem may be particularly serious as neither donor nor donee may have sufficient cash available to pay the inheritance tax. However, if the *donee* is paying the tax it is possible in respect of certain types of property to elect to pay the tax by instalments (see para.4-091 and following) and this will mitigate the problem.

Grossing-up is required on lifetime gifts whenever the *donor* pays the tax. The parties may agree that the donee will pay but, if the donee fails to do so and the donor in fact pays, grossing-up is required.

Grossing-up is not normally required on the transfer of property forming part of the estate on death. The reason for this is that the tax on death is on the full value of the estate (subject to exemptions) not on the loss to the donor's estate. In very limited circumstances grossing-up is required to calculate the tax on death (see para.4-096).

Where a potentially exempt or a chargeable transfer has been made and death occurs within seven years, tax may be payable as a result of the death. This is primarily the liability of the donee. As the donee will be paying the tax, the gift to the donee is a gross gift and no grossing-up is required.

Gifts involving more than one tax band

If a transferor makes a transfer of value part of which is taxed at nil per cent and part of which is taxed at 40 per cent, only the part falling within the 40 per cent tax band needs to be grossed-up. **4-028**

Gifts within seven years of death—changes in value

If the asset increases in value, the increase is ignored so tax is calculated on the initial value. **4-029**

Example 26

Geraint gives an investment property worth £300,000 to Donna. He dies three years later when the property has increased to £500,000. Tax is-calculated on £300,000 not £500,000.

An expected future increase in value is often the impetus for making a lifetime gift rather than holding on to the asset until death.

However, in a rare win/win for the taxpayer, a relief is available where the value of an asset falls between the date of the gift and the date of death, where the value of the property transferred has declined between the transfer and the death. The rules which provide this relief are, in detail, very complex but their broad effect is to allow a decline in value of an asset to be deducted from the amount liable to the extra tax where the donee still owns the asset at the donor's death (see IHTA 1984 s.131).

Where the asset has been sold before the donor's death by the donee (or their spouse) at a loss in a qualifying sale (which broadly means in a genuine commercial transaction) the decline in value between the date of the gift and the date of sale may be deducted from the amount liable to extra tax. No relief is given where the asset was tangible moveable property which had a predictable useful life of 50 years or less immediately before the transfer to the donee.

Example 27 (taken from IHTM14621)

Joel transfers a house to his son, Philip, on 1 November 2009. At that date it was valued at £400,000. Joel dies on 1 March 2012. The house at that date is valued at £375,000.

Without the relief (inheritance tax of £30,000 (£400,000 – £325,000 (the inheritance tax nil-rate band at the date of death) = £75,000 × 40 per cent) would be payable on the transfer.

If Philip makes a claim for fall in value relief the date of death value of £375,000 will be used to calculate the tax instead. The inheritance tax payable by Philip is reduced to £20,000.

The reduction in value is solely for the purpose of calculating the tax payable on the lifetime transfer. It does not affect:

- the transferor's cumulative total, which remains at its original figure for the purpose of taxing any later lifetime transfers and the transfer on death; or

- the tax originally charged at lifetime rates on an immediately chargeable lifetime transfer.

Example 28 (taken from IHTM14622)

Frances transfers a portfolio of quoted shares to her son David on 1 February 2010 valued at £100,000. On 1 February 2011 she transfers a house to her daughter Jane, valued at £250,000. Frances dies on 1 April 2013, when the inheritance tax nil-rate band was £325,000.

There is no inheritance tax due on the gift of quoted shares as the value is less than the nil-rate band. Inheritance tax of £10,000 is payable on the gift of the house (£250,000 – £225,000 (the remaining nil-rate band after deducting the first gift of £100,000) = £25,000 × 40 per cent).

At the date of death the house was valued at £230,000 and Jane makes a claim for fall in value relief. The inheritance tax payable is reduced by £8,000 (£20,000 × 40 per cent) from £10,000 to £2,000.

However, the original value of the gifts of £350,000 is still used when calculating the tax due on Frances's estate at the date of death.

There is no particular form for the claim, but the claim

- must be signed by one or more of the persons liable for the tax (or additional tax); and
- must be made within four years of the date of the donor's death.

The claim must also:

- identify the transfer and the transferred asset;
- confirm that the asset has been retained by the transferee (or their spouse or civil partner or has been sold by a qualifying sale (details of which should be provided); and
- confirm that the asset is in all respects the same at the date of death or sale as at the time of the transfer or give details of the changes which have taken place.

The person making the claim should also provide an estimate of the relief sought, which may normally take the form of an estimate of the market value at the date of death or sale.

Gifts within seven years of death—changes of rate

4-030 When a potentially exempt transfer or chargeable transfer become taxable as the result of death within seven years, the rate of tax chargeable will be the rate in force at the date the gift was made except to the extent that rates have been reduced (IHTA 1984 Sch.2). This is quite a useful tax planning tool since it means that a transferor who fears that rates of tax may rise can make a gift now and guarantee that no increases in the rate of tax will affect the transfer. The transfer will, however, get the benefit of any reductions in rate—a rare example of having your tax cake and eating it.

Gifts with a reservation

What is a gift with reservation?

4-031 The Finance Act 1986 contains special provisions in respect of property subject to a reservation.

Section 102(1) provides that property is regarded as subject to a reservation where an individual transfers property by way of gift and:

(a) *either* the donee does not bona fide assume possession and enjoyment within the relevant period;
(b) *or* at any time in the relevant period the property is not enjoyed to the entire, or virtually the entire, exclusion of the donor and of any benefit to him by contract or otherwise (Finance Act 1986 s.102).

The relevant period is the period ending with the date of death of the deceased and beginning seven years earlier or at the date of the gift if it was made within seven years of the death.

A simple example of a gift with reservation under (a) would be a father giving his daughter a picture but keeping it. The picture will be treated as part of the father's death estate if he still retains it at death.

A simple example of a gift with reservation under (b) would be a father giving a picture to his daughter and borrowing it back 10 years later. The picture will be treated as part of the father's death estate if he still retains it at death. If he gives it back to his daughter before death, he is treated as making a new potentially exempt transfer.

According to the Court of Appeal in *Buzzoni v RCC* (2013) a donee's enjoyment is to "*the entire exclusion*" of benefit to the donor within the meaning of s.102(1)(b) even where the donor retains a benefit provided that benefit is not obtained at "*the expense of*" the donee.

In *Buzzoni* the taxpayer had a long lease of a valuable flat in Knightsbridge. She granted an under-lease of the flat to commence in 10 years' time. The head lease which she retained was valued at £50,000. Without the under-lease, it would have been worth £2.1 million. The grant of the under-lease required the landlord's consent. The consent was granted subject to a requirement that the under-tenant enter into a covenant with the landlord to observe all the covenants and obligations of the tenant. The under-lease contained covenants and obligations mirroring those in the lease apart from the requirement to pay rent. HMRC contended that the under-lease gave rise to a reservation of benefit because it had the effect of transferring to the trustees liabilities which would otherwise have been borne by the donor. HMRC were successful before the first-tier and Upper Tribunal but lost in the Court of Appeal which held that, in construing s.102(1)(b), the focus is not primarily on the question whether the donor had obtained a benefit from the gifted property, but whether the donee's enjoyment of that property remained exclusive. If the benefit to the donor had no impact on, was irrelevant to and made no, or virtually no, difference to the donee's enjoyment, that enjoyment was to the entire, or virtually entire, exclusion of any benefit to the donor. In *Buzzoni* any benefit which the donor had obtained from the positive covenants did not affect or make any difference to the donee's enjoyment of the under-lease; the donees' obligations under those covenants precisely matched the obligations which they already owed to the head lessor under the sub-letting licence. Even if the donor could be said to have obtained a benefit which she had not previously enjoyed, it had not been obtained at the expense of the donee's enjoyment of the sub-lease and had neither added to nor subtracted from that enjoyment.

In *Hood v RCC* (2016) on similar facts there was held to be a reservation of benefit because, unlike *Buzzoni*, the under-lessees were under no pre-existing obligation to the head lessor meaning that the covenants entered into did provide a benefit to the donor.

In *Sillars v IRC* (2004) the deceased had put a bank account into the joint names of herself and her two daughters. Her personal representatives argued that only one third of the balance should be included in her estate at death but HMRC contended successfully that she should be treated as entitled to the whole for inheritance tax purposes. There were two grounds for the decision. First, the deceased had a general power or authority to deal with the account as she thought fit and, therefore, the account was part of her estate under IHTA 1984 s.5(2). Secondly, the account was part of her estate under the reservation of benefit rules because the gift was a gift of the chose in action of the whole account and she was clearly not excluded from benefit.

Membership of a class of discretionary beneficiaries will inevitably amount to a reservation of benefit. See *IRC v Eversden* (2002) and *Lyon's PRs v HMRC* (2007).

The double charges regulations

4-032 If a donor gives away property and retains a benefit, there is a potentially exempt transfer at the date of the gift so there is the possibility of a charge to tax if death occurs within seven years of the gift.

If the donor dies while retaining a benefit, the property is treated for the purpose of inheritance tax as if it was part of their estate on death.

If the property ceases to be subject to a reservation within seven years of death the donor is treated as making a potentially exempt transfer at that date. This means that tax will be payable on the property which was subject to a reservation if the donor dies within seven years of the property ceasing to be subject to a reservation.

There is clearly the possibility of double charges to tax on the same property.

Example 29

A transferor gives a country cottage to his son in 2020 stipulating that he retains the right to spend holidays there for three months in the summer for the next four years. He dies in 2025. The initial transfer in 2020 is a potentially exempt transfer, a "PET" (arguably the value transferred is reduced because of the transferor's entitlement to occupation). The termination of the right to holidays after four years in 2024 is a PET equal in value of the property. Because this is a "deemed" PET it cannot be reduced by annual exemptions. When the transferor dies in 2025 both PETs become chargeable.

Had the transferor died before the right of occupation ceased, the continued reservation of benefit would mean that the entire value of the cottage would have been included in his estate for inheritance purposes despite the fact that the initial PET has become chargeable. Note that the-inclusion in the estate is a fiction and is only relevant for inheritance tax purposes. The house would not be treated as part of the transferor's estate for capital gains tax purposes so there would be no uplift in value on the death of the transferor; nor would main residence relief be available on a lifetime disposal.

The Inheritance Tax (Double Charges Relief) Regulations 1987 (SI 1987/1130) provide a measure of relief in the case of double charges. They require alternative calculations to be made and unsurprisingly the taxpayer is required to pay on the basis of the calculation which produces the highest figure. It is necessary to consult the Rules carefully since the procedure varies according to the types of transfer involved.

Exceptions to the reservation of benefit rules

There are exceptions to the reservation of benefit rules. The gifted property must be enjoyed to the entire or *virtually* the entire exclusion of the donor so *de minimis* benefits can be ignored. HMRC's views on what amounts to de minimis are set out in the *IHT Manual* at para.IHTM14333. **4-033**

Under the Finance Act 1986 ss.102A(3), 102B(3)(b) and Sch.20 para.6(1)(a) the reservation of benefit rules do not apply to an interest in land or enjoyment of a chattel if the donor provides full consideration (rent) for the use of the asset. The consideration must be full throughout the relevant period so rent review clauses should be included in any agreement and the rent must be increased appropriately.

Under Finance Act 1986 Sch.20 para.6(1)(b) in the case of land, there will be no reservation of benefit if a donor has to go into occupation

- (i) because there has been an unexpected change in circumstances which was not brought about by the donor to receive the benefit of this provision; and
- (ii) it occurs at a time when the donor has become unable to maintain himself through old age or infirmity or otherwise, the donor is unable to maintain themselves; and
- (iii) it represents a reasonable provision by the donee for the care and maintenance of the donor; and
- (iv) the donee is a relative of the donor or his spouse or civil partner.

Section 102B of the Finance Act 1986 contains two further "get outs" from the reservation of benefit rules where the donor makes a gift of an undivided share or interest in land.

Section 102B(3) provides that there is no reservation of benefit where the donor makes a gift of an undivided share land and does not occupy the land. This exception would apply where the donor gives away let land and continues to enjoy the rental income.

Section 102B(4) provides that there is no reservation of benefit where:

- (i) the donor makes a gift of a share in land;
- (ii) the donor and donee both occupy the land; and
- (iii) the donor receives no benefit connected with the gift other than a negligible one.

This exception is designed to cover the situation where, for example, an elderly parent gives an interest in the family home to an adult child and both occupy the property. It is fatal if the whole house is given away or if the child moves out. In both cases the requirements of the section are no longer fulfilled and the reservation of benefit rules will apply (unless the donor can pay full consideration for the occupation). Because the donor must not receive a benefit connected with the gift, the donee must not pay more than a fair share of the running costs. The section replaces an earlier, more restricted, exception based on a statement made in parliament in 1986 when the reservation of benefit rules were first introduced.

"Schemes " to avoid the gift with reservation provisions

The reservation of benefit rules are very troublesome to taxpayers who are trying to enjoy their assets while reducing their exposure to inheritance tax and there have been a number of ingenious attempts to capitalise on loopholes in the legislation. **4-034**

Taxpayers have largely been successful in court but have then found the loophole blocked by legislation.

Section 102(5) of the Finance Act 1986 provides that the reservation of benefit rules have no application where there is a disposal to a spouse which is exempt under IHTA 1984 s.18. In *IRC v Eversden* (2003) the Court of Appeal held that if a gift is exempt *at the time it is made*, the reservation of benefit rules cannot have any application at a later date. The duration of the proprietary interest gifted to the spouse is irrelevant. This meant, for example, that a wife could settle property on her husband for life but subject to an overriding power of appointment in favour of a class of beneficiaries including herself. After a short period (say six months) the trustees could terminate the husband's interest so that the discretionary trusts came into effect. The reservation of benefit rules would not apply to the trusts following the husband's life interest. This loophole was closed in relation to disposals made on or after 20 June 2003. A new s.102(5B) provides that the effect of the spouse exemption is limited to the period that the spouse retains an interest in possession. If the interest is terminated, the settlor is treated as making a disposal immediately after the spouse's interest comes to an end. Hence, if H gives W a terminable life interest followed by discretionary trusts and W's interest is terminated, H will be treated as making a transfer on discretionary trusts and the spouse's interest in possession will be ignored.

In *Ingram v IRC* (1999) Lady Ingram successfully divided her interest in property into a 20-year lease and a freehold reversion. The reversion was transferred to trustees to hold for the benefits of persons other than Lady Ingram. Lord Hoffman said that decided cases show that while the legislation prevents a man having his cake and eating it, there is nothing to stop him from "carefully dividing up the cake, eating part of it and having the rest". The House of Lords accepted that a contemporaneous lease and gift of freehold was possible without creating a reservation of benefit.

The effect of the decision was reversed by very narrowly targeted legislation. Section 102A of the Finance Act 1986 provides that a donor will be treated as making a gift with a reservation if he:

(i) makes a gift of an interest in land; and
(ii) retains a "significant" right or interest in the land or is party to a "significant arrangement" in relation to the land in which the gifted property is an interest.

A retained right or interest is not "significant" if the interest was obtained at least seven years before the gift (s.102A(5)). The result is that the section would appear not to apply where a taxpayer grants a reversionary lease more than seven years after acquiring the freehold land. However, pre-owned assets tax may be chargeable. See para.4-035.

Pre-owned assets tax

4-035 Taxpayers continued to develop ways round the reservation of benefit rules. For example, there are no provisions in Finance Act 1986 s.102 for tracing a gift of cash. Hence a taxpayer could give cash to a donee who would use the cash to buy property. The donor could benefit from the property without reserving a benefit.

In response to the ingenuity of taxpayers s.84 of and Sch.15 to the Finance Act 2004 introduced an entirely new charge to income tax, called pre-owned assets tax, where a person gives away assets and enjoys benefits derived from those assets. The rules apply from 2005/2006 and only catch benefits not within the reservation of benefit rules and the exceptions to them. Taxpayers who are liable to pay the pre-owned assets charge can opt out of that regime and into the inheritance tax reservation of benefit provisions (Finance Act 2004 Sch.15 paras 21(2), 22(2) and 22(3)) by making an election.

The election must be made (using Form IHT 500) on or before the relevant filing date which is 31 January of the year of assessment that immediately follows the first year in which the taxpayer would otherwise be chargeable (unless they can show a reasonable excuse—Sch.15 para.23(3)). Once made, the election can be withdrawn or amended by the taxpayer but only before the relevant filing date (Sch.15 para.23(5)). It cannot be withdrawn by the taxpayer's personal representatives.

4. VALUATION OF PROPERTY

General principles of valuation

Section 160 of the IHTA 1984 provides that **4-036**

> "the value at any time of any property shall for the purposes of inheritance tax be the price which the property might reasonably be expected to fetch if sold in the open market at that time; but that price shall not be assumed to be reduced on the grounds that the whole property is to be placed on the market at one and the same time".

The market value of any property is a question of fact. If property is actually sold within a short period after death on the open market the price received will be evidence (though not conclusive evidence) of the market value at the date of death.

The qualification which prohibits the assumption that all the property is to be sold at the same time will not affect valuation in most cases but would be relevant in valuing a large holding of shares in a private company (or even in a public company if the holding was a significant proportion of the share capital).

Valuation of lifetime transfers

On a lifetime transfer the loss to the donor or on death the value of the estate will depend on the valuation of particular items of property. However, it is important to bear in mind that the question is "*what is the reduction in value of the transferor's estate?*" and not "*what is the value of the asset given?*" The answer is frequently not the same. **4-037**

For example, if a taxpayer had a 51 per cent shareholding and gives away two per cent, the transfer of value is the difference between the value of a majority shareholding and a minority shareholding and not the value of two per cent of the shares.

For a real life example of a failure to appreciate this, see *Green v Revenue and Customs Commissioners.* (2015) where a taxpayer transferred 85 per cent of a property, valued at £1,650,000, to a trust in two tranches. The first tranche was 23 per cent of the property and the taxpayer valued this at 23 per cent of £1,650,000 (£379,500); the taxpayer reduced this further by a 10 per cent co-ownership discount to £341,550. However, the basis of calculation was wrong. The loss to the estate was the difference between the initial value of 100 per cent and the value of the 77 per cent remaining. This was agreed by the parties to be £583,000.

The following principles have been developed:

(a) *The sale on the open market is a hypothetical one between a vendor and purchaser* It is assumed that the hypothetical purchaser would make the proper enquiries but would not appear too eager to buy; they embody the demand at the particular time for the property concerned (see *IRC v Gray (surviving executor of Lady Fox)* (1994)).

(b) *No deduction for notional expenses of hypothetical sale* The notional expense of the hypothetical sale in the open market cannot be deducted from the open market price (see *IHT Manual* para.IHTM09703). The open market value is the *gross* amount payable by a purchaser without deduction of any notional expenses: *Duke of Buccleuch v IRC* (1967) and *Executor of Price deceased v HMRC* (2010).

A partial exception to the "no expenses" rule is that allowance is made for additional costs of administration or realisation actually incurred in respect of foreign assets when valuing an estate on death: IHTA 1984 s.173.

(c) *The buyer is not a speculator* The hypothetical vendor and purchaser are serious prudent men of business of the kind who buy and sell the asset in question. If in the real world there are no speculators in the kind of asset under consideration, it is not permissible to invent "*a hypothetical willing speculator*" (see *Bower v HMRC* (2008)).

(d) *Effect of restrictions on sale attached to the particular asset* Restrictions on sale are ignored and the asset is deemed capable of being freely sold. However, the restrictions on a future sale by the purchaser would be taken into account in determining the price which that purchaser would be likely to pay (*IRC v Crossman* (1937)).

In other words, the question is "*what would a purchaser have paid to enjoy the rights attached to the property at the relevant date?*"

(e) *The hypothetical vendor acts to get the largest price possible* For this purpose the estate may be divided into units for the purposes of sale or items of property may be lotted together for sale provided that such splitting or joining does not entail undue expenditure of time and effort (see *IRC v Gray (surviving executor of Lady Fox)* (1994) and *Executor of Price deceased v HMRC* (2010)).

(f) *Price which a "special" purchaser may be prepared to pay should be taken into account* A special purchaser is a person to whom the property has special value and is therefore willing to pay more than an ordinary purchaser. Although the special purchaser is taken into account, there is no certainty that the special purchaser would succeed in buying the property.

Valuation on death

General principles

4-038 On death there is a transfer of value equal to the value of the estate immediately before death. Section 160 of the Inheritance Tax Act 1984 applies so it is important that assets are valued at *market* value. HMRC will normally want to see a statement in a professional valuation that it has been prepared on this basis or a letter instructing the valuer to prepare a valuation on this basis.

Careful valuation on the basis of market value is particularly significant in the case of land. HMRC's guidance to completing IHT 400 states that the valuer should be asked to take into account any development or hope value.

It also says that if, when the property is marketed at the valuation price, offers are received in excess of that valuation, this would suggest that the true value is higher than the marketed price.

In its *Newsletter for Estates and Trusts Practitioners* (2010) HMRC recommended that in such cases taxpayers should

> "ask the valuer to reconsider and, if appropriate, amend the date of death value, taking into account such things as the length of time since the death and movements in the property market".

The December 2004 *IHT Newsletter* announced that from January 2005 the Revenue would be "paying close attention" to the values included for household and personal goods. Personal representatives should normally obtain a professional valuation of such items or be able to explain the basis on which they have determined that such assets are valueless.

There may be cases where personal representatives need to obtain a grant of representation urgently and do not have time to obtain a professional valuation. In *Robertson v CIR* (2002) the Revenue demanded a penalty from a taxpayer who had estimated a value at substantially less than the final figure despite the fact that the taxpayer submitted a corrective account and paid the correct amount before the due date for payment. The Revenue argued that the executor had not fulfilled his obligation under IHTA 1984 s.216(3) to make the fullest inquiries that were reasonably practicable in the circumstances. The Special Commissioner held that the taxpayer had acted perfectly properly and in *Robertson v IRC (No.2)* (2002) the taxpayer was awarded his expenses on the basis that the Revenue had acted "wholly unreasonably" in connection with the hearing.

HMRC publish guidance on avoiding risks of errors in relation to IHT, The IHT Toolkit' which says this in relation to estimates:

> *"To enable you to gather all the necessary information and valuations and to submit as complete a form IHT400 as possible, use as much of the allowable time for submission of the form as necessary. If there is still a problem and, for example, you are unable to get exact values, you can enter a reasonable estimate of value. But you must tell us which figures are estimates. Tell us how you have arrived at the values and why you had to use them, preferably on pages 15 and ¬16 in form IHT400, or in a covering letter or note. You should only use estimates on form IHT400 if you have no other option."*

It is important that taxpayers follow these instructions. In *Cairns v HMRC* (2009) a taxpayer completed the inheritance tax account on the basis of an estimated valuation but did not describe it as provisional or estimated. HMRC demanded a penalty when the property was sold for an amount substantially in excess of the valuation. The Special Commissioners agreed that the failure to describe the valuation as an estimate was an error, but held that on the facts it was "minor, technical and of no consequence". Clearly, however, it is preferable to avoid arguments with HMRC.

Changes in value resulting from death

The transfer of value on death is a transfer of all property owned by the deceased **4-039**
immediately before their death. However, IHTA 1984 s.171(1) provides that:

> "changes in the value of [the] estate which have occurred by reason of the death ... shall be taken into account as if they had occurred before the death".

The effect of this provision is to take into account changes in the market value of property which *result* from the death. Sometimes this will lead to an increase in the value of the estate, sometimes to a decrease.

For example, if the deceased is the managing director of a private company and owns a majority shareholding in it, then the value of the shares may well decline because of the director's death. Such a decline is likely to occur wherever the goodwill of the company is dependent on the personal ability of the deceased and is particularly likely in cases where the deceased has no successor able and willing to continue to run the company's business.

An example of an increase in the value of property resulting from the death of the owner is where the deceased owned a life insurance policy on their own life payable to their estate. Clearly, the value of the policy will increase as a result of the death from the surrender value of the policy to its capital value.

It is important to remember that the transfer on death is a transfer of the deceased's "estate", that is property to which the deceased was beneficially entitled (IHTA 1984 s.5). Thus, any item not in the deceased's beneficial enjoyment will not be part of the estate and will not attract inheritance tax. Always look at insurance policies closely to see whether or not they are part of the estate. A policy on the deceased's life owned beneficially by a third party does not form part of the deceased's estate and so no inheritance tax is payable on the proceeds of the policy on their death. Examples of policies not beneficially owned by the deceased are policies taken out under the Married Women's Property Act 1882 or written in trust for a third party.

The co-ownership discount

4-040 Section 171 only allows changes in the *market* value of property to be taken into account; it does not allow changes in the value of the property *to the deceased* to be taken into account. For this reason, the deceased's share in joint property (which passes to the remaining joint tenant by survivorship) is fully taxable. Although it is true that the value to the deceased's *estate* of the joint property is nil once the deceased is dead, this does not affect the market value of the *property*. However, where the deceased was a co-owner of land, it is normal when valuing the deceased's interest in residential property to allow a 15 per cent discount to reflect the fact that the surviving co-owner will have the right to continue in occupation—see *Wight v Commissioners of the Inland Revenue* (1982).

Where the property is a commercial investment, this factor is not relevant and the discount should be no more than 10 per cent unless the interest is a minority interest or there are other complicating factors—see *St-Clair Ford v Ryder* (2006).

Note, however, that where property is co-owned by spouses or civil partners, the related property rules apply and a discount is not available. See para.4-046.

Special valuation rules

Quoted shares

4-041 Quoted stocks and shares are normally valued by taking the lower of the two prices quoted in the Stock Exchange Daily Official List for the relevant day and adding to it one-quarter of the difference between the lower and higher prices there quoted (for example, if the Daily List shows 200p/205p the value will be 201.25p for inheritance tax purposes) or if it produces a lower figure by taking a figure halfway between the lowest and highest prices at which bargains were struck on the relevant day. The "relevant day" is the day of death or the last or next trading day before or after death. "Quoted" means listed on a recognised stock exchange (IHTA 1984 s.272).

Unquoted shares

In the case of shares not listed on the Stock Exchange, although recent bargains will be taken as a starting point, other factors may lead to a different value being adopted (SP 18/80). **4-042**

The valuation of unquoted shares is factually very difficult but will take into account: the dividend record of the company, the retained earnings (especially where earnings have been retained with a view to increasing the share value), the profitability of the company even if profits have not been used to pay dividends (this is especially relevant where profits have been used to pay high director's fees to a controlling shareholder) and the value of the assets owned by the company (this is especially relevant where the company is likely to be wound up or taken over).

Three special rules apply to the valuation of unquoted shares:

(a) A reduction in value resulting from the death cannot be taken into account if it arises from the fact that the rights attached to the shares are varied as a result of the death (for example, because the articles of the company provide that the shares are then to lose their right to dividend or to vote) (IHTA 1984 s.171(2)).
(b) If the shares are subject to pre-emption rights the market value is to be assessed on the basis that the pre-emption rights do not apply to the hypothetical sale on the open market at the time of death but that they will apply to the hypothetical purchaser (in other words the value is the price which a purchaser would pay knowing that they would be subject to the pre-emption rights in the future). This was established in *IRC v Crossman* (1937) an estate duty case decided on legislation which was in this respect similar to the inheritance tax legislation.
(c) The value on death is calculated on the assumption that a prospective purchaser would have all the information which a prudent prospective purchaser might reasonably require if they were purchasing from a willing vendor by private treaty and at arm's length (IHTA 1984 s.168(1)).

Other assets subject to restrictions on sale

The *Crossman* principle referred to at para.4-037 has been extended to other assets sold, subject to restrictions. For example in *Alexander v IRC* (1991) a flat which had been purchased by the deceased under the "Right to Buy" scheme was subject to an obligation to repay the discount if sold within five years of its purchase. The deceased died one year after purchase. The Court of Appeal held that the property was to be valued on the basis of the amount a purchaser would pay to stand in the shoes of the deceased, i.e. to obtain the property subject to the obligation of repaying the discount if the property was sold within five years. **4-043**

There has been a series of cases on the correct valuation of non-assignable agricultural tenancies, e.g. *Baird's Executors v IRC* (1991); *Walton v IRC* (1996). It has been accepted that such tenancies have a value and therefore the question of deciding on the value is simply a matter of evidence. The Court of Appeal in *Walton* confirmed that there are no hard and fast valuation rules. It is incorrect to proceed on the basis that the landlord is a "special purchaser" if in fact the freeholder is not interested in acquiring the tenancy. The taxpayer should be careful in such a case to gather adequate information on the value of the property. In the absence of such evidence from the taxpayer the view of HMRC will go unchallenged.

Sale within one or four years of death

4-044 If quoted shares are sold within one year of death or an interest in land within four years of death for less than the value at death, then a reduction of the tax may be claimed in certain circumstances (see paras 12-017–12-020).

Commorientes

4-045 Section 184 of the Law of Property Act 1925 provides that where two or more people die in circumstances such that it is uncertain which of them survived, for the purposes of succession to property the deaths are deemed to occur in the order of seniority so that the elder is deemed to die first. Consequently if the elder has left property to the younger, the younger will inherit that property which will then pass under the terms of the will or intestacy of the younger (for a detailed discussion of this rule, see para.16-024).

However, for inheritance tax purposes, s.4(1) provides that the value transferred on death is equal to the value of the deceased's estate immediately before his death and s.4(2) of the IHTA 1984 provides that

> "where it cannot be known which of two or more persons who have died survived the other or others they shall be assumed to have died at the same instant".

Hence, the inheritance tax estate of a person inheriting property as a result of s.184 will not include the value of that inherited property. This avoids a double charge to tax. Where the elder person has left property to the younger it will be taxed as part of the elder's estate (unless an exemption is available) but the younger will not be deemed to have survived for tax purposes and so the property will not be taxed as part of their estate.

Example 30

A and her son B are killed in a car accident. A's will leaves everything to B. B's will leaves everything to X. It is uncertain whether A or B died first; therefore, for the purposes of succession to property the deaths are deemed to occur in order of seniority and A's property passes to B.

B's property (including that which has been inherited from A) then passes to X. For the purposes of inheritance tax, A and B are deemed to die at the same instant. Thus, when calculating inheritance tax payable on B's estate, B's estate is deemed not to include the property received from A.

If A and B in the above example were husband and wife instead of mother and son, the whole of A's estate will be exempt as it is passing to a spouse. B's estate is deemed not to include the property inherited from A. A's property is, therefore, not charged to inheritance tax. B will have the benefit of A's unused nil-rate band and residence nil-rate band. This is an extremely beneficial result but, since it is impossible to guarantee dying in circumstances where s.4(2) would apply, it is difficult to use the provision for effective tax planning. However, when drafting wills for spouses who are agreed on the identity of the default beneficiaries, it may be preferable not to include a survivorship clause at all or to provide that a survivorship clause is not to apply if the order of deaths is uncertain. This ensures that the benefit of the spouse exemption is retained if deaths occur *commorientes*.

Related property

Certain assets are more valuable when owned in conjunction with other assets of the same type than when owned individually. For example, a share in a company owned as part of a majority shareholding in the company will be more valuable than a share owned as part of a minority shareholding. There is a possibility that spouses and civil partners might try to avoid inheritance tax by using the spouse exemption (available on transfers between spouses and civil partners: see IHTA 1984 s.18 and para.4-049) to split the ownership of such items between themselves. In order to prevent this, special rules applying to the valuation of "related property" exist. Section 161(2) of the IHTA 1984 provides that property is related to other property owned by the transferor's spouse or civil partner at the time of the transfer. Property is also related to property which was transferred by the transferor by an exempt transfer to a charity, political party or certain national bodies (as defined by IHTA 1984 Sch.3), and is owned by the charity, etc. at the time of the transfer or has been owned by it within five years before the transfer. This provision is designed to prevent abuse where a person makes an exempt transfer to a charity of property from which they can benefit or which they control. **4-046**

On a transfer of related property the transferred property and the property related to it are valued according to the rules set out in IHTA 1984 s.161.

Sub-section (1) provides that the value of related property is the "appropriate" proportion of the value of the whole. To calculate the appropriate proportion of a property s.161(3) requires the property as a whole to be valued (the aggregate value). The deceased's interest and the related property are then valued separately as if they did not form part of the aggregate. Those two values are then used to establish a ratio. That ratio is then applied to the aggregate. If (and only if) the value of the deceased's share in the aggregate is greater than the value of their separate share, the related value will be substituted.

Sub-section (4) provides that in the case of shares, stock, debentures and units of any other type of property (for example one of a set of items) the individual units are valued as a mathematical proportion of the whole shareholding or total units.

Example 31

A owns 40 per cent of the shares in a private company and A's spouse owns another 30 per cent. If A dies and makes a chargeable transfer of the shares his estate will be taxed not on a 40 per cent holding but on four-sevenths of a 70 per cent holding. This figure is likely to be considerably higher than the value of a 40 per cent holding since a 70 per cent holding usually gives control of the company.

All property held by spouses and civil partners is related but in most cases the value will not be affected (for example, if a husband and wife each owns a motor car neither car will be more highly valued as the values of the two properties are factually entirely independent). Apart from shares in private companies, the most likely types of property which may be more highly valued because of the related property rule are collections of chattels and land held as beneficial joint tenants or as tenants-in-common.

The case of *Arkwright v CIR* (2004) considered the application of s.161 to an interest in land held as beneficial tenants in common by a husband, who was terminally ill, and his wife. On the husband's death HMRC argued that the husband's interest in the land should be valued in accordance with s.161(4) as a fractional share of the whole. Hence his interest should be valued at 50 per cent of the whole. The Special Commissioner found that, whilst that measure was appropriate for separate units of property such as unit trusts or a set of furniture (for example 12 dining chairs), it did not apply to fractions of a single unit such as land. The taxpayers argued successfully that land should be valued in accordance with s.161(1) and (3) where, to establish the related value, it is necessary to:

- value the property as a whole (the aggregate value);
- value the deceased's interest and the related property separately as if they did not form part of the aggregate;
- use those two values to establish a ratio;
- apply that ratio to the aggregate.

The related value is substituted if (and only if) the value of the deceased's share in the aggregate is then greater than the value of their separate share. This means that a deceased co-owner's share of land will only be an exact half of the total where the values of the deceased's property and the related property are identical. Otherwise the value of the deceased's interest will always be more or less than half of the aggregate. The taxpayers contended that when one co-owner was terminally ill, the value of his interest would be less than the value of the healthy co-owner's. This issue was referred to the Lands Tribunal but the case was settled by agreement.

HMRC issued a Revenue and Customs Brief 71/07 stating that it had received legal advice that in some circumstances s.161(4) may, in fact, apply to a fractional share of a single unit and that in future it would apply s.161(4) when valuing shares of land as related property. However, in *Price v HMRC* (2010) HMRC referred to their failure in *Arkwright* to establish that s.161(4) applied to jointly owned land and accepted that s.161(1) and (3) applied as explained in *Arkwright*. The question of the valuation of the deceased's interest in the property valued on that basis was referred to the Upper Tribunal (Lands Chamber) if the parties were unable to agree. HMRC says in the IHT Manual at para.IHTM09737

> "there is still some question whether IHTA1984/S161(4) can apply to shares of land. For this reason, any cases that involve the application of IHTA1984/S161(4) should be referred to Litigation."

When property is valued as related property on death, it is that value which is taxed (unless an exemption applies). However, if that property is sold within three years of death by the personal representatives or a person in whom the property concerned vested immediately after the death in an arm's length sale, it can be revalued as if there had been no related property (IHTA 1984 s.176). This may result in a repayment of tax. Such a revaluation is not permitted where the sale is made in conjunction with a sale of the related property.

Apportionment of income attributable to a period falling partly before and partly after death

4-047 In order to calculate the value of the estate for inheritance tax purposes it is necessary to include any income which accrued prior to death even if it is not paid until after death. The pre-death portion of such income is chargeable to inheritance tax and must be shown on the Inheritance Tax Account (if one is required) while the post-death portion is not chargeable to inheritance tax and will not be shown on an Inheritance Tax Account.

Income which is paid before death and which relates to a period falling wholly or partly after death is not apportioned. It is all treated as a capital asset of the estate. A direction in the will that no apportionments of income should be made, while relevant for the purposes of distribution amongst beneficiaries, is entirely irrelevant for the-purposes of inheritance tax. Similarly, the disapplication of the apportionment rules in trusts created on or after 1 October 2013 introduced by the Trusts (Capital and Income) Act 2013 is irrelevant for inheritance tax purposes: see para.16-062. The following examples illustrate the way in which types of income may have to be apportioned when calculating the value of the estate for-inheritance tax.

Example 32

(a) *Interest.* Interest which has accrued *up to* the date of death on assets such as money in a building society account or deposit bank account is treated as capital and is chargeable to inheritance tax. Interest on such assets which accrues *from* the date of death is treated as income and is not chargeable to inheritance tax.

(b) *Rent.* If the rent is payable in arrear for a period which falls partly before and partly after death it is necessary to apportion the rent. The pre-death portion is included as an asset on the Inheritance Tax Account and is chargeable to inheritance tax, the post-death portion is not.

(c) *Dividends.* Shares maybe valued "cum div." or "ex div.". If they are valued "cum div." this means that the share price has been calculated on the basis that a purchaser buying the stocks or shares would be entitled to the *whole* of the next dividend. The share price is, therefore, increased to compensate the vendor for the loss of that part of the year's interest or dividend that has already accrued. For inheritance tax purposes if the probate valuation is made "cum div." that value is entered on the Inheritance Tax Account and no further reference need be made to the dividend, since the value of the dividend or interest is included in the share price.

As the date for payment of interest or of a dividend approaches companies close their transfer books. This means that if shares are sold after that date the next interest payment or dividend will be sent to the *old* registered owner. If shares are valued after this date they will be valued "ex div.". This means that the basic share price is reduced to compensate the purchaser for the fact that if they buy they will receive no benefit from the next dividend payment. For inheritance tax purposes if the probate valuation is made "ex div." the ex div. price is entered on the Inheritance Tax Account but so is the whole of the dividend payment which will be paid to the estate by the company.

We will see in para.6-016 that for income tax purposes if a dividend is declared after death or interest paid after death for a period which falls partly before and partly after death the whole of such a receipt will be treated as income and will, therefore, be liable to income tax. This could lead to an element of double taxation since the receipt would already have been apportioned and a part of it made chargeable to inheritance tax. There is, therefore, a limited income tax relief (Income Tax (Trading and Other Income) Act 2005 s.669) whereby residuary income is treated as reduced, for the purposes of income tax liability in excess of the basic rate only, by an amount equal to the inheritance tax liability on that income, grossed up at the basic rate.

(d) *Government securities.* A holder of securities receives interest rather than dividends. Just as the price of company shares can be quoted "cum" or "ex div." so the price of securities can be quoted "cum interest" (that is with the right to receive accrued interest) or "ex interest" (that is without the right to receive any of the next interest payment). For inheritance tax purposes if the valuation is "cum interest" that value is entered on the Inheritance Tax Account and no further reference is made to the interest. If the valuation is "ex interest" the capital value of the security and the whole of the next interest payment payable to the estate are included as separate items.

5. EXEMPTIONS

Introduction

4-048 Certain transfers are exempt from inheritance tax as a result of the IHTA 1984 ss.18–29 and other parts of the inheritance tax legislation.

An exempt transfer is not liable to tax nor is it included in the cumulative total of the transferor (so that it does not affect the rate of tax on later transfers). All the exemptions will be considered in this chapter although they are not all relevant on death. The exemptions which are relevant only to transfers made *before* death are included since lifetime gifts are sometimes a suitable (and from the tax point of view beneficial) alternative to disposing of property by will.

Compensation for wrongs suffered during World War II such as payments to slave or forced labourers or other victims of the German Nationalist Socialist (Nazi) regime are exempt. Under IHTA 1984, s.153ZA (replacing Extra Statutory Concession F20 for deaths on or after 1 January 2015) where the payment has been made, or the personal representatives include a value for the right to make a claim, the payment or value for the right is effectively left out account for Inheritance Tax purposes. Section 153ZA (and, before it, the ESC) applies whether or not the money can actually be traced in the deceased's assets and irrespective of when the money is received. If the payment is made, the estate is entitled to the deduction. See para.IHTM04422.

The legislation also extends extended the scope of the existing concession to cover one-off compensation payments of €2,500 (two thousand five hundred euros) made under a recently-created scheme known as the Child Survivor Fund.

Finance Act 2020 added one-off payments made by the German government to Jewish refugees who travelled to the UK on the Kindertransport (Children's Transport) between 1938 and 1940 to the payments exempt from inheritance tax included in s.153ZA. The relief applies to all payments from the Kindertransport fund whenever made and takes effect in relation to deaths on or after 1 January 2019 when the scheme first opened.

If the deceased received a compensation payment during their lifetime for personal harm suffered at the hands of the Japanese or Nazi governments, the amount of tax charged on the estate is reduced by the smaller of either:

- 40 per cent of the payments received;
- the amount of tax payable before allowing the deduction (in other words the

credit is subject to an upper limit of the amount of IHT chargeable on the death).

Example 33

The deceased received a payment of £10,000, which would give a deduction of £10,000 x 40% = £4,000. The Inheritance Tax on the estate before the deduction was £5,000. The tax can be reduced by £4,000.

The figure for the reduction in tax is entered in the Quick Succession Relief ("QSR") section of form IHT400 "Calculation". Applying the reduction can only reduce the tax liability to nil, it cannot result in a repayment of tax. A suitable note explaining the deduction should be provided. The subsequent calculations will automatically apportion the benefit of the reduction across the estate as a whole. In the rare event that QSR is also due, simply add the figures together. See IHTM04423.

If the deceased died having made a claim but before receiving the payment, include the amount claimed in box 76 on form IHT400 and then reduce the tax as above.

Copies of any correspondence showing details of the deceased's claim should be sent with form IHT400. If no correspondence exists, give details in the "Additional information" boxes on pp.15 and 16 of form IHT400.

HMRC guidance for the reliefs can be found in the Inheritance Tax Manuals IHTM4422 and IHTM04423.

Finance Act 2020, s.102 and Sch.15 also introduced inheritance tax exemption (as well as exemptions for income tax and capital gains tax) for payments made under:

(a) the Windrush Compensation Scheme on or after 3 April 2019. This compensation scheme was introduced on 3 April 2019 and compensates those who have suffered loss as a result of being unable to demonstrate their lawful status in the UK;
(b) the Troubles Permanent Disablement Payment Scheme. This compensation scheme was introduced in May 2020 to support victims injured in the Northern Ireland Troubles.
(c) other compensation payments made by or on behalf of a government, public authority or local authority.

A number of compensation schemes have been brought within the exemption by Regulations:

- London Capital and Finance Compensation Scheme (Chargeable Gains Exemption) Regulations 2021 (SI 2021/1385).
- Post Office Horizon Compensation and Infected Blood Interim Compensation Payment Schemes (Tax Exemptions and Relief) Regulations 2023 (SI 2023/184).
- Post Office Horizon Shortfall Scheme Top-Up Payments (Tax Exemptions) Regulations 2023 (SI 2023/772).
- Post Office Horizon Shortfall Scheme and Group Litigation Order Compensation Payments (Inheritance Tax Relief) Regulations 2023 (SI 2023/1009).
- War Widows Recognition Payment Scheme (Income Tax Exemption) Regulations 2023 (SI 2023/1171).

HMRC guidance for the reliefs can be found in the Inheritance Tax Manual at IHTM04142.

The exemption for transfers between spouses and civil partners

4-049 This exemption is equally available for lifetime transfers and on death.

Section 18 of the IHTA 1984 provides that a transfer of value is exempt "to the extent that the value transferred is attributable to property which becomes comprised in the estate of the transferor's spouse or civil partner ...".

This means that gifts to the transferor's spouse or civil partner, before death or on death, are completely exempt. The exemption is lost if the gift does not take effect immediately so that a gift by a testator "to my mother for life, remainder to my spouse" is not an exempt transfer. However, the exemption is not lost if the gift is conditional and the condition is satisfied within 12 months of the transfer. Thus, if property is left to a spouse or civil partner, provided they survive for a period of up to 12 months, the exemption will be available provided that the spouse or civil partner survives the specified period. However, there are other considerations which make a survivorship period exceeding six months inadvisable. Such a gift will be treated as creating a relevant property settlement (see Ch.7) and will result in an immediate chargeable transfer from the deceased to the settlement.

The exemption is available for interests created on death even though the gift to the spouse or civil partner is not absolute, provided the interest is immediate. The exemption applies, therefore, if a testator makes a gift by will "to my spouse for life, remainder to my son".

The exemption was available for lifetime transfers made before 22 March 2006 to a settlement in which a spouse or civil partner had an interest in possession as these were treated as a gift "to" the spouse or civil partner. In the case of transfers made on or after that date (apart from those covered by the transitional provisions—see Ch.7) the exemption is not available as such settlements are relevant property settlements.

For inheritance tax purposes (unlike income tax and capital gains tax) "spouse" and "civil partner" has a normal meaning so that the exemption is available even though the parties are separated. Same sex marriages have been possible since 13 March 2014, the date on which the bulk of the Marriage (Same Sex Couples) Act 2013 came into force. Opposite sex civil partnerships have been possible since 31 December 2019, under the Civil Partnerships, Marriages and Deaths (Registration etc) Act 2019 and the Civil Partnership (Opposite-sex Couples) Regulations 2019.

In *Executor of Holland deceased v IRC* (2003) the special commissioners held that the exemption was limited to married couples and was not available to cohabitees. This was not contrary to the Human Rights Act. Cohabitees are not analogous to married couples and, in any event, the difference in treatment was objectively and reasonably justifiable. Married persons have mutual rights and obligations relating to maintenance during their lives and after their deaths. These interlocking property rights and obligations justify the special tax treatment of spouses.

In *Burden v UK* (2008) two elderly, unmarried sisters who had lived together their whole lives, and for the last 30 years in a house built on land inherited from their parents, complained to the European Court of Human Rights that that their inability to benefit from the spouse exemption from inheritance tax amounted to discriminatory treatment in respect of their right to peaceful enjoyment of their possessions. They lost both at first instance and on appeal. The Grand Chamber of the European Court of Human Rights held that the relationship between adult siblings on the one hand and between spouses or civil partners on the other was qualitatively different. The relationships of marriage and civil partnership involve a public undertaking carrying with it rights and obligations of a contractual nature, which set those relationships apart from other types of cohabitation. There had therefore been no discrimination.

Non-domiciled spouses and civil partners

Only a limited exemption is available

Section 18(2) of the IHTA 1984 limits the amount of the exemption in the case of transfers from a UK-domiciled spouse or civil partner to a spouse or civil-partners who is domiciled elsewhere: for transfers on or after 6 April 2013 the first £325,000 transferred is exempt. The exemption is linked to the level of the nil-rate band so will increase automatically as and when the nil-rate band increases. For transfers before 6 April 2013 only the first £55,000 transferred was exempt. **4-050**

Example 34

Fred who is domiciled in England and Wales is married to Isabella who is domiciled in Spain. He dies in 2024/25 leaving her his £1 million estate. Under s.18(2) only the first £325,000 is exempt. However, if he has a full nil-rate band available there will be no tax on a further £325,000. The excess will be chargeable at 40 per cent.

The election to be UK domiciled

Finance Act 2013 introduced a further change (contained in IHTA 1984 ss.267ZA and 267ZB) to the position of non-domiciled spouses and civil partners. They can now elect to be treated as UK domiciled in order to benefit from an unrestricted spouse exemption on gifts from the domiciled spouse. **4-051**

There is a downside to making such an election as all their non-UK assets will cease to be excluded property and will become chargeable to UK inheritance tax. The election is irrevocable although there are circumstances in which it will lapse (see below).

There are two types of election:

- *A lifetime election.* The person electing must have had a UK domiciled spouse or civil partner at any time on or after 6 April 2013 and during the period of seven years before the election is made.
- *A death election.* The person electing must at any time on or after 6 April 2013 and within the period of seven years ending with the date of death have been the spouse or civil partner of a person who died domiciled in the UK or the personal representative of such a person.

Note that the marriage or civil partnership does not have to be continuing at the date of the election.

Both types of election can be backdated to a specified date which can be up to seven years before:

(i) the date of the election in the case of lifetime elections;

(ii) the date of the spouse's death in the case of death elections.

However, the specified date cannot be before 6 April 2013.

If no date is specified, the lifetime election takes effect on the date it is made and the death election is treated as taking effect immediately before the death of the spouse or civil partner.

The death election must be made within two years of the death of the spouse or such longer period as an officer of HMRC may in the particular case allow (IHTA 1984 s.267ZB(6)).

The first opportunity to make an election was on 17 July 2013 (the date when the Finance Act 2013 received Royal Assent).

Example 35

Fred (UK domiciled) gives £500,000 to Isabella (Spanish domiciled) on 1 December 2016. She can make a lifetime election at any point within the next seven years and specify that it is to take effect as from the day of the gift. If Isabella has substantial assets in Spain, she should not rush to make the election as those assets will become chargeable to inheritance tax. Fred's gift is a potentially exempt transfer so there is no tax to pay unless he dies within seven years. If he does, she can make a death election and backdate it to the day of the transfer death. If she dies without making an election, her personal representatives can make one on her behalf (IHTA 1984 s.267A(2)).

The election cannot be revoked. However, if the person making it is not UK resident for the purposes of income tax for a period of four successive tax years beginning at any time after the election is made, the election ceases to have effect at the end of that period.

Hence if Isabella in the example above returns to Spain a few weeks after Fred's death (say January 2019), her election will cease to have effect after four full tax years. Her non-UK assets will, therefore, be free of the UK inheritance tax net at the start of tax year 2024/25.

Gifts to charities, etc.

4-052 "Transfers of value are exempt to the extent that the values transferred ... are attributable to property which is given to charities or registered clubs (that is community amateur sports clubs". (IHTA 1984 s.23)

There is no limit to the amount which is exempt under this provision. As with the spouse exemption the gift must be immediate and, if conditional, any condition must be satisfied within 12 months. In addition a gift to a charity must normally be absolute if the exemption is to be available.

The relief had been limited to UK charities but s.30 of and Sch.6 to the Finance Act 2010 gave the same UK tax reliefs to any charity (UK or EU) which met the four conditions set out in Pt 1 Sch.6. However, following the UK's withdrawal from the European Union, Finance (No. 2) Act 2023 amended the conditions to limit relief to charities within the jurisdiction of UK courts. The change took effect from 15 March 2023 although this was extended to 1 April 2024 in the case of charities that had previously established their status for UK charitable tax reliefs. To qualify as a charity, from 1 April 2024, an organisation must now meet the following conditions:

(a) *It must be established for charitable purposes only* Charitable purposes are defined by reference to s.2 of the Charities Act 2011; i.e. to be entitled to

UK charitable tax reliefs, a charity must have charitable purposes as defined in that Act, and be of public benefit according to English charity law principles.

(b) *It must meet a "jurisdiction condition"* A charity must be subject either to the jurisdiction of the High Court (in England and Wales), the Court of Session (in Scotland) or the High Court in Northern Ireland.

(c) *It must meet a "registration condition"* Charities established in England and Wales must have complied with "*any requirement*" to register with the Charity Commission; other charities must have satisfied "*any requirement*" to be registered in a corresponding register under the law of its own.

(d) It must meet a "management condition"

An organisation meets the management condition if "*its managers are fit and proper persons to be managers of the body or trust*". "Managers" are those having general control and management over the running of the charity. "Fit and proper" is not defined. HMRC guidance suggests that those with a history of tax fraud or other fraudulent behaviour including misrepresentation and/or identity theft would probably not be regarded as fit and proper.

When drafting a will which directs that funds are to be used for charitable purposes, it is important to limit those purposes to the UK. If funds could be applied for non-UK charities, the exemption will not be available. See *Withers Trust Corp Ltd v Goodman's Estate* (2023) for an example.

Transfers of value to exempt political parties are entitled to relief in the same way as transfers to charity. A political party qualifies for exemption if it had two members elected to the House of Commons at the last general election or one member if the party's candidates generally got at least 150,000 votes.

Transfers of value to certain national bodies are entitled to relief in the same way as transfers to charities. The IHTA 1984 Sch.13 contains a list of the national bodies to which this rule applies; they include, for example, national museums and art galleries, universities and their libraries, local authorities and government departments.

Transfers of value to non-profit-making bodies (other than charities, political parties and national bodies) are also exempt if the property transferred is within certain specified categories (which may broadly be described as covering scenic, historic or scientifically important land, buildings, books, papers or objects) and the Treasury direct that an exemption is to be available.

Transfers to charities, etc. are only exempt if the money or other property given is to be used exclusively for the purposes of a charity, political party, national or non-profit-making body. The exemptions are not available if "the property or any part of it *may* become applicable for (other) purposes ..." (IHTA 1984 ss.24(3), 25(2), 26(7)).

The "annual" exemption

This exemption is only available on transfers made *before* death. Section 19 of the IHTA 1984 provides for an annual exemption of £3,000. This exemption applies to the first £3,000 of transfers in each tax year (6 April to 5 April inclusive). This exemption is available in addition to other exemptions so that a transferor can give as much property as they like to their spouse or civil partner and still have the annual exemption available for gifts to others. **4-053**

To the extent that the annual exemption is not used in a particular year the unused part may be carried forward for one year but no longer. For example, a transferor who made no transfer last year will be entitled to a £6,000 exemption this year. To ensure that the carry forward is limited to one year the exemption of the current year must be used first and only after the whole of that exemption is exhausted can anything brought forward from the previous year be used.

Example 36

If A transfers nothing in year one, £6,000 of relief will be available in year two. If only £4,000 is transferred in year two, this will use up the whole of year two's exemption and £1,000 from year one. Thus, in year three only an exemption of £3,000 will be available.

If more than one transfer is made in a tax year, the annual exemption must be allocated to the first chargeable transfer made in that tax year. If more than one transfer is made on the same day the exemption is apportioned pro rata irrespective of the order in which the gifts are made.

The annual exemption must be allocated to the *first* transfer in a tax year even though that transfer would otherwise be potentially exempt. This means that it is more tax efficient to make a lifetime chargeable transfer earlier in the tax year than a potentially exempt transfer.

Example 37

Arshad has never made any transfers of value. In the tax year 2024/25 he gives £331,000 to Bhopal and then gives £331,000 to a discretionary trust. He survives seven years.

The annual exemption must be allocated to the first transfer which is therefore exempt as to £6,000 and potentially exempt as to £325,000; the second transfer is a lifetime chargeable transfer of £331,000. As Arshad survives seven years, the potentially exempt transfer becomes fully exempt and Arshad derives no benefit from the annual exemption.

Small gifts exemption

4-054 In addition to the annual exemption, outright lifetime gifts worth up to £250 per donee are exempt (IHTA 1984 s.20). This exemption does not apply to the first part of a gift which exceeds £250 (for example, a donor who gives three people £250 each does not pay any tax and does not use up any of the £3,000 exemption but, if £600 is given to one donee, £600 of the £3,000 exemption is used up).

Normal expenditure out of income

4-055 The relief for normal expenditure is only available for lifetime transfers. The IHTA 1984 s.21 provides that a transfer of value is exempt to the extent that:

(a) It is made as part of the normal expenditure of the transferor. (It is a question of fact whether this requirement is satisfied. Expenditure may be "normal" if the donor has entered into a commitment to make payments on a regular basis or if payments are actually made on a regular basis without any commitment.
(b) It is (taking one year with another) made out of income.
(c) It is such that the transferor's usual standard of living is not affected by it.

Bennett v IRC (1995) shows how useful this exemption can be in tax planning.

Mrs Bennett was an elderly widow and the life tenant of a trust which had always produced a very modest income (£300 p.a. approximately). In 1987 the income of the trust increased enormously as a result of the sale of trust assets. Mrs Bennett instructed her trustees to continue to pay her £300 p.a. and to use the surplus income, for which she had no need, to her sons. The trustees paid £9,300 in 1989 to each of the three sons and £60,000 the following year. She then died. The Revenue contended that the transfers were potentially exempt transfers which became chargeable on her death within seven years. The personal representatives contended that they were exempt as normal expenditure out of income.

The court agreed that the transfers were exempt. It said that "normal expenditure" required a demonstration of a settled pattern of giving. This could be demonstrated by a pattern of giving over a period of time or by the individual assuming a commitment.

> "There is no fixed minimum period during which the expenditure should have occurred ... if the prior commitment or resolution can be shown, a single payment implementing the commitment or resolution may be-sufficient ... the amount of expenditure need not be fixed in amount nor indeed the individual recipient be the same. As regards quantum, it is sufficient that a formula or standard has been adopted by application of which the payment (which may be of a fluctuating amount) can be identified ...."

In *McDowall v IRC* (2004) an attorney made a number of gifts to family members from accumulated surplus income which had been placed on deposit. Although the gifts were held to be invalid as being beyond the attorney's powers, the court accepted that the exemption would otherwise have applied. The gifts were made out of retained income which remained income in character rather than capital; it was identifiably money which was essentially unspent income and which had been placed on deposit, but not invested in any more formal sense.

The question of when income ceases to be income and becomes capital remains contentious. HMRC states in the *IHT Manual* that there are no hard and fast rules, but:

> "If there is no evidence to the contrary, we consider that income becomes capital after a period of two years. Evidence to the contrary could impact either way as income:
>
> - may immediately be invested in a capital product and become capital, or
> - may be retained as income for more than two years with a specific purpose in mind.
>
> Each case will depend on its own facts but, in general, the longer the period of accumulation, the more likely it is that the income has become capital."

Income is not defined for this purpose. HMRC states at para.IHTM14250 that it should be determined for each year in accordance with "normal accountancy rules". It is not necessarily the same as income for income tax purposes. Income is the net income after payment of income tax.

It is usually clear whether payments received are income in nature. However in the same paragraph of the *IHT Manual* HMRC states that payments received on a regular basis which appear to be income may in fact be capital in nature. It gives the example of capital withdrawals from a discounted gift scheme.

Gifts in consideration of marriage or civil partnership

4-056 This exemption is only available on lifetime transfers. Section 22 of the IHTA 1984 provides that a gift in consideration of marriage or civil partnership is exempt to the extent of:

(a) £5,000 if made by a parent of one of the parties to the marriage or civil partnership;
(b) £2,500 if made by a remoter ancestor of one of the parties or by a party to the prospective marriage or civil partnership; and
(c) £1,000 in any other case.

The limits apply to each marriage or civil partnership, not to each donee (so that a parent cannot give £5,000 to his child and £1,000 to his future child-in-law and obtain exemption for £6,000).

Family maintenance

4-057 This exemption is only available on lifetime transfers. Section 11 of IHTA 1984 provides that a disposition is not a transfer of value (and so is effectively exempt) if it is made by one party to a marriage or civil partnership in favour of the other party and is for the maintenance of the other party. There would usually be a spouse exemption anyway (see para.4-049) but the family maintenance exemption applies to transfers made on the dissolution or annulment of a marriage or civil partnership (and variations of such dispositions) and to those to spouses or civil partners domiciled outside the UK whereas the normal spouse exemption does not.

In *PRs of Phizackerley v HMCR* (2007) the taxpayer argued that Mr Phizackerley's lifetime gift of a half interest in the house to his wife was not a transfer of value because it fell under s.11 as a disposition for family maintenance. Had it done so, Mr Phizackerly's estate would have escaped Finance Act 1986 s.103 which makes a debt non-deductible if it was incurred in consideration of property derived from the deceased; s.103(4) provides that s.103 does not apply if the initial disposition was not a transfer of value. The Special Commissioner agreed that the ordinary meaning of maintenance is wide enough to cover the transfer of a house or part interest in a house if it relieves the recipient from income expenditure, for example rent. Sadly for the taxpayers he considered that the reason married couples put their house into joint names, is not to provide for the maintenance of the other party but to give the other party security. When a husband put a house into the joint names of himself and his wife during their marriage it is not within the ordinary meaning of maintenance. The disposition had, therefore, not been for maintenance and the taxpayer's argument failed.

The exemption is also available for dispositions for maintenance, education or training of a child for a period ending not later than the year in which he attains the age of 18 or, after attaining that age, ceases to undergo full-time education or training. The disposition can be made by:

- either party to a marriage or civil partnership children to a child of either party;
- the parent of an illegitimate child; or
- a non-parent where the child is not in the care of its parents although, if the disposition is for education or training after the age of 18, the child must have been in the care of the person making the disposition for substantial

> periods (this prevents grandparents making use of the exemption to fund the costs of university education for grandchildren living away from home).

There is scope for s.11 to be used by single parents (who have no spouse exemption available) to make death bed provision for the maintenance of their children. However, the section requires the provision to be limited to the minority of the child or the termination of full time education or training whichever is the earlier.

There is an oddity here. The relief is available under s.11(4) to the parent of an illegitimate child who makes gifts for the appropriate purpose. It is available to people who are married or in a civil partnership under s.11(1). However where a marriage or civil partnership has ended whether by death, divorce or dissolution, the exemption will not apply where a parent makes a disposition in favour of his or her own legitimate child other than by way of divorce provision or variation of divorce provision.

Section 11(3) provides that dispositions in favour of dependent relatives other than spouses and children are not transfers of value to the extent that they are "reasonable provision for care or maintenance".

Where a disposition satisfies the conditions of the preceding provisions of this section to a limited extent only, for example because the amount given is excessive, s.11(5) provides that the gift is to be apportioned and treated as two separate dispositions. In *McKelvey v RCC* (2008) a taxpayer who was terminally ill gave two investment properties to her elderly mother intending that they would be sold after her death and the proceeds used to pay for residential care for her mother. In fact the properties were never sold as the mother was cared for at home by other family members until her death. HMRC considered the gift to be a potentially exempt transfer made by the daughter within seven years of her death and, therefore, chargeable. The taxpayers contended that the properties were given for maintenance of a dependant and fell within s.11.

The Special Commissioner decided that the question of whether or not the gift was made for maintenance had to be determined at the date the gift was made and that subsequent events were irrelevant. Here, the gift was clearly made for maintenance. The next question was whether the gift was "reasonable" provision for maintenance. Reasonable imports an objective standard. Taking into account the mother's age and the cost of care, the bulk of the gift (£140,500) fell within s.11(3) and was not a transfer of value. The balance (£28,500) was excessive and was, therefore, chargeable.

Cumulative effect of exemptions

All the exemptions set out above (other than the small gifts exemption dealt with at para.4-053) are cumulative with each other. After the exemptions have been claimed the transferor is entitled to a certain amount (£325,000 for tax year 2024/25) taxed at a nil-rate. For example, a transferor who has made no previous gifts and who wishes to benefit their child who is about to be married as much as possible without a potential liability to inheritance tax if they die within seven years could give the following: **4-058**

Annual exemption from last year	£3,000
Annual exemption for this year	£3,000
Marriage exemption	£5,000
Nil-rate band	£325,000

The transferor's spouse could make similar provision immediately and both could give further sums of £3,000 annually. Seven years after these gifts the potentially exempt transfer of £325,000 will prove to be exempt and the transferor will be free to make further transfers up to the limit of the then nil-rate band without any liability to inheritance tax.

Death while responding to emergency circumstances

4-059 Section 153A introduced a new exemption which applies for deaths on or after 19 March 2014. It provides that no inheritance tax will be charged on the death estate or on lifetime transfers made within seven years of death where a person:

(a) dies from an injury sustained, accident occurring or disease contracted at a time when that person was responding to emergency circumstances in that person's capacity as an emergency responder; or
(b) dies from a disease contracted at some previous time, the death being due to, or hastened by, the aggravation of the disease during a period when that person was responding to emergency circumstances in that person's capacity as an emergency responder.

"Emergency circumstances" are defined in s.153A(3) as circumstances which are present or imminent and are causing or likely to cause:

(a) the death of a person;
(b) serious injury to, or the serious illness of, a person;
(c) the death of an animal;
(d) serious injury to, or the serious illness of, an animal;
(e) serious harm to the environment (including the life and health of plants and animals);
(f) serious harm to any building or other property; or
(g) a worsening of any such injury, illness or harm.

Section 153A(4) provides that a person is "responding to emergency circumstances" if the person:

(a) is going anywhere for the purpose of dealing with emergency circumstances occurring there; or
(b) is dealing with emergency circumstances, preparing to do so imminently or dealing with the immediate aftermath of emergency circumstances.

"Emergency responder" is defined in s.153A(5):

(a) a person employed, or engaged, in connection with the provision of fire services or fire and rescue services;
(b) a person employed for the purposes of providing, or engaged to provide, search services or rescue services (or both);
(c) a person employed for the purposes of providing, or engaged to provide, medical, ambulance or paramedic services;
(d) a constable or a person employed for police purposes or engaged to provide services for police purposes;
(e) a person employed for the purposes of providing, or engaged to provide, services for the transportation of organs, blood, medical equipment or medical personnel; or
(f) a person employed, or engaged, by the government of a state or territory,

an international organisation or a charity in connection with the provision of humanitarian assistance.

It is immaterial whether the employment or engagement is paid or unpaid.

Example 38

Faheem, a fireman, is killed when the fire engine in which he is travelling to deal with a fire overturns. The exemption applies to tax becoming due on lifetime transfers made within seven years of his death as well as to his death estate.

Death on active service

Section 154 of the IHTA 1984 provides that no inheritance tax will be charged on the death estate of or, in the case of deaths on or after 19 March 2014, on lifetime transfers made within seven years of death by a person certified by the Ministry of Defence or the Secretary of State as having died from: **4-060**

(a) a wound inflicted, accident occurring or disease contracted while acting as set out in s.154(2); or
(b) a disease contracted at some previous time, the death being due to or hastened by the aggravation of the disease while acting as set out in s.154(2).

Section 154(2) provides that at the time the wound was inflicted or the disease was contracted or aggravated, the deceased must have been a member of the armed forces of the Crown or a civilian subject to service discipline within the meaning of the Armed Forces Act 2006:

(a) on active service against an enemy; or
(b) on other service of a warlike nature or which in the opinion of the Treasury involved the same risks as service of a warlike nature; or
(c) responding to emergency circumstances in the course of the person's duties as a member of any of the armed forces or as a civilian subject to service discipline.

The person must be responding to emergency circumstances "in the course of their duties" and so must be on duty. A soldier who dies assisting at an incident whilst on leave, or who was on duty, but whose unit was not assigned to respond to emergency circumstances, would not qualify.

In *Barty-King v Ministry of Defence* (1979) (decided on an earlier section) May J said:

> "the purpose and nature of the legislation seem to me to require a benevolent interpretation in favour of the estate of the deceased".

In *Barty-King* the fourth Duke of Westminster had died of cancer in 1967 after sustaining a wound in 1944 while on active service. May J held that the proper question to ask was

> "whether the wound was a cause of the deceased's death, and not whether the wound was the direct cause of the death".

In order to claim the exemption it is essential to obtain a certificate. Paragraph IHTM11304 of HMRC's *IHT Manual* deals with the procedure for claiming exemption.

Death of constables and service personnel targeted because of their status

4-061 The death in service exemption set out at para.4-060 was extended by s.155A of the IHTA 1984 to apply where it is certified by the Defence Council or the Secretary of State that a person:

(a) died from an injury sustained or disease contracted in circumstances where the person was deliberately targeted by reason of his or her status as a service person or former service person; or
(b) died from a disease contracted at some previous time, the death being due to, or hastened by, the aggravation of the disease by an injury sustained or disease contracted in circumstances mentioned in para (a).

Conditional exemption for heritage property

4-062 "Conditional" exemption is available on death and on certain lifetime transfers in respect of assets designated by the Treasury as being of national, scientific, historic or artistic interest (IHTA 1984 ss.31–35 as amended). Claims must be made within two years of the transfer of value or such longer period as the Board may allow (s.30(3BA) inserted by Finance Act 1998). The exemption is only available if suitable undertakings are given. The taxpayer must undertake to take reasonable steps to preserve the asset, to secure reasonable access to the public and to keep objects permanently in the UK.

There were concerns that proper access for the public was not always made available. The Finance Act 1998, therefore, provided that access by prior appointment is not sufficient. There must be extended access and also greater disclosure of information about items. See IHTA 1984 s.31(4FA) and (4FB). The exemption is "conditional" on these undertakings. Tax becomes payable if an undertaking is broken or if there is a disposal and similar undertakings are not given. Tax will normally become payable in any event if the asset is sold. Existing undertakings can be varied as regards extended access and publication by agreement or, where no agreement has been reached on a variation proposed by HMRC within six months, by the direction of a tribunal. The tribunal must be satisfied that the proposed variation is "just and reasonable". See *Re A and B's Undertakings* (2005) for a discussion of the matters it is appropriate to consider.

It was not possible for owners of heritage assets to meet all their undertakings during the Covid pandemic. HMRC issued guidance in May 2020 to confirm that where properties could not be opened or access could not be given to assets due to social distancing issues, this would not be treated as a breach of the conditions.

HMRC's guidance was further updated in June and December 2021 to confirm that HMRC would not consider agreements broken where reasonable public access could not be provided when following guidance on social distancing.

The temporary rules surrounding the closing or delayed opening of properties due to the pandemic ceased on 1 April 2022.

6. RELIEFS

Introduction

4-063 A relief may reduce the tax payable on a particular asset in whole or in part if the required conditions are satisfied. A variety of reliefs are available such as quick succession relief under s.161 of the IHTA 1984 (where a *death* occurs within five years of a chargeable transfer), relief on the value of growing timber under the IHTA 1984 ss.125–130 (where within two years of a death an election claiming relief is made) and, most importantly, reliefs for business and agricultural property under IHTA 1984 ss.103–114 and ss.115–124A.

Quick succession relief and timber relief are only available on death, not on transfers made before death.

The reliefs on business and on agricultural property are available on both lifetime and death transfers. They take effect by means of a percentage reduction in the value transferred. A reduction in the value transferred will have the effect of reducing the tax payable. The relief will prevent any charge to tax arising, where it brings the value transferred within the nil-rate band.

The object of these reliefs is to ease the burden of taxation on businesses and agricultural land. To ensure that taxpayers cannot take unfair advantage of them there are rules requiring a minimum period of ownership before the relief becomes available. Further mitigation of the hardship of paying tax out of business and agricultural property (which might otherwise lead to the forced sale of such property) is provided by the instalment option (as to which see para.4-091 and following).

Agricultural relief

When is agricultural property relief available?

Agricultural relief is available in respect of "agricultural property". **4-064**

Section 115(2) defines "agricultural property". The definition has three limbs and says that agricultural property:

(a) means "agricultural land or pasture" ("Limb 1");
(b) it includes "woodland and any building used in connection with the intensive rearing of livestock or fish if the woodland or building is occupied with agricultural land or pasture and the occupation is ancillary to that of agricultural land or pasture" ("Limb 2");
(c) it also includes "such cottages, farm buildings and farmhouses, together with the land occupied with them, as are of a character appropriate to the property" ("Limb 3").

In order to get relief, there must be agricultural land or pasture. The assets mentioned in Limbs 2 and 3 are essentially ancillary to the land.

The definition has been extended (in the case of transfers made on or after 6 April 1995) to include land used for short-term coppice.

Farm buildings and cottages must have been occupied for the purposes of agriculture (IHTA 1984 s.117). However an ESC dated 13 February 1995 extends the relief to cottages by retired farm employees or their surviving spouses in certain circumstances. See *IHT Manual* at para.IHTM24034.

Agricultural relief takes the form of a percentage reduction in the "agricultural value" of the property which is defined as "the value of the property if the property were subject to a perpetual covenant prohibiting its use otherwise than as agricultural property" (s.115(3)). The effect of this definition is that relief is available to the extent of the value of a farm or other agricultural property *as a farm* but any other value attached to it, such as development value, is not relieved (although business property relief may be available on that value—see para.4-072 and following).

In the case of charges to tax arising on or after 10 March 1992, the reduction in value is either 100 per cent or 50 per cent.

The percentage reduction in the agricultural value of the property is 100 per cent:

(i) if the taxpayer has the right to vacant possession or the right to obtain it within the next 12 months. This applies to in-hand farming (including contract farming) and (usually) to land let on grazing licences;

(ii) if the property let on a tenancy beginning on or after 1 September 1995 (either a farm business tenancy or a successor Agricultural Holdings Act tenancy).

In other cases (typically to Agricultural Holdings Act 1986 tenancies), the relief is at 50 per cent. It may be possible to "convert" a pre-1995 tenancy into a new tenancy thereby securing relief at 100 per cent for the landowner. See Regulatory Reform (Agricultural Tenancies) (England and Wales) Order 2006.

The right to agricultural relief only arises if certain requirements are satisfied. First, the transferor must have *occupied* the land for the purposes of agriculture "throughout the period of two years ending with the date of the transfer" or it must have been *owned* by them throughout the period of seven years ending with the date of the transfer and was occupied by them *or another* for the purposes of agriculture throughout that period (s.117). This means that farmers who buy their own farm qualify for relief (at 100 per cent) after two years if they continue to occupy it up to the time of transfer. A person who buys a farm and puts in a tenant qualifies for relief (at 100 per cent) only after seven years. A tenant who purchases their farm qualifies for relief (at 100 per cent) immediately if they have been in occupation for two years. Any break in the periods of ownership or occupation is fatal to the availability of the relief.

Special rules apply in relation to the occupation requirement where a farmer moves from one farm to another (s.118), where a farm is owned by the spouse of a former owner, or where there is a transfer within two years of a previous transfer, provided one transfer is on death (s.120).

A transfer of shares in a company which owns agricultural property is eligible for relief to the extent that the value of the shares reflects the agricultural value of land and provided the shareholder is in control of the company. Occupation by the company is deemed to be occupation by the controlling shareholder (s.119).

What is agriculture?

4-065 The Inheritance Tax Act 1984 does not contain a definition of "agriculture". There is a definition in the Agricultural Holdings Act 1986, s.96 and the Agricultural Tenancies Act 1995, s.38 which is *"horticulture, fruit growing, seed growing, dairy farming and livestock breeding and keeping, the use of land as grazing land, meadow land, osier land, market gardens and nursery grounds, and the use of land for woodlands where that use is ancillary to the farming of land for other agricultural purposes".*

Paragraph 24062 of the Inheritance Tax Manual says that the position has to be considered carefully where land is used other than for arable or pastoral farming.

An example of non-agricultural use is the cutting of reeds for thatching on the basis that there is no tilling, sowing or cultivating. The reeds are simply cut.

The grazing of land by horses other than those connected with agriculture is not occupation of land for an agricultural purpose. The breeding and grazing of racehorses on a stud farm is made an agricultural purpose for the purposes of agricultural relief by IHTA 1984, s.115(4).

There is much discussion at the time of writing of the changing nature of agriculture. Many farmers are diversifying and there are various schemes available some but not all of which attract agricultural property relief.

- *Habitat schemes* These schemes (for example, salt marshes, water fringes, former set-aside land) tend to prevent agricultural production for long periods of up to 20 years and so land managed under these schemes would not qualify for agricultural relief without being brought into scope by the specific provisions. IHTA 1984, s.124C provides that for deaths on or after 26 November 1996 land in specified habitat schemes is deemed as agricultural land, with the result that the management of the land is deemed as agriculture, and buildings (including farmhouses) used in connection with such management are regarded as farm buildings.
- *Environmental Land Management Schemes* Schemes, such as Countryside Stewardship and Landscape Recovery pay farmers to provide environmental and climate goods and services. Land which been taken out of agricultural production over an extended period for an environmental scheme or project is unlikely to qualify for agricultural relief. However, owner-occupiers may continue to benefit from business property relief if the land is still used in the business and the overall business is not one of wholly or mainly making or holding investments.

Example 39

> An individual owns a 300 acre farm used for raising cattle and growing root crops. They decide to remove 80 acres of the land from agricultural production and enter it into an agri-environment scheme for which they receive grant payments. As the 80 acres is no longer being used for the purposes of agriculture it will not qualify for agricultural property relief. However, as the individual's business is still mainly one of farming, providing the income from the agri-environmental scheme is received by and used in the business, the land will qualify for business property relief as it is used in a business that is not wholly or mainly one of making or holding investments.

- *Carbon and Peatland Codes* The government is investing in *"Nature Markets"* to enable farmers and land managers to attract private investment to increase the provision of ecosystem services such as carbon sequestration and biodiversity. This is not agriculture. However, land registered and validated to the Woodland Carbon and Peatland Codes to generate units will, in principle, qualify for business property relief in its own right. HMRC consider that the activities necessary to create, manage and maintain the land for the purposes of generating units for use or sale mean the business is not an investment business. This means that owner-occupiers continue to benefit from business property relief provided the overall business is not one of wholly or mainly making or holding investments. However, a land owner who has let property to a tenant who abandons conventional agriculture in favour of the provision of such services will not be entitled to business property relief as their business will be regarded as an investment business (but see the response to the Consultation Paper "*Taxation of environmental land management and ecosystem service markets*" below).

In 2023 the Conservative government issued a Consultation Paper "*Taxation of environmental land management and ecosystem service markets*", which looked at the tax treatment of land management schemes, including the woodland Carbon Code and Peatland Code. Then Conservative government responded in 2024 proposing that it would:

- establish a joint HM Treasury and HMRC working group with industry representatives to try to provide clarity on the taxation of ecosystem service markets where existing law or guidance is lacking;
- extend the existing scope of agricultural property relief from 6 April 2025 to land managed under an environmental agreement with, or on behalf of, the UK government, devolved administrations, public bodies, local authorities or approved responsible bodies;
- not introduce the suggested restriction of agricultural property relief to tenancies of at least eight years.

The new Labour government has not made any firm proposals at the time of writing.

Occupation for the purposes of agriculture

4-066 Section 117 requires occupation to have been for the purposes of agriculture In *Atkinson v RCC* (2011) the Upper Tribunal had to decide whether a farm cottage had been occupied for the purposes of agriculture where the elderly partner who lived in it had been in residential care for four years before his death, though his possessions remained in the cottage. It said that in such cases there had to be an "objective connection" with the agricultural activities on the farm. Use of a dwelling house can be occupation for the purposes of agriculture even if the occupant is not engaged in physical agricultural work; for example the farm bookkeeper. The partner's use of the bungalow before moving into the home could be seen as occupation for agricultural purposes. Once he had gone into residential care the connection between the use of the bungalow and the activities on the rest of the farm, was broken. Relief was not available.

What is a farmhouse?

4-067 The increase in residential property values over the last few years means that the availability of 100 per cent relief on a farmhouse is extremely valuable. As a result farmhouses have become something of a battle ground between taxpayers and HMRC.

There have been a number of cases where HMRC has declined to allow relief on farmhouses because they have not been occupied for the requisite period or have not been occupied *with* the land. *Starke v IRC* (1995) was an example of a house which was not occupied *with* land. The house was situate with some substantial outbuildings and one or two small areas of enclosed land and, as a result, failed to qualify for relief. *Harrold v IRC* (1996) is an example of a house which was not occupied for the requisite period. The taxpayer had bought a farm and started working it but could not live in the farmhouse which was in a dilapidated state until essential repairs were carried out. The Special Commissioners found that despite the taxpayer's care for the property and work on it, he was not in occupation until he actually moved in.

It is fatal if farming activities are not being conducted from the property in question. To be a farmhouse, the property must be occupied by the farmer and according to *Lloyds TSB Private Banking Plc v Twiddy* (2006) at [49]:

> "The farmer is the person who lives in the farmhouse in order to farm the land comprised in the farm and who farms the land on a day to day basis. ... We do not think that a house occupied with a farm is a farmhouse merely because the person living there is in overall control of the agricultural business conducted on the land, and, in particular, we think that the lifestyle farmer, the person whose bid for the land is treated by the appellant as establishing the agricultural value of the land, is not the farmer for the purpose of the provisions.,"

The same point was made in *Arnander v RCC* (2006) where the Special Commissioner refused to accept that a residence was a "farmhouse" on the basis that day to day management was in the hands of an agent who lived elsewhere.

Given that the farmhouse is the house from which the farming business is managed on a day to day basis. It follows that if no farming is carried on, there can be no farmhouse. Elderly farmers are advised not to let land on grazing licences because they are then likely to be simply taking an income from land and not farming so there will be no farmhouse. See for example *McCall v RCC* (2008) where the deceased farmer had let all land on grazing. The decision was that the deceased was merely taking an income from the land.

However, the granting of grazing licences may not be fatal to the availability of relief. See *Charnley v RCC* (2019) where the elderly farmer was regarded as "farming" despite having granted grazing licences. The facts were unusual in that the landowner, on behalf of the licensee, carried out the day to day care of the animals and made decisions on the use of the land. The first tier tribunal accepted the licensee's description of the two of them "working together" and found this was analogous to a partnership. Part of the deceased's work could be described as mere "maintenance" of the land or keeping it in good order, but his activities went so far beyond this that to use the term "maintenance" would be an over-simplistic description which did not accurately describe the position.

The tribunal was wholly satisfied that the deceased did not occupy the house solely as a residence but rather as a dwelling from which he farmed and managed the farm. He had always been a farmer and, although the manner in which he farmed was modified with time and age, he did not cease to be a farmer; his activities did not cease to be "for the purposes of agriculture" nor did they become those of an investor. Relief was available on both the land and the house.

Character appropriate

It is frequently difficult in practice to determine whether or not a farmhouse is of a character appropriate to the property. *Lloyds TSB as personal representative of Antrobus (Deceased) v IRC* (2002) summarised the relevant principles as follows: **4-068**

(1) one should consider whether the house is appropriate by reference to its size, content and layout with the farm buildings and the particular area of farmland being farmed;
(2) one should consider whether the house is proportionate in size and nature to the requirements of the farming activities conducted on the agricultural land or pasture in question;
(3) although one cannot describe a farmhouse which satisfies the "character appropriate" test, one knows one when one sees it;
(4) one should ask whether the educated rural layman would regard the property as a house with land or a farm; and
(5) one should consider the historical dimension and ask how long the house

in question has been associated with the agricultural property and whether there was a history of agricultural production.

Applying these tests the house in question was "of a character appropriate to the property".

Executors of Higginson v IRC (2002) confirmed that there is no single test. In that case the house was of such value that it was the predominant element of the unit. It was a house with farmland going with it (and not vice versa). In *Arnander v Revenue and Customs Commissioners* (2006) the tribunal held that even if the day to day farming had been managed from the residence in question (which it had not), the house was not of a character appropriate being too large and grand for the comparatively small amount of land being farmed. The commissioner also held that even if the claim had not failed on those grounds, it would still have failed because the property had not been occupied for the purposes of agriculture for the two previous years. The elderly owners were too old and frail in their final two years of ownership to carry out any farming activities. The same point had been fatal in *Rosser v IRC* (2003) where the special commissioner held that a property which had clearly been a farmhouse for many years had changed in the years before death from a farmhouse to a retirement home for the deceased and her husband.

Many farmers continue farming at a reduced level as they grow older. There is a danger that the farmhouse ceases to be of a character appropriate to the amount of farming that is carried on at the date of death. HMRC argued that this was the case in *Golding v RCC* (2011). The deceased had farmed the same land since 1940 but at the date of his death (aged 81) the level of activity had dwindled and the profits were tiny. However, the tribunal found that the property was of a character appropriate to the land farmed with it. Given the deceased's age it would have been unreasonable to expect his farming to be an extensive activity. On the facts, he had been farming the land to the best of his ability up until his death and he had relied on its produce to supplement his meagre income. Farms do make losses from time to time and the lack of a substantial profit was not detrimental to a decision that the farmhouse was "character appropriate".

Hanson v RCC (2012) is a helpful decision for taxpayers. The first tier tribunal decided that when deciding whether a farmhouse is character appropriate, all the land farmed from it can be taken into account, not just the land owned by the transferor. In this case agricultural property relief was available on a property owned by the deceased which was occupied by his son, a working farmer, who farmed 128 acres of land which he owned plus a much smaller area owned by the deceased and 20 acres owned by a third party. The farmhouse was clearly not character appropriate if only the father's land was considered but it was character appropriate when all the land farmed was taken into account.

Agricultural value of farmhouse

4-069 Relief is available only on the agricultural value of the property. The *Antrobus* case was referred to the Lands Tribunal to determine the value of the farmhouse. The taxpayer argued that the deemed perpetual covenant that the property could be used only for agricultural purposes would not reduce the price significantly because a new owner could employ someone to do the day-to-day management of the farm. In the course of its determination of value, the Lands Tribunal expressed the opinion that:

"A farmhouse is ... the house in which the farmer of the land lives .... The question is:

> who is the farmer of the land for the purpose of the definition in section 115(2)? In our view it is the person who lives in the farmhouse in order to farm the land comprised in the farm and who farms the land on a day to day basis .... We do not think that a house occupied with a farm is a farmhouse simply because the person living there is in overall control of the agricultural business conducted on the land."

It determined that a working farmer would pay 15 per cent less than someone who simply wanted to buy a house with land and let others manage the property (a so-called "lifestyle farmer"). The relief was, therefore, granted on the discounted figure. Taxpayers should, therefore, expect to get relief only on a discounted figure.

More important, though, was the finding that a farmer had to be a "hands-on" working farmer. Many people thought that the Lands Tribunal approach was wrong. However, in *Arnander v HMRC* (2006) the Special Commissioner held that

> "the principle that the farmer of the land is the person who farms it on a day-to-day basis rather [than] the person who is in overall control of the agricultural business conducted on the land is a helpful principle".

Farm buildings

According to *Williams v HMRC* (2005) buildings used for intensive rearing of livestock or fish only qualify for agricultural property relief if they are used as part of a farm. Section 115(2) requires the occupation of the buildings to be ancillary to the agricultural use. This requires there to be a common purpose between the use of the agricultural land or pasture and the intensive buildings, with the buildings as the "junior partner" in the enterprise. **4-070**

Claw back of relief on lifetime transfers

Where a transfer is made before death, whether chargeable or potentially exempt, and the transferor dies within seven years, the relief is available only if the property originally given, or qualifying property representing it, has remained as agricultural property in the ownership of the transferee from the date of transfer to the date of death of the transferor. If the transferee dies before the transferor within the seven-year period, relief is only available on the death of the transferee if the same conditions are satisfied. This is more fully discussed in connection with business property relief. **4-071**

If only a proportion of the property originally given or qualifying property representing it remains in the ownership of the transferee at the date of death, relief is available on the proportion of the property owned at that date (s.124A).

Clawback is discussed more fully in connection with business property relief.

Business property relief

When is business property relief available?

This relief is available in respect of "relevant business property". The relief is a reduction in the value transferred by a particular percentage depending on what type of property is being transferred (IHTA 1984 s.104). Relevant business property is property falling into one of the following six categories: **4-072**

(a) Property consisting of a business or an interest in a business (this includes the interest of a sole proprietor or of a partner in a business) (s.105(1)(a)).

(b) Unquoted securities which alone or with other shares owned by the transferor or with related property gave the transferor control of the company (s.105(1)(b)). A person has control if they control more than 50 per cent of the votes exercisable in the general meeting.

In deciding whether or not one person has control it is not possible to ignore votes attaching to shares held by another person who lacks capacity: *Walding v IRC* (1996). It is sufficient for the transferor to control a majority of shares *immediately before* the transfer. A company may buy back and cancel some shares with the result that after the cancellation a shareholder may have more than 50 per cent of the remaining shares. A transfer by the shareholders at that point will attract 100 per cent relief even if more shares are issued shortly afterwards.

The transfer of one share from an 80 per cent shareholding will attract 100 per cent relief on the transfer of that one share.

(c) Shareholdings in unlisted companies (s.105(1)(bb)). Again it is not necessary for the transfer to cause the transferor to lose control. Shares dealt with in or on the Alternative Investment Market are unquoted for this purpose. Investments of this type are often bought by elderly people anxious to minimise the inheritance tax bill on their death.

In the three cases above the relief is 100 per cent.

(d) Shareholdings in listed companies which alone or with other shares owned by the transferor or with related property gave the transferor control immediately before the transfer. Again control is exercising more than 50 per cent of the votes in general meeting. Temporary control will suffice. Relief is available until the size of the holding dips below the crucial point. Where a person intends to make a number of gifts of shares from such a holding, it is desirable to make the smaller gifts first to try to ensure that control is maintained for as long as possible.

(e) Land or buildings, machinery or plant used immediately before the transfer wholly or mainly for the purposes of a company controlled by the transferor or of a partnership of which they were a member. Notice the distinction between partnerships and companies for this purpose. An asset used by a company will attract no relief if the owner has a minority shareholding whereas an asset used by a partnership will attract relief however small an interest in the partnership the owner of the asset has.

(f) Land or buildings, machinery or plant used immediately before the transfer for the purposes of a business carried on by the transferor and which was settled property in which the transferor had an interest in possession. Perhaps surprisingly no changes were made to the legislation by Finance Act 2006, so it does not matter whether the person with the beneficial interest in possession is treated as the owner of the underlying trust capital or not.

In the three cases above, the relief is 50 per cent.

"Business"

4-073 The term "business" includes a profession or vocation but does not include a business carried on otherwise than for gain (s.103(3)). Agriculture is regarded as a type of business so that business property relief may be available to the extent that agricultural relief cannot be claimed (that is business property relief is available for any non-agricultural value of agricultural property and on stock and plant and machinery). It used to be thought that business property relief was only available where the taxpayer transferred "a business or an interest in a business" and that no relief was available, for example, on the transfer of a single field or business asset. However, in *Trustees of the Nelson Dance Settlement v HMRC* (2009) the Special Commissioner held that this was wrong. On a correct reading of all the relevant sections, it was clear that there is no need for the transfer to be *of* a business; all that is required is that the transfer of *value* is attributable to the value of the business. Hence, relief is available on the transfer of single items.

Non-qualifying businesses

Businesses which consist wholly or mainly of dealing in securities, stocks, shares, land or buildings or of holding investments are specifically excluded from relief (s.105(3)). **4-074**

Phillips v HMRC (2006) held that a company which lent money to other companies owned by the taxpayer was a trading company not an investment company and shares, therefore, qualified for relief.

A person who derives income from land or a building is to be treated as having a business of holding an investment, notwithstanding that in order to obtain the income they carry out incidental maintenance and management work, find tenants and grant leases.

In *McCall v RCC* (2009) the Court of Appeal denied business property relief to a land owner who had let out her land on a grazing licence. She was simply deriving income from land. In *McCall* there was no doubt that agricultural property relief was available but that relieved only the agricultural value of the property and the land had substantial development value which could only escape tax if business property relief was available.

A series of cases involving land-based businesses such as holiday lettings, office blocks and business parks have been decided against taxpayers on the basis that the businesses consisted "mainly" of taking an income from land and thus were investment businesses (see "mixed businesses" at para.4-075). However, some recent cases have been more encouraging.

Mixed businesses

Notice that the relief is all or nothing. Many businesses carry on a range of mixed activities. Once the business crosses the line and becomes mainly a business carrying out one of the forbidden activities, it loses all relief. There have been a number of cases on the availability of relief for mixed businesses, many involving static caravan sites and holiday lettings where a range of services are provided. In *Hall v IRC* (1997) the greater part of the income came from rents and standing charges and it was held that the business was "mainly" that of making or holding investments. In *Furness v IRC* (1999) the taxpayer obtained relief where net profit from caravan sales exceeded that from net rents. **4-075**

The question is always one of fact to be decided by an "intelligent businessman" (see *Weston v IRC* (2000), *McCall v RCC* (2009) and *Brander v RCC* (2010)).

In *IRC v George (Executors of Stedman) deceased* (2003) Carnwath LJ made it clear that, in the case of a business of letting a building, the provision of additional services is "unlikely to be material" because they will not be enough to prevent the business remaining mainly one of property investment.

In *Farmer v IRC* (1999) the Special Commissioner concluded that a business which comprised farming and letting of former farm buildings was one business consisting mainly of farming. The case is interesting because the net profit from lettings exceeded that from farming but that was held not to be conclusive. What was actually relevant was the amount of time spent on the various activities, the allocation of capital employed between the activities and the fact that farming turnover often exceeded turnover from rents.

A similar approach was taken by the Upper Tribunal in *Brander v RCC* (2010) which involved a landed estate which carried on a mixture of farming and letting activities. It was necessary to look at the business in the round and consider the relative importance of the investment activities to the business as a whole; that involves looking at the business over a period of time. On the facts the business fell on the "right" side of the line and relief was available.

In *RCC v PRs of Pawson deceased* (2013) the taxpayers argued unsuccessfully that a holiday letting business should attract relief. While some additional services were provided, they were largely incidental to the letting. The-implication is that in any normal case an actively managed property letting business will be denied relief because any additional services provided will be relatively insignificant and the business will remain "mainly" an investment business.

Taxpayers were similarly unsuccessful in the case of an actively managed office block in *Trustees of Zetland Settlement v RCC* (2013) *and* a business centre in *Best v RCC* (2014) where despite the provision of a number of services the business was held to be "mainly" that of investment.

Recent cases have made the point that it is necessary to take a purposive approach to the construction of s.105 which has resulted in rather more success for taxpayers. In *PRs of Vigne v RCC* (2017), a case concerning a livery stables where relief was granted, Judge Geraint Jones QC said (at [16]):

> "[w]e keep in mind that section 105 of the 1984 Act is essentially driving at businesses which can properly be characterised as investment businesses, that is, where there is little or no element of trading or the provision of services in consideration of monies received".

Similarly, Judge Hellier in *Graham v RCC* (2018) agreed that the question to ask is "is the business mainly one of holding investments?" *Graham* was a case of a holiday letting business which the tribunal accepted provided such a high level of services that it qualified for relief. The tribunal accepted that only an exceptional letting business will fall on the non-investment side of the line. However, *Graham* was such a case. An intelligent businessman would regard the business as more like a family-run hotel than a holiday-let. It is clear that the business must be exceptional. In *Cox (Deceased) v Revenue and Customs Commissioners* (2020) the taxpayer was unsuccessful in her claim for business property relief on the holiday letting business (Crail House) run by her father, despite a valiant attempt to argue that the services provided made the business more akin to providing suites in a luxury hotel. This got short shrift as the tribunal determined that none of the services typically provided in a luxury hotel were on offer.

The taxpayers were similarly unsuccessful in *Firth v HMRC* (2022). Four properties were run as "aparthotels" described by the owners as offering "accommodation with the quality of a boutique hotel with the freedom and privacy of apartment living". Apartments were available to let on a night-by-night basis but were not serviced for stays of less than a week other than on request. Welcome packs with tea, coffee, milk etc were provided, as well as Wi-Fi, bedding and towels. Guests could request additional packs for a fee including items such as flowers, cakes, prosecco etc. The majority of guests were corporate customers staying for one to three nights. The tribunal refused an application for relief on the basis that the services offered were very limited.

Whilst some apart-hotels would be categorised as providing services with occupation of the accommodation as ancillary, looked at in the round, this business could not. The services provided did not take the business over the line into the non-investment side of the spectrum. Taxpayers were similarly unsuccessful in *Marks v HMRC* (2024). This was a holiday letting which catered for Kosher guests. The tribunal accepted that the provision of a Kosher flat as a holiday let was not common and that it required certain services to be provided that would not be provided for a non-Kosher holiday let. However, the taxpayers had failed to demonstrate that the Kosher related services supplied, either alone or in conjunction with the non-Kosher related services, were sufficient to move the business from being a typical holiday let to a non-investment business.

In *Butler v HMRC* (2023) the first tier tribunal refused business property relief to a wedding event business. The business actually consisted of three strands: (i) farming; (ii) commercial lettings; and (iii) a wedding venue business operating from an historic barn on the farm, called Clock Barn. It was common ground that:

(1) the commercial lettings element was an investment activity and the farming element was non-investment.
(2) the wedding business was the most significant aspect of the activities, so, if it was wholly or mainly an investment activity, then BPR would not be available.

Tribunal judge Aleksander made the point that a "*broad spectrum of activities*" exists in relation to the exploitation of land. In the case of holiday lets, this ranges from the bare letting of furnished accommodation to a room in an hotel. He suggested that a corresponding spectrum existed for event venues, ranging from the hire of a community hall at one end of the spectrum to a fully serviced conference venue offering a complete wedding package at the other.

In this case virtually all services were provided by an outside contractor. The terms of the hire agreement were that in consideration of the payment of the facility fee, the business would "*make available*" the premises to the customer for a specific period. The facility fee was the only fee paid by customers to the business. The terms of the agreement specified that payments were applied solely for the hire of the venue, and include no other services or facilities. Customer were required to use a specified firm of caterers but they contracted separately with that firm.

The tribunal judge said, "*Stepping back and looking at the business as a whole, I find that the Clock Barn business has always fallen on the village or community hall side of the spectrum, and away from the fully-serviced conference venue.*"

In *Charnley v RCC* (2019) HMRC had refused business property relief on the basis that the business was mainly an investment business consisting of the exploitation of a capital asset, the land, through the use of grazing licences. The first tier tribunal disagreed with HMRC: the issue of where a particular business falls is a question of fact and degree which requires a qualitative assessment of the facts as found in each case. In *Charnley* it was clear from the evidence that the deceased was not a landowner holding an investment in respect of which he carried out incidental work; an intelligent businessman would view the asset as a farming business being turned to account by the day-to-day farming carried out by the deceased with the additional component of some investment income being received. The existence of that component, namely receiving income in the form of income from the grazing licences by the use of land, did not automatically exclude the business from relief. In the tribunal's view, in looking at the components of the business and then at the whole picture the statutory requirements of either "wholly or mainly" were not satisfied. The business was not one of holding land as investment with the provision of additional services incidental to that business.

Businesses change their activities over time and a business which started out as a trading business may become mainly an investment business and vice versa: see *Executors of Clark deceased v HMRC* (2005). It may be preferable to divide businesses into separate entities so as to guarantee relief on the part of the activities rather than gambling on getting relief on the whole range carried on in one single business.

The value of the business

4-076 Business property relief is given on the net value of business property (s.110). This is the value after deducting liabilities incurred for the purposes of the business (for other inheritance tax purposes in the case of death liabilities are deducted from *the whole estate* unless charged on particular property). The value of property qualifying for relief cannot be increased by charging business debts on non-business property. The fact that a guarantee in support of a business has been charged over a particular asset does not mean that the asset is a business asset. See *IRC v Mallender* (2001).

Period of ownership

4-077 The transferor must have owned the relevant business property throughout the period of two years before the transfer (s.107(1)). Property which replaces other relevant business property qualifies for relief even though not owned for two years provided that the aggregate period of ownership exceeds two years in the five years before the transfer. Until the new property has been owned for two years the relief is limited to the value of the original property (s.107(2)).

Relief is available on shares owned for less than two years where the new shares are obtained as a result of a company reorganisation and can be identified, under TCGA 1992 ss.126–136, with other shares owned for the requisite period. The TCGA provisions require the new shares to be issued in proportion to the existing holding, for example as a rights issue or bonus issue. For an illustration see *Executors of Dugan-Chapman (deceased) v RRC* (2008).

Where a transfer of value of relevant business property is followed by another transfer of the same property, the second owner need not own the property for two years before becoming entitled to the relief, provided that the relief was available on the first transfer and one of the transfers was a transfer on death (s.109(1)).

The ownership requirement can be a trap, as the facts of *Burrell & Sharman v Burrell* (2005) demonstrate. A beneficiary of an accumulation and maintenance trust obtained a qualifying interest in possession which the trustees terminated within two years in order to appoint the property on discretionary trusts. The termination of the interest in possession was immediately chargeable to inheritance tax and, because the beneficiary had not fulfilled the two-year ownership requirement, business property relief was not available.

A person who receives property on the death of their *spouse or civil partner* may aggregate their period of ownership with their own so as to make up a two-year period of ownership (s.108).

When a business (or other relevant business property) has been owned for two years then business property relief is available on its full value at the time of the transfer (at the appropriate percentage). It is not, therefore, necessary to show that particular assets of the business have been owned for two years. However, the value of an asset is excluded from relief if it has not been used wholly or mainly for the purpose of the business throughout the two years before the transfer or throughout the period since it was acquired, if later.

Excepted assets

In order to prevent taxpayers "parking" private assets in a business and then seeking to obtain business property relief on them, s.112 provides that relief is not available on "excepted assets". There are assets which were neither: **4-078**

(a) used wholly or mainly for the purposes of the business concerned throughout the whole of the previous two years; nor
(b) required at the time of the transfer for future use.

These are alternative requirements. An asset which fulfils either one of the requirements will not be an excepted asset. Assets which are excepted do not qualify for relief. However, their existence does not prejudice the eligibility of the rest of the business for relief.

Contract for sale

Relief is not available if property is subject to a binding contract to sell. It is important, therefore, that partnerships and companies do not require the personal representatives of deceased partners or shareholder to sell their share(s) and the survivors to purchase them. Pre-emption rights and options to purchase do not present the same problems as there is no binding agreement. HMRC accepts that automatic accruer clauses do not constitute binding contracts for sale. See *IHT Manual* at para. IHTM25292. **4-079**

Clawback of relief on lifetime transfers

As with agricultural relief, where a transfer is made before death, whether chargeable or potentially exempt, and the transferor dies within seven years, the relief is available only if the property originally given or qualifying property representing it has remained as relevant business property in the ownership of the transferee from the date of the transfer to the date of death of the transferor. If the transferee dies before the transferor within the seven-year period, relief is only available on the death of the transferee if the same conditions are satisfied. **4-080**

The property must remain relevant business property in the hands of the donee. This may be beyond the control of the donee. For example, a donor with a controlling holding may give a donee 20 per cent of the shares in an unquoted trading company, thus qualifying for 100 per cent relief. A year later the donor may sell the assets of a trading company and decide to keep the cash in the company using the company as an investment company. If the transfer becomes chargeable, the donee will have no relief available because the shares are no longer in a trading company and no longer qualify as relevant business property.

If only a proportion of the property originally given or qualifying property representing it remains in the ownership of the transferee at the date of death, relief is available on the proportion of the property owned at that date (s.113A).

In the case of both agricultural and business property relief it is sufficient if "property representing" the original property is in the hands of the donee at the relevant date. There are some rather strange limitations:

(a) The *whole* of the consideration must have been applied on acquiring the replacement property.
(b) The replacement property must be acquired within three years *after* the disposal of the original property. Note that there is no provision as with roll over relief for the replacement property to be obtained *before* the disposal.
(c) The provision applies only to the first replacement and not to subsequent ones.

The December 1994 Tax Bulletin gives guidance on two matters relating to agricultural and business property relief:

(1) If agricultural property is replaced with business property (or vice versa) shortly before the owner's death, the periods of ownership can be amalgamated.
(2) Where the donee of agricultural property has sold the gifted property and replaced it with business property, agricultural property relief is denied by s.124A(1). Consequently s.114(1) does not exclude *business* property relief if the conditions for relief are satisfied. In the reverse situation, a farming business acquired by the donee can be relevant business property for the purposes of s.113B(3)(c).

Woodland relief

4-081 A relief is available on the value of growing timber for transfers made on death but not for lifetime transfers (IHTA 1984 ss.125–130). The relief is only available if a written election is made within two years of death. Where an election is made no tax is payable on the value of the timber provided that the deceased was either beneficially entitled to the land on which the timber is growing for five years before their death or acquired it otherwise than for consideration in money or money's worth within the five years.

The relief for timber is merely a deferral since tax becomes payable on a later sale or lifetime gift of the timber. The tax is payable at the deceased's death rate and treating the value as the highest part of the value of their estate. Tax is paid on the value of the timber at the date of the later disposal, not on its value at the date of death, and is payable by the person entitled to the proceeds of sale or who would be so entitled if the disposal had been a sale. The effect of this relief is that no tax is payable on timber until it is sold or given away by lifetime transfer; the tax payable is calculated by reference to the estate of the last person to die owning it. Where the value of the timber is low at the date of death, it may be preferable not to claim the relief.

Timber relief is not available where the woodlands qualify for agricultural property relief (short rotation coppice) and commercial woodlands will often qualify for business property relief.

Quick succession relief

Where a person dies within five years of a transfer to them (whether lifetime or on death) a relief commonly called quick succession relief is available (IHTA 1984 s.141). The relief takes the form of a reduction in the amount of tax payable on death equal to a percentage of the tax paid on the *net* amount of the increase in the value of the deceased's estate caused by the transfer within five years. **4-082**

The percentage relief is:

100 per cent if the death is within one year;
80 per cent if more than one but not more than two years;
60 per cent if more than two but not more than three years;
40 per cent if more than three years but not more than four years; and
20 per cent if more than four years but not more than five years.

Example 40

A dies and leaves B £12,500 worth of property. A's estate pays £2,500 in tax. B dies three years and three months later. The reduction of tax on B's death is 40 per cent of the tax on the net amount of the increase in B's estate. This can be calculated in the following way:

$$\frac{\text{net amount}}{\text{gross amount}} \times \text{tax} \times \text{percentage} = \text{Reduction}$$

i.e. in this case:

£10,000/£12,500 x £2,500 x 40/100 = £800

The reduction produced by quick succession relief is available whether or not the deceased still owned the property transferred to them within the five years before death. Where the amount of quick succession relief is more than the amount of tax to which the deceased would otherwise have been liable, no tax will be payable on the death (although no reclaim of the wasted relief from HMRC is possible—the excess may be carried forward to be set off against the liability of the deceased's beneficiary on their death if it is within five years of the original transfer to the deceased).

7. LIABILITY FOR INHERITANCE TAX ON DEATH

Introduction

The inheritance tax legislation includes rules to determine who is liable to account to HMRC for inheritance tax due as a result of death. Where inheritance tax is payable on an estate no grant of representation can be obtained until the amount due is paid. HMRC wants to maximise its chances of collecting the tax due. Accordingly, s.200(1) sets out four categories of people who are concurrently "accountable" or "liable" to HRMC for the inheritance tax due on death. **4-083**

HMRC is not concerned with who actually bears the burden of inheritance tax and it may be that the person who is accountable to HMRC for the tax (for example, the personal representative of the deceased) has a right to recover the money paid from individual beneficiaries. The question of where the burden of inheritance tax eventually falls is dealt with at paras 4-086–4-090. It is possible for a testator to change the statutory implied rules on where the burden of inheritance tax falls by express direction in the will but the rules on accountability cannot be altered.

Since inheritance tax must normally be paid before the grant of representation is obtained, the persons accountable to HMRC (for example, the personal representatives) frequently encounter difficulty in realising assets of the estate to raise cash to pay the amount due (See Ch.12).

Persons liable for inheritance tax on death (IHTA 1984 s.200(1))

4-084 The four categories of persons accountable for inheritance tax on death are set out in s.200(1):

(a) The personal representatives of the deceased are accountable for the inheritance tax attributable to property which was not comprised in a settlement immediately before the death or was comprised in a settlement and was land in the UK which devolves upon or vests in the personal representatives. This includes foreign property, property passing by survivorship, nomination and a donatio mortis causa even though this property does not vest in the personal representatives. It also includes property subject to a reservation of benefit but only if the tax remains unpaid 12 months after the end of the month of death.

The liability of ordinary personal representatives for inheritance tax is limited to the value of assets which they received or would have received but for their own neglect or default (s.204(1)).

The term personal representative includes an executor *de son tort*, i.e. a person who has made themselves liable as executor by intermeddling in the estate (see paras 8-010). The liability for inheritance tax of such a person is limited to the value of assets that have come into his hands: *IRC v Stype Investments* (1982).

(b) The trustees of a settlement are accountable for inheritance tax attributable to property comprised in the settlement immediately before the death. Their liability is limited to the value of assets which they received or disposed of or which they have become liable to account for to the beneficiaries and to the extent of any other property available in their hands for the payment of tax or which might have been available but for their own neglect or default (s.204(2)).

(c) Any person in whom property is vested (whether beneficially or not) or who is entitled to an interest in possession is accountable for the inheritance tax attributable to such property. This category includes beneficiaries under a will, persons entitled to property under the intestacy rules, a beneficiary with an interest in possession in property settled after death and a purchaser. A purchaser for money or money's worth of property is not, however, liable where the property is not subject to an HMRC charge (see para.4-112).

Liability of such persons is limited to the value of the property (or any property which represents it) (s.204(3)). This is a rather draconian provision for a beneficiary with an interest in possession as the beneficiary is entitled only to income and yet has a liability limited only by the capital value of the property in which they have an interest in possession. HMRC confirmed in correspondence with the Society of Trust and Estate Practitioners and the Chartered Institute of Taxation on 8 May 2007 that this was the position and that it had no intention of changing it.

(d) Where property was settled prior to death, a beneficiary for whose benefit settled property or income therefrom is applied thereafter is accountable for the inheritance tax attributable to such property. A beneficiary of a discretionary trust would be an example of such a person. Liability is limited to the amount of the property or income received (less any income tax) (s.204(5)).

Liability for additional tax on lifetime gifts

Where death occurs within seven years of a potentially exempt transfer, inheritance tax may become payable. Where death occurs within seven years of a chargeable transfer extra tax may become payable. In such circumstances the following are liable for the tax or extra tax: **4-085**

(a) The personal representatives of the transferor (but only to a limited extent—see below).
(b) Any person the value of whose estate is increased by the transfer.
(c) So far as the tax is attributable to the value of any property, any person in whom the property is vested (whether beneficially or otherwise) at any time after the transfer, or who at any such time is beneficially entitled to an interest in possession in the property.
(d) Where by the chargeable transfer any property that becomes comprised in a settlement, any person for whose benefit any of the property or income from it is applied.

A person liable as a trustee is liable only to the extent of property which they have actually received or disposed of or have become liable to account for to the beneficiaries and to the extent of any other property available in their hands for the payment of tax or which might have been so available but for their own neglect or default.

A person liable for tax as a person in whom property is vested or as a person entitled to a beneficial interest in possession in property is liable only to the extent of that property.

A person liable for tax as a person for whose benefit property or income has been applied is liable only to the extent of that property or income (less any income tax).

The personal representatives of the transferor are liable only to the extent that as a result of the limitations of liability relevant to the other categories no one falling within any of the other categories is liable *or* the tax remains unpaid 12 months after the end of the month in which the death of the transferor occurred. In such a case their liability is limited to the value of assets which they received or would have received but for their own neglect or default.

In a case where potentially exempt or chargeable transfers were made within seven years of death and inheritance tax is due, personal representatives would be wise to refrain from completely distributing the assets of the estate until satisfied that the tax has been paid. If they do not, they may find themselves personally liable for unpaid tax. This is, of course, easier said than done, as there will often be cases where the personal representatives are unaware of lifetime gifts. Personal representatives may be unaware of their possible liability for additional inheritance tax when they distribute assets to the beneficiaries of the estate. They can obtain indemnities from the beneficiaries, but these will be useless if the beneficiary becomes bankrupt. They can try to obtain insurance, but this is often difficult or expensive.

Personal representatives who pay inheritance tax on lifetime transfers have no statutory right of recovery against the donees who were primarily liable for the tax.

Section 212 of IHTA 1984 gives power to persons liable for tax to sell, mortgage or charge assets to raise money to pay the tax even if the assets are not vested in them. It is important for personal representatives to make full enquiries to establish any lifetime transfers or property subject to a reservation of benefit. There is a letter from the Revenue to the Law Society dated 11 February 1991 which states that the Revenue will not "usually" pursue personal representatives for inheritance tax who:

"• after making the fullest enquiries that are reasonably practicable in the circumstances to discover lifetime transfers, and so
• having done all in their power to make full disclosure of them to the Board of Inland Revenue
• have obtained a certificate of discharge and distributed the estate before a chargeable lifetime transfer comes to light".

The issue of course is "what is reasonably practicable". Personal representatives may well be expected to look at bank statements going back seven years as well as asking friends and family. Those who give misleading information to personal representatives may face a penalty under para.1A of FA 2007 Sch.24.

In any event the letter affords no help to personal representatives who are aware that lifetime gifts have been made but who cannot persuade the transferee to provide funds to meet the liability. Such a situation can arise where the transferee is outside the UK and has not been left anything in the will. The liability to tax on the lifetime transfer may exhaust the death estate so that the beneficiaries of the will take nothing. HMRC recognises the problem. It says at IHTM3004:

> "The liability of the transferor's personal representatives is a sensitive area of the legislation. You must alert the personal representatives at an early stage where recourse to them might occur. In cases where the transferee is not resident in the UK we are likely to be aware of that fact from the replies on the schedule IHT403, but nevertheless we should still warn the personal representatives of their potential liability, if the transferee and any other persons who may be liable under IHTA84/S199 (1) do not pay ...
>
> You must remember that the facility to have recourse to the transferor's personal representatives is not to be regarded as a soft option. We are to make all the attempts at recovering from the persons liable under IHTA 1984 s.199(1) that we would presently contemplate in a similar situation against any liable person. But having warned the personal representatives that we may look to them to discharge the tax liability, we must ensure firstly that they are kept fully in the picture and secondly that a decision actually to collect from them is not delayed for years."

There is a similar danger for personal representatives in relation to the inheritance tax on property given away during the deceased's lifetime but subject to a reservation of benefit (see para.4-031). The transferee is primarily liable but the personal representatives will become liable if the tax is unpaid after 12 months from the death. Here, though, the personal representatives do have a statutory right of recovery under IHTA 1984 s.211(3). Personal representatives should be particularly careful to check for property subject to a reservation of benefit as a result of the rules on pre-owned assets.

Taxpayers who are liable to pay the pre-owned assets charge (Finance Act 2004 s.84 and Sch.15 and see para.4-035) can opt out of the regime and into the inheritance tax reservation of benefit provisions within the relevant time limit (Sch.15 para.21). The donee, who is the person primarily liable for the inheritance tax on the gifted property, has no say in the matter and may not even know that the election has been made.

The election is sent not to the local Inspector of Taxes but to the Pre-Owned Assets Section at Nottingham. The section will inform the local tax office *and record the election.* There will be a check on death for any elections made by the taxpayer with a view to the collection of inheritance tax. It is, therefore. important for personal representatives to try to establish whether or not the deceased made such an election so that the information given to HMRC is accurate. Once made, the election can be withdrawn or amended by the taxpayer but only before the relevant filing date (Sch.15 para.23(5)). It cannot be withdrawn by the taxpayer's PRs.

8. Burden (or Incidence) of Inheritance Tax

Introduction

When inheritance tax is due on death, the beneficiaries of the estate will be very concerned to discover on which part of the estate the burden of the tax will fall since this may affect the size of their entitlement. The following example illustrates this. **4-086**

Example 41

T leaves a house to A, a pecuniary legacy to B, jewellery to C and the residue of the estate to D. There is substantial inheritance tax to pay. The personal representatives are liable for the inheritance tax and before obtaining a grant of representation must pay the tax due to HMRC. The personal representatives may borrow the money from a bank or from a beneficiary or may arrange for a bank or building society to release funds directly to HMRC. Whichever course they follow, they will have to decide where the burden ultimately falls. If the entire burden falls on residue, D's benefit from the estate will be much reduced; whereas, if the burden is divided proportionately amongst the beneficiaries, D will receive rather more but the benefits received by A, B and C will be reduced.

A testator may include an express direction in the will as to whether or not assets are to bear their own tax. In the absence of such a direction there are statutory rules as to burden.

Express direction in the will as to burden

The testator may state in the will that certain gifts are to be "free of inheritance tax" while others are to bear their own; if such a direction is included, it is conclusive (with one exception: see para.4-097) and the inheritance tax payable on gifts made "free of tax" will be a testamentary expense paid from the property available to pay other debts of the estate (primarily undisposed-of property and residue). Any professionally drawn will should include an express direction as to the burden of inheritance tax since this not only avoids future disputes but leads the testator to consider whether the proposed disposition of property is satisfactory having regard to the burden of inheritance tax. However, as we shall see in paras 4-097–4-099, a direction that an exempt share of residue is to bear inheritance tax attributable to a non-exempt share of residue must be disregarded. **4-087**

No express direction in will

In order to remove uncertainties which had arisen, IHTA 1984 s.211 makes express provision for the burden of inheritance tax in relation to deaths occurring on or after 25 July 1983. Section 211 provides that where personal representatives **4-088** are liable for inheritance tax on the value transferred by a chargeable transfer made on death the tax:

- shall be treated as part of the general testamentary and administration expenses of the estate and therefore payable primarily from undisposed of property, followed by residue,
- but only in so far as it is attributable to the value of property which:
  (a) is situate in the UK;
  (b) vests in the deceased's personal representatives; and
  (b) was not, immediately before the death, comprised in a settlement.

The provision is subject to any contrary intention shown by the deceased in their will.

As we shall see in Ch.15, general testamentary and administration expenses of the estate (and debts) are paid primarily from undisposed-of property and, if none, from the residue of the estate. Thus, where under s.211(1) inheritance tax is to be treated as a general testamentary and administration expense, the burden of it falls primarily on the undisposed-of property and then on the residue. Section 211(3) provides that:

> "where any amount of tax paid by personal representatives on the value transferred by a chargeable transfer made on death does not fall to be borne as part of the general testamentary and administration expenses of the estate, that amount shall, where occasion requires, be repaid to them by the person in whom the property to the value of which the tax is attributable is vested".

The effect of s.211(3) is that whenever personal representatives are liable to pay inheritance tax (as they are on all of the deceased's free estate and on settled land which devolves on them), they have a right to recover it from the particular beneficiary receiving the property to which it relates *unless* the tax is a general, testamentary and administration expense under s.211(1); that is *unless* the property to which the inheritance tax is attributable was situate in the UK, vested in the personal representatives and was not comprised in a Settled Land Act settlement immediately before the death. As a result of s.211(3) the personal representatives can recover from the particular beneficiary concerned (subject to contrary intention) inheritance tax attributable to:

(a) non-UK property;
(b) property not vesting in the personal representatives (that is, joint property passing by survivorship, property subject to a nomination or to a *donatio mortis causa*); and
(c) property which was immediately before the death comprised in a Settled Land Act settlement.

(The personal representatives will only have accounted for inheritance tax in respect of trust property where the property was settled land devolving on them. They are not *liable* for inheritance tax in respect of other types of trust property and so will not generally be involved in the payment or recovery of inheritance tax relating to it.)

Practical problems

4-089 In practice, where personal representatives have accounted to HMRC for inheritance tax for which they were liable, they may encounter difficulties in obtaining repayment for the residuary estate from the person in whom the property is vested. The personal representatives should take all possible steps to minimise such difficulties.

If a pecuniary legacy has been left to a legatee and the will declares that the legatee is to bear the burden of inheritance tax attributable to it, the personal representatives should deduct an appropriate amount and pay the net legacy to the legatee. Obviously if an asset is left, rather than cash, no deduction can be made. However, the personal representatives should not vest the asset in the beneficiary until arrangements have been made for reimbursement of the amount due.

If the beneficiary has possession of the asset (for example, because the property has passed by survivorship) there is nothing the personal representatives can do to prevent problems arising unless other assets due to the beneficiary under the will or intestacy rules are in the hands of the personal representatives. If the personal representatives have got possession of other assets due to the beneficiary they should ensure that all repayments of inheritance tax due to the residuary estate are made before they part with the assets.

Personal representatives have power under s.212 to sell, mortgage or charge property *whether or not it is vested in them* to raise money for tax for which they are liable. It would obviously be difficult to do this where the property is not vested in them but the fact that they have such a sanction may persuade the person in whom it is vested to pay them the amount due.

The same problem arises in relation to foreign property. Such property is unlikely to go through their hands. In a civil law country, it will be transferred to the heir by a notary and in other jurisdictions may pass under a separate will to separate personal representatives. How will the UK personal representatives in practice recoup that tax from a beneficiary who has no other entitlement to assets which pass through their hands?

Example 42

Fred, who is domiciled in England and Wales, dies with assets in UK and a house and contents in Spain. He appoints a solicitor as executor and leaves everything in Spain to his son and everything in the UK to his sister. IHT is payable on the estate and the executor is liable for it. The Spanish property should bear its own share of IHT (after allowing for a deduction for any Spanish tax) but the executor has no access to it.

The son, as heir, will be able to claim the Spanish property without reference to the executor. The executor may not be able to recover the tax paid on the foreign asset from the son and his sister may complain that the residue is wrongly depleted.

The s.212 power to raise tax from assets may be useful in theory, but it does not provide any clue as to how to recover the tax from a beneficiary who is outside the jurisdiction and refuses to pay. PRs could assign rights under s.212 to residuary beneficiaries. The easiest option is to provide that IHT on foreign property is to be treated as a testamentary expense. If the client does not wish to reduce the share of the residuary beneficiary in this way, consider insurance or giving the residuary beneficiary a share of the foreign asset (but this may not be possible if forced heirship rules apply).

Apportioning the burden of inheritance tax

Where the burden of inheritance tax due is to be divided amongst different **4-090**
people, it is necessary to apportion the inheritance tax amongst the various assets

comprised in the estate. This can be done in one of two ways. *Either* calculate an average rate of inheritance tax for the estate and apply that rate to the assets each beneficiary is to receive; *or* (more simply) allocate a proportionate part of the total inheritance tax to each beneficiary. The result of the two methods will be identical.

Example 43

A dies having made chargeable lifetime transfers which leave £300,000 of the nil-rate band remaining. Her estate comprises:

	£
Land	500,000
Liquid Assets	300,000

Her will directs that the land is to bear its own tax and is to pass to B, that a pecuniary legacy of £60,000 bearing its own tax is to pass to C, and that residue is to pass to D. No exemptions apply.

Band		**Rate**	
£	£	%	£
0 -	300,000	0	0
301,000 -	800,000	40	200,000
Total Inheritance	Tax Bill		200,000

The tax must then be apportioned.

Using method 1: Calculate an estate rate

$$\frac{\text{Total Tax}}{\text{Value of Estate}} \times 100 = \%$$

£200,000/£800,000 × 100 = 25%

This rate can then be applied to the property bearing its own tax passing to each beneficiary:

B's share of tax burden

£500,000 × 25% = £125,000

C's share of tax burden

£60,000 × 25% = £15,000

The rate will also be applied to the residue passing to D. The residue amounts to £240,000 that is the liquid assets of £300,000 less the £60,000 legacy:

D's share of tax burden

£240,000 × 25% = £60,000

The total tax payable on the whole estate is £200,000.

Using method 2: Allocate a proportion of the total tax to each beneficiary:

B's share of tax burden

£500,000/£800,000 × £200,000 = £125,000

C's share of tax burden

£60,000/£800,000 × £200,000 = £15,000

D's share of tax burden

£240,000/£800,000 × £200,000 = £60,000

The total tax payable on the whole estate is £200,000.

9. Time for Payment

General position

The tax on a transfer on death is payable six months after the end of the month in which death occurred. The tax on a chargeable transfer made before death is payable six months after the end of the month in which the transfer is made or, if the transfer is made after 5 April and before 1 October, at the end of April in the next year. Where tax or extra tax is payable on a lifetime transfer because of the death of the donor it is payable six months after the end of the month of death. **4-091**

Where tax is paid after the date on which it should have been paid interest is chargeable on it. The rate of interest is prescribed by statutory instrument and is linked to the Bank Rate. The inheritance tax on certain types of property may be paid by instalments over a 10-year period in certain circumstances (IHTA 1984 ss.227–228).

Instalment option on death

(a) Land of any description (this term is not further defined but clearly freehold and leasehold interests are included). **4-092**

(b) Shares or securities in a company giving the deceased control of the company immediately before death.

(c) Unquoted shares or securities which did not give the deceased control provided that HMRC are satisfied that the payment of the tax in one sum would cause undue hardship.

(d) Unquoted shares or securities which did not give the deceased control where at least 20 per cent of the tax payable on the death by the person paying the tax on those shares is either tax on those shares or on those shares and other instalment option property.

(e) Unquoted shares which did not give the deceased control and the value of which exceeds £20,000 at the time of death provided that either:
  (i) they are at least 10 per cent (by nominal value) of all the shares in the company; or
  (ii) they are ordinary shares and are at least 10 per cent (by nominal value) of all the ordinary shares in the company.

(f) A business or an interest in a business including a profession or vocation. Liabilities incurred for the purposes of the business must be deducted in computing what is the value of the business for this purpose (normally liabilities are deducted from the whole rather than from particular assets unless the assets are charged with payment of the liabilities).

"Unquoted" means not listed on a recognised stock exchange. Unquoted shares include those dealt in on the Alternative Investment Market. Shareholders have control for this purpose if they (with the benefit of any shares or securities which are related property) have voting control on all questions affecting the company as a whole (IHTA 1984 s.269).

In cases where business property relief or agricultural property relief is available at 100 per cent the instalment option will be irrelevant. However, the instalment option will be useful in cases where the qualifying ownership period has not been fulfilled or where relief is not available because of the nature of the business.

Instalment option on lifetime transfers

4-093 Inheritance tax on chargeable transfers made before death may be paid by instalments in respect of the same types of property as in the case of transfers on death. However, this relief is only available where the inheritance tax is *paid by the donee*. In the case of tax payable on the value transferred by a potentially exempt transfer which proves to be chargeable (or extra tax payable where the transferee dies within seven years of a chargeable transfer), the instalment option is available only to the extent that one of the following conditions is fulfilled:

(a) the transferee owns the qualifying property throughout the period from transfer until the death of the transferor (or, if earlier, of the transferee);
(b) in the case of property eligible for business or agricultural relief, the transferee has disposed of the original property but has applied the proceeds in acquiring replacement property; or
(c) in the case of unquoted shares the shares remain unquoted up to the date of death of the transferor (or, if earlier, of the transferee).

The instalment option is also available on transfers on the termination of an interest in possession in settled property and when tax becomes payable in the case of settlements without an interest in possession. In the case of-woodlands tax, this can always be paid by instalments even if paid by the donor.

Procedure for payment by instalments

4-094 The payment of tax by instalments is only possible where the person paying the tax gives notice in writing to HMRC that he wishes to pay in that way (on death, notice is given in the IHT 400). Where the election is made, tax is payable in 10 equal annual instalments. The first instalment is due on the date on which the tax would be due if not paid by instalments (in the case of death six months after the end of the month of death).

The taxpayer may pay off all remaining instalments at any time within the 10 years and must do so if the assets are sold. In the case of tax paid by instalments on non-agricultural land, not comprised in a business, interest on the whole of the outstanding tax is payable and is added to each instalment. In the case of tax paid by instalments on shares (other than shares in investment companies), business or interests in businesses interest is only payable to the extent that an instalment of tax is overdue.

It is common for personal representatives to choose to exercise the option initially even if they feel they may wish to pay off the outstanding amount in one lump sum at a later stage. The reason for considering a temporary exercise of the option is that it reduces the amount of inheritance tax falling due for payment six months after the end of the month of the death and so keeps to a minimum the amount of money which may have to be borrowed to pay the inheritance tax due. Once the personal representatives have obtained the grant of representation, they are able to realise assets of the estate and may then decide (particularly if interest is payable on the amount outstanding) to use the money to pay off any outstanding inheritance tax.

Personal representatives should remember that they remain personally liable for the inheritance tax on the death estate until it has been paid in full. Thus, if they transfer property on which the instalment option has been claimed to beneficiaries, they should consider what steps, if any, they can take to ensure that full payment is made. This may well mean retaining assets as security.

The case of *Howarth's Executors v IRC* (1997) indicates the perils which can exist for the unwary. The deceased's will was proved by her son, H, and his wife, who were both beneficiaries, and by S, an employee of a firm of solicitors, who was not a beneficiary.

The executors elected to pay tax in instalments. The deceased's assets were transferred to the two beneficiaries. Initially instalments were paid by H but these ceased and H was eventually declared bankrupt. The Revenue served notices of outstanding tax and interest on the three executors.

The Special Commissioner held that, although H was primarily liable for the payment of tax, the co-executor, S, remained personally liable. He had joined in the election to pay by instalments and had then consented to transfer all the assets to the beneficiaries. In so doing he had taken an obvious risk.

A more recent example is *Harris v RCC* (2018). Mr Harris was the administrator of Helena McDonald's estate. The value of the estate was £1.1 million and the tax payable was £341,278.76.

Following the sale of the deceased's home, Mr Harris gave the proceeds of sale to Whitfield Harewood (the deceased's brother and a beneficiary of the estate), on the understanding that Whitfield would pay the estate's bills and taxes. Whitfield subsequently returned to his home in Barbados and did not discharge the outstanding inheritance tax liability. Mr Harris was unable to make contact with Whitfield. HMRC issued a demand for the money. Mr Harris appealed on the basis that he did not have the money and HMRC applied-successfully for the appeal to be stuck out on the basis that it had "no reasonable prospect of success". The tribunal judge (Nicholas Aleksander) said (at [24]):

> "It is no defence to any inheritance tax determination that Mr Harris may have transferred the assets of the estate to a beneficiary on the basis that the beneficiary would be responsible for payment of the inheritance tax due. Nor is it a defence that Mr Harris was ignorant of his obligations, as a personal-representative, to pay the inheritance tax owing. Inevitably it follows (and I find) that Mr Harris's appeal has no reasonable prospects of success."

10. PARTIALLY EXEMPT TRANSFERS

Introduction

The transfer of value on death is for inheritance tax purposes one transfer of the whole of the deceased's estate. This transfer may be fully taxable, fully exempt or it may be partly taxable and partly exempt (for example, because part but not all of the property is given to a spouse, charity, political party or exempt body). **4-095**

If it is partly taxable and partly exempt IHTA 1984 contains rules for calculating the amount of inheritance tax and as to the burden of tax. These rules can give rise to rather complicated arithmetical computations. The three rules are dealt with at paras 4-096–4-098. Similar problems arise where property eligible for relief is included in an estate which is partially exempt. There are statutory rules as to the way the reliefs are allocated, which are dealt with at para.4-102 and following.

"Specific" gifts not bearing their own tax to non-exempt beneficiary residue to exempt beneficiary

4-096 For this purpose any gift is "specific" if it is not a gift of residue (IHTA 1984 s.42). If a specific gift is not exempt, the tax in respect of it will normally be paid from residue (see para.4-088). The specific legatee is treated as having received an amount *net* of tax (IHTA 1984 s.3B) and, therefore, the net gift must be grossed up at the death rate to calculate the amount of the tax borne by residue.

Example 44

Aidan has made lifetime chargeable transfers which have exhausted his nil-rate band and has died with a death estate of £500,000. On his death he gives £120,000 to his son, Sam, and *does not provide that this gift is subject to tax*; Aidan leaves the residue of his estate to his wife. Since the gift of £120,000 is not made to bear its own tax, the tax will come out of exempt residue so grossing-up is required.

£120,000 grossed up at the death rates with a cumulative total which has exhausted his nil-rate band is:

$$£120,000 \times 100/60 = £200,000$$

The tax is the difference between the gross and net gifts.

$$£200,000 - £120,000 = £80,000$$

The estate is therefore divided as follows:

	£	£
Tax		80,000
Legacy to Sam		120,000
Residue to widow	500,000	
	(200,000)	
		300,000
		500,000

Residue partly to exempt and partly to non-exempt beneficiaries

4-097 Section 41 states that "notwithstanding the terms of any disposition" none of the tax attributable to residue shall fall on an exempt share of residue. Thus, if residue is left "to pay debts and tax and then to be divided between" an exempt and a non-exempt beneficiary, the share of the non-exempt beneficiary is diminished by tax while the share of the exempt beneficiary is not. Note that the effect of s.41 cannot be varied by the will.

Example 45

Ted dies with a nil cumulative total leaving an estate of £900,000 to be divided equally between son and spouse. The half of the estate passing to the son bears its own tax irrespective of any direction to the contrary.

The case of *Re Benham* (1995) caused problems for practitioners. For a discussion of the problems raised by *Benham* see para.4-099.

Specific gifts not bearing their own tax to non-exempt beneficiaries residue partly to exempt and partly to non-exempt beneficiaries

In this situation the tax on the "specific" gifts is borne by the whole of the residue unless the will provides otherwise. The tax on the non-exempt part of residue *must* however be borne by that part of the residue only. This is because IHTA 1984 s.41 provides that exempt residue is not to bear the tax on any other part of the *residue*. Calculating the tax is difficult because the rate of tax at which the legacies are to be grossed-up cannot be known until the total tax payable on the estate is calculated. To deal with this problem HMRC requires a two-stage calculation called "double grossing-up". The procedure is as follows: **4-098**

(1) gross-up the specific gifts not bearing their own tax as if they were cumulated with any chargeable lifetime transfers but were the only taxable part of the estate on death;
(2) add this figure to any other parts of the estate which are in fact taxable (i.e. specific gifts bearing their own tax and non-exempt residue) to give the taxable estate;
(3) calculate an "assumed rate" of tax;
(4) gross-up the specific gifts not bearing their own tax at the assumed rate;
(5) the tax on the estate is tax on the figure at (3) plus tax on any other non-exempt parts of the estate (e.g. residue).

Example 46

Tessa dies in tax year 2024/25 leaving an estate of £800,000. She has made lifetime transfers which leave £300,000 of her nil-rate band available. In her will she gives £315,000 to her daughter, residue to be divided between her husband and her sister. The will contains no directions as to the burden of inheritance tax.

(1) Gross-up the gift to the daughter as if it were the only taxable gift on death. On this assumption, £300,000 is within the nil-rate band so only £15,000 has to be grossed-up at 40 per cent. £15,000 grossed-up at 40 per cent is £25,000. The gross legacy is therefore £300,000 + £25,000 = £325,000.
(2) Add the grossed-up legacy to the other taxable parts of the estate. Only half of the residue is taxable, as the other half is going to the husband (and so is exempt). To calculate the taxable half of residue it is necessary to deduct the grossed-up legacy:

	£
Value of estate	800,000
Less: grossed-up legacy	(325,000)
"Residue"	475,000
Half residue	237,500

The taxable estate is the grossed-up legacy plus the taxable half of residue:

Grossed-up legacy	325,000
Taxable half of residue	237,500
Taxable estate	562,500

(3) Calculate the assumed rate. This is the rate of tax which would be charged on an estate of £562,500 with £300,000 of nil-rate band available. The tax would be:

Band	**Rate**	
£	%	£
First 300,000	nil	nil
Next 262,500	40	105,000
Inheritance Tax		105,000

The assumed rate would therefore be:

$$£105{,}000/£562{,}500 \times 100 = 18.67\%$$

(4) Gross-up the specific gift not bearing its own tax at the assumed rate:

$$\frac{£315{,}000 \times 100}{100 - 18.67}$$

$$£315{,}000/81.33 \times 100 = £387{,}310.95$$

(5) Tax is now payable on the grossed-up specific gift and half the residue. To calculate half the residue, it is necessary to deduct the grossed-up legacy from the value of the estate:

	£
Value of estate	800,000.00
Less: grossed-up legacy	(387,310.95)
"Residue"	412,689.05
Half residue	206,344.52

Tax is therefore payable on:

Grossed-up legacy	387,310.95
Taxable half of residue	206,344.52
Taxable estate	593,655.47

Tax is therefore:

Band	**Rate**	
£	%	£
First 300,000.00	nil	nil

Band	Rate	
£	%	£
next 293,655.47	40	117,7462.18
Tax		117,7462.18

The portion of the £117,7462.18 attributable to the specific legacy is borne by the residue as a whole. The balance of the residue is then split into two equal parts and the portion of the £117,7462.18 attributable to the non-exempt residue is borne entirely from the non-exempt part of residue. In apportioning the inheritance tax bill either of the two methods explained in para.4-090, can be used.

Of course, if Tessa had no nil rate band available to her death estate, double grossing up would not be necessary as we would know that the rate for grossing up would be 40 per cent.

Section 41 and Re Benham's Will Trusts (1995)

The decision

In *Re Benham* the deceased left the residue of the estate to pay debts and then to pay to those beneficiaries **4-099**

> "as are living at my death and who are listed in List A and List B ... in such proportions as will bring about the result that the aforesaid beneficiaries named in List A shall receive 3.2 times as much as the aforesaid beneficiaries named in List B ...".

Some of the beneficiaries were charities and some were not.

The deputy judge hearing the case held that

> "the plain intention of the testatrix is that at the end of the day each beneficiary whether charitable or non-charitable should receive the same as the other beneficiaries ...".

He found that this was to be achieved by grossing-up the shares of the non-charitable legatees so that *after payment of tax* charitable and non-charitable legatees ended up with the same amount.

The effect was that more of the estate had to be allocated initially to the non-exempt beneficiaries so that after the payment of tax they retained the same net amount that the exempt beneficiaries received. The Revenue received more tax than it would have had the initial division been equal. The exempt beneficiaries received less.

Initially it was not clear whether the case was to be interpreted as of very limited importance turning on the particular words used by the testatrix which demonstrated an intention that residue was to be divided unequally or whether it was to be interpreted as of general application wherever residue was left to be divided "equally" between exempt and non-exempt beneficiaries. There was uncertainty and practitioners and charities were unhappy.

There was an exchange of correspondence between the Revenue and the British Heart Foundation (P. Twiddy, "Re Benham—the Revenue's view" [1996] 5 P.C.B. 295). The charity was concerned that the decision would result in a reduction in the amount of property passing to exempt beneficiaries.

The Revenue's response stated that in their view *Benham* is a decision "primarily concerned with ascertaining the intention of the testatrix and ... does not directly involve the Inland Revenue". It confirmed that the decision followed from the particular facts of the case and that

> "if the Will is drafted in 'common form' with a direction to ascertain residue after payment of funeral and testamentary expenses and debts followed by a bequest of that residue, then it is focusing on the ascertainment and division of disposable residue rather than on what each beneficiary is to receive. Accordingly a will so drafted would not appear to involve Benham-style grossing up computations."

The decision in *Re Ratcliffe, Holmes v McMullan* (1999) largely alleviated the uncertainty raised by the decision in *Re Benham.*

In *Re Ratcliffe* the testatrix left her residue after payment of debts, funeral and testamentary expenses to be divided equally between exempt and non-exempt beneficiaries. Blackburne J was of the view that, on a true construction of the will, the testatrix intended to divide her residue equally before payment of tax between the beneficiaries. The non-exempt beneficiaries then had to pay tax from their share without grossing-up.

He accepted that a will could direct that residue be divided unequally between exempt and non-exempt beneficiaries so that after payment of tax they were each left with the same amount. However, he said that to achieve this result "much clearer wording would be needed than the common form wording actually used". He said that he did not regard *Re Benham* as laying down any principle and, accordingly, did not feel bound to follow it.

The decisions leave two problems for practitioners:

(1) How to draft a will in the light of *Benham* and *Ratcliffe*?
(2) How to deal with the administration of an estate where the will contains a standard gift of residue dividing it between exempt and non-exempt beneficiaries?

Will drafting

4-100 This is relatively simple. Ask the testator whether they want their residue to be divided equally between the exempt and non-exempt beneficiaries. Explain that the result will be that the non-exempt beneficiary will "end up" with less because their share will be reduced by inheritance tax. The alternative is that the residue is divided unequally. The result of an unequal division is that the initial share of the non-exempt beneficiary is bigger, leaving the two shares of equal size once the tax has been deducted. Obviously more of the estate will be lost in tax since more of it is being given to a non-exempt beneficiary.

Once the testator has decided on the type of gifts they want the will must be drafted to give clear effect to their wishes. There are many suitable precedents; the following is taken from *Butterworths Wills Probate and Administration Service* Form 1A, 22.1.

> "*My trustee shall hold the Trust Fund ON TRUST*
>
> (a) as to one share absolutely for my Wife (Husband) (*or give name if not already defined as such*) if she (he) survives me for 28 days.
> (b) as to another share (or as to the whole if the preceding gift fails) absolutely for such of my children as are alive at my death (and reach the age of [18]) and if more than one in equal shares PROVIDED that if any child of mine [is already dead or] dies before me [or before reaching that age] but leaves a child or children alive at the death of the survivor of my child and me who reach the age of [18]

or marry under that age then such child or children shall take absolutely and if more than one in equal shares so much of the Trust Fund as that child of mine would have taken on attaining a vested interest AND the shares given by (a) and (b) above shall be such shares as before [after] the deduction of any inheritance tax attributable to them 2:1] the larger share being that given by [a] [b]]."

Administration of an estate

It is necessary to construe the will to determine the testator's intention. If the will contains a common form residuary gift directing division of residue after payment of debts and inheritance tax, it would seem safe in the light of *Re Ratcliffe* to divide the residue equally before payment of tax. However, if there is any ambiguity or unusual wording, the correct construction may be uncertain. In such a case it would be desirable to get the agreement of the beneficiaries as to the method of division, but they may not be united. Application to court to confirm the correct construction would then be required. The cost of such applications means that it would be beneficial for the parties to make strenuous efforts to reach agreement. **4-101**

Partly exempt transfers and agricultural and business property relief

Prior to the Finance Act 1986 anomalous results sometimes arose where a partly exempt transfer included property qualifying for agricultural or business property relief. The Finance Act 1986 therefore inserted s.39A to ensure that the reliefs are available in a consistent manner. Section 39A cannot be varied by the terms of a will. **4-102**

Where there is a specific gift of property qualifying for relief, the relief attaches to that property irrespective of whether the specific beneficiary is an exempt or non-exempt beneficiary (s.39A(2)).

Example 47

T dies with an estate of £1 million including a business worth £600,000 qualifying for 100 per cent relief. T has exhausted his nil-rate band. T leaves the business to his wife and the residue to his son. Tax will be payable at 40 per cent on all the assets passing to the son.

Had the business been left to the son, no tax would have been paid on the estate at all. It is clearly more tax efficient to leave property attracting 100 per cent relief to non-exempt beneficiaries.

Note that an appropriation of property on which a relief is available by the personal representatives to a residuary beneficiary is not a specific gift for this purpose. However, the disposition of the estate can be varied by the-beneficiaries under IHTA 1984 s.142 to produce a specific gift eligible for relief.

Where property eligible for relief passes as part of the residue of the estate, the relief does not attach only to the residue. Instead it is allocated pro rata to all the assets transferred (s.39A(3)) using the statutory formula:

R/U

where R is the value of the estate as reduced by agricultural and business relief less the value of any specific gifts qualifying for relief and U is the unreduced value of the estate less the value of any specific gifts qualifying for relief.

Example 48

T dies with an estate of £1 million including a business worth £600,000 qualifying for 100 per cent relief. T has exhausted his nil-rate band. T leaves a pecuniary legacy of £200,000 to his son, specific assets worth £100,000 and not qualifying for relief to his daughter and the residue which includes the business to his wife. Since the business has not been left specifically to anyone the benefit of the relief must be apportioned pro rata through the estate.

R is £1 million less £600,000 = £400,000

U is £1 million

Thus, the value for inheritance tax purposes of the property transferred will be:

Pecuniary legacy

$$£200,000 \times £400,000/£1m = £80,000$$

Specific legacy

$$£100,000 \times £400,000/£1m = £40,000$$

Residue

$$£700,000 \times £400,000/£1m = £280,000$$

While some of the relief is "wasted" on the gift passing to the spouse, the gifts passing to the son and daughter derive some benefit from the relief.

The effect of s.39A can cause problems where the testator has used a formula clause to pass a legacy to a non-exempt beneficiary "equal to the maximum amount that can pass without payment of inheritance tax". If the residuary estate includes property eligible for relief, the amount passing under such a gift will be increased. If this is not what the testator wants, the will should either leave the property eligible for relief by specific gift or impose a "cap" on the amount that can pass under the gift, for example, "the legacy is not to exceed the value of the nil-rate band in force at my death".

It is rarely certain at the time that a will is drafted whether or not assets will qualify for relief at the date of the death. The nature of the trading activities of a business may change or a farmhouse may cease to be occupied for the purposes of agriculture before the death. It is, therefore, normally advisable to leave assets which may be eligible for relief to a discretionary trust. Appointments from such a trust within two years of death will be read back into the will under IHTA 1984 s.144—see paras 19-029 and following. Personal representatives will, therefore, be able to decide how best to deal with the business assets once they know whether or not relief is available.

11. SOME PARTICULAR PROBLEMS

Inter-relationship of inheritance tax and capital gains tax

4-103 Capital gains tax, like inheritance tax, is a tax charged on movements of capital assets. It is not payable on death (except in certain circumstances in respect of settled property). However, a lifetime transfer may give rise to capital gains tax liability, as well as to inheritance tax liability. Such liability must be taken into account when deciding between lifetime gifts and gifts on death. To ensure that one tax is not paid on the amount of the other tax, two rules apply:

(1) Capital gains tax paid by the transferor is not treated as a loss to the transferor's estate for inheritance tax purposes.

(2) Capital gains tax paid by the transferee reduces the value transferred for inheritance tax purposes.

Example 49

Ann makes a chargeable lifetime transfer to a relevant property trust of shares acquired for £10,000; the current value of the shares is £24,000. We will assume that capital gains tax is £2,800 (i.e. 20 per cent of the £14,000 gain—this will in fact be the amount of tax if there are no exemptions or losses available and Ann's income is equal to or exceeds the limit for basic rate income tax). We will assume that the rate of inheritance tax is half of 40 per cent. This would be the appropriate rate if the transferor had no annual exemption or nil-rate band available. Remember that the value transferred is grossed up where the transferor pays the inheritance tax.

(a) If transferor pays both taxes:
  (i) Capital gains tax (£2,800) is not a loss to the transferor's estate.
  (ii) Inheritance tax is payable on the grossed-up gift.
  Gross gift for inheritance tax purposes

$$£24,000 \times 100/80 = £30,000$$

Inheritance tax = £6,000

		£
(iii) Total cost to transferor:	CGT	2,800
	Gift	24,000
	IHT	6,000
		32,800
Amount added to cumulative total		£30,000
Benefit to transferee		£24,000

(b) If transferee pays both taxes:
  (i) Capital gains tax (£2,800) reduces value transferred to £21,200
  (ii) Inheritance tax is payable on gift (not grossed up) less £2,800 (the capital gains tax)
  Inheritance tax £21,200 × 20% = £4,240
  (iii) Total cost to transferor £24,000
  Amount added to cumulative total £21,200
  Net benefit to transferee £16,960

(c) If transferor pays inheritance tax and transferee pays capital gains tax:
  (i) Capital gains tax (£2,800) reduces value transferred.
  (ii) Inheritance tax is payable on grossed up amount of gift less capital gains tax:

$$£21,200 \times 100/80 = £26,500$$

Inheritance tax

$$£26,500 \times 20\% = £5,300$$

(iii) Total cost to transferor

Gift	£24,000
IHT	£5,300
	£29,300
Amount added to cumulative total	£26,500
Benefit to transferee	£21,200

(d) If transferee pays inheritance tax and transferor pays capital gains tax:
  (i) Capital gains tax (£2,800) not a loss to transferor's estate
  (ii) Inheritance tax payable on gift (not grossed-up)

£24,000 × 20% = £4,800

(iii) Total cost to transferor	£26,800
Amount added to cumulative total	£24,000
Benefit to transferee£	19,200

Where capital gains tax hold-over relief is claimed on a gift (see para.5-019) a different rule applies to deal with the overlap between the two taxes. The amount of inheritance tax paid on the transfer of value is deducted in computing the donee's chargeable gain on a later disposal by them. Where the donor dies within seven years of the gift the inheritance tax may have to be recalculated. In such a case the transferor's estate is entitled to a refund of capital gains tax paid, if appropriate. However, the deduction is only permitted to the extent that it will wipe out the chargeable gain and so cannot give rise to an allowable loss.

Example 50

Arshad buys a business asset for £18,000 and makes a chargeable lifetime transfer of it to a relevant property trust when it is worth £20,000. Hold-over relief is claimed. We will assume that the rate of inheritance tax is half of 40 per cent. This would be the appropriate rate if the transferor had used up his annual exemption and the nil-rate band. If Arshad pays the inheritance tax, it will be £5,000 (with grossing-up); if the trust pays the inheritance tax, it will be £4,000 (without grossing-up).

The trust then sells the business asset for £22,500. Assuming that there are no incidental costs of disposal, the gain according to normal capital gains tax principles would be £4,500 (£22,500 – £18,000 = £4,500) since the trust is allowed to deduct Arshad's acquisition cost from the disposal consideration. However, as hold-over relief was claimed the amount of inheritance tax paid on the original transfer can be deducted in computing the gain for capital gains tax purposes.

(a) Chargeable gain where the donee paid the inheritance tax:

	£
Gain	4,500
Less	(4,000*)
	500

* Note: The whole of the inheritance tax is deducted, thus leaving a

chargeable gain of £500 on which capital gains tax will be payable unless there is an exemption available (for example, the annual exemption).

(b) Chargeable gain where the donor paid the inheritance tax:

	£
Gain	4,500
Less	(5,000**)
	Nil

** Note: A deduction is permitted only to the extent that it is necessary to extinguish a gain. It cannot be used to create a loss.

In the above example had the transfer been to Arshad's daughter, Bashira, it would have been potentially exempt, hence no inheritance tax would have been payable at the time of the transfer. Therefore, if Bashirah had sold the business asset for £22,500 before Arshad's death then capital gains tax would have been payable on the full gain of £4,500. Assuming Bashirah has already exhausted her basic rate income tax band, the capital gains tax would be calculated as follows:

$$28\% \times £4,500 = £1,260$$

However, if Arshad then died, say, four-and-a-half years after the transfer to Bashirah, inheritance tax would become payable at 60 per cent of the full rate. Assuming that Bashirah paid the inheritance tax there would be no grossing-up and the inheritance tax would be 60 per cent of the full rate of 40 per cent (assuming the rates remain identical to the current rates):

$$60\% \times 40\% \times £20,000 = £4,800$$

The £4,800 of inheritance tax now due would be deducted from the gain of £4,500 and would extinguish it. Thus the capital gains tax already paid could be reclaimed.

Anti-avoidance

Changing attitudes to tax avoidance

It used to be the case that taxpayers were entitled to arrange their financial affairs so as to avoid paying tax unnecessarily. However, the growth of highly sophisticated tax avoidance arrangements (particularly by global corporations) has led to increasing public criticism of tax avoidance. Lord Walker said in *Futter v Futter; Pitt v Holt* (2013): **4-104**

> "Since the seminal decision of the House of Lords in *WT Ramsay Ltd v IRC* [1982] AC 300 there has been an increasingly strong and general recognition that artificial tax avoidance is a social evil which puts an unfair burden on the shoulders of those who do not adopt such measures."

In the 1980s there was a strong judicial movement to counter artificial tax avoidance schemes. The House of Lords held in the *Ramsay* case that a court was not required to look at documents or transactions in blinkers, isolated from the context to which it belongs. If it is clear that a document or transaction is intended to have effect as part of a nexus or series of transactions, it can be regarded as such.

Furniss v Dawson set out the conditions required for the application of the so-called *Ramsey* principle: where a taxpayer achieves a purpose either by using a preordained series of transactions or a single composite transaction and steps are inserted which have no commercial purpose apart from the avoidance of a liability to tax, the inserted steps are to be disregarded for tax purposes.

These decisions caused some unease as being little short of judicial legislation. HMRC tended to respond to what it perceived as tax avoidance with targeted legislation to close loopholes, or even in the case of the pre-owned assets legislation, to introduce a new charge to tax. However, so much money was being lost to the Treasury that more general legislative measures were felt to be necessary.

DOTAS

4-105 The disclosure of tax avoidance schemes (DOTAS) regime was introduced in Pt 7 of Finance Act 2004. The regulations require certain arrangements designed to secure a tax advantage to be reported to HMRC. This gives HMRC warning of the schemes that are being developed and an opportunity to decide whether or not they work, to comment on why a particular scheme does not work and to introduce amending legislation for those that do.

The primary legislation setting out the DOTAS regime applies to the taxes included in the definition of "tax" in FA 2004 s.318(1). In practice, however, the regime does not apply to a particular tax until the government makes regulations introducing one or more "hallmarks" for that tax for the purposes of the notifiability test.

Failure to notify is not a criminal offence but gives rise to penalties. Notifying does not, of itself, produce any direct consequence for the taxpayer. Once reported, an arrangement is given a reference number and those using the arrangement must include that reference number on their tax returns.

There are several separate sets of regulations, some of which apply to more than one tax and some only to one specific tax. These regulations have been amended over time. Hallmarks are not mutually exclusive, so more than one may apply to particular arrangements.

DOTAS was extended to inheritance tax as from 6 April 2011 but only to a limited extent. The DOTAS reporting requirements, as originally introduced in the Inheritance Tax Avoidance Schemes (Prescribed Descriptions of Arrangements) Regulations 2011 (SI 2011/170), apply only to schemes which are designed to avoid an entry charge when property is settled on relevant property trusts (see para.7-016, for entry charges).

There were generous grandfathering provisions as a result of which it was not necessary to disclose arrangements which were the same, or substantially the same, as arrangements made available for implementation before 6 April 2011.

HMRC became concerned that there was inadequate reporting in relation to inheritance tax, partly because the hallmark was too narrow and partly because grandfathering was being claimed for schemes inappropriately.

With effect from 23 February 2016, the confidentiality and premium fee hallmarks were extended to inheritance tax. Hence arrangements designed to achieve an inheritance tax advantage which require the client to sign a confidentiality agreement or to pay a premium fee have to be reported.

On 16 July 2015, HMRC published draft regulations extending the inheritance tax hallmark. The conditions were extremely wide ranging. The draft hallmark required disclosure in relation to all death and lifetime transfers or events where an informed observer, having studied the arrangements and having regard to all the relevant circumstances, could reasonably be expected to conclude that "*securing an inheritance tax advantage was a main benefit*".

The draft hallmark attracted widespread criticism from professional bodies in the light of HMRC's stated intention to retain tightly targeted rules that would not catch the straightforward use of exemptions and reliefs.

HMRC recognised the criticisms and withdrew the draft. However, it said that it "*remained committed to updating the inheritance tax provisions in DOTAS to ensure that the regime operates more effectively*". On 20 April 2016 the draft Inheritance Tax Avoidance Schemes (Prescribed Descriptions of Arrangements) Regulations 2016 were published for consultation on the technical detail. They contained a requirement that an informed observer, having studied the arrangements could reasonably be expected to conclude that (1) the main purpose, or one of the main purposes, of the arrangements was that a person might reasonably be expected to obtain an advantage in relation to inheritance tax; and (2) that one or more elements of the arrangements would be unlikely to have been entered into but for the obtaining of the tax advantage; and (3) that the arrangements involved one or more contrived or abnormal steps without which the tax advantage could not be obtained.

The Consultation Paper accompanying the draft regulations says:

> "4.10 The Government recognises that the purpose of obtaining a tax advantage has a wide meaning in the context of inheritance tax. Therefore the approach taken in the redrafted hallmark is to link the tax advantage much more clearly to arrangements which are abnormal or contrived. Consequently ordinary tax planning arrangements which result in a tax advantage yet are not contrived or abnormal are not caught by the revised hallmark."

The draft regulations were amended and finally emerged as the Inheritance Tax Avoidance Schemes (Prescribed Descriptions of Arrangements) Regulations 2017 (SI 2017/1172) which came into effect as from 1 April 2018. Arrangements must be notified if it would be reasonable to expect an informed observer (having studied the arrangements and having regard to all relevant circumstances) to conclude that condition 1 and condition 2 are met.

Condition 1 is that the main purpose, or one of the main purposes, of the arrangements is to enable a person to obtain one or more of the following advantages in relation to inheritance tax (the "tax advantage"):

(a) the avoidance or reduction of a relevant property entry charge;
(b) the avoidance or reduction of:
- a 10-year anniversary or exit charge (IHTA ss.64, 65); or
- exit charges from employee/newspaper trusts (IHTA s.72); or
- charge on a gift made by a close company that is treated as having been made by the participators (IHTA s.94);

(c) the avoidance or reduction of a charge to inheritance tax arising from the application of s.102, 102ZA, 102A or 102B of the Finance Act 1986 (gifts with reservation) in circumstances where there is also no pre-owned assets charge to income tax under Sch.15 to the Finance Act 2004);
(d) a reduction in the value of a person's estate without giving rise to a chargeable transfer or potentially exempt transfer.

Condition 2 is that the arrangements involve one or more contrived or abnormal steps without which the tax advantage could not be obtained.

Guidance is available in HMRC's Guidance: Disclosure of tax avoidance schemes (DOTAS) available on the *gov.uk* website. It contains a number of examples of "straightforward" inheritance tax planning which will not be notifiable and a rather smaller number of notifiable arrangements.

There are no grandfathering provisions in the 2017 Regulations but there is an "established practice" exemption in reg.4 designed to remove from the scope of the hallmark established inheritance tax planning schemes whose workings are well understood and agreed. Arrangements are excepted if they:

(a) implement a proposal which has been implemented by related arrangements; and
(b) are substantially the same as the related arrangements.

"Related arrangements" means arrangements which were entered into before 1 April 2018 and, at the time they were entered into, accorded with established practice of which HMRC had indicated their acceptance.

Note that even if a particular proposal has been implemented before 1 April 2018, it is still necessary to test the proposal or arrangements against the premium fee and confidentiality hallmarks, which means the proposal or scheme may be notifiable by virtue only of one or both of those hallmarks.

"Established practice" is not defined in the legislation and, therefore, takes its ordinary meaning. HMRC's guidance (Guidance: Disclosure of tax avoidance schemes (DOTAS) available on the gov.uk website) says that it may be demonstrated by reference to published material (whether from HMRC, or text books or articles in journals) or by other written evidence of what had become a common practice by the relevant time (that is, when the arrangements were entered into).

It is then necessary to consider whether the arrangements actually carried out were the same or substantially the same as the related arrangements. HMRC says in its guidance that the "*substantially the same*" requirement relates to the arrangements being implemented and the related arrangements, not to the proposal that the arrangements are implementing. For the exception to apply, the current arrangements have to implement the same proposal that was implemented by the "*related arrangements*". Minor changes, for example to reflect the different personal details of users, will not stop arrangements from being substantially the same.

However, where the arrangements being implemented are altered beyond merely making the necessary changes to effect the proposal for that individual, the arrangements will no longer be "substantially the same" and will not be capable of being related arrangements.

The "informed observer" test is crucial as this provides the context in which the conditions are to be judged. In relation to the informed observer the guidance makes the following points:

- The informed observer is to be contrasted with an "uninformed observer", but is not an expert or necessarily a tax practitioner.
- The informed observer is independent, has all the relevant information about the scheme and has sufficient knowledge to understand both the scheme and the relevant statutory context.
- The informed observer is assumed to have the appropriate knowledge and skillset to reach the conclusions that the hallmark requires.
- While the promoter is not an informed observer for this purpose, the

informed observer should be presumed to have access to all of the information that is available to the promoter of the scheme.

The guidance includes the following examples of non-notifiable arrangements, with explanatory notes.

1. Ordinary outright gifts are not notifiable, even where they are exempt *Example 1: A lifetime gift to a spouse or civil partner*

Condition 1: Such a gift is caught by condition 1(d) as at least a main purpose of the gift is to reduce the value of the person's estate without giving rise to a chargeable transfer or a potentially exempt transfer. Instead the reduction gives rise to an exempt transfer.

But to be notifiable condition 2 must also be met.

Condition 2: It is not reasonable to expect that an informed observer would conclude a straightforward gift or transfer of assets to a spouse or civil partner includes either contrived or abnormal steps. This is simply the use of an exemption provided for by the legislation.

Although condition 1 is met, condition 2 is not, so these arrangements are not notifiable under this hallmark.

Example 2 Regular gifts out of income

Condition 1: If these are gifts to an individual, they may be caught by condition 1(d) as a main purpose of the gifts is to reduce the value of the person's estate without giving rise to a chargeable transfer or a potentially exempt transfer – they give rise to a series of exempt transfers.

If these are gifts into trust, they may also be caught by condition 1(a) in that they avoid or reduce a relevant property entry charge.

Again, although condition 1 may be met, to be notifiable condition 2 must also be met

Condition 2: It is not reasonable to expect that an informed observer would conclude it is either contrived or abnormal for a person to make regular gifts to those the person wants to benefit from their generosity where they are straightforward gifts to an individual or gifts into trust. This would just be the use of an exemption provided for by the legislation.

Although condition 1 is met, condition 2 is not, so these arrangements are not notifiable under this hallmark.

Example 3: Transfers of value equal to the available nil-rate band into trust, which may be repeated every seven years

Condition 1: These gifts are chargeable but within the available nil-rate band, so they are taxed at zero per cent. There is no reduction or avoidance of any charge set out in condition 1, so condition 1 is not met.

Condition 2: Even if the arrangements met condition 1, it would not be reasonable to expect an informed observer to conclude a gift of a sum equal to the available nil-rate band on its own was either contrived or abnormal, or contained contrived or abnormal steps.

Neither condition 1 nor condition 2 is met, so these arrangements are not notifiable under this hallmark.

Example 4: Making a lifetime transfer to a bare trust for a minor beneficiary

Condition 1: The transfer is a gift into a bare trust from which the donor cannot benefit. Although the transfer reduces the value of the transferor's estate, it gives rise to a potentially exempt transfer. Condition 1(d) is therefore not met and the arrangement does not give rise to any of the other tax advantages set out in condition 1. This analysis would apply whether or not the trustees were able to defer actual payments to the beneficiary beyond the age of 18. As condition 1 is not met there is no need to consider condition 2.

2. Executing a will, deed of variation or disclaimer which gives rise to exemption from inheritance tax *Example 5: Executing a will that leaves property to an exempt beneficiary such as the spouse or a charity*

Condition 1: Executing a will does not meet any of the elements of condition 1. Although a will may be executed to reduce or avoid the inheritance tax charge on death by use of exemptions, the will does not reduce the person's estate. Rather the will determines how the estate devolves on death and it is this devolution which secures any inheritance tax exemption. As there is no reduction in the person's estate without giving rise to a chargeable transfer, condition 1(d) is not met.

As condition 1 is not met there is no need to consider condition 2.

Example 6: Executing a deed of variation to which s.142 IHTA 1984 applies to transfer assets on death to an exempt beneficiary

Condition 1: Executing a deed of variation may reduce the inheritance tax charge on a person's death, but it does not meet any of the elements of condition 1 with regard to the person who has died as their estate is not reduced

A deed of variation is a lifetime transfer by the donor (the beneficiary) who originally inherited the property on the death. The property is treated as never being comprised in the donor's estate, so there is no reduction in the donor's estate and condition 1(d) is not met with respect to the donor. This is not therefore a notifiable arrangement under this hallmark.

As condition 1 is not met there is no need to consider condition 2.

Example 7: Disclaiming an entitlement under a will to which s.142 IHTA 1984 applies where there is an exempt residuary beneficiary

Condition 1: Disclaiming an entitlement under a will where there is an exempt residuary beneficiary may reduce the inheritance tax charge on a person's death, but it does not meet any of the elements of condition 1 with regard to the person who has died.

The beneficiary who makes the disclaimer is making a lifetime transfer of the property, but the property is treated as never being comprised in the beneficiary's estate, so there is no reduction in the value of the beneficiary's estate and condition 1(d) is not met. This is not therefore a notifiable arrangement under this hallmark.

As condition 1 is not met there is no need to consider condition 2.

3. Acquisition of property which qualifies for a statutory relief or a transfer which is specifically provided for in the inheritance tax legislation. There are a number of examples given. Some of the more important are set out below.

Example 8: Purchase of shares which will qualify for business property relief after they have been owned for two years

Condition 1: The purchase of shares does not reduce the value of a person's estate. If it becomes available, business property relief only has the effect of reducing the value transferred by a transfer of value, it does not remove the value of the shares from the estate. The act of purchasing shares in order to qualify for business property relief after two years does not, on its own, meet condition 1. It is not therefore a notifiable arrangement under this hallmark.

As condition 1 is not met there is no need to consider condition 2.

Example 9: Gift of land where the donor continues to use that land but pays full consideration for their use

Condition 1: The gift of land which the donor continues to occupy or use would normally be a gift with reservation of benefit, but the payment by the donor of full consideration in money or money's worth for that use prevents s.102 FA 1986 applying. It would be reasonable to expect an informed observer to conclude that at least a main purpose of this arrangement is to reduce or avoid a charge to inheritance tax as a gift with reservation of benefit. As there is also no pre-owned assets income tax charge under Sch.15 to the Finance Act 2004, this arrangement meets condition 1(c).

Condition 2: Even though condition 1 is met, the gift of land followed by payment of full consideration for use of that land would not, on its own, be regarded as contrived or abnormal, or involving contrived or abnormal steps. Sale and leaseback arrangements are not unusual in either the commercial world or for individuals (equity release).

Example 10: Gift of an undivided share of property which is subsequently used by both the donor and donee

Condition 1: The gift of land from which the donor continues to enjoy the benefit of occupation would be a gift with reservation of benefit, but where the donee has taken up possession and enjoyment of the property by occupying the property with the donor, s.102B Finance Act 1986 prevents this being a gift with reservation of benefit. There is no pre-owned assets income tax charge under Sch.15 to the Finance Act 2004. Depending on all the relevant circumstances it is likely that an informed observer would conclude that obtaining the inheritance tax advantage was the main reason, or one of the main reasons for the arrangements. It would therefore be reasonable to expect an informed observer to conclude that condition 1(c) was met.

Condition 2: If condition 1 was met, the gift of a share in land followed by the donee occupying that land with the donor could not be said to be contrived or abnormal. The analysis might be different where the donor only retained a very small proportion of the property in comparison to their level of occupation.

4. Arrangements which may not result in a reduced Inheritance Tax liability, but which cap the value subject to Inheritance Tax *Example 14: loan trusts and gift and loan trusts*

Gift and loan trusts involve the creation of a trust by a person by way of gift, followed by the person making an interest free loan to the trustees which is repayable on demand. The settlor is excluded from benefiting from the trust. Loan trusts are similar except that the trust is established by the granting of the interest free loan without the separate initial gift. The trustees invest the borrowed money.

The person may or may not require repayment of some or all of the loan in their lifetime. Any part of the loan which has not been repaid by the person's death is included within their estate.

Condition 1: The person's estate is not reduced by the granting of the loan, so condition 1 is not met. The hoped for Inheritance Tax saving arises only if the value of the Investment rises, but if it falls no Inheritance Tax saving is achieved. As condition 1 is not met there is no need to consider condition 2.

Example 15: loans to companies or other entities from which the lender cannot benefit

Condition 1: The granting of a loan which is repayable on demand, or on which a commercial rate of interest is charged, does not reduce the value of the lender's estate, so condition 1 is not met. As condition 1 is not met there is no need to consider condition 2.

The guidance goes on to deal with arrangements which might be notifiable. It makes the point that, because conditions 1 and 2 have to be evaluated taking all relevant circumstances into account, there will be some arrangements and proposals where it is difficult to be definitive. The guidance suggests that where arrangements include multiple steps in order to achieve the intended tax advantage however, there becomes an increased likelihood that they may be notifiable, either by reason of the inheritance tax hallmark or because they fall within the confidentiality or premium fee hallmarks. It gives this example:

Arrangement to gift shares which qualify for business property relief into trust and subsequently sell the shares back to the transferor

Condition 1: In isolation the transfer of shares qualifying for business property relief into a trust, or the sale of trust assets by the trustees, would not meet condition 1. Where arrangements are entered into with the intention that all of these steps take place, the arrangements have the effect of placing cash into a relevant property trust, but without incurring a relevant property entry charge. As one of the main purposes of these arrangements is to reduce or avoid a relevant property entry charge it would be reasonable to expect an informed observer to conclude that condition 1(a) is met.

This can be contrasted to a situation where, for example, family company shares are transferred into trust for succession planning purposes, at which time there is no intention of the trustees selling those shares. If the trustees later took an independent decision to sell the shares it is unlikely that an informed observer would conclude these separate steps form part of a single overall arrangement, or to conclude that condition 1(a) was met.

Condition 2: It would not normally be possible to transfer cash into a relevant property trust without incurring a relevant property entry charge, which is what has been achieved. To achieve this outcome and to gain this tax advantage, contrived steps are necessary, that is the transfer or shares qualifying for relief followed by their sale back to the transferor rather than the simple transfer of cash which would be the non-contrived way of achieving the same result. Without these contrived steps the tax advantage would not arise. It would therefore be reasonable to expect an informed observer to conclude, considering the arrangements as a whole, that condition 2 was met.

Where new proposals for arrangements involve contrived or abnormal steps in order to obtain the inheritance tax advantages set out in condition 1 these proposals will be notifiable. Because the "grandfathering" provisions in the 2011 Regulations ceased to apply from 1 April 2018, arrangements which would have previously been excepted from disclosure will be notifiable if the two conditions in the new hallmark are met.

The guidance includes the following example of a notifiable arrangement.

Creation of a reversionary lease

A person owning a freehold grants a lease to a trust or to their children. The lease starts in 21 years' time, longer than the person expects to survive. The person continues to live in the property until the sub-lease begins.

Condition 1: The arrangements avoid or reduce a charge to inheritance tax arising from the application of the gift with reservation of benefit rules. The person continues to benefit from the property, but the whole value of the property is no longer in the estate. If, in addition, no charge arises under Sch.15 to the Finance Act 2004, it would be reasonable to expect an informed observer to conclude that this arrangement meets condition 1(c).

Condition 2: The creation of a lease which only takes effect several years in the future and which in the meantime allows the owner of the property to continue in occupation at no cost is a contrived and/or abnormal step. The tax advantage would not be achieved without this contrived or abnormal step. It is therefore reasonable to expect an informed observer to conclude that this arrangement meets condition 2 and is notifiable under this hallmark.

GAAR

In addition, a general anti-abuse rule (GAAR) was introduced by Finance Act 2013. The provisions apply to all taxes including inheritance, although inheritance tax has always had its own anti-avoidance measures: the associated operations rules (see para.4-107). **4-106**

The rule is aimed at "tax advantages arising from tax arrangements that are abusive" (FA 2013 s.206(1)). It came into operation on 17 July 2013. The overriding objective is to target abusive arrangements. It is not aimed at the "centre ground" of responsible tax planning.

Finance Act 2013 s.207(2) states that tax arrangements are "abusive" if they are arrangements the entering into or carrying out of which cannot reasonably be regarded as a reasonable course of action in relation to the relevant tax provisions, having regard to all the circumstances. This is sometimes referred to as the double reasonableness test. The test does not ask whether entering, etc. into the arrangements was a reasonable course of action. It asks whether there can be a reasonably held view that it was reasonable. It therefore appears that although, looked at in isolation, the arrangements might not *be* reasonable, they might still *seem* a reasonable course of action: s.209 provides that it is for HMRC to show, on the balance of probabilities, that the tax arrangements are abusive. When deciding, a court or tribunal must take into account: HMRC's guidance about the general anti-abuse rule that was approved by the GAAR Advisory Panel at the time the tax arrangements were entered into, and any opinion of the GAAR Advisory Panel about the arrangements.

If tax arrangements are abusive and are successfully challenged under GAAR, such adjustments are to be made as shall be "just and reasonable". This may be straightforward (for instance, the disallowance of a loss) or may involve a redefinition of the arrangement to identify the arrangement that would have been carried out to achieve the same objective but without the abusive tax advantage. It may simply result in the arrangement being ignored altogether (as will be the case with circular self-cancelling arrangements).

Associated operations

Section 268 of IHTA 1984 provides that where a transfer of value is made by "associated operations" carried out at different times it shall be treated as made at the time of the last of them. "Associated operations" are defined very widely as being: **4-107**

> "any two or more operations which affect the same property ... or any two operations of which one is effected with reference to the other or with a view to enabling or facilitating the other to be effected whether effected by the same or different people and whether or not they are simultaneous".

The object of these provisions is to prevent donors avoiding inheritance tax by making artificial arrangements.

Obviously many individuals wish to arrange their financial affairs so as to provide the maximum benefit for members of their family and so as to avoid unnecessary tax; this may well involve arrangements which *could* be regarded as associated. In particular, it is common, where one spouse is much wealthier than the other, for the wealthier spouse to make use of the spouse exemption to transfer assets to the poorer spouse. This enables the poorer spouse to make transfers to the issue of the couple which will attract lifetime exemptions and/or prove to be fully exempt if the donor survives seven years. When the associated operations provisions were discussed in Parliament in 1975 the Chief Secretary to the Treasury said that transfers between spouses would only be attacked in blatant cases where a transfer was made *on condition* that the recipient would at once use the money to make gifts to others.

In *Rysaffe Trustee Co (CI) Ltd v IRC* (2003) a taxpayer had set up a series of £10 pilot trusts on different days to which substantial funds were later transferred. The Revenue sought to charge tax on the basis that there was just one single settlement. A unanimous Court of Appeal rejected the Revenue's arguments. Associated operations are only relevant if in substance there is a single disposition which has been divided into a number of separate "operations". In *Rysaffe*, while each transfer was part of one scheme, the transfer of each amount made no reference to the other transfers. Each transfer was effected in the knowledge that the others were being effected as well, but that is not the same as effecting transfers "with reference to the other" which is what the section requires.

The difficulty of deciding whether or not the associated operations rule applies is illustrated by *RCC v Parry* [2018] EWCA Civ 2266, reversing the decision of the Upper Tribunal in *Parry v RCC* [2017] UKUT 4 (TCC). A deceased taxpayer, Mrs Staveley, had transferred funds from one pension scheme to another and omitted to draw funds from the new pension thus benefiting her sons who were nominated to receive any surplus funds. Under the first scheme Mrs Stavely's estate would have received the funds as of right, apart from an over-funding element which would have been returned to the employer company which was owned by her ex-husband and would have therefore benefited him. The new pension scheme was discretionary and gave Mrs Stavely no right to control the destination of the funds. The Upper Tribunal held that, although this represented a loss to her estate it was not a transfer of value because it fell under IHTA 1984 s.10 which provides that a transaction is not a transfer of value if there is no gratuitous intent. It was accepted that her motive was to put the funds beyond reach of her ex-husband and, therefore, there was no gratuitous intent. However, s.10(2) states that "transaction" includes "any associated operations". HMRC contended that the transfer and omission to draw funds were associated operations and that the omission to draw did have a gratuitous intent. The Upper Tribunal did not agree. Both a transaction and any associated operations require intention to confer gratuitous benefit. The scheme, comprising all its elements, must be intended to confer the benefit. In this case, the necessary intention had to be shown for both the initial transfer and the omission to take lifetime benefits. The transfer, and the motivation for it, was entirely separate from the omission to take lifetime pension benefits. That was sufficient for the transfer not to be an associated operation with the omission. The transfer was not part of any scheme with the omission which had that collective intention.

The Court of Appeal held that the tribunal had been mistaken in considering that there was no intent linking the omission and the transfer. Both were motivated by a desire on the deceased's part that her sons should have the death benefits payable if she did not draw a pension. Although she did not see the transfer as improving their position, the only reasonable conclusion was that she also intended the personal pension plan to be a means by which the death benefits could be passed to them. It was implicit in the tribunal's decision that the deceased intended her sons to benefit from the personal pension plan. The transfer to the plan and the failure to take pension benefits were properly to be seen as forming part of and contributing to a scheme intended to confer gratuitous benefits.

12. Reduced Rate of Inheritance Tax

When is the reduced rate available?

The Finance Act 2012 contains provisions (s.209 and Sch.32) reducing the rate of inheritance tax from 40 per cent to 36 per cent for taxpayers who leave 10 per cent or more of their net estate to charity. Schedule 32 inserts a new Sch.1A into IHTA 1984. The reduced rate applies where death occurs on or after 6 April 2012. **4-108**

For the purposes of the 10 per cent test a deceased's estate is divided into three components:

1. the survivorship component (the deceased's interest in assets owned as beneficial joint tenant);
2. the settled property component (assets in which the deceased had a qualifying interest in possession);
3. the general component (all other assets within the deceased's inheritance tax estate except for property treated as part of the estate because of the reservation of property rules).

The 10 per cent test is normally applied separately to each component (subject to a merger election—see para.4-109).

When calculating whether the 10 per cent test is met for any component, it is necessary to compare the amount given to charity with "the baseline amount" for each component. The "baseline amount" is the net value (i.e. after debts) of the assets included in the component after deducting:

- any available nil-rate band (or transferred nil-rate band);
- any exemptions (other than the charity exemption); and
- any reliefs.

The nil-rate band is allocated proportionally amongst the components of the estate.

Any additional residence nil-rate band available to the estate is ignored when calculating the baseline amount.

Example 51

Fred dies with a chargeable estate of £800,000 plus property eligible for business property relief of £1 million. He has unused nil-rate band of £300,000. He leaves a legacy to charity, his house worth £400,000 to his wife and the residue to his son. If his estate is to benefit from the reduced rate, how large must the charitable legacy be?

The spouse exemption and property eligible for business property relief are deducted leaving £400,000 (the gift to charity is included when calculating the baseline amount). After deducting the available nil-rate band of £300,000 the baseline amount of the general component is £100,000 so the charitable legacy must be at least £10,000.

Without the legacy Fred's son would take £400,000 less inheritance tax at 40 per cent on £100,000 (£40,000) so £360,000.

With the legacy and the benefit of the reduced rate Fred's son will take £390,000 less inheritance tax at 36 per cent on £90,000 (£32,400) so £357,600.

Notice that in the above example Fred's son takes less than he would have taken had no legacy at all been given. However, where a will contains a charitable legacy of less than 10 per cent, increasing it to reach the magic 10 per cent can actually increase the amount taken by the non-exempt beneficiaries. For example, if Fred had given a legacy of say nine per cent to charity, it would benefit Fred's son to increase the legacy to 10 per cent by means of a post-death variation (for post-death variations see Ch.19). There is a useful calculator on the HMRC website at *https://www.gov.uk/inheritance-tax-reduced-rate-calculator* [Accessed 6 March 2020] which can calculate the size of legacy required to obtain the rate reduction.

Opt-out and merger elections

4-109 An opt-out election (contained in IHTA 1984 Sch.1A para.8) is included because there may be cases where the cost of claiming the reduction (for example additional valuations) may exceed the benefit obtained from the rate reduction.

Who makes the opt-out election? It varies according to the component being considered:

- the survivorship component: those taking by survivorship (or their PRs);
- the settled property component: the trustees;
- the general component: the deceased's PRs;
- property subject to a reservation of benefit: the person in whom the property is vested.

Although the reduced rate normally applies only to components for which the 10 per cent test is met and not for any other component, it is possible under IHTA 1984 Sch.1A para.7 to elect to merge components. The merger election is made by those who would make the opt-out election for each component being merged.

An election to merge components would, typically, be made where one component more than meets the 10 per cent test while another component fails. The merged components will be treated as a single component and the reduced rate will be available if the deemed single component satisfies the test.

Example 52

Tom owns a house as beneficial joint tenants with his brother, Bert. The value of his interest in the house is £400,000. He has other assets not eligible for relief worth £600,000 and has exhausted his nil-rate band. He leaves his entire estate to charity and appoints Bert as his executor.

The joint property is a separate component so no reduction of rate is-possible unless a merger election is made. If Bert makes the election, the baseline amount is £1 million and, given that £600,000 is passing to charity, the reduced rate will become available on the property passing by survivorship.

In the above example, had Tom had nil-rate band available, it would have been apportioned between the two components.

It is possible to elect to merge property subject to a reservation of benefit with one of the other components (IHTA 1984 Sch.1A para.7(5)(b)).

Formula clauses

Introduction

4-110 It is not possible to calculate the size of the legacy required to meet the 10 per cent test before death. This is because the amount required to meet the requirement will depend on matters such as the amount of nil-rate band available at death, the value of the estate and the availability of reliefs and-exemptions. It is possible to draft a legacy by reference to a formula giving the amount required to gain the benefit of the reduced rate. HMRC has included a clause in the *IHT Manual* at para.IHTM45008 which it says achieves the desired result.

Technical provisions

The schedule includes provisions dealing with various technical problems, for example if a grossing-up calculation has to be done, the initial calculation is done at 36 per cent making it easier to meet the 10 per cent test (IHTA 1984 Sch.1A para.6(1)). Where property eligible for business or agricultural property relief is included in the residue the normal apportionment of relief required by IHTA s.39A does not apply, making it easier to meet the test. There are also specific provisions dealing with the situation where there are deferred inheritance tax charges (assets that attract conditional exemption from inheritance tax are ignored), but any recapture charge cannot benefit from the reduced rate. Successive charges relief (under IHTA 1984 s.141) has been appropriately amended by the insertion of a new s.141A. **4-111**

13. Discharge from Liability for IHT

If HMRC are satisfied that the tax attributable to a chargeable transfer has been, or will be, paid in instalments they can (and, if the transfer is one made on death, must) give a certificate to that effect (s.239(1)). The effect is to discharge all persons (unless there was fraud or non-disclosure of material facts) from liability for any further claim for tax. It also extinguishes any HMRC charge on property for that tax. **4-112**

It is possible to obtain a more limited certificate which extinguishes an HMRC charge on property which is to be purchased but which does not discharge any accountable person.

An HMRC charge for unpaid inheritance tax attaches to property other than UK personal property beneficially owned by the deceased before death which vests in the personal representatives.

Where property subject to an HMRC charge is disposed of, that property ceases to be subject to the charge (although the property representing it becomes subject to the charge) if:

(a) in the case of land the charge was not registered; or
(b) in the case of UK personalty the purchaser had no notice of the facts giving rise to the charge.

It frequently happens that adjustments have to be made to the inheritance tax value of the estate during the administration (for example, because-estimated figures are finalised or additional assets are discovered). Where inheritance tax is due as a result of the increase, the personal representatives must submit a corrective account to HMRC giving full information of all changes in value. Pressure on resources at HMRC led to the following request in the *Trusts & Estates Newsletter* for April 2018 in relation to changes to estates:

> "*Telling us about changes*
> We know that you need to tell us about changes to most estates after you have the grant.

> On average, you tell us three times on each case. However, some agents report small changes much more often. Responding to correspondence and recalculating the tax on these cases takes up a disproportionate amount of time.
>
> We would like you to tell us about smaller changes to the values in the estate all in one go.
>
> Do this when you believe the values in the estate are final or when 18 months have passed since the date of death, whichever is earlier. Before this, you only need to tell us if:
>
> - the changes relate to the value of land, buildings or unlisted shares
> - you want to claim relief when you have sold land or shares at a loss
> - you have sold assets on which you were paying tax by instalments
> - the total increase or decrease in the value of the estate is more than £50,000, before any exemptions or reliefs
> - we have told you that we are carrying out a compliance check on the estate
> - the person who died made a gift with reservation of benefit or had the right to benefit from a trust when they died
>
> We will not charge you a penalty for not telling us about amendments as long as you follow these guidelines. We have added new guidance to the *IHT Manual* at Accountability: telling us about amendments to reflect this.
>
> We expect agents to calculate the additional tax due as a result of changes to the estate. You can make a payment on account if you want to reduce or stop interest."

In fact the list of exclusions is such that taxpayers frequently will have to inform HMRC of changes in value as they occur.

Until the personal representatives have obtained a certificate of discharge they cannot safely complete the distribution of the assets comprised in the estate since further tax may become due as a result of adjustments to the value of the estate.

A certificate of discharge does not affect any further tax which becomes payable as a result of the discovery of additional assets or as a result of increases in the amount of property passing to non-exempt beneficiaries.

Where inheritance tax is not paid in full on the death, for example, on timber, on blocked foreign assets or where there is a conditional exemption for heritage property, HMRC will issue a limited certificate expressed to be "save and except" those items.

HMRC used to send a standard clearance letter when it had finished its checks. However the *Trusts & Estates Newsletter* for April 2018 announced a change:

> "We will no longer issue our standard clearance letter when we have finished our checks. If you want to apply for clearance, you should use form IHT30 'Application for a clearance certificate'. Only do this when you are sure there will be no further changes that will affect the tax position on the estate. You can also use the form IHT30 to report any changes to the estate.
>
> IHTA84 S239 (2) suggests that it is appropriate to apply for clearance once two years have passed since the date of death. In practice, we will consider clearance earlier than this, but only if you are sure that there will be no more changes to report. We would not normally expect you to apply until at least a year has passed since the date of death."

Neither certificates of discharge nor clearance letters are issued in relation to excepted estates which receive automatic clearance after the expiry of the specified period unless selected for investigation (see Ch.10).

Chapter Five

CAPITAL GAINS TAX

1. Introduction

The *death* of an individual does not give rise to a liability to capital gains tax (save in very limited circumstances where there is settled property). However, capital gains tax may have to be considered in connection with all or any of the following: **5-001**

(a) disposals made by the deceased up to the date of death;
(b) disposals made by the personal representatives after the date of death during the period of administration; and
(c) disposals made by beneficiaries of assets they have received from the estate.

Before considering these three situations, a brief outline of the capital gains tax system contained in the Taxation of Chargeable Gains Act 1992 is necessary. All references are to that Act unless otherwise stated.

The Finance Act 2008 substantially simplified the calculation of capital gains tax for tax year 2008/09 onwards by, inter alia, introducing a single rate of tax, abolishing indexation and taper relief. It also introduced entrepreneurs' relief which became increasingly valuable over the years but has now been replaced by a much more limited relief called business asset disposal relief.

In tax year 2010/11 further changes were made by the coalition government in the Finance (No.2) Act 2010 which reintroduced differential rates of tax part way through the tax year in an attempt to increase tax revenue.

The rate charged on a disposal made on or after 23 June 2010 depends on the level of income of the taxpayer with further changes introduced from 6 April 2016 (see para.5-013).

Capital gains tax was originally a territorial tax: UK tax residents are subject to UK capital gains tax on their worldwide assets, whereas non-UK tax residents originally escaped the tax. However, changes have been introduced to increase their-liability for the tax and further changes are proposed.

Finance Act 2013 introduced an annual tax on enveloped dwellings (ATED) which is an annual tax on high value residential UK property owned by non--natural persons such as companies (NNPs). The Act also introduces a capital gains tax charge on disposals on or after 6 April 2013 of such properties by both resident and non-resident NNPs. It was part of a package of measures that the government announced in the 2012 budget to ensure that individuals and companies pay a fair share of tax on residential property transactions and to tackle avoidance, including the wrapping of property in corporate and other "envelopes".

Finance Act 2019 introduced significant changes. The non-resident capital gains tax regime was significantly expanded by new sections substituted in Pt 1 of the Act and a new Sch.1A. Non-residents became subject to tax on all UK real estate gains not just residential property and ATED gains.

In the Spring 2024 Budget, Jeremy Hunt, who was at that time the Chancellor of the Exchequer, announced that from 6 April 2025, the remittance basis regime will be abolished and replaced with a new residence-based tax system. The Labour government will implement a version of the proposals. See 5-005 below.

2. Capital Gains Tax Generally

Introduction

5-002 Capital gains tax is payable when a *person* makes a disposal of *chargeable assets* giving rise to a *chargeable gain* unless an *exemption or relief* applies. The tax is charged on a "current year basis" by reference to gains made in a "tax year", from 6 April to the following 5 April (officially called a "year of assessment").

Taxable person pre-tax year 2019/20

5-003 For 2013/14 and later years, a person is chargeable to capital gains if he meets the *"residence condition"* set out in s.2(1A) which is as follows:

"(a) in the case of an individual, he is resident in the UK for the year;
(b) in the case of personal representatives of a deceased person, the deemed single and continuing body is resident in the UK;
(c) in the case of the trustees of a settlement, the deemed single person is resident in the UK during any part of the year; or
(d) in any other case, the person is resident in the UK when the gain accrues."

Personal representatives are treated as being a single and continuing body of persons (distinct from the persons who may from time to time be the personal representatives) under s.62(3). Trustees are treated as if they were a single person (distinct from the persons who are trustees of the settlement from time to time under s.69(1).

Trustees are treated as resident in the UK at any time when a condition in s.69(2A) or (2B) is satisfied.

(2A) Condition 1 is that all the trustees are resident in the United Kingdom.
(2B) Condition 2 is that:

"(a) at least one trustee is resident in the United Kingdom,
(b) at least one is not resident in the United Kingdom, and
(c) the settlor in relation was resident ... or domiciled in the United Kingdom immediately before death if the settlement was created on death and, in any other case, the time when the settlor made the settlement."

If an individual is domiciled in the UK, they are liable in respect of gains arising from assets situated anywhere in the world. If the individual is not domiciled in the UK, they may claim the remittance basis of taxation for the year. If successful, they are liable on gains arising from assets situated in the UK but not liable on gains arising from assets located outside the UK except to the extent that those gains are remitted to the UK (s.12).

Taxable person 2019/20 onwards

2019/20 to end of 2024/25

Finance Act 2019 s.13, Sch.1, Pt 1, paras 1, 2 have made significant changes to the taxation of gains made by non-residents. 5-004

A person who is UK resident for a tax year is chargeable to capital gains tax on chargeable gains accruing to the person in the tax year on the disposal of assets wherever situated (TCGA 1992 s.1A(1)). For these purposes, a person is "UK resident" for a tax year if the person is resident in the UK during any part of the tax year. The position of personal representatives and trustees continues unchanged.

Under s.1A(3) a person who is not UK resident for a tax year is chargeable to capital gains tax on chargeable gains accruing to the person in the tax year on the disposal of:

(a) assets situated in the UK that have a relevant connection to the person's UK branch or agency and are disposed of at a time when the person has that branch or agency (see s.1B);
(b) assets not within para.(a) that are interests in UK land; and
(c) assets (wherever situated) not within para.(a) or (b) that derive at least 75 per cent of their value from UK land where the person has a substantial indirect interest in that land (as defined in s.1D and Sch.1A). For this purpose, a person is "UK resident" for a tax year if resident in the UK during any part of the tax year.

Schedule 1A broadly provides that an asset derives at least 75 per cent of its value from UK land if it consists of a right or an interest in a company and, at the time of the disposal, at least 75 per cent of the total market value of the company's qualifying assets derives (directly or indirectly) from interests in UK land. A person has a substantial indirect interest in UK land if, at any time in the period of two years ending with the time of the disposal, the person has a 25 per cent investment in the company.

Thus, from 6 April 2019 the scope of UK tax is broadened for non-UK tax residents to include disposals of all real estate located in the UK, not just residential property and disposals of entities such as companies deriving at least 75 per cent of their value from UK land.

There is an exclusion for UK property-rich entities where all (or almost all) of the property has been used for trading purposes (TCGA 1992 Sch.1A para.5). In addition, HMRC will only be able to apply UK capital gains tax to the disposal of UK property-rich entities if the tax treaty with the vendor's country of residence gives taxing rights to the UK for this type of disposal—currently not all UK tax treaties include this clause, so there will have a gradual replacement of all those treaties which do not give such taxing rights to the country where real estate is located.

2025/26 onwards

In the Spring 2024 Budget, the then Conservative Chancellor, Jeremy Hunt, announced that from 6 April 2025, the remittance basis regime would be abolished and replaced with a new residence-based tax system under which new arrivers to the UK, or individuals returning to the UK after at least 10 years overseas, would be able to elect not to be taxed on their foreign income or gains during the first four years of UK tax residence (the FIG regime). Electing into the FIG regime would 5-005 result in the loss of personal allowances and the capital gains tax annual exempt amount as is the case for remittance basis users. However, those electing to be taxed on the FIG regime will only be taxable in the UK on their UK-sourced income and gains. They will not be taxable on their overseas income and gains—regardless of whether these are remitted to the UK.

Individuals who have already been resident in the UK for four tax years on 6 April 2025 will not be eligible for the FIG regime and will be subject to UK taxation on their worldwide income and gains as it arises.

The proposals include fairly generous transitionary terms.

Following the General Election in June 2024, the new Labour government announced that it will implement the basic proposal but with fewer transitional provisions.

Disposals

5-006 The Act does not provide an exhaustive definition of the term, but it is clear that a sale or gift amounts to a "disposal". Furthermore, s.21(2) provides that the term "disposal" covers part disposals. Thus the sale of part of a plot of land is a disposal as is the grant of a lease or an easement. In addition, there are statutory provisions by which certain transactions are treated as disposals (such as the total loss or destruction of an asset or the granting of an option). If an asset is disposed of under a contract, the date of disposal is the date of the contract, not the date on which the asset is eventually transferred (s.28(1)). If a contract is conditional, the operative date is the date on which the condition is satisfied (s.28(2)).

Chargeable assets

5-007 The definition of *assets* for capital gains tax purposes is set out in s.21(1), which provides that:

> "All forms of property shall be assets for the purposes of this Act, whether situated in the United Kingdom or not, including:
>
> (a) options, debts and incorporeal property generally,
> (b) any currency other than sterling, and
> (c) any form of property created by the person disposing of it or otherwise coming to be owned without being acquired (such as goodwill in a business)."

All *assets* are *chargeable assets* subject to a few exceptions including sterling and motor cars.

Chargeable gains

The basic rule

5-008 A gain arises if the "consideration for disposal" exceeds the "allowable deductions" provided for in the Act.

The "consideration for disposal" is the sale price if the asset is sold in an arm's length transaction or the market value if there is a gift or a gift element. The market value is the price which the asset might reasonably be expected to fetch on a sale in the open market. Section 272(2) provides that no reduction in the value can be made by assuming that the assets would be placed on the market at the same time.

Once the "consideration for disposal" has been calculated, the allowable expenditure is deducted to calculate the chargeable gains. The allowable expenditure is defined by s.38(1) and falls into three categories:

(a) Initial expenditure, which is the original purchase price (or market value if the asset was acquired by way of gift) plus incidental costs incurred in acquiring the asset, such as solicitors' fees and stamp duty. If the asset was not acquired by the taxpayer from anyone else (because, for example, it is the goodwill of a business they have set up) the initial expenditure is that wholly and exclusively incurred in providing thc asset.
(b) Subsequent expenditure, which is expenditure wholly and exclusively incurred for the purpose of enhancing the value of the asset (the expenditure being reflected in the state or nature of the asset at the time of disposal) and expenditure incurred in establishing, preserving or defending title to, or a right over, the asset.
(c) Incidental costs of disposal such as solicitors' fees, estate agents' fees, the cost of advertising, etc.

There must be excluded from the calculation any sum that is charged to income tax (such as portions of premiums on certain leases which are taxable under Income Tax (Trading and Other Income) Act 2005 s.276 and following)) or any expense that is deductible for income tax purposes (such as the cost of *repairs* to an asset as opposed to the cost of improvements).

With regard to the allowable deductions, special rules apply if part only of an asset is disposed of since it would clearly be unfair for the taxpayer to be able to deduct expenditure laid out on the whole asset against the sale price of only part. In these circumstances s.42(2) provides that the allowable expenditure to be deducted from the sale price (or market value if appropriate) of the part sold or given away is found by multiplying the total expenditure on the whole asset by:

$$\frac{A}{A + B}$$

where A is the consideration received for the part disposed of and B is the market value of the part retained.

Example 1

Terence buys a plot of land for £40,000 (his only allowable expenditure). He sells part for £45,000; the value of the remainder is £15,000. From the £45,000 sale proceeds he can deduct:

$$\frac{£40,000 \times £45,000}{£45,000 + £15,000}$$

$$\frac{£40,000 \times £45,000}{£60,000} = £30,000$$

He therefore has a chargeable gain of £15,000.

The indexation allowance

5-009 An indexation allowance to offset the effects of inflation was introduced for disposals made on or after 6 April 1982 (1 April in the case of companies). The effect of the allowance was to "index link" allowable expenditure so that only "real" profits were potentially taxable on a subsequent disposal. For disposals by individuals, personal representatives and trustees the allowance was abolished for months after April 1998 and taper relief was introduced. The Finance Act 2008 completely abolished the indexation allowance and taper relief but at the same time introduced a lower rate of tax.

Special rules for assets held on 6 April 1965 and 31 March 1982

5-010 Capital gains tax came into force on 6 April 1965 and tax has never been levied on gains arising before that date.

In March 1988 it was announced that the base date for capital gains tax would be altered. In respect of disposals made on or after 6 April 1988 no tax is levied on gains arising prior to 31 March 1982. Taxpayers are treated as having disposed of assets on 31 March 1982 and as having acquired them at market value at that date (s.55(1)).

Example 2

A acquires an asset in 1980 for £2,000; on 31 March 1982 it is worth £8,000; on 1 September 2024 he disposes of the asset for £19,000. Ignoring exemptions for the purposes of this example he will be treated as making a chargeable gain of £11,000 (£19,000–£8,000).

Taper relief

5-011 Taper relief came into effect on 6 April 1998 and gave relief once assets had been held for a minimum period of three years for non-business assets and one year for business assets. The relief increased with each year the asset was owned until, after 10 years of ownership in the case of non-business assets, the maximum relief (60 per cent of the gain being chargeable) was reached.

"Business assets" (as defined in Sch.A1) were treated more generously; from 6 April 2002 only 50 per cent of the gain was chargeable once the asset had been owned for one year, reducing to only 25 per cent for assets owned for two or more years.

Taper relief is not available for disposals made on or after 6 April 2008.

Losses

5-012 If deducting the allowable expenditure from the sale proceeds or market value of the asset shows that the taxpayer has made a loss, it may be set off against all gains made during the current tax year. If this year's gains are insufficient to absorb the whole loss, it may be carried forward and set off against all future gains as they arise. The losses can be carried forward indefinitely until such gains arise (s.2(2)).

It is important to note that in the tax year in which the loss arises, it must be set against that year's gains to reduce them as far as is possible. This is so even if the loss would reduce the gains below the annual exemption limit (£6,000 in 2023/24 and £3,000 in 2024/25—see para.5-016). However, if there are unabsorbed losses which are carried forward, in the future years they are used only to the extent necessary to reduce the gains of those later years to the level of the annual exemption (s.3(5)).

Example 3

During the tax year 2023/24, X sells two assets; one disposal gives rise to a gain of £6,000 and the other disposal shows a loss of £8,000. The loss must be set against the gain reducing it to nil and leaving £2,000 unabsorbed loss that can be carried forward to set against future gains.

If X in 2024/25 sells an asset making a gain of £3,500, only £500 of the loss brought forward is used to reduce the gain to the level of the annual exemption (£3,000), leaving £3,000 of the unabsorbed loss to be carried forward to set against future gains.

A loss is only allowable in circumstances where, had a gain been made on the disposal of the asset, it would have been *chargeable*. Thus the sale of a private motor car at a loss does not give rise to an allowable loss.

Rates of tax

For tax years before 2008/09 the rates of capital gains tax applicable to individuals were equivalent to the rates of income tax which would apply if gains were treated as the top slice of income. The rate of tax for disposals made in 2009/10 and up to 23 June 23 2010 was a flat 18 per cent. **5-013**

For disposals made by individuals on or after 23 June 2010 and before 6 April 2016 the rate remains 18 per cent where total taxable gains *and income* are less than the upper limit of the income tax basic rate band for the relevant tax year. Gains or parts of gains above that limit are taxed at 28 per cent.

For disposals made by individuals on or after 6 April 2016, the rate was reduced to 10 per cent and 20 per cent except for gains on residential property (although such gains will often be exempt; see para.5-015) and carried interest where the rates are higher, 18 per cent for gains within the basic rate band and 28 per cent for those above. The 28 per cent rate was reduced to 24 per cent for disposals made on or after 6 April 2024. The 18 per cent rate remains unchanged. The policy objective was stated as follows:

> "*Cutting the 28% rate of CGT to 24% is expected to incentivise earlier disposals of second homes, buy-to-let property and other residential property where accrued gains do not fully benefit from PRR. This will generate more transactions in the property market, benefitting those looking to move home or get onto the property ladder.*"

The change is presumably linked to the abolition of the favourable furnished holiday let tax regime—although that will not take effect until April 2025 (see 5-013). Properties meeting the qualifying tests for the regime are taxed under special rules and owners of such properties can access specific tax advantages not available for other lettings, including:

- entitlement to plant and machinery allowances on items of fixtures, furniture, furnishings and equipment. The relief also allowed utilisation of the 100 per cent annual investment allowance.
- CGT reliefs for traders such as rollover relief and business asset disposal relief on sale which reduces the rate of CGT to 10 per cent;

- finance and interest restrictions do not apply to loans and mortgages on FHL properties.

Where business asset disposal relief (formerly entrepreneur's relief) is available (see para.5-016) the rate is reduced.

Losses and the annual exemption can be allocated in the way most beneficial to the taxpayer.

Example 4

In 2024/25 Colin's taxable income is £1,000 below the limit for higher rate tax.

He disposes of shares and makes a gain of £21,000. Ignoring the annual exemption (see para.5-016), the first £1,000 will be taxed at 10 per cent and the remaining £19,000 at 20 per cent. If he made the same gain on the disposal of a residential property, the rates would be 18 per cent and 24 per cent.

Disposals made by personal representatives and trustees on or after 23 June 2010 and before 6 April 2016 are taxed at 28 per cent whatever the level of income.

Disposals made by personal representatives and trustees on or after 6 April 2016 are at the higher rates whatever the level of income.

Exemptions and reliefs

Introduction

5-014 Certain exemptions and reliefs are available. In some cases they extinguish, and in others they reduce, the taxpayer's liability.

Exemptions

5-015 The main exemptions are:

(a) The taxpayer's only or main residence together with gardens and grounds up to, normally, 0.5 of a hectare (s.222). The property must normally have been the taxpayer's main residence throughout their period of ownership and not have been bought with a view to making a gain on the disposal (s.224(3)). Certain periods of absence are disregarded under s.223(3) including:

(i) a period of absence not exceeding three years;

(ii) any period of absence during which the taxpayer was employed, or held an office, all the duties of which were performed outside the UK; and

(iii) a period of absence, not exceeding four years, throughout which the taxpayer was prevented from residing as a result of the situation of their place of work or as a result of their employer requiring them to reside elsewhere, the condition being reasonably imposed to secure the effective performance of their duties.

The last 36 months of ownership is disregarded in any event for contracts exchanged before 6 April 2014. The taxpayer may still claim full relief whether or not the property was occupied as their main residence during that period: s.223(1). For contracts exchanged on or after 6 April 2014 the disregarded period is reduced to 18 months and is further reduced to nine months for disposals on or after 6 April 2020. In recognition that a person moving into care may take longer to decide to dispose of their former home, the period remains at 36-months for this group of people.

If the taxpayer occupies more than one residence, they can choose which is to be treated as their main residence by an election made within two years of acquiring the additional property (s.222(5)). If no election is made within that period, the question will be decided on the basis of the facts. Following a change in the properties owned, a new two-year election period starts.

Section 225A provides that personal representatives can claim the exemption where they dispose of a property which before and after the deceased's death has been used as their only or main residence by individuals who under the will or intestacy are entitled to at least 75 per cent of the proceeds of the house either absolutely or for life.

(b) Items of tangible moveable property having a predictable useful life not exceeding 50 years (s.45), such as most yachts.
(c) Chattels where the *consideration* for disposal does not exceed £6,000 (s.262). Marginal relief exists if the consideration exceeds £6,000.
(d) National savings certificates and premium bonds (s.121).

There are other exemptions including:

(a) damages for personal injuries and betting winnings (s.51);
(b) interests under trusts, unless the interest was acquired for money or money's worth (s.76);
(c) gains made on the disposal of certain government securities (s.115(1));
(d) decorations for valour unless acquired for consideration in money or money's worth (s.268);
(e) foreign currency purchased for personal use abroad (s.269);
(f) life assurance policies and deferred annuity contracts (s.210);
(g) works of art in certain circumstances (s.258).

Reliefs

If the assets disposed of do not come within any of the categories in para.5-015, there may be relief from liability to tax as a result of one of the following: **5-016**

(a) The annual exemption: The first £12,300 of gains arising on the disposals made by an individual during tax year 2022/23 reducing to £6,000 in 2023/24 and £3,000 in 2024/25 (s.1K). Married couples and civil partners are taxed independently on their capital gains and have separate annual exemptions.
(b) Venture capital trusts: In respect of disposals taking place on or after 6 April 1995 gains made on the disposal of shares in an approved venture capital trust are exempt. The shares disposed of must not have been acquired in excess of the permitted maximum. A qualified exemption for shares acquired under the Enterprise Investment Scheme is also available.
(c) Business asset disposal relief (formerly entrepreneur's relief): Sections 169H–169VY of the Taxation of Chargeable Gains Act 1992 provide that for disposals made on or after 6 April 2008 relief is available on gains arising on or in connection with disposals of the whole or part of a business up to a certain figure. As the original name suggests, the relief was intended to stimulate entrepreneurial activity, but it became apparent that it was not working as intended. Changes were introduced in the Finance Act 2019, and much more far-reaching changes in the Finance Act 2020, s.23 and Sch.3. The 2020 changes have severely limited the value of the relief. The name

of the relief was changed at the same time to "business asset disposal relief". See below.

Business asset disposal relief

The relief is available under s.169I where an individual makes a disposal of:

(a) The whole or part of a business owned for at least two years before the disposal;
(b) Assets owned by an individual but used by a partnership or trading company which was the transferor's personal company and of which the transferor was an officer or employee; the disposal of the assets must be associated with a qualifying disposal of the transferor's interest in the partnership or company arising from the withdrawal of the transferor from the business. From 18 March 2015, the associated disposal must be of at least 5 per cent of the partnership assets or 5 per cent of the shares in the company (TCGA 1992, s.169K as amended by Finance Act 2015, s.41); or
(c) Shares in a trading company (or the holding company of a trading group) which was:
    (i) the individual's personal company; and
    (ii) the individual is an officer or employee of the company or a company within the group,

    for at least two years before:
    (i) the disposal;
    (ii) the time when the company ceased to be a trading company (or the holding company of a trading group) and the disposal is within three years of the cessation.

For disposals made on or after 6 April 2008 and before 6 April 2019 the period of required ownership is only one year.

"Business" includes a business carried on in partnership. Only those assets used for the purposes of the business carried on by the sole trader or partner are eligible for relief. Shares and other assets held for investment purposes are not eligible.

"Personal company" is defined in s.169S(3). For disposals prior to 29 October 2018, a company is a personal company if the transferor holds at least five per cent of the ordinary share capital and that holding gave at least five per cent of the voting rights in the company.

From 29 October 2018 in addition to the existing conditions the holding must also give an entitlement to either at least five per cent of the:

(a) profits available for distribution and five per cent of the distributable assets on a winding up of the company, or
(b) proceeds in the event of a company sale.

The limit for gains on which entrepreneur's relief was available had risen significantly since its introduction, as follows:

(i) disposals before 6 June 2010: £1 million;
(ii) disposals on or after 6 April 2010: £2 million (less any of the previous limit used up); and
(iii) disposals on or after 23 June 2010: £5 million (less any of the previous limits used up);

(iv) disposals on or after 6 April 2011: £10 million ((less any of the previous limits used up).

Finance Act 2020 changed the name of the relief to business asset disposal relief and reduced the level of relief to £1 million. The lifetime limit must take into account the value of entrepreneurs' relief claimed in respect of qualifying gains in the past. The new limit took effect immediately (i.e. it applies to disposals made on or after 11 March 2020). See TCGA 1992, s.169N.

There were forestalling provisions to catch arrangements entered into before Budget day. The reduction in the limit means that any individual who had already claimed relief on gains of £1 million or more is unable to claim relief on any future disposals of business assets.

Gains up to the limit are taxed at 10 per cent. Above that the normal rates apply. Gains eligible for business assets disposal relief are taxed before other gains, which means that the gains not eligible for relief are likely to be taxed at the higher rates.

The relief is not available to personal representatives.

The relief is available under s.169J where trustees of a settlement dispose of shares in a trading company (or the holding company of a trading group) or assets used in a business which are part of the settlement assets provided certain conditions are fulfilled:

(i) there must be a beneficiary with an interest in possession (other than for a fixed term) in the whole of the settled property or in the business assets disposed of (a "qualifying" beneficiary);
(ii) in the case of company shares, the company must for a period of at least two years ending not earlier than three years before the disposal have been the beneficiary's personal company and the beneficiary must have been an officer or employee of the company or a company within the group business; and
(iii) in the case of business assets, the assets must have been used in the business for a period of at least two years ending not earlier than three years before the disposal and the beneficiary must cease to carry on the business on the date of the disposal or within the previous three years.

For disposals before 6 April 2019 the qualifying period was one year.

In *Quentin Skinner 2005 Settlement L v Revenue and Customs Commissioners* (2019) the first tier tribunal held that s.169J did not require the interest in possession to have existed throughout the qualifying period. The company simply had to be a personal company and a trading company throughout that period. However,

HMRC appealed successfully. In *Revenue and Customs Commissioners v Quentin Skinner 2005 Settlement L* (2021) the Upper Tribunal held that in order for relief to be available, a beneficiary must have been a qualifying beneficiary throughout the required period. In

Quentin Skinner 2015 Settlement L v Revenue and Customs Commissioners (2022) the Court of Appeal overruled the Upper Tribunal. It accepted that the drafting of s.169 is confusing in parts, but considered that the drafting of s.169J "pointed strongly" away from the idea that an individual who is a qualifying beneficiary at the date of disposal must also satisfy the requirements of that definition throughout the stipulated holding period. "The identification of a qualifying beneficiary depends on an examination of the trusts of the settlement as at the date of the disposal. There is no requirement … that the individual should have had the interest in possession for any minimum period, but only that the interest should exist at the time of the disposal."

The individual making the disposal (or in the case of trust assets the trustees and beneficiary with the interest in possession jointly) must claim the relief by the second 31 January following the tax year in which the disposal was made.

Letting property, whether residential or commercial, will not qualify as a trade for this purpose except for furnished holiday lettings in the UK or European Economic Area (EEA). See s.169S and s.241(3A) and (5). But note that the favourable furnished holiday letting regime will cease in 2024/35.

Selling an asset in isolation will not attract the relief. There must be a disposal of a business or part of a business or the disposal of assets on cessation of a business. See *Russell v RCC* (2012) for a disposal of farming land which was held to be merely a disposal of an asset and *Rice v RCC* (2014)for a disposal held to be made on cessation.

Investors' relief

5-017 To encourage an investment culture and help companies access the capital they need to expand and create jobs, the Finance Act 2016 amended Pt V of the TCGA 1992 to extend entrepreneurs' relief to gains accruing on the disposal of ordinary shares in an unlisted trading company held by individuals. It is referred to as "investors" relief'. When available, the relief reduces the rate of capital gains tax to 10 per cent. At the time it was introduced, there was a lifetime cap of £10 million and this has not been reduced.

The relief is available to trustees of a settlement with an interest in possession (other than one for a fixed term) subject to certain conditions (ss.169VH, 169VI and 169VL). Personal representatives can only claim if the disposal took place whilst the deceased person was alive.

The investor must not be a remunerated director or employee of the company in question at any time during the period of share ownership, and nor can any person connected with them be an officer or employee. This restriction—which applies throughout the share-holding period for the shares in question—was modified to exclude only "relevant employees". The position is set out in s.169VB(2)(g) and s.169VW—the latter defining the term "relevant employee". Broadly, non-executive directors who had no pre-existing connection with the company, and people who become employees after acquiring the shares where there was no reasonable prospect that this would occur, are not relevant employees. The shares must be newly issued to the claimant and acquired for new consideration on or after 17 March 2016, and have been held for a period of at least three years starting from 6 April 2016. When the relief was introduced, a person's qualifying gains for investors' relief was subject to a lifetime cap of £10 million. At the time of writing, this limit had not been reduced despite the reduction in the limit for business asset disposal relief.

Deferments

5-018 The final group of reliefs are those which have the effect of deferring the payment of tax.

When a transfer is made by way of gift or sale at under-value, the donor and donee may in certain circumstances elect to "hold over" any gain so that the donee is treated as acquiring the asset at the donor's acquisition value.

When an owner sells certain types of assets, they may elect to "roll over" any gain into new assets purchased so that the acquisition cost is reduced by the amount of the rolled-over gain. If an election is made either to hold over or roll over a gain, the whole of the gain must be held over or rolled over. It is not-possible to elect to hold over or roll over a portion of a gain allowing the balance to be covered by the annual exemption.

While tax can eventually become payable on the "held-over" or "rolled-over" gain, it will not be payable until sometime in the future. These reliefs may offer advantages beyond the mere postponement of the payment of tax but the possible advantages differ depending on whether the gain is "held over" on a gift or "rolled over" on a sale.

Hold-over relief

Considering "held-over" gains first, the advantages are that: **5-019**

(a) when tax is paid by the donee in the future it will be paid with money that may have been reduced in value by inflation; and
(b) if the donee dies while owning the property the gain will be effectively extinguished (see para.5-023).

There is, however, the disadvantage that the donor will lose the benefit of their annual exemption.

The circumstances in which hold-over relief applies include:

(a) *Transfers between spouses and civil partners.* Any transfer of an asset between a husband and wife or between civil partners who are living together is treated as taking place for such consideration as will give neither a gain nor a loss to the transferor. The effect is that any gain is *automatically* "held over" into the hands of the new owner (s.58).
(b) *Gifts to charities.* The donor is treated as having made the disposal for a consideration which gives rise to neither a gain nor a loss (s.257). Gains made by charities are normally exempt if applicable and applied for charitable purposes (s.256).
(c) *Business assets.* Where a taxpayer disposes (otherwise than under a bargain at arm's length) of "business assets" a joint election can be made by the transferor and transferee (or by the transferor alone if the disposal is to the trustees of a settlement) that any gain be held over (s.165). Business assets for this purpose are, broadly, assets used for the purposes of a trade, profession or vocation carried on by the transferor or their personal company (s.165(2)). The term also covers shares, provided the shares are in an unquoted company or in the transferor's personal company.
(d) *Transfers chargeable to inheritance tax.* Where a disposal is made which is chargeable to inheritance tax or would be but for the existence of the annual exemption, a joint election can be made by the transferor and transferee (or by the transferor alone if the disposal is to the trustees of a settlement) that any gain be held over (s.260(2)). The relief is available only to disposals which are initially chargeable to inheritance tax, and not to those which are initially potentially exempt but which become chargeable as a result of the death of the transferor within the seven years. Paragraph 7-029 and following, deal more fully with chargeable transfers but they are broadly transfers to and from settlements without an interest in possession. Note that a transfer is technically chargeable to inheritance tax even though it is within the transferor's nil-rate band (s.260 (2)(a)).

(e) *Transfers exempt from inheritance tax.* Where a disposal is made which is exempt from inheritance tax because it is a transfer either to a political party, for the public benefit, to a maintenance fund for historic buildings or of property designated by the Treasury as of outstanding national interest, a joint election can be made by the transferor and transferee (or by the transferor alone if the transfer is to the trustees of a settlement) that the gain be held over (s.260(2)(b)).

(f) *Transfers from an accumulation and maintenance trust, a trust for a bereaved minor or a trust for a bereaved young person.* Where a-beneficiary becomes absolutely entitled to assets from one of these trusts the trustees and beneficiary may jointly elect that any gain be held over (s.260(2)). Chapter 7 deals more fully with these trusts.

Roll-over relief

5-020 The roll-over relief which is available on the sale of assets offers the same-advantages and suffers the same disadvantages as hold-over relief. The relief applies:

(a) *On the replacement of business assets.* When a trader sells certain business assets (including land, buildings, plant and machinery) and reinvests the proceeds of sale in new business assets within certain time limits, any gain realised on the sale can be "rolled over" into the new asset. The effect of this is to reduce the trader's acquisition price of the asset by the "rolled-over" gain (ss.152–159).

(b) *On the incorporation of a business.* If the taxpayer transfers an unincorporated business (and all assets other than cash) as a going concern to a company in exchange for shares, the gain realised on the disposal to the company can be "rolled over" into the newly acquired shares. The effect is that the shares (subject to certain conditions) are treated as having been acquired for the same value as the assets transferred instead of at market value at the date of the disposal (ss.162 and 162A).

(c) Deferral relief under the Enterprise Investment Scheme (s.150C and Sch.5B). This deferral relief allows an investor to defer a charge to capital gains tax on a gain arising on the disposal of a qualifying Enterprise Investment Scheme (EIS) investment where the gain is rolled over into another qualifying investment within the qualifying time. There are a number of conditions which must be satisfied for the investment to be a "qualifying investment". However, the key ones are that the investment must be wholly in cash to subscribe for ordinary, non-preferential shares in a company which qualifies for the purposes of EIS income tax relief and the shares must be issued to fund a "qualifying business activity".

The date for payment of tax

5-021 Capital gains tax due from individuals and trustees is payable on a current year basis on 31 January following the year of assessment (Taxes Management Act 1970 s.59B as substituted). Interest is charged on tax remaining unpaid after the due date.

If the sale price is paid by instalments over a period exceeding 18 months, HMRC may allow the person making the disposal to opt to pay the tax by-instalments also. There is no requirement for him to satisfy HMRC that he would otherwise suffer undue hardship (s.280).

Where hold-over relief is not available on a disposal by way of gift (or deemed disposal under s.71(1) see para.7-051) tax on certain assets can be paid in 10 equal yearly instalments (s.281). An election must be made in writing by the person paying the tax. Payment by instalments is possible only where hold-over relief is *not available* and not where it is available but the taxpayer chooses not to claim it.

The assets in relation to which an election can be made are land or an interest in land, any shares or securities which, immediately before the disposal gave the person disposing of the shares control of the company, and any shares in a company not listed on a recognised stock exchange.

3. THE CAPITAL GAINS TAX LIABILITY OF THE DECEASED

Prior to the date of death, the deceased may have made disposals which gave rise to capital gains tax liability. If this liability has not been discharged prior to the death, the personal representatives must discharge it on the deceased's behalf. The personal representatives calculate tax in accordance with the principles outlined in Pt 2, and will be able to claim, on behalf of the deceased, the benefit of any exemptions or reliefs the deceased could have claimed. Once these exemptions and reliefs have been claimed, the personal representatives will pay tax on behalf of the deceased at the appropriate rate(s). **5-022**

The deceased may have unrelieved losses in the tax year of death. Section 62(2) provides that such losses can be carried back and set against the gains realised by the deceased in the three tax years preceding the tax year of death, taking later years first. If tax was paid in any of those earlier years, a rebate will be claimed.

If there are still unrelieved losses, these cannot be taken over by the-personal representatives to set off against gains they make. If the deceased made a-disposal by way of a *donatio mortis causa,* no chargeable gain arises (s.62(5)).

4. THE CAPITAL GAINS TAX LIABILITY OF THE PERSONAL REPRESENTATIVES

The position on death

There is no disposal of assets on death. Section 62(1)(a) provides that the assets of which a deceased person was competent to dispose shall be deemed to be *acquired* on their death by the personal representatives for a consideration equal to their market value at the date of the death. Since there is a deemed acquisition but no deemed disposal, no capital gains tax liability arises as a result of the death. The same rule applies to a person who takes property held jointly with the deceased. **5-023**

If the value of a deceased's assets have been ascertained for inheritance tax purposes s.274 requires that value to be the asset's value for capital gains tax purposes. This will then determine the acquisition cost of the personal representatives and of the legatee, if the asset is transferred to a legatee.

The revaluation at death can be beneficial to taxpayers where, for example, an asset owned by the deceased receives a high inheritance tax value as a result of the related property rules. However, s.274 only has this result if the inheritance tax value has actually been *ascertained.* The *Capital Gains Tax Manual* states at para.CG32222 that a value is not ascertained where:

- all the assets pass to a surviving spouse or civil partner and the entire estate is exempt;

- all the assets pass to charities, political parties or other persons listed in Sch.3 to IHTA and the estate is thus exempt;
- the estimated value of the estate is well below the threshold on which tax is to be payable and it can be accepted that the estate is non-taxpaying;
- the assets of the estate are all covered by the reliefs for agricultural and business assets in a period when the rates of relief for such assets are 100 per cent;
- some combination of the above factors and/or other exemptions makes the estate non-taxpaying.

In all these cases the values will not have been considered in any detail or are not considered at all and are not "ascertained". CG32224 adds: " *Furthermore in cases where the liability to IHT is relatively small, in order to avoid the need for expensive valuations which have little effect, HMRC – Trusts and Estates IHT may make it clear to the personal representatives or agents that the value has not been agreed, and therefore has not been 'ascertained'.* "

In the *Trusts and Estates Newsletter* for December 2016 HMRC complained that where property included in an excepted estate was sold for more than its probate value, taxpayers were asking them to agree to treat the sale price as the inheritance tax value of the property at the date of death, even though the sale was much later.

HMRC reminded taxpayers that it only considers the value of assets in a person's estate when inheritance tax is due. Where an estate is returned to HMRC as an excepted estate and no inheritance tax is due, HMRC does not consider values. The District Valuer does not agree or "ascertain" the values for tax purposes. The *Newsletter* said:

> "We have accepted the figure reported in the IHT205 Return without any further investigation. We will not amend the value of the property previously reported to us in the IHT205 for a subsequent sale price."
>
> Where a property has increased in value between death and sale, the issue is capital gains tax. As the PRs have not agreed the value of a property for inheritance tax purposes at the date of death, they don't have an agreed value for the purposes of calculating whether there is any capital gain between the date of death and the date of the eventual sale. The Newsletter suggested that they should apply for a post-transaction valuation check.
>
> If the personal representatives wish to check the valuation of the-property at the date of death for capital gains tax purposes in relation to the sale of a property after the date of death, HMRC offers a post-transaction valuation check for capital gains purposes. This is a free service. You should refer to the form CG34 'Post-transaction valuation checks for capital gains'."

In cases where the value has not been ascertained for IHT the market value of the asset at the date of death must be established and agreed with HMRC using normal principles and procedures. The market value that will be required is that of the holding or interest passing to the personal representatives even if the value is needed for the purposes of a computation relating to a legatee to whom only part of the interest or holding passed: see CG32230.

The fact that inheritance *reliefs* (such as business, agricultural or woodland) are available will not reduce the capital gains tax valuation.

If quoted shares and securities are sold within 12 months from the date of death, at less than market value at the date of death, the personal representatives can elect that, for inheritance tax purposes, the sale price be substituted for the probate value (see paras 12-017–12-018). If the reduced value is taken for inheritance tax purposes, it becomes the acquisition price of the personal representatives for capital gains tax purposes as well. The personal representatives cannot keep the original acquisition value for capital gains tax purposes once they have elected for the inheritance tax reduction. The result is that the sale will show only a small loss for capital gains tax purposes equal to the costs of disposal.

If land or an interest in land is sold within four years of death at less than market value at the date of death, the personal representatives can elect that the sale price be substituted for the probate value (see paras 12-019–12-020). The reduced value will become the acquisition value for capital gains tax purposes as if it has been ascertained; see s.274.

Property given away before death may be treated as part of the death estate as a result of the gift with reservation rules. However, those rules are fictitious treatments created only for inheritance tax purposes. They do not affect the actual devolution of the property in real life, so the gifted property does not actually pass on death under the will or intestacy, neither was any gift actually made at the time the reservation ceased. Therefore, the date of acquisition of the asset for capital gains tax purposes is the occasion of the gift, and the base cost of the asset is its market value on that date (subject to any adjustments required for example for hold-over relief for business assets under TCGA1992, s.165).

Disposals by the personal representatives

In the course of administering the estate, the personal representatives may have **5-024**
to sell assets. If they do so, they will be liable to capital gains tax calculated on the difference between their acquisition value (the value at the date of death) and the value at the date of the disposal after deducting any losses they have incurred on other disposals. The calculation of liability has been-outlined in Pt 2. Business asset disposal relief is not available to personal representatives.

Prior to 6 April 2008 personal representatives paid capital gains tax at a flat rate of 40 per cent. From that date until 23 June 2010 they paid at a flat rate of 18 per cent. For disposals made on or after 23 June 2010 they paid at a flat rate of 28 per cent. From 6 April 2016, personal representatives pay 20 per cent on disposals unless they are disposing of non-exempt residential property or carried interest in which case the rate is 28 per cent for disposals before 6 April 2024 and 24 per cent for disposals after that date.

Where beneficiaries are basic rate taxpayers or not taxpayers at all (for charities are exempt from capital gains tax) it will be better for personal representatives to appropriate assets showing increases in value to the beneficiaries and make the disposal on their behalf, benefiting from the lower rate of tax.

In addition to the normal deductions for incidental selling expenses, personal representatives are entitled to deduct a proportion of the costs of making title (*IRC v Richards' Executors* (1971)). HMRC publishes a scale of permitted deductions (Capital Gains Tax Manual para CG65040). However, the personal representatives are free to claim more than the scale deduction where they can show that the actual cost was higher.

The rights of personal representatives to claim exemptions and relief are limited. In the tax year of death, and the two following tax years, the personal representatives can claim the annual exemption £3,000 in tax year 2024/25 (s.1K). Thereafter all the gains they realise (other than on exempt assets within para.5-015) are taxable. The only or main residence exemption cannot apply to personal representatives since a continuing body of persons cannot have a residence. However, s.225A provides that the exemption will be available to personal representatives on the disposal of a residence if the residence has been used as the only or main residence—before and after the death—by individuals who, under the will or intestacy, are entitled to 75 per cent or more of the proceeds of sale of the house either absolutely or for life, then the exemption can be claimed.

If the personal representatives have made losses on their disposals but have no, or insufficient, gains to set them against, these unabsorbed losses cannot be passed on to the beneficiaries.

Where personal representatives are proposing to sell an asset which has fallen in value since death and have no gains against which the loss can be set, it may be preferable for them to consider appropriating the asset to a beneficiary and selling on behalf of the beneficiary. Even if the beneficiary has no gains in the current tax year, the loss can be carried forward indefinitely; see para.5-012.

Transfers to legatees

5-025 For capital gains tax purposes, s.64(2) defines the term "legatee" as including

> "any person taking under a testamentary disposition or on an intestacy or partial intestacy, whether he takes beneficially or as trustee, and a person taking a *donatio mortis causa* shall be treated ... as a legatee and his acquisition as made at the time of the donor's death."

Section 62(4) provides that when the personal representatives transfer an asset to a legatee under the terms of a will, or the intestacy rules, no chargeable gain accrues to the personal representatives. The personal representatives' acquisition is treated as the legatee's acquisition. The position is the same if the personal representatives appropriate an asset in or towards satisfaction of a pecuniary legacy or a share in residue. Therefore, such transfers cannot give rise to capital gains tax liability if the asset has risen in value since the date of death. Similarly, the personal representatives cannot have the benefit of a loss where the asset has fallen in value since the date of death.

If the personal representatives vest assets in trustees (even if they themselves are the trustees) the trustees are treated in the same way as legatees and so acquire the asset at market value at the date of death. When the beneficiaries of the trust become absolutely entitled to the trust assets there will be a charge to capital gains tax if the assets have risen in value since the death.

When the personal representatives are deciding which assets to sell and which to vest in beneficiaries, they should take into account their own and the beneficiaries' present and future tax liability. The rate payable by beneficiaries may be lower than the higher rates payable by the personal representatives or they may have losses available to offset gains.

Personal representatives should be particularly careful when dealing with charities. Charities benefit from a capital gains tax exemption in respect of gains realised on the disposal of assets if the gains are applicable and applied forcharitable purposes (s.256). However, the exemption will only apply if the property disposed of is beneficially owned by the charity. During the administration of an estate beneficiaries have only a chose in action to compel due administration. They have no rights to individual assets until the personal representatives either

- vest individual assets in or appropriate assets to those entitled; or

- the residue is ascertained at which point the personal representatives hold the residuary assets as bare trustee for the residuary beneficiary.

If the personal representatives sell before the residue is ascertained and without vesting or appropriating the asset, they will make a disposal and will be liable for capital gains tax on any gain in excess of their annual exemption even if a charity is entitled to the proceeds of sale.

Hence, if personal representatives wish to sell an asset included in residue which has increased in value since the date of death and distribute the proceeds to charity, they should appropriate the asset to the charity absolutely using a declaration of trust and record an instruction to sell on the charity's behalf.

The need to consider appropriation before sale is a good reason for consulting charities early in the administration.

If claiming an appropriation before sale, it is important to have written evidence. HMRC are quick to take this point. See para. CG30781:

> "the personal representatives and legatees may claim that administration has ceased and residue has been ascertained at an early date if:
>
> - the legatees would be liable at a lower rate of Capital Gains Tax than the personal representatives on the disposal of assets in the estate
> - have any unused annual exemption that could be used to cover the gains
> - the legatee is a charity and any gain on the disposal would be exempt.
>
> Applying the rule that assets remain vested in the personal representatives until residue has been ascertained unless specific steps have been taken to vest the assets in advance of ascertainment of residue usually defeats unwarranted claims in this area."

The Institute of Legacy Management has a helpful booklet, *Charities as Beneficiaries*, produced by the Law Society and available on online. It has a useful memorandum of appropriation at Appendix E.

5. The Capital Gains Tax Liability of Beneficiaries

As has already been explained, all legatees receive the property at market value at the date of the death, whether they are entitled under a will or the intestacy rules, whether they receive a specific legacy, an asset in satisfaction of a pecuniary legacy or a residuary legacy or whether they are beneficially entitled or are merely entitled as trustees. **5-026**

This means they take the asset with the benefit of any unrealised losses that may have accrued since the death and subject to any unrealised gains that have arisen since that date. They cannot, however, take over any unrelieved losses which the personal representatives realised.

On subsequent disposals by beneficiaries the gain or the loss must be calculated on the basis of the market value at the date of death. It is therefore helpful if personal representatives provide beneficiaries with details of market value at the time the assets are transferred.

A beneficiary who purchases an asset from the personal representatives takes as a purchaser not a legatee. Thus, the personal representatives make a disposal and will be liable for any gain between date of death and sale.

6. REPORTING REQUIREMENTS FOR CHARGEABLE GAINS

Disposals of assets other than residential land

5-027 For personal representatives the procedure for dealing with capital gains tax (and income tax) normally depends on whether the estate is simple or complex. If the estate is complex, the personal representatives must complete a self-assessment tax return for each tax year of the administration. If the estate is simple, they can use the informal procedure.

The position is dealt with in para.7410 of HMRC's *Trusts, Settlements and Estates Manual*. A useful summary is contained in the *Trusts and Estates Newsletter* for August 2018 which contains a reminder of the two different procedures. An estate is considered complex if:

- the probate value of the estate is more than £2.5 million, or
- income tax and/or CGT for the whole of the administration period exceeds £10,000, or
- the proceeds of assets sold by the personal representative in any one tax year for date of deaths up to 5 April 2016 exceeds £250,000 or £500,000 for date of deaths after 5 April 2016.

The Newsletter summarised the position as follows. Where the estate is simple:

> "*Informal Payment Arrangements*
> Personal representatives (executors or administrators) provide HMRC with a calculation of the amount of tax due. HMRC will then provide a payment slip with a reference number, for this payment only, for the Personal Representative to then make a one-off informal payment of the total tax liability for the whole period of administering the deceased's estate, without the personal representatives having to complete a Self-Assessment return
>
> All informal payments made for the administration period, should include the reference number provided by HMRC for payment of the administration period tax due. Any payments made by cheque should include on the reverse the following information:
>
> - the name of the deceased
> - the last private address of the deceased
> - the deceased's National Insurance number or Self-Assessment UTR or reference which has been provided by HMRC for this payment
> - the reason for this payment indicating Administration Period
>
> The covering letter with the cheque for payment of the tax due should be sent to HMRC. Informal payments should normally be accepted by the office that handled the deceased's tax affairs."

If the estate is complex, the Newsletter explains that a tax return will be needed for each tax year of the administration and that details of the estate will-therefore have to be registered on the Trusts Register as this is how the issue of self-assessment tax returns is now triggered:

> "*Complex Estates*
> HMRC Administration of Estates Cardiff is responsible for dealing with all aspects of the period of administration where the case is regarded as a complex case (subject to the exceptions at TSEM7366)... If an estate is considered complex, Self-Assessment Trust & Estate tax return SA900 will be required for each year of the Administration period.

Self-Assessment deadlines for the late submission of tax returns and penalties for late payment of tax apply.

It should be evident when gathering assets and if dealing with the Inheritance Tax account if the probate or confirmation value of the estate is over £2.5 million and the estate is therefore considered by HMRC as complex for the Income Tax and Capital Gains Tax of the administration period. Equally, the value of an asset will be required at date of death, which should give some indication if the value is likely to exceed £500,000 when the Executor is selling the asset.

For Income Tax due over £10,000 the estate would be in receipt of gross income exceeding £50,000 during the whole of the administration period which could be from one or various sources: bank and building society interest, dividends, property related income and many more. Again, this should be evident from assets held in the estate but may not be clear early in the administration period. The informal payment procedures can only be used once and only when the administration period has ended. If the £10,000 Income Tax due is exceeded HMRC should be notified as a Self-Assessment Trust & Estate tax return SA900 will be required to be submitted.

Only rarely, should an estate be reported as informal at the end of the administration period and then subsequently, a criterion for complex estate is triggered. This could be a previously unknown assets comes to light which exceeds the informal criterion values. In these circumstances, the estate should be registered on the TRS in order to request a UTR and a Self-Assessment Trust & Estate tax return SA900 will be required for each year of the administration period to declare all the income and, or capital gains information. Any payment previously made using the informal route will be transferred and used against the total tax now due and included in the Self-Assessment statement of account."

There are a few situations where informal payments are not accepted, for example, where part of the tax due is the recovery of income or capital gains tax wrongly refunded to the taxpayer and repayable under Taxes Management Act (TMA) 1970 s.30.

Capital gains tax (CGT) is normally dealt with through a self-assessment tax return. For tax returns for tax year 2003/04 onwards it is not necessary for individuals, trustees and personal representatives (in the tax year following death and the following two tax years) to complete the capital gains pages of a tax return where the total of disposal proceeds does not exceed four times the annual exemption which applies to individuals provided:

- the gains do not exceed their annual exemption; or
- there are no allowable losses to be deducted from chargeable gains and there is no CGT liability after any available taper has been deducted.

Disposals of assets from spouse to spouse will not count towards the four times annual exemption limit if they are treated as giving rise to neither a gain nor a loss under s.58(1) because they are "living together". For earlier tax years there was a more limited concession.

Accelerated payment of CGT on UK residential land

Financial Act 2019, s.14 and Sch.2 introduced accelerated reporting and payment dates for capital gains tax on UK land disposed of by non-residents starting in tax year 2019/20. **5-028**

The change was extended to all disposals of UK residential land on or after 6 April 2020 *where tax is due*. (In the case of disposals by non-UK residents a report is required even if there is no tax due.)

The change applies to disposals made by PRs and trustees as well as to disposals by individuals.

The date of disposal is fixed by reference to the date of unconditional exchange of contracts. The return and payment must be submitted within 60 days of completion of the disposal for completions on or after 27 October 2021. For completions before that date the time period was only 30 days.

No returns are required for disposals where no tax is due, for example because the gain is:

- within the annual exemption,
- covered by existing losses,
- attracts main residence relief, or
- to a spouse or civil partner (no gain/no loss disposal).

The calculation of tax is made on the basis of events so far in the tax year with an approximation of the level of income expected during the year. The payment made is on account of the tax due at the end of the year. However, it is not necessary to submit a self-assessment tax if the tax paid was correct and there is no other need for a return.

If the personal representatives are ready to finalise the tax affairs of the estate within 60 days, they do not need to make a separate report but can deal with the payment of capital gains tax as part of the normal final payment procedure. So, if the estate:

- meets the "complex estate" criteria, the personal representatives will complete a self-assessment return for the final year of the administration period;
- is a simple estate, the personal representatives will use the "informal arrangements" and make payment in one lump sum.

This will potentially be of benefit in those cases when the property sale occurs just before the estate administration is completed. More frequently the PRs will not be in a position to finalise the estate's tax affairs within the 60 day period.

HMRC has guidance for personal representatives dealing with the procedure themselves at CG Manual App18. A personal representative can use their own UK property account if they have one or open one. They then select the option to complete the return for someone else or someone who has died.

Personal representatives can authorise an agent to submit the digital return on their behalf but if the personal representative already has an agent to deal with their personal tax affairs, this is not possible. They can authorise a separate agent, but the agent will have to download a paper form. See HMRCs' *Trusts and Estates Newsletter* April 2024.

Chapter Six

INCOME TAX

1. Introduction

In the illustrations given in this chapter, it is assumed (except where the contrary 6-001
is stated) that rates and thresholds will remain as they are for 2024/25 for all future tax years.

Many people regard income tax as the bane of thMartha is entitled to income for life from her mother's estate. The personal representatives receive various items of income and payeir lives and would be distressed to discover that HMRC can pursue them beyond the grave.

When a person dies, income tax must be considered in respect of three different periods:

(1) the period up to death;
(2) the administration period; and
(3) the period after the completion of administration.

The purpose of this chapter is to consider the rules that apply to these different periods but, before looking at the detailed rules, a brief explanation of the types of receipt on which income tax is levied and the methods of calculating the tax is necessary.

2. Income Tax Generally

Matters to consider

A detailed discussion of the income tax system is beyond the scope of this book. 6-002
Instead we intend merely to make some simple basic points to put the particular rules relevant on death into context.

It is necessary when considering income tax to ask the following questions:

(1) What is income?
(2) What income is taxable?
(3) In what year of assessment will income be taxed?
(4) How is the tax liability calculated?
(5) When is the tax payable?

What is income?

The first problem that arises is to define the kind of receipt which attracts the 6-003
charge to income tax. Most people would probably not be able to define income but no doubt would hope to recognise it when they receive it.

As there is no statutory definition of "income", over the years, lawyers have attempted to define the nebulous concept of "income" which is subject to tax. In the case of *London County Council v Attorney General* (1901) Lord MacNaughten said "*income tax, if I may be pardoned for saying so, is a tax on income*". As a definition this is of little assistance. However, more precise guidelines have developed and it can now be said that the tax is paid on profits of an income nature, as opposed to profits arising on the disposal of a capital asset (although there are cases where capital receipts can be treated as income, such as certain premiums on leases). The distinction between these two types of receipt is, broadly speaking, that to be of an income nature, the receipt should be recurrent.

What income is taxable?

6-004 The charging statute for income tax is the Income Tax Act 2007 (ITA 2007) as amended by later Finance Acts. The statutes which specify the sources of income subject to income tax are the Income Tax (Trading and Other Income) Act 2005 (ITTOIA 2005) and the Income Tax (Earnings and Pensions) Act 2003 (ITEPA 2003).

The most important sources of income taxed under ITTOIA 2005 and ITEPA 2003 are:

(a) Under ITTOIA 2005:
  Part 2 Trading income (so profits from a trade, profession or vocation);
  Part 3 Property income (so rents and other profits from receipts from land in the UK);
  Part 4 Savings and investment income (so interest, annuities and dividends);
  Part 5 Other miscellaneous income (such as other annual income not otherwise charged to tax).

(b) Under ITEPA 2003:
  Employment and pensions income.

A few types of income are specified in Pt 6 ITTOIA 2005 as being exempt (for example, interest on certain National Savings products and scholarship income) and so are tax-free.

Each part of ITTOIA 2005 and ITEPA 2003 lays down its own rules for the particular type of income dealt with. For example, the rules as to what expenses can be deducted to determine taxable income vary according to the type of income. The tax year in which the income will be taxed is determined by the basis of assessment relevant to the particular part of ITTOIA 2005 or ITEPA 2003.

What is the relevant year of assessment?

6-005 Tax is calculated by reference to years of assessment (commonly called "tax years"). A new tax year commences on 6 April each year. The charging statutes lay down the basis of assessment—the current year basis. This requires that tax is assessed in each year on the income of that tax year.

Different rules applied for unincorporated businesses; they were taxed on the profits of the accounting period ending in the previous tax year. However, from 6 April 2024, there are changes to the basis of assessment for individual traders and partnerships which mean that business profits are assessed and taxed in the tax year in which they arise.

How is the tax liability calculated?

General

Section 23 of ITA 2007 provides that there are five main steps necessary to calculate income tax: **6-006**

Step 1: calculate "total income".
Step 2: deduct any allowable reliefs (e.g. interest on a loan qualifying under ITA 2007 s.383).
Step 3: deduct any personal reliefs.
Step 4: calculate tax payable at the appropriate rates on total income less allowable and personal reliefs.
Step 5: add together the sums calculated at step 4.

A taxpayer who is entitled to any tax reduction deducts it from the amount of tax calculated at step 5 and a taxpayer required to pay additional tax, for example where an unauthorised payment has been made from a pension scheme, adds it.

What is "total income"?

The taxpayer's "total income" is the aggregate of the taxpayer's income from all sources (after deducting allowable expenses) which is chargeable to income tax. The sources are listed at para.6-004. Total income is reduced by reliefs at steps 2 and 3 to give the net income on which tax is calculated. **6-007**

Total income includes sums received gross (such as trading income) and the grossed-up amounts of sums which are received net of tax (for example, a beneficiary of a trust usually receives trust income net of tax paid by the trustees). Salaries will have tax deducted under the PAYE scheme. The rate at which tax is deducted under the PAYE system varies depending on the personal circumstances of the employee.

Banks and building societies used to deduct basic rate tax from interest paid on accounts but ceased to do so from 6 April 2016. Individuals receive a tax-free personal savings allowance (see para.6-009) but personal representatives and trustees do not.

The rules on dividends were also changed from 6 April 2016. They are now received gross instead of with a basic rate tax credit.

Individuals receive a tax-free dividend allowance (see para.6-009) but personal representatives and trustees do not.

There are also tax-free allowances for individuals (but not personal representatives) for £1,000 from trading activities—such as selling items on eBay or offering a small freelance service and £1,000 for income from land, for example, renting out a garden for an event or letting out a room for a week.

Income tax is calculated on the basis of a person's gross income and so it is necessary to gross up any sums received net of tax (credit is then given for the tax paid or tax credit). To gross-up a net sum where tax has been deducted, simply multiply the sum actually received by:

$$\frac{100}{100 - \text{tax rate}}$$

If tax has been deducted at the rate of 20 per cent and £160 is received net of tax, then the £160 is 80 per cent of the gross figure (20 per cent of the gross figure having already been deducted). To calculate 100 per cent of the receipt, simply divide by 80 to find one per cent and then multiply by 100 to find 100 per cent. Follow the same steps whatever rate of tax has been deducted.

Example 1

A life tenant of a trust fund receives £4,000. Tax at the basic rate of 20 per cent has already been deducted. When calculating the beneficiary's statutory income the interest is grossed up to £5,000.

$$£4{,}000 \times \frac{100}{100 - 20} = £5{,}000$$

£5,000 is included in the taxpayer's income tax return as part of gross income.

However, it must be remembered that in the above example £1,000 in tax has already been paid. This sum is a "tax credit" so that, when calculating what tax (if any) is due to HMRC, an allowance must be made for the £1,000 already paid on behalf of the taxpayer by the trustees.

If a taxpayer with a 20 per cent tax credit is only liable to basic rate tax on the receipt, then no additional tax need be sent to HMRC since the "right" amount of tax has already been paid. If the taxpayer is liable to higher rate tax, additional tax will have to be sent.

If the taxpayer from whom income tax has been deducted is not liable to even basic rate tax (because of their entitlement to reliefs at step 2 and/or step 3), they can reclaim, from HMRC, the excess tax already paid on their behalf.

What are allowable reliefs deductible at Step 2?

6-008 Certain specified commitments to make payments, known as allowable reliefs, are deducted from total income. These reliefs remove sums from the income tax calculation completely so that the income is not regarded as the taxpayer's. Interest payments on qualifying loans (such as loans to buy an interest in a partnership) are allowable reliefs under s.383 of ITA 2007. Other allowable reliefs are set out in s.24 and include payments to trade unions or police organisations and certain payments to pensions.

There are special provisions for gifts to charities which qualify for relief under the gift aid provisions in Ch.2 of Pt 8.

What are personal reliefs deductible at Step 3?

6-009 There are a variety of personal reliefs available. The availability of these allowances depends not on the type of income or payment involved but on the personal circumstances of the taxpayer. Everyone whose total income from all sources is less than £100,000 is entitled to a personal allowance £12,570 in 2024/25 (frozen until the end of 2027/28). If a taxpayer's total income is over £100,000, the personal allowance is reduced by £1 for every £2 in excess of that limit.

There are other allowances, for example, a blind person's allowance (£3,070 in tax year 2024/35).

Spouses and civil partners are normally treated as separate single people with their own personal allowances. However, a married couple's allowance is available where at least one member of the couple was born before 6 April 1935—it is also available to civil partners. The requirement that one member is born before 6 April 1935 means that the allowance is now only available to couples where one party was at least 89 on 5 April 2024. It differs from all the other personal allowances as it is given as a reduction to the tax bill. The reduction is worked out as 10 per cent of the amount of the allowance which is £11,080 for 2024/25. The maximum reduction for 2024/25 is £1,108. It is reduced by £1 for every £2 of income over the income limit of £37,000 although there is a minimum of £4,280 payable irrespective of income. For marriages before 5 December 2005, the husband's income is used to work out any reduction. For marriage and civil partnerships after this date, it's the income of the highest earner. The income of the wife (for marriages before 5 December 2005) or the lower-income spouse or civil partner (for marriages or civil partnerships formed after that date) is never taken into account.

For the tax year 2015/16 and subsequent tax years a transferable tax allowance for married couples and civil partners is available (ss.55A–55F of ITA 2007). To be eligible for the transfer neither of the spouses or civil partners must be liable to income tax at the higher or additional rate. The transferred allowance (£1,260 for 2024/25) will be given as a deduction from the income tax liability of the transferee.

Example 2

In 2024/25 Civil Partner 1 earns £10,000 and has no other income. This is within the personal allowance for 2024/25 which is £12,570 so taxable income is nil.

Civil Partner 2 earns £30,070 and has no other income so after deduction of the personal allowance, taxable income is £17,500.

Civil Partner 1 can transfer £2,570 in unused personal allowance to Civil Partner 2.

There are two additional allowances available to individuals: a dividend allowance and a savings allowance'.

- The dividend allowance was first introduced in 2016/17 and was £5,000. Since then, it has been reduced significantly. From 6 April 2018 it was reduced to £2,000. From 6 April 2023 it was reduced to £1,000 and from 6 April 2024 it is only £500.
- The level of savings allowance depends on the individual's tax band.
  Income Tax bandPersonal Savings Allowance:

Basic rate	£1,000
Higher rate	£500
Additional rate	£0

What are the rates of tax used at Step 4?

The rates of tax payable depend on the type of income being taxed. Therefore, the type of income must first be identified and there are three categories: **6-010**

Non-savings income: this is not separately defined in ITA 2007 but broadly covers earnings, pensions, taxable social security benefits, trading profits and income from property.

Savings income: defined in ITA 2007 s.18 and broadly bank and building society interest.

Dividend income: defined in ITA 2007 s.19.

Non-savings income is normally received gross apart from wages and salaries which frequently have tax deducted under the PAYE system.

Banks and building societies used to deduct basic rate income tax from interest paid on accounts but ceased to do so from 6 April 2016. Tax credits in respect of such interest are no longer available.

There is a starting rate for savings income of 0 per cent available only to taxpayers whose other income is less than £17,570. The starting rate for savings is a maximum of £5,000. Every £1 of other income above the personal allowance reduces the starting rate for savings by £1.

Example 3

An individual earns £16,000 of wages and gets £200 interest.

The personal allowance of £12,570 is used up by the first £12,570 of wages.

The remaining £3,430 of wages (£16,000 minus £12,570) reduces the starting rate for savings by £3,430.

The starting rate for savings is therefore available on £1,570 (£5,000 minus £3,430). This means that no tax is payable on the £200 savings interest.

The treatment of dividends also changed with effect from 6 April 2016. Before that date dividends were paid with an irrecoverable tax credit of 10 per cent which was treated as satisfying a taxpayer's basic rate tax liability. Since that date dividends are paid gross. However, there is a dividend allowance of £500 for 2024/25 for dividends received by individuals. The first £500 is charged to tax at 0 per cent.

Rates charged on dividend income

6-011 Dividends received which total more than dividend allowance amount are taxed at the following rates in 2024/25:

- 8.75 per cent for basic rate taxpayers;
- 33.75 per cent for higher rate tax payers;
- 39.35 per cent for additional rate taxpayers.

Dividends within the allowance still count towards an individual's basic, higher or additional rate band and so may affect the rate of tax paid on dividends above the £500 allowance. To determine which tax band dividends fall into, dividends are treated as the highest part of a taxpayer's income.

Section 16 of ITA 2007 sets out the order in which different types of income are taxed. Dividends are to be treated as the highest part of a taxpayer's income, then savings income and finally other income. The non-dividend/non-savings income is, therefore, always taxed first. The rates charged on dividends are different from those charged on savings and other income (see below).

Rates charged on non-dividend taxable income

6-012 The rates payable on taxable income (i.e. income in excess of the personal allowance) for 2020/21 are:

	£
"Basic rate" of 20 per cent	0–37,700
"Higher rate" of 40 per cent	37,701–125,140
"Additional rate" of 45 per cent	125,140 and more

Note that the basic rate band for taxpayers who are resident in Scotland will be different for that applicable to taxpayers who are resident elsewhere in the UK.

Example 4

(1) In 2024/25 Peter has earned income of £70,570 and receives net interest of £20,000 and a dividend of £6,000. The earned income will be the first part of his income. Part of it will not be liable to tax at all because Peter has a personal allowance. The balance will be taxed partly at the basic rate and partly at the higher rate. The savings income will be taxed next; it will all fall into the higher rate tax band. As a higher rate taxpayer, Peter is entitled to a personal savings allowance of £500 so he will be liable to tax at 40 per cent on £45,800. The dividend will be taxed last and will all fall into the higher rate tax band. Peter is entitled to the dividend allowance of £500 and the excess over that limit (£5,500) will be taxed at 33.75 per cent. None of Peter's income falls into the additional rate band.

(2) If Peter had no earnings, the interest would be taxed first. Part of it would escape tax because of the personal allowance; the next £1,000 would fall within the personal savings allowance which, as he is a basic rate taxpayer will be £1,000, and the balance would be taxed at 20 per cent. The first £500 of dividends would fall within the dividend allowance rate and the balance (of £5,500) would be taxed at 8.75 per cent.

(3) In 2024/25 Thomas receives interest of £1,000, a dividend of £1,500 and a payment from a trust of which he was the life tenant of £800 (grossed up to £1,000 with a £200 tax credit). His personal allowances exceed his income and so he is not liable to pay tax at all. He can recover the tax already paid on the trust income.

(4) *An example of a simple calculation of a taxpayer's liability* may be helpful.

Anoop, who is single, has the following income on which he is liable to tax in the year 2024/25.

(a) £50,070 from his share of the profits of the firm of solicitors in which he is a partner for the tax year.
(b) £16,000 gross director's fees from XYZ Ltd, from which the company has deducted £686 under the PAYE system.
(c) £8,000 from a trust fund paid to him net of basic rate tax.

He has paid £5,000 interest on a £50,000 loan to buy an interest in the firm of solicitors.

His tax liability will be calculated as follows:

	£
Step 1: Calculate total income	
Practice receipts	50,070
Salary (gross)	16,000
Income from trust fund grossed-up	

	£
£8,000 × 100/80	= 10,000
	76,070
Step 2: Deduct allowable reliefs (interest paid)	(5,000)
Step 3: Deduct personal allowance	(12,570)
	58,500

Step 4: Calculate tax on net income

All of his income is non-savings income:

	£	£
On first	£37,700 tax at 20%	7,540
On next	£20,800 tax at 40%	8,320
Tax Bill		15,860

However, some tax has already been deducted at source and Anoop is credited with this. The trustees of the trust fund deducted £2,000 and XYZ Ltd deducted £686. Therefore, HMRC will require £13,174 direct from Anoop.

When is the tax payable?

6-013 The due date for the payment of tax is 31 January following the year of assessment. However, there are two interim payments due on 31 January in the year of assessment and 31 July immediately following that year. Tax under ITEPA 2003 on employment and pension income is deducted before the employee receives it under the PAYE system.

3. INCOME OF THE DECEASED

Introduction

6-014 We will now look at the rules which are particularly relevant to death.

It is the responsibility of personal representatives to deal with the income tax affairs both of the deceased and of the estate during the administration period, to ensure that a full declaration of income, arising before and after the death, is made and that tax, at the appropriate rates, is paid. When performing this duty the personal representatives must make self-assessment returns both in respect of the income of the deceased up to the date of death and in respect of the administration period.

The tax due on many estates during the administration period is often so small that it is not worth dealing with under normal self-assessment procedures. To minimise costs and administrative burdens for personal representatives, HMRC allow tax liabilities to be settled informally by a one-off payment in all cases where the estate is not regarded as "complex". The position is dealt with in para.7410 of HMRC's *Trusts, Settlements and Estates Manual* (TSEM) details of which are set out at para.5-027.

If the informal procedure is used for estate income, there is no time limit and, therefore, no interest on "late" tax and no penalties and there is no need to request formal clearance.

However, in cases where self-assessment returns are required for estate income, the time limit for submission of the self-assessment form is 31 January, following the end of each tax year.

Income of the deceased

The personal representatives must ascertain the total income of the deceased for the tax year of death. Only income received or receivable before death is included. Income receivable after death is income of the estate (see para.6-016). They will calculate the tax liability in the usual way by deducting any charges on income payable before the death together with a *full* year's personal reliefs, regardless of the date of death. **6-015**

Once the deceased's taxable income has been calculated, the appropriate rates of tax are applied and any extra tax due is paid or a rebate claimed where relevant.

Example 5

Betty, unmarried, died on 6 May 2024 aged 59 and her personal representatives find her share of the profits from a solicitor's practice taxable in the tax year 2024/25 is £65,570. She received £5,000 interest from a building society account. They find that she was entitled to a dividend of £500 from A Plc (declared on 1 May 2023) and that a dividend of £1,500 on shares which she owned in B Plc was declared on 1 June 2025.

The dividend from B Plc is treated as income of the estate (see para.6-016).

The tax calculation is as follows.

	£
Step 1: Calculate Total income	
Practice receipts	65,570
Interest	5,000
Dividend	500
	71,070
Step 2: Deduct allowable reliefs	
(Personal savings allowance)	(500)
Step 3: Deduct personal allowance	(12,570)
	58,000
Step 4: Calculate tax on net income	

The practice receipts are taxed first. Everything except the dividend income will be taxed at the basic or higher rate.

The tax on the practice receipts and interest is:

	£	£
On first	37,700 tax at 20%	7,540
On the next	20,300 tax at 40%	8,120

The dividend income of £500 is considered last as the highest part of Betty's income and it attracts the 0 per cent dividend allowance as it is does not exceed the £500 limit

Tax Bill	15.660

Distinguishing income of the deceased from income of the estate

6-016 The personal representatives must differentiate between the deceased's income and that of the administration period and this is done by ascertaining when the particular receipt arose. This causes few problems when considering salary or profits from a trade or profession since these sources of income will normally cease with the death. However, other types of income which continue to arise after the death, such as rent, interest or dividends, will cause greater problems since they are often attributable to a period which falls partly before and partly after the death.

Income which is *due* before the death is part of the deceased's income (for example, a dividend on shares due and payable on a date before death) even if paid after death. Income which is *due* after the death is income of the estate (for example, a dividend due and payable after death or interest which becomes due and payable on a date after the death).

The Apportionment Act 1870 (see para.16-062), which in some cases provides for the apportionment of income on a day-to-day basis for the purposes of distribution, does not apply for income tax purposes (*IRC v Henderson's Executors* (1931)). A limited income tax relief is available where income received after death has been apportioned for inheritance tax purposes and some of that income has been included as an asset of the estate at death attracting inheritance tax (ITTOIA 2005 s.669).

Practical problems

6-017 The income tax liability of the deceased may take a considerable length of time to finalise. This is particularly likely to be the case where the deceased was a sole trader or a partner as there may be delays in preparing the accounts on which the tax liability is to be calculated. There may be additional tax due to HMRC or there may be repayments of tax due to the deceased as the result, for example, of excessive PAYE tax paid by an employer on the taxpayer's behalf. Where personal representatives cannot pay tax until they have obtained a grant of representation, HMRC treats any charge to interest on unpaid tax as running from 30 days after the grant (Finance Act 2009 Sch.53 Pt 2 para.12).

The personal representatives are normally required to submit an inheritance tax account at the latest within 12 months of the death detailing the assets and liabilities of the deceased and showing the amount of inheritance tax due calculated on the basis of the net value of the estate. At the same time they are required to pay any inheritance tax due except where the instalment option is claimed. The value of the estate cannot be accurately determined until all the assets and liabilities are ascertained so any delay in finalising the income tax position of the deceased will prevent the final calculation and payment of inheritance tax due.

Personal representatives are usually anxious to pay inheritance tax promptly, partly because interest starts to run after six months from the end of the month of death but, more importantly, because they cannot get a grant of representation and therefore cannot start administering the estate until the inheritance tax due has been paid. To prevent delays, personal representatives will frequently estimate the income tax liability of the deceased and pay inheritance tax due on the basis of that estimated figure. When they obtain the final income tax figure, they can, if necessary, submit a corrective account and make any adjustments to the inheritance tax which prove necessary. In a press release of 4 April 1996, HMRC announced their willingness to issue self-assessment tax returns before the end of the tax year at the request of personal representatives. HMRC will then give early confirmation if they decide not to enquire into the return. The details are now contained in TSEM 7280.

4. Income Arising after Death

Income taxed during the administration period

There are special rules dealing with income received by the estate during the "administration period". This period starts with the day after the date of death and continues until the completion of the administration of the estate (ITTOIA 2005 s.653). It is generally accepted that completion of the administration occurs on the date the residue is ascertained for distribution. Personal representatives cannot claim any personal reliefs since these are only available to individuals. They can deduct interest on a loan (but not an overdraft) to pay inheritance tax when calculating the taxable income of the estate but only in so far as the loan is to pay tax on personalty vesting in the personal representatives to which the deceased was beneficially entitled. Further, this interest is only deductible for one year. Other expenses incurred by the personal representative in administering the estate are not deductible. **6-018**

Investments held in an Individual Savings Account (ISA) wrapper were originally only tax free during the lifetime of the holder individual. However, the Individual Savings Account (Amendment) Regulations 2017 (SI 2017/186) extend ISA tax advantages to investments held within an account after the death of the account holder. This means there is no income tax (or capital gains tax) on investments retained in an ISA during the administration of a deceased saver's estate or for three years whichever is the shorter.

The ISA Regulations have been amended to allow the spouse or civil partner of an ISA saver who died on or after 3 December 2014 to invest additional amounts in ISAs equal to the value of the deceased's ISA savings at the date of their death.

Rates of tax

The rate of tax which personal representatives pay is determined by the type of income they receive. They do not pay tax at the higher rate(s) irrespective of the amount of income they receive. Hence personal representatives are only ever liable at the following rates: **6-019**

- *Dividends:* The dividend allowance (see para.6-010) is only available to individuals so personal representatives will be liable to tax on any dividends received. Dividends declared before 6 April 2016 were received with a tax credit of 10 per cent which satisfied the basic rate tax liability of the personal representatives in its entirety. However, if the dividend is declared on or after 6 April 2016, it is paid gross. The personal representatives will pay tax at the dividend ordinary rate of 8.75 per cent.
- *Interest:* Personal representatives do not qualify for the savings allowance (see para.6-009) available to individuals. Therefore, they will have to pay tax pay at the basic rate (20 per cent). Interest attributable to tax year 2015/16 and earlier tax years had basic rate tax deducted so the personal

representatives did not need to make any further payment. In the HMRC *Trusts and Estates Newsletter* of April 2016 HMRC recognised that the change meant more work for personal representatives, who would now have to actually pay income tax on all income of the estate instead of being able to rely on deduction of tax at source. As a concession HMRC said it would not require tax returns where the only source of income was savings interest with a tax liability below £100. The concession was extended several times to 2023/24, is the concession was very limited applying only to estates where the only source of income is savings interest. If there was any other income, for example, a dividend, the concession does not apply. For tax years 2024/25 onwards the concession has been formalised and extended. See para.6-020 below.
- *Other income:* Personal representatives are assessed to basic rate tax applying the rules relevant to the particular type of income. So, for example, if the deceased was carrying on a business and the personal representatives continue to carry it on (either preparatory to winding it up or to passing it on to beneficiaries), the profits during the administration period form part of the assessable income of the personal representatives as trading income under ITTOIA 2005 Pt 2.

Special treatment of low income estates

6-020 HMRC consulted (Income Tax: Low income trusts and estates 25 April 2020) on amendments to Income Tax Act 2007 to allow the concessionary treatment of interest not exceeding £500 to be extended to allow other income to be included. Finance (No. 2) Act 2023, Sch.2 provides that ITA 2007 is amended for tax year 2024 to 2025 onwards as follows:

- Where the income of an estates does not exceed £500, personal representatives will pay tax at 0 per cent on that income whatever its nature.
- Beneficiaries of UK estates will not pay tax on income distributed to them that is within the £500 limit. However, beneficiaries of trusts will (see paras 7-068–7-069).

HMRC say in the Trusts, Settlements and Estates manual at TSEM7410:

> "From 6 April 2024, estates with income of all types up to £500 will not pay income tax on that income as it arises. Where income exceeds that amount, tax will be payable on the full amount. s24B ITA2007.
>
> The £500 tax-free amount will apply:
>
> - for every tax year of administration, but unused amounts do not roll over to subsequent years when reporting under informal procedures
> - to all types of income, after taking off ISA income which continues to be exempt after a person has died until closure or up to 3 years following the death
>
> If an estate has no chargeable income and no chargeable gains then there is no need to notify HMRC, either formally via the Trust Registration Service and Self-Assessment, or under informal procedures."

There will be an issue in relation to deciding which year's income beneficiaries are receiving. This may not be easy to establish, as the administration of an estate may span more than one tax year—so, for example, a payment may be made in a tax year in which the £500 de minimis limit applied but may be paid wholly or partly out an earlier year's income. The basic rule is that a payment is treated as made first out of income subject to the basic rate, then the dividend rate, followed by income bearing income tax at 0% (e.g. stock dividends and loans to participators), followed lastly by income bearing income tax at 0% because of the de minimis (ITTOIA 2005, s.679, as amended).

Income paid to beneficiaries where estate is not a low income estate

UK or foreign estate?

To the extent that income is paid to beneficiaries, further rules are relevant. These differ depending on whether the estate is a UK estate or a foreign estate (and also on the beneficiaries' interests in the estate). **6-021**

The residence status of the personal representatives determines the status of the estate. If they are all resident in the UK, then the estate is UK resident. The residence status of the deceased is irrelevant. Similarly, if none of the personal representatives is a UK resident, then the estate is non-UK resident. If the personal representatives have mixed residence, the residence of the deceased acts as a "tie-breaker". If the deceased was UK resident or domiciled here then all of the estate is UK resident. If not, the estate is non-resident. As with individuals, if the estate is not UK resident, it is only assessable on income arising in the UK (see ITA 2007 s.834 and ITTOIA 2005 s.651).

Income received by beneficiaries is grossed up

A beneficiary is charged to income tax on the estate income applicable to their interest, grossed up by reference to the rate at which the personal representatives have paid income tax. Personal representatives are required, if so requested by residuary beneficiaries, to provide a written statement setting out the amounts of income paid to the residuary beneficiary in any year of assessment and the amount of tax and the rates which the amounts are deemed to have borne (Income Tax (Trading and Other Income) Act 2005 s.682A). **6-022**

Note that where the estate income does not exceed £500, the beneficiaries are not required to pay tax.

Specific legatees

Income arising from property which is the subject of a specific disposition by will belongs to the beneficiary from the date of death, subject to anything in the will to the contrary. The legacy itself does not give rise to tax liability, being a payment out of capital. But if there is delay in vesting the property in a beneficiary who is absolutely entitled, any income arising to the personal representatives belongs to the beneficiary and if it is paid to them will form part of their estate income. The income received will be grossed up at the appropriate rate and included in the beneficiary's tax return. The beneficiary will have credit for the tax paid by the personal representatives. **6-023**

Suppose there is an income-producing asset such as a house which has been let and is producing rental income. The beneficiary only becomes liable to *pay* tax after the personal representatives have made an assent of the asset to the beneficiary. However, the liability relates back to the date of death so the beneficiary's assessments for intervening tax years will be reopened and tax will be reassessed for the years in which the income arose. The beneficiary will have the benefit of the 20 per cent tax paid by the personal representatives. If the beneficiary is a higher (or additional) rate taxpayer, they will have to pay the difference between the 20 per cent deducted and the 40 (or 45) per cent liability. If they are not a taxpayer, then they can reclaim the tax.

A specific legatee of shares will be liable to tax at the appropriate rate (see para.6-011) to the extent that the dividend, treated as the highest part of the taxpayer's income and when aggregated with any other dividends the specific legatee has received, exceeds his or her £2,000 dividend allowance.

Pecuniary and general legatees

6-024 Such legatees may be entitled to be paid interest on the value of their legacies (see para.16-065). The question of their liability to income tax on such interest then arises. In many circumstances income tax is chargeable on income even if not accepted but, in the case of interest, tax is only payable on sums actually received. Thus, if a beneficiary disclaims entitlement to interest payable to them on a pecuniary or general legacy or the personal representatives cannot pay it, they are not liable to tax: *Dewar v IRC* (1935) (unless a sum has been specifically set aside to pay the legacy in which case tax must be paid even if the legatee fails to draw the interest: *Spens v IRC* (1970)). If interest is paid to the beneficiary, it is taxed as savings income in their hands. Payment will be made gross (i.e. without deduction of any tax).

Residuary beneficiaries

6-025 The rules relating to residuary beneficiaries are themselves sub-divided into those which relate to beneficiaries with:

- limited interests;
- absolute interests;
- discretionary interests; and
- successive interests

in the residue of the estate.

Where there are different interests in different parts of the residue, each part is treated as a separate estate (ITTOIA 2005 s.649(4)). Residuary beneficiaries are charged to tax on their share of the residuary income of the estate.

Broadly speaking the income on which residuary beneficiaries may be taxed is their share of the "aggregate income" of the estate less various deductions set out in ITTOIA 2005 s.666 such as:

- interest (other than interest on unpaid inheritance tax);
- higher rate income tax relief available under ITTOIA 2005 s.669 where income of the estate has been included in the calculation of inheritance tax; and
- management expenses which are properly chargeable to income under the general law (as opposed to under a direction in the will).

Aggregate income is income of the estate which is chargeable to income tax less allowable deductions and excluding income to which a specific legatee is entitled (ITTOIA 2005 s.664).

Amounts treated as income of the beneficiary are "grossed up" at the basic rate or dividend ordinary rate, as applicable for the tax year of receipt. The estate income is then treated as having borne income tax at that rate or rates. In determining the rate applicable it is assumed first that amounts are paid to beneficiaries out of the different parts of the aggregate income of the estate in such proportions as are just and reasonable for their different interests, and then that payments are made from those parts bearing tax at the basic rate before they are made from those parts bearing tax at the dividend ordinary rate (ITTOIA 2005 s.679).

Because payments to a beneficiary of an estate are deemed to be made out of their share of income bearing tax at the basic rate in priority to their share of income bearing tax at the dividend ordinary rate, administration expenses chargeable to income are effectively relieved primarily against-dividend income.

Beneficiary with a limited interest in residue

A beneficiary who has an entitlement to income once the residue is ascertained, **6-026**
but not to capital, has a limited interest (ITTOIA 2005 s.650(3)). An example of such a beneficiary is a person who has a life interest in residue.

All sums received by the beneficiary will be liable to income tax in the year of receipt. In the final tax year of the administration, the beneficiary is assessed on all receipts before the end of the administration period plus any amounts payable to them at the end of the administration period (ITTOIA 2005 s.654(3)).

In the case of income received gross, the personal representatives will deduct tax from the income received.

They will deduct basic rate tax from non-savings income or interest and the dividend ordinary rate from dividend income. They pay the tax deducted to HMRC on behalf of the beneficiary. The beneficiary is liable to tax on income received in each tax year. The beneficiary will gross up the income at the appropriate rate and then deduct the tax credits. The personal-representatives are treated as paying out income taxed at basic rate first (see para.6-025).

Example 6

Martha is entitled to income for life from her mother's estate. The personal representatives receive various items of income and pay all the income to Martha in tax year 2024/25. Martha is an additional rate taxpayer. She is therefore not entitled to a savings allowance (see para.6-009). She has received dividends which have used up her dividend allowance (see para.6-009).

Martha grosses up the receipts

	Net		**Gross**
Rent	£3,200 × 100/80	=	£4,000
Interest	£4,800 × 100/80	=	£6,000
Dividend	£5,475x 100/91.25	=	£6,000

As an additional rate taxpayer, she is liable at 45 per cent on the rent and interest but has the benefit of the tax already paid by the personal representatives.

		£
Tax @ 45% on £10,000	=	4,500
Less Tax Paid	=	(2,000)
Tax to pay		£2,500

Martha has already used up her dividend allowance. Therefore, as an additional rate taxpayer she is liable to tax at 39.35 per cent but has the benefit of the tax already paid by the personal representatives.

Tax @ 39.35 on £6,000	=	2,361
Less Tax Paid	=	(480)
Tax to pay		1,821

In the above example, had the personal representatives paid only £5,000 of the income received to Martha in 2024/25, this would have been treated as a payment net of basic rate tax (see para.6-025). The delayed income would be paid to Martha in the following tax year so that she would receive additional income that year. Because she is already an additional rate taxpayer in both tax years, this is not significant (unless the additional rate changes). However, had Martha been a basic or higher rate taxpayer, receiving more income in one tax year might have pushed her into the higher or additional rate band in that tax year.

If income payments can be spread evenly across the tax years of the administration the beneficiary may remain below the higher or additional rate threshold. Personal representatives should, if practicable, discuss with the beneficiary the strategy for making payments.

Beneficiary with an absolute interest in residue

6-027 A beneficiary has an absolute interest in residue if the capital is properly payable to them, or would be so payable if the residue had been ascertained (ITTOIA 2005 s.650(2)). Such a beneficiary is entitled to both income and capital; income tax is, of course, only payable on income receipts. Therefore, when a beneficiary receives a cash sum from the estate it is necessary to distinguish income from capital receipts.

All payments to the beneficiary are treated as income up to the level of their " *assumed income entitlement* " for the tax year in question. Assumed income entitlement is the beneficiary's share of the residuary income for all the years of the administration in which they had the interest, less income tax at the appropriate rate and any payments already made to them via ITTOIA 2005 s.665. Payments to a beneficiary of an estate are deemed to be made out of their share of income bearing tax at the basic rate in priority to their share of income bearing tax at the dividend ordinary rate.

For the year in which the administration period ends (the "final tax year"), income is treated as arising if the beneficiary has an assumed income-entitlement for the year (whether or not any payments are made).

Example 7

Personal representatives are administering the estate of Theo who died in January 2024 leaving his residuary estate to Rosa absolutely.

(1) In tax year 2023/24 the personal representatives receive the following:

Interest	£1,000
Rent	£2,000
Total	£3,000

The personal representatives pay income tax at 20 per cent (£600) leaving net income of £2,400.

They make no payments to Rosa.

(2) In tax year 2024/25 the personal representatives receive the following:

Interest	£3,000
Rent	£6,000
Total	£9,000

The personal representatives pay income tax at 20 per cent (£1,800) leaving net income of £7,200.

They complete the administration and pay £500,000 to Rosa.

(3) In tax year 2023/24 Rosa's assumed income entitlement is £2,400. As she receives nothing from the estate, she includes nothing on her tax return.

(4) In tax year 2024/25 Rosa's assumed income entitlement is £2,400 + £7,200 = £9,600. All receipts will be treated as income up to that figure. Rosa will include on her tax return:

Net		**Gross**
£9,600 × 100/80	=	£12,000

She will have credit for the 20 per cent tax paid on the income received gross by the personal representatives and the 20 per cent deducted from the interest.

The balance of the payment to her is capital and as such is not included in her statutory income.

Again, so far as is practicable, personal representatives should discuss with the residuary beneficiary the strategy for making payments. It may be possible for the beneficiary to avoid paying higher (or additional) rate tax on the estate income in some tax years if payments can be staggered suitably.

Beneficiary with a discretionary interest

A person has a discretionary interest in all or part of the residue of an estate if a discretion may be exercised in their favour and (if the residue had been ascertained at the beginning of the administration period) on the exercise of the discretion any of the income of the residue would be properly payable to them (ITTOIA 2005 s.650(3)). The person in whose favour the discretion is exercised is charged income tax on the total payments made in a tax year in exercise of the discretion, grossed up, where appropriate (ITTOIA 2005 s.655). **6-028**

Successive interests

Special rules apply to the calculation of estate income where there are two or more successive absolute or limited interests during the period of administration to ensure that account is taken of income payments and tax deductions made on behalf of earlier beneficiaries. See ITTOIA 2005 ss.671–676. **6-029**

Successive interests arise most frequently where the disposition of an estate is varied (see Ch.19). Although the variation can be read back to the date of death for inheritance tax and capital gains tax, there is no reading back for income tax purposes.

(1) *Successive absolute interests.* Where there are successive absolute interests, each person is taxed on amounts received in each tax year up to the level of the assumed income entitlement.

In the final tax year of the administration for the purpose of calculating the final holder's assumed income entitlement, his share of the residuary income is treated as including the share of any person with a previous absolute interest. Hence, his assumed income entitlement will only include residuary income that has not been paid out earlier in the administration.

(2) *Successive limited interests.* A person with a life interest obviously cannot vary the disposition of the capital but can redirect the right to income during their lifetime. Where a beneficiary redirects a limited interest to create a new limited interest, this results in a succession of limited interests. Each successive beneficiary is taxed on the income to which he is entitled and actually receives in the relevant tax year (ITTOIA 2005 s.674 and s.675).

Example 8

Residue is left to Livia for life, remainder to Rizzo. Livia varies to give the right to income to Igor. Igor receives income during Livia's lifetime. On her death the right to income ceases and the capital passes to Rizzo.

(3) *Limited interest followed by absolute interest.* For the purpose of calculating the assumed income entitlement of the beneficiary with the absolute entitlement, any sums paid out to the prior limited interest beneficiaries are treated by ITTOIA 2005 s.672 as being included in the amounts relating to the absolute interest.

Example 9

Residue is left on trust to pay the income to Lana for life with remainder to Raoul. Lana surrenders her life interest by variation before administration is complete. Any sums paid to Lana will be taxed as her income; but for the purpose of calculating Raoul's assumed income entitlement, the sums paid to Lana will be treated as though they were sums paid as income to Raoul.

Completion of the administration

6-030 HMRC state at para.7418 of the *Trusts and Settlements Manual* that to help personal representatives settle the tax affairs of the administration period quickly it will, on request, issue a tax return before the end of the tax year in which the administration is completed. This practice is not statutory, but was included in the Budget announcement for Finance Act 2007.

Whether the tax return is issued before or after the end of that tax year, HMRC will, on request, give early written confirmation if they do not intend to enquire into that return. This confirmation does not preclude subsequent enquiries if it turns out that the return was incomplete or incorrect. Again this practice is not statutory, but was included in the Budget announcement for the Finance Act 2007.

Chapter Seven

TAXATION OF TRUSTS AND SETTLEMENTS

1. Introduction

Where property is held on trust the legal and beneficial interests are often held by different people and HMRC find it convenient and, in some cases, necessary, to impose liability on both the trustee and the beneficiary. Where the beneficial interest in property is divided between several people, either at a particular time or successively, special rules are required to ensure that the creation of the -settlement cannot be used as a means of saving tax. **7-001**

The definition of "settlement" differs for the three taxes. The definitions for tax purposes are not the same as for other purposes.

Settlements may be created by lifetime transfer, by the intestacy rules or by will.

We will deal with each tax separately for the sake of clarity, but it is important to realise that in deciding whether or not to create a settlement each tax must be taken into account. Furthermore, the non-tax consequences of creating a settlement should always be regarded as the first consideration. A gift is unwise, even if it saves tax, if it leaves the settlor or their dependants with insufficient income or capital for their needs.

It is also necessary to consider the administrative requirements of running a trust, for example, the need to register details of beneficial owners on the Trust Register operated by HMRC.

2. Settlements and Inheritance Tax

For inheritance tax purposes the term "settlement" is defined by s.43(2) of the Inheritance Tax Act 1984 (IHTA 1984) as: **7-002**

> "any disposition or dispositions of property … whereby the property is for the time being—
>
> (a) held in trust for persons in succession or for any person subject to a contingency; or
>
> (b) held by trustees on trust to accumulate the whole or part of any income of the property or with power to make payments out of that income at the discretion of the trustees or some other person, with or without power to accumulate surplus income; or
>
> (c) charged or burdened (otherwise than for full consideration …) with the payment of any annuity or other periodical payment payable for a life or any other limited or terminable period … ."

Section 43(3) adds to the definition a lease for life or lives or for a period ascertainable only by reference to a death which is not granted for full consideration.

It is important to note that a settlement is "any disposition or dispositions of property ... whereby the property is *for the time being*" held in one of the various ways listed in the definition. Whether or not property is settled must, therefore, be considered each time that a potential charge to tax arises. Property ceases to be settled once it ceases to be held in one of the various ways listed in the definition even though it may still be held by trustees (for example, where they have not yet vested it in a beneficiary who has become absolutely entitled).

A "bare" trust (where one person holds the legal title on trust for another person who is absolutely entitled) is not within the definition of a settlement for inheritance tax purposes. The beneficiary of such a trust is treated as an absolute owner.

The statutory trust imposed where property is held by co-owners is not a settlement for inheritance tax purposes. The co-owners are treated as absolute owners.

The following are examples of inheritance tax settlements:

(a) Trustees are holding property for "A for life remainder to B" (successive interest, see s.43(2)(a)).
(b) Trustees are holding property for "A if he reaches 25" (subject to a contingency, see s.43(2)(a)).
(c) Trustees are holding property "to accumulate the income therefrom for 10 years and then to pay capital to A" (trust to accumulate until the 10-year period expires, see s.43(2)(b)).
(d) Trustees are holding property "to pay the income therefrom for 10 years from [date] to such of my children as they shall in their absolute discretion from time to time appoint and thereafter to pay the capital to A" (discretion to pay income until the 10-year period expires, see s.43(2)(b)).
(e) Property is being held by someone subject to the payment of an annuity to someone else and full consideration was not given for the annuity. For example, the will of a testator leaves Blackacre "to my son charged with the payment to X of an annuity of £1,000 per annum for the rest of X's life". In this case there will be a settlement of Blackacre from the death of the testator until the death of X (see s.43(2)(c)).

3. INTERESTS IN POSSESSION

Qualifying interests in possession

7-003 It is often important for inheritance purposes to know whether or not a settlement has an interest in possession and, if so, whether the interest is a -"*qualifying*" interest in possession for inheritance tax purposes. This is because a person with a *qualifying* interest in possession is treated for inheritance tax purposes as owning the underlying trust capital. Hence, the value of the trust assets is aggregated with the free estate of the beneficiary on death and if the beneficiary surrenders or assigns the interest, it is a transfer of value.

Since the changes to the taxation of trusts introduced by Finance Act 2006 far fewer interests in possession are qualifying interests.

A qualifying interest in possession is defined in IHTA 1984 s.49 as:

- an interest in possession created before 22 March 2006 (see para.7-010);
- a disabled person's interest (see para.7-045);
- a transitional serial interest, (see para.7-014); or
- an immediate post-death interest (see para.7-037).

With the exception of transitional serial interests and trusts for the disabled no new qualifying interests in possession can be created by lifetime transfer on or after 22 March 2006. However, they can still be created on death in the form of immediate post-death interests and, interests in possession created pre-22 March 2006 trusts continue to be qualifying interests in possession.

What is an interest in possession?

The term "interest in possession" is not defined in the legislation. However, the House of Lords in *Pearson v IRC* (1980) defined it as "a present right to present enjoyment". In most cases it is clear whether or not there is an interest in possession. A beneficiary who has an immediate right to receive income or to use and enjoy trust property has such an interest. Thus, the life tenant of a settlement usually has an interest in possession (although in the case of a minor Trustee Act 1925 s.31 will remove the right: see the discussion at para.7-070). A beneficiary whose right to capital is contingent on reaching a specified age may obtain an interest in possession at an earlier age if the terms of the settlement (or Trustee Act 1925 s.31) gives them a right to income at an earlier age. Trustees may have power under the terms of a settlement to give beneficiaries a right to income for specified periods. In the case of an ordinary discretionary trust no one has such an interest unless, and until the trustees exercise their powers to give such a right, since no one has a *right* to income under the terms of the trust. There are, however, some marginal cases where the position is less clear. **7-004**

For example, in *Pearson v IRC* (1980) a trust fund was held for three beneficiaries (all adults) who were entitled to the property subject to powers of appointment and a power to accumulate; they would each receive one-third of the income unless the trustees exercised the power to accumulate or the power of appointment. The House of Lords by a majority of three to two (and overruling the decisions at first instance and in the Court of Appeal) held that there was no interest in possession. The majority held that an interest in possession is one giving "a present right to present enjoyment" and that on these facts there was no such right since the beneficiaries would not receive the income to the extent that the power to accumulate was exercised.

In *Douglas's Trustees v HMRC* (2007) trustees were to pay the deceased's widow the whole of the income of a trust fund or such part of it as they "may consider proper and expedient". Had the settlement said no more, the widow would not have had an interest in possession. However, the trust deed said that the trustees could only withhold income "with the concurrence of" the widow. The addition of these words converted the interest into an interest in possession since the widow would receive all the income unless and until she agreed to give up part of it.

In *Judge (PRs of Walden deceased) v HMRC* (2005) a rather unclear trust deed was held to provide that trustees had power to permit a widow to occupy a property "for such period or periods as they shall in their absolute discretion think fit". On that basis the widow did not have an interest in possession. This case also suggested that in order for trustees to create an interest in possession where one does not already exist, they must do something positive. Mere inactivity will not suffice.

Effect of administrative and dispositive powers on interests in possession

Distinction between the two

In theory, a beneficiary with an interest in possession is entitled to trust income as it arises. However, trustees will always have an administrative power to pay **7-005** management expenses of the trust from that income leaving only the balance for the beneficiary. In *Pearson*, Viscount Dilhorne said that there was a distinction between powers which were merely administrative and powers which were dispositive in their nature. A beneficiary with an interest in possession is entitled to all the net income of the trust once the expenses of the trust have been paid. If the trustees have power to withhold that net income from a beneficiary, there is no interest in possession. The difficulty lies in identifying expenses of the trust. Management expenses clearly fall into that category but what if trustees have power to pay items which would be normally be paid from capital (for example, capital gains tax) from income? There are cases where it will be difficult to draw the line.

Power to allow beneficiaries of a discretionary trust to occupy a dwelling house

7-006 The mere existence of such a power is of no significance. However, the exercise of the power may create an interest in possession. HMRC's view is set out in Statement of Practice 10/79:

> "if the power is drawn in terms wide enough to cover the creation of an exclusive or joint residence, albeit revocable, for a definite or indefinite period, and is exercised with the intention of providing a particular beneficiary with a permanent home, the Revenue will normally regard the exercise of the power as creating an interest in possession".

The statement continues with the following:

> "no interest in possession arises on the creation of a lease for a term or a periodic tenancy for less than full consideration".

It is, therefore, open to trustees to grant a lease to a member of the class at less than a market rent without creating an interest in possession.

Note that principal private dwelling house relief will be available to the trustees under TCGA 1992 s.225 where a beneficiary occupies a trust asset whether as of right under the terms of the trust or as the result of the exercise of a trustees' discretion: see *Sansom v Peay* (1976).

Will expressing wish that a beneficiary be allowed to reside in a dwelling house

7-007 Provided the will expresses a mere wish and confers no rights on the beneficiary, there is no interest in possession. However, testators frequently try to protect the position of the beneficiary by directing that the trustees *must* allow the beneficiary to occupy the property. If the beneficiary has a right to occupy, there is an interest in possession.

In *IRC v Lloyds Private Banking* (1998) a wife left her half share in the matrimonial home on trust directing that while her husband:

- was alive;
- wanted to reside in the property;
- kept it in repair; and
- indemnified the trustees against rates, taxes and other outgoings,

her trustees would not:

- make any objection to such residence;
- disturb or restrict it in any way;
- take any steps to enforce the trust for sale on which the property is held; or

- obtain any rent or profit from the property.

Subject to this, the property was held for her daughter absolutely.

The husband was held to have an interest in possession in the property. The terms of the gift elevated him to the status of a sole occupier of the whole -property, free from the possibility of a claim that he compensate the daughter for her exclusion or that an application be made to court for sale.

In *Faulkner (Trustee of Adams, deceased) v IRC* (2001) a testator directed in his will that a married couple, H and W, (or the survivor of them) should be permitted to live in a house which formed part of his estate for as long as they so wished.

The Special Commissioner agreed with the Revenue that there was an interest in possession. The will did not give the trustees any dispositive powers to decide whether or not H and W should occupy the property. The trustees had no discretion to refuse any request by H and W that they be permitted to occupy the property. It followed that the will created a settlement in favour of H and W and that H (the survivor of the couple) had an interest in possession at the date of his death.

In *Vincent v HMRC* (2019) the testatrix left her three-eighths share in a residence to the trustees of her will upon trust to permit her brother (who owned five-eighths of the residence) to reside there:

> "for so long as he shall desire free of rent but he being responsible for general rates, water rates, insurance and maintenance repairs of an income nature"

and subject thereto she gave her estate to her daughter. The brother continued in occupation of the property until he died. The first tier tribunal agreed with HMRC's contention that the brother had an interest in possession. The drafting of such an interest may be expressed as a right to occupy or in terms of restrictions on the trustee, but the issue is whether the substance of the clause creates a present right to present enjoyment of the property. The drafting in this case had to be read as creating an interest in possession in the testatrix's share of the property. It was a direction to the trustees to permit her brother to occupy the property subject to paying all the income expenses, and the substance was to confer a right on him "for so long as he shall desire". It was not simply a request that the testatrix's daughter should permit her uncle to reside, nor was the right to occupy left at the discretion for the trustees to permit the testatrix's brother to reside.

Co-owner in exclusive occupation

The Revenue has sometimes suggested that where one co-owner is in sole occupation, that co-owner may have an interest in possession in the whole property. **7-008**
In *Woodhall v CIR* (2000) such an argument failed. The testator left his house on trust for sale with a direction that the sale should be postponed so long as any of his children wished to live there. Until sale the trustees were to permit "all or any of them to occupy". All three of the testator's children lived there for a time but two moved out in the 1950s. The third child (Eric) occupied the property until his death.

The Revenue argued that Eric had had an interest in possession in the whole. Eric's executors argued that he had not had an interest in possession at all because he had had no right to exclusive possession. The Special Commissioner found that Eric and the other surviving child each had an interest in possession, being able to claim to occupy the property jointly. The trustees could not exclude them. Eric's estate, therefore, included half of the value of the property.

4. The Significance of Finance Act 2006

7-009 On 22 March 2006 the Chancellor introduced huge changes to the way in which settlements are treated for inheritance tax purposes. The Treasury had formed the view that settlements were being used primarily to escape inheritance tax and was determined to make them less attractive. Their intention was to encourage people to make outright gifts rather than to use trusts. There was concerted opposition from professional advisers and the press who pointed out that trusts are used for all kinds of tax-neutral reasons. The Treasury backed down to some extent in relation to settlements created on death but made very few concessions in relation to lifetime settlements. The date, therefore, remains a significant watershed in the tax treatment of settlements.

For settlements created before that date the important question was whether or not the settlement created had an interest in possession. The two types of settlement were subject to different inheritance tax regimes.

For settlements created on or after 22 March 2006 the important question is whether the settlement is created by lifetime transfer or on death. Settlements created by lifetime transfer are virtually all subject to the regime that previously applied only to settlements without an interest in possession: the "relevant property" regime. There are limited exceptions, for example settlements which create a "disabled person's interest" or those with a transitional serial interest.

Settlements created on death are subject to that regime unless they fall into one of the privileged categories.

5. Settlements Created before 22 March 2006

Classification

7-010 In the case of settlements created before 22 March 2006 the crucial question is whether or not the settlement has an interest in possession (see paras 7-004–7-008). This is because the inheritance tax treatment of a settlement with an interest in possession created before 22 March 2006 is entirely different from the treatment of a settlement without such an interest.

Settlements created before 22 March 2006 can be divided as follows:

a) *Settlements with a qualifying interest in possession.* Typically such a settlement is a life interest trust for an adult beneficiary, but it is possible to have short-term interests in possession, for example where a beneficiary becomes entitled to income at 18 under the Trustee Act 1925 s.31 before becoming entitled to capital. Before 22 March 2006 it made no difference whether the settlement was created by lifetime transfer or on death.

b) *Relevant property settlements.* Before 22 March 2006 relevant property settlements were those without an interest in possession which did not attract privileged inheritance tax treatment. Typically such a settlement would be a discretionary trust. It could also be a settlement in which beneficiaries had an interest contingent on reaching a specified age which failed to fulfil the requirements for privileged inheritance tax treatment.

   The property in such a settlement is referred to in IHTA 1984 s.58 as relevant property and hence such settlements are described as relevant property settlements.

c) *Settlements attracting privileged inheritance tax treatment.* A number of settlements without a qualifying interest in possession attracted privileged inheritance tax treatment; for example trusts for the disabled, accumulation and maintenance trusts (IHTA 1984 s.71), charitable trusts (IHTA 1984 s.58), employees trusts (IHTA 1984 s.86), and maintenance funds for historic buildings (IHTA 1984 s.77).

Settlements with a qualifying interest in possession

Tax arising on creation of a settlement with a qualifying interest in possession

Section 49 of IHTA 1984 provides that a person with an interest in possession created before 22 March 2006 is treated as being beneficially entitled to the property in which the interest subsists. This is referred to as a "qualifying" interest in possession. **7-011**

A transfer to any type of settlement is a transfer of value by the settlor. Assuming that no exemptions apply, the transfer will be either exempt, potentially exempt or chargeable.

A person with a qualifying interest in possession is deemed to own the trust assets beneficially. This has a number of inheritance tax implications. Before 22 March 2006 if taxpayers created settlements by lifetime transfer in which they were the first life tenant there was no charge to tax. This was because before the creation they *actually* owned the property beneficially; after the creation they were *deemed* to own it beneficially, so for tax purposes the value of their estate has not gone down. Similarly, if the settlor's spouse or civil partner was the first life tenant, the creation of the settlement (whether by lifetime transfer or on death) did not give rise to tax because it was spouse exempt.

A settlor who made a lifetime transfer to a settlement in which a non-exempt beneficiary had an interest in possession on or after 17 March 1987 and before 22 March 2006 was treated as making a potentially exempt transfer. Thus, no inheritance tax was payable unless the settlor died within seven years of the transfer. If the settlor dies within that period, then the transfer becomes chargeable at the full rates in force at the date of death (subject to the possibility of tapering relief).

Example 1

On 5 February 2006, Sayeed gave £335,000 to trustees to hold on trust for Arshad for life, and the remainder to Bhopal. No exemptions or reliefs apply. Sayeed's cumulative total was nil. Sayeed died on 15 February 2011.

No tax was payable on creation as the transfer was potentially exempt. However, on Sayeed's death in February 2011, when the nil-rate band was £325,000, the transfer became chargeable. The first £325,000 was within the nil-rate band; the remaining £10,000 was taxed at 40 per cent (with the benefit of tapering relief as Sayeed survived five complete years after making the transfer).

If Sayeed had transferred property to the settlement on death, the property transferred would have been taxed as part of his death estate before being transferred to the trustees of the settlement.

Note that if by lifetime transfer Sayeed transferred £335,000 to trustees to hold for Arshad for life on or after 22 March 2006, the settlement would be a relevant property settlement and the transfer would be immediately chargeable to inheritance tax at half the death rates.

Chargeable events after creation of settlement with a qualifying interest in possession

7-012 Since a person with a qualifying interest in possession is treated as owning the trust property (or a proportion of it if they are entitled to part only of the income) it follows that a termination of the interest in possession is taxable as a disposition *of the trust property* by that person. Tax may thus become chargeable:

(a) on the death of the person entitled to the interest;
(b) on an actual disposal of the interest (for example, the beneficiary gives their interest away, surrenders it or sells it at an undervalue); or
(c) on the termination of the interest in any other way (for example, where the interest is determinable at a particular date or on the happening of a particular event, or at the discretion of the trustees).

Since the termination of the interest is treated as a transfer of the trust property by the person entitled to the interest, the tax payable, if any, will depend on that person's cumulative total and on whether the termination is on death or during their lifetime, to an individual absolutely or on continuing trusts.

Example 2(1)

(1) Trustees of a trust created before 22 March 2006 are holding a trust fund of £300,000 on trust for Larry for life remainder to Roger. Larry dies having made chargeable lifetime transfers in the seven years preceding his death which have exhausted his nil-rate band, and owning £150,000 worth of unsettled property. Larry's estate on death is £450,000 (i.e. the trust fund and the unsettled £150,000). The whole £450,000 is subject to tax at 40 per cent. The tax is, therefore, £180,000 (that is £450,000 at 40 per cent). This tax will normally be paid by the trustees of the settlement and the personal representatives in the same proportions that the trust property and the unsettled property bear to the whole estate on death. In this case the trustees will pay two-thirds of the tax and the personal representatives one-third.
(2) Trustees of a trust created before 22 March 2006 are holding a trust fund of £500,000 for Anya for life, remainder to Barack for life, remainder to Casimir absolutely.

Example 2(2)

In February 2006 Anya surrendered her life interest so accelerating Barack's life interest. Anya is deemed to have made a potentially exempt transfer of £500,000 to Barack.

Note that if Anya did the same thing after 22 March 2006, she would make a lifetime chargeable transfer. Lifetime transfers on continuing trusts on or after 22 March 2006 are lifetime chargeable transfers unless they fall within very limited exceptions.

Where a pre-22 March 2006 interest in possession comes to an end and at that time the person with the interest in possession becomes beneficially entitled to the trust property there is no tax to pay. This is because, as we saw at para.7-011, before the interest ends they are treated as owning the trust property, after it ends they actually own it so that for tax purposes there is no loss to their (or anyone else's) estate.

Example 3

Trustees of a trust created before 22 March 2006 hold property on trust to pay the income to Anup until 25 and thereafter for Anup absolutely. When Anup reaches 25, no tax will be payable.

There is no tax on the termination of a pre-22 March 2006 interest in possession if the property then reverts to the settlor during the settlor's lifetime or to the settlor's spouse or civil partner during the settlor's lifetime or within two years of their death (IHTA 1984 s.53).

Example 4

In 2004 Salazar settles property on Brigitte for life with a reversion to himself. No tax is payable when the property reverts to Salazar on Brigitte's death.

The exception from charge on the termination of interests in possession with reverter to settlor under IHTA 1984 s.53 is of much less significance since 22 March 2006. Very few interest in possession settlements are qualifying settlements. The most common are immediate post-death interests in relation to which there can be no reverter to settlor (because the settlor of an immediate post-death interest is necessarily dead). Relief from charge is only required for the few remaining qualifying interests in possession: disabled person's interest or transitional serial interests.

An advance of capital to anyone other than the person with the interest in possession does give rise to tax since it brings the interest in possession in that property to an end.

Various exemptions and reliefs are available on the termination of a pre-22 March 2006 interest in possession including the following:

(a) The annual exemption of £3,000 (unless already used to exempt other transfers) is available where the termination occurs as a result of a lifetime transfer.
(b) The spouse exemption applies unless the spouse has acquired the reversion for money or money's worth. (For example, settlement to A for life remainder to B—no tax on A's death if A is then married to B. Settlement to A for life remainder to X; B (A's spouse) buys X's reversion and then A dies—tax will be payable.)
(c) Business and agricultural property relief. The relief is available provided the person with the pre-22 March 2006 interest in possession fulfils the ownership requirement. This is a potential pitfall. See *Burrell v Burrell* (2005) where trustees terminated the interest in possession of a beneficiary of a trust of unquoted shares. The beneficiary had acquired an interest in possession at the age of 18 and would have received very substantial dividends. The trustees used their powers to terminate the interest in possession by appointing the property on discretionary trusts. This was a lifetime chargeable transfer by the beneficiary which would give rise to a substantial inheritance tax charge unless business property relief was available. The trustees believed that it was but overlooked the fact that the beneficiary had acquired the interest in possession in the shares less than two years earlier and, therefore, the ownership requirement of IHTA 1984 s.106 was not fulfilled.

The exemptions for small gifts and normal expenditure out of income cannot be used in relation to transfers from settlements.

Reversions

7-013 A reversionary interest (that is a future interest) in settled property is usually excluded property and so no tax is payable on a transfer (lifetime or on death) of such an interest. This rule is really just a consequence of the fact that the person with an interest in possession is deemed to own the trust property absolutely.

Example 5

Property is settled before 22 March 2006 on Lashmi for life remainder to Rohan. No tax is payable on Rohan's remainder interest if Rohan dies or gives away his interest during Lashmi's lifetime.

To prevent tax avoidance a reversionary interest is *not* excluded property (so that tax will be payable on the death of its owner or on a lifetime transfer by them) in certain special cases, for example where the reversionary interest was purchased.

Transitional serial interests

7-014 A beneficiary who had a qualifying interest in possession on 22 March 2006 continues to be treated as being beneficially entitled to the underlying trust assets. The tax treatment on the ending of that interest in possession may be different because it is no longer generally possible to create new qualifying interests in possession. Hence if, on the ending of the interest in possession, the property continues to be settled, the new beneficiary will normally not have a qualifying interest in possession.

However, new qualifying interests in possession could be created in the transitional period which for this purpose ran from 22 March 2006 to 5 April 2008. These replacement interests are called transitional serial interests. The person with a transitional serial interest is treated in exactly the same way that any other person with a qualifying interest in possession is treated.

Example 6

Ben had a life interest in a substantial family trust. On 22 March 2006 he was 72 and did not need the income. The trustees terminated his interest on 1 January 2007 and appointed the fund to his son, Jack, for life. Jack obtained a transitional serial interest and Ben made a potentially exempt transfer to him.

A transitional serial interest normally only arises when it replaces an interest which was in existence on 22 March 2006. In the above example if Jack asked the trustees to terminate his interest in favour of his daughter, Dana, for life and the trustees did so on 30 January 2008, i.e. before the end of the transitional period. Dana would not have a transitional serial interest; she would have an interest in a relevant property trust and Jack would be treated as having made a lifetime chargeable transfer to that relevant property trust.

There is one case where a transitional serial interest can arise outside the transitional period. This is where a spouse or civil partner with an interest in possession in existence on 22 March 2006 *dies* and their spouse or civil partner takes an interest in possession following their death. The surviving spouse or civil partner takes a transitional serial interest even though the beneficiary's death occurs outside the transitional period. This is not the case, however, if the replacement interest in possession arises outside the transitional period as a result of a *lifetime* transfer.

Example 7

Alan has a life interest in a family trust. His interest was in existence on 22 March 2006. In 2020 he marries, appoints his wife a life interest in the settlement on his death and dies shortly afterwards. His wife has a transitional serial interest (so that she is treated as owning the capital in the settlement) and so the spouse exemption applies.

By contrast if in 2023 he divorces and creates an interest in possession for his wife as part of the divorce agreement: (a) the interest of the wife is not a transitional serial interest, and (b) the continuing trust falls within the relevant property regime. He will be treated as making a lifetime chargeable transfer to the relevant property settlement.

Relevant property settlements

Introduction

The rules which before 22 March 2006 applied only to non-privileged settlements without an interest in possession are described in this section. As we shall see at para.7-034 and following, these rules now apply to all settlements created on or after that date unless they fall within certain limited exceptions so these rules have become extremely important. **7-015**

There is no interest in possession in a settlement if no individual has "a present right to present enjoyment" of the trust property (*Pearson v IRC* (1980); see para.7-004 and following). A typical example is a discretionary settlement.

Where there is a qualifying interest in possession, tax is chargeable once for each individual beneficiary's period of enjoyment of the property.

The rules for settlements without an interest in possession were designed to achieve the equivalent of one full tax charge every generation thus establishing rough parity of treatment with other settlements and with circumstances where the property is not settled at all.

The settlement itself is treated as a taxable entity. It inherits the cumulative total of the settlor but, thereafter, has its own cumulative total. It is always taxed at lifetime rates even if the initial creation was on death. The main feature is the "anniversary charge" which is charged on the 10th anniversary of the creation of the settlement. It is charged on "relevant property" defined in s.58 as settled property (other than excluded property) in which there is no qualifying interest in possession. There is also an exit charge which is levied when property leaves the settlement between 10-year anniversaries.

Inheritance tax arising on creation of a relevant property settlement

If the settlement is created by lifetime transfer, the transfer of property to the settlement is an immediate chargeable transfer and tax will be charged initially at half the death rates. Tax will become chargeable at the full death rates if the settlor dies within seven years of the transfer, although credit is given for any tax already paid. Tapering relief will be available if the settlor survives three years from the transfer. Grossing up will be required if the settlor pays the tax. **7-016**

Example 8

Sam made a lifetime transfer of £400,000 to a discretionary trust on 1 January 2006. The nil-rate band at that time was £275,000. He had made chargeable transfers of £200,000 and so had £75,000 of his nil-rate band available. He had exhausted his annual exemptions. The trust paid the inheritance tax (so no grossing up was required). The first £75,000 was taxed at 0 per cent and the remaining £325,000 at 20 per cent.

$$20/100 \times £325,000 = £65,000$$

(Had the transfer been made on death, the property would have been taxed as part of the death estate before being transferred to the trustees of the settlement.)

Where a transfer is made to a discretionary trust, there is no reduction in the amount of tax if the settlor or their spouse is one of the discretionary beneficiaries since a discretionary beneficiary has no interest in the trust property for tax -purposes. If the settlor is included in the class of beneficiaries, this will amount to a reservation of benefit leading to a possible charge on their death (see para.7-029).

The settlement inherits the cumulative total of the settlor immediately before creation of the settlement. That cumulative total forms part of the settlement's cumulative total throughout its life. It is, therefore, beneficial for the future taxation of the settlement if it is created at a time when the settlor has a low cumulative total.

Settlements created on the same day are "related settlements". For chargeable events arising on or after 18 November 2015, the value of any relevant property contained in a related settlement immediately after creation of that settlement has to be added to the value of the settlement being taxed and will increase the rate of tax paid. It is therefore advisable to avoid having substantial amounts of relevant property in a related settlement at creation. (For chargeable events arising before 18 November the rule was more draconian and the value of any property in the related settlement immediately after creation had to be added, whether or not it was relevant property.)

It is only settlements created on the same day which are related. In *Rysaffe Trust Company (Cl) v IRC* (2002) a settlor signed five identical discretionary settlements on the same day. His solicitors dated them on different days. He sent a cheque for £50 to his accountants who credited £10 to each settlement. At a later date he transferred five parcels of shares in the same company to the five trusts. HMRC argued that the initial creation of the settlements and the subsequent transfers were associated operations and, therefore, there was one settlement not five separate settlements. The taxpayer successfully appealed. As a matter of general trust law there were five separate settlements not one. Although they were initially identical, they each contained powers of appointment and powers to appoint new trustees so that eventually they might be very different. The associated operations rules were held to be inapplicable.

Inheritance tax chargeable after creation of relevant property settlements

7-017 After creation, there are three possible occasions of charge to inheritance tax:

(a) when property ceases to be "relevant property" between creation and the first 10-year anniversary;
(b) on each 10-year anniversary; and
(c) when property ceases to be "relevant property" between 10-year anniversaries.

(a) Property ceasing to be relevant property before the first 10-year anniversary A charge is imposed on the value of the property ceasing to be relevant property (s.65). Property will cease to be relevant property when the trustees appoint capital to a beneficiary, an "exit" charge.

The charge is always based on lifetime rates and is calculated on the basis of a hypothetical chargeable transfer. The actual rate of tax charged is 30 per cent of the rate of tax calculated on the hypothetical chargeable transfer. As the maximum rate of tax payable on a lifetime transfer is 20 per cent, the maximum rate payable on a settlement is 30 per cent of 20 per cent, i.e. 6 per cent but the rate will be lower if the settlement has nil rate band available to it.

Step one is, therefore, to calculate the hypothetical chargeable transfer.

For exits in the first 10 years on or after 18 November 2015 the hypothetical chargeable transfer is calculated by adding together the following:

- the value of relevant property in the settlement immediately after commencement;
- value of subsequent additions (at time added); and
- value of any relevant property in a related settlement (immediately after it commenced; subsequent increases in value are ignored); and
- for chargeable events arising on or after 18 November 2015 the value of a same-day addition. For same-day additions see para.7-024.

Step two is to calculate the tax at lifetime rates on the hypothetical chargeable transfer by joining the table of rates at the point reached by the settlor in the seven years before the creation of the settlement. Other chargeable transfers made on the same day are ignored (s.68(4)). The settlor's cumulative total remains relevant to the rate of tax charged on the settlement throughout its life so as a matter of tax planning settlors should create relevant property settlements at a time when they have a full nil-rate band available. No account is taken of any earlier transfers from the settlement.

Step three is to convert the tax calculated into an average rate (equivalent to an estate rate). The relevant property in the settlement is charged to tax at 30 per cent of that average rate. This is referred to as the "settlement rate".

Step four is to calculate what proportion of the settlement rate will be applied to the transfer. One-fortieth of the settlement rate is charged for each complete successive quarter that has elapsed from creation of the settlement to the date of the transfer. This is referred to as the "effective rate". There is no charge if property ceases to be relevant property in the first quarter. There is a calculator available on the *gov.uk* website which will calculate the number of quarters that have elapsed.

Example 8.1 (continued from para.7-016)

Let us assume that the trustees of the trust created by Sam on 1 January 2006 appointed £30,000 to one of the discretionary beneficiaries on 1 April 2009 when the nil-rate band was £300,000.

Step one: Find value of hypothetical transfer—In our example the value of the hypothetical transfer is £400,000 as there is nothing to add to the initial transfer.

Step two: Calculate tax at half rates on hypothetical transfer—In our example the settlor's cumulative total was £200,000 at the time the settlement was created. The nil-rate band in tax year 2008/09 is £300,000 so tax will be charged at 0 per cent on the first £100,000 of the settled property and 20 per cent on the last £300,000 giving a tax figure of £60,000.

Step three: Convert the tax to an average rate and then take 30 per cent which will be the "settlement rate"

$$\frac{\text{Tax}}{\text{Value of Settlement}} \times 100 = \text{Settlement Rate}$$

£60,000 / £400,000	×	100 = 15%

Settlement rate is 30 per cent of 15 per cent, i.e. 4.5 per cent.

Step four: Calculate the "effective" rate by reference to the number of quarters completed since the settlement was created—In our example there are nine completed quarters since the date the settlement was created on 1 January 2006, so we take 9/40 of the settlement rate of 4.5 per cent and apply this to the fall in value of the trust property.

9 / 40	×	4.5 / 100	×	£30,000 = £303.75

If the tax comes from the trust fund the transfer will have to be grossed-up.

(b) The first 10-year anniversary Tax is charged on the value of the relevant property in the settlement immediately before the first 10-year anniversary (s.64). The term "anniversary" in the definition of "ten-year anniversary" in s.61 has its usual meaning of the recurrence of a particular date, so that, for example, if the first property to be transferred into a settlement was so transferred on 16 June 1992, the 10-year anniversaries of that settlement are 16 June 2002, 16 June 2012, etc. A settlement is treated as commencing when property first becomes comprised in it (s.60). This means that where a settlement is initially made of £100, and substantial property is added to it at a later date, the 10-year anniversaries (on which the periodic charge occurs) for that settlement are calculated from the date on which the £100 became comprised in it.

Relevant property used to consist only of trust capital and income which had become capital by being formally accumulated. Accumulation occurs when the trustees take an irrevocable decision to accumulate it although it can also occur when income has been held for a sufficiently long period. The Revenue became concerned that many trusts were holding large amounts of income for substantial periods and claiming that, in the absence of a formal decision to accumulate, the funds retained their character as income. To put the matter beyond argument, Finance Act 2014 included provisions which deem income held within a settlement for five years to be treated as capital for the purposes of the anniversary charge even though not formally accumulated by the trustees. The change applies to anniversary charges arising on or after 6 April 2014. Income is not treated as capital for the purposes of exit charges. This is beneficial for income tax purposes as it allows any available income tax credits to be set against the income.

As with charges on exits before the first 10-year anniversary *step one* is to calculate the value of a hypothetical chargeable transfer. On 10-year anniversaries it is calculated by adding together the following:

- current value of relevant property (including income formally accumulated or deemed to be accumulated for this purpose) in the settlement immediately after commencement; and

- value of relevant property in a related settlement (immediately after the settlement commenced, subsequent increases in value are ignored); and
- for chargeable events arising on or after 18 November 2015 the value of a same-day addition. For same-day additions see para.7-024.

For anniversaries occurring before 18 November 2015 it was necessary to include the value at the date the settlement commenced of any other property in the settlement which had not subsequently become relevant property. This was an anti-avoidance provision but has been removed in the interests of simplification.

Step two is to calculate the tax at lifetime rates on the hypothetical chargeable transfer by joining the table of rates at the point reached:

- by the settlor in the seven years before the creation of the settlement; plus
- any chargeable transfers made from the settlement in the previous 10 years.

Step three is to convert that tax into an average rate and to take 30 per cent of that average rate as the "settlement rate" to be applied to the relevant property in the settlement.

Example 8.2 (continued from para.7-016)

The first 10-year anniversary falls on 1 January 2016. Assume the assets remaining in the trust fund are worth £595,000 on that date. The nil-rate band is £325,000.

Step one: Find value of hypothetical transfer—assume that in our example the current value of the relevant property is £595,000.

Step two: Calculate tax at half rates on hypothetical transfer—In our example the settlor's cumulative total was £200,000 and £30,000 was appointed from the settlement so transfers to be taken into account are £230,000 leaving £95,000 of the nil-rate band available. Tax will be at 0 per cent on the first £95,000 and 20 per cent on the last £500,000, i.e. £100,000.

Step three: Convert the tax to an average rate and then take 30 per cent which will be the "settlement rate"

$$\frac{\text{Tax}}{\text{Value of Settlement}} \times 100 = \text{Settlement Rate}$$

£100,000/£595,000 × 100 = 16.806%

Settlement rate is 30 per cent of 16.806 per cent, i.e. 5.042 per cent.

Step four: The settlement rate is applied to the property to be taxed to produce the tax payable

5.042/100 × £595,000 = £29,999

(c) Property ceasing to be relevant property between 10-year anniversaries Tax is charged on the property ceasing to be relevant property. The rate of tax is a proportion of the effective rate charged at the first 10-year anniversary. The proportion is one-40th for each complete successive quarter that has elapsed from the date of the first anniversary to the date of the transfer. There is no charge if property ceases to be relevant property in the first quarter.

Example 8.3 (continued from para.7-016)

Assume the trustees appoint £200,000 to a discretionary beneficiary on 1 December 2018.

Step one: Calculate the property ceasing to be relevant property—In our example the fall is £200,000.

Step two: Calculate the effective rate by reference to the quarters completed since the previous anniversary—There are 11 completed quarters since the last 10-year anniversary so take 11/40 of the settlement rate (5.042 per cent) and apply this to the fall in value of the trust property.

11	×	5.042	×	£200,000 = £2,773.10
40		100		

If the tax comes from the trust fund the transfer will have to be grossed up.

(d) Subsequent 10-year anniversaries The charge is calculated in the same way that it was calculated on the first 10-year anniversary.

Points to be aware of in connection with the taxation of settlements without an interest in possession

7-018 **Agricultural and business property relief** Agricultural and business property relief will reduce the value of relevant property if the trustees meet the conditions necessary for relief.

7-019 **Importance of review before each anniversary** Where asset values are rising, it is preferable for trustees to appoint capital out of a trust immediately before an anniversary rather than immediately after one. This is because the charge to tax will be calculated at the rate calculated on the previous anniversary. That rate will be based on the value of the trust property when the trust was created or on the previous anniversary rather than on its current value.

It is particularly important to review nil-rate band settlements before the first 10-year anniversary. Where the property settled was within the settlor's available nil-rate band at creation, all exits in the first 10 years will be taxed at 0 per cent no matter how much the trust property increases in value. This is because the rate is based on the value of the property originally settled and this was within the settlor's available nil rate band. On the first 10-year anniversary the property remaining in the settlement is revalued.

Example 9

Ahmed died on 30 June 2017 with a nil cumulative total. He left a nil-rate band legacy (£325,000) on discretionary trusts for his children and the residue to his wife so no inheritance tax was payable on his death.

By May 2027 the trust fund is worth £900,000.

Up to 30 June 2027 the trustees can appoint the whole of the fund to the children and there will be no inheritance tax liability.

If they wait until 30 July 2027 to make the appointment, tax will be calculated on the new value of the fund so there will be a tax liability on everything in excess of the current nil-rate band.

Transfers from the settlement in the previous 10 years are cumulated when calculating the rate of inheritance tax to be charged on the next 10 year anniversary but then drop out of cumulation so the settlement reverts to its original nil rate band.

50 per cent business and agricultural relief There is one case (possibly the result of defective drafting of the IHTA 1984) where appointments should not be made before the first 10-year anniversary. This is where property is settled which qualifies for 50 per cent business or agricultural relief. When calculating the *rate* of tax on an exit before the first 10-year anniversary under s.68, it is necessary to take "the value, immediately *after* the settlement commenced, of the property then comprised in it". Valuing the property immediately after the creation of the settlement for the purposes of calculating the rate of tax means no business or agricultural property relief is available because the property has not been owned for the requisite two-year period. If the property leaves the settlement after the necessary two-year -ownership period the value of the property will be reduced by the 50 per cent relief but the rate of tax will remain relatively high for the whole of the first 10-year period. The problem does not arise where relief is available at 100 per cent as the value of the property being charged will be reduced to zero so the rate of tax will be irrelevant. On the 10-year anniversary the 50 per cent relief is taken into account when calculating the rate to be charged under s.66 and subsequent exits in that 10-year period will be a proportion of that rate. It is, therefore, preferable to wait until after the expiry of the first 10-yearanniversary before making the distribution. **7-020**

Appointments within three months following creation or within three months of an anniversary There is no exit charge if an appointment is made within three months of creation of the settlement or within the first three months following an anniversary (IHTA 1984 s.65(4)). This is because no completed quarters of the year have elapsed. **7-021**

Additions of property to the settlement by the settlor If the settlor adds property to the settlement by means of a chargeable transfer special rules apply (s.67(1)). The special rules do not apply where the transfer is exempt, for example because it is covered by the annual exemption. **7-022**

Where the rules apply, the calculation of the periodic charge following the addition will be modified. When calculating the tax on the hypothetical -chargeable transfer the settlor's cumulative total will be taken as the higher of the totals:

- immediately before creating the settlement plus transfers made by the settlement before the addition; and
- immediately before transferring the added property deducting from this latter total, the transfer made on creation of the settlement and a transfer to any related settlement.

Whenever the modification would result in higher rates of tax, the settlor should consider whether it will be preferable to create a new settlement rather than adding property to an existing one.

Inheritance tax planning using pilot trusts

Before the Finance (No.2) Act 2015 it was common for settlors to reduce inheritance tax by creating a number of small trusts on consecutive days (typically transferring £10 to each settlement so that the amount transferred was within the **7-023** annual exemption) at a time when they had an unused nil-rate band. These lifetime settlements are referred to as pilot trusts.

Because the settlements were created at a time when the settlor had a full nil-rate band, each settlement inherited a full nil-rate band from the settlor. The settlements were not related to each other because they were created on different days. If the settlor added property to all the settlements on the same day, the rules on additions dealt with at para.7-022 did not apply. Provided the settlor still had a full nil-rate band available on the date of the transfers, each settlement continued to have a full nil-rate band available from the settlor. This reduced anniversary and exit charges. It was therefore possible for taxpayers to create a number of trusts each of which would have a full nil-rate band available to it and so avoid anniversary and exit charges.

Example 10

In 2013 Wily wants to leave £675,000 by will on discretionary trusts for his children and grandchildren. He has a full nil-rate band available. If he creates one settlement it will have one nil-rate band available and there will be anniversary and exit charges. If he creates three settlements of £10 on separate days and leaves £225,000 to each by will, each settlement benefits from a full nil-rate band so anniversary and exit charges will be at 0 per cent.

HMRC, understandably, became concerned about "*the leakage of IHT through the use of multiple trusts*" and in Finance (No.2) Act 2015 introduced amendments to the rules to catch what it calls "same day additions.

Same-day additions

7-024 **Introduction** The new rules do not affect the availability of nil-rate bands. Instead, a new s.62A requires relevant property added, after commencement, to two or more trusts on the same day (a "*same-day addition*") to be brought into account when calculating the rate of charge for 10-year anniversaries and exit charges.

Same-day additions will be included in the calculation of the hypothetical chargeable transfer for all charges arising on or after 18 November 2015 in respect of relevant property trusts created on or after 10 December 2014.

7-025 **Anti-forestalling provisions** To prevent forestalling, the Act provided that the new provisions would apply to relevant property trusts created before 10 December 2014 where additions were made to more than one trust on the same day on or after that date. But there was one exception for "protected settlements".

7-026 **Protected settlements** The anti-forestalling provision did not apply where death occurred before 6 April 2017 and additions were made to existing trusts under "*provisions of the settlor's will that at the settlor's death are, in substance, the same as they were immediately before 10 December 2014*". This was intended to give taxpayers who had already created plot trusts with the intention of leaving property to them by will a breathing space which would allow them to review their wills and decide whether or not to amend them in the light of the new provisions.

Example 11

In January 2014 Sam created three pilot trusts transferring £10 to each on consecutive days. Sam had a full nil-rate band available. At the same time he made a will leaving £250,000 to each settlement.

(1) Assume that Sam dies in January 2017 with his will unchanged and

£250,000 is transferred to each settlement. In January 2024 the first anniversary charge has to be calculated.

Assume the value of the settled property in each settlement at that date is £325,000 and the nil-rate band has remained at £325,000.

The same-day addition rule will not apply so the hypothetical chargeable transfer for each settlement is £325,000. All three settlements have a full nil-rate band available so the anniversary rate of tax on each is nil.

(2) If instead Sam died in January 2018, the same-day addition rule will apply so in 2024 the hypothetical chargeable transfer for each settlement is £325,000 + £250,000 + £250,000.

All three settlements have a full nil-rate band available. The anniversary rate is calculated on a hypothetical chargeable transfer of £825,000.

There is a full nil-rate band available to each settlement so 20 per cent is charged on £500,000 = £100,000.

This is an average rate of £100,000/£825,000 x100 = 12.12 per cent.

The rate actually charged is 30 per cent of that, so 3.6 per cent.

Note that, where asset values rise, there is still a benefit to using three settlements rather than putting the whole lot into one big settlement. If Sam had used one settlement, the rate of tax would have been calculated on a hypothetical chargeable transfer of £975,000. One nil-rate band would have been available so tax at 20 per cent would be charged on £650,000 = £130,000.

This is an average rate of £130,000/£975,000 x100 = 13.33 per cent. The rate actually charged is 30 per cent of that, so 3.9 per cent.

Additional points

- The same-day addition can be an increase in value as opposed to a transfer of property (e.g. a settlor releasing his loan to the settlement or paying a 10-year anniversary charge when the trust is "dry". 7-027
- If the value of an addition is £5,000 or less the same-day addition rule does not apply. There are anti-fragmentation provisions to prevent individuals avoiding the same-day addition rules by transferring amounts in excess of £5,000 to settlements in multiples of £5,000.
- Death benefits paid to a lifetime trust from a pension scheme operated via a trust remain in the original trust for inheritance tax purposes (s.81) so are not same-day additions in relation to relevant property trusts created on death (or payments other pension scheme)

Summary

- Pilot trusts created and filled with assets before 10 December 2014 are unchanged and do not have to take into account the value of same-day additions. 7-028
- Pilot trusts created before 10 December 2014 and "empty" on that date will have to take into account "*same-day additions*" unless assets were transferred on death before 6 April 2017 under wills executed before 10 December 2014 (or contained in a later will replicating such provisions).
- All other trusts will have to take into account the value of "*same-day additions*".

- Property added on different days is obviously not subject to the "*same-day additions*" rule. Hence every seven years a settlor could create a settlement with a full nil-rate band.
- If property is exempt or attracts 100 per cent relief, it does not affect the settlor's cumulative total so multiple settlements can be created using the normal expenditure from income exemption all of which will have a full nil-rate band available.

Reservation of benefit

7-029 Settlors who create settlements without an interest in possession may wish to be beneficiaries of the settlement (e.g. one of the objects of a discretionary trust). In such a case they make a gift "subject to a reservation" and tax will, therefore, be payable *on their death* in respect of that property unless they have been excluded from benefit for seven years before they die: see *IRC v Eversden* (2002) and *PRs of Lyon v HMRC* (2007).

When trustees terminate a beneficiary's interest in possession, the beneficiary makes a transfer of value (see para.7-012) but would not normally be regarded as making a gift. This gave the possibility of avoiding the gift with reservation rules. Trustees could terminate an interest in possession to create a discretionary trust which would include the original beneficiary in the class of beneficiaries. The original beneficiary would be treated as making a lifetime chargeable transfer but so long as the transfer was limited to the nil-rate band, there would be no tax to pay. The beneficiary could benefit from the trust funds which would be outside their estate for inheritance tax purposes. To prevent this useful technique, a new s.102ZA was introduced into the Finance Act 1986. This provides that a person whose interest in possession in property is terminated on or after 22 March 2006 is to be regarded as making a gift of the property in which the interest was terminated. This means that the reservation of benefit rules can apply to property in which a person had an interest in possession which was terminated.

Settlements with no interest in possession which qualify for privileged treatment

Introduction

7-030 A number of pre-22 March 2006 settlements attract privileged inheritance tax treatment. We will only consider accumulation and maintenance settlements here. These are settlements which satisfy the requirements of IHTA 1984 s.71 as amended.

The purpose of accumulation and maintenance settlements was to enable a settlor to give property without any tax penalty to young people with conditions attached which prevent them having access to income and/or capital at too young an age. They are settlements without an interest in possession, but they are not subject to anniversary charges or exit charges. The creation of an accumulation and maintenance settlement by lifetime transfer before 22 March 2006 was a potentially exempt transfer.

The government formed the view that these settlements were being used to avoid inheritance tax and in 2006 changed the rules that apply to such settlements.

Settlements created on or after 22 March 2006 cannot qualify as accumulation and maintenance settlements. Transitional provisions were made for accumulation and maintenance settlements in existence on 22 March 2006.

If the terms on which the beneficiaries took the capital complied with the requirements of the new s.71A, the settlement was converted on 22 March 2006 to a bereaved minor trust (see para.7-038 and following).

Settlements which did not qualify as s.71A settlements were allowed to continue as accumulation and maintenance settlements until 6 April 2008. On that date the definition of an accumulation and maintenance settlement contained in IHTA 1984 s.71 changed. Settlements which did not meet the new definition became relevant property trusts, unless the terms on which the beneficiaries took the capital complied with the requirements of the new s.71D, in which case the settlement was converted to a s.71D settlement (see para.7-041 and following below).

Definition in IHTA 1984 s.71

The amended requirements of s.71 are as follows: **7-031**

(a) one or more persons will, on or before attaining a specified age not exceeding 18, become beneficially entitled to the settled property;
(b) no interest in possession subsists in the settled property;
(c) the income from the settled property is to be accumulated so far as not applied for the maintenance, education or benefit of a beneficiary (i.e. one of the persons who will become entitled under (a)); and
(d) *either:*
    (i) not more than 25 years have elapsed since the beginning of the settlement (or later time when it satisfied the three requirements above); *or*
    (ii) all of the beneficiaries had a common grandparent (or are the children, widows or widowers of the original beneficiaries who die before achieving the specified age).

Originally the age specified in condition (a) was 25 and it was sufficient for beneficiaries to take an interest in income; they did not need to become entitled to capital. The government felt that this was too generous and as from 6 April 2008 beneficiaries must become entitled to *capital* at or before *18*.

Relatively few settlements in existence on 22 March 2006 fulfilled the requirements of the amended sub-section (a). However, the benefits in retaining privileged status (no anniversary or exit charges) meant that a number of accumulation and maintenance settlements were amended to meet the requirements of the new s.71. Some trustees had powers which enabled them to amend the terms of the settlement and some trustees made applications to court under the Variation of Trusts Act 1958 to allow a variation of the terms of the trust. As a result practitioners will continue to meet accumulation and maintenance settlements for some years to come.

We will consider each of the requirements of the amended s.71 in turn. Some of them are relevant to settlements fulfilling the requirements of s.71A and s.71D as we will see later.

(a) Entitlement to the trust property at 18 or some lower specified age A settlement only satisfies this requirement if the beneficiaries *will* be entitled at 18 or some lower specified age. It is not sufficient that a beneficiary *may* be entitled at 18 or some lower specified age. Thus a settlement which gives "*capital and income at 18 or on earlier marriage*" satisfies the requirement since the beneficiary will get the property at 18 at the latest. A settlement which gives "*capital and income on* *marriage or at 18 whichever is the later*" does not satisfy the requirement. Strictly speaking it is impossible to have absolute certainty because death can always prevent a beneficiary becoming entitled. However, the -possibility of death intervening is ignored. The section is construed to mean "*will, if at all*".

The requirement is that "*one or more persons*" will be entitled at a specified age. The "*persons*" can include unborn persons. This is useful as it means an accumulation and maintenance settlement can have an open class of beneficiaries. However, s.71(7) provides that the condition is not satisfied "*unless there is or has been a living beneficiary*". Thus a settlement on "*the children of A at 18*" is not an accumulation and maintenance settlement if A was childless when the settlement was created. If the settlement was to the children of A and A had a child living at the time that the settlement was made, then the settlement would remain an accumulation and maintenance settlement even if that child subsequently died since there would then "*have been*" a living beneficiary.

The possibility that trust funds may go to someone who does not qualify as a beneficiary of the accumulation and maintenance trust is usually fatal to accumulation and maintenance status. Thus, settlements had to be drafted without powers of appointment which, if exercised, could result in entitlement being postponed beyond 18 or in property passing to non-qualifying beneficiaries.

Thus, the mere *existence* of a power of appointment which will enable trustees to pay capital or income to non-qualifying beneficiaries will cause loss of accumulation and maintenance status even if there is never any exercise of the power.

Example 12

Prior to 22 March 2006 A set up a trust for the benefit of her grandchildren contingent on them reaching 18 with power for the trustees to appoint capital or income to A's brother. The trust does not qualify for privileged status as there is no certainty that A's children will become entitled.

There would be no problem if the overriding power allowed the trustees to appoint capital or income amongst A's children as they saw fit while the children were under 18. The power does not infringe the s.71 requirement. It cannot be used to benefit anyone other than the class members and cannot postpone their entitlement.

To avoid the danger of trusts losing privileged status by oversight, accumulation and maintenance settlements often include a direction that no power shall be exercised in such a way as to prevent the trust qualifying as an accumulation and maintenance trust or to direct that appointments and advances shall not be made to any possible beneficiary who is above the age limit.

In *Lord Inglewood v IRC* (1983) it was accepted that the mere *existence* in a trust of a common form power of advancement did not compromise the privileged status of a trust even though it could be used to postpone the vesting of property in a beneficiary beyond the age limit (then 25). However, the *exercise* of such powers inappropriately might do so.

For the avoidance of doubt the Revenue confirmed (see "Payment of school fees out of an accumulation and maintenance trust" [1996] P.C.B. 76) that the payment by trustees of an accumulation and maintenance trust of trust funds direct to a school in payment of school fees will not compromise the privileged status of a trust.

(b) No interest in possession Once there is an interest in possession in settled property it ceases to be subject to the rules for an accumulation and maintenance settlement. However, where there is more than one beneficiary each part of the settled property must be considered separately.

Example 13

A settlement was created in 2003 for "*such of the children of Ann as reach 25*"; when the settlement was created Ann has been dead for some time and had left two children, Ben, aged 16, and Colin, aged 10. The whole of the settled property was an accumulation and maintenance settlement for two years. When Ben reached 18 in 2005, s.31 of the Trustee Act 1925 gave him a right to the income from half of the settlement. He obtained an interest in possession in half the settled property. The other half of the property remained an accumulation and maintenance settlement. If Ben dies before reaching 25, there will be tax to pay on his half share (since he has an interest in possession).

Note that on 22 March 2006 Ben's half of the fund was not an accumulation and maintenance settlement. He had already acquired an interest in possession. Colin's half was an accumulation and maintenance settlement. On 6 April 2008 the settlement did not fulfil the requirements of the new s.71 and so Colin's half of the fund was converted into a s.71D settlement (as to bereaved young person trusts, see para.7-041).

(c) Income to be accumulated so far as not applied for maintenance, etc. The income must be either accumulated or used for the maintenance, education or benefit *of the beneficiaries*.

This requirement will not be satisfied if the trustees are given power to apply the income for other purposes (such as maintenance of persons other than the beneficiaries).

(d) Common grandparent or less than 25 years since settlement became an accumulation and maintenance settlement This requirement is satisfied where all the beneficiaries are children of the same person or grandchildren of the same person. The common grandparent need not be the settlor. This requirement is also satisfied where the settlement provides for the replacement of beneficiaries who have a common grandparent but die before obtaining a vested right to capital by their own children, widows or widowers.

Example 14

A settlement "*to the children of Jay equally at 18 or, if any of them shall die before that age, such deceased child's share shall go to the children of such deceased child at 18*" will be an accumulation and maintenance settlement.

Where the settlement is on persons without a common grandparent it will retain its status as an accumulation and maintenance settlement for 25 years. Inheritance tax will become payable at the end of 25 years under s.71(3)(a). The rate at which tax is payable is dependent solely on the length of time the property has been in the settlement and is usually much higher than the rate for other settlements with or without an interest in possession. It is, therefore, important, where beneficiaries do not have a common grandparent, to ensure that all property vests in the beneficiaries within 25 years.

Capital gains tax and income tax

There are no special rules for capital gains tax and income tax in relation to accumulation and maintenance settlements save that hold-over relief may be avail- **7-032** able under s.260 of the Taxation of Chargeable Gains Act when a beneficiary becomes absolutely entitled to capital.

What of settlements which did not satisfy the requirements of the amended s.71?

7-033 Settlements which had not been converted into s.71A settlements on 6 April 2006 continued until 6 April 2008. They became relevant property settlements on that date if they did not satisfy the requirements of the amended s.71 (unless they qualified as s.71D settlements—see para.7-041). There was no charge to inheritance tax either on ending of the accumulation and maintenance settlement or on its conversion to a new form of settlement. The settlement simply changed its nature.

A settlement which converted to a relevant property settlement became liable to anniversary charges and exit charges. Anniversary charges are payable on each 10-year anniversary of the conversion of the original creation of the settlement (not its conversion to a relevant property settlement). There is a reduction in the tax charge for each quarter that the settlement was not a relevant property settlement.

Example 15

Sandip created an accumulation and maintenance settlement on 1 January 2000 with £400,000. There were no related settlements, and this was Sandip's first transfer (apart from transfers using up his annual exemptions).

The settlement became a relevant property settlement on 6 April 2008 because it did not satisfy the requirements of the new s.71 (or those of s.71A or s.71D).

The first 10-year charge arose on 1 January 2010 when the funds were worth £500,000 and the nil-rate band was £325,000.

Tax was calculated on £500,000 (using the method explained at para.7-017) with a reduction for the number of complete quarters that the property was not relevant property, that is the period 1 January 2000 to 6 April 2008 which is 33 quarters.

The value of the hypothetical chargeable transfer is £500,000. Sandip had a full nil-rate band available and the settlement has made no transfers so the tax payable on the hypothetical transfer is 0 per cent on the first £325,000 and 20 per cent on the remaining £175,000 giving £35,000.

The average rate of tax is

$$\frac{£35,000}{£500,000} \times 100 = 7\%$$

The settlement rate is 30 per cent of 7 per cent which is 2.1 per cent.

This is applied to the value of the settled property:

$$£500,000 \times 2.1\% = £10,500.$$

But this is reduced by 33/40 for the time the property was not relevant (pre-6 April 2008) so the tax payable is:

$$£10,500 - (33/40 \times £10,500) = £1,837.50$$

The tax charged on the first 10-year anniversary will in many cases, be -substantially less than a full charge.

6. Settlements Created on or after 22 March 2006 by Lifetime Chargeable Transfer

All lifetime settlements created on or after 22 March 2006 (with the exception of those for disabled beneficiaries—see para.7-045 and following) are treated in the same way. They are all subject to the relevant property regime described at paras 7-016–7-017. It is irrelevant whether or not there is an interest in possession or whether they are for young beneficiaries. **7-034**

Example 16

Sam creates the following settlements on 22 March 2006. They are all relevant property settlements. The initial transfer is a lifetime chargeable transfer by Sam and the settlements are subject to anniversary charges and exit charges.

(1) "*To myself for life, remainder to my children absolutely.*"
(2) "*To my wife for life, remainder to my children absolutely.*"
(3) "*To my son, Jeff, for life, remainder to his children absolutely.*"
(4) "*To my children contingent on reaching 25.*"
(5) "*To my children contingent on reaching 18.*"
(6) "*To my trustees on discretionary trusts for my children and grandchildren.*"

However, it does not follow that inheritance tax will actually be payable on the creation of a relevant property settlement. The initial transfer may be within the settlor's nil-rate band. The property transferred may attract 100 per cent agricultural or business property relief or be exempt as normal expenditure out of income.

Example 17

On 6 April 2020, a married couple, Harry and Wanda, each settle £331,000 on discretionary trusts for the benefit of their grandchildren. Neither has made any previous transfers so they each have a full nil-rate band available.

No inheritance tax is payable on the initial transfers because the first £6,000 is covered by two years' annual exemptions and the balance is within their nil-rate bands.

No inheritance tax will be payable on exits in the first 10 years because the rate will be 0 per cent. No anniversary charge will be payable unless the value of the property has increased beyond the nil-rate threshold.

In addition they could transfer any property that they had which was eligible for 100 per cent relief.

After seven years the transfers will fall out of the cumulative totals for Harry and Wanda and, should they so wish, they can make further transfers.

After creation, all relevant property settlements will be subject to anniversary and exit charges as explained at paras 7-016–7-017.

7. SETTLEMENTS CREATED ON OR AFTER 22 MARCH 2006 ON DEATH

Settlements not subject to the relevant property regime

The main types

7-035 Many settlements created on death will be subject to the relevant property regime. However, on death it is possible to create four types of settlement which will not be subject to the relevant property regime. These are:

(a) immediate post-death interests (IHTA 1984 s.49A);
(b) trusts for bereaved minors (IHTA 1984 s.71A);
(c) trusts for bereaved young people (IHTA 1984 s.71D);
(d) trusts for the disabled escape the relevant property regime and can be created on death. However, these trusts can also be created by lifetime transfer so they are dealt with separately at para.7-045.

A "pecking" order

7-036 There is a possibility of overlap between immediate post-death interests and trusts for bereaved minors and bereaved young persons. If a settlement fulfils the conditions for a bereaved minor's trust and an immediate post-death interest, it is a bereaved minor's trust. If it fulfils the requirements for a bereaved young person's trust and an immediate post death interest, it is an immediate post-death interest: see IHTA 1984, s.49A and s.71D(5).

Immediate post-death interests

7-037 To qualify as an immediate post-death interest a person must become beneficially entitled to an interest in possession in created on death and must continue to have such an interest at all times since the death (IHTA 1984 s.49A). Provided the interest in possession takes effect immediately on death, it is irrelevant that trustees have power to terminate it. If the interest does come to an end at any point, for example as a result of the trustees exercising a right to appoint the property elsewhere, then the immediate post-death interest ceases. It cannot restart even if the original beneficiary reacquires the interest in possession.

A survivorship clause is ignored provided it does not exceed six months. The dispositions actually taking effect are treated as if they had had effect from the beginning of the period. An immediate post-death interest can arise as a result of a post-death variation under IHTA 1984 s.142 or of an appointment from a will trust within two years of death under IHTA 1984 s.144 because in both cases the interest will be treated as arising on death as a result of the reading back effect of the two sections (see Ch.12).

A person with an immediate post-death interest is treated as if beneficially entitled to the underlying trust property (as explained in relation to pre-22 March 2006 settlements with a qualifying interest in possession at para.7-011 and following). There are no anniversary or exit charges. Instead the property is aggregated with the beneficiary's own estate on death. If the interest comes to an end before death, the beneficiary will be treated as making a lifetime transfer of value. The type of transfer depends on whether the property passes to someone absolutely entitled in which case there is a potentially exempt transfer (to the extent that the transfer is not exempt) or whether the property passes on trust in which case there is a lifetime chargeable transfer.

Example 18

(1) By will Terri leaves property to Lara for life, remainder to Raj absolutely. When Lara dies, the trust property is aggregated with her free estate in order to calculate the inheritance tax payable on her death.
(2) By will Terri leaves property to Lucy for life, remainder to Rohan absolutely. If Lucy surrenders her lifetime interest, the trust property will pass to Rohan absolutely. Lucy will make a potentially exempt transfer. If, however, she was married to Rohan, the transfer would be exempt.
(3) By will Terri leaves property to Larry for life, remainder to Linda for life, remainder to Rocco. If Larry surrenders his life interest and Linda's life interest takes effect, he will make a lifetime chargeable transfer, not a potentially exempt transfer, because the transfer is on continuing trusts.

Trusts for bereaved minors

What is a trust for a bereaved minor?

A trust for a bereaved minor is one which satisfies the conditions set out in IHTA 1984 s.71A. **7-038**

(1) The trust must be created by will or on intestacy or established under the Criminal Injuries Compensation Scheme or the Victims of Overseas Terrorism Compensation Scheme for the deceased's own child (the bereaved minor).
(2) The bereaved minor must on or before attaining 18 become entitled to the settled property, any income arising from it and any income that has already arisen and been accumulated.
(3) While the bereaved minor is living and under 18:
    (a) any capital applied must be applied for the benefit of the minor, and
    (b) the bereaved minor must be entitled to all the income arising from the settled property or no such income may be applied for any other person.

(Condition 1 does not have to be satisfied in the case of an accumulation and maintenance settlement converted on 22 March 2006.)

Unlike an immediate post-death interest, it is not necessary for the property to be held on bereaved minor trusts immediately on death. There can be a preceding immediate post-death interest, relevant property trust or bereaved young person's trust.

Where a settlement satisfies the s.71A requirements, there are no anniversary charges and s.71B(2) provides that there is no exit charge when:

(a) the bereaved minor becomes entitled to capital at 18 (or earlier);
(b) the bereaved minor dies before becoming entitled to capital; or
(c) capital is advanced to the bereaved minor.

Example 19

Mandy, who is divorced, dies intestate on 30 April 2010 leaving three children aged four, three and two. Her estate is £900,000. Under the terms of the statutory trusts applying on intestacy the children become entitled to the capital at 18 (or earlier marriage or formation of a civil partnership). If they all die before obtaining vested interests, the property held on the statutory trusts will pass to Mandy's father.

(1) There will be no anniversary charge on 30 April 2020.
(2) There will be no exit charge as and when each beneficiary reaches 18 and becomes entitled to a share of the capital.
(3) There will be no exit charge if capital is advanced to a child before 18.
(4) If all the children die before 18 and the property passes to Mandy's father, there will be no exit charge.

Points on s.71A

7-039 The power to advance capital under s.32 of the Trustee Act 1925 allows trustees to advance capital for the "*benefit*" of a beneficiary. "*Benefit*" is a wide word and could include settling capital for the beneficiary and close family members. This would seem to conflict with the requirement that capital must be applied for the bereaved minor. However, s.71A(4) makes specific provision for this problem. It provides that a settlement can still satisfy the capital condition if s.32 applies. In the case of trusts created or arising before 1 October 2014 the statutory power of advancement is limited to one-half of a vested or presumptive entitlement and it was normal for settlements to remove that restriction. Section 71A(4)provides that the capital condition is satisfied if there is an express clause widening the statutory power to allow up to the whole of the beneficiary's interest to be advanced.

This means that if the trustees are unhappy at the prospect of a beneficiary becoming entitled to capital at 18, they can use their power of advancement to settle the beneficiary's share on continuing trusts. There will be no exit charge, but the property will then be held on relevant property trusts so thereafter there will be anniversary and exit charges.

Finance Act 2013 amended s.71A to provide that a settlement can satisfy the requirements of s.71A even though the trustees' have powers that enable them to apply limited sums otherwise than for the benefit of the bereaved minor. The sums must not exceed an annual limit (whether consisting of income or capital, or both). The current annual limit is the lesser of £3,000 and three per cent of the maximum value of the trust fund during the relevant year. The change was introduced as part of a harmonisation of provisions applying to trusts for "*vulnerable beneficiaries*", that is settlements created for bereaved young people and disabled beneficiaries.

As was the case for accumulation and maintenance settlements (see para.7-031) the word "*will*" does not require absolute certainty. Death can prevent the beneficiary taking an interest. The word should be read as meaning "*will, if at all*".

Notice that these trusts are very restricted. A grandparent cannot create a s.71A trust for a grandchild. A parent may leave property to their children contingent on reaching 18 with a substitutional gift to a grandchild if a child predeceases; the trust for the children will fulfil the requirements of s.71A but if a grandchild is substituted that part of the settlement will be subject to the relevant property regime.

Example 20

Trevor dies in 2024 with an estate of £600,000 which he leaves on trust for his three children, Ann, Ben and Clare contingent on reaching 18 with a substitutional gift to children of a child who predeceases also contingent on reaching 18.

On Trevor's death Ann is 24, Ben died, aged 22, but has left a child, Brady who is aged two, and Clare is 17.

Ann has a vested interest and is immediately entitled to her share. Clare's interest fulfils the requirements of s.71A; the portion held for Brady is subject to the relevant property regime.

Oddly, IHTA 1984 s.71A provides that where the trusts arise *on intestacy*, a substituted grandchild will be a beneficiary of a trust for a bereaved minor. Had Trevor died intestate in the above example, Brady would have been a beneficiary of a trust for a bereaved minor.

Section 71A is drafted by reference to a single beneficiary called the bereaved minor suggesting that each bereaved minor must become entitled to their own "share" of the trust capital. If this was the correct interpretation, it would be fatal to the status of the settlement for the trustees to have a power to alter the shares of individual beneficiaries to give one more than the other. However, *HMRC issued guidance in June 2007 (HMRC guidance on ss 71A, 71D and accumulation and maintenance trusts 20 June 2007* available on the websites of the Society for Trusts and Estates Practitioners and Chartered Institute of Taxation) which said that this was not the correct interpretation. It is possible to include a power for trustees to appoint capital in unequal shares or even all to one at the expense of another.

Example 21

Fred died and left £400,000 to trustees to hold for his three children contingent on reaching 18 but with a power for the trustees to appoint capital to the children in such proportions as they see fit, equally in default of appointment. The trustees decide to appoint £300,000 to the youngest child and the rest equally to the two older children. Despite the power to vary the shares of the beneficiaries this settlement fulfils the requirements of s.71A.

According to HMRC guidance the power must not permit the trustees to vary the share of a child who has *already* reached 18. HMRC also takes the view that once a child has been excluded from benefit, even revocably, the power cannot afterwards be used to benefit the excluded child. In HMRC's view it is not possible under the s.71A regime for someone who is not currently benefiting to become entitled in the future. Trustees should therefore consider carefully before excluding a child from benefit or making a revocable appointment of all the trust funds to one child. The mere possibility of trustees exercising the power in this way will not affect the status of the settlement.

To prevent problems the power of appointment should be limited in the following way:

> "PROVIDED that no such appointment shall be made and no such appointment shall be revoked so as to either diminish or to increase the share (or the accumulations of income forming part of the share) of or give a new share (or new accumulations of income) to a child who at the date of such appointment or revocation has reached the age of 18 nor to benefit a child who has been excluded from benefit as a result of the exercise of the power."

Capital gains tax and income tax and s.71A trusts

Note there is no special treatment for capital gains tax or income tax except that when a beneficiary becomes absolutely entitled as against the trustees, hold-over relief is available under TCGA 1992 s.260. **7-040**

Trusts for bereaved young people

What is a trust for a bereaved young person?

7-041 Many people regard an age of 18 as too young for entitlement to capital. As a result of public criticism of the very restricted trusts afforded privileged treatment for inheritance tax in the Finance Bill 2006, the government amended it at a late stage and introduced a new s.71D into the 1984 Act. This allows entitlement to capital to be deferred beyond the age of 18 while still offering some inheritance tax privileges. However, the privileges are more restricted than those available to a trust for a bereaved minor.

The following conditions set out in s.71D must be satisfied:

(1) The trust must be created by will or established under the Criminal Injuries Compensation Scheme or the Victims of Overseas Terrorism Compensation Scheme for the deceased's own child (B).
(2) B must at or before 25 become entitled to the settled property, any income arising from it and any income that has already arisen and been accumulated.
(3) While B is living and under 25:
    (a) any capital applied must be applied for the benefit of B; and
    (b) B must be entitled to all the income arising from the settled property or no such income may be applied for any other person.

(Condition 1 does not have to be satisfied in the case of an accumulation and maintenance settlement converted on 6 April 2008.)

Unlike an immediate post-death interest, it is not necessary for the property to be held on bereaved young person trusts immediately on death. There can be a preceding immediate post-death interest, relevant property trust or bereaved minor's trust.

As was the case with trusts for a bereaved minor a settlement can still satisfy the capital condition if s.32 applies or if the settlement widens the statutory power to allow up to the whole of the beneficiary's interest to be advanced. It can also satisfy the requirements if the trustees have power to apply income sums within the annual limit. See para.7-039.

Where a settlement satisfies the s.71D requirements, there are no anniversary charges and s.71E(2) provides that there is no exit charge when:

(a) a beneficiary becomes entitled to capital at 18 (or earlier);
(b) a beneficiary dies before becoming entitled to capital; or
(c) capital is advanced to a beneficiary before 18.

If the capital remains settled after the age of 18 there will be an exit charge on any of the above events, but it will only be calculated for the period from 18 to the exit.

Example 22

Adele dies after 21 March 2006 and leaves property on trust for her two children contingent on reaching 25. If the trustees appoint the capital to the children at or before 18, there will be no charge to inheritance tax. If the trustees appoint capital to the first child at 21 there will be a charge for the period 18–21 and if they appoint to the second child at age 25, there will be a charge for the period 18–25.

The calculation of the exit charge is similar to the calculation of an exit charge in the first 10 years of a relevant property settlement. However, it is based on the value of the property originally settled not on the value of the property at the time the beneficiary becomes entitled to capital (s.71F(9)). Hence the charge may be calculated on the basis of a value which differs substantially from the value of the property at the date of the exit.

Example 23

Assume that Adele in the previous example died on 9 July 2015 and that the property she left to her two children contingent on reaching 25 was worth £400,000. Her first child reached 18 on 12 May 2017. The trustees decided to allow the trust to continue but on 19 August 2021 they appoint that child his share of capital (now worth £300,000).

The settlement rate is calculated on the basis of the property originally settled (£400,000). Assume that the nil-rate band remains £325,000. Tax is calculated at 20 per cent on the balance above the nil-rate band and 30 per cent of the resulting rate will be applied to the appointment of capital.

Assumed chargeable transfer = £400,000 – £325,000 = £75,000

Tax on £75,000 × 20% = £15,000

Settlement rate = £15,000/£400,000 × 100 × 30% = 1.125%

However, there is a reduction because tax is only chargeable for the number of complete quarters in the period from the day that the beneficiary attained 18 and ending with the day before the chargeable event (from 12 May 2017 to 18 August 2021). In this example the number of complete quarters is 17, so the amount of tax under s.71F(3) is:

£3,375 × 17/40 = £1,434.37

Points on s.71D

As was the case for accumulation and maintenance settlements the word "*will*" does not require absolute certainty. Death can prevent the beneficiary taking an interest. The word should be read as meaning "*will, if at all*". 7-042

Settlements satisfying the s.71D requirements can only be created by parents. The existence of a substitutional gift to issue of the testator's predeceased child will not prevent the settlement qualifying as a s.71D trust. However, if the substitution takes effect, the substituted beneficiary will be a beneficiary of a relevant property trust not a s.71D trust.

Section 71D is drafted by reference to a single beneficiary referred to as "B". However, HMRC guidance issued in July 2007 (referred to at para.7-039) takes the same approach in relation to s.71D settlements as to s.71A settlements. Trustees can have a power to appoint capital unequally amongst the beneficiaries without affecting the status of the settlement. As with s.71A settlements the power must not be exercisable in favour of a child who has reached 25 and the trustees must not make an appointment to a beneficiary who has been excluded.

Most people making wills who want to benefit their children without paying continuing inheritance tax charges will probably choose a s.71D settlement in preference to a s.71A one. The trustees of a s.71D settlement are free to advance the trust funds to the beneficiaries at 18 if they choose. This will mean no charges to inheritance tax. If, however, the beneficiary is too immature to deal with the funds at 18, the trustees can allow the settlement to continue until 25. There will be an exit charge at that point.

If the trustees are still doubtful as to the maturity of the beneficiary they could apply any power of advancement they may have to settle the trust funds on discretionary trusts for the benefit of the beneficiary. The same exit charge will be payable as if the property went to the beneficiary absolutely. There will be subsequent anniversary charges and an exit charge, but this may be worthwhile if the beneficiary cannot be trusted to deal sensibly with the funds.

Capital gains tax and income tax and s.71D trusts

7-043 Note there is no special treatment for capital gains tax or income tax except that when a beneficiary becomes absolutely entitled as against the trustees, hold-over relief is available under TCGA 1992 s.260.

Accumulation and maintenance settlements converted into s.71D trusts

7-044 Accumulation and maintenance settlements which did not fulfil the requirements of the amended s.71 of IHTA 1984 (see para.7-030) on 6 April 2008 will normally be converted into a relevant property settlement. However, they can qualify as s.71D trusts despite the fact that they may have been created by lifetime transfer and may not be for the settlor's own children: see IHTA 1984 s.71D(3) and (4). The beneficiaries must become entitled to capital at or before 25.

HMRC takes the view that in order to fulfil the requirements of s.71D the class of beneficiaries must be closed (see Guidance issued in June 2007). This is because in the case of an ordinary s.71D trust created for the deceased's own children, the class must, by definition, be closed. So if, for example, an existing accumulation and maintenance settlement in favour of the settlor's grandchildren provides that the class closes only when the eldest becomes 25 and the trust currently benefits only two existing grandchildren, aged eight and nine, in order to qualify as a s.71D settlement, the terms of the trust had to be amended to exclude any future born beneficiaries.

8. SETTLEMENTS FOR THE DISABLED

7-045 Settlements for a disabled beneficiary present a problem. Those creating such settlements will often want them to be discretionary in form so as not to prejudice means-tested benefits. However, a discretionary settlement is subject to the relevant property regime under which 10-year anniversary and exit charges would erode the value of the settled funds.

The legislative solution is to allow the creation of a special form of settlement which deems the disabled person to have a qualifying interest in possession. The effect is that there are no anniversary or exit charges but any funds remaining on the death of the disabled person will be treated as part of their estate for inheritance tax purposes. Such settlements can be created by lifetime transfer or on death. The creation of a settlement for a disabled beneficiary by lifetime transfer will be a potentially exempt transfer in so far as not exempt.

"*Disabled person*" for this purpose has the meaning given by Sch.1A to the Finance Act 2005 which is a person who by reason of mental disorder within the meaning of the Mental Health Act 1983 is incapable of administering his or her property or managing his or her affairs or a person who is in receipt of one of the following allowances:

(a) attendance allowance;

(b) disability living allowance by virtue of entitlement to the care component at the highest or middle rate;
(c) personal independence payment by virtue of entitlement to the daily living component;
(d) an increased disablement pension;
(e) constant attendance allowance; or
(f) a person in receipt of armed forces independence payment.

This definition applies for transfers into settlement on or after 8 April 2013. For transfers before that date the definition was slightly different.

There are four types of disabled person's interest. The original is contained in IHTA 1984 s.89 and is the most common. The definition was changed by Finance Act 2013 for property transferred into settlement on or after 8 April 2013. Transitional provisions preserve the status of settlements created before the change.

As from 8 April 2013 s.89(1) required that the property is held on trusts:

(a) under which, during the life of a disabled person, no interest in possession in the settled property subsists; and
(b) which secure that, if any of the settled property or income arising from it is applied during the disabled person's life for the benefit of a beneficiary, it is applied for the benefit of the disabled person.

Note that it is not necessary for the disabled person to receive anything, whether income or capital, but if either or both is applied then it must be used for the benefit of the disabled person during their lifetime.

Section 89(3) provides that the trusts on which the settled property is held are not to be treated as falling outside s.89(1) by reason only of the trustees having the statutory power to advance capital or a widened express power. The trustees can also have power to apply income and/or capital up to the "annual limit" to persons other than the disabled person without affecting the status of the settlement. The annual limit is the lesser of £3,000 and three per cent of the maximum value of the trust fund during the relevant year. The provision would, for example, allow a payment from the trust fund of holiday expenses for those caring for the disabled person without the trustees having to establish that the payment was for the benefit of the disabled person (although such a payment almost certainly is). The terms of the settlement have to authorise limited payments to others.

The 2006 changes in the inheritance tax treatment of settlements introduced three further types of disabled trust: (1) a trust under which the disabled person has an interest in possession; (2) a self-settlement by a person with a condition expected to lead to disability which meets the requirements of s.89A -(essentially the same as s.89); (3) a self-settlement again by a person with a condition expected to lead to disability under which he has an interest in possession.

These 2006 extensions benefit from the same inheritance tax treatment as s.89 trusts; i.e. the disabled person is treated as the beneficial owner of the settled property.

Example 24

(1) Karim has a condition likely to lead to disability. He establishes a trust for himself in accordance with the provisions of s.89A. He is treated as having an interest in possession with the result that the creation of the settlement is not a transfer of value (i.e. his estate does not fall in value).
(2) Moira sets up a s.89 disabled trust for her civil partner Mona. Because Mona

is treated as the inheritance tax owner of the settled property, the gift by Moira is spouse exempt under s.18.

The 2013 changes harmonised the rules for the different taxes with the same definition of disabled person and the same conditions for the settlement to qualify for special treatment. In essence:

(a) the full capital gains tax annual exemption applies to the settlement (and not the usual 50 per cent)—see para.7-050;
(b) relief is given in the taxation of the income by limiting the tax to what it would be if the income was the beneficiary's (the beneficiary's rate of tax instead of the 45 per cent trust rate normally payable when trustees have discretionary powers over income—see para.7-060 and
(c) similarly, the capital gains tax charge on trust disposals will be calculated as if the disposal was by the beneficiary.

In order for the special income and capital gains tax treatment set out above to apply, an election, called a "vulnerable person's election" must be made by the trustees and the beneficiary.

There used to be a capital gains tax disadvantage to trusts for the disabled. On death there was no revaluing of the trust assets for capital gains tax as is normally the case when a beneficiary with a qualifying interest in possession dies (see para.7-053). Finance Act 2014 amended TCGA 1992 s.72 to allow for revaluation on death with effect in relation to deaths occurring on or after 5 December 2013.

9. Capital Gains Tax and Settlements

7-046 The basic structure of capital gains tax was explained in Ch.5. In this section we will consider the possible liability to capital gains tax, in relation to disposals of trust assets or interests in a trust, of:

(a) the settlor;
(b) the trustees; and
(c) the beneficiaries.

The capital gains tax legislation draws distinctions between settlements which are UK resident and those which are non-resident. Residence depends on the residence of the trustees. In this book, we will only consider the rules applicable to the former.

"Settled property" is defined, by Taxation of Chargeable Gains Act (TCGA) 1992 s.68, as any property held on trust other than property to which s.60, applies. A trust may be created without formal language so long as the intention is clear: see *Wagstaff v RCC* (2014).

The property excluded from the definition of settled property by s.60 is property held by a person:

(a) as nominee for another person;
(b) as trustee for another person absolutely entitled as against the trustee. Such a bare trust often arises where property has been held on trust for a life tenant who has recently died and the trustees are holding the property while arranging to vest it in the remainderman. Another example of such a bare trust is where the trustees are preparing to transfer the assets to a beneficiary who has satisfied a contingency. The test for deciding whether a person is absolutely entitled as against the trustees is whether they have the exclusive

right (subject only to paying the expenses of the trust) to direct how those assets shall be dealt with (TCGA 1992 s.60(2)). The beneficiary must, therefore, have the right to demand that the assets be handed over to them; or

(c) as a trustee for any person who would be so entitled but for being a minor or other person under disability. Thus, where land has been left to a minor, since a minor cannot hold a legal estate in land, trustees will have to hold the property until the minor reaches 18. If they must satisfy a contingency (such as reaching 18) before they can become absolutely entitled to the property, the exception does not apply (*Tomlinson v Glyn's Executor and Trustee Co* (1970)).

Where the "trust" falls within one of the s.60(1) exceptions, the Taxation of Chargeable Gains Act applies as if the property were vested in the beneficiary and any acts of the nominee or trustee are treated as acts of the beneficiary. Thus, for example, when the trustees transfer assets to the remainderman after the death of the life tenant, no capital gains tax liability can arise.

Property held by two or more persons as joint tenants or tenants in common is not "settled property" provided they are together absolutely entitled to the property.

In 2010/11 trustees of settlements, like individuals, paid capital gains tax at a flat rate of 18 per cent on disposals before 22 June 2010. Disposals on or after that date and before 6 April 2016 by trustees are all taxed at a flat rate of 28 per cent irrespective of the level of trust income. Disposals by trustees on or after 6 April 2016 are all taxed at 20 per cent apart from disposals of residential property and carried interest which are taxed at 28 per cent. The 28 per cent rate on residential land was reduced to 24 per cent from 6 April 2024.

10. CAPITAL GAINS TAX—THE LIABILITY OF THE SETTLOR

Creating a settlement by lifetime transfer

If the settlor transfers assets to trustees (whatever the terms of the settlement), this is a disposal. The gain or loss will be calculated in the normal way by deducting from the market value of the assets at the time of disposal the deductions permitted by TCGA 1992 (see para.5-008). The trustees will in turn acquire the assets at market value at the date of the disposal unless hold-over relief is claimed. **7-047**

Should the disposal give rise to a loss, that loss can only be set against gains made by the settlor on other transfers to trustees of the same settlement since settlors and their trustees are "connected persons" (TCGA 1992 ss.18(3) and 286).

The potential liability to capital gains tax can arise even if the settlor has an interest as a beneficiary or is a trustee, or the sole trustee, of the settlement (TCGA 1992 s.70).

In certain cases hold-over relief may be claimed on the creation of a settlement so that no immediate charge to capital gains tax arises. Hold-over relief is available under TCGA 1992 s.165 where the assets put into settlement are business assets. Hold-over relief is also available under TCGA 1992 s.260, regardless of the nature of the assets which are settled, where the creation of the settlement is a chargeable transfer for inheritance tax purposes. Since 22 March 2006 all lifetime transfers to settlements will be chargeable transfers unless to a trust for the disabled. Where hold-over relief is available on the creation of a settlement, it is the settlor alone who makes the election for relief; the trustees of the settlement are not required to agree.

Section 169B provides that hold-over relief is not available under either TCGA 1992 s.165 or s.260 if the settlement is settlor interested. Section 169F of TCGA 1992 sets out the situations in which a settlor will be regarded as having an interest for this purpose.

A settlor has an interest if settled property could be paid or applied to the settlor or their spouse or civil partner or for their dependent child or if any of them derive a benefit directly or indirectly from the property. A dependent child is one who is under the age of 18 and is unmarried and without a civil partner. "Child" includes stepchild for this purpose. If a settlement becomes settlor interested within six years of the end of the tax year in which the disposal was made, any hold-over relief is lost and capital gains tax becomes payable (TCGA 1992 s.169C). Where a settlor wants to claim hold-over relief, it is advisable to exclude children and stepchildren during their minority. Even if the settlor has none at the time of creation, there is a risk of acquiring an unexpected child or step-child which would lead to clawback of the relief.

Creating the settlement on death

7-048 If the settlement is created on death there will be no disposal and so no capital gains tax liability will arise. The deceased settlor's personal representatives will acquire the assets at their market value at death. This will also be the acquisition value for the trustees.

11. Capital Gains Tax—The Liability of the Trustees

Changes in trustees

7-049 During the "life" of the settlement the persons holding office as trustees may change, whether by reason of death, retirement or removal. Whenever a new trustee is appointed the assets will have to be transferred to the newly constituted body of trustees. Section 69(1) of TCGA 1992 provides that settlement trustees are a continuing body of persons and disposals to the new trustees do not give rise to capital gains tax liability.

Actual disposals

7-050 The trustees may wish to dispose of items of trust property and replace them with new items. They may wish to sell assets to raise cash, whether to meet expenses or to be able to make a cash advance to a beneficiary. Whatever the reason for the disposal, if the trustees make an actual disposal of trust property they may become liable to capital gains tax.

Whether a gain or loss arises will be determined in the usual way. The trustees can set the exemptions and reliefs they are entitled to claim against any -chargeable gains realised. The exemptions and reliefs to which they are entitled include:

(a) The annual exemption which is normally half the exempt amount available to an individual (so that trustees in tax year 2024/25 get £1,500). However, if the settlement is one of a number created by the same settlor the annual exemption is divided equally amongst the settlements subject to a minimum exemption per settlement of one-tenth of the annual exemption, so £300 for tax year 2024/25. Hence if a taxpayer created 12 settlements, each would have an annual exemption of £300. Trustees of a disabled person's trust have a full annual exemption. See para.7-045.

(b) The principal private dwelling house exemption given in TCGA 1992 ss.222 and 223, provided the house disposed of has been the only or main residence of a person entitled to occupy it under the terms of the settlement (TCGA 1992 s.225). The exemption will apply, whether the beneficiary has an interest in possession or has been permitted to occupy by the trustees exercising their powers under the trust instrument (*Sansom v Peay (Inspector of Taxes)* (1976)). A trust for the purpose of occupation may be created without formal language so long as the intention is clear: see *Wagstaff v RCC* (2014).

Note that principal private dwelling house exemption is not available for disposals on or after 10 December 2003 if the gain includes a gain that was held over on one or more previous disposals. The relief will continue to apply to that part of the gain referable to the period before 10 December 2003: see s.226A of TCGA 1992. This is an anti-avoidance provision designed to prevent taxpayers transferring second homes to a trust for the benefit of their children, allowing one child to occupy it as their principal private dwelling house and then selling and claiming principal private dwelling house relief.

If a disposal gives rise to a loss, the trustees may set that loss against any gains they have made in the year of disposal and may carry forward unabsorbed losses to set against gains made in future years.

Deemed disposals

Persons becoming absolutely entitled as against the trustees

Where a person becomes absolutely entitled to trust property as against the trustees, TCGA 1992 s.71(1) provides that **7-051**

> "all assets forming part of the settled property to which he becomes so entitled shall be deemed to have been disposed of by the trustee, and immediately reacquired by him in his capacity as a trustee within section 60(1) ..., for a consideration equal to their market value".

Any capital gains tax payable is assessed at this point and thereafter the trustee holds as a bare trustee. Section 71(1) of TCGA 1992 applies where:

(a) the trustees advance assets to a beneficiary (where they are a life tenant or a discretionary beneficiary);
(b) a beneficiary satisfies a contingency and so becomes entitled to all or part of the trust property; or
(c) the settlement comes to an end as a result of the death of a person with an interest in possession and the remainderman becomes absolutely entitled to the property. (However, no tax is payable in this circumstance: see para.7-053.)

The deemed disposal and reacquisition takes place as soon as the beneficiary becomes absolutely entitled as against the trustees, even though the assets may not be transferred for some time afterwards. Thus, if a person is entitled to property provided they reached the age of 25, on their 25th birthday the trustees are deemed to dispose of the assets as settlement trustees and immediately to reacquire them as bare trustees for the beneficiary. Capital gains tax will be payable if a gain has arisen after taking account of exemptions, reliefs and allowances but there is no further liability when the assets are subsequently vested in the beneficiary.

There are cases where the date of the deemed disposal is unclear. In *Figg v Clarke (I.O.T.)* (1997) there was a trust for the children of X who reached 21. In 1964 X had been paralysed from the chest down and was, consequently, incapable of fathering any more children. It was argued that the class closed at that point creating a deemed disposal, rather than on X's death. The court held that this was not so and that the class remained open until X's death. It would be unworkable to have to enquire into the exact date on which a person became incapable of fathering children.

Where property is left contingently to several beneficiaries, beneficiaries who attain a vested interest will not be absolutely entitled as against the trustees unless they are able to call for distribution. They may not be able to do so until the interests of all the beneficiaries have vested. This is because beneficiaries with an entitlement to a share of a trust fund cannot insist on receiving their shares if the effect of distribution would be to damage the interests of other beneficiaries whose interests have not yet vested. Nor can they insist on receiving their shares if the trustees have an express power of appropriation unless the trustees make an appropriation. Until this power is exercised, the beneficiary cannot claim any specific asset and therefore it cannot be said that they are absolutely entitled to a fractional share of everything.

If the settled property is land in England or Wales, the decision of Goff J in *Crowe v Appleby* (1975) suggests that there is no occasion of absolute entitlement until the final contingency is fulfilled. The land as a whole remains settled property, and any actual disposal of it is a disposal entirely by the trustees. The beneficiary has no right to call upon the trustees to transfer a divided share of the land or to create a tenancy in common.

Reliefs

7-052 Hold-over relief is available under TCGA 1992 s.260 where a beneficiary becomes absolutely entitled as against the trustees in the following cases:

(1) There is a transfer chargeable to inheritance tax. This will be the case where a beneficiary of a relevant property settlement becomes absolutely entitled.
(2) A beneficiary of an accumulation and maintenance trust or a s.71A or s.71D trust becomes absolutely entitled.

Hold-over relief is claimed by a joint election of trustees and beneficiary.

Business assets' disposal relief is available to trustees in limited circumstances. TGCA 1992 s.169J provides that there must be a "*qualifying beneficiary*" and the trustees must dispose of "*settlement business assets*".

A qualifying beneficiary is one with an interest in possession in the whole of the settled property, or the part of it which includes the "settlement business assets" being disposed of. Relief is not available if the interest in possession is for a fixed term.

"*Settlement business assets*" are:

(a) company shares; or
(b) assets (other than investment assets) used or previously used for the purposes of a business, which are part of the settled property.

Where the disposal is of shares the company must be a trading company and the qualifying beneficiary's "personal company" (as defined in s.169S). In addition the qualifying beneficiary must be an officer or employee of the company.

Where the disposal is of assets, they must have been used for a period of at least two years ending not earlier than three years before the disposal and the qualifying beneficiary must cease to carry on the business on the date of the disposal or within the period of three years before that date.

In the case of a trust holding shares the Court of Appeal in *Quentin Skinner 2015 Settlement L v Revenue and Customs Commissioners* (2022) overruled the Upper Tribunal, holding that it is not necessary for the individual to have had the interest in possession for any minimum period, but only that the interest should exist at the time of the disposal.

The lifetime limits which apply to individuals also apply to trustees: see para.5-016.

Death of person with qualifying interest in possession where settlement ends

Where a beneficiary with a qualifying interest in possession who is treated as owning the underlying trust capital (for example because the interest is an immediate post-death interest or an interest in existence on 22 March 2006) dies and, on their death, the remainderman becomes absolutely entitled to the settled property, there is a deemed disposal and reacquisition but no chargeable gain arises (see TCGA 1992 s.73(1)(a)). This is in accordance with the general principle that death does not give rise to capital gains tax. It means that if the assets have increased in value since the date the trustees acquired them, the remainderman has the benefit of a tax-free uplift in their base value. For deaths occurring on or after 5 December 2013 the rule applies on the death of a person with a disabled person's interest (TCGA 1992 s.72(1B)). **7-053**

If the disposal gives rise to a loss, TCGA 1992 s.71(2) provides that such a loss is first available to the trustees to set off against capital gains realised by the settlement in that tax year. If they cannot utilise the loss it is treated as accruing to the beneficiary. However, the loss is not generally available for set off against gains of the beneficiary. Instead, it is ring-fenced and can only be set against gains arising on the subsequent disposal of the asset.

Where a claim for hold-over relief was made on the transfer of assets to the settlement, the gain held over on the acquisition becomes chargeable on the death of the beneficiary with a qualifying interest in possession.

Example 25

In 2012 Saleema settled assets worth £100,000 for her daughter for life, remainder to her grandson absolutely. She elected to hold over gains of £30,000. When her daughter dies there is no capital gains tax charge on the increase in value since creation of the settlement but the held-over gain of £30,000 is chargeable.

Death of person with qualifying interest in possession where the settlement continues

Where a beneficiary with an interest in possession who is treated as owning the underlying trust capital (for example because the interest is an immediate post-death interest or an interest in existence on 22 March 2006) dies and on their death, the settlement continues, there is a deemed disposal and reacquisition at market value of the assets but no chargeable gain accrues on the disposal (subject to tax becoming payable on gains held-over when assets were transferred to the trustees): see s.72(1) of TCGA 1992. **7-054**

Thus, if property is held on trust for persons in succession, for example "*to A for life, remainder to B for life, remainder to C absolutely*" and A's interest is an immediate post-death interest, on A's death there is a deemed disposal and reacquisition. However, no tax is payable on accrued gains unless gains were held-over when the trustees were originally given the assets. The trustees acquire the assets as trustees for B at the market value at the date of A's death. During B's lifetime, the settlement will be a relevant property settlement unless B is A's spouse or civil partner and acquires a transitional serial interest (see para.7-014).

Death of a beneficiary of a relevant property settlement

7-055 Where a beneficiary of a relevant property settlement dies, there are no capital gains tax implications unless a beneficiary becomes absolutely entitled as a result of the death.

Example 26

Cassandra transfers assets to a lifetime settlement in 2019. The trustees are to hold the trust assets for Lamia for life and then for Roxanne. Lamia's death will not give rise to a deemed disposal and reacquisition because she is not treated as owning the underlying trust assets.

If, following Lamia's death, the property is held for Roxanne for life, her death will have no capital gains tax implications whatsoever. If on Lamia's death the property passes to Roxanne absolutely, there will be a deemed disposal and reacquisition.

Trustees ceasing to be resident in UK

Section 80(1) of the Taxation of Chargeable Gains Act 1992 provides that if the trustees of a settlement become not resident in the United Kingdom, they shall be deemed to have disposed of the defined assets immediately before the relevant time, and immediately to have reacquired them, "Trustees" are a continuing body so this situation normally arises where the resident trustees retire in place of non-resident trustees. The retiring trustees should ensure that they have funds available for the payment of any tax due.

12. Capital Gains Tax—The Liability of Beneficiaries

7-056 If a beneficiary is entitled to an interest in settled property, no chargeable gain arises on the disposal of the interest unless it was acquired by the beneficiary (or a predecessor in title) for consideration in money or money's worth, other than consideration consisting of another interest under the settlement (TCGA 1992 s.76(1)). Thus, if a life tenant sells their interest, no gain arises but the purchaser may face a tax liability on any subsequent disposal.

If the beneficiary is entitled under one of the types of trusts within s.60 of the TCGA 1992 (i.e. broadly speaking where they are the beneficiary of a bare trust—see para.7-046), they are treated as if the assets were vested in them and so any disposals made by the trustees are taxed as if the beneficiary had disposed of the property. This means that the normal rules for calculating capital gains tax liability will apply and exemptions, reliefs and allowances the beneficiary is personally able to claim will be available; losses realised by the trustees can be used by the beneficiary (TCGA 1992 s.71(2)). Furthermore, if the disposal by the trustees is to the beneficiary themselves then there is no capital gains tax liability.

13. SETTLEMENTS AND INCOME TAX—INTRODUCTION

In Ch.6 we considered the general rules for the taxation of income and the particular rules that apply when a person dies. We saw that it is the personal representatives' responsibility to pay any outstanding income tax liability of the deceased and to pay tax on income that arises in the course of administering the estate. Once the administration period is complete the personal representatives' liability ceases. **7-057**

If the beneficiaries have absolute interests in the residue, the capital of the residue will be transferred to them (see para.6-027, for the income tax rules applying in these circumstances). However, if the will creates any type of trust which is to continue after the administration period the property will be vested in trustees and special tax rules will apply.

Will trusts are basically taxed in the same way as other trusts but, since the settlor is dead when the trust becomes operative, the special anti--avoidance provisions relating to settlements contained in Ch.5 of the Income Tax (Trading and Other Income) Act 2005 (income treated as the settlor's where the settlor has retained an interest or where income is paid to minor children of the settlor who are neither married nor in a civil partnership) cannot apply.

Trust income is taxed in two stages. The trustees are liable to tax on all the income of the trust (the rate depends on the type of trust). There are special rules for low income trusts. See below.

Beneficiaries who are entitled to income or who receive income from the trust are then assessed to tax. They may be charged further tax or have tax refunded to them, depending on their particular circumstances.

14. INCOME TAX—LIABILITY OF TRUSTEES

General principles

The income of trustees is calculated in the same way as for an individual by applying the rules set out in Ch.3 of Pt 2 of the Income Tax Act 2007. In calculating this figure, the trustees may deduct permitted expenses. **7-058**

Thus, if the trustees are carrying on a trade, the income derived from the trade is assessed in accordance with the provisions of the Income Tax (Trading and Other Income) Act 2005 and they can deduct allowable business expenses.

There are two income tax regimes. One applies where beneficiaries have a right to income and the other where no beneficiary has such a right. The former is much more straightforward, as the trustees are liable only for basic rate tax. Trustees of trusts where beneficiaries have no right to income are liable to the trust rate of tax.

If income is paid directly to the beneficiary, a beneficiary with a right to income from its source, bypassing the trustees (often referred to as "mandating the income"), it is taxed in the hands of the beneficiary without the trustees paying tax (such a situation would arise where, for example, trustees ask a tenant of land owned by the trust to pay the rent to the beneficiary or where the trustees authorise a financial institution to pay income to the beneficiary).

Until tax year 2016/17 interest was received with basic rate tax deducted and dividends were received with an irrecoverable tax credit which satisfied liability to basic rate tax. As a result, trustees who were not liable to the trust rate of tax only had to pay tax on income received gross.

The fact that interest and dividends are received gross from 2016/17 onwards means that many trustees have more work in relation to income tax. A limited concession was introduced to help trustees of low income trusts. The concession applied until the end of 2023/24 when it was replaced by statutory provisions. Low income trusts are considered below.

Trustees are not liable to higher or additional rates of tax regardless of the amount of the income. However, trustees of trusts where income is to be accumulated or is paid at the discretion of the trustees are liable at the trust or dividend trust rate: see para.7-060.

Trustees will incur trust management expenses (for example accountancy and legal fees) and must debit each item of expenditure either against income or capital. *Carver v Duncan (Inspector of Taxes)* (1985) states the general rule in trust law which is that capital "*must bear all costs, charges and expenses incurred for the benefit of the whole estate*". Only expenses incurred exclusively for the benefit of the income beneficiaries are chargeable to income. Even when trust management expenses are properly set against income for trust purposes, they cannot normally be deducted for income tax purposes (*Aikin v MacDonald's Trustees* (1894)). There is an exception for trusts where income is to be accumulated or is paid at the discretion of the trustees. Here trustees are liable at the trust or dividend trust rate: see para.7-060. Trust management expenses are deductible when calculating liability at the trust rate provided the expenses are properly attributable to income.

Where beneficiaries have a right to income

7-059 Having calculated the income of the trust the trustees are liable to pay income tax at the basic or dividend ordinary rate on *all* of the rest of the income without the deduction of any personal reliefs (which are only available to "individuals" and for these purposes trustees are not "individuals") and without the deduction of trust management expenses. Trustees do not benefit from the starting rate or from the tax-free allowances for dividend and savings income.

Example 27

In tax year 2024/25 trustees have trust management expenses of £90 which are properly attributable to income. The trust is not required to pay the trust rate of tax as a beneficiary has an interest in possession. It receives the following income.

	£
Rent	1,000
Interest	500
Dividends	400

Unless they have mandated the income to the beneficiary the trustees will pay income tax at 20 per cent on the rent and interest (£200 and £100) and at 8.75 per cent on the dividend (£35). They will be left with £1,565 net income.

The trust management expenses do not reduce the basic rate tax liability of the trustees. Trustees are liable to basic rate income tax on all the income of the trust. However, because the expenses reduce the income available to the beneficiary, expenses which are properly chargeable to income will reduce the beneficiary's liability to tax. In the case of settlements where a beneficiary has a right to income, "properly" includes expenses whose final incidence falls on income by virtue of the terms of the trust deed. (See Income Tax Act 2007 s.500(2) and para.7-058.)

The trustees will pay the trust management expenses of £90 from the £1,565 of net income in their hands. They will pay the remaining £1,475 to the beneficiary and must provide a certificate of deduction of income tax at the appropriate rates. The beneficiary will receive the trust income net of tax at basic and dividend ordinary rate and net of expenses. Expenses are set first against income taxed at the dividend ordinary rate and then against income taxed at basic rate (ITA 2007 s.503(2)).

Liability of trustees of accumulation and discretionary trusts

Section 479 of the Income Tax Act 2007 requires trustees who have income: **7-060**

(a) which must be accumulated; or
(b) is payable at the discretion of the trustees or any other person,

to pay tax at the trust or dividend trust rate on trust income in excess of the first £1,000.

For tax year 2016/17 onwards the trust rate is 45 per cent and the dividend trust rate was 38.1 per cent until 2023/24 when it was increased to 39.35 per cent (see Income Tax Act 2007 s.9).

Until 2024/25, the first £1,000 of trust income was not liable to the special trust rates. This basic rate tax band was abolished by Finance (No.2) Act 2023 as part of the changes introduced for low income trusts and estates. Where a trust receives income of different types, Income Tax Act 2007 s.491 (now repealed) provided that income which would be charged at basic rate is to be allocated to the £1,000 band before dividend income. This basic rate tax band was abolished from 6 April 2024 as part of the changes to the treatment of low income trusts.

Example 28

In 2024/25 a trust receives interest of £2,000 and dividends of £100.

The interest will be taxed at 45 per cent. The dividend income will all be taxed at the dividend trust rate of 39.35 per cent.

The trust and dividend trust rate are not payable:

(a) where a beneficiary has a right to income;
(b) where income is treated as that of the settlor;
(c) on income of a charitable trust; or
(d) on income properly used for trust expenses (Income Tax Act 2007 s.484).

By comparison with individuals who only pay tax at 45 per cent if their taxable income exceeds £150,000, the trust rate of tax starts at a very low figure. There is, therefore, an incentive to set trust expenses against income rather than capital wherever possible.

For this purpose, expenses "properly" chargeable to income are those so chargeable as a matter of general law and not those made chargeable to income by the trust instrument (*Carver v Duncan* (1985)). In *Carver v Duncan* the House of Lords held that the general rule was that:

> "income must bear all ordinary outgoings of a recurrent nature, such as rates and taxes, and interest on charges and incumbrances. Capital must bear all costs, charges and expenses incurred for the benefit of the whole estate."

This was confirmed by the Court of Appeal in *HMRC v Clay's Trustees* (2007) where the taxpayers had contended that expenses which were for the benefit of the whole estate should be apportioned. However, the Court of Appeal did concede that apportionment of an expense is possible if it can be shown that an identified part of an expense is for work carried out for the benefit of the income beneficiaries alone. The onus of showing that an element of an expense relates to income rests on the trustees so in the absence of time records and minutes of what was considered at each trustees' meetings, it will be almost impossible to establish a basis for apportionment.

Section 486(1) of the Income Tax Act 2007 provides the order in which expenses are to be set against income for the purposes of the trust or dividend trust rate. This is first against income chargeable to the dividend trust rate, then against income chargeable to the trust rate.

When calculating liability to the trust or dividend trust rate, the trust management expenses are grossed up (at basic or dividend ordinary rate). The reason for this is that the trust and dividend trust rates are only chargeable on income which can be accumulated or is payable at the discretion of the trustees or some other person. The income which can be accumulated is the trust income *after* the trust expenses have been paid. The expenses are grossed up to reflect the fact that they were paid from taxed income.

The trust and dividend trust rates are applied to "income". Thus, they would not be applied to sums treated as income under particular provisions. However Income Tax Act 2007 s.481 expressly provides that the trust and dividend trust rates are to apply to certain sums treated as income which are listed in s.482 (e.g. to sums received on company buy backs).

The application of these rules on expenses can be seen in the following example.

Example 29

In 2024/25 a discretionary trust receives interest of £2,000 and dividends of £400.

It has spent £425 on allowable trust management expenses. The expenses are set first against the dividend income and will exhaust it. The portion of expenses to be set against the gross dividend income is grossed up at 8.75 per cent

£365 of expenses grossed up at 8.75 per cent is £400.

$$£365 \times 100/91.25 = £400$$

The balance of the expenses (£425 – £365 = £60) grossed up at 20 per cent is set against the interest. £60 of expenses grossed up at 20 per cent is £75.

$$£60 \times 100/80 = £75$$

After deducting the grossed-up expenses from the interest of £2,000, there is income available for distribution of £1,925.

Having deducted the expenses it is then necessary to calculate tax at 45 per cent on the remaining £1,925 of trust income.

$$£1,925 \times 45/100 = £866.25$$

The income available for distribution to the beneficiaries is, therefore, the gross income £2,400 less the expenses of £425 (£1,975) and tax of £866.25. The amount available for distribution is therefore £1,108.75.

Trustees' liability under Income Tax Act 2007 s.496

Section 494 of the Income Tax Act 2007 provides that trustees who make a discretionary payment to a beneficiary are to be treated as making a payment all of which has borne tax at the trust rate (45 per cent). They will provide beneficiaries with a certificate of deduction of income tax at 45 per cent (s.495). To the extent that the beneficiaries are not 45 per cent taxpayers, they can recover the tax treated as paid from HMRC. **7-061**

The trustees will not have paid 45 per cent tax on income liable to the dividend trust rate (and before 2024/25, they would not have paid 45 per cent tax on the first £1,000 of trust income). There is, therefore, a mismatch between the tax treated as paid by the trustees and the tax actually paid.

Section 496 of the Income Tax Act 2007 provides that the trustees will be assessed to tax on the difference between the tax treated as paid and the tax actually paid. This may be satisfied by tax credits available in the tax pool.

The tax pool consists of tax actually paid by the trustees plus any recoverable tax credits. Prior to 6 April 1999 dividends from UK companies were paid with a recoverable tax credit of 20 per cent. From that date until 5 April 2016 the tax credit was reduced to 10 per cent and was irrecoverable. Dividend tax credits, therefore, no longer entered the tax pool. From 6 April 2016 dividends are paid gross and trustees will actually pay tax on them. Trusts which have been in -existence for many years and which have accumulated income will have substantial tax pools. Others may have little or nothing in their tax pool. Trusts with no tax pools will have to satisfy any s.496 liability from trust funds. Trustees need to take their liability to tax under s.496 into account when deciding how much to distribute to beneficiaries.

Example 30

In 2024/25 the trustees of the ABC trust and the XYZ trust each receive dividends of £10,000. The ABC trust has substantial tax credits available in the tax pool; the XYZ trust does not. In each case the £10,000 of gross income is taxed as follows:

(a) £10,000 is taxed at 39.35 per cent (£3,935).
(b) The trustees, therefore, have available for distribution £6,065.

Whatever the trustees distribute to the beneficiaries will be treated as having borne tax at 45 per cent and will be grossed up in the hands of the beneficiaries at that rate. If the trustees distribute all the available income to a beneficiary, they will be treated as paying the beneficiary:

$$£6,065 \times 100/55 = £11,027.27$$

The tax treated as paid will be 45 per cent of £11,027.27 which is £4,962.27. The beneficiary will have a credit for that amount of tax. To the extent that the beneficiary is not a 45 per cent taxpayer, they can recover the tax treated as paid from HMRC.

As the trustees have only paid £3,935, they have an additional liability under s.496 of £1,027.27. The ABC trust can satisfy this from the tax pool but the XYZ trust will have to use capital.

If the XYZ trustees wish to meet the additional liability from the dividend income of the current year, they cannot distribute all of the £6,065. They should only distribute 55 per cent of the cash dividend received as follows:

Distribution to beneficiary:

£10,000 × 55% = 5,500

The beneficiary will be treated as receiving:

£5,500 × 100/55 = £10,000

with tax paid at the rate of 45 per cent (£4,500).

The trustees will be liable for the difference between the tax treated as paid at 45 per cent on the £10,000 (i.e. £4,500) and the £3,935 actually paid which amounts to £565. They have this amount available.

Where the trustees of accumulation and discretionary trusts choose to distribute all available dividend income and have no unused additional tax credits in the "tax pool", they will lose the benefit of the lower dividend rate. The problem can be alleviated by giving beneficiaries a right to income.

Since the introduction of the Finance Act 2006, giving beneficiaries a right to income normally has no inheritance tax consequences since trustees can no longer create qualifying interests in possession. There is one case where giving a right to income will have inheritance tax consequences. This is where the trust is a will trust and the appointment is within two years of death. The appointment will be read back to the date of death under Inheritance Act 1984 s.144 (see Ch.12) and will retrospectively create an immediate post-death interest.

15. INCOME TAX—LIABILITY OF BENEFICIARIES

Beneficiary with a right to income

General principles

7-062 A beneficiary with a right to trust income is entitled to all the trust income less trust expenses. The income paid to the beneficiary retains its original nature and is included on the beneficiary's tax return under the appropriate heading grossed up at basic or dividend ordinary rate. The beneficiary is entitled to require a certificate of deduction of income tax at the appropriate rate under Income Tax Act 2007 s.495.

When calculating the tax liability, the beneficiary is assessed on the income calculated in accordance with the rules appropriate to the source of the income (*Baker v Archer-Shee* (1927)). Most trust income will be derived from sources which would be savings or dividend income in the hands of an individual. However, some trusts may derive their income from property or from a trade carried on by the trustees.

If the gross trust income from a trade is £10,000 and there are allowable trading expenses for tax purposes of £2,000, the trustees are taxable on the net profit of £8,000, which is the trust income from the trade. The beneficiary is entitled to the income of the trust (not to the gross receipts). The trust income is £8,000 not £10,000, so the beneficiary is assessed to tax on £8,000. If the net profit after allowable trading expenses is £8,000 and the trustees can claim £3,000 capital allowances for tax purposes, the beneficiary's income for tax purposes is reduced by £3,000 to £5,000. If the trustees have trading or rental losses that they can use against trading or rental income in any year to reduce the trust's taxable income, the beneficiary's taxable income for that year is consequently reduced.

How to decide whether a beneficiary has a right to income

A beneficiary who has a right to trust income is taxed on the income when it arises irrespective of whether or not it is paid over to them. Such a right arises when the beneficiary has a vested interest in the income of the trust. A direction to accumulatc income will not destroy a vested interest in it provided the accumulated income *must* be paid to the beneficiary or to the estate of the beneficiary at some time. **7-063**

Three examples of trusts where beneficiaries have vested interests in the income are where the beneficiary has:

(a) A life interest in a trust fund, for example "to A for life" (however, if A is under 18 and s.31 of the Trustee Act 1925 applies there will be no right to income and A will effectively have only an interest contingent on reaching 18).
(b) A right to income conferred by s.31 of the Trustee Act 1925 (for example, where a beneficiary has an interest in the capital of the fund contingent on reaching an age greater than 18 and has reached 18).
(c) A vested interest in accumulating income, for example "to A but the income to be accumulated for 10 years and then paid to A or A's estate". A has no right to receive the income immediately but it is certain that A or A's estate will receive it in 10 years' time.

Trust management expenses

A beneficiary with a right to receive income is assessed to tax on all the income of the trust to which they are entitled less expenses properly chargeable to income. For income tax purposes this is all the trust income net of tax at basic or dividend ordinary rate less trust management expenses properly chargeable to income. **7-064**

Section 500(2) of the Income Tax Act 2007 provides that in the case of settlements where a beneficiary has a right to income "properly" includes expenses whose final incidence falls on income by virtue of the terms of the trust deed. This is in contrast with discretionary and accumulation trusts, where Income Tax Act 2007 s.484 specifically excludes provisions in the trust deed.

So if a trust deed allows the trustees to pay what are normally capital expenses out of income, those expenses reduce the measure of the beneficiary's income. If a trust deed allows trustees to pay what are in general trust law income expenses out of capital, again the trust deed has priority over general trust law.

Section 503(2) of the Income Tax Act 2007 provides the order of set-off for trust management expenses to reduce the income of a beneficiary with a right to income. The order of set-off is the same as that used for accumulation/-discretionary trustees. Expenses are set first against income taxed at the -dividend ordinary rate, then income taxed at basic rate.

Example 31

This is the same example we used at para.7-059, where the trust had expenses properly attributable to income of £90 and the following income:

	£
Rent	1,000
Interest	500
Dividends	400

The trust expenses will be treated as paid first from the dividend income of £400 which will be reduced to £310.

The beneficiary's gross income will be:

	£
Rent	1,000
Interest	500
Dividends	310

The beneficiary will include each category of income on the appropriate section of the income tax return because the income retains its original nature. Beneficiaries who are higher or additional rate taxpayers will have to pay the difference between the tax already paid on their behalf and the higher rate tax for which they are liable. Beneficiaries who are basic rate taxpayers will have no further liability to tax. Beneficiaries who are not taxpayers at all will be able to recover all the tax paid on the income.

Income and capital

7-065 A beneficiary's income is usually based on a share of what was assessed to income tax in the hands of the trustees. However, this does not apply to items that are capital in trust law and only deemed to be income for tax purposes. An example of such an item is a premium for a lease not exceeding 50 years. This is treated as rent (Income Tax (Trading and Other Income) Act 2005 s.276). Deemed rent of the trustees is chargeable on them but is not regarded as the beneficiary's income. This is because, under trust law, it is capital.

If a beneficiary with an entitlement to income receives a payment that is income in their hands, they may be liable to income tax on it even if the trustees make the payment from capital (*Michelham's Trustees v IRC* (1930)). The case of *Stevenson v Wishart* (1986) is interesting in that the Revenue failed in their contention that regular capital payments for nursing home fees should be treated as income. The position now appears to be that capital payments will not be treated as income payments unless:

(a) they are designed to make income up to a fixed amount or a certain defined level; or
(b) the trust instrument authorises the use of capital to maintain the beneficiary's standard of living.

Beneficiary receiving income from an accumulation or discretionary trust

7-066 A beneficiary whose entitlement to receive income depends on satisfying a contingency or on the trustees exercising a discretion in their favour has no income tax liability unless and until the trustees make a payment to them. The income is treated as the income of the trustees who will pay tax as described at para.7-060 and following. The most common examples of trusts falling within this category are discretionary trusts and trusts where the income is being accumulated for a person with only a contingent interest in capital.

When trustees exercise their discretion to pay income to a beneficiary, a new source of income comes into existence: trust income. The original source of the income is not relevant: see *Cunard's Trustees v CIR* (1946).

Any payments made to a beneficiary must be treated as part of the -beneficiary's income. The receipts of trust income must be grossed up on the beneficiary's tax return at 45 per cent. The beneficiary will have a 45 per cent tax credit and can claim a refund if not a higher rate taxpayer. The income paid from the trust loses its original nature and is treated as a new source of income: trust income. This means that the income cannot be set against a beneficiary's dividend or savings allowance.

The following example illustrates these points.

Example 32

In 2024/25 a discretionary trust receives interest of £2,000 and dividends of £400.

It has spent £425 on allowable trust management expenses. After the payment of expenses and income tax, £1,108.75 is available for -distribution. (See para.7-060 for the calculation.)

The trustees pay the whole amount to one of the beneficiaries, Fred, who has no other source of income.

Fred will gross up the £1,108.75 at 45 per cent:

£1,108.75 × 100/55 = £2,015.90

He will have a certificate of deduction of income tax at 45 per cent from the trustees. As a non-taxpayer he will be able to recover the whole 45 per cent (£907.16) from HMRC.

The trustees will have an additional tax liability under Income Tax Act 2007 s.496 for the difference between the tax they paid (£866.25) and the tax Fred has reclaimed.

Note that where beneficiaries are taxpayers, they suffer an income tax disadvantage. Because they receive a new source of income, trust income, they do not benefit from the tax-free allowances available on interest and dividends, nor from the lower rate of tax payable on dividends.

16. Low Income Trusts

Position before 6 April 2024

From 2016/17 by concession HMRC have not required notification from trustees **7-067**
and PRs where the only source of income of a trust or estate is savings interest which does not exceed £500. The trustees pay the gross interest to the beneficiaries who include it as part of their own taxable income.

The concession is very limited. If any income other than interest is received or if the interest exceeds £500, it is not available.

Position from 6 April 2024

HMRC consulted (*Income Tax: Low income trusts and estates* 25 April 2020) on **7-068**
amendments to Income Tax Act 2007 to allow the concessionary treatment of inter-

est not exceeding £500 to be extended to allow other income to be included. Finance (No.2) Act 2023 Sch.2 provides that ITA 2007 is amended for tax year 2024 to 2025 onwards as follows:

- Trusts and estates with income up to £500 will not pay tax on that income. Where a settlor has a number of accumulation and discretionary trusts, the £500 limit will be proportionately reduced by the total number of the current trusts to a minimum of £100. Interest in possession trusts, settlor-interested trusts, vulnerable beneficiary trusts and heritage maintenance trusts will not be taken into account.
- Beneficiaries of UK estates do not pay tax on income distributed to them that is within the £500 limit but beneficiaries of trusts do.

As a result of the change there will no longer be a tax credit attaching to the income of beneficiaries where income of the trust or estate is below the threshold.

- Non-tax paying beneficiaries will no longer have to make a repayment claim to receive the gross amount.
- Tax paying beneficiaries will no longer receive a tax credit since no tax has been paid.

A simplification?

7-069 Beneficiaries of an estate who receive income that falls below the low income exemption will not need to report this and will be exempt from tax on this income so this is a genuine simplification.

However, this is not so true for trusts, particularly those where there is no right to income.

- *Trusts where beneficiaries have a right to income* The beneficiary will receive the income gross without a tax credit. If they are not liable to income tax on the income, they need do nothing (whereas before the change, they would have to reclaim the tax paid) but if they are liable to income tax, they will now have to pay because of the lack of a tax credit.

  Example 33

  An "interest in possession" trust receives dividend income only, totalling £480.

  In 2023/24, the trustees would be liable to income tax at the dividend ordinary rate of 8.7 per cent, the tax payable being £42. Assuming there are no management expenses chargeable to income, the £438 balance would be distributed to the income beneficiary.

  If the income beneficiary has unused dividend allowance available to cover the receipt, they will make a claim to HMRC for the £42 paid by the trustees.

  In 2024/25, the trustees will not be liable to income tax; the full £480 of income will be distributed; and the beneficiary will have no tax to pay or claim in respect of that income because of available allowances. The tax outcomes will be the same as now but with reduced administrative burdens for both the trustees and the beneficiary.

  If the beneficiary has no tax free dividend allowance available, they will have to pay HMRC the tax due without any tax credit.

- *Trusts where beneficiaries have no right to income* Beneficiaries will continue to be treated as receiving income on which 45 per cent tax has been paid, as set out in Income Tax Act 2007 s.9 and s.494.

  The beneficiaries will have to include the income on their tax returns, and they will be treated as having a 45 per cent tax credit.

  Trustees will continue to have to make up any shortfall so, unless there are unused tax credits in the tax pool from previous years, they will have to pay cash to HMRC. This also means that the trustees have to do tax calculations even though they are within the de minimis limit.

  Example 34

  In year 1, a trust has rental income of £350. Assuming a £500 de minimis amount, the trustees have no tax liability, and no tax enters the tax pool.
  In year 2, the income is £400. Again, the trustees have no tax liability, and no tax enters the tax pool.
  In year 2, the trustees make a discretionary payment of £110 to a beneficiary.
  The beneficiary is treated as having a gross receipt of £200, (£110 x 100/55 = £200) with an accompanying £90 tax credit (£200 at 45 per cent). As no tax has entered the tax pool, the trustees are liable to pay £90 to fund the beneficiary's tax credit (unless they have credits left from earlier years).
  Without the proposal, the trustees would have paid tax on the income each year. In year 1, £70 (£350 x 20 per cent) and in year 2, £80 (£400 x 20 per cent). As £150 has entered the tax pool, it could be used to cover the additional liability and there would be no need for the trustees to pay anything further.

17. Income Tax and Trustee Act 1925 s.31

Section 31 of the Trustee Act 1925 is not a tax provision. However, in some circumstances it gives beneficiaries a right to income which they would not otherwise have and, in other circumstances, removes a right to income which would otherwise exist. Changes to a beneficiary's right to income can affect the income tax liability of trustees and beneficiaries. **7-070**

Section 31 (see para.11-017 and following, for a full discussion) provides that where there is income available to a minor (whether they have a vested or a contingent interest) the trustees of the trust may at their sole discretion apply the whole or part of such income for or towards the minor's maintenance, education or benefit and, to the extent that they do not, they must accumulate the whole or part of such income.

If, after reaching the age of 18, the beneficiary has not attained a vested interest in such income the trustees *shall* thereafter pay the income (together with any income produced by investments bought with accumulated income) to the beneficiary until the beneficiary either attains a vested interest or dies or until their interest fails.

What happens to income that has been accumulated? In all cases, except one, the accumulated income is added to capital and devolves with it. Thus, whoever takes the capital takes the accumulations. The exceptional case is that of a minor with a life interest, or other income entitlement. If the minor reaches 18, any income which has been accumulated is paid to them. However, if the minor dies before reaching 18 the accumulated income is added to capital and devolves with it. A minor given a life interest or other income entitlement under the terms of the trust, therefore, has no *right* to receive income until they reach the age of 18 (since the trustees may decide to accumulate it) and cannot be certain of ever receiving the accumulations (since they may die before reaching 18).

Section 31 can, therefore, *give* certain beneficiaries a right to income where prima facie they had no such right under the terms of the trust. It can also *prevent* beneficiaries having a right to income which under the terms of the trust they would otherwise have enjoyed. The effect, if any, of s.31 on income tax liability can be illustrated by examples.

Example 35

(a) *T's will gives 20,000 shares to Ayesha for life (Ayesha is aged six).* If s.31 did not apply, Ayesha would have *a right* to receive the income from the shares and the trustees would pay only the dividend ordinary rate. Ayesha would include the grossed-up income on her income tax return and might be liable to higher rate tax or a tax refund depending on the level of income from other sources.

However, if s.31 applies the trustees have a discretion whether to apply income for Ayesha's benefit and Ayesha, therefore, has no *right* to receive current income until they reach 18. She has no right to receive accumulated income unless and until she reaches 18. Ayesha effectively has an interest contingent on reaching 18. The trustees therefore pay the dividend trust rate on all the income in excess of the first £1,000. Ayesha includes income actually applied for her maintenance on her tax return. (Liability to higher rate tax or a right to a tax refund may arise depending on her other income.) Once Ayesha reaches 18 she will obtain a right to current income. The trustees will then pay tax at the dividend ordinary rate. A settlor may want to give a minor a right to income; for example a grandparent may wish to leave property to grandchildren by will and secure the residence nil-rate band for the estate but may not want the grandchildren to have access to capital at too young an age. The only way to achieve this is to create an immediate post-death interest for the grandchildren. The will must vary s.31 by providing that any unapplied capital is to be held exclusively for the beneficiary, effectively a bare trust, with a right to capital at an appropriate age state.

(b) *T's will gives 20,000 shares to Ben if he reaches* 25 *(Ben is aged six).* If s.31 did not apply Ben would have no *right* to the income until reaching 25 and the trustees would pay the dividend higher rate on all the income in excess of £1,000. Nothing would be included on Ben's tax return in respect of the trust income unless the trustees chose to apply income for their benefit.

However, if s.31 applies the above will only be correct *until* Ben's 18th birthday. From 18 to 25 Ben will have a right to the income. The trustees will then pay no further tax. The tax credit on the dividends will satisfy their liability at dividend ordinary rate. Ben will include the grossed-up amount on his tax return (grossed up at 10 per cent) and again may be liable to extra tax depending on their circumstances.

18. Demergers and Scrip Issues

Introduction

Demergers can present serious problems for trustees. A demerger is a series of transactions which have the effect and purpose of dividing the trading activities carried on by a single company or group of companies between two or more companies or groups of companies. **7-071**

There have been some complex demergers during which companies have divided themselves up. Probably the most complex was the Hanson demerger where four separate holdings were created, while the biggest was probably the demerger of Zeneca from ICI.

In a simple direct demerger the company declares a dividend from distributable profits and proceeds to satisfy it with an allocation of shares in the demerged company. It follows that the shares represent income so if they are paid to an interest in possession trust, the life tenant will be entitled to them.

From the point of view of the trust fund the consequences can be very serious. The capital value of the trust fund can be greatly reduced and the life tenant can receive a huge income benefit. The trustees may not be happy with this result. They can sell shares before the demerger but this, being a disposal, may lead to an unwelcome capital gains tax liability.

An indirect demerger includes a further step absent from a direct demerger; at the same time as declaring a dividend, Company A transfers all its shares in Company B to another (wholly separate) holding company (Company C). In consideration for this transfer of shares Company C satisfies Company A's dividend by issuing its own shares to the shareholders of Company A.

In *Sinclair v Lee* (1993) a testatrix bequeathed shares in ICI Plc (ICI) to her husband for life with the remainder to her son. After her death, ICI resolved to demerge its bioscience activities. In preparation it consolidated its bioscience activities into a wholly owned subsidiary company. ICI proposed to transfer the shares of this subsidiary company to a newly created holding company called Zeneca Group Plc (Zeneca). Zeneca was then to issue its own paid-up shares to ICI shareholders. Sir Donald Nicholls VC, as he then was, conceded that the line of cases on direct demergers required him to treat the Zeneca shares as income but this was such an unsatisfactory result that he felt able to distinguish the indirect demerger. He held that the ICI transaction was to be characterised not as a distribution at all, but as a company reconstruction resulting in a single capital asset in the trustees' hands being replaced by two such assets.

The Law Commission said of this decision, in its report *Capital and Income in Trusts: Classification and Apportionment*, Law Com. No.315 that, while helpful, it had:

> "given rise to an unprincipled distinction between direct and indirect demergers. The formalistic ground for distinction adopted by the Vice-Chancellor enabled him to avoid what he considered to be an 'absurd' result, but did not affect the equally absurd result that arises from direct demergers."

What is the tax position?

The tax treatment of shares received on a demerger depends on whether or not the demerger fulfils the requirements of Corporation Tax Act 2010 Pt 23, Ch.5 to **7-072** qualify as an exempt demerger. An exempt demerger is not a distribution for the purposes of corporation tax and does not give rise to tax liabilities for the recipients. Direct demergers falls within s.1076 of CTA 2010. Indirect demergers fall within s.1077 of CTA 2010.

Where a demerger is not exempt, the position is as follows.

- On a direct demerger there is no charge under s.71 of TCGA 1992 (beneficiary becoming absolutely entitled) because the shares belong to the beneficiaries from the very beginning. They never form part of the capital of the estate and there is no disposal by the personal representatives, etc. Their base value is the market value at the time of the demerger (TCGA 1992 s.17). The income beneficiaries will not be assessed to income tax.

  If the personal representatives or trustees retain the new shares on a direct demerger then they will purchase them from the income beneficiaries. Unless the gain made by the beneficiaries exceeds their annual exemption, etc. there will be no tax consequences. This may well mean that, in most cases, this is what happens.
- On an indirect demerger the income beneficiaries get nothing and all that happens is that the personal representatives, etc. have to split their base value for the original holding between the holdings which emerge. HMRC's view is fully explained in the *Capital Gains Manual*, paras CG33900–CG33936.

Stock or scrip

7-073 Scrip dividends are dividends which offer shareholders the choice of being paid in the form of cash or shares. When a company declares a conventional scrip dividend each shareholder has the option to take the dividend in cash or in additional shares of equal value. For income tax purposes scrip dividends are subject to income tax as "stock dividend income" under Income Tax (Trading and Other Income) Act 2005.

If trustees receive a scrip dividend, they are treated as receiving income if a cash dividend paid to them in respect of the shares would have been (to any extent) accumulated income or discretionary income within the meaning of s.480 of Income Tax Act 2007 (ITTOIA 2005 s.410(3)). They are, therefore, liable to income tax on scrip dividends at the dividend trust rate (see *Howell v Trippier (HM Inspector of Taxes)* (2004)).

In *Pierce v Wood* (2009) the High Court held that the effect of *Howell v Trippier* was that scrip dividends received by trustees and treated as income for income tax purposes had to be treated as income for all tax and trust law purposes. Hence, such dividends were not capital (unless formally accumulated) and were not liable to inheritance tax charges as part of the capital of the trust fund.

However, the Upper Tribunal in *Gilchrist v HMRC* (2014) declined to follow *Pierce v Wood*. It considered that the decision in *Howell v Trippier* was only relevant for the purposes of income tax. The Court of Appeal had not considered whether the deeming provision might apply for wider purposes. Therefore, as a matter of trust law and for inheritance tax purposes, the scrip dividend proceeds were capital and so relevant property for the purposes of the 10-year -anniversary charge.

Trusts (Capital and Income) Act 2013

The Law Commission, in its report *Capital and Income in Trusts: Classification and Apportionment*, Law Com.No.315, was critical of the current law on the basis of its inappropriate and unpredictable results, complexity and its uncertainty in application to novel arrangements. **7-074**

It recommended that trustees should have a power of allocation. This power would allow trustees, taking the trust's receipts over a given period, to allocate all or part of one or more trust receipts as necessary in order to ensure that a balance was kept between classes of beneficiaries entitled to capital and to income. This would be coupled with a statutory requirement to balance investment returns arising under a power of allocation, applying solely in the context of the exercise of the power of allocation.

It also recommended that shares distributed in a tax-exempt demerger should be classified as capital for trust law purposes. This would classify as capital shares received as a result both of direct and indirect demergers. It also recommended that when such a distribution is made, trustees should have a power to make a payment of capital to beneficiaries interested in income where otherwise there would be prejudice to those beneficiaries. The Law Commission would have preferred to make a recommendation in relation to all demergers but was unable to do so because the introduction of flexibility in treatment of receipts would have impacted on the tax treatment of interests in possession and might have caused an interest in possession trust to lose its status as such for both income tax and, where relevant, inheritance tax purposes.

The Trusts (Capital and Income) Act 2013 came into force on 1 October 2013 and rationalised the trust law classification of receipts from tax-exempt corporate demergers by ensuring that all such receipts are treated as capital, together with a power for trustees to redress an income beneficiary's position in -appropriate circumstances.

Chapter Eight

GRANTS

1. Introduction

A grant of representation is an order of the High Court. The High Court has exclusive jurisdiction to make grants in England and Wales. Since 1 October 1971 the Family Division of the High Court has exercised the jurisdiction to make grants (Administration of Justice Act 1970 s.1(4)). The Chancery Division and the county court have certain powers in probate cases but these do not include a power to make grants; these powers will be considered in Ch.9. **8-001**

The procedure for applying for a grant at the time of writing is governed by the Non-Contentious Probate Rules 1987 (SI 1987/2024) as amended (the 1987 Rules). Various amendments have been made most significantly by the Non-Contentious Probate (Amendment) Rules 2018 (SI 2018/1137) and the Non-Contentious Probate (Amendment) Rules (SI 2020/1059) in relation to online applications:

(a) online applications for a grant can be made by any unrepresented applicant but can also be made on paper,
(b) all applications for a grant probate by a solicitor or probate practitioner (with some exceptions such as grants of double probate) are required to be made online.

From 27 November 2018 all applications (can be verified by a statement of truth (instead of an oath) and without the will having to be marked (signed by the applicant).

The explanatory memorandum published by the Ministry of Justice to accompany the Rules says:

> "As the present pilot scheme for online applications through solicitors and probate practitioners under rule 4A is continuing and further reform and pilot schemes may follow as the modernisation of the probate process continues, the department does not propose to consolidate the NCPR as amended by the instrument at this stage."

The on-line pilot scheme has now been extended to all solicitors and probate practitioners.

From 18 May 2020, Statements of Truth are replaced by Probate Application Forms: PA1P where there is a will and PA1A where the deceased died intestate.

2. Types of Grant

There are three basic types of grant of representation: **8-002**

(1) a grant of probate;
(2) a grant of letters of administration with will annexed; and

(3) a grant of letters of administration (commonly called a grant of simple administration).

A grant, once made, serves two main purposes. First, it establishes the -authority of the personal representative. Secondly, it establishes either the validity of the deceased's will (in the case of probate or administration with will annexed) or that the deceased died without a valid will (in the case of simple administration).

Certain types of property do not devolve on the personal representatives when their owner dies. This applies to property which is the subject of a statutory nomination, property subject to a *donatio mortis causa*, certain payments from pension funds and insurance policies and, most importantly, property held by the deceased and another person (or persons) as joint tenants in equity. Such property is not included in the grant of representation. The ways in which it is dealt with on death are described in Ch.21.

3. CAPACITY TO TAKE A GRANT

8-003 Any person, including an alien, a minor, a corporation, a bankrupt, a convicted criminal, or a mentally disordered person may be *appointed* an executor by a will. Similarly, any such person may prima facie be entitled to a grant of letters of administration.

However, a minor cannot *take* a grant of representation and therefore the grant is made to an adult for the use and benefit of the minor. Such a grant will usually be limited to the period of incapacity so that the minor may take out a grant on attaining majority. Similar rules apply to mentally disordered persons (that is persons who lack the mental capacity to act as personal representatives).

Where an alien resident outside the jurisdiction, a bankrupt or a criminal is entitled to a grant no special rules apply. However, in each case the court may exercise its discretion to pass over the person entitled and make a grant to some other person entitled (Senior Courts Act 1981 s.116). The court will also exercise its powers to pass over a person who is unsuitable; for a recent example see *Adepoju v Akinola* (2016) where the person with the best right had lied to the court and had possibly misappropriated estate assets.

After the coming into force of the Family Law Reform Act 1987 the fact that a person's parents were not married to each other at the time of his or her birth is irrelevant for the purposes of succession to property and is therefore irrelevant for the purpose of entitlement to a grant of representation (unless a contrary intention has been expressed in a will left by the deceased). Section 21 of the 1987 Act does provide, however, that for the purpose of determining who is entitled to a grant of probate or administration, a deceased person shall be presumed not to have been survived by any person whose parents were not married to, or civil partners of, each other at the time of that person's birth (or who is related through such a person). The presumption can be rebutted by evidence to the contrary.

4. GRANT OF PROBATE

The executor appointed by will

8-004 Normally the only person who may obtain a grant of probate is the executor appointed by the deceased in his or her will (or in a codicil validly supplementing or amending the will). An executor is a person appointed by the will to administer the deceased's property. The will may *appoint* any number of executors but not more than four persons may take out a grant in respect of the same part of the estate (power may be reserved to any others—see para.8-011).

Since most testators want to choose a person to administer the estate, a properly drafted will should expressly provide for the appointment of an executor; for example, by including a clause which says "I appoint X of [address] to be the executor of this will". The person named should be someone suitable to act as executor and who is willing to take a grant. The appointment may describe rather than name the executor; for example, "I appoint the Vicar of St James's Church in the parish of [...] to be the executor of this will" but such appointments are unwise since they may be ambiguous.

The appointment of an executor may be implied in cases where the will shows an intention that a particular person should perform the functions of an executor even though not expressly described as an executor. Such a person is described as "an executor according to the tenor of the will". For example, in *In the Goods of Baylis* (1865) the will directed that named persons should pay the debts of the estate and then hold the estate on trust for sale for the deceased's children. Lord Penzance held that since the "trustees" were to get in the whole estate, pay the debts and distribute the property the clear intention was that they should act as executors; therefore they were entitled to a grant.

The appointment of trustees without a direction that they are to pay the debts of the estate is not sufficient to make them executors according to the tenor (*In the Estate of McKenzie* (1909)).

A firm (for example, of solicitors) may be named as executors. However, since the office is a personal one this is treated as an appointment of all the individual partners in the firm. Great care should be taken with such appointments since, in the absence of clear words to the contrary, the partners in the firm at the date on which the will is made (rather than the partners at the date of death) are the executors and they may be unavailable or unwilling to act at the time of the death (the drafting problems connected with appointment of a firm are considered in para.22-019).

Appointment other than by will

A will may validly appoint someone to nominate an executor (in such a case the **8-005**
person appointed may nominate themselves). Such a provision in a will would seldom be advantageous but, if included, a time limit should be imposed on the making of the appointment.

One executor is always sufficient even where there is a minority or life interest. However, the court has a rarely exercised power to appoint an additional personal representative to act with a sole executor in the administration of the estate (Senior Courts Act 1981 s.114(4)). Such a person is not described as an executor but would seem to have the same powers as an executor.

Under the Administration of Estates Act 1925 s.22 trustees of settled land of which the deceased was tenant for life and which remains settled land after his or her death are deemed appointed executors in respect of the settled land alone. However, in accordance with r.29 of the 1987 Rules, they will act as administrators not executors.

Under s.50(1)(a) of the Administration of Justice Act 1985 the court may appoint a person to be a personal representative in substitution for an existing personal representative. If the substitute is to act with an existing executor, he or she is also an executor; in any other case he or she is an administrator.

In *Goodman v Goodman* (2013) the section was used to remove a person named as an executor in a will who had not yet been granted probate. It would be more natural to use Senior Courts Act 1981 s.116, but Newey J held that because an executor derives his authority from the will (unlike an administrator who derives it from the grant) there was nothing to prevent s.50 being used before a grant of probate was made (see para.8-023).

Chain of representation (Administration of Estates Act 1925 s.7)

8-006 Where the sole or last surviving executor dies before completing the administration of the estate a grant of letters of administration *de bonis non administratis* may be made to the person entitled under r.20 of the 1987 Rules (see para.8-013). Where one of a number of executors dies there is no need for a further grant; the remaining executor or executors having full power to complete the administration.

However, where a sole or last surviving proving executor (other than an executor substituted under s.50(1)(a) of the Administration of Justice Act 1985) dies *having appointed an executor themselves*, the latter, on taking a grant of probate in respect of the executor's estate, automatically becomes the executor of the original testator as well so that a grant of administration to the original estate is not needed (Administration of Estates Act 1925 s.7).

Example 1

A appoints B to be his executor and B appoints C. On A's death B will become his executor and may take a grant of probate. If B dies having taken a grant but without having completed the administration of A's estate and C takes a grant of probate of B's estate, C will automatically become executor of A as well as B.

This is called the chain of representation. There may be more than two links in the chain. To continue the same example, if C appoints D to be his executor and C then dies without completing the administration of the estates and D takes out a grant of probate in respect of C's estate, D will automatically become the executor of A and B as well as of C.

The chain of representation only applies where there is a grant of *probate* to the executor of a person who had taken out a grant of probate themselves in respect of someone else's estate. Thus, the chain of representation is broken (and a grant of administration *de bonis non* is required) where:

(a) an executor dies intestate or without appointing an executor;
(b) an executor dies having appointed an executor but that executor has predeceased; or
(c) an executor dies having appointed an executor but that executor fails to take out a grant in respect of the original executor's estate.

The chain of representation can be said to pass from *proving executor* to *proving executor*. There is, therefore, no chain of representation where no executor has been appointed. For example, A dies intestate, B takes out a grant of letters of administration and then B dies having appointed C to be his executor. C does not become the executor of A.

The appointment of an administrator will usually break the chain of representation. However, a temporary appointment does not do so.

Example 2

A appoints B to be his executor, B appoints C and dies. C is a minor when B dies. A grant of administration is made in respect of B's estate to D. D does not become A's executor. When, however, C reaches majority he may take out a grant of probate in respect of B's estate. If he does so he will then automatically become A's executor.

Similarly a person who becomes executor through the chain of representation may cease to be executor when someone else takes out a grant of probate in respect of the deceased's estate.

Example 3

A appoints B and C to be his executors: when A dies B is an adult and C a minor. A grant will be made to B alone, but C is said to have "power reserved", i.e. he can take out a grant when he reaches majority. If B dies without completing the administration of A's estate appointing D his executor while C is still a minor, D will become A's executor on taking out probate of B's estate. However, if on reaching 18 C takes out a grant in respect of A's estate, D will cease to be A's executor. This is because the chain of representation can only operate on the death of the *last proving* executor and C has now become a proving executor.

Limited, conditional and substitutional appointments

Most wills appoint one or more persons to act as executor for the whole of the deceased's estate and without limit as to time. However, an appointment may be limited. For example, an appointment may: **8-007**

(a) be limited in time (the appointment may, for example, appoint one person until another person reaches the age of majority);
(b) be limited to certain property (for example, one executor may be appointed to deal with the deceased's general estate and another to deal with business property or literary effects); and
(c) be limited as to purpose (for example, to conduct litigation).

Limited grants are dealt with in more detail in paras 8-024–8-032.

An appointment may also be conditional. For example, "I appoint A to be my executor provided he is a partner in the firm of A, B and Co at the date of my death."

A will may also validly provide for a substitutional appointment. For example, "I appoint A to be my executor but if he is unable or unwilling to act then I appoint B." B may take out a grant once A has renounced probate or died. Care should be taken when wording a substitutional appointment. For example, if a person is appointed as a substitute if the executor has died, the substitution will not take effect if the original executor renounces or is incapable of acting.

Effect of grant of probate

Conclusive proof of content and execution of will

A grant of probate in respect of a particular will is conclusive evidence as to the terms of the will of the deceased and that it was duly executed. If a will is found to be invalid (for example, because it is found not to have been properly executed or a later will is discovered) after a grant of probate, the grant must be revoked (see paras 8-035–8-040). **8-008**

A copy of the will (and any codicils to it) used to be attached to the grant. This was useful as it provided an "authorised version" of the will. In 2019 the probate registries stopped doing this although they will issue a copy on application. Professional bodies have made the point that the change facilitates fraud.

Confirmation of executors' authority

8-009 A grant of probate merely confirms the authority of the executor conferred by the will. The authority derives from the will. An executor may, therefore, deal with the estate of the deceased without first taking out a grant (see para.11-006). However, a grant is in practice necessary to prove to other people that the executor has authority to deal with the property of the deceased and to pass a good title to any land in the estate.

Executor de son tort

8-010 The term executor *de son tort* means literally executor as a result of his or her own wrong. The expression is unfortunate since the noun is wholly misleading and the adjectival phrase almost as much so. An executor *de son tort* is a person who deals with the estate of a deceased person by intermeddling with it as if he or she were an executor or administrator. Acts which have been held to amount to intermeddling include selling property, paying debts, collecting debts and carrying on the business of the deceased. However, acts of charity, humanity or necessity are not sufficient. Thus, arranging the deceased's funeral, ordering necessary goods for the deceased's dependents and protecting the deceased's property by moving it to a safe place have been held not to amount to intermeddling. In *Pollard v Jackson* (1995) it was held that a tenant of part of the deceased's house, who kept the parts formerly occupied by the deceased clean and who burnt rubbish found there was not an executor *de son tort*. The steps he had taken could not be regarded as characteristic of executorship.

An executor *de son tort* has no authority to act in the estate of the deceased and can obtain no rights by intermeddling. However, a person who is in fact the deceased's executor and who intermeddles loses the right to renounce probate and so can be cited to take a grant (see para.10-062).

The effect of being an executor *de son tort* is that such a person becomes liable to the creditors and beneficiaries to the extent of the real and personal estate coming into his or her hands as if he or she were an executor (Administration of Estates Act 1925 s.8). He or she is also liable for inheritance tax to the extent of such property.

An executor *de son tort* can bring his or her liability to creditors and beneficiaries to an end by delivering the assets received (or their value) to the lawful executor or administrator before the creditors or beneficiaries bring an action against them.

Power reserved to prove at a later date

8-011 A will may appoint several people to act as co-executors. It is unnecessary for them all to join in taking the grant if they do not wish to. Those who do not take the grant may renounce their rights, but if they prefer not to renounce they may have power reserved to them to take the grant at a later date if it proves desirable. Where an application for probate is made and power is to be reserved to some executors to prove at a later date, notice of the application must be given to the non-proving executors. The oath for executors, filed when the application for the grant is made, must state that this notice has been given unless the court otherwise orders (1987 Rules r.27(1)). Where the other executors are not named in the will and are partners in a firm of solicitors with the proving executors, the persons to whom power is reserved need not be given notice (1987 Rules r.27(1A)).

5. Grant of Letters of Administration with Will Annexed

Circumstances in which a grant is made

A grant of letters of administration with will annexed is made when the deceased has a valid will and a grant of probate cannot be made to an executor. Such a situation arises where the will makes no appointment of an executor, where the executor predeceases, where the executor has validly renounced probate, where the executor is passed over by order of the court and where the executor has been cited but has not taken a grant of probate (see para.10-062, for the citation procedure). A grant of administration with will annexed is also made in certain cases where an earlier grant of probate or administration with will annexed has been made but the personal representative appointed by the earlier grant has been unable to complete the administration of the estate (see para.8-034 and following). **8-012**

Persons entitled to take a grant

Rule 20 of the 1987 Rules contains a list of the persons who are entitled to take out a grant of administration with the will annexed. The list follows the order of entitlement to property under the will. Persons who come earlier in the list will take a grant in preference to those who come later. If there is no executor able and willing to act, the following are entitled: **8-013**

(i) *Any residuary legatee or devisee holding in trust for any other person.* For example, residue is given to X and Y on trust for A and B. X and Y are the residuary legatees holding on trust and so have the first right to a grant. This is logical since the testator by appointing X and Y as trustees has shown that he or she is willing that they should deal with the property.

(ii) *Any other residuary legatee or devisee (including one for life), or where the residue is not wholly disposed of by the will, any person entitled to share in the undisposed of residue (including the Treasury Solicitor when claiming bona vacantia on behalf of the Crown).* For example, residue is given to A, B, C and D in equal shares; each will be entitled to take the grant. If D predeceased the testator and X was entitled to take the quarter of residue undisposed of, X would be equally entitled to the grant.

There are two provisos to this category:

(a) unless a district judge or registrar otherwise directs, a residuary legatee or devisee whose legacy or devise is vested in interest shall be preferred to one entitled on the happening of a contingency; and

(b) where the residue is not in terms wholly disposed of, the district judge or registrar may, if satisfied that the testator has, -nevertheless, disposed of the whole or substantially the whole of the known estate, allow a grant to be made to any legatee or devisee entitled to, or to share in, the estate so disposed of, without regard to the persons entitled to share in any residue not disposed of by the will.

For example the will says "I leave my home, Blackacre, all its contents and my bank account to my friend X." When the testator dies the property described in the will is substantially everything owned by the deceased. X can take a grant in preference to those family members who would be entitled to take residue under the intestacy rules.

(iii) *The personal representative of any residuary legatee or devisee (but not one for life, or one holding in trust for any other person), or of any person entitled to share in any residue not disposed of by the will.* For example, residue is given to A and B in equal shares; A predeceases the testator and X is entitled to take the half share of residue undisposed of. If X and B both die before taking a grant the personal representatives of either will be entitled to the grant.

(iv) *Any other legatee or devisee (including one for life or one holding in trust for any other person) or any creditor of the deceased.* For example, a house is left to A and £1,000 to B. Either is entitled to the grant unless a registrar otherwise directs. A legatee or devisee whose legacy or devise is vested in interest shall be preferred to one entitled on the happening of a contingency.

(v) *The personal representative of any other legatee or devisee (but not one for life or one holding in trust for any other person) or of any creditor of the deceased.* For example, if A and B in the previous example survive the testator but die before taking a grant the personal representatives of either will be entitled to the grant.

Rule 27(4) and (6) of the 1987 Rules provide that where two or more persons are entitled in the same degree (i.e. come into the same paragraph above) a grant may be made to any of them without notice to the others (contrast the position with grants of probate: see para.8-011) and that disputes between persons entitled in the same degree are to be decided by a district judge or registrar.

Living beneficiaries are to be preferred to the personal representative of deceased beneficiaries entitled in the same degree and adults to minors entitled in the same degree unless a district judge or registrar directs to the contrary (r.27(5) of the 1987 Rules). If the whole estate of the deceased is assigned by the beneficiaries, the assignees have the same right to a grant as the assignors (r.24 of the 1987 Rules).

The effect of a grant

Conclusive proof of content and execution of will

8-014 A grant of administration with will annexed is like a grant of probate in that it is conclusive evidence as to content and execution of the will.

Conferral of authority on administrator

8-015 A grant of probate merely confirms the authority of executors. However, a grant of letters of administration *confers* authority on the administrator and vests the deceased's property in him. Until the grant is made the property of a deceased who appoints no executor is technically vested in the Public Trustee (Administration of Estates Act 1925 s.9, as substituted). Once made the grant does not relate back to the date of death of the deceased except to the extent that relation back would (at the time of the grant) be beneficial to the estate (see para.11-006).

6. GRANT OF SIMPLE ADMINISTRATION

Circumstances in which a grant is made

A grant of simple administration is made when there is no will capable of being admitted to probate (or of being annexed to letters of administration). **8-016**

Simple administration is appropriate in the vast majority of cases where there is a total intestacy. However, if there is an admissible will which does not deal with property (for example, a will merely appointing executors) a grant of probate may be made. Similarly, a will is admissible to probate (or may be annexed to letters of administration) where it purports to deal with property, but all the gifts fail.

Persons entitled to take a grant

Rule 22(1) of the 1987 Rules contains the order of the persons who are entitled to take out a grant of simple administration. The order follows the order of entitlement to the estate on intestacy and says that the persons entitled are, in the order listed and provided that they have a beneficial interest in the estate: **8-017**

(a) the surviving spouse or civil partner of the deceased;
(b) children of the deceased (and the issue of a child who has predeceased);
(c) the parents of the deceased;
(d) the brothers and sisters of the whole blood of the deceased (and the issue of any brothers or sisters who have predeceased);
(e) brothers and sisters of the half blood of the deceased (and the issue of any who have predeceased);
(f) grandparents;
(g) uncles and aunts of the whole blood (and the issue of any who have -predeceased); and
(h) uncles and aunts of the half blood (and the issue of any who have predeceased).

Rule 22(2) of the 1987 Rules provides that if no-one is entitled as being in any of the above categories then the Treasury Solicitor may take out a grant when claiming bona vacantia on behalf of the crown.

Since a beneficial interest is required under r.22(1) the entitlement to a grant depends in part on the size of the estate. For example, if an intestate died leaving a spouse or civil partner and adult issue, the issue would have no entitlement to a grant under r.22(1) if the estate was £180,000 since it would all go to the spouse or civil partner but would be entitled if it was £600,000. They would however have a right under r.22(3).

Rule 22(3) of the 1987 Rules provides that a grant may be made to a creditor of the deceased or to a person who would be entitled to a beneficial interest in the estate if there were an accretion to the estate provided that all those who would otherwise be entitled are cleared off.

Thus, in the example given above (a deceased with an estate of £180,000 and personal chattels who is survived by spouse or civil and adult issue) the issue (if surviving at the date of the accretion) would have a right to a grant if the spouse or civil partner had been cleared off.

The personal representative of a person who survives the deceased but dies before taking a grant is entitled in the same degree as the person whom he represents (r.22(4) of the 1987 Rules).

However, unless a district judge or registrar directs otherwise, where a number of persons are entitled in the same degree, a person of full age is to be preferred to the guardian of a minor and a living person is to be preferred over the personal representative of a dead person (r.27(5) of the 1987 Rules).

Furthermore, relatives who are entitled to part of the estate are to be preferred to the personal representative of a spouse unless the spouse's estate is entitled to the *whole* of the estate as ascertained at the time of application for the grant (r.22(4) of the 1987 Rules).

Example 4

H dies in April 2024 when the statutory legacy is £322,000. He is survived by spouse and children. The spouse dies before obtaining a grant. The spouse's personal representative will be able to take a grant if the estate is not more than £322,000 plus personal chattels but if it is, the children will have priority.

The effect of a grant

8-018 The effect of a grant of simple administration is the same as that of a grant of administration with will annexed except that it provides conclusive evidence of intestacy rather than as to the contents and terms of the will.

7. Renunciation

8-019 Persons who are entitled to a grant of probate or administration may renounce their entitlement unless they have lost the right to renounce. Renunciation is made in writing to the registry. The most convenient way to deal with any renunciation is to submit it with the papers submitted by a person who does wish to take a grant.

An executor accepts office and thereby loses the right to renounce if he or she intermeddles in the estate (the principles are the same as those applying to a person becoming an executor *de son tort* so that the performance of acts of charity, humanity or necessity does not deprive the executor of their right to renounce). A potential administrator does not lose the right to renounce if he or she intermeddles. Both an executor and an administrator lose the rights to renounce if a grant is made in his or her favour.

A renunciation of probate by an executor does not operate as a renunciation of any right to administration which he or she may have unless that right is also renounced (r.37(1) of the 1987 Rules). However, a renunciation of administration in one capacity in effect operates to renounce *all* rights to a grant of administration.

Once a renunciation has been made it may only be retracted on the order of a district judge or registrar (r.37(3) of the 1987 Rules). The court will only allow the retraction of a renunciation if it can be shown to be for the benefit of the estate or of the persons interested in the estate (*Re Gill* (1873)).

8. Number of Personal Representatives

8-020 Section 114(1) of the Senior Courts Act 1981 provides that

> "probate or administration shall not be granted … to more than four persons in respect of the same part of the estate of a deceased person".

This means that if more than four executors are appointed to administer the estate a grant can be made to only four of them. Power may be reserved to the others so that they can take a grant if a vacancy occurs (for example on the death of one of the four who has taken a grant). Similarly if more than four persons are equally entitled to a grant of administration (of either type) the grant cannot be made to more than four. If any dispute arises as to which of more than four persons are to take a grant it is resolved by a hearing before a district judge or registrar (r.27(6) of the 1987 Rules). It is possible to appoint executors whose powers are limited to only part of the estate in which case up to four people can take each limited grant.

The minimum number of executors is always one, although the court has a discretion to appoint one or more additional personal representatives to act with the sole executor while there is a minority of a beneficiary or life interest subsisting in the estate (Senior Courts Act 1981 s.114(4)). An application for such an appointment may be made by any person interested in the estate or the guardian or receiver of any such person.

The minimum number of administrators is generally one, unless there is a minor beneficiary or a life interest in the estate where the appointment must normally be made to a trust corporation (with or without an individual) or to not less than two individuals (Senior Courts Act 1981 s.114(2)). However, the court has a discretion to appoint a sole administrator where there is a minority or life interest if it appears to the court "to be expedient in all the circumstances" (Senior Courts Act 1981 s.114(2)).

Where two administrators are necessary they may often be persons who have different entitlements to a grant.

Example 5

T dies with a will which leaves a number of pecuniary legacies to his grandchildren who are minors, a specific legacy to his adult son and residue to his wife. No executor is appointed. His wife has the best right to take a grant because she is a residuary beneficiary, but a second administrator is required because of the minority interest. The adult son is entitled to take a grant as a non-residuary beneficiary so he can be appointed as a co-administrator.

There is no requirement in cases of a minority or life interest that the numbers be maintained. Thus, if one of two administrators dies, the survivor can continue alone.

9. SPECIAL RULES AS TO APPOINTMENT OF PERSONAL REPRESENTATIVES

After renunciation

It may appear from what has been said so far that the choice of executor or administrator is automatic. However, this is far from being the case in all circumstances. The person with the best entitlement to a grant may renounce (see para.8-019) in which case the person(s) with the next best right become entitled. Thus, if a will appoints an executor who renounces, makes some specific gifts and leaves the residue equally to two people, either or both of the two residuary beneficiaries can apply for a grant of administration with will annexed as they are the people with the best entitlement to a grant under r.20 of the 1987 Rules. If they renounce, the specific legatees can apply. In the case of an intestacy if the people with the best entitlement under r.22 of the 1987 Rules renounce, the person next in the list will have a right to a grant. 8-021

Passing-over

8-022 The High Court has power under the Senior Courts Act 1981 s.116(1) to pass over the person entitled to a grant if

> "If by reason of any special circumstances it appears to the High Court to be necessary or expedient to appoint as administrator some person other than the person who, but for this section, would in accordance with probate rules have been entitled to the grant, the court may in its discretion appoint as administrator such person as it thinks expedient.".

It had become common to divide the test in s.116 into two stages: (1) whether there are any special circumstances and, if so, (2) whether it is necessary or expedient to appoint some person as administrator other than the person who would normally be entitled (see for example *Oldham MBC v Makin* (2017)).

However, in *Ganoun v Joshi* (2020) Robin Vos sitting as a deputy High Court judge considered that the two-stage approach was hard to justify. The court must determine whether it is necessary or expedient to appoint an administrator as a result of the existence of special circumstances. The special circumstances are therefore only relevant to the question as to whether it is necessary or expedient to appoint a particular person as administrator.

When this power is exercised the court may appoint any person to be the administrator, so that it does not necessarily appoint the person with the next best right to a grant or indeed a person with any right. Frequently the appointment will be to an independent professional or to a person agreed upon by the parties involved.

Under s.115(1)(b) the court also has power to grant administration to a trust corporation either solely or jointly with another person.

The power to pass over the person entitled to a grant is discretionary so that no exact rules can be laid down as to when the power will be exercised. However, two types of case may be recognised.

First, where the persons entitled request the appointment of their nominee. In *Teague and Ashdown v Wharton* (1871) Lord Penzance held that a mere request was insufficient to enable the court to pass over those entitled since

> "persons entitled to grants ... are many of them persons who have no opportunity of knowing their own rights, and are not aware of the dangers that may beset them if they transfer these rights to other persons".

In *Re Potter* (1899) Gorell Barnes J made a grant at the request of the persons who were entitled to a grant. It should be noted that in that case there were other special circumstances and that in his remarkably short judgment the judge seemed to place reliance on the fact that the appointment was made with the agreement of all the persons *interested* in the estate and not merely with the agreement of the persons entitled to a grant. It would seem, therefore, that the court will not pass over those entitled merely because they request that course.

Secondly, the court may pass over a personal representative who is unsuitable for that office either in general or in the circumstances of the case. For example, in *In the Estate of Crippen* (1911) the deceased had been murdered by her husband; she had died intestate and normally he would have taken her property. He would also have been entitled to take a grant to her estate and, as he was dead, his personal representatives would have taken the grant. However, there is a rule of public policy that a person who slays another loses their entitlement to that person's property (see para.16-045). The husband had, therefore, lost his beneficial entitlement to her estate and so his personal representative was passed over in favour of the wife's next-of-kin. In *Adepoju v Akinola* (2016) the person who would have been entitled to the grant was passed over on the basis that her evidence was not to be trusted and that she had lied. In *Oldham Metropolitan Borough Council v Makin* (2017) the deceased was an "*infamous murderer*", the executor had not made arrangements for the disposal of the body five months after the death and there was a concern that whatever arrangements might be made could cause public unrest.

In *In the Estate of Hall* (1914) an executor who was in prison was passed over. In *Re Hall* (1950) the person entitled to administration was passed over on the ground that she could not be traced. In *In the Estate of Biggs* (1966) an executor had dealt with property in the estate without taking a grant (and was therefore debarred from renouncing probate—see para.8-010) but was now unwilling to continue acting despite the fact that he had been ordered to take a grant and that proceedings for contempt of court had been started against him. The court passed him over.

In *A.B. v Dobbs* (2010) the court emphasised that, although the power is discretionary, it should only be exercised to pass over executors in extreme cases such as where the executor is in prison, demented, bankrupt or refuses to act. The intentions of the testator should not be set aside "unless the persons chosen had, more or less, disentitled themselves from carrying out the task".

Finally, the case of *In the Goods of Edwards-Taylor* (1951) shows that the power to pass over is designed to control the appointment of personal representatives and cannot be used for a collateral purpose. In that case there was an application to pass over a beneficiary who was alleged to be mentally and physically immature. The application was made so that she would not be able to get possession of the deceased's estate immediately. The court refused to pass her over since the reason for the application was not concerned with the administration of the estate.

Administration of Justice Act 1985 s.50

Under s.50(1)(a) the court has power to remove an existing personal representa- **8-023**
tive and appoint a substitute. Under s.50(1)(b) where there are two or more existing personal representatives it can terminate the appointment of one or more of those persons. The jurisdiction under s.50 is contentious business and accordingly is dealt with in the Chancery Division. The application must be made by a beneficiary (*Re Thomas and Agnes Carvel Foundation* (2007)).

In *Goodman v Goodman* (2013) the court allowed the removal of an executor under s.50 before probate had been granted. Section 50 confers a power to replace or remove a "personal representative". The term encompasses both an executor and an administrator. While an administrator derives title from his appointment as such by the court so that there can be no question of his being replaced or removed in advance of the grant of letters of administration, an executor derives title from the will.

Three recent decisions illustrate the approach that the court is likely to take in deciding whether to exercise its discretion to remove a personal representative under s.50. In *Kershaw v Micklethwaite* (2010) the court refused to remove executors where there was simply a breakdown in relations between them and the residuary beneficiary. Removal under s.50 should only be ordered where the hostility interferes with the administration of the estate. Contrast *Re Steele* (2010) where the court removed an executor because the evidence was that the mistrust between the beneficiaries and the executor was likely to affect the proper administration of the estate even though the executor had been guilty of no wrongdoing. In *Aikin v Raymond* (2010) one of the two executors allegedly invoiced the estate for work done for the deceased. The beneficiaries disputed the invoice. The court held that it did not "*bear scrutiny*" and the work was not properly calculated. The court ordered the removal of the executor and of his co-executor who, although not involved in the work or the drawing up of the invoice, had supported him in the dispute with the beneficiaries. The court refused to allow the beneficiaries to take a grant but appointed two neutral individuals to replace the executors.

10. LIMITED GRANTS

Introduction

8-024 Most grants are general in their effect. That is, they give the personal representative authority (or, in the case of probate, confirm their authority) to act for all purposes in the administration of the estate and extend to all the property in the estate without time limit.

There are, however, three ways in which grants may be limited in their effect:

(a) they may be limited in time (for example, "until X reaches majority");
(b) they may be limited to part of the estate (for example, "limited to settled land"); or
(c) they may be limited as to a purpose, that is they may give the personal representative authority to deal with one particular aspect of the administration (for example, "limited to conducting or defending litigation").

Grants limited as to time

Grants on behalf of minors

8-025 A minor cannot take a grant of probate or of administration. Where one of several executors appointed by a will is a minor the adult executors may take a general grant of probate immediately. Power is reserved to the minor who may take a grant of double probate on reaching 18. Where one of several potential administrators entitled in the same degree is a minor the grant will usually be made to the adults in preference to the guardians of the minor (r.27(5) of the 1987 Rules).

Where, however, the executors or the persons with the best entitlement to be administrators are all minors, it is necessary to make a grant of letters of administration to some other person until the minors reach 18. This type of grant may be a grant of administration with will annexed or a grant of simple administration. It confers on the administrator a general power to deal with the estate but is limited in time until the minor reaches 18. The grant will usually expire automatically on the minor reaching 18 although it is possible for some other time limit to be fixed (for example, the grant may be effective until the minor himself takes a grant). A grant of this type is made "*for the use and benefit of the minor*" and is therefore, made to the guardian of the minor (subject to the exceptions mentioned below) rather than to others entitled to the estate of the deceased.

The persons entitled to take a grant on behalf of a minor are set out in r.32 of the 1987 Rules:

(a) a parent of the minor who has or is deemed to have parental responsibility under the Children Act 1989 as amended, a guardian or special guardian appointed under that Act, or in certain circumstances a step-parent, adoption agency or local authority;

(b) an "appointed" guardian; that is someone appointed by a district judge or registrar under r.32(2) of the 1987 Rules either because there is no one eligible under (a) above or because the registrar decides to pass over those persons; and

(c) where there is a minority in the estate so that two administrators are required but there is only one person competent and willing to take a grant under (a) or (b) above, that person may nominate a second administrator.

A Practice Direction of 26 September 1991 (see [1991] 4 All E.R. 562) details the evidence of entitlement required for applications for grants on behalf of minors.

Lack of mental capacity to take a grant

Where the executors or administrators lack mental capacity within the meaning of the Mental Capacity Act 2005, they *may* in some cases be passed over in favour of other applicants, but normally a grant will be made to some other person for the use and benefit of the person lacking capacity (r.35 of the 1987 Rules). The grant is made in the following order of priority unless the district judge or registrar otherwise directs: **8-026**

(a) to the person authorised by the Court of Protection to apply for a grant;

(b) where there is no person so authorised, to the lawful attorney, acting under a lasting power of attorney or a registered enduring power of attorney, of the person who lacks capacity; and

(c) where there is no person authorised under (a) or (b), the grant is to the person or persons entitled to the residuary estate of the deceased. In this case a medical certificate from a doctor who is responsible for the patient is required to prove incapacity.

Unless a district judge or registrar otherwise directs, no grant shall be made under this rule unless all persons entitled in the same degree as the person who lacks capacity have been cleared off.

In 2019 Winchester District Registry (via the Private Client Section of the Law Society) published a list of common errors it encountered in probate applications. Failure to supply supporting medical evidence was one of the errors identified.

Grants limited as to property

Appointment of executors

A will may appoint different executors to deal with different parts of the estate. One example of this is an appointment of a literary executor to deal with literary effects and of a general executor to deal with the rest of the estate. The grant of probate taken by the literary executor will be limited to literary effects only. The grant taken by the general executor, if taken before the grant to the limited part of the estate, is described as a grant "*save and except*" the limited part; if taken after the grant of the limited part it is limited to the rest of the estate. There is no practical difference between these two types of grant. Where a grant is made limited to **8-027** certain property, up to four personal representatives may join in that grant and up to four in the grant made in respect of the rest of the estate.

The court's discretion

8-028 The court can make a grant limited to part of the estate in exercise of its discretion under s.116 of the Senior Courts Act 1981. However, the court will not make such a grant unless there are very exceptional circumstances and will usually pass over the person entitled to a grant altogether rather than make a limited grant.

Settled land

8-029 The legal title to settled land is vested in the tenant for life not in the trustees of the settlement. When the tenant for life dies and the settlement continues after his or her death, a grant limited to settled land is required in order that the settled land vests in the trustees of the settlement rather than the general personal representatives.

A grant of letters of administration is made to the trustees at the date of death or, where they fail to take a grant to the trustees, at the date of grant or where no such trustees take a grant by the deceased's general personal representatives.

Where the property passes to a person absolutely entitled after death of the tenant for life the settlement comes to an end and the property devolves on the general personal representatives of the deceased tenant for life. There is, therefore, no need for special personal representatives in such a case (*Re Bridgett and Hayes Contract* (1928)). Similarly no special personal representatives are needed where a settlement is *created* by the will of the deceased.

The above rules requiring a separate grant for settled land apply only to strict settlements under the Settled Land Act 1925. Where a person is entitled to a life interest under a trust of land (under the Trusts of Land Act 1996) or a trust for sale, whether or not of land, the property is vested in the trustees and continues to be vested in them despite the death of the life tenant. The trust property does not, therefore, pass to any personal representative of the life tenant. Where a trust of land is created by will or intestacy, the general personal representatives will deal with the property and will vest it in the trustees.

Grants limited as to purpose

Grants for dealing with certain assets

8-030 These grants, called grants *ad colligenda bona* under the 1987 Rules enable collection and preservation of the assets in the estate before a general grant is made so that any assets in danger may be preserved. There are no particular rules as to who may apply for the grant; application is made to a district judge or registrar ex parte (r.52(b) of the 1987 Rules).

Although a grant *ad colligenda bona* is usually limited to collecting in the estate the court may grant power to sell or otherwise deal with the assets so as to preserve their value.

Grant for purposes of litigation

8-031 Such grants (called *ad litem* under the 1987 Rules) are made to enable proceedings in court to be begun or continued on behalf of the estate of the deceased or against it. Any person interested in the litigation may apply ex parte to a district judge or registrar.

Temporary grant while probate action taking place

Where there is a probate action in relation to an estate (for example, because the validity of an alleged will is in question), the court may appoint an administrator to act until the probate action is concluded. Any person who is a party to the probate action or interested in the estate may apply for the grant to be made but the grant will usually be made to an independent third party. The administrator will not usually be given authority to distribute any of the estate. Parties involved in disputes should consider such an application, as loss can easily be caused to the estate if steps are not taken to deal with the assets. See, for example, *Crabbe v Townsend* (2016) and *Sifri v Clough Willis* (2007). **8-032**

11. INCOMPLETE ADMINISTRATION

Introduction

In most cases the executor or administrator who first takes out a grant will complete the administration of the estate. Sometimes, however, the original personal representative will die or otherwise cease to hold office without completing the administration. In such a case, if there is no chain of representation, a grant to some other person will be required. This will either be a grant *de bonis non administratis* or a cessate grant depending on the circumstances. Sometimes before the administration is completed an executor is added by means of a grant of double probate. A grant of double probate is made where one or some of a number of executors have taken a grant with power reserved to others to take at a later stage and one of those others now obtains a grant. **8-033**

Grant of administration where estate incompletely administered

Where *all* the previous personal representatives die or lack mental capacity to act and the estate is incompletely administered, a grant limited to the unadministered portion of the estate is made to enable the administration of the estate to be completed. **8-034**

There are three requirements which must be satisfied before such a grant can be made:

- (i) *The administration is incomplete.* Administration is complete once the debts and legacies have been paid, accounts have been prepared and any land or other assets remaining in the estate have been vested in the beneficiaries by means of assents.
- (ii) *There is no remaining personal representative.* No additional grant is required so long as one personal representative remains. That personal representative will have full power to complete the administration. Similarly no additional grant is required following the death of the last surviving executor if he or she has appointed an executor who proves his or her will and so becomes an executor by representation (see para.8-006).
- (iii) *There has been a previous grant.* An original, not a limited, grant is appropriate where an executor has acted without a grant or someone has

partly administered the estate without any authority.

The limited grant may be a grant of administration with will annexed or a grant of simple administration. The order of priority for taking the grant is governed by the normal rules of priority which were explained at paras 8-013 and 8-017.

Usually the person (or persons) to whom the grant is made will be the person who was entitled to a grant equally with the previous grantee or who was next entitled after them. Where the previous personal representative was entitled to the whole of the estate the grant will usually be made to his or her personal representatives (the rule that living persons are to be preferred to the personal representatives of deceased persons only applies as between persons entitled in the same degree).

Where there is a minority or a life interest in the estate at the time when the application for the limited grant is made, two administrators will be required unless the court orders to the contrary or makes a grant to a trust corporation.

Grant to follow expiry of a time limited grant

8-035 Such a grant is required where the original grant was limited in time and has ceased to be effective because the time has expired. The most common circumstances in which such a grant is required is where a grant of administration (with will or of simple administration) has been made to a guardian "for the use and benefit" of a minor who would be entitled to a grant but for minority. When the minor reaches 18 the limited grant to the guardian automatically ceases to be effective and the minor is entitled to apply for a "follow-on" grant. The follow-on grant may be a grant of probate, administration with the will annexed or simple administration depending on the nature of the minor's entitlement.

A follow-on grant is also appropriate in other circumstances where a grant is limited in time and the time expires. Thus if a will appoints an executor for life the executor's office ceases altogether on death and so the chain of representation cannot provide the estate with an executor. A follow-on grant is then made to any executor appointed in substitution for the deceased executor by the will (for example, the will may have appointed "A for life and thereafter B"). If no substitutional appointment has been made a follow-on grant of administration with will is made to the person entitled under the normal priority rules. If a grant of simple administration is made for the use and benefit of a minor a follow-on grant of simple administration is made to the minor on reaching 18.

Double probate

8-036 A grant of double probate is made to an executor who applies for a grant after a grant of *probate* has already been made to another executor. There are three types of case in which a grant of double probate is appropriate:

(i) Where one of a number of executors does not wish to take a grant immediately, does not wish to renounce and has not been cited to take or renounce probate, power will be reserved to take a grant later. Such an executor may then apply for double probate at any time.

(ii) Where one of a number of executors is a minor at the time of the original grant of probate to the others, power is reserved automatically and the executor can apply for double probate on reaching 18. If the original grant had been a grant of administration the application would be for a follow-on grant not a grant of double probate. Thus where a will appoints several executors of whom some are adults and some minors a grant of probate will be made to the adults immediately and a grant of double probate to the minors on reaching majority. Where a will appoints a minor as the only executor, a grant of administration with will annexed will be made to the guardians of the executor (or to the person entitled to residue if the minor executor was not so entitled) and a follow-on grant of probate to the infant on reaching majority.

(iii) Where executors are prevented from taking a grant by the rule which restricts a grant to four persons in respect of any part of an estate (Senior Courts Act 1981 s.114(1)) one of them may apply for a grant of double probate if a vacancy occurs (for example on the death of one of the four proving executors) since power is reserved to them in the original grant.

It should be noted that there is no possibility of double grants of *administration*. A potential administrator who does not prove in the original grant will only be able to take a grant later if a grant or a follow-on grant is needed or if a second administrator is needed because a life interest or minority arises.

When applying for a grant of double probate the oath must set out, in addition to the usual matters, particulars of the former grant. An office copy of the original grant should accompany the application.

12. CIRCUMSTANCES IN WHICH NO GRANT IS REQUIRED

Since an executor's authority derives from the will rather than the grant of probate, certain steps may be taken without a grant. However, in nearly all circumstances a grant is eventually, in fact, required so that it can be produced to prove title to the assets of the estate. **8-037**

There are a number of statutory provisions which enable certain assets to be dealt with without production of a grant but they are all concerned with relatively small amounts of property (see paras 12-010 and 21-002).

13. REVOCATION OF GRANTS

Jurisdiction

In certain circumstances a grant may be revoked by the Chancery Division (or county court) in contentious cases or by a district judge or registrar of the Family Division in non-contentious cases. **8-038**

Where there is a dispute as to whether a grant should be revoked the case is contentious and every personal representative must be a party to the action. The original grant must be lodged with the court. If there is no dispute as to the need for revocation the case is non-contentious. However, a grant cannot normally be revoked in non-contentious proceedings except on the application of the person to whom the grant was made.

Grounds for revocation

A grant will be revoked where: **8-039**

(1) It is subsequently found that it ought not to have been made to the person to whom it was in fact made. This may arise in many ways: for example, where a fraudulent application is made by a person with no right to a grant;

where a person thought to have predeceased is subsequently found to be alive and better entitled to a grant than the person to whom the original grant was made; where the grant was made despite the entry of a caveat; where a grant was made even though contentious probate proceedings were pending.

(2) A subsequent will is discovered (and in most cases where a subsequent codicil is discovered) or where it is found, after a grant, that the will was invalid or had been revoked before death.

(3) A personal representative loses mental or physical capacity, or disappears or wishes to retire and the court agrees to this.

(4) The "deceased" is not in fact dead.

Consequences of revocation

8-040 Section 27 of the Administration of Estates Act 1925 protects an original personal representative who makes or permits payments or dispositions in good faith. A person who makes a payment to a personal representative in good faith is also protected. Section 39 of the same Act provides that contracts for sale remain binding on and enforceable by the estate despite the revocation of the grant. Section 37 provides that a conveyance of any type of property remains valid despite revocation of the grant provided the conveyance is to a purchaser who gave valuable consideration in good faith (a conveyance is widely defined in this context and includes almost all dealings with property).

If property is transferred to the wrong beneficiary under a grant which is later revoked (for example, the property is distributed as on intestacy and then a will is found) the beneficiary is liable to return the asset or to refund its value. The true beneficiary is also entitled to trace the asset or its proceeds and to recover it from the person now in possession so long as it remains identifiable. However, there is no right to trace into the hands of a bona fide purchaser for value without notice.

Chapter Nine

PROBATE JURISDICTION

1. Jurisdiction—Territorial Limits

Grants of representation are made by the English courts where property of the deceased is situated in England and Wales and either an executor is appointed or such property is disposed of in England and Wales. A will which neither appoints an executor nor disposes of English property is not usually admitted to probate although the court has a discretion to issue a grant in such cases. **9-001**

2. Nature of Probate Jurisdiction—Contentious and Non-Contentious Business

Probate jurisdiction is concerned with three things only. First, the decision as to whether a document may be admitted to probate or annexed to a grant of administration as a testamentary document; secondly, the decision as to who is entitled to a grant of representation in respect of the estate of a deceased person; and, thirdly, the decision to amend or revoke a grant. **9-002**

Since 1970 probate business has been divided between the Family Division (which deals with non-contentious business), the Chancery Division (which deals with contentious business) and the county court (which has concurrent jurisdiction to deal with contentious business where the value of the estate of the deceased does not exceed a limit laid down by rules of court. The present limit is £30,000 for contentions probate and £350,000 increased from £30,000 for the purposes of equity jurisdiction only. See the County Court Jurisdiction Order 2014 (SI 2014/503). However, Chancery Masters and Deputies have power to order the transfer of claims out of the Chancery Division in London where another court, such as the county court (particularly the Central London County Court which has are two circuit judges who are specialised in Chancery work), is more suitable for case management and trial of a claim.

The objective is to ensure that only cases which may properly be regarded as being suitable for management and trial in the Chancery Division of the High Court in London are retained there. The monetary value is taken into account but is only one factor. The *Chancery Masters' Guidelines For The Transfer Of Claims* says that "*for probate and equity claims, the figures of £30,000 and £350,000 respectively are not determinative*".

Non-contentious business (which is also called common form business) is defined by the Senior Courts Act 1981 s.128 as:

> "the business of obtaining probate and administration where there is no-contention as to the right thereto, including—

(a) the passing of probates and administrations through the High Court in contentious cases where the contest has been terminated, and
(b) all business of a non-contentious nature in matters of testacy and-intestacy not being proceedings in any action, and
(c) the business of lodging caveats against the grant of probate or administration."

The vast majority of probate cases are non-contentious and are dealt with entirely by the Family Division. Non-contentious probate may involve a hearing before a district judge or registrar; for example, a hearing may be required to decide between persons entitled to a grant in the same degree, or where the court is asked to pass over a person entitled to a grant in favour of some other person.

Where there is a dispute as to what document or documents should be admitted to probate, or as to who is entitled to take out a grant, or as to whether a grant should be revoked, contentious (or solemn form) proceedings may be necessary and will be brought in the Chancery Division or county court. In most cases non-contentious proceedings will begin first and the case will only become contentious when the dispute arises.

A grant of representation in common form does not prevent a probate claim for proof in solemn form from being brought later. Thus if, after the Family Division has granted probate, someone wishes to challenge the validity of the will, they may start contentious proceedings.

Frequently, where there is a dispute, a caveat or citation will be entered but neither of these steps is, of itself, sufficient to start a contentious probate action.

After a probate claim is started, the case remains contentious until the dispute is finally decided by the Chancery Division or the county court. Once the dispute is disposed of, the case becomes non-contentious and so is returned to the Family Division which is responsible for the issue of the grant (the Family Division is the only court which actually makes grants).

3. FINANCIAL LIMITS

9-003 The jurisdiction of the High Court (Family and Chancery Division) is unlimited as to the amount of the estate. The county court's jurisdiction in contentious cases is limited to cases where the estate is less than the county court limit at the time of death. (In valuing the estate for this purpose debts, funeral expenses and incumbrances are deducted as is property vested in the deceased as trustee and not beneficially.) Once proceedings have been commenced in the county court the Principal Registry should be informed so that no grant is made in common form in the estate.

4. PROBATE JURISDICTION AND OTHER JURISDICTION CONCERNING WILLS

9-004 Probate jurisdiction is concerned only with what documents are admissible as testamentary documents and to whom grants should be made. Litigation-concerning wills and administration of estates may, however, arise in at least three other ways:

(a) there may be no dispute as to what should be admitted as a testamentary document but a dispute as to what it means (that is, a question of construction may arise);
(b) there may be a dispute as to how the estate should be administered by the

personal representatives (so that an administration action becomes necessary); or

(c) there may be a claim against a personal representative who is alleged to have acted improperly (and so may be liable for the *devastavit* which has been committed).

Proceedings in each of these three types of case will usually be brought in the Chancery Division. When a question of construction is before the court, it is bound by the decision of the Family Division (or of the Chancery Division in earlier probate proceedings) as to the wording of the testamentary instrument. Questions of construction are not generally decided in probate proceedings except to the extent that it is necessary for the purpose of the probate action. Thus, it is appropriate for the court to decide, in probate proceedings, who the testator intended to appoint as executor and what parts of earlier wills or codicils have been revoked by a later testamentary document.

5. SOLEMN FORM PROCEDURE

We have already outlined the distinction between common form and solemn form probate. We intend to give no more than an outline of the solemn form procedure in the High Court (Chancery Division) (the procedure for obtaining a grant in common form cases is dealt with in Ch.10). Probate claims are dealt with in Pt 57 of the Civil Procedure Rules 1998 (SI 1998/3132) and the CPR PD 57 (Probate and Inheritance) which deal with rectification of wills, the removal of personal representatives, claims under the Inheritance (Provision for Family Dependents) Act 1975, proceedings under the Presumption of Death Act 2013 and Guardianship of Missing Persons Act 2017, as well as contentious probate. **9-005**

The probate action is started by issuing a claim form under CPR Pt 7 in a Chancery District Registry or Chancery Chambers at the Royal Courts of Justice (or in the county court office if the case is in the county court). A defendant served with the claim must file an acknowledgement of service within 28 days (or within 28 days of service of the particulars of claim if later). Any testamentary documents in the possession of the claimant must be lodged in the court when the claim form is issued, any in the possession of the defendant must be lodged when they acknowledge service (CPR r.57.5). If service is not acknowledged the claimant can proceed with the action as if it had been acknowledged.

The claim form must contain a statement of the nature of the interest of the claimant in the estate and of the nature of each defendant's interest (CPR r.57.7(1) and (2)). A party who disputes any such statement must say so in the statement of case. Similarly a party claiming that the will was not duly executed or that the testator did not know or approve of the contents of the will, lacked capacity or was subject to undue influence or fraud must say so and give particulars of the facts relied upon (CPR r.57.7(3) and (4)).

A default judgment cannot be obtained in a probate action. This is because the court has to make a positive decision as to whether the will is valid or not.

A defendant may give notice in his defence that he does not raise any positive case, but insists on the will being proved in solemn form and, for that purpose, will cross-examine the witnesses who attested the will. If a defendant gives such a notice, the court will not make an order for costs against him unless it considers that there was no reasonable ground for opposing the will (CPR r.57(5)). This offers valuable protection against exposure to costs. However, costs will be ordered if there were no reasonable grounds for opposing the will. This happened in *Elliott v Simmonds* (2016) where costs were ordered but only from the date on which the deceased's daughter, with her advisers, had sufficient material on which to form a view about whether there was any reasonable ground on which the will could be opposed.

It is a common misconception that in probate actions costs come out of the estate but this is not the case. The normal rules about costs contained in CPR Pt 44 apply to probate claims. Thus the court has discretion as to who pays costs and the amount of costs. Costs of litigation are, therefore, borne by the unsuccessful party (CPR r.44.3(2)(a)) unless the court orders otherwise (CPR r.44.3(2)(b)), e.g. from the other side in whole or in part, or from the estate.

There are two exceptions to the general rule that costs follow the event which were identified by Sir Gorell Barnes P in *Spiers v English* (1907) as follows:

(1) if a person who makes a will or persons who are interested in the residue have been really the cause of the litigation a case is made out for costs to come out of the estate;
(2) if the circumstances lead reasonably to an investigation of the matter, then the costs may be left to be borne by those who have incurred them.

Kostic v Chaplin (2007) contains an extremely helpful modern summary of the rules.

Executors who successfully prove a will are entitled to take their own costs out of the estate.

Chapter Ten

OBTAINING THE GRANT (NON-CONTENTIOUS CASES)

1. Who Deals With Grants?

A grant of representation is an order of the High Court. Applications used to be dealt with at one of the following: **10-001**

- the Principal Probate Registry;
- a District Probate Registry;
- a Sub-Probate Registry.

The London Probate Department at the Principal Registry formerly situated at First Avenue House, 7th Floor, 42–49 High Holborn, London WC1V 6NP closed at the end of 2020. Sub-Probate Registries have all been closed and District Registries have been reduced to eight in a move towards centralisation and modernisation of the system. All probate registries now utilise a central address which is HMCTS Probate, PO Box 12625, Harlow, CM20 9QE.

Applications can be made either in person by those entitled to take a grant or through a solicitor or probate practitioner (Non-Contentious Probate Rules 1987 r.4(1)).

Personal applications can be made by post or online. Strenuous efforts have been made to make the process simple and user-friendly. It is no longer necessary to swear an oath. Applications are made by completing a form PA1P if there is a will and a form PA1A if there is no will. Postal applications are sent to: HMCTS Probate, PO Box 12625, Harlow, CM20 9QE.

A probate practitioner is defined by r.2(1) of the Non-Contentious Probate Rules 1987 as a person who for the purposes of the Legal Services Act 2007 is an authorised person in relation to probate activities. Probate activities are defined in Legal Services Act 2007 Sch.2, para.6 as "*preparing any probate papers for the purposes of the law of England and Wales*" and probate papers are defined as "*papers on which to found or oppose a grant of probate or administration*". It is an offence for anyone to carry out probate activities who is not authorised under the Legal Services Act 2007. A probate practitioner includes a barrister, a duly certificated notary public, the Public Trustee or the Official Solicitor. A -solicitor should be duly certificated in accordance with the Solicitors Act 1974 s.13. Similarly, a barrister must have a practising certificate issued in accordance with the Practising Certificate Regulations of the General Council of the Bar. A practising certificate for a notary public is given by the Faculty Office of the Archbishop of Canterbury.

The Council for Licensed Conveyancers and the Association of Certified Chartered Accountants are designated as approved regulators for the purpose of granting to licensed conveyancers and certified chartered accountants authority to carry on probate activities.

In this chapter we are concerned only with the procedure where a solicitor or probate practitioner is obtaining a grant on behalf of the personal representative.

Online applications are now dealt with from the Courts and Tribunals Service Centre in Birmingham. Bulk scanning of supporting documents takes place at HMCTS Probate in Harlow. The scanned supporting documents are then transmitted to Birmingham.

Paper applications made by professionals are sent to the Newcastle District Probate Registry (or Cardiff if a copy of the grant is required in Welsh). Paper applications made by non-professionals are sent to Harlow. All applications are then allocated to whichever District Registry has the most capacity.

The judicial officers of the Principal Registry are called district judges and those of the district registries are called registrars. In cases of doubt or uncertainty a district judge or registrar may refer a matter to a judge of the Family Division (Non-Contentious Probate Rules 1987 (SI 1987/2024) (the 1987 Rules) r.61(1)).

2. ONLINE APPLICATIONS BY PROBATE PRACTITIONERS

10-002 The Courts and Tribunal Service (HMCTS) is moving towards a digital process for obtaining all grants. On 2 November 2020, the Non-Contentious Probate (Amendment) Rules 2020 (SI 2020/1059) came into force.

The SI inserts a new r.4 into the Non-contentious Probate Rules 1987 making it obligatory for professionals to apply online unless the application is listed in a new Third Schedule to the 1987 Rules. Even in the case of applications listed in the schedule applications can be made online if the HMCTS system is able to accept it. The current applications which cannot be made online are set out in *Guidance: Apply for probate on paper as a practitioner* available on the gov.uk website.

At the time of writing applications cannot be made online for the more complex applications for probate and for most grants of administration. HMCTS is planning to extend the online capability so it is always worth checking the list of exclusions.

By way of illustration the following types of applications for probate are excluded:

- for a second grant for the same estate;
- where the person entitled has been convicted of murder or manslaughter of the deceased or has otherwise forfeited the right to apply;
- in respect of a foreign will;
- accompanied by an application to prove a copy of the will;
- accompanied by an application for rectification or fiat copy of the will (a reproduction of a will in its state as at the time of execution, as is required, for example, where a will contains alterations which are not admissible to probate).

In the case of an application for letters of administration on intestacy it is only possible to apply online in the following very limited cases:

- there is only one applicant, and they are the only person entitled to the estate;
- the applicant is a spouse/civil partner or sole child/adopted child of the deceased;
- where the deceased was domiciled outside of England and Wales, the estate in England and Wales only consists of immovable property;

- there is no other claim on the estate;
- there is no minority interest;
- the applicant is able to make their own decisions;
- the deceased died after 1 October 2014.

It is not possible to apply online if any of these apply:

- the applicant is represented by an Attorney, under NCPR 1987 r.31;
- where all those entitled are deceased and their legal personal representatives are making the application;
- the application relates to resealing under Colonial Probates Acts 1892 and 1927, under NCPR 1987 r.39;
- for administration under the court's discretionary powers under NCPR r.52 (Administration of Justice Act 1982 s.116 to pass over those entitled and grants *ad colligenda bona*);
- where the person entitled has been convicted of murder or manslaughter of the deceased or has otherwise forfeited the right to apply.

In the case of applications for letters of administration with will annexed it is only possible to apply online in the following very limited cases:

- there is only one applicant, and they are the only person entitled to the estate;
- all the beneficiaries in the will and/or codicils (both who receive a specific gift and who get the residue) are over 18;
- the applicant is named in the will and/or codicils as the only residuary legatee or devisee or residuary legatee and devisee;
- all executors, residuary legatees and devisees holding the estate in trust have died or chosen not to apply.

It is not possible to apply online if the application is:

- for a second grant for the same estate;
- for a foreign will;
- accompanied by an application to prove a copy of the will;
- accompanied by an application for rectification or fiat copy of the will;
- for joinder of administrator, under NCPR 1987 r.25;
- for two or more persons who are entitled in the same degree, under NCPR 1987 r.27(3)–(8);
- where there is a life interest.

It is also possible to apply for a caveat online as well as by post.

It is only the application which is made online. Supporting documentation such as the Will, any codicils, any statements of truth must be sent to the Harlow Bulk Scanning Centre.

It is necessary to register to use the service and a pay by account (PBA) account is required in order to use the Courts and Tribunal Service Fee Account System to pay for online applications.

3. THE PAPERS LEADING TO A GRANT

The following are required by HMCTS: **10-003**

(a) The will (if there is one) and any codicils to it.
(b) Probate fees. Probate fees are £300 from May 2024 (increased from £273)

£273 for estates exceeding £5,000. Estates which do not exceed £5,000 pay no fee. The "estate" consists of all assets requiring a grant after deduction of debts of the estate. The fee is not payable on property which passes by survivorship or under a trust without need for a grant.

(c) An application from the personal representatives. This will be an online form unless the application is one which must be made on paper in which case it will be a PA1P if there is a will and a PA1A if there is no will. All applications include a legal statement confirming that those making the application will carry out their obligations as personal representatives, will provide full details of the estate and how it has been distributed, if required by the court, and that they understand that criminal proceedings can be brought if they are deliberately untruthful or dishonest.

(d) If inheritance tax is payable, the personal representatives must complete and submit an IHT400 with supporting schedules and pay the tax which is due with the application. The IHT421 sets out the tax due. HMRC will receipt it and transmit it to HMCTS as proof that IHT has been paid. When this has been done, HMRC issues the applicant with a code and details of the estate values needed to submit a grant application to HM Courts and Tribunals Service. The application for a grant cannot be made until the Code and confirmation of the values are received.

(e) Any written evidence supported by a statement of truth that may be required, for example to prove due execution where there is no attestation clause or it is defective, or to explain any damage or crossings out on the will which might suggest an attempt to revoke it by destruction. On 17 April 2020 the President of the Family Division issued *Guidance as to the replacement of affidavits with statements of truth in non-contentious probate processes* which said that because of social distancing requirements resulting from the coronavirus pandemic, he had authorised Registrars to allow statements of truth to be used as an alternative to affidavits for all non-contentious probate applications until 30 July 2020. The change was made permanent by Non-Contentious Probate (Amendment) Rules 2020 (SI 2020/1059) as from 2 November 2020.

(f) Any renunciation by a person who would have been entitled to a grant in priority to the applicant.

Further information on these items is contained in this chapter.

Once the application has been made, HMCTS will carry out searches; one to ensure that no caveat has been entered against the estate and one to ensure that no grant of representation has already been issued. Searches are also made to ensure that no will has been deposited with the registry.

The papers are examined. If there are defects in the papers HMCTS will contact the applicant to resolve the queries.

If the papers are in order the grant of representation is prepared. A photographic copy of the will and codicils (if any) is no longer attached to the grant. This is unpopular with practitioners. The grant is returned to the applicant by post together with any office copies which have been requested. The fee is £1.50 per copy.

4. The Will and Copies

10-004 The will (if there is one) and any codicils to it must be submitted to HMCTS.

If the will has been damaged in any way, an explanation should be provided and if there are any staple or paper clip marks HMCTS will require an explanation. The concern is that a later will or codicil may have been attached and become detached.

NCPR 1987 r.11 provides that where a district judge or registrar considers that a copy of the original will would not be satisfactory for purposes of record, they may require an engrossment suitable for reproduction to be lodged. Where a will contains alterations which are not to be admitted to proof; or has been ordered to be rectified under the Administration of Justice Act 1982, s.20(1), an engrossment of the will in the form in which it is to be proved must be lodged. The engrossment must reproduce the punctuation, spacing and division into paragraphs of the will and follow continuously from page to page on both sides of the paper. In such circumstances, as an alternative to an engrossment the registrar has discretion to allow a facsimile copy produced by photography in certain circumstances including:

(i) where a complete page is, or complete pages are, to be excluded; and
(ii) where the original has been altered but neither re-executed nor republished and there is in existence a photocopy of the original executed document.

If the original will has been lost or destroyed it may be possible to obtain an order admitting to proof the will as contained in a copy or reconstruction (r.54(1) of the 1987 Rules).

If the original will is lodged in a foreign court a duly authenticated copy of the will may be admitted to proof without need for an order (r.54(2) of the 1987 Rules).

If the will incorporates standard clauses, such as the STEP Standard Provisions, these need not be produced provided that the forms or clauses are contained in published documents and have previously been lodged with the senior district judge of the principal registry and accepted as sufficient lodgment for these purposes (Practice Direction issued by Senior District Judge Angel, 10 April 1995).

5. Forms PA1P and PA1A and Online Applications

Introduction

It used to be necessary for applications for a grant of representation to be supported by an oath sworn or affirmed by the personal representatives before an independent solicitor. The move to online applications together with the Covid pandemic made this requirement inappropriate. A declaration is now included at the end of the application. **10-005**

Before the changes to the Rules, PRs completed different applications for each of the three main grants of representation: probate, administration with will and simple administration.

There are now only two types of paper application:

- Form PA1P where there is a will, irrespective of whether it will lead to a grant of probate or administration with will; and
- Form PA1A where there is no will.

The two PA1 applications are similar but differ in points of detail. Online applications are made using one form which has different sections depending on whether the application is for a grant of probate, administration with a will or administration on intestacy. It is very similar to the paper forms.

What the application forms do

10-006 The purpose of the application forms is to:

(a) establish the basis of the applicants' claim to be entitled to take the grant (for example, in the case of an executor it identifies the applicant as the person named as executor in the will).
(b) confirm that the personal representatives will carry out their statutory duty (contained in Administration of Estates Act 1925 s.25 to:
  - collect and get in the real and personal estate of the deceased and administer it according to law;
  - when required to do so by the court, exhibit on oath in the court a full inventory of the estate and when so required render an account of the administration of the estate to the court;
  - when required to do so by the High Court, deliver up the grant of probate or administration to that court.
(c) In the case of applications where there is a will, identify the will and any codicils to it. The date of the will must be included.

Items (b) and (c) are included on the application forms as a legal statement signed by the personal representatives. Where the application is made online by a professional, the personal representatives can authorise the professional to sign the legal statement on their behalf. The professional must also sign the statement of truth. Typed and handwritten signatures are acceptable.

Points common to both the PA1P and the PA1A

Commencement page

10-007 The application starts with a checklist of enclosures to accompany the form. The only difference is that in the case of the PA1P the last original will and any codicils must be included. In both cases if there is a foreign will or wills or any wills dealing with assets held outside England and Wales, a copy must be provided (together with an English translation and if not in English). This allows HMCTS to check whether the foreign will has any effect on UK succession.

Section A

10-008 **Identifying the applicants** The names, postal and email addresses of all applicants for the grant must be entered. A maximum of four can apply. Where there is more than one applicant, HMCTS will treat the first applicant as nominated by all applicants to apply on their behalf. HMCTS will send all correspondence and the Grant of Representation to the first applicant or to their legal representative, if named at the end of Section 1.

The first applicant is asked to provide telephone numbers (land line and mobile). Other applicants are not.

The marginal notes state that the names provided must be the same as those on the applicants' identification documents such as their Passport or Driving Licence, although identification documents are not required to be submitted. If the applicant is a firm, company, or corporation, the full name of the organisation must be given.

10-009 **Name differs from name in will (in the case of the PA1P)** If the name written in the will differs from any applicant's name, the name written in the will or codicil must be included on the form.

Minimum number of applicants The guidance notes in the margin make the point that where the application is not made by executors and there are minor beneficiaries, at least two applicants are required. The guidance does not deal with the need for two applicants where there is a life interest. Presumably this will be picked up by the Registry, if necessary. 10-010

If the application is made as an attorney, details of the attorney are provided in Section A as the applicant and details of the donor of the power in Section B at Question 5 of the PA1P and Question 4 of the PA1A.

Section B

Identifying the deceased The form requires the name, address, date of birth and date of death of the deceased together with their marital status and domicile at the date of death. 10-011

Name: The name of the deceased is normally the name in which the birth was registered or in the case of a married or divorced woman the surname of her husband (if she has adopted her husband's name). A person may change their name by:

(a) deed poll; or
(b) habit and repute; however, a name is only regarded as changed by habit and repute if the former name has been completely abandoned over a period of time.

If the deceased was known by any other name, that name must be included if the deceased held assets in that name. It will then be included on the grant. There is no need to include another name if no assets were held in that name. There is no need to identify the assets.

Date of birth and death: These must be set out as they appear in the certificate of death. In cases where the precise date of death is uncertain the following wording is used: "who was known to be alive on … and whose dead body was found on …"

A person may have disappeared and be believed dead. As from 1 October 2014, the date on which the Presumption of Death Act 2013 came into force, the High Court makes one declaration of death under s.2 which will be effective for all purposes. The court will only make a declaration if it is satisfied that the person has died, or the person has not been known to be alive for a period of at least seven years.

The declaration must include a finding as to the date and time of the missing person's death. Where the court is satisfied that the missing person has died, but is uncertain at which moment during a period the missing person died, it will state that the missing person is presumed to have died at the end of that period. Where the court is satisfied that the missing person has not been known to be alive for a period of at least seven years, but is not satisfied that they are dead, it will state that the missing person is presumed to have died at the end of the period of seven years beginning with the day after the day on which he or she was last known to be alive (s.2(4)).

The wording used in the declaration should be repeated in the statement.

Marital status: The deceased's marital status at death must be provided. The form has separate tick boxes for:

— Never married
— Widowed, their lawful spouse or civil partner having died before them
— Married/in a civil partnership – the date is required
— Divorced/civil partnership is dissolved – the date is required
— Judicially separated – the date is required

The form asks for the name of the court where the decree absolute, decree of dissolution of civil partnership or decree of Judicial Separation was issued. Checking on this is important as, reasonably frequently, people die after a decree nisi or conditional dissolution order but before the decree absolute or final dissolution order is made. In such a case the person is still married or in a civil partnership at the date of death.

Domicile: Although the form does not require this, if there is any doubt as to whether the deceased died domiciled in England or Wales, an affidavit or witness statement setting out the fact should be filed in support of the application to avoid later problems.

The Administration of Estates Act 1971 provides that where a grant of representation is issued in England and Wales, Scotland or Northern Ireland in respect of the estate of a person who died domiciled in one of these countries, the grant will be recognised in the other two countries provided it contains a statement of the deceased's domicile. Thus, if a person dies domiciled in Scotland owning assets in England and Wales, provided the Scots confirmation contains a reference to the domicile of the deceased it will be recognised as the equivalent of an English grant.

Other information: This section of the form continues with questions about more unusual matters.

If the deceased owned any foreign assets, the total value of their foreign assets (not including houses or land) must be provided.

The form asks whether there was any land vested in the person who has died which was settled previously to their death and which remained settled land not withstanding their death. If the answer is yes, personal applicants are told to obtain legal advice.

10-012 **Settled Land Act settlements** These settlements are relatively unusual as, since the Trusts of Land Act 1996 no new Settled Land Act settlement can be created. Old settlements continue and present particular problems in relation to grants of representation. Normally such settled land devolves not on the general personal representatives but on the trustees of the settlement who take out a special grant of representation limited to the settled land. Therefore in such a case the general personal representatives take out a grant which excludes the settled land. If, however, the settled land devolves on the general personal representatives (for example, where they happen to be the trustees of the settlement) the grant will be made "including settled land".

10-013 **Adopted relatives** If the application is not made by executors, Question 2.13 requires the applicants to give details of any legally adopted relatives of the deceased. This includes persons adopted into the deceased's family and out of it. The guidance notes say:

"We use this information to work out who is eligible to make the application. This information will become public record when probate is granted."

This will obviously not be relevant if the estate is fully disposed if the whole estate is left to named individuals but may become relevant if gifts fail.

Type of grant Questions 2.15 and 2.16 are only to be answered by legal professionals. They ask for the type of application to be identified: this could be one of the main three grants or one of the limited grants. If the application is not for probate or there are limitations to be applied, for example, reseals, double probate, grants *de bonis non* the form asks for the type of grant required, details of the grounds for the application and any relevant information (for example, limitations required). Practitioners are referred to *Tristram and Cootes Probate Practice* for guidance on the information that is required and wording that should be used. We will consider the wording that is required for a grant of letters of administration with will. **10-014**

Grant in Welsh Question 2.17 asks whether or not a grant is required in Welsh. **10-015**

Applications as an attorney It is quite common for persons to apply for a grant as an attorney on behalf of the person entitled to take out the grant (for example where the person entitled is elderly). Attorneys provide identification information for themselves in the first section of the form and then later identify the person or persons on whose behalf they are applying (Question 5 in the PA1P and Question 4 in the PA1A). They must enclose the signed attorney form with this application. The attorney of one executor and an executor acting in their own right may not jointly apply for a grant of representation. **10-016**

Where a person lacks capacity to manage their own affairs, medical evidence may be required as will the enduring or lasting power of attorney appointing the applicant to act.

Where no attorney has been appointed and there are no persons entitled in the same degree to take out a grant, a grant will be made to another person for the use and benefit of the incapacitous person.

Foreign domicile Question 2 on both forms includes sub-questions asking whether the deceased was domiciled outside the UK and whether there are any foreign assets. If there are, the value must be given, not including houses or land. **10-017**

In order to obtain a grant for a person domiciled abroad, it is necessary to demonstrate who is entitled to deal with the assets. NCPR 1987 r.30(1) provides that where a person dies domiciled outside England and Wales, a registrar may issue a grant to any of the following:

(a) to the person entrusted with the administration of the estate by the court having jurisdiction at the place where the deceased died domiciled; or
(b) where there is no person so entrusted, to the person beneficially entitled to the estate by the law of the place where the deceased died domiciled or, if there is more than one person so entitled, to such of them as the registrar may direct; or
(c) if in the opinion of the registrar the circumstances so require, to such person as the registrar may direct.

Paragraph 3 provides that probate may issue without an order:

(a) if the will is in the English or Welsh language, to the executor named in it or to a person described in such a way that they are an executor according to the tenor of the will; and
(b) where the whole or substantially the whole of the estate in England and Wales consists of land, a grant in respect of the whole estate may be made in accordance with the law which would have been applicable if the deceased had died domiciled in England and Wales.

To make provision for grants under r.30(1) the form asks whether there is an entrusting document or a succession certificate or inheritance certificate confirming who is entitled to the deceased's estate.

If there are, the documents must accompany the application. In the absence of such documents, evidence of entitlement will have to be provided.

10-018 **Inheritance tax and value of estate** A grant cannot be issued until the required amount of inheritance tax has been paid. The final set of questions relates to the value of the deceased's assets and the tax due (if any).

The applicant must state whether an IHT400 was completed. This is required unless the estate fulfils the requirements to qualify as an excepted estate (see para.10-039 below).

From 17 January 2044 the application cannot proceed until the applicant receives a letter from HMRC with a unique code. The code indicates that the tax due on delivery of the IHT account has been paid. It must be included on the application together with the gross and net probate values of the estate provided by HMRC in the letter. For applications before that date, applications could not proceed until HMRC sent HMCTS a receipted IHT421 certifying that the tax due had been paid.

If the estate is excepted, a form IHT207 must be completed if the deceased was not UK domiciled. If the deceased was UK domiciled, no IHT form is required unless the death was before 1 January 2022 in which case an IHT205 is required.

In the case of excepted estates where no IHT form was completed, applicants must provide three inheritance tax values:

- gross value of the estate;
- net value of the estate (after deduction of liabilities);
- net qualifying value of the estate (after deduction of exemptions and reliefs)

These terms are defined in the Inheritance Tax (Delivery of Accounts) (Excepted Estates) Regulations 2004 (SI 2004/2543) as amended. They are considered below at para.10-039 but it is worth noting that "estate" for this purpose is defined to include specified chargeable and exempt transfers made in the seven years before death: see reg.4(6).

In the case of applicants who completed an IHT207 or IHT205 gross and net values of the estate are taken from the IHT207 or IHT205.

In all case applicants must also provide the gross and net values of the estate for the purposes of probate. The probate value will frequently differ from the inheritance tax value of the estate. The probate application is not concerned with the value of any part of the estate which does not pass under the grant whereas this is relevant for inheritance tax purposes. The following property does not pass under the grant: a life interest, joint property devolving by survivorship, a property which is the subject of a *donatio mortis causa* or nomination. The test is whether the grant is necessary to establish a claimant's right to the property.

The inheritance tax value of the estate may be reduced by business and agricultural property relief, but such reliefs are irrelevant for probate purposes.

The gross value of property passing under the grant must be stated, in addition to the net value, because the personal representatives undertake to duly administer the estate and due administration of the estate includes the payment of debts; therefore, they must refer to gross figures not merely to net ones.

Legal statements Both forms end with a series of declarations and undertakings. **10-019**
On the PA1P the applicants confirm that the last will and any codicils referred to in this application is the last will and testament of the person who has died.

On both forms the applicants confirm (as required by Administration of Estates Act 1925 s.25) that:

- they will collect the whole estate;
- they will keep full details (an inventory) of the estate;
- they will keep a full account of how the estate has been distributed;
- if appropriate, the estate is an 'excepted estate' and that the person who died was domiciled in the UK.

If required by the court, they will:

- provide the full details of the estate and how it has been distributed;
- return the grant of representation to the court.

They understand that:

- the application will be rejected if the information is not provided (if asked);
- criminal proceedings for fraud may be brought against the undersigned if it is found; that the evidence provided is deliberately untruthful or dishonest.

The applicants confirm that they will administer the deceased's estate in accordance to law, and that the application is truthful.

Form PA1P: Applications where there is a will

Introduction

This form is completed whenever there is a will and irrespective of whether the **10-020**
grant sought is a grant of probate (in the case of executors) or a grant of letters of administration with will (in the case of non-executors). Because one form is being used for differently entitled applicants, not all of the questions asked are relevant but, unless the form says otherwise, all should be answered.

Identification of the will

The original will, and any codicils must accompany the application. The date **10-021**
must be entered, and details must be provided of any foreign wills in case they revoke the UK will. The form asks whether the deceased married or formed a civil partnership after making the will for the same reason.

Question 3.8 asks whether there any features of the will that the applicant wishes to highlight, such as the condition of the will, or if it has been separated, why, who by and when? Where there are oddities about the appearance of the will, it is important to provide as much information as possible to avoid additional queries which will inevitably delay the issue of the grant.

Question 3.9 asks for confirmation that the will consisted of the pages being submitted and that no other pages or documents of a testamentary nature or other nature were attached.

Question 4 asks about relatives of the deceased. This section is only likely to be relevant where there is a partial intestacy not where the application is made by executors or by administrators taking by reason of a gift in the will. However, it appears that all applicants must complete it.

The application must state whether there is a surviving spouse or civil partner and how many of the following blood and adoptive relatives the deceased had and whether they are under or over 18:

(a) Surviving sons or daughters;
(b) Predeceased sons or daughters;
(c) Children of predeceased sons and daughters.

The person applying for the grant must explain their relationship to the deceased or whether they are applying as an attorney. This section of the form seems a little oddly constructed as there is no place to explain that the application is made by a person who is a beneficiary of the estate but not a relative.

Application by executors

10-022 **Introduction** Executors have the best right to take a grant which will be a grant of probate. They are appointed by will (which must, of course, be valid). One executor may obtain a grant and act alone. However, it is necessary to explain what has happened to any executor who is not applying. Details of executors not applying for the grant must be given at question 3.6. The options are:

A They died before the person who has died.
B They died after the person who has died.
C They wish to have power reserved to apply at a later date.
D They have renounced.
E They have appointed an attorney to take the grant on their behalf.
F They lack capacity to act as executor.

One executor is always sufficient. This is not the case for administrators.

10-023 **Power reserved** There is no limit on how many executors can be appointed by the will, but probate will be granted to a maximum of four executors in respect of the same property. Power may be reserved to the other(s) to take out a grant in the future if a vacancy arises.

There is no need for every executor to act. A person appointed as one of several executors may not wish to act initially but may not want to take the irrevocable step of renouncing the right to a grant of probate.

Where the applicant states that an executor wishes to have power reserved, they are required to give written notice of their application to that executor and to declare that they have done so.

10-024 **Renunciation** Persons appointed as executors may renounce their right to take the grant, provided they have not intermeddled in the estate. Intermeddling consists of doing tasks a PR might do, for example notifying the deceased's bank of the death. By intermeddling, executors accept their appointment. Once executors have intermeddled, they must take the grant because they are treated as having accepted office.

If executors renounce their rights, the administration of the estate proceeds as if the executor had never been appointed.

The renunciation must be made using Form PA15, signed by the person renouncing (the signature must be witnessed), and the renunciation must be filed with the application.

Executors who are also appointed as trustees will remain trustees despite renouncing the executorship. They will have to disclaim the trusteeship as well if they want to act in neither capacity.

Attorneys The executor appointing the attorney must complete a PA11 attorney form. **10-025**

If an executor lacks mental capacity, they cannot take a grant. If they have an attorney appointed under an enduring or lasting power of attorney, the attorney may be able to take a grant on their behalf. See below.

The attorney of one executor and an executor acting in their own right may not jointly apply for a Grant of Representation.

Executor lacking capacity to act Capacity to act as executor is judged at the time of the application for the grant. A person appointed as an executor by the will but who, at the testator's death, lacks capacity to make decisions, cannot apply for the grant. Where one of several executors lacks capacity, the others will take the grant. Where the only executor lacks capacity, NCPR 1987 r.35 provides that a grant can be made for the use and benefit of that person to: **10-026**

- (a) the person authorised by the Court of Protection to apply for a grant or, where there is no such person,
- (b) the attorney of the person who lacks capacity appointed under a registered enduring power of attorney or lasting power of attorney, or where there is no attorney or the attorney renounces,
- (c) the person entitled to the residuary estate of the deceased.

Minors There is no prohibition on a testator naming a minor as their executor. However, an executor who is still a minor at the testator's death cannot act as an executor nor obtain a grant of probate until attaining majority. **10-027**

Where one of several executors is a minor, the other(s) being adults, probate can be granted to the adult executor(s) with power reserved to the minor to take a grant at a later date. If the administration of the estate has not been completed by the time the minor attains 18 years, an application for a grant of double probate can be made to enable the former minor to act as executor alongside the other proving executor(s).

Example 1

George dies appointing his wife, Ingrid and his son Harry (aged 16) as his executors.

Ingrid will take a grant of probate with power reserved to Harry to take a grant of probate at 18. Harry may choose to do so if the administration of the estate has not been completed at that date.

Where the minor is the only executor appointed by the will (or the adult executors are not able or willing to act), someone must take the grant on behalf of the minor as it would be impracticable to leave the testator's estate unadministered until the executor reaches 18 years. A grant of letters of administration with will annexed for the use and benefit of the minor will be made, usually to the parent(s) or guardian(s) of the minor, until the minor attains 18 years. On obtaining majority, the executor may apply for a cessate grant of probate if the administration has not been completed.

10-028 **A former spouse or civil partner** If the testator appointed their spouse or civil partner as their executor and the marriage or civil partnership subsequently ends, that appointment will fail unless the testator has shown a contrary intention in the will (Wills Act 1837 s.18A: see para.2-054).

If the spouse or civil partner was one of several executors, the others may apply for the grant of probate without the spouse or civil partner. If the spouse was appointed as a sole executor, application should be made for a grant of letters of administration with will annexed. In either case, details should be provided of the fact and date of the divorce.

Applications by administrators

10-029 **Need for clearing off** Where the application is not made by executors, those wanting to obtain a grant of administration with will must explain:

(1) that the applicant is the person entitled in priority to take the grant, and
(2) how persons with prior rights (for example, persons appointed executors in the will) have been cleared off.

The text box 2.16 should be worded to clear off all persons having a prior right to the grant and show the capacity in which the intended administrator is entitled. Some elements that would previously have been included in the clearing off paragraph will be captured by other questions on the form. For example, applicants must state at question 3.6 that no executors were appointed, or that they are dead or have renounced. Despite this, practitioners may prefer to provide all the necessary information at question 2.16.

10-030 **Necessary elements of clearing off** The explanation of priority should include the following elements:

Whether minority or life interests exist

> "that [] ... minority [] life interests in [his/her] estate".

If a minority or life interest exists no matter how small it may be (but see below for details of certain permitted deductions that may extinguish an apparent minority or life interest) the grant will usually have to be made to at least two individuals or to a trust corporation. Therefore, the applicant must state whether or not there is a minority or life interest.

If no minority interest arises, the applicant confirms by tick box at section 3.5 that there is no one under the age of 18 years who receives a gift. If there is a minor who takes a benefit, the applicant confirms this by the tick box and if appropriate by completing box 4.2 (relatives under 18 years). The form (in box 3.5) includes provision for the name of the child and person who has parental responsibility to be inserted but it is suggested that this is unnecessary if there are two applicants entitled in their own right to the grant.

Clearing off persons with prior rights Priority is governed by r.20 of the 1987 Rules.

The applicant must state why any other person with a prior right is not seeking a grant. The reasons are likely to be:

(a) death;
(b) renunciation; or
(c) failure to appear to citation.

The precise wording of such a recital will vary according to the circumstances, the following is a specimen:

> "That A, the sole surviving executor and trustee appointed in the will, predeceased the deceased [or survived the deceased but has since died without having proved the will] and that B, the residuary legatee and devisee for life named in the will, has renounced letters of administration with the will annexed and that C, the ultimate residuary legatee and devisee, has been duly cited to accept or refuse letters of administration with the will annexed. That in default of appearance of the said C to the said citation it was ordered by District Judge [...] of this Division on the ... day of ... 20 that letters of administration with the will annexed be granted to [me/us]."
>
> The information about A is unnecessary as the form itself asks for details of non-proving executors. It is not necessary to clear off persons entitled in the same degree as the applicant. For example, if there are three specific legatees one of whom wishes to take a grant he or she must clear off persons with a prior right but not the other two specific legatees.

Recital of applicant's right to grant After clearing off any person with a prior right the statement must set out the exact capacity in which the applicant claims the grant. If the applicant is claiming as a person entitled under a partial intestacy, the relationship (if any) must be given.

Example 2

"One of the residuary legatees and devisees named in the will."

"One of the specific legatees and devisees named in the will."

"A brother of the whole blood of the deceased and one of the persons entitled to share in the undisposed of estate of the said deceased."

Person entitled a minor If the person entitled to the grant is a minor and the applicants are taking a grant for their use and benefit, the statement must recite this and must also show the applicants' authority to take such a grant. Suitable wording would be:

> "That A is the residuary legatee and devisee named in the said will and is a minor, the said A being the age of ... and that there is no other person appointed or deemed to be appointed guardian of the said minor and that I, C, am the father and statutory guardian of the said minor and I, D, am the person nominated by an instrument in writing dated the ... day of ... 20 ... under the hand of the said C, for the purpose of joining with him in taking a grant of letters of administration with will annexed of the estate of the said deceased."

Person entitled lacks capacity Similarly if a grant is to be taken out for the use and benefit of a person who lacks the mental capacity to take a grant, the applicant should state this is the case and should show the basis of the applicant's right to take the grant; for example, that the applicant is the person authorised by the Court of Protection.

Permitted deductions "Permitted deductions" from the value of the estate may reduce the value of property undisposed of by the will to less than the level of the statutory legacy payable to a surviving spouse or civil partner under the intestacy rules. This is done, for example, where the effect of such deductions will be to reduce the value of the property passing under the intestacy rules to such an extent that no minority interest arises so that it is possible for the grant to issue to a sole administrator. The permitted deductions are:

(a) the value of personal chattels;
(b) debts;
(c) inheritance tax payable from the estate without a right of recovery from any other person or property;
(d) fair and reasonable costs incurred and to be incurred; and
(e) probate fees.

10-031 **Renunciation** Any person entitled to apply for a grant of letters of administration with will annexed can renounce in the same way as an executor (though using a Form PA16), except that an administrator does not lose the right to renounce by intermeddling. Renunciation does not affect any beneficial entitlement of the administrator or any appointment as a trustee.

PA1A: Applications where there is no will

Need for clearing off

10-032 The application follows the same general format as the PA1P. We will only consider the parts that differ.

Entitlement to a grant where there is no will is governed by r.22 of the 1987 Rules and depends on the relationship of the applicant to the deceased. The explanation of the applicant's right to a grant at para.2-016 must therefore show that there are no persons with a prior right and set out the relationship of the applicant to the deceased.

Clearing off is done either by stating that the deceased left no-one in the prior categories set out in r.22 or by stating that there were such people at the time of the intestate's death but they have since renounced their rights, failed to appear to a citation or died without taking a grant.

A surviving spouse or civil partner has first claim to a grant so if the intestate left no spouse or civil partner the oath must first state that the deceased died intestate "a bachelor" or "a spinster" or "a widower" or "a widow" or "a single man" or "a single woman".

Any other persons entitled are cleared off by stating that the deceased died without "issue", or "parent", or "brother or sister of the whole [or half] blood" or "their issue", or "grandparent", or "uncle and aunt of the whole [or half] blood" or "their issue".

If a person with a prior right has renounced, an example of the wording is as follows:

> "died intestate, a widow, without issue or parent (or any other person entitled in priority to share in her estate by virtue of any enactment) leaving B her brother of the whole blood and the only person entitled to her estate surviving her and that the said B has duly renounced letters of administration".

If a person with a prior right has survived the intestate but died before taking a grant, that person's personal representatives can apply for the grant and the wording is as follows:

> "died intestate leaving W his lawful widow and the only person now entitled to his estate

> surviving him and that the said W has since died without having taken letters of administration of the said estate".

It is not necessary to clear off persons entitled in the same degree as the applicant. For example, if there are three children of the deceased one child does not need to clear off the other two.

> "[I am/we are] ... of the deceased".
>
> The applicant must here show the precise relationship to the deceased and state whether they are "the only person entitled to the estate of the deceased", "one of the persons entitled to share in the estate of the deceased", or "a person who may have a beneficial interest in the estate of the said deceased in the event of an accretion thereto".

A surviving spouse is described as "the lawful surviving husband" or "the lawful widow". Section 11 of and Sch.3 to the Marriage (Same Sex Couples) Act 2013 provide that in existing legislation in England and Wales references to marriage, married couple, spouse, etc. in existing legislation for England and Wales will be read as including marriage of a same sex couple. Hence when referring to a same sex husband or wife it is not necessary to say anything like "surviving same sex spouse" or "surviving widow or widower in a same sex marriage". It will be sufficient to say "surviving widow or widower".

Equally, civil partners of the deceased will simply describe themselves as "lawful surviving civil partners" without needing to specify whether they are opposite or same sex civil partners.

Since the Family Law Reform Act 1987 it is no longer necessary to describe a child as either "lawful" or "natural".

An adopted child should be described as "lawful adopted". A child of a deceased uncle or aunt can be described as "a cousin german".

A surviving civil partner is described as "the lawful civil partner". If the application is made by a grandchild, nephew or niece or cousin german the statement must recite that the parent through whom the claim is made died in the lifetime of the deceased.

Permitted deductions

As with the PA1P details of permitted deductions may be shown to bring the entitlement of a surviving spouse or civil partner below the level of the statutory legacy payable on intestacy. **10-033**

Relatives of the deceased

Introduction There is obviously no section corresponding to Question 3 of the PA1P which dealt with the will and codicils. Question 3 of the PA1A starts in identical terms to Question 4 of the PA1P although if the applicant is a child of a predeceased child, the application must state that the applicant's parent predeceased the deceased. Grandchildren are equally entitled with the deceased's children if, and only if, their parent predeceased the deceased. Step-children (i.e., children of the deceased's spouse or civil partner) are not children for this purpose unless the deceased adopted them. **10-034**

In addition to asking about the surviving spouse, civil partner, children and children of a predeceased child, where there are no such relatives, additional questions are asked about other surviving relatives.

The applicant must specify:

(a) Any surviving parents of the person of the deceased;
(b) The number of surviving whole-blood brothers or sisters of the deceased;
(c) The number of predeceased whole-blood brothers or sisters;
(d) The number of surviving children of predeceased whole-blood brothers or sisters;
(e) The number of surviving half-blood brothers or sisters of the deceased;
(f) The number of predeceased half-blood brothers or sisters;
(g) The number of surviving children of predeceased half -blood brothers or sisters.

Brothers and sisters of the deceased are also known as "siblings". A sibling is of the "whole blood" where they share both parents in common with the deceased, and of the "half blood" where they have only one common parent. If the applicant is a child of a predeceased sibling (whether whole-blood or half-blood, the application must state that the applicant's parent predeceased the deceased.

If there are no relatives in any of the above categories, the application must give the same information in relation to grandparents, uncles and aunts of the whole-blood, uncles and aunts of the half-blood and any children of a predeceased uncle or aunt of the whole or half blood.

If the application is by a child of a predeceased uncle or aunt (whether whole-blood or half-blood), the application must state that the applicant's parent predeceased the deceased.

10-035 **Minors** A minor cannot act as administrator, neither can they apply for a grant. The same procedure as that discussed above in relation to administrators with the will annexed should be followed.

10-036 **Renunciation** A person entitled to a grant under NCPR 1987 r.22 can renounce their right to the grant in the same way as an administrator with the will annexed. If they are the only relative of the deceased with a beneficial entitlement, the grant will be made to a creditor of the deceased.

Renunciation does not affect any beneficial entitlement of the administrator.

It is common for a creditor to take the grant if the estate is insolvent.

Example 3

Graeme dies intestate survived by one brother, Henry, and an uncle, Jack. Graeme owes Kalya £100.

Henry has the best right to a grant under r.22. As Jack has no beneficial interest in the estate under the intestacy rules, he cannot apply for the grant if Henry fails to do so.

Completing the Online Application

10-037 Completing the application online is fairly intuitive, but there is helpful guidance provided by HMCTS at "*Apply for probate with MyHMCTS*". There is a drop down menu to indicate which of the three grants is required. The questions will then be appropriate for the grant which has been selected. The questions correspond to those on the paper forms.

The legal statement confirming that the information is correct and that the personal representatives will carry out their duties can be emailed to them, in which case they will add their typed signature, or printed for them to sign in pen.

Alternatively, if the applicants wish to, they can authorise the practitioner to sign on their behalf. The legal statement can be uploaded with the application or sent by post.

Once the application is submitted, a summary appears followed by information about what needs to be done next. This includes a list of the documents that need to be sent. A coversheet can be downloaded which has the list of documents, the case number and where to send them (currently HMCTS Probate at Harlow). Once sent, the documents are scanned. The scanned documents are then made available to the case workers who work on the applications.

There is an optional box where additional details can be provided about the application. It is helpful to point out if supporting documentation is double-sided, as this is sometimes missed when documents are scanned. Since case workers work out of the processing centre in Birmingham, they cannot access the physical documents. Hence scanning errors will significantly delay the application.

6. Inheritance Tax Accounts and Payment of Tax

Introduction

A grant of representation will not, normally, be issued until the personal representatives have dealt with the question of inheritance tax. An account giving full details of the deceased's estate is required unless the estate is excepted (see para.10-049 and following). If any inheritance tax is immediately due, it must normally be paid before the grant can be issued (Senior Courts Act 1981 s.109(1)) as amended by the Finance Act 2004 s.294(1)(a)). In certain circumstances HMRC will allow a grant to issue on credit. See para.12-011 below. **10-038**

The account, where it is required, must generally be delivered within 12 months of the end of the month in which the death occurred or within three months after the applicant begins to act as personal representative if later. The inheritance tax accounts are available online at the gov.uk website.

The purpose of the account is to enable the applicant to list the deceased's assets and to calculate the inheritance tax liability, if any. HMRC will then check the "self-assessment" to tax to determine whether or not it is correct.

An account must be delivered whether or not there is any tax to pay either on delivery of the account or at any time in the future unless the estate fulfils the requirements to qualify as an excepted estate (see para.10-039 and following).

If tax is payable on delivery of the account, it can be paid in a variety of ways:

- directly using your online or mobile bank account.
- online or telephone bank transfer.
- at a bank or building society by cash or cheque.
- by cheque payable to 'HM Revenue and Customs only.

Where tax is payable it is necessary to apply for a reference and a payslip. This can be done by post using IHT422 or online at *https://www.gov.uk/paying-inheritance-tax/get-a-reference-number* [Accessed 6 March19 April 20202024] which also provides full details of each method of payment.

HMRC retains the IHT400. From 17 January 2024, there is a change of practice for applications in England and Wales. When HMRC write to confirm receipt and processing of the IHT400, they include a unique code and the details of the estate values which the applicant will require when making the application for a grant to HMCTS. Before that date applicants completed an IHT421 which set out the tax due and the probate values. HMRC receipted it and sent it to HMCTS. It was not possible to apply to HMCTS until they had received the IHT421.

If it is discovered at a later date that the inheritance tax account does not reflect the true circumstances of the deceased's estate, a corrective account must be filed within six months of the discovery.

Where tax is payable it is necessary to apply for a reference and a payslip. This can be done by post using IHT 422 or online at *https://www.gov.uk/paying-inheritance-tax/get-a-reference-number* [Accessed 19 April 2024].

The reference should be written on the top right-hand corner of form IHT400.

Normally payment will be made electronically. If, unusually, payment is made by post using a cheque, the payslip and cheque must be sent to HMRC Banking, St Mungo's Road, Cumbernauld, Glasgow G70 5WY. This is the only address that will deal with cheques.

If tax is to be paid out of the deceased's bank account or building society account under the Direct Payment Scheme it is necessary to complete a copy of form IHT423 for each bank or building society that will be transferring funds and send it to the relevant banks and building societies.

"Excepted estates" where no inheritance tax account need be filed

Introduction

10-039 The obligation to file an IHT400 account does not apply to "excepted estates" under the Inheritance Tax (Delivery of Accounts) (Excepted Estates) Regulations 2004 (SI 2004/2543) as amended. Since 1 January 2022, the person applying for the grant will include inheritance tax values in the application for a grant submitted to HMCTS. In the case of excepted estates of non-domiciled deceased persons, an IHT207 must be submitted.

For deaths before 1 January 2022 in the case of estates of UK domiciled deceased persons a short IHT205 had to be completed.

What estates are excepted depend on the date of death of the deceased. We will only consider the position for deaths on or after 1 January 2022.

There are three types of excepted estates:

- low value estates—gross value of estate does not exceed nil-rate band;
- exempt estates—value of estate after deduction of spouse and charity exemptions does not exceed nil-rate band and gross value before deductions does not exceed £3 million;
- foreign domiciliaries' estates—deceased never domiciled in UK and UK estate limited.

Definitions

10-040 Regulation 4(6) of (SI 2004/2543) as amended in 2022 introduces three defined terms for the purposes of the excepted estates regulations: gross value of the estate for inheritance tax, net value of the estate for inheritance tax and net qualifying value of the estate.

"Gross value of the estate for inheritance tax" is given an unusually wide definition. It is:

- the death estate, plus;
- specified transfers made in the seven years before death, plus;

- specified exempt transfers made in the seven years before death.

"Net value of the estate for inheritance tax purposes" is gross estate less deductible liabilities of the estate.

"Net qualifying value of the estate" is the net value less amounts transferred on death which are exempt by reason of the spouse or charity exemption.

Regulation 6 also contains definitions of specified lifetime chargeable transfers and specified exempt transfers.

"Specified transfers" are chargeable transfers made by a person during the period of seven years ending with that person's death where the value transferred is attributable to:

(a) cash;
(b) personal chattels or corporeal moveable property;
(c) quoted shares or securities; or
(d) an interest in or over land, save to the extent that ss.102 and 102A(2) of the Finance Act 1986 apply to that transfer (gifts with reservation of benefit or the land became settled property on that transfer).

As we will see when we consider the conditions required to qualify as an excepted estate, where there are lifetime transfers of other assets, such as unquoted shares, within seven years of death, the estate cannot qualify as an excepted estate.

"Specified exempt transfers" are transfers of value made by a person during the period of seven years ending with that person's death which are exempt transfers by reason of one of the following provisions of Inheritance Tax Act 1984:

(a) section 18 (transfers between spouses [or civil partners]),
(b) section 23 (gifts to charities),
(c) section 24 (gifts to political parties),
(d) section 24A (gifts to housing associations),
(e) section 27 (maintenance funds for historic buildings, etc), or
(f) section 28 (employee trusts).

Notice that the annual exemption and small gifts exemption are not included as a specified exempt transfer and therefore do not need to be added when calculating the gross value of the estate. Transfers which are exempt under the normal expenditure from income exemption are treated as chargeable for this purpose if they exceed £3,000.

Example 4

T died on 2 January 2024 leaving assets worth £275,000. Everything is left to T's daughter apart from a charitable legacy of £1,000. T gave away £10,000 above the annual exemption two years before death, there are debts of £15,000 and funeral costs of £5,000.

Gross value of estate	£285,000 (death estate plus gifts other than those covered by annual exemption)
Net value of estate	£265,000 (gross value less debts of £20,000)
Net qualifying value of estate	£264,000 (net value less charitable legacy)

HMRCs' Online Inheritance Tax Checker' available on the gov.uk website will produce these three figures.

Time limits

10-041 HMCTS must transmit information on values to HMRC within one month from the issue of the grant.

HMRC has 60 days from the issue of the grant of representation to ask for additional information.

HMRC do not issue clearance letters on excepted estates. An excepted estate is automatically discharged from any liability at the end of the 60 day period unless there was fraud or failure to disclose material facts. Clearance does not affect any tax that may be payable if further property is later shown to form part of the estate and, in consequence of that property, the estate is not an excepted estate.

Low value estates and exempt estates

10-042 These are similar. Both must fulfil the following conditions:

(a) The deceased died on or after 6 April 2004 domiciled in the UK.
(b) The deceased's estate consists wholly of property passing by will or intestacy, under a statutory nomination, under a single settlement in which he was entitled to an interest in possession in settled property, or by survivorship in a beneficial joint tenancy.
(c) Of the deceased's estate no more than £100,000 was immediately before death situate outside the UK.
(ca) The deceased was not a person by reason of whose death one of the alternatively secured pension fund provisions applies.
(d) The deceased made no lifetime chargeable transfers other than specified transfers not exceeding £250,000. Business and agricultural reliefs are ignored when determining the value of specified transfers.

For each type of excepted estate there are limitations on the value of settled property which can be included in the estate. They are similar but not identical.

For low value estates no more than £250,000 of the deceased's estate was immediately before death settled property.

For exempt estates no more than £1,000,000 of the deceased's estate was immediately before death settled property, and of that settled property, not more than £250,000 not more than £250,000 must pass to anyone other than a UK domiciled spouse or civil partner or charity.

If those conditions are fulfilled:

(a) An estate will be excepted from the need to deliver an IHT400 as a low value estate if the gross value of the estate (gross value includes specified transfers and specified exempt transfers) before deducting inheritance tax exemptions does not exceed the nil-rate threshold. For deaths before 6 April 2011 the nil-rate threshold was a single nil-rate band. For deaths on or after that date and before 1 January 2022 the threshold can be increased by 100 per cent where the deceased inherited a full nil-rate band from a single predeceased spouse or civil partner. In the interests of simplicity HMRC did not allow the nil-rate threshold to be increased where a portion of a nil-rate band was inherited. For deaths on or after 1 January 2022 the nil rate threshold can be increased where a portion of nil rate band is inherited but only one predeceased spouse or civil partner can be taken into account for this purpose.

(b) An estate will be excepted from the need to deliver an IHT400 as an exempt estate if the gross value of the estate (gross value includes specified transfers and specified exempt transfers) before deducting inheritance tax exemptions does not exceed £3 million and the net value of the estate after deducting liabilities and spouse and charity exemptions does not exceed the nil-rate threshold. As for low value estates the nil-rate threshold gain can be increased by any portion of nil rate band (up to 100 per cent) inherited from a single predeceased spouse or civil partner.

Foreign domiciliary estates

These are estates where: **10-043**

- the deceased was never domiciled nor treated as domiciled in the UK,
- the deceased was not a person by reason of whose death one of the alternatively secured pension fund provisions applies,
- the UK assets consist only of cash, quoted shares or securities passing by will, intestacy or survivorship with a gross value not exceeding £150,000.

Personal representatives must complete and submit an IHT207 to HMRC.

IHT Form 400

Introduction

If the estate does not fall within the Excepted Estates Regulations, the intending personal representatives will have to complete and deliver form IHT400. This form can be obtained at the gov.uk website. Form 400 and its supplements together form a formidably long document. The IHT400 itself consists of 16 basic pages which summarise details of the assets of the estate and the tax calculation. Details of the deceased and of the personal representatives are also included and a declaration as to the accuracy of the form. Depending on the circumstances of the estate, supplementary pages selected from a suite of 19 such documents giving details of particular assets and exemptions are also required. **10-044**

The rules as to calculation of inheritance tax and as to the liability to pay the tax were explained in Ch.4.

Form 400 is designed to allow self-assessment of the tax liability taking into account:

(a) the amount of tax payable on the death estate taking into account any lifetime chargeable transfers and any exemptions and reliefs available on death;
(b) the amount of tax payable by the personal representatives on the one hand and trustees of any settlement in which the deceased had an interest on the other hand. (It will be recalled that personal representatives are responsible for the tax on joint property, property given away by a *donatio mortis causa* or nomination and foreign assets even though they do not vest in them and so are not part of the estate for probate purposes.); and
(c) the amount of tax payable on delivery of the account as opposed to tax payable by instalments.

The form also allows calculation of the value of the estate for probate purposes.

IHT 400 pp.1–4

10-045 The first two and a half pages of IHT400 consist of details of the deceased and of the probate practitioner who is making the application for the personal representative (personal applications for probate or administration are permitted and are quite common but the procedure for dealing with inheritance tax is then quite different and is not dealt with further in this book) and of the will if any.

The bottom half of page three asks for details of any will. Page 4 requires details of assets referred to in the will which do not form part of the estate, for example, because they have been sold or given away during the lifetime of the deceased. Pages 5 and 6 are a checklist to enable the person completing the form to decide which of the supplementary schedules are needed in this particular estate.

IHT 400 pp.5–6

10-046 Pages 5 and 6 enable the person completing the form to work out what supplementary pages are required to deal with particular types of assets and with any exemptions which are available. If any such pages are required, they should be completed first as they contain information which will be summarised in form IHT400 itself.

IHT 400 pp.7–11

10-047 Pages 7 and 8 contain lists of the various assets included in the estate as set out in the various supplementary schedules and on which the personal representatives must pay the tax if any is due. There are separate columns for assets with and without the instalment option. Pages 9–11 list deductions from the taxable total arising from liabilities of the deceased, exemptions and reliefs. Page 11 also lists assets which are to be taken into account in calculating tax but on which the personal representatives are not liable for the tax (such as interests in trusts).

IHT 400 pp.12–17

10-048 Page 12 is used to calculate the tax actually payable on the estate. At the top of p.13 there is a space to indicate if the direct payment scheme is to be used. The rest of p.13 and p.14 contain a declaration by the applicants that the form has been correctly completed. Page 15 is a checklist to enable the person completing the form to ensure that all necessary information has been supplied. Finally, room is left at the end of the form for the inclusion of further explanations and information.

Reduced Form 400

10-049 Where the estate is not an excepted estate but no tax is payable then a reduced form IHT 400 may be submitted. This is a form of the 400 in which only some of the form has to be completed. Details are included on pp.5 and 6 of "Guide to completing your Inheritance Tax account" "form IHT Notes" available from the HMRC website. The most common type of case where a reduced account can be submitted is where the estate is too substantial to be excepted but all or most of the estate is exempt because it is being given to a spouse, civil partner or charity so that no tax is payable.

Further forms—Corrective accounts and direct payments

In addition to the forms already described, other forms may have to be completed. **10-050**

If the information originally provided by the personal representatives proves to be incorrect, whether as a result of a mistake or because they discover additional property or liabilities, a corrective account, Form C4, will have to be sent to HMRC. If the alteration is trivial, they may dispense with the requirement.

Late payment, penalties and estimated accounts

A failure to deliver an accurate account within the prescribed time limits may lead to the assessment of a penalty. The main provision relating to late delivery of an account is IHTA s.245 which provides for a penalty of £100 plus £60 for each day that the account is late once the case has been referred to the First Tier Tribunal. The penalty does not apply if there is a reasonable excuse for the failure to comply with the time limit. HMRC guidance contained in "Disagree with a Tax Decision" available on the gov.uk website says that: **10-051**

> "A reasonable excuse is normally something unexpected or outside your control that stopped you meeting a tax obligation, for example:
>
> - your partner or another close relative died shortly before the tax return or payment deadline
> - you had an unexpected stay in hospital that prevented you from dealing with your tax affairs
> - you had a serious or life-threatening illness
> - your computer or software failed just before or while you were preparing your online return
> - service issues with HM Revenue and Customs (HMRC) online services
> - a fire, flood or theft prevented you from completing your tax return
> - postal delays that you couldn't have predicted.
> - delays related to a disability or mental illness you have
> - you were unaware of or misunderstood your legal obligation
> - you relied on someone else to send your return, and they did not"

It says that the following will not be accepted as a reasonable excuse:

> "• your cheque bounced or payment failed because you didn't have enough money
> - you found the HMRC online system too difficult to use
> - you didn't get a reminder from HMRC
> - you made a mistake on your tax return."

The fact that a taxpayer is owed money by a third party and, therefore, does not have sufficient funds to pay the tax due was held not to be a reasonable excuse for late payment in *Gebbie v RCC* (2014).

Penalties are also imposed by Finance Act 2007 Sch.24 as amended in cases where the account proves inaccurate and leads to an underpayment of tax. In this case the amount of the penalty depends in part on whether the error was deliberate or made without due care and on the amount of the tax which could have been lost to HMRC if the inaccuracy had not been discovered.

A particular problem arises in cases where a personal representative wishes to avoid delay in obtaining a grant but does not have complete information available. This is well illustrated by the case of *Robertson v IRC* (2002). In that case the testatrix had left part of her property in Scotland to the Church of Scotland which was anxious for a quick sale. The executor submitted an account which dealt fully with most of the property. However, a cottage in Hertfordshire was yet to be valued. An estimated figure was included in the account which turned out to be far too low. A corrective account was submitted almost immediately and the correct amount of tax on the estate was paid within six months of the death (i.e. before the time when the tax would have become due if no account had been submitted). The Revenue were not therefore out of pocket as a result of the inaccurate estimate in the original account. Nevertheless, they imposed a penalty of £10,000 on the basis that the executor had not made "the fullest enquiries reasonably practicable" about the value of the property as required by IHTA s.216(3A). The executor was successful on his appeal to the Special Commissioners on the basis that what he had done was in accordance with accepted practice, the fact that the original figure was an estimate was disclosed and there was no negligence involved. At a later hearing the executor was awarded his expenses of and relating to the hearing on the basis that the Revenue had acted wholly unreasonably.

In the light of the *Robertson* case the Revenue issued the following guidelines as to how they will deal with such cases in future (in their *IHT Newsletter*—Special Issue May 2002):

> "The Revenue is keen to provide assistance to personal representatives to enable them to fulfil their obligations without incurring penalties. In most circumstances we would expect the exact value of property to be given when form IHT 400 is submitted and not merely an estimate. However we accept that if there is a proven need to obtain a grant urgently personal representatives may find themselves in a position where they think that they need to submit an estimated account of the value of a particular item of property. In such circumstances they should ensure that they have made the fullest enquiries that are reasonably practicable before doing so, and the estimate should be as accurate as possible. The Personal Representative should, for example, contact the professional who is going to value the property formally to ensure that the estimate is a reasonable one."

Personal representatives need to be very careful when completing the inheritance tax accounts as HMRC is increasingly quick to impose penalties. Given that they are calculated as a percentage of the underpaid tax, they can be substantial amounts. Claiming business or agricultural property relief in circumstances where it is clearly not available will generally lead to a penalty. Undiscovered lifetime gifts may also lead to penalties. In the "IHT Toolkit", available on the gov.uk website, HMRC recommends that, in addition to questioning family members, personal representatives should check the deceased's bank and building society accounts for at least three years, and preferably seven for indications of possible gifts.

As from 1 April 2009 HMRC has had power to impose penalties on third parties who deliberately give false information to or withhold information from personal representatives who in consequence submit an inaccurate account. However, personal representatives may also be liable to a penalty in such cases. HMRC warned in the April 2009 *Inheritance Tax and Trusts Newsletter* that -personal representatives could face penalties themselves

> "If the withheld or false information gave rise to inconsistencies in the information they had received about the estate and they did not question those inconsistencies; the liable person may still be charged a penalty for failing to take reasonable care as well."

In *Hutchings v HMRC* (2015) the residuary beneficiary did not disclose a lifetime gift of over £400,000. He received a penalty of (£87,533.80, which was 50 per cent of the underpaid tax). HMRC also raised a penalty enquiry with the executors but having inspected the file relating to the administration were satisfied that the executors had acted properly. Hence although the inheritance tax account did contain an inaccuracy, the error was not due to carelessness or deliberate behaviour of the executors. No penalty was imposed on the executors.

7. Additional Evidence

Introduction

The Non-contentious Probate Rules 1987 originally required supporting evidence to be provided in affidavit form. However, as explained at para.10-005 above, the President of the Family Division announced on 17 April 2020 that because of the problems resulting from the Covid-19 pandemic, evidence would be accepted in the form of witness statements verified by a statement of truth until 30 July 2020. The change was made permanent by Non-Contentious Probate (Amendment) Rules 2020 (SI 2020/1059) which amended the 1987 Rules to allow evidence to be presented either in an affidavit or in a witness statement. **10-052**

Evidence of due execution

Before a will or codicil can be admitted to probate the district judge or registrar must be satisfied that it was duly executed. **10-053**

If a will or codicil contains an attestation clause, which recites that the proper formalities were complied with, a presumption that the will was duly executed arises. If the will contains no attestation clause or the attestation clause is insufficient or where it appears to the district judge or registrar that there is some doubt about the due execution of the will evidence is required as to due execution before the will can be admitted to probate in common form. Rule 12.1(1) of the 1987 Rules requires an affidavit or witness statement should be from one of the attesting witnesses or, if no attesting witness is conveniently available, from any other person who was present at the time the will was executed. If no such evidence is obtainable, the district judge or registrar may (under r.12(2)) accept evidence from any person thought fit to show that the signature on the will is in the deceased's handwriting or on any other matter which may raise a presumption in favour of due execution. The district judge or registrar may require notice of the application to be given to any person who may be prejudiced by the will. If the district judge or registrar after considering the evidence is satisfied that the will was not duly executed he or she must refuse probate and mark the will accordingly.

The maxim *omnia praesumuntur rite ac solemniter esse acta* may assist when actual evidence of due execution cannot be obtained. In certain circumstances it allows the inference to be drawn that the necessary formalities have been complied with. Per Lord Lindley LJ in *Harris v Knight* (1890):

> "The maxim expresses an inference which may reasonably be drawn when an intention to do some formal act is established; when the evidence is -consistent with that intention having been carried into effect in a proper way; but where the actual observance of all due formalities can only be inferred as a matter of probability."

The presumption can only be of use where the appearance of the document in question is consistent with the formalities having been complied with. The presumption applies very strongly where there is a formal attestation clause and less strongly where there is an informal clause or no clause at all. *In the Estate of Denning* (1958) is an example of the application of the presumption in the absence of an attestation clause. The dispositive part of a will, together with the testator's signature, was contained on one side of a piece of paper. On the reverse side two signatures were written in different handwriting, one below the other. Sachs J applied the presumption and declared that the will was duly executed. He said:

> "that there is no other practical reason why the names should be on the back of the document unless it was for the purpose of attesting the will".

However, the presumption will not apply where the evidence suggests that the "will" was not executed in accordance with the formalities required by law even though the testator intended to execute a will. For example, it will not validate a document where there is only one witness to the testator's signature.

Evidence as to knowledge and approval

10-054 Under r.13 of the 1987 Rules, before admitting to proof wills which appear to have been signed by blind or illiterate testators or by another person by the testator's direction or which for any other reason give rise to doubt as to the testator having had knowledge of the contents of the will at the time of its execution, the district judges or registrars must satisfy themselves that the testator had such knowledge. Evidence in the form of an affidavit or witness statement may be required for this purpose under r.16 of the 1987 Rules.

A person preparing a will for a client in such circumstances should amend the attestation clause states that the will was read over to or explained to the testator and that the testator appeared to understand and approve the contents.

Evidence of alteration and date of execution

Alteration

10-055 If a will appears to contain an unexecuted alteration (other than the completion of a blank space) the district judge or registrar must require evidence to show whether the alteration was present at the time the will was executed (r.14(1) of the 1987 Rules) and may require evidence in the form of an affidavit or witness statement for this purpose (r.16 of the 1987 Rules). In the absence of evidence to the contrary the alteration is presumed to have been made after execution. The district judge or registrar may, however, disregard an alteration which is of no practical importance (for example, an alteration to a legacy which has lapsed).

Incorporation

10-056 If a will contains a reference to another document in such terms as to suggest that it ought to be incorporated in the will, the district judge or registrar may require the document to be produced and may call for such evidence in regard to the attaching or incorporation of the document as he or she may think fit in the form of an affidavit or witness statement (r.14(3) of the 1987 Rules).

Date of execution

10-057 If there is doubt as to the date on which a will was executed, the district judge or registrar may require such evidence as he or she thinks necessary to establish the date (r.14(4) of the 1987 Rules) and may require evidence in the form of an affidavit or witness statement for this purpose (r.16 of the 1987 Rules).

Evidence relating to attempted revocation

Any appearance of attempted revocation by burning, tearing or otherwise destroying must be accounted for to the district judge or registrar's satisfaction (r.15 of the 1987 Rules) and he or she may require evidence in the form of an affidavit or witness statement for this purpose (r.16 of the 1987 Rules). It is not desirable to attach anything to an original will since the existence of marks, pin holes, staple holes or clip impressions may suggest that there has been an attempted revocation in which case the district judge or registrar may call for evidence to explain the apparent interference with the will. **10-058**

8. PREVENTING A GRANT

Caveats

A person who wishes to stop another person obtaining a grant of representation (usually because they wish to challenge the validity of the will) can inform the probate registry and place a "stop" on the issue of the grant. The procedure is called "entering a caveat" and is dealt with under r.44 of the 1987 Rules. **10-059**

A caveat is a notice. Application for a caveat can be made online by personal applicants or entered at any probate registry by post or in person. The purpose of a caveat is to prevent a grant of probate or administration being made without notice first being given to the person who enters the caveat, called the caveator (r.44 of the 1987 Rules). The caveat can be completed online, or using form PA8A, which can be posted to Harlow. There is an application fee of £3.

Once a caveat is entered it is effective for a period starting with the day after the day on which it is entered and ending six months after the day on which it was entered. A caveat may be renewed for an additional six months during the last month of the six-month period and again in the last month of each successive six-month period. A form PA8B should be used. No grant can be made while the caveat is effective. The caveat must contain the name and address of the deceased, the date and place of death and the name and address for service of the caveator.

Any person interested may issue a "warning" to the caveat under r.44(5). The index to caveats has been kept since 1 August 1988 at the Leeds District Probate Registry and not at the Principal Registry. As a consequence, warnings must be issued either personally, through the post or through the document exchange at Leeds District Probate Registry. The "person warning" must state the nature of his or her interest and the date of the will (if any) in the warning which must then be served on the caveator. The warning must also require the caveator to state the nature of the interest. A person whose application for a grant was blocked by a caveat may issue a warning as a "person interested".

Once the warning has been served on the caveator one of four things will happen depending on what right the caveator is alleging and what steps he or she chooses to take:

(a) *The caveator may withdraw the caveat* (r.44(11)). A caveator is free to withdraw the caveat at any time whether a warning has been issued or not. A caveator who withdraws after receiving a warning must give notice to the person warning. Once the caveat is withdrawn it becomes ineffective and the person warning is free to proceed with the application for a grant (unless, of course, there is another caveat in force).

(b) *The caveator may enter an appearance* (r.44(10)). An appearance should be entered within 14 days of the service of the warning on the caveator. If it is not the person warning may thereafter take steps to "warn off" the caveator (see (d)). An appearance can only be entered by a caveator who has an interest contrary to that of the person warning. For example, entry of an appearance would be the appropriate step to take where the caveator claims to be an executor under a valid will and the person warning claims to be entitled to letters of administration on the grounds that the will is invalid. The appearance must be entered at the Leeds District Probate Registry.

Once an appearance has been entered, the caveat remains in force until a district judge (or, where the parties consent to the discontinuance of the caveat, a registrar) otherwise directs (r.44(13)). Often the entry of the appearance will be followed by the commencement of a probate action (although neither the warning nor the entry of the appearance itself amounts to the commencement of such an action). Where this happens the caveat is no longer necessary, since the fact that a probate action has been started has the effect of preventing a grant being made (r.45(3)).

(c) *The caveator may issue and serve a summons for directions* (r.44(6)). This step must be taken within 14 days of service of the warning, otherwise the caveator risks being warned off. A summons for directions may only be issued by a caveator who has no interest contrary to that of the person warning. It is, therefore, the appropriate step to take where the caveator is entitled to a grant in the same degree as or a lower degree than the person warning but wishes to show cause why that person should not take a grant (for example, because he or she is unsuitable and the caveator wishes the court to pass him or her over).

After a summons for directions has been issued there will be a hearing before a district judge (or in case of difficulty a High Court judge) who will decide to whom a grant should be made.

(d) *The caveator may do nothing*. In this case the person warning may file an affidavit or witness statement after the time limit for entering an appearance (eight days) has expired (r.44(12)). The affidavit or witness statement must show that the warning was served on the caveator. The caveat is then said to be "warned off" and is no longer effective so that the person warning is now free to proceed with an application.

9. Compelling Action

Introduction

10-060 Sometimes the people with the best right to take a grant will neither take out a grant nor renounce their rights leaving the person with the next best right unable to apply for a grant. There is a procedure for requiring a person to take a grant or lose their right to do so. Similarly, a person in possession of a will may refuse to take action to prove it (called "propounding" the will). There is a procedure for requiring them to do so. Under the 1987 Rules these procedures are called citations and are dealt with in rr.46–48.

Types of citation

Introduction

Citations are issued by the principal or district registry. **10-061**
There are three types of citation:

(a) a citation to take probate;
(b) a citation to accept or refuse a grant (of probate or letters of administration); and
(c) a citation to propound a will.

Citation to take probate

An executor may normally renounce the right to take a grant. However, once he or she has "intermeddled" (so as to constitute him or herself an executor *de son tort*) in the estate he or she is no longer free to renounce and so may be cited to take probate. The citation may be issued at the instance of any person interested in the estate but cannot be issued until at least six months after the testator's death nor at any time while proceedings as to the validity of the will are pending (r.47(3) of the 1987 Rules). An administrator does not, by intermeddling, lose the right to renounce and so cannot be cited to take administration; (an administrator who intermeddles will, however, be liable up to the limit of assets coming into his or her hands as an executor *de son tort*). **10-062**

Citation to accept or refuse a grant

A citation to accept or refuse a grant may be issued at the instance of any person who would be entitled to a grant if the person were to renounce (r.47(1) of the 1987 Rules). This type of citation is, therefore, used where a person with an inferior right to a grant wishes to force the person or persons better entitled to make up their minds whether to apply or not. Where there are several persons with a superior right, they must all be cited before the person with the inferior right can take a grant. Where power has been reserved to a person to take a grant of probate, the proving executor may cite them to take or refuse probate (r.47(2) of the 1987 Rules). It is not necessary or possible to cite a person with an equal right to take a grant since the court can issue a grant to any of the persons equally entitled. **10-063**

A citation to accept or refuse a grant may be issued to a person with a right to either a grant of probate (unless they have lost the right to renounce) or letters of administration. A citation of this type may be made at any time after the death of the testator or intestate.

Citation to propound a will

The object of this type of citation is to force the persons interested in the alleged will to seek probate of it if they can. The application may be made by any person with a contrary interest (which in effect means a person who is entitled on intestacy or under an earlier will). The citation must be directed to all the persons interested under the alleged will and not only to the executors of it (r.48(1) of the 1987 Rules). **10-064**

An executor of a will who doubts the validity of a later codicil is not entitled to cite the beneficiaries of the alleged codicil to propound it. The proper course is to bring a probate action in which he or she will seek to establish the validity of the will and the invalidity of the codicil.

Procedure on citation

10-065 A person (called a citor) who wishes to obtain a citation must first issue a caveat (r.46(3) of the 1987 Rules). The citor must then swear an affidavit or make a witness statement confirming every averment in the citation (r.46(2) of the 1987 Rules). The district judge or registrar must settle the form of citation before it is issued (r.46(1) of the 1987 Rules). Any will referred to in the citation must be lodged in a registry before the citation is issued unless it is not in the citor's possession and it is impractical to lodge it (r.46(5) of the 1987 Rules). The citation will set out the steps which the court will take if the person cited does not show cause to the contrary.

A citation must normally be personally served on the person cited (r.46(4)) but other modes of service, including advertisement, may be ordered by the registrar (this will be done, for example, where the difficulty in obtaining the grant has been caused by the disappearance of the person entitled).

A person cited must enter an appearance within eight days of service (r.46(6) of the 1987 Rules). If this is not done the citor may apply for an order for a grant if the citation was a citation to accept or refuse a grant (r.47(5)(a) of the 1987 Rules). Where the person cited was cited to take probate he or she can be ordered to do so within a stated time on failing to enter an appearance (r.47(5)(c) of the 1987 Rules), although the court may exercise its discretion to pass over the person cited (see, for example, *In the Estate of Biggs* (1966); see para.8-022). If the person cited was cited to propound a will and has failed to enter an appearance, the citor may apply for a grant in common form as if the will were invalid.

Where the person cited does enter an appearance he or she may show cause why the steps contemplated by the citation should not be taken. Alternatively, if he or she is now willing to take a grant an ex parte application to a registrar for an order for a grant (r.47(4) of the 1987 Rules) to him- or herself can be made.

Where power to take a grant has been reserved to an executor, a citation to accept or refuse a grant may be made at the instance of the proving executors (or the person who is executor by representation) against that person.

10. Standing Searches

10-066 People with an interest in the estate may wish to be informed when an application for a grant of representation is made. A caveat (or objection) will ensure that notice of an application is given to the caveator (or objector). However, it is an abuse of the process of the court for a person to enter a caveat or objection where there is no dispute as to an issue concerned with a probate matter (such as the validity of a will or a right to a grant of probate or administration).

A person who merely wishes to know when a grant is made so as to make a claim against the estate should not therefore enter a caveat. Such a person could, in most cases, enter a citation, since a creditor is entitled to a grant of administration on clearing off the beneficiaries. However, it will usually be more appropriate for them to make a "standing search".

A standing search is made by sending a completed form PA1S together with the prescribed fee (£3) to the Postal Copies and Searches Department at Leeds District Probate Registry. An office copy of any grant made within 12 months before or six months after the search will then be given to the applicant. The period of search can be extended by further periods of six months on payment of a fee for each extension.

11. GUARANTEES

Before 1972 almost all administrators were required to enter into bonds for the due administration of the estate of the deceased. This requirement was repealed by the Administration of Estates Act 1971 and replaced by a much less stringent provision requiring a guarantee in certain limited circumstances and no guarantee or bond at all in most circumstances. **10-067**

The present law is contained in s.120(1) of the Senior Courts Act 1981 which provides that:

> "the High Court may ... require one or more sureties to guarantee that they will make good, within any limit imposed by the court on the total liability of the surety or sureties, any loss which any person interested in the administration of the estate of the deceased may suffer in consequence of a breach by the administrator of his duties as such".

Chapter Eleven

POWERS AND DUTIES OF PERSONAL REPRESENTATIVES

1. Duties of Personal Representatives

Duty to collect assets

The first duty of a personal representative is "to collect and get in the deceased's real and personal estate" (Administration of Estates Act 1925 s.25 as amended by Administration of Estates Act 1971 s.9). Once the assets are collected the personal representative must administer the estate by paying debts and legacies and by disposing of the residue (these duties are dealt with in Chs 15, 16 and 18). All duties of personal representatives must be performed with "due diligence". The personal representative must: therefore: **11-001**

(a) take reasonable steps to collect money due to the deceased (by bringing proceedings if necessary); and
(b) collect the assets as quickly as is practical (money which is due to the deceased and which is secured by mortgage or other charge need not be collected immediately unless the security is in danger).

No absolute rule can be laid down as to what is a reasonable time for collection of assets nor as to what steps must be taken in order to collect assets. In each case the personal representative will only be liable for loss resulting from failure to act if he or she has acted unreasonably.

Assets devolving on personal representatives

The personal and real property of the deceased devolves on the personal representatives at death, in the case of an executor or on the making of the grant, in the case of an administrator. **11-002**

This only applies to interests in property which continue notwithstanding the death so that property held on life interest trusts does not devolve on the personal representatives of the life tenant. The legal title to property held by the deceased as a trustee devolves on the personal representative if the deceased was a sole trustee but on the remaining trustees if there are any at the time of death.

If the deceased owned an interest as a tenant in common in equity, it will devolve on the personal representatives, unless it was a life interest in which case it will cease to exist on death. An interest held as beneficial joint tenant will not devolve on the personal representatives but will pass by right of survivorship to the surviving joint tenant(s).

Property subject to a nomination or *donatio mortis causa* will not devolve on the personal representatives, it can be claimed by the nominee or donee immediately after death.

Insurance policies on the deceased's life written in trust for third parties or taken out under the Married Women's Property Act 1882 are not assets of the estate. Such policies are payable to the trustees on proof of death; a grant of representation is not required. The personal representatives will not be concerned in the collection of the proceeds of such policies (unless there is no trustee named in which case the proceeds will be paid to them—even so the proceeds will still not be assets of the estate).

A lump sum payable under a discretionary pension scheme is not an asset of the estate and the personal representatives are not concerned in its collection. The trustees of the pension scheme will pay direct to the person(s) they have selected.

Proof of title to assets

11-003 In order to collect the assets which devolve on them, personal representatives will have to prove their entitlement to the people who are in possession of the assets at the time of death. This can be done by production of the original grant of probate or administration or of an official copy of the grant. Copies can be obtained from HMCTS on payment of a small fee (£1.50 per copy). Personal representatives should apply for sufficient copies to enable them to deal with the estate of the deceased promptly—the more items of property included in the estate the greater the number of copies which should be obtained. It is not, however, necessary to have a copy for each item of property. A person in possession of estate assets must hand over the assets on production of the original or official copy grant which they must then return to the personal representatives.

Enforcement of personal representatives' duties

11-004 A personal representative who accepts office (by taking a grant or by acting as executor) is liable for loss resulting from any breach of duty which he or she commits. A breach of duty by a personal representative may consist of misappropriating the property of the deceased for his or her own benefit, maladministration (such as distributing to the wrong people even though in good faith) or negligence (such as an unreasonable delay in dealing with the collection or distribution of the estate). Any breach of duty by a personal representative is called a *devastavit*.

An action may be brought against the personal representative by a-beneficiary or creditor who is not paid in full as a result of a *devastavit* by a personal-representative. Personal representatives can protect themselves against certain types of breach of duty in a number of ways (see para.14-002 and following). In particular, a personal representative cannot be held liable to an adult who has consented to the way in which he or she has performed duties with full knowledge of the circumstances.

Where several personal representatives are appointed, each is liable for his or her own breach of duty but not for breaches by a co-executor or co-administrator. However, a personal representative who permits a breach of trust by another personal representative will be liable since he or she has then failed to perform his or her own duty of safeguarding the estate. They may also be liable in negligence if they fail to attend to their duties and thus allow a breach by another personal representative to go unnoticed.

Duty of care

The Trustee Act 2000 provides for a single duty of care which applies to trustees. Under s.35 the duties set out in the Act apply to personal representatives as well as to trustees. **11-005**

Section 1 provides:

> "(1) Wherever the duty under this subsection applies to a trustee, he must exercise such care and skill as is reasonable in the circumstances, having regard in particular—
> (a) to any special knowledge skill or experience that he has or holds himself out as having, and
> (b) if he acts as trustee in the course of a business or profession to any special knowledge or experience that it is reasonable to expect of a person acting in the course of that kind of business or profession."

Schedule 1 provides that the duty applies to personal representatives and trustees when:

1. exercising any power of investment whether conferred by the act (as to which see para.11-023) or otherwise (for example under the terms of the will);
2. exercising a power to acquire land: see para.11-024;
3. entering into arrangements appointing agents, nominees or custodians (see para.11-021) or reviewing such agents' arrangements; and
4. exercising the power to insure (see para.11-012).

Schedule 1 para.7 allows exclusion or restriction of the duty (in the case of personal representatives, the exclusion or restriction must be in the will).

2. Powers of Personal Representatives before the Grant

The authority of an administrator derives from *the grant*. The powers of an administrator before the grant is made are, therefore, very limited. In *Caudle v L.D. Law Ltd* (2008) Wynn Williams J recognised (in an obiter dictum) that a person entitled to a grant of letters of administration **11-006**

> "has an immediate right to possession of personal property owned by the deceased if it is necessary that he takes possession to safeguard the estate ... such a person also has the right to take legal action to enforce that right".

It should be emphasised that this right allows the potential administrator to do no more than preserve the property.

Administrators may not otherwise bring any action before grant and if they purport to do so a later grant does not cure the defect in the original proceedings (*Ingall v Moran* (1944)). A new action must be brought once the grant has been made. For a modern example, see *Millburn-Snell v Evans* (2011) where an action brought by claimants purportedly as administrators of a deceased's estate but who had not obtained a grant of letters of administration was struck out as a nullity. The same point arose in *Ali Abdullah Alesayi Will Establishment v Ali Alesayi* (2023) where proceedings issued before administrators obtained a grant were dismissed as a nullity.

In order to protect an estate from wrongful injury in the period between death and the obtaining of the grant the authority of an administrator will relate back for the limited purpose of giving validity to acts done before letters of administration were obtained. However, such relation back occurs only in those cases where the acts done are for the benefit of the estate. The test of whether or not an act is for the benefit of the estate is entirely objective. Thus in *Mills v Anderson* (1984) an "administrator" agreed before the grant to accept on behalf of the estate a sum in full and final settlement of a claim for damages. It later became apparent that the settlement was too low. It was held that there could be no question of the administrator's authority relating back to validate the agreement as it would not be to the benefit of the estate.

An administrator has no power to vest property in any person before obtaining a grant. In the period between death and grant of administration the property of the deceased vests in the Public Trustee (see Administration of Estates Act 1925 s.9 as substituted).

The power of an executor derives from *the will* of the deceased and not from the grant which merely confirms their authority. An executor can therefore, in principle, exercise all powers without obtaining a grant. An executor can sue or be sued before obtaining a grant. If an executor brings an action (for example, against a creditor) the action is valid even though no grant has been issued. However, before judgment is entered in his or her favour a grant must be obtained since the court will, at that stage, require proof of authority to act as executor if the action depends on title to act in that capacity.

In *Jennison v Jennison* (2022) the Court of Appeal had to consider the position of an executor who had obtained a grant of probate in New South Wales but did not reseal the grant here until after the issue of proceedings. The court held that resealing was not retrospective but that was irrelevant because under the law of England and Wales an executor's authority derives from the will. The position under the law of New South Wales was different. It does not consider an executor who has not obtained probate to have legal title to the testator's estate. However, the executrix derived title to collect assets here from law of England and Wales and therefore was deemed to have authority from the deceased's death.

An executor is also entitled to deal with the collection and distribution of the estate without first obtaining a grant. In practice, collection of assets without a grant may prove impossible since the persons in possession may refuse to hand them over without proof of the executor's title. Similarly, as far as distribution is concerned, a purchaser will require proof of title before paying for assets. A beneficiary in whose favour an assent or conveyance of a legal estate in land is made is entitled to have a notice of the assent or conveyance endorsed on the original grant of representation; thus, the grant will have to be obtained before the assent can be made.

Certain assets can be dealt with without the production of a grant (see para.12-010).

3. Implied Administrative Powers

Introduction

11-007 Trustees are given many powers by the Administration of Estates Act 1925, the Trustee Act 1925 and the Trustee Act 2000. The powers of "trustees" under these acts are also given to personal representatives. The Trustee Act 2000 came into force on 1 February 2001; it extends the powers of trustees and personal representatives and removes many of the restrictions contained in earlier legislation as well as imposing a statutory duty of care on trustees and personal representatives (see para.11-005). The Trustee Act 2000 applies to wills made before as well as after the commencement date.

It is always possible for a testator to exclude an implied power by stating in the will that it is not available to the personal representatives or trustees.

Powers of personal representatives to sell, mortgage and lease

Section 39 of the Administration of Estates Act 1925 (as amended by the Trusts of Land and Appointment of Trustees Act 1996) gives the personal representatives very extensive powers. Section 39(1)(i) preserves the common law powers of personal representatives to sell and mortgage personal property included in the estate. In relation to realty they are given (by s.39(1)(ii)) all the functions of a trustee of land under the Trusts of Land and Appointment of Trustees Act 1996. This provision effectively gives them the same powers as an absolute owner. **11-008**

A receipt given by a personal representative for money, securities or other personal property is a sufficient discharge to the person paying or transferring (Trustee Act 1925 s.14) unless that person acts in bad faith (for example, by purchasing property at a fraudulent undervalue) in which case the transaction is vitiated and a beneficiary or creditor of the estate may have the transaction set aside. If trustees sell land, it is necessary for a receipt to be given by at least two trustees or a trust corporation. However, a sole personal representative may give a good receipt for capital money (Law of Property Act 1925 s.27(2)).

The personal representatives obviously have very wide powers to sell assets and raise money. These powers are necessary since cash is required for a number of purposes in connection with the administration—for example, the payment of funeral, testamentary and administration expenses, inheritance tax, debts and pecuniary legacies. Deciding *which* assets to sell is a complex decision and the personal representatives have to consider a number of matters—for example, which assets have been specifically given to beneficiaries, which assets occur first in the statutory order for property available for payment of debts (see para.15-011 and following), which assets will fetch the best price and which assets will attract the least liability to tax for the estate and for the beneficiaries. These matters are discussed more fully in Ch.12.

Power to appropriate

Section 41 of the Administration of Estates Act 1925 gives the personal representatives power to appropriate any part of the estate in or towards satisfaction of any legacy or interest or share in the estate of the deceased, provided that such an appropriation does not prejudice any specific beneficiary. **11-009**

Example 1

T leaves X a pecuniary legacy of £1,000 and the residue of the estate to Y. The residue includes a clock valued at £750. The personal representatives can allow X to take the clock in partial satisfaction of the legacy.

A statutory appropriation can only be made by the personal representatives if the appropriate consents are obtained. There are two situations to consider.

(a) *If the beneficiary is absolutely and beneficially entitled to the legacy* the consent required is that of the beneficiary or, if the beneficiary is a minor or lacks capacity to manage his or her own affairs, the consent must be that of the beneficiary's parent or guardian or receiver.

(b) *If the legacy is settled* the consent must be that of the trustees (provided they are not also the personal representatives) or of the person for the time being entitled to the income provided such a person is of full age and capacity. If the personal representatives are the only trustees and there is no person of full age or capacity for the time being entitled to the income then no consents are required. However, in this case the appropriation must be of an investment authorised by law or by the will. This limitation as to the type of property appropriated does not exist in other cases.

It is common for wills to include an express power to appropriate without obtaining any formal consents.

For the purpose of ascertaining the entitlement of beneficiaries to appropriated assets, values are taken as at the date of the appropriation, not at the date of death (*Re Collins* (1975)); if the asset is rising in value, therefore, a pecuniary legatee will be anxious that the appropriation be made as quickly as possible. The personal representatives will have to ascertain and fix the value of assets for this purpose as they see fit but must strive to be fair to all beneficiaries. A duly qualified valuer should be employed where necessary. Thus, in *Re Bythway* (1911) it was held that an executrix was not entitled to appropriate to herself shares in an unquoted company at her own valuation.

It is possible for the will to provide that the personal representatives are to have power to appropriate at death value rather than at the date of the appropriation. This saves on the cost of an additional valuation but has the potential to work unfairly as between beneficiaries.

If the asset is worth more than the legacy to which the beneficiary is entitled, it would appear that the power granted by s.41 cannot be exercised since in such a case the asset cannot be said to be appropriated "in or towards satisfaction" of the legacy (*Re Phelps* (1980)). The personal representatives can, however, exercise their power of sale under s.39 of the Administration of Estates Act 1925 to sell the asset to a beneficiary in consideration of a part payment of cash and the satisfaction of the legacy. However, a sale may trigger a charge to capital gains tax as personal representatives will be making an actual disposal (see para.5-024)

Stamp duty used to be an important consideration in relation to appropriations, but this is no longer the case. Because of the consent required by s.41, HMRC regard an appropriation as a "conveyance or transfer on sale" (this can be beneficial as it allows personal representatives to claim inheritance tax loss on sale relief (see para.12-017) where quoted shares are appropriated to a pecuniary legatee). In the days when ad valorem stamp duty was chargeable, instruments, giving effect to the appropriation, therefore, attracted duty (*Jopling v IRC* (1940)). For that reason it was common for wills to provide that the personal representatives need not obtain the consent of a legatee to an appropriation.

Finance Act 1985 s.84 removed ad valorem stamp duty from appropriations in satisfaction of a pecuniary legacy or in satisfaction of any interest of a surviving spouse or civil partner in an intestate's estate. Appropriations in favour of residuary legatees who received no more than their entitlement were regarded by HMRC as outside the scope of ad valorem duty although they were subject to fixed duty. Finance Act 2008 s.99 abolished fixed duty in relation to such appropriations for instruments executed on or after 13 March 2008 except in relation to land transactions. Prior to that date it was normally possible to certify the instrument as exempt from stamp duty in accordance with the Stamp Duty (Exempt Instruments) Regulations 1987 (SI 1987/516).

In relation to land transactions stamp duty was replaced by stamp duty land tax as from 1 December 2003. However, Finance Act 2003 Sch.3 para.3A(1) provides that stamp duty land tax does not apply to the acquisition of property in or towards satisfaction of an entitlement under a will or on intestacy (unless the person acquiring the property gives any consideration for it, other than the assumption of secured debt so a sale of land to a beneficiary partly in satisfaction of a legacy and partly in consideration of an additional cash payment will give rise to a liability).

Stamp duty and stamp duty land tax are, therefore, normally not an issue in relation to appropriations so it is no longer necessary to exclude the need for consent to avoid liability to these taxes. Indeed, it may be preferable not to exclude the need for consent. Where the need for consent has been excluded, the personal representatives cannot claim inheritance tax loss relief if quoted shares are appropriated to a pecuniary legatee at a time when their value is less than their value at the date of death: see para.12-017.

Power to appoint trustees of a minor's property

When a personal representative vests property in a beneficiary absolutely entitled (or person otherwise entitled to assets, for example, a trustee) the personal representative obtains a discharge from liability by means of a receipt signed by the person entitled. It is often said that parents and guardians cannot give a good receipt on behalf of the minor without authority in the will. However, the Children Act 1989 s.3 defines parental responsibility as including: **11-010**

> "in particular, the right to receive or recover in his own name, for the benefit of the child, property of whatever description and wherever situated which the child is entitled to receive or recover".

Testators may not wish this to happen, in which case they should include a direction in the will that the legacy is to be held on trust by the personal representatives or a stated person until such time as the beneficiary can give a good receipt. The will can authorise the personal representatives to accept a receipt from a minor at a stated age, say 16.

The Administration of Estates Act 1925 s.42 gives personal representatives power, where a minor is absolutely entitled to property, to appoint a trust corporation or two or more individuals, not exceeding four (whether or not including one or more of the personal representatives) to be trustees of the property for the minor. The personal representatives may transfer property to the trustees and a receipt signed by those trustees will be a good discharge to the personal representatives. However, the power is not available where the minor merely has a contingent interest.

Power to postpone distribution

Section 44 of the Administration of Estates Act 1925 provides that the -personal representatives are not bound to distribute the estate of the deceased before the expiration of one year from death. This does not affect their duty to pay debts with due diligence and simply means that a beneficiary cannot insist on earlier payment of a legacy, even if a testator directed payment within a short period after the death. In a case where such a direction for payment is included in the will a pecuniary or general legatee is merely entitled to interest from the date fixed for payment (there are also cases where there is a right to interest from the date of death—see para.16-066). **11-011**

The personal representatives cannot necessarily be compelled to pay a legacy even after the 12-month period has expired although they may thereafter be required to explain the delay and all pecuniary and general legatees (other than contingent ones) will thereafter be entitled to interest at the basic rate payable for the relevant time on funds in court or such other rate as the court shall direct (see para.16-064).

Power to insure

11-012 The statutory power of insurance is contained in s.19 of the Trustee Act 1925 as substituted by s.34 of the Trustee Act 2000. The substituted section gives a much wider power to personal representatives than did the original s.19. Personal representatives now have power to insure any property in the estate against risks of loss or damage due to any event and power to pay the premiums out of the estate. The duty of care under s.1 of the Trustee Act 2000 applies to the "exercise of the power to insure".

Power to run a business

Introduction

11-013 A deceased person may have run a business either as a sole trader, a partner or through the medium of a limited company. The personal representatives of such a person must consider their position in relation to the business and determine what powers and duties, if any, they have.

Sole traders

11-014 Where the will is silent the personal representatives have implied power to continue the business *for the purpose of realisation only*, that is to enable it to be sold as a going concern. Such a period will not usually exceed one year (*Re Crowther* (1895)). It is preferable to give the personal representatives express power to continue the business so long as they see fit (thus avoiding the possibility of a forced sale in a poor market).

Unless the will makes express provision, the personal representatives will only have authority to use those assets which were used in the business at the date of the deceased's death. It may be desirable to give them power to use other assets of the estate if they see fit.

When the personal representatives have authority to carry on a business, they are personally liable for any debts they incur. However, they are entitled to an indemnity from the estate. If the business is being carried on for the purpose of *realisation only*, the right of indemnity may be exercised in priority to all creditors of the deceased and beneficiaries. If the business is being carried on under authority given by the will the right of indemnity may be exercised in priority to beneficiaries but not in priority to creditors of the deceased. The reason for this is that the beneficiaries are bound by the terms of the will, but the creditors of the deceased are not (unless a creditor has expressly assented to the carrying on of the business). In this case the indemnity extends only to assets which the will authorised them to use.

Partnerships and limited companies

Where a partner or shareholder in a limited company dies the personal representatives of the deceased normally have no power to intervene in the management of the business. Death dissolves a partnership unless, as is usually the case, the partnership agreement provides otherwise. **11-015**

A company is a legal person which continues to exist despite the death of shareholders or directors. In the case of a "one-man" company there may, however, be difficulties in directing its activities once the major shareholder/director dies. Articles of Association may give the personal representatives of the last shareholder a right to appoint a person to be a director (Companies (Model Articles) Regulations 2008 (SI 2008/3229) and subsequent Regulations do so but the old Table A regulations do not).

In either case the personal representatives will be mainly concerned with ascertaining the beneficial entitlement to the deceased's interest in the business and, if appropriate, arranging a sale of the interest. It is important that personal representatives should be aware that a partnership agreement frequently contains provisions relating to death of partners. For example, many agreements provide for automatic accruer of a deceased's share of goodwill and/or for the exercise by surviving partners of an option to purchase the deceased's share in the capital assets. Similarly, the articles of association of a company or an agreement between the shareholders may give other shareholders pre-emption rights or options to purchase a deceased shareholder's shares. Personal representatives should discover whether or not such rights exist and should not look only at the deceased's will.

Power to maintain minors

What happens to income—the general rule

Where a testator directs that property is to be held on trust for beneficiaries (for example, "to A if A becomes a solicitor"), the question arises of what happens to any income produced by the property after death. If the testator has left express directions, they must be carried out. If not, there are general rules (see Ch.16). We can summarise these rules by saying that most testamentary gifts carry with them the right to intermediate income. This means that income produced by the property is added to capital and devolves with it, so that whoever becomes entitled to the capital also becomes entitled to the intermediate income. Certain gifts do not carry with them the right to intermediate income; the most common example of such a gift is a contingent pecuniary legacy (apart from certain-exceptional contingent pecuniary legacies dealt with at para.16-066). A contingent pecuniary legatee is entitled to nothing but the capital (unless there is a delay in payment after the contingency has been fulfilled, in which case the legatee becomes entitled to interest). In such a case, if the legacy fund is invested any interest produced is paid to the residuary beneficiary or, if there is none, to the person entitled on intestacy. It is normally preferable to provide that the gift carries intermediate income or, if it is a significant amount, to create an express trust with appropriate provisions. **11-016**

The effect of s.31 of the Trustee Act

Section 31 of the Trustee Act provides that where property is held for a minor beneficiary who is unmarried and not a civil partner and the gift carries with it the **11-017** right to intermediate income the trustees have a discretion as to what they do with that income, whether the minor's interest is vested or contingent. The trustees are entitled under s.31 to choose to apply the income for the maintenance, education and benefit of the minor but, to the extent that they do not, they must accumulate it. Accumulated income may be applied during the minority of the beneficiary as if it were income of the current year.

Example 2

T makes two settlements. T gives his shareholding in X Co. to trustees to hold for A if A reaches 25 and his shareholding in Y Co. to trustees to hold for B for life, remainder to C. At T's death both A and B are minors. A has a contingent interest, B has a vested interest. The trustees may choose to apply the income from the respective shares for the benefit of A and B but, in so far as they do not apply it, they must accumulate it.

In exercising this discretion the original wording of the section directed trustees to consider the age and requirements of the minor, the circumstances of the case generally and in particular what other income, if any, is applicable for the same purposes. If they had notice that more than one trust fund was available for those purposes the trustees were required, so far as was practicable, unless the entire income of the funds was applied or the court otherwise directed, to apply only a proportionate part of each trust fund. It was common for wills and trusts to remove these requirements to give the trustees an unfettered discretion when exercising their power to apply income.

For trusts created or arising on or after 1 October 2014 (the date on which the Inheritance and Trustees' Powers Act 2014 came into force) the wording of s.31 is amended to give trustees an unfettered discretion. Explanatory Note 53 to the Bill says that if a trust is created by will, it is the date of death not the date of execution which is significant.

Section 31(1) provides that if the minor reaches 18 and still has an interest which is contingent the discretion of the trustees ceases and from that date they *must* pay the income to the beneficiary until the contingency is fulfilled or the gift fails. In the above example, therefore, as soon as A reaches 18 the trustees must pay current income to A until A reaches 25 or dies without fulfilling the contingency. B will be entitled to current income at 18 and until death.

Once the minor reaches 18 (or marries or enters a civil partnership earlier) the trustees must consider what is to happen to income which has been accumulated. Section 31(2) provides that with one exception (dealt with below) such accumulations are to be added to capital and will devolve with it. Thus, if a gift is contingent on reaching 21 the beneficiary will be entitled to both capital and accumulations if they reach 21 but, if they do not, both pass to the person entitled in substitution.

The exceptional case where accumulations do not devolve with capital is that of a minor with a right to income who reaches 18 (or marries or forms a civil partnership earlier). Section 31(2) provides that such a minor is entitled to any income that has been accumulated. If he or she fails to reach 18 (or marry or form a civil partnership earlier), the accumulations will devolve with the capital. The effect is that a minor with a life interest has no right to receive income until reaching 18 (or marrying or forming a civil partnership earlier); he or she can neither insist on receiving income as it arises, nor can he or she be certain of receiving the accumulations.

Example 3

T gives his shareholding in Y Co to trustees to hold for A for life remainder to B. A is aged six at the time the settlement comes into effect. Until A reaches 18 the trustees must accumulate the income to the extent that they do not choose to apply it for the benefit of A. If A dies before reaching 18 the accumulated income (together with the shares in Y Co.) will pass to B. If A reaches 18 the trustees must pay the accumulated income to A.

The effect of s.31(2) is significant where the intention is to create an immediate post-death interest for inheritance tax purposes. If it is not amended, there will not be an immediate post-death interest. This has caused problems in a number of cases such as *Fine v Fine* (2012), *Price v Williams-Wynn* (2006) and *Bullard v Bullard* (2017).

Express clauses varying s.31

Where a gift is contingent on reaching an age greater than 18 (for example, 25) the person drafting the will may consider removing the right to income at 18 and allowing the trustees' discretion to continue. Historically it has been common to remove the right to income at 18 for the following reasons: **11-018**

(a) Beneficiaries who were already 18 at the testator's death, would have an immediate post-death interest. If a beneficiary with an immediate post-death interest dies aged between 18 and the vesting age for capital, the value of the trust property is included in their estate when calculating inheritance tax payable even though the beneficiary had no right to capital: see para.7-012. The same result will occur if a beneficiary becomes entitled to income within two years of the testator's death as a result of the reading back effect of IHTA 1984 s.144.
(b) Hold-over relief for capital gains tax will not be available under TCGA 1992 s.260 when a beneficiary with an immediate post-death interest becomes absolutely entitled to capital because the vesting is not chargeable to inheritance tax.
(c) Testators may be unwilling in the case of large trusts to give 18-year-olds a right to income.

Conversely a testator may want to create an immediate post-death interest for the following reasons:

(a) to avoid anniversary and exit charges that are payable if the settlement is a relevant property settlement (see para.7-017);
(b) to secure the residence nil-rate band for the testator's estate. Immediate post-death interest trusts are one of the few trusts that qualify for the residence nil-rate band (see para.4-019).

If an immediate post-death interest is desired, s.31 must be varied to provide that accumulated income will be held for the minor and will be paid to the minor at 18 or to his estate if he dies before 18. Failure to make this change will mean that the minor has no certainty of receiving income and the settlement is a relevant property settlement. See *Fine v Fine* (2012) for an example.

Power to advance capital

Introduction

Section 32 of the Trustee Act provides that trustees (and personal representatives) have an absolute discretion to apply capital for the advancement or benefit **11-019** of any person who has either a vested or contingent interest in capital. Property may be advanced under this section to new trustees to be held upon new trusts containing powers and discretions not contemplated by the original instrument.

If a beneficiary with a contingent interest dies after receiving an advance and without fulfilling the contingency the trustees have no right to recover property from the estate of the deceased beneficiary. The section does not apply to land or capital money under a Settled Land Act settlement (it does, however, apply to the proceeds of sale of land held upon trust for sale).

The Inheritance and Trustees' Powers Act 2014 amended the wording of s.32 to make it clear that trustees can apply capital assets not merely cash. Existing case law suggested that this was the case (see *Re Collard's Will Trusts* (1961)). The change to the wording simply clarifies the position. The amended wording applies to all trusts whenever created.

As originally drafted the section was subject to three limitations:

(a) The trustees could advance only up to one-half of the beneficiary's vested or presumptive share. Once the trustees had advanced half the value of a beneficiary's interest the power was exhausted and nothing more could be advanced even if the fund increased in value (see *Re Marquess of Abergavenny's Estate Act Trusts* (1981)). The Inheritance and Trustees' Powers Act 2014 amended s.32 to remove the one-half limit, allowing the advance of the whole of a beneficiary's vested or presumptive entitlement. The amendment applies to all trusts created or arising on or after 1 October 2014 (the date the Act came into force). Explanatory Note 53 to the Bill says that if a trust is created by will, it is the date of death not the date of execution which is significant.

(b) Any advance made must be brought into account when the beneficiary becomes absolutely entitled. This limitation is not altered by the Inheritance and Trustees' Powers Act 2014.

(c) Any person with a prior interest (e.g. the right to receive income from the trust property) must consent to the advance. This limitation is not altered by the Inheritance and Trustees' Powers Act 2014.

When an advance is brought into account, it is normally brought in at its nominal value at the date of the advance. This can work unfairly where assets increase substantially in value after the date of an advance. The beneficiary who received the advance will benefit disproportionately if the advance is brought into account at nominal value. *Re Leigh's Settlement Trusts* (1981) suggests that trustees may be able to choose the basis on which they make an advance.

Example 4

Suppose that a trust fund is held for the settlor's four children equally at 21. When the trust fund is worth £400,000, the trustees advance £50,000 to the eldest, A. The trustees later distribute the remainder of the trust fund, now worth £1,400,000, to the four beneficiaries. If the trustees made the advance to A:

> *On the nominal value basis* On this basis, the nominal value of the advance is added back in to the current value of the trust fund (£1,450,000). A is then entitled to one-quarter of that value less the advance, that is, £312,500. The other beneficiaries will each receive £362,500. If A's advance has grown in value at the same rate as the trust fund, it will now be worth £200,000 and so A will have received £512,500 in total.

On the proportionate basis On a proportionate basis, it represents half of A's share at the time of the advance. Therefore, the trust fund is now held as to one-seventh for A and six-sevenths for the other three beneficiaries. A is now entitled to £200,000 and the other beneficiaries £400,000. If A's advance has grown in value at the same rate as the trust fund, all the beneficiaries will have received £400,000 in total.

The Inheritance and Trustees' Powers Act 2014 inserted a new sub-section 1A into s.32 to provide expressly that trustees of all trusts (whenever created) are free to choose the basis on which they make an advance.

Express clauses varying s.32

Historically it has been common for a will to include an express clause removing the three limitations. **11-020**

Since 1 October 2014 it has become unnecessary to provide that trustees have power to apply the whole of a beneficiary's vested or presumptive share as this is the statutory position. Explanatory Note 53 to the Bill says that if a trust is created by will, it is the date of death not the date of execution which is significant.

Power to delegate—Trustee Act 2000

The power of personal representatives to delegate is now contained in Pt IV (ss.11–27) of the Trustee Act 2000. Under s.11 personal representatives may delegate any or all of their "delegable functions" to an agent. The delegable functions are defined as any functions except: decisions as to how or whether assets should be distributed; decisions as to whether fees or payments due should be made out of income or capital of the trust fund; exercise of powers under other enactments or under the will (which must be dealt with under those enactments or in accordance with the terms of the will); and the appointment of nominees and custodians (ss.16 and 17). The power to delegate is further restricted in the case of charitable trusts. **11-021**

More than one agent may be appointed (s.12(2)) but if two or more agents are to exercise the same function they must do so jointly. A personal representative may be appointed as agent, but a beneficiary may not be (s.12(1) and (3)). The terms on which the agent is appointed are set by the personal representatives and may include provision for remuneration (s.14(1)). Sub-delegation by the agent, any restriction on the agent's liability and any permission for the agent to act where a conflict of interest might arise are only permitted if "reasonably necessary" (s.14(2) and (3)).

Section 15 imposes special restrictions on the appointment of agents in the case of asset management. Asset management is defined as the investment of assets, and the acquisition and disposal of property (s.15(5)). In these cases the agreement authorising the exercise of the functions must be in writing or evidenced in writing (s.15(1)). The personal representatives must supply the agent with a policy statement giving guidance as to how the asset management functions should be exercised (s.15(2)(a)) and the agreement must require the agent to comply with the policy statement or any replacement of it (s.15(2)(b)).

Section 16 contains provisions which allow personal representatives to appoint nominees to hold property. This power enables personal-representatives, for example, to vest shares in a nominee to facilitate management of the investments.

Section 17 enables personal representatives to appoint "custodians" to undertake the safe custody of assets, documents or records. A nominee or custodian must be carrying on business as such for these appointments to be made (unless it is a body corporate controlled by the personal representatives).

Section 22 requires personal representatives to keep under review the appointments of agents, nominees or custodians and the terms under which they act. Provided that the personal representatives comply with the duty of care in appointing and reviewing agents, nominees and custodians, they are not liable for any acts or defaults of the agents, nominees or custodians. They would, of course, be liable for their own act in making the appointment or in deciding the terms of appointment if they were negligent in doing so.

When drafting a will, the implication of the rules and the restrictions contained in the statutory provisions should be considered. In some cases it may be appropriate to provide for the delegation of all powers of personal representatives not just the "delegable functions" as defined by the Act. It may also be appropriate to dispense with the need for a policy statement, to allow sub-delegation by the agent, restriction on the agent's liability and permission for the agent to act where a conflict of interest might arise whether or not "reasonably necessary". In particular it may be appropriate to allow delegation to a beneficiary.

Indemnity

11-022 Section 31 of the Trustee Act 2000 provides that personal representatives are entitled to reimbursement from the estate for expenses properly incurred. Similarly, under s.32, they are entitled to reimburse agents nominees and custodians.

Powers of investment

11-023 Part II (ss.3–7) of the Trustee Act 2000 simplifies and liberalises the law relating to investment by personal representatives. Section 3(1) provides that a personal representative "*may make any kind of investment that he could make if he were absolutely entitled to the assets*" of the estate. This is called the "*the general power of investment*". It does not include a power to invest in land (but s.8 does contain such a power—see para.11-024 and loans secured on land are permitted under s.3). In exercising the general power of investment or any other power of investment (such as one provided in the will) personal representatives must, under s.4, have regard to "standard investment criteria". These criteria are the suitability to the estate of the kind of investment chosen and the need for diversification of investments in so far as is appropriate to the circumstances of the estate.

Under s.5 personal representatives must take advice in making and reviewing investments. The advice must be (s.5(4)):

> "*the advice of a person who is reasonably believed by the [personal representative] to be qualified to give it by his ability in and practical experience of financial and other matters relating to the proposed investment*".

However, under s.5(3) advice need not be taken if the personal representatives "*reasonably conclude that in all the circumstances it is unnecessary or inappropriate to do so*". The personal representatives owe their duty to all the beneficiaries of the estate. A personal representative cannot normally assert an adverse claim to assets of the estate. See, for example, *Re Exler deceased* (2017) where the administrator attempted to claim the major asset of the estate under a *donatia mortis causa*. Charles Hollander QC, sitting as a deputy judge, said that the administrator should never have been permitted to act as sole personal representative as his interests were diametrically opposed to the interests of the beneficiaries as a whole.

These provisions apply to wills made before as well as after the commencement of the Act on 1 February 2001. The power to invest may be restricted in the will. The overall effect of these provisions is to free personal representatives from the restrictions formerly imposed on them by the Trustee Investment Act 1961. However, there is a potential liability for negligence where speculative investments are chosen. It is arguable that a failure to consider making investments could also be a failure to have regard to the "*standard investment criteria*" and so could give rise to a claim for negligence. However, it is also arguable that a failure to consider making investments is not an exercise of a power at all and so falls outside the scope of Pt II altogether.

Power to purchase land

Section 8 of the Trustee Act 2000 gives personal representatives the power to buy land in the UK (freehold or leasehold) as an investment, for occupation by a beneficiary or for any other reason. The power can be restricted by the will. The general duty of care applies to the exercise of the power. **11-024**

4. ADMINISTRATIVE POWERS GRANTED BY WILL

As indicated in the previous section it is common to extend many of the statutory powers of trustees and personal representatives. It is also common to confer on them certain additional powers such as the power to make loans to beneficiaries or to advance capital to a surviving spouse to whom a life interest has been given. These matters are dealt with more fully in Ch.22. **11-025**

5. RIGHTS OF BENEFICIARIES DURING THE ADMINISTRATION

Introduction

As we have seen it is the function of the personal representatives to administer the deceased's estate by collecting the assets, paying off the debts and liabilities and distributing the estate to the beneficiaries under the will or the intestacy rules. The beneficiaries may wish to know what rights they have against the personal representatives during the administration period. **11-026**

The right to compel due administration

Beneficiaries have no equitable interest in assets

The assets of the deceased vest in the personal representatives and those assets come to the personal representatives "in full ownership without distinction between legal and equitable interests" (*Commissioner of Stamp Duties (Queensland) v Livingston* (1965)). In view of this, until the administration of the estate is complete, the beneficiary, whether under a will or intestacy, can have neither a legal nor an equitable interest in the deceased's assets (*Dr Barnardo's Homes National Incorporated Association v Commissioners for Special Purposes of the Income Tax* **11-027**

Acts (1921)). Until the administration has been completed, it is impossible to say which assets will be available to the beneficiaries and which will have to be used to pay debts and administration expenses. The effect of this is that the beneficiaries cannot claim the assets until the administration has been completed because until then the beneficiaries cannot be certain of entitlement to any assets. They cannot object simply because the personal representatives sell, or intend to sell, an asset given to them in the will. They can only object if the asset should not be sold because, for example, there is no need to sell the asset in the circumstances. Personal representatives are not trustees of the estate in the strict or narrow sense that any beneficiary can claim to be specifically entitled to any particular property of the estate. But in many respects they can be regarded as holding on trust the assets of estate that have come to them for the purpose of carrying out their duties of administration. The position was explained in the judgment of the Privy Council in *Commissioner of Stamp Duties (Queensland) v Livingston* (1965) (at 707) in terms of a chose in action to compel due administration. See para.11-028.

The beneficiaries' chose in action

11-028 Although the beneficiaries have no legal or equitable interest in the deceased's individual assets, they do have something. They have a chose in action; that is a right to ensure that the deceased's estate is properly administered. Although the personal representatives own the whole legal and beneficial interests in the assets of the estate, they hold them for the purpose of carrying out the functions and duties of administration, not for their own benefit; and those duties would be enforced by the court. "An executor", said Kay J in *Re Marsden* (1884), "is personally liable in equity for all breaches of the ordinary trusts which in Courts of Equity are considered to arise from his office." He is a trustee in this sense. Viscount Radcliffe said in *Commissioner of Stamp Duties (Queensland) v Livingston* (1965)) that:

> "It may not be possible to state exhaustively what those trusts are at any one moment. Essentially, they are trusts that preserve the assets, to deal properly with them, and to apply them in the due course of administration for the benefit of those interested according to that course, creditors, the death duty authorities, legatees of various sorts, and the residuary beneficiaries."

Effectively the "*trusts*" are the duties that the personal representatives must carry out and the beneficiaries can compel them to do so.

The chose in action can be transmitted to another person, as is illustrated by the case of *Re Leigh's Will Trusts* (1970). In this case the testatrix left "*all shares which I hold and any other interest ... which I may have*" in a named company. She did not hold any shares in that company but at the date of her death she was the sole beneficiary of her husband's estate which included shares in that company. It was held that the gift took effect as a gift of her chose in action in her husband's estate.

In *Re Bernstein* (2008) it was accepted that, while there was no trust in the narrow sense during the administration period, the fiduciary obligations owed by the executor to the beneficiaries meant that there was a trust in a wider sense which was sufficient to allow the court to exercise its powers under the Variation of Trusts Act 1958 to consent to variations of trust on behalf of beneficiaries unable to consent for themselves.

The position of specific legatees

While the general rule is that beneficiaries acquire merely a chose in action, in *IRC v Hawley* (1928) it was suggested that a specific legatee takes an equitable interest in the property given under the terms of the will from the date of death, even though the property may be used to discharge the debts and liabilities of the estate by the personal representatives in whom the legal estate will vest. **11-029**

However, this decision is inconsistent with the personal representatives receiving both the legal and equitable interests, as suggested in *Commissioner of Stamp Duties (Queensland) v Livingston* (1965): see para.11-028. In *Re Hayes' Will Trusts* (1971) Ungoed-Thomas J said "*no legatee, devisee or next of kin has any beneficial interest in the assets being administered*". In view of this conflict it seems likely that even a specific legatee has only a chose in action to ensure due administration.

General administration actions

Introduction

Where difficulties arise while the estate is being administered, whether because of a problem which the personal representatives have encountered or a dispute arising over the conduct of the administration (for example, where the beneficiaries allege that the personal representatives have committed a *devastavit*) an application can be made to the court to have the difficulty resolved. These proceedings, which are intended to ensure that the administration is conducted properly, are called "*administration proceedings*". There are two types of administration proceedings: **11-030**

(a) actions for general administration of the whole or part of the estate by the court. If the court makes such an order the personal representatives cannot exercise their powers to sell or distribute the assets without the consent of the court. The order stops time running under the Limitation Act for creditors' claims; or
(b) actions for specific relief, such as the determination of one specific problem.

Administration proceedings are not necessarily the result of any wrongdoing. The court's help may be sought by the personal representatives themselves if they are anxious about a particular point; this is particularly likely in the case of an action for specific relief and this is, therefore, dealt with at para.14-017 and following, which are concerned with protection of personal representatives. Alternatively, the beneficiaries may seek the help of the court; this is more likely in the case of a general administration action and, therefore, the rest of this section deals with such actions. These days the most common action taken by unhappy beneficiaries is to have the personal representatives removed under Administration of Justice Act 1985 s.50 and replaced by someone else. See paras 8-023 and 11-036.

Jurisdiction

The Chancery Division of the High Court has jurisdiction in these matters, but the following also have jurisdiction: **11-031**

(a) the county court if the estate does not exceed in amount or value the county court limit (increased for this purpose from £30,000 to £350,000 by the County Court Jurisdiction Order 2014 (SI 2014/503)), and

(b) the bankruptcy court if the estate is insolvent.

The parties

11-032 The action can be commenced by any personal representative, any beneficiary under the will or intestacy or any creditor. All the personal representatives must be made parties to any action; those who consent are made claimants and those who do not are made defendants: CPR Pt 64.4.

The order for administration

11-033 If the whole estate is to be administered under the court's direction (a very unusual step) the court can order that an account be taken of:

(a) property that forms part of the residue of the estate which has come into the possession, either of the personal representatives or of some other person by the order or for the use of the personal representatives;
(b) the deceased's debts and funeral and testamentary expenses. If the deceased died more than six years before the date of the order the court can order that an enquiry be made as to whether any such liability of the deceased remains outstanding;
(c) legacies and annuities; and
(d) any parts of the deceased's estate that have not yet been collected or distributed after enquiries have been made and any charges attaching to such property have been ascertained.

If an instance of wilful default is established against the personal representative, the account may be ordered on the footing of wilful default, that is that the personal representatives account for property which would have come into their possession but for their wilful default.

Once accounts and enquiries have been taken and made, the court will order distribution to the beneficiaries.

As an alternative to making a general order the court can order that:

(a) specific accounts and inquiries be taken and made to deal with particular problems that have arisen; or
(b) the personal representative should produce particular accounts within a stated period of time.

Costs

11-034 The personal representatives are entitled to have their costs paid from the assets of the estate, unless they have acted unreasonably or unless the result of such an order would be to diminish the estate to such an extent that claimants to it would be unfairly prejudiced (*Evans v Evans*). The costs of other parties are in the court's discretion.

Appointing a judicial trustee

11-035 Where the personal representatives cannot administer the estate and are unwilling to incur the expense of an administration action, they (or a beneficiary) can apply for a judicial trustee to be appointed. The trustee will be appointed to act either alone or with others and can be appointed to replace the existing personal representatives. Since they are officers of the court, once appointed, they do not need the court's consent to exercise their powers.

Substitution or removal of personal representative

The High Court has a discretionary power under s.50 of the Administration of Justice Act 1985 on an application made by a beneficiary of an estate (or by or on behalf of a personal representative): **11-036**

(a) to appoint a substitute to act in place of an existing personal representative; or
(b) where there are two or more existing personal representatives to terminate the appointment of one or more, but not all, of these persons.

The s.50 power can be used before an executor has taken a grant: see *Goodman & Goodman v Goodman & Goodman* (2013). These applications are becoming increasingly common. For a fuller discussion see para.8-023.

6. OTHER REMEDIES OF BENEFICIARIES

A personal action against personal representatives

When a personal representative accepts office he or she accepts the duties of the office. A failure to carry out those duties properly is a *devastavit* for which the personal representative will be personally liable to the disappointed beneficiaries (or next of kin). The court may, however, grant relief either wholly or partly from personal liability to a personal representative for a breach of trust where it appears that a personal representative acted honestly and reasonably and ought fairly to be excused (Trustee Act 1925 s.61). **11-037**

The right to trace

A beneficiary (or next-of-kin or creditor) has the right to trace and recover *property* of the estate (or property representing property of the estate) from the personal representative or from any recipient of it other than a bona fide purchaser for value (or person deriving title from such a purchaser). The right to trace is lost where the property of the estate has been dissipated or where tracing would produce an inequitable result. **11-038**

Example 5

X, a personal representative, takes £1,000 belonging to an estate he is administering and spends it on a car which he gives to Y. The beneficiaries can recover the car from Y. If Y sells the car for £900 to Z, a bona fide purchaser for value, the beneficiaries have no right to trace the car into the hands of Z. They can, however, recover the £900 from Y. If Y dissipates the £900 by spending it on a holiday the right to trace is lost.

In some cases a beneficiary may prefer to rely on tracing rather than on bringing a personal action against the personal representatives (for example, where they are anxious to recover a particular asset rather than its value). In some cases the personal remedy may be valueless (for example, where the personal representative is bankrupt) so that tracing may be the only effective remedy.

A full discussion of the law on tracing is beyond the scope of this book and the reader is referred to any standard equity textbook.

A personal action against recipients of assets of the estate

11-039 Where all the other remedies of a beneficiary, next-of-kin or creditor have been exhausted a personal action may be brought against a person who has wrongly received assets of the estate. This was established by the judgment of the House of Lords in *Ministry of Health v Simpson* (1951). In this case, personal representatives had paid large sums of money to various charities in the mistaken belief that they were entitled to do so under the terms of the will. The next-of-kin of the deceased had established that the personal representatives were not so entitled and had exhausted their personal remedies against the personal representatives. They had been able to trace some of the payments into the hands of the charities and to recover them. However, some of the charities had dissipated the money with the result that the right to trace was lost. It was held that the next-of-kin were able to bring an action against the recipients personally to recover an amount equal to that which had been wrongly paid to them.

Chapter Twelve

PRACTICAL CONSIDERATIONS DURING ADMINISTRATION

1. Introduction

In previous chapters we have studied the legal rules that are relevant to the administration of an estate. When applying the legal rules the circumstances of the estate and of the beneficiaries must be borne in mind. In this chapter we will consider some of the practical problems which can arise during an administration. **12-001**

2. Raising Money to Pay Debts and Inheritance Tax

Introduction

Before the personal representatives can obtain a grant of representation, they will need to pay any inheritance tax that is due. However, the problem which faces them is that in order to get access to money in the deceased's bank or building society or to raise money by selling assets they will normally need the grant. They will therefore need to find a way of raising money to pay the tax which does not require a grant of representation. **12-002**

Borrowing from a bank or other commercial lender may seem the obvious solution but it is expensive and it may prove difficult to obtain funds, depending on the nature of the estate assets. It is sensible for personal representatives to explore other options first. Since 1 April 2024, HMRC has allowed grants on credit in certain circumstances which is helpful to taxpayers although interest runs on the unpaid tax from six months after the end of the month of death.

Whatever method of payment is used, personal representatives will need to apply for an IHT reference number. The application can be made online or by post using form IHT422. HMRC advises allowing at least three weeks in their guidance note "Pay your inheritance tax bill" available on the gov.uk website.

Borrow money from commercial providers

Lenders normally insist on an undertaking being given by the personal representatives to the effect that they will account to the lender from the first realised assets of the estate. If the personal representatives have appointed solicitors to act for them, the bank may require a further undertaking to be given by the solicitors. In this case the solicitor should obtain the personal representatives' irrevocable authority to give an undertaking. **12-003**

The disadvantage of borrowing from a commercial provider is that the loan will carry interest. Therefore, irrespective of any undertaking that has been given, the loan should be outstanding for as short a time as possible. It is advisable to arrange the loan immediately before the application for the grant is to be made and, once the grant has been obtained, to use it to realise sufficient assets to repay the debt quickly.

The Income Tax Act 2007 ss.383 and 403 provide that the personal representatives may, for the purposes of calculating income tax liability, deduct interest paid as a charge on their income to the extent that it is paid on a loan which is used to pay inheritance tax that they are obliged to pay under IHTA 1984 s.226(2) (i.e. all the tax for which they are liable on delivery of their inheritance tax account). Even if the loan satisfies this requirement, the interest is only deductible to the extent that it is paid in respect of a period ending within one year from the making of the loan. Furthermore, the personal representatives must open a separate loan account, and not merely allow the deceased's bank account to become overdrawn. The liability to pay interest may make this method unattractive to personal representatives and to beneficiaries.

Banks releasing funds of the deceased

12-004 Many banks are willing to release funds from the deceased's bank accounts before the grant is obtained. It is clearly always worth contacting the deceased's bank to find out whether they will release funds for this purpose. Although this practice is generally helpful to personal representatives and family members, there are obvious dangers. There have been reported examples of family members obtaining funds to which they were not entitled in this way. It is sensible to inform all banks at which the deceased is known to have had an account as quickly as possible of the death and of who is entitled to deal with the estate.

A banking practices protocol dealing with estate administration has been agreed between the British Bankers' Association, the Law Society of England and Wales and the Society of Trust and Estate Practitioners. The purpose is to bring clarity to probate-related dealings between advisors and banks. It covers the handling of current, savings, credit card and unsecured loan accounts. It sets out the information banks are likely to require from solicitor/STEP member and information that the solicitor/STEP member is likely to require from the bank together with an outline of how the bank might normally respond to such requests.

Para.15 of the Banking Practices Protocol Estate Administration (3 November 2012) (available on The Law Society's website) says:

> "Where a specific request is made, confirmation that the bank will allow the balance on accounts to be used before production of the grant of representation for payment of inheritance tax and the funeral bill.
>
> The bank may also:
>
> - allow these funds to be used for the payment of probate fees
> - require copies of relevant documentation, in accordance with the individual bank's procedures
> - require an indemnity or solicitor's undertaking
>
> In all cases, confirmation is subject to the exercise of the bank's right to set-off to the extent permitted by law where there are also debts due to the bank."

(*https://www.lawsociety.org.uk/topics/private-client/banking-practices-protocol-estate-administration*)

Direct payment scheme

The direct payment scheme allows funds to be paid from the deceased's bank, building society or National Savings and Investments accounts directly to HMRC for inheritance tax due on delivery of IHT400. The scheme is voluntary so personal representatives should check whether the particular bank or building society is part of the scheme. The procedure is set out in the Guidance Notes to IHT423 and in "Pay your Inheritance Tax bill" available on the gov.uk website. **12-005**

Personal representatives must complete and sign a separate IHT423 for each paying institution from which they wish to transfer money, adding the reference number obtained from HMRC. They send the completed IHT423 to the relevant institution which will then transfer the sum requested to HMRC. Once HMRC receives notice of the payment it will link the payment to IHT400. In England and Wales HMRC will then send the personal representatives a unique code which is included in the application for a grant of representation. In Northern Ireland HMRC will stamp and return the Probate Summary form IHT421. The whole process will take longer than paying from other funds. However, this should be offset by the saving in time and cost of arranging a loan.

British Government stock proceeds paid direct to HMRC

Where an estate includes British Government stock on the Bank of England register (for example War Loan, Treasury Stock and Exchequer Stock), it is possible to arrange for the payment of inheritance tax from such products direct to HMRC without the need to encash them. However, in its guidance "Pay your Inheritance Tax bill" (available on the gov.uk website) HMRC says *"Don't pay this way if you need to get probate quickly."* **12-006**

The first step is to write to Computershare Investor Services (who run the British Government Stock scheme) at British Government Stocks (Gilts), Computershare Investor Services Plc, The Pavilions, Bristol BS99 6ZW, telling them you want to pay inheritance tax and how much of the stock you want to use. Enclose a copy of the death certificate and the stock reference number (if available).

At the same time, send HMRC:

- A letter saying how much tax you want to be paid out of the stock;
- Inheritance Tax Account form IHT400 including Inheritance Tax payment reference number on the form;
- Probate Summary form IHT421 if you're in Northern Ireland.

HMRC will contact Computershare and ask for the money to be transferred. This can take up to four weeks.

If any additional tax is due after the transfer of funds, HMRC will give information as to the amount of the shortfall. Once all the tax is paid in England and Wales HMRC will send the personal representatives a unique code. In Northern Ireland they will send the receipted IHT421.

Borrow from a beneficiary

Beneficiaries may object to the personal representatives borrowing money from banks to meet the inheritance tax liability since the interest paid will reduce the income from the estate available to them. The beneficiaries may have to accept the **12-007** payment as unavoidable but, in some cases, it is possible to borrow money from a beneficiary interest-free.

Since the loan will facilitate the administration, beneficiaries will often be amenable to such a suggestion, provided they have the money available. This may come from their own resources or from the proceeds of an insurance policy taken out by the deceased and payable direct to the beneficiary. Such a policy may be a Married Women's Property Act 1882 s.11 policy or one written in trust for a particular person. In such cases the insurance company will simply require proof of death, in the form of a death certificate and will not require production of a grant.

If the deceased was a member of a pension scheme and a death in service lump sum is paid by the trustees to a beneficiary on the death, the beneficiary may be willing to use such a sum to make an interest-free loan.

Where easily realisable property (such as money in a building society account) was held jointly with the deceased, the survivor may be willing to lend to the personal representatives out of such property. The beneficiary will be reimbursed from the assets of the estate once the grant has been obtained.

Sale of assets before grant

12-008 An executor's authority derives from the will, whereas an administrator's authority derives from the grant. An executor, therefore, has power to sell assets before a grant of representation is made whereas an administrator has no such power. However, an executor may find that it is, in fact, difficult to sell some types of assets since a prospective purchaser may insist on seeing the grant in order to confirm that the person claiming to be the executor is, in fact, the person entitled to the grant. Moreover, while the executors may be able to sell items of moveable personal property such as clothes, paintings and furniture, such items may not raise sufficient funds. Land cannot be sold without the grant because the purchaser will want to examine the original grant and endorse a memorandum of the sale on the original grant.

Assets handed direct to HMRC

12-009 HMRC has discretion to accept certain assets in total, or partial, satisfaction of the tax liability on an estate (IHTA 1984 s.230).

It can accept:

(a) land (which includes any building on the land) agreed upon between HMRC and the person liable to pay the inheritance tax together with any objects which are or have been kept in a particular building and which the Secretary of State considers should remain associated with it;
(b) any picture, print, book, manuscript, work of art, scientific object or other thing which the Secretary of State is satisfied is pre-eminent for its national, scientific, historic or artistic interest;
(c) any collection or group of pictures, prints, books, manuscripts, works of art, scientific objects or other things (such as stamps), if the Secretary of State is satisfied that the collection or group, taken as a whole, is pre-eminent for its national, scientific, historic or artistic interest.

Land and buildings of outstanding interest will only be accepted if an -appropriate recipient for them can be found (for example the National Trust or national park authorities) and they are capable of being used for the public benefit.

Sums payable without a grant

Small payments

12-010 Various provisions permit small sums to be paid or transferred on death without the need to produce a grant of representation. In all cases this power is discretionary, not obligatory and orders made under the Administration of Estates (Small Payments) Act 1965 place an upper limit on these payments of £5,000. If the sum due to the deceased is in excess of £5,000 the grant is needed for the *whole amount*, not just the excess over £5,000.

Subject to the £5,000 limit the payment can be made to the person appearing to be entitled to the grant or to be beneficially entitled to the sums in respect of inter alia:

(a) Money held in the National Savings Bank, Trustee Savings Bank, savings certificates or premium bonds. It should, however, be noted that despite these rules the Director of Savings will, in practice, require sight of a grant if the deceased held more than £5,000 *in total* in the National Savings Bank, savings certificates and premium bonds. In certain circumstances, the Director of Savings must obtain a statement from HMRC to the effect that either no inheritance tax is payable or that it has been paid, before they will make the payment without the production of the grant.
(b) Monies payable on the death of a member of a trade union, an industrial or provident society or a friendly society.
(c) Arrears of salary, wages or superannuation on benefits due to employees of government departments.
(d) Police and Fire Service pensions, Army and Air Force pensions.

Schedule 7 para.1 of the Building Societies Act 1986 contains corresponding provisions in respect of monies invested in a building society. These small payments may be a useful source of funds to pay inheritance tax for personal representatives and may be preferable to seeking loans from beneficiaries.

Obtaining a grant on credit

12-011 Although IHTA 1984 s.226(2) clearly states that all personal representatives who are liable for inheritance tax "shall" on delivery of their account pay all the tax for which they are liable, HMRC acknowledges that in exceptional circumstances it may be appropriate to allow taxpayers to obtain a grant before paying the tax due. The *IHT Manual* at para.IHTM05120 says

> "In certain circumstances (IHTM05123), HMRC will allow a PR to postpone payment of all or part of the tax and interest due on delivery of an account. This is referred to as a grant on credit. It is important to note that late payment interest will accrue as usual on any unpaid tax."

Personal representatives are personally liable for the inheritance tax due on the deceased's estate and HMRC expect them to consider all financial sources, including their own assets. However, from 1 April 2024, they are not expected to seek commercial loans to pay the tax before applying to obtain a grant on credit from HMRC.

Paragraph IHTM05123 sets out the circumstances in which HMRC consider that a grant on credit could be issued:

- when the personal representative is unable to raise all the funds to pay the tax due;
- when it is not in the interests of the Exchequer for the issue of a grant to be delayed.

In relation to inability to pay IHTM05123 says:

> "Sometimes there may be insufficient liquid assets in the estate to allow the PR to pay the tax due. In this situation we may consider postponing payment on delivery. Although the PR is expected to make every effort to raise the funds, from 1 April 2024 they are not required to seek commercial loans to pay the Inheritance Tax before applying to obtain a grant on credit from HMRC.."

In relation to the interests of the Exchequer IHTM05123 says there may be cases where the precise details of the value of the estate cannot be obtained without the authority of the grant. In such a case:

> "there might be significant delay in settling the tax debt. This may put the Exchequer at risk of losing the tax, especially if the nature of the estate assets could alter in value. A grant on credit could be the key to breaking the deadlock and we should consider it as an option."

HMRC say that each case must be considered on its own merits but a grant on credit will only be agreed where the personal representative is experiencing genuine difficulty paying the tax and has exhausted the alternative sources of funding listed and the grant on credit does not put the Exchequer at risk. When seeking a grant on credit IHTM05126 says that personal representatives should:

- Send a signed and completed IHT400, if they have not already done so.
- State the maximum amount of tax they can raise.
- Provide a statement explaining what steps they and their advisors have taken so far to fund the tax liability. This should include confirmation that all the sources of funding mentioned at para.IHTM05122 have been pursued or, if that is not the case, an explanation why not.

HMRC used to require taxpayers to provide copies of correspondence with banks or other financial institutions that had refused to provide funding or had attached onerous conditions. From 1 April 2024, personal representatives of estates no longer need to have sought commercial loans to pay inheritance tax before applying to obtain a grant on credit from HMRC. As a result, HMRC have therefore dropped this requirement.

The sources of funding mentioned at para.IHTM05122 are direct payments, assets that can be realised before the issue of the grant and the resources of the personal representatives.

3. Sale of Assets—Which to Sell?

Introduction

12-012 When the personal representatives have to sell assets, whether to raise money to pay inheritance tax or in the course of administering the estate after the grant has been obtained, they must bear in mind a number of considerations:

(a) the terms of the will,
(b) the wishes of the beneficiaries, and

(c) the tax consequences of selling individual items.

The terms of the will and the wishes of the beneficiaries

When deciding which assets to sell first, the personal representatives must have due regard to the statutory order for payment of debts (see para.15-011 and following); so, for example items which have been specifically given by the will should only be taken if assets comprised in residue have been exhausted. Should the personal representatives use the wrong items to satisfy the debts then "marshalling" may be necessary so that the appropriate beneficiary bears the burden of the debt. Therefore, if the will gives specific items of property to beneficiaries, these items should not be considered for sale until the other assets in the estate have been exhausted. **12-013**

When the personal representatives are choosing which assets to sell, the wishes and needs of the beneficiaries should be considered. For example, if the residuary beneficiary wants a valuable antique which has not been specifically dealt with in the will, their wishes should be respected if at all possible.

Future destination of property

If the terms of the will or the intestacy rules create a trust, the personal representatives should ensure that any property retained is suitable in view of the nature of the trust. **12-014**

The sale of shares

The sale of shares in a quoted company should cause few problems, but if the shares are in an unquoted company it may be less easy to find a market for the shares. In this circumstance, the personal representatives could seek a buyer among the other members of the company. The company itself may be willing to buy the shares under Pt 18 of the Companies Act 2006. When a payment is made by the company in these circumstances to the deceased member's personal representatives any profit made on the sale may attract income tax liability (the details of these rules are beyond the scope of this book). **12-015**

Clearly, where unquoted shares are concerned, the personal representatives must take professional advice as to the price they should obtain for the shares. They should also be aware of the fact that the company's Articles of Association may contain pre-emption rights.

Tax considerations—inheritance tax

Introduction

The sale of assets does not normally affect the amount of inheritance tax payable. However, IHTA 1984 ss.178–198 contains provisions giving relief where certain assets of the estate are sold for less than their market value at the date of death. **12-016**

Relief for sales of shares at a loss

If "qualifying investments" are sold by the "appropriate person" within 12 months of the death at less than their market value at the date of death, the sale price **12-017** can be substituted for the market value at the date of death. Depending on the size of the death estate and the deceased's cumulative total, this may lead to a repayment of tax. The relief also applies to qualifying investments held in a settlement of which the deceased was a life tenant.

"Qualifying investments" are defined in IHTA 1984 s.178(1) as

- shares and securities which are quoted at the date of death,
- units in authorised unit trusts,
- shares in an open-ended investment company, and
- shares in any common investment fund established under s.42 of the Administration of Justice Act 1982 (these are rare; they relate to funds in court that are administered by the Public Trustee and are comparable to unit trusts).

Quoted holdings include shares quoted on the London Stock Exchange and shares quoted on recognised foreign stock exchanges (para.IHTM34140).

Unquoted shares and shares traded on the Alternative Investment Market (AIM) do not qualify for relief.

The "appropriate person" is defined in s.178(1) as

> "*the person liable for tax attributable to the value of those investments or, if there is more than one such person, and one of them is in fact paying the tax, that person*"."

In view of the wording of the definition, it is important that the sale be made by the person who is liable for, and who has actually paid, the tax (usually the personal representatives or trustees) if the relief is to be available. For example, if the personal representatives paid the inheritance tax on quoted shares, they must be the ones to sell those shares. The relief would not be available if the shares were vested in a specific legatee even if the legatee sold the shares at a loss within 12 months.

A sale is an essential element of the relief but, in addition to straightforward sales of shareholdings, an appropriation of shares can be treated as a sale in certain circumstances. The *IHT Manual* at para.IHTM34153 states that an appropriation made by the personal representatives is treated as a sale for the purposes of this relief if it is made:

- in satisfaction of a pecuniary legacy,
- with the consent of the legatee, where there is no power of appropriation without that consent.

Where the will allows appropriation of assets in satisfaction of a pecuniary legacy without consent, HMRC will not treat the appropriation as a sale even if is made with consent.

It is common, when drafting wills, to exclude the need for consent but where estates include qualifying investments, it may be preferable not to do so. There are no longer any stamp duty disadvantages to appropriations with consent.

The loss is calculated by deducting the sale price from the market value of the shares at death. However, HMRC have the power to substitute the best consideration which could reasonably have been obtained (s.179(1)(b)). Expenses incurred as a result of the sale, such as stockbrokers commission and stamp duty, cannot be used to increase the loss.

Example 1

On X's death he had made chargeable transfers up to the limit of his nil-rate band and had a death estate of £500,000 including shares in a public quoted company worth £3,000. Inheritance tax was paid on the estate. If X's personal representatives sell the holding for £2,500 within 12 months of the death, they can claim relief and so receive a rebate equal to the tax paid on the £500 reduction in value.

If a number of sales of qualifying investments are made within the 12-month period the sale proceeds of all transactions must be aggregated to discover the overall gain or loss. If, overall, a loss has arisen the claim for the relief may be made. If, overall, a gain has been made, HMRC cannot demand extra inheritance tax but no loss relief can be claimed on the particular shares sold at a loss.

Example 2

The figures for X's estate are the same as for the previous example save that X held shares in three separate public companies, each holding being worth £1,000 at his death. If X's personal representatives sell the three holdings for £500, £750 and £1,250 respectively within 12 months of the death, they must aggregate the three sale prices to calculate the overall loss of £500. It is not possible to take account only of the first two sales.

The relief is available whenever a sale is made by the appropriate person within the specified period but, if the appropriate person purchases other qualifying investments within two months of the last such sale, the loss relief available will be reduced or extinguished (s.180). This is because the purpose of the reliefs is to give assistance where shares are sold to raise money to pay inheritance tax or other debts. If the sale is to improve the estate's portfolio of investments, the relief will not be available to the personal representatives.

Where, as is usually the case, the appropriate person is a personal representative or trustee, the restriction applies if during the period beginning on the date of death and ending two months after the date of the last sale, they purchase any qualifying investments in the same capacity in which he makes the claim, (s.180(1)).

However, where the appropriate person is not a legal personal representative or a trustee (for example, a beneficiary who has paid the tax), the restriction only applies if during the period beginning on the date of death and ending two months after the date of the last sale, they purchase qualifying investments *of the same description* as one of the investments included in the claim (s.180(2)).

In considering whether two investments are of the same description s.180(3) provides that two investments are not the same if they are separately quoted on a stock exchange.

A personal representative may also be a beneficiary or a trustee. A purchase in the capacity of a beneficiary or trustee will not impact on a claim for loss relief made by the same person in their capacity as personal representative. However, it is important to have evidence of a change in status.

IHTM34213 says:

> "In general the major change in capacity from PR to trustee/legatee will only occur when the estate has been fully administered and the residue is ascertained.
>
> However, a change of capacity will occur if an irrevocable appropriation of assets – including cash from the proceeds of shares – is made under either
>
> - specific powers included in the will, or
> - the general authority of s 41 Administration of Estates Act 1925.
>
> So for example, if
>
> - the PRs appropriate investments to the trustees of an existing trust, and

- the trustees then make purchases of qualifying investments using the proceeds from the sale of these investments

then the purchases are not taken into account by the appropriate person when considering an application for a loss on sale relief and the restrictions imposed by IHTA84/s 180.

If, however, the trust was established by the Will of the deceased and the executors were also the trustees, in the absence of an assent to the trustees, it is likely that the purchases will be by the appropriate persons in the same capacity. In this case, s 180 will apply."

If the sale is to be eligible for the relief, it must occur within 12 months of the death. The operative date is the sale date unless there was a contract to sell, in which case, the contract date determines whether the sale qualifies for relief.

A problem existed for personal representatives who found themselves at the end of the 12-month period from death holding shares where the quotation had been suspended or cancelled. Clearly the personal representatives could not sell the shares and, therefore, no relief was available. However, the Finance Act 1993 s.199 inserted new ss.186A and 186B into the IHTA 1984 to deal with these situations.

Section 186A provides that cancelled shares are to be treated as having been sold by the appropriate person for a nominal consideration (one pound) -immediately before cancellation.

Section 186B provides that suspended shares are to be treated as sold by the appropriate person immediately before the end of the 12-month period for their value at the time.

A claim for relief must be made not more than four years after the end of the 12-month period starting with the date of death (s.179(2A)).

The inter-relation of inheritance tax loss relief on shares and capital gains tax

12-018 When sales which can potentially give rise to claims for inheritance tax loss relief, take place, the personal representatives also realise a loss for capital gains tax purposes. However, if the personal representatives claim the inheritance tax relief, the sale price becomes the personal representatives' acquisition value for capital gains tax (IHTA 1984 s.187 and TCGA 1992 s.274). The personal representatives will then be treated for capital gains tax purposes as selling for the same amount as the acquisition value and will not be able to claim a capital gains tax loss, other than for costs of disposal.

Inheritance tax is chargeable at 40 per cent (or 36 per cent if a sufficiently large part of the estate is left to charity: see para.4-108 and following) on the value of the portion of an estate exceeding the nil-rate band (after cumulation). Since capital gains tax payable by personal representatives on quoted shares is charged at 28 per cent of the chargeable *gain*, it will always be preferable to claim inheritance tax loss relief unless the amount of the capital gains tax loss is more than the amount by which the nil-rate band is exceeded and there are (or are likely to be) future gains against which the loss can be set in excess of any exemption or relief the personal representatives can claim.

Relief for sales of land at a loss

12-019 If the deceased was entitled to an interest in land at the time of death and that interest is sold for less than the market value at death, the personal representatives can claim to have the sale price substituted for the market value at death, provided the sale takes place within four years of death, the operative date being the date of the contract for sale (ss.190–198 of the IHTA 1984). This can lead to a rebate in much the same way that sales of quoted shares can.

Section 191 provides that small decreases in value are ignored. Thus, the relief is not available if the reduction in the value of the interest is less than either £1,000 or five per cent of its value on death, whichever is the lesser.

As with sales of quoted shares the sale must be by "the appropriate person" which has the same meaning as in para.12-017.

Section 191(3) prevents a claim being made if the sale is by a personal representative or trustee to:

(i) a person who, at any time between the death and the sale, has been beneficially entitled to, or to an interest in possession in, property comprising the interest sold, or
(ii) the spouse or civil partner or a child or remoter descendant of a person within sub-para.(i) above, or
(iii) trustees of a settlement under which a person within sub-para.(i) or (ii) above has an interest in possession in property comprising the interest sold.

The word "comprising" is used here to mean "including" or "made up of". So, the interest sold must be the same as the beneficiary's original interest for the relief to be denied. The *IHT Manual* gives these examples at para.IHTM33082:

> "*Example 1*
>
> A house is left to Angela, Brian and Carol. Angela buys the house from the executors. The property 'comprising' the interest sold is the whole house. Angela's beneficial interest was in a one third share only. Her beneficial entitlement was included in the interest sold but was not the interest sold, which was the whole. As a result the sale qualifies for relief.
>
> *Example 2*
>
> A house is left to Aarif and Basheera. Basheera's half share of the house is sold to Aarif's son. The relief is allowable because the sale is to the child of a beneficiary of a different share.
>
> *Example 3*
>
> A house is left to Chandra as sole beneficiary. The house is sold to Chandra's daughter. IHTA84/s.191(3)(a)(ii) will prevent the relief from applying, as the sale is of the same interest (the whole) to the child of the original beneficiary of the interest."

Sections 192–195 require certain adjustments to be made which may reduce the amount of loss relief that can be claimed. For example, where the appropriate person, acting in the same capacity, purchases an interest in land during the period beginning on the date of death and ending not later than four months after the last qualifying sale, the relief may be reduced or extinguished.

Where several interests in land are *sold* within three years of death, if one is revalued in order to claim loss relief, all the interests sold must be revalued. If any interest has increased in value, there may be more inheritance tax to pay as a result. Care must, therefore, be taken when deciding whether to make the claim in these circumstances since if the personal representatives make an overall *gain*, additional inheritance tax *can* be levied. (This is an important distinction as compared with the position on shares. A disadvantageous claim cannot be withdrawn.)

In the case of sales in the fourth year after death, sales for more than value at date of death are ignored.

Where the deceased was a co-owner of land, the personal representatives should consider carefully before making a claim. The discount normally available on co-owned land will be lost if a claim is made to substitute the sale proceeds and the result may be to increase the inheritance tax payable. See *IHT Manual*, para.IHTM33182.

Example 3

Ann dies owning a half-share of Blackacre as beneficial tenant. Blackacre is valued at £200,000 at the date of Ann's death and the value of her one-half-share is discounted by 10 per cent to £90,000. A year after the death, the whole property is sold for £190,000. The sale value of the property for these purposes is an arithmetic half-share of the gross proceeds of sale, £95,000. Any claim is, therefore, disadvantageous as additional inheritance tax would be payable.

The inter-relation of inheritance tax loss relief and capital gains tax

12-020 Unlike the provisions which deal with loss relief on the sale of qualifying investments, the provisions which deal with loss relief on the sales of interests in land contain no section which states expressly that the capital gains tax acquisition value is to be reduced in the event of a claim for inheritance tax loss relief. However, s.274 of the TCGA 1992 provides that where a value has been "ascertained" for inheritance tax purposes, that figure will become the acquisition value for capital gains tax purposes. In cases where land is sold for more than death value but no inheritance tax is payable (e.g. because the property passes to an exempt beneficiary), it would be beneficial to elect to substitute the sale price for capital gains tax purposes. However, an attempt to do this was held to be impossible in *Stonor v IRC* (2001). The appropriate person to make the claim under s.191 is the person liable for the inheritance tax on the asset sold. There is no such person if no tax is payable so no claim can be made.

Where land is sold for less than probate value, personal representatives will have to choose whether to claim the capital gains tax loss or the reduction in inheritance tax value. As explained at para.12-018 above, in relation to qualifying investments, it is usually preferable to claim the inheritance tax reduction.

Tax considerations—capital gains tax

12-021 Personal representatives are chargeable only on gains arising since death and have the same annual exemption that individuals have for the tax year of death and two following tax years. The successive reductions in the level of the annual exemption mean that capital gains tax is more of an issue for personal representatives than it was previously.

For disposals on or after 6 April 2016 personal representatives pay capital gains tax on all disposals in excess of the annual exemption at higher rates. Beneficiaries may not be liable to capital gains tax at all or be able to pay at the lower rates or have losses available. It is, therefore, important for personal representatives to consider carefully whether planning the disposal can minimise the tax bill.

If the personal representatives vest assets in the beneficiaries, or appropriate them to beneficiaries before sale, the beneficiaries acquire the assets at their market value at the date of death.

If the personal representatives wish to sell assets, they should consider the following factors:

(a) *Will a chargeable gain arise?* The assets may have risen in value since the date of death. However, the personal representatives will be able to claim an annual exemption in the tax year of death and the two following tax years. The amount of this exemption is the same as that available to individuals. Where possible, sales of assets which have risen in value during the administration should be spread over two or more tax years so that more than one annual exemption may be claimed.

(b) *Will a loss arise?* A loss must be set off against any gains which the personal representatives realise in the same tax year. To the extent that the loss cannot be set off against gains of the same tax year, it is carried forward and set off against gains made by the personal representatives in future tax years. If the personal representatives are unlikely to make future gains they may wish to consider vesting the loss-making asset in a beneficiary, thus allowing the beneficiary to sell the asset. The beneficiary can then set the loss off against any gain that they may make in the future. If the assets sold are shares or land, the inheritance tax loss relief discussed at paras 12-017–12-020 should be considered.

(c) *Is it better to sell an appreciating asset or a depreciating one?* Selling an asset that is increasing in value may avoid the payment of tax but equally will deprive the estate of a valuable asset. Selling a depreciating one will give rise to a loss which may lead to a tax saving but the personal representatives must not delay too long before selling since the value of the estate may be unnecessarily reduced. However, it would be foolish to sell if there is any possibility of the asset recovering its value in the near future.

(d) *What are the wishes of the beneficiaries?* When choosing which assets to sell and which to retain, the personal representatives should consult with the beneficiaries to obtain their views. Most beneficiaries will want to ensure that the value of their entitlement is maintained so will advocate selling assets which are falling in value and retaining assets which are increasing. However, a beneficiary with a substantial capital gains tax liability from other disposals might agree to receive an asset which has fallen in value since death so as to sell it, thus realising a loss that can be set against gains. Similarly, beneficiaries with unrelieved losses can have assets which have increased in value since death vested in them. These assets can be sold by the beneficiaries, the gains being reduced by their allowable losses.

(e) *Are any beneficiaries charities?* Where assets are held for a charity, it is likely that the charity will want the asset to be appropriated to it and sold on its behalf as bare trustee. This is because charities are exempt from capital gains tax on gains made and applied for charitable purposes. An appropriation can, therefore, result in a saving of capital gains tax as compared to the position where the assets are sold by the personal representatives and the proceeds transferred to the charity. It is -important to comply with the necessary formalities. There should be a written appropriation and a record of the instruction to sell. Most major charities are familiar with the necessary steps and many have helpful leaflets and precedents available. It is well worth talking to charities early in the administration and keeping them informed of developments.

(f) Has the inheritance tax value of assets been "ascertained"? Where an estate is an excepted estate for inheritance tax purposes, values are not agreed with HMRC. HMRC simply accepts the figures reported (unless the estate is selected for a check). Following a sale, personal representatives may feel that the value reported for inheritance tax purposes was too low. It is not appropriate to ask HMRC to amend the inheritance tax valuation. In *Trusts & Estates Newsletter* for December 2016 HMRC complained that taxpayers were doing this, often some considerable time after the death, in the hope that the revised value would become the capital gains tax acquisition value. The Newsletter suggested that personal representatives who sell in such circumstances and wish to expedite settlement of the capital gains tax liability should apply for a post-transaction valuation check:

> "If the personal representatives wish to check the valuation of the property at the date of death for capital gains tax purposes in relation to the sale of a property after the date of death, HMRC offers a post-transaction valuation check for capital gains purposes. This is a free service. You should refer to the form CG34 'Post-transaction valuation checks for capital gains'."

There is no obligation to use a post-transaction check. Where there is no check, values will have to be agreed with HMRC.

4. NEED TO COMPLY WITH THE GENERAL DATA PROTECTION REGULATION

Introduction

12-022 The purpose of the General Data Protection Regulation (EU) 2016/679 (GDPR) is to harmonise data privacy laws across Europe. Anyone who processes personal data must comply with the requirements of the GDPR. The breadth of the definitions means that personal representatives will inevitably process personal data of beneficiaries.

(Solicitors are also subject to the GDPR in relation to beneficiaries and clients and their obligations are dealt with in Ch.13.)

Following the UK's departure from the European Union on 1 January 2021, the UK took the decision to incorporate the EU GDPR into its own data protection regime, effectively incorporating a slightly modified version of the EU GDPR into the UK's domestic law such that a new "UK GDPR" took effect from 1 January 2021, with the UK GDPR becoming retained law in the UK and continuing to apply after the "transition period" ended on 31 December 2020.

At the time of writing, the UK data protection landscape is currently made up of the Data Protection Act 2018, the UK GDPR (as defined in s.3(10) of the Data Protection Act 2018) and the Privacy and Electronic Communications Regulations 2003 (SI 2003/2426) (together, the "Data Protection Legislation").

There are currently very few differences between the EU GDPR and the UK GDPR and for the purposes of most PRs the transition between the two was not a material change of law. Given the UK has incorporated the previous GDPR regime directly into English law, there is currently no material difference between the two. To that extent, the obligations which applied to PRs prior to 1 January 2021 shall continue to apply after that date. The Data Protection and Digital Information Bill, which was scheduled to begin its House of Lords report stage on 10 June 2024, was lost as a result of the 2024 General Election. The new Labour Government will pass into law a Digital Information and Smart Data Bill, as announced in the King's Speech on 17 July, to "harness the power of data for economic growth".

Processing personal data

12-023 The definition of "processing" contained in art.4 of the GDPR is "any operation or set of operations which is performed on personal data or on sets of personal data, whether or not by automated means, such as collection, recording, organisation, structuring, storage ...".

"Personal data" is defined as "any information relating to an identified or identifiable natural person, an identifiable natural person is one who can be identified, directly or indirectly".

Personal representatives will at the very least be recording and storing information on beneficiaries. The reference to "natural" beneficiaries means that there are no obligations owed to non-natural beneficiaries such as charities.

Lack of remuneration does not provide an exception. Recital 18 says:

> "This Regulation does not apply to the processing of personal data by a natural person in the course of a purely personal or household activity and thus with no connection to a professional or commercial activity. Personal or household activities could include correspondence and the holding of addresses, or social networking and online activity undertaken within the context of such activities."

Acting as a personal representative or trustee would appear to fall outside such a limited exception. However, on 24 January 2020, following discussion with the Information Commissioner's Office (ICO), STEP published guidance for those dealing with the processing of personal data relating to beneficiaries of trusts and estates. It sets out STEP's views on what it considers to be reasonable positions for members to take in the absence of any further clarifications from either the Courts or the ICO. At the time of writing the ICO had not expressed any disagreement.

STEP considers that a trustee or personal representative is within the scope of the "purely personal or household activity" exemption (and therefore not subject to the GDPR) if they are:

(a) acting in their personal capacity as opposed to a professional capacity; and
(b) unpaid (for these purposes, expenses do not qualify as payment).

In its view, treating lay people as processing data would lead to "*innumerable accidental breaches of data protection laws and a reduction in the willingness of individuals to accept these roles*". It notes that this approach would be in line with the view of the Court of Appeal expressed in *Ittihadieh v 5-11 Cheyne Gardens RTM Company Ltd* that the courts should "*be cautious about criminalising what, for many people, are their ordinary activities*".

Professional and paid personal representatives will not be within the scope of the exemption.

General principles of data protection

Article 5(1) sets out the principles governing the processing of personal data. **12-024**
Personal data shall be:

(a) processed lawfully, fairly and in a transparent manner in relation to the data subject ("lawfulness, fairness and transparency");
(b) collected for specified, explicit and legitimate purposes and not further processed in a manner that is incompatible with those purposes;
(c) adequate, relevant and limited to what is necessary in relation to the purposes for which they are processed ("data minimisation");
(d) accurate and, where necessary, kept up to date; every reasonable step must be taken to ensure that personal data that are inaccurate, having regard to the purposes for which they are processed, are erased or rectified without delay ("accuracy");

(e) kept in a form which permits identification of data subjects for no longer than is necessary for the purposes for which the personal data are processed;
(f) processed in a manner that ensures appropriate security of the personal data, including protection against unauthorised or unlawful processing and against accidental loss, destruction or damage, using appropriate technical or organisational measures ("integrity and confidentiality").

The "integrity and confidentiality" principle means that personal representatives and trustees must consider how they are keeping data. Papers should be locked away and electronic data should be password protected.

Legal ground for processing data

12-025 A person holding personal data must have a legal ground for doing so. The grounds are set out in art.6 of the GDPR. Consent is a legal ground under art.6(a). However, data will normally be supplied to personal representatives, trustees and professional advisers (at least, initially) by the testator or settlor, so consent will not be available as a ground. The most relevant ground is probably art.6(c) which is "*processing is necessary for compliance with a legal obligation to which the controller is subject*". Personal representatives, trustees and their advisers need to hold personal data to carry out their legal obligations.

There is a further complication in relation to "*special category*" data. Processing data about a person's race, ethnic origin, politics, religion, trade union membership, genetic and biometric data, health, sex life or sexual orientation is prohibited under art.9 of the GDPR unless certain conditions apply. Trustees and personal representatives will sometimes hold such information.

For example, a testator or settlor might create a discretionary trust for the benefit of family members and give a letter of wishes which refers to the drug problems of one of her children and the mental or physical health problems of another. Holding such information is prohibited unless one of the conditions set out in art.9 applies.

Consent of the data subject is a sufficient condition, but it will not always be possible to obtain such consent. Article 9 also allows such data to be processed where it is necessary to establish, exercise or defend legal claims.

There is pre-GDPR case law (decided in relation to the Data Protection Act 1998) which held that a more "*natura,*" way of expressing legal claims was to express it in terms of processing that is necessary for the purposes of establishing, exercising or defending "*legal rights*". STEP expressed the view in the Guidance referred to at para.12-023 above that this continues to be a relevant authority.

In the context of trusts and estates, the beneficiaries of a trust or estate have a legal right to see a trust or estate properly administered and may gain further legal claims or rights during the course of its administration (such as becoming absolutely entitled to assets from the trust or estate).

STEP's view is that, in order for the legal claims/rights of beneficiaries to be established, exercised and defended, trustees and personal representatives must be permitted to process special category data to the extent necessary to comply with their fiduciary duties. The Guidance continues:

> "While, as with the other positions set out in this note, the ICO has not expressly confirmed its agreement with STEP's view, guidance published after STEP's discussions with the ICO appears to offer it considerable support. Specifically, the revision to the ICO's guidance on special category data that was issued on 14 November 2019

includes the following example:

> A professional trust and estate practitioner advises a client on setting up a trust to provide for a disabled family member. The advisor processes health data of the beneficiary for this purpose. Although there is no active legal claim before the courts, this is still for the purpose of establishing the legal claims of the trust beneficiary for the purposes of this condition."

The ICO's guidance of 14 November 2019 states that

> "Legal claims in this context is not limited to current legal proceedings. It includes processing necessary for:
>
> - actual or prospective court proceedings;
> - obtaining legal advice; or
> - establishing, exercising or defending legal rights in any other way."

Privacy notices

Article 13 of the GDPR applies where information has been provided by the data subject and art.14 where the information has been supplied by a third party. Both articles require data controllers to give a data subject specified -information. For example, where personal data has not been obtained from the data subject, the information required includes the following: **12-026**

- the identity and the contact details of the controller and, where applicable, of the controller's representative;
- the purposes of the processing for which the personal data are intended as well as the legal basis for the processing (if the controller proposes to use data for a further purpose, the data subject must be notified in advance—hence the purposes should be stated broadly, for example "the proper administration of the estate");
- the period for which the personal data will be stored or, if that is not possible, the criteria used to determine that period;
- the existence of the right to request from the controller access to and rectification or erasure of personal data or restriction of processing concerning the data subject and to object to processing as well as the right to data portability;
- the right to lodge a complaint with a supervisory authority;
- the source the personal data originate and, if applicable, whether it came from publicly accessible sources.

Article 14(5) applies a proportionality filter to privacy notices so that it is not necessary to provide information if providing it would:

- be impossible (art.14(5)(b)),
- involve disproportionate effort (art.14(5)(b)),
- seriously impair the achievement of the objectives behind the processing (art.14(5)(b)),
- breach confidentiality obligations (including professional or statutory secrecy obligations) (art.14(5)(d)),

In addition, article 14(5)(c) provides an exception if obtaining or disclosure is expressly laid down by Union or Member State law to which the controller is subject and which provides appropriate measures to protect the data subject's legitimate interests.

The STEP guidance referred to at para.12-023 above states that in relation to article 13 privacy notices should normally be supplied as a matter of course.

However, it gives examples of situations where, in relation to article 14, it would not be appropriate to do so, for example where a discretionary trust has a class of secondary beneficiaries who are intended to benefit only if the whole of the primary class is wiped out, or where a family trust exists for the benefit of minor children and the parents do not want the children to be disincentivised from pursuing a career.

In STEP's view the two relevant exceptions are disproportionate effort (art.14(5)(b)) and art 14(5)(c). It considers that UK trust law already contains sufficient protection for beneficiaries' interests.

Personal representatives and trustees will normally have to provide privacy notices to the beneficiaries. Article 14(3) requires information to be provided "within a reasonable period after obtaining the personal data but at the latest within one month" and, where data

> "are to be used for communication with the data subject, at the latest at the time of the first communication to that data subject".

Many firms do not contact beneficiaries until the grant has been obtained which would normally exceed the one-month limit. However, it should be possible to argue that providing the information more quickly would involve disproportionate effort.

5. GENERAL DUTIES

12-027 In addition to the detailed points set out in this chapter, the personal representatives must bear in mind more general considerations when administering the estate. The personal representatives must ascertain the deceased's debts and liabilities, obtain the grant, pay debts and distribute the assets to the beneficiaries. While administering the estate they must ensure that the value of assets are maintained. This obligation will be discharged in a number of ways. The personal representatives must ensure that when any asset is damaged or falls into disrepair it is repaired. This can be expensive and so they should take out insurance cover. If the deceased had taken out property insurance the personal representatives should as soon as possible after the death notify the insurance company and either have their interest noted on the policy or a fresh policy issued. If a property is empty, they should inform the insurers as this may affect the validity of the policy.

For estates which include shares, personal representatives must regularly review their portfolio, taking expert advice as appropriate, and ensuring as far as possible that the portfolio maintains its value. Therefore, the personal representatives must consider selling shares that are dropping in value with a view to replacing them with a better investment. Equally the personal representatives should avoid speculative investments even though they might realise substantial profits. Any investments other than stocks and shares of the deceased should also be looked at critically. In *Crabbe v Townsend* (2016) an executor was held to be liable for losses caused by lack of active management of a share portfolio comprised in the estate.

Finally, the personal representatives should ensure that they complete their task quickly and efficiently by anticipating difficulties before they arise (so far as possible) and not delaying the performance of their duties.

Personal representatives will also have obligations where there are grounds for suspecting that an estate includes the proceeds of crime or money-laundering. As these also apply to professionals dealing with the administration, they are dealt with in Ch.13.

CHAPTER THIRTEEN

DUTIES OF SOLICITORS

1. INTRODUCTION

Many duties arise from the contractual relationship between the client and the solicitor. Breach of that duty can result in contractual or tortious liability. Increasingly, however, there are duties imposed by statute which are regulatory in nature. We will look at both in this chapter. **13-001**

2. THE EXTENT OF THE RETAINER

Introduction

The starting point for a discussion of a solicitor's duty to a client is the well-known dictum of Oliver J in *Midland Bank Trust Co Ltd v Hett Stubbs and Kemp*, a firm: **13-002**

> "The extent of a solicitors duties depends upon the terms and limits of that retainer and any duty of care to be implied must be related to what he is instructed to do."

In relation to the preparation of a will a solicitor will normally be expected to prepare a will which carries out the client's testamentary intentions and to take any other steps which are necessary to give effect to those wishes. A failure by the solicitor to draft a will complying with the client's wishes is an especially serious matter since the mistake which has been made is not likely to become apparent until the client is dead or may never be discovered at all.

It is too late to correct certain types of mistake once the client is dead. The will (or part of it) may be refused probate on the grounds that the client did not have knowledge and approval of the contents, but this will not necessarily ensure that the testator's true wishes are put into effect. It may be possible to interpret the words wrongly written in the will to give effect to the testator's true intentions but only if there is sufficient evidence to demonstrate clearly what those intentions were. Section 20 of the Administration of Justice Act 1982 allows rectification of a will to correct clerical errors or failure to understand the client's instructions but, as we saw at paras 2-034–2-037, this does not enable every type of mistake to be corrected. Even if rectification is possible the mistake will cause considerable delay and expense.

A beneficiary who suffers loss as a result of the failure of the solicitor to carry out his duty is all too likely to sue the solicitor who acted for the testator. In *White v Jones* (1995) the House of Lords held that the solicitor's assumption of responsibility towards his client should be held in law to extend to the intended beneficiary in circumstances where the beneficiary would otherwise have no remedy. The result of this decision has been a proliferation of cases alleging breach of duty on the part of solicitors in relation to the drafting and execution of wills.

Similarly a personal representative may sue solicitors retained to act in the administration of the estate. In *Chappell v Somers and Blake* (2004), the retained solicitors delayed obtaining probate for five years with the result that two properties were left vacant with consequent loss of income. The solicitors were held to be liable to pay damages to the executor for the benefit of the estate even though she had suffered no personal loss. In an obiter dictum the judge said that the beneficiaries could not have sued personally because they were not the clients of the defendant.

The solicitor must clarify the terms of the retainer

13-003 Any ambiguity will be resolved in favour of the client. In *Gray v Buss Murton* (1999) a trainee solicitor believed that he was being asked to give an opinion as to whether a will had been validly executed (which it had). The clients believed that he was advising them on whether the will was effective (which it was not). The firm was held liable to the clients on the basis that it was for the solicitor to establish the extent of the retainer.

In *Hurlingham Estates Ltd v Wilde & Partners* (1997) Lightman J said that, in the absence of a retainer limiting liability, it was necessary to consider whether the solicitor "should reasonably have appreciated" that the client "needed his advice and guidance" on the tax aspects of the transaction. Any limitation on the retainer would have to be in writing to enable the client to consider it and give informed consent.

3. Duties Relating to the Preparation of the Will

The solicitor must prepare the will with reasonable speed

13-004 In *White v Jones* itself solicitors received a letter on 17 July instructing them to prepare a new will but had not prepared the will for execution by the time the testator died on 14 September. The firm had to compensate the disappointed beneficiaries.

In *X v Woollcombe Yonge* (2001) a solicitor prepared a will for a terminally ill client within a week but the client died before it was ready. Neuberger J, as he then was, suggested that seven days would be a sufficiently short period "*in most cases*" where the client was "*elderly or likely to die*". In this case the testatrix, although terminally ill, was not expected to die within the next couple of weeks. She was planning to move to a hospice and raised no objection when told that the solicitor would bring the will some time in the following week. The amount of time taken was not unreasonable. However, he said

> *"[w]here there is a plain and substantial risk of the client's imminent death, anything other than a handwritten rough codicil prepared on the spot for signature may be negligent".*

It is beneficial to agree a timeframe with the client for preparation of the will and keep to it. This is good practice in itself but, beyond that, may be of assistance if the client dies before the will is ready for execution. The duty owed by the solicitor is to the client to produce a legally effective will which carries out the client's intentions. If the solicitor has carried out the terms of the agreement, it will be much more difficult (though not necessarily impossible) for the beneficiaries to allege breach of duty. In *Hooper v Fynmores (A Firm)* (2002) a solicitor who postponed a visit to a client in hospital to execute a new will was held liable in negligence: see para.13-016.

Perhaps inevitably this is an area of law where narrow distinctions are made between different sets of facts. For example, in *Atkins v Dunn and Baker* (2004), solicitors sent a will was to a client for approval but it was not returned to them. They did not send the client a reminder, and the client died with the will unexecuted. The firm was not held to be negligent as the client had understood the importance of making a new will.

The solicitor must take instructions from the client in person wherever possible

It is possible to take instructions in writing or via the internet but there may be misunderstandings as a result of the lack of face-to-face contact: see *Sifri v Clough & Willis* (2007) and, more recently, *Wales v Dixon* (2020). In this case instructions were taken by telephone. Residue was left to the great-nieces and nephews of the testator whereas extrinsic evidence established that the intention had been to include those of the testator's wife. Master Teverson said this: **13-005**

> "The manner in which the Deceased's instructions were taken for the Will greatly increases the likelihood that the Deceased's intention with regard to residue was not understood. His instructions were taken by telephone. The draft will was prepared and sent out on the same day.
>
> The striking feature of the communications between the Deceased and [the will drafter] is .... the complete lack of any attempt to establish by name or parent who was intended to receive a share of residue. This illustrates graphically the dangers of taking instructions by telephone from an elderly widower without sight of his prior will or knowledge of his family tree."

It is difficult for the solicitor to assess the client's mental capacity and whether there is any possibility of fraud or undue influence.

Ideally solicitors should not accept instructions from an intermediary particularly one who has an interest in the disposition of the estate. The court was extremely critical of the solicitor in *Richards v Allen* (2001) who accepted instructions from his sister-in-law without ever seeing the testatrix. More recently, see *Bond v Webster* (2024), where the court was similarly critical of a will drafter who took instructions from one of the deceased's four children.

Be careful of conflicts of interest. It is common to see married couples together when taking instructions for their wills, but many solicitors are not happy doing this and there may be tensions particularly in the case of second marriages. In *Hines v Willans* (2002) a solicitor was held liable for breach of duty as a result of acting for a husband to the detriment of the wife whom he had already agreed to represent. He had an appointment to see the wife on the following Monday, but made a will for her husband disinheriting her and (at his own suggestion) prepared a notice of severance of the couple's joint tenancy.

The solicitor must try to establish that the client has testamentary capacity

Where a solicitor fails to check a testator's capacity and prepares a will which later turns out to be invalid, there may be a claim from the estate that it has been reduced by the costs of the dispute: see *Worby v Rosser* (1999) and *Corbett v Bond Pearce* (2001). Even if there is no such claim, being involved in disputed wills is **13-006** an anxious and time-consuming business. It is, therefore, important to minimise the chances of dispute, so far as possible.

The so-called "Golden Rule" was articulated by Templeman J (as he then was) in *Kenward v Adams* (1975) and *Re Simpson (Deceased)* (1977). It was referred to with approval in *Buckenham v Dickinson* (1997) and by Rimer J in *Re Morris (Deceased), Special Trustees for Great Ormond Street Hospital for Children v Rushin* (2001). Templeman J said:

> "In the case of an aged testator or a testator who has suffered a serious illness, there is one golden rule which should always be observed, however straightforward matters may appear, and however difficult or tactless it may be to suggest that precautions be taken: the making of a will by such a testator ought to be witnessed or approved by a medical practitioner who satisfies himself of the capacity and understanding of the testator, and records and preserves his examination and findings."

The purpose of the "Golden Rule" is merely to provide evidence to the court to help it decide the legal question of whether or not the testator had capacity. Complying with the "Golden Rule" does not guarantee that the will is valid and failure to do so does not invalidate it. It simply means that there will be less evidence available in the event of a dispute.

A lack of evidence may be extremely important. If those challenging a will can establish a doubt as to capacity, the burden of proof shifts to those putting forward the will. If there is insufficient evidence to prove capacity on the balance of probabilities the will fails.

It is fair to say that it is often difficult to get medical evidence, particularly in urgent cases. Norris J said in *Wharton v Bancroft* (2011):

> "A solicitor so placed cannot simply conjure up a medical attendant ... I do not think [the solicitor] is to be criticised for deciding to make his own assessment (accepted as correct) and to get on with the job of drawing a will."

General practitioners are often not expert in assessing mental capacity so the value of their report will be limited. It is usually preferable to obtain an expert's report but this is expensive and the client may be unwilling to incur that expense. It is the client's choice. However, so that the choice is an informed one, the solicitor should explain the grounds on which a will can be challenged and the reasons why a report may be helpful.

A positive capacity report is obviously useful in deterring challenges to the will on the basis of lack of capacity. However, another reason for obtaining a report is that the lack of one may have adverse costs consequences. Normally in probate litigation, the usual litigation rules apply and costs follow the event. However, as explained at para.9-005, there are two exceptions to this general rule. The second exception is that if the circumstances lead reasonably to an investigation of the matter, the costs may be left to be borne by those who have incurred them. In *James v James* (2018) the judge did not order costs against the unsuccessful challenger of a will made by a testator who had been diagnosed with dementia some years earlier; instead he allowed costs to lie where they fell. He said of the claimant:

> "He pursued the challenge to the will because there was a reasonable basis for doing so. There was medical evidence and factual evidence tending to suggest that the testator's capacity was doubtful. The expert medical evidence (on both sides) reinforced that view. The fact that the so-called 'golden rule' was not followed was also significant. There being no contemporary medical evidence, all that was left was for the court to decide. In my

> judgment, it was reasonable for the claimant to pursue the will challenge, even though, at the end of the day I have held that the testator had capacity to make his will when in fact he made it."

The more out of line with previous wills the proposed will is, the more care the solicitor should take in trying to gather evidence of capacity.

What should a solicitor do if uncertain of a client's capacity? Nicholas Strauss QC in *Sharp v Adam* (2005) addressed this question at [226] in relation to a solicitor who had taken instructions from a testator who was suffering from advanced multiple sclerosis. He appeared perfectly rational but insisted that he wanted to leave nothing to his two daughters even though he was on very good terms with them. The solicitor had found these instructions troubling. The judge was very complimentary about the way in which she had proceeded, saying (at [226]) that she had done exactly what a solicitor should do when uncertain as to capacity:

> "She was satisfied, in relation to those elements of the *Banks v. Goodfellow* test on which she could judge, that her client was competent. She had no practical means of reaching a judgment on the other elements of the test, whether by lengthy further examinations by specialists or by further enquiries into the family history (which by themselves would not have sufficed anyhow). In such circumstances, her duty was to warn her client that the will might be challenged and, if he ignored the warning, implement his instructions without further delay, both of which she very properly did. To have acted otherwise would have risked depriving her client right to make a will, when he might well have had testamentary capacity. It is only if he clearly did not that she would have been justified in refusing to act."

He went on to say that a will drafter who has acted correctly is not to be blamed if litigation ensues.

It is always important to prepare a full attendance note detailing the questions you asked to establish testamentary capacity and the client's replies. The solicitor's own attendance note can be extremely helpful to the court (see *Sharp v Adam* (2006)). However, it is particularly important where it is clear that the will is not going to be well received by certain family members.

In *Re Bascoe deceased* (2019) Deputy Master Linwood mentioned how helpful an attendance note had been, saying (at [44]):

> "I would also commend the file as an exemplar of a properly maintained solicitor's will file. It is easy to follow and the attendance notes are dated, detailed, timed and indicate who the author is. The manuscript note of the important meeting to take Mrs Bascoe's instructions has been retained. The instructions to Dr Funnel are comprehensive. The file has a clear beginning and end as it starts with a formal file opening sheet and concludes with a "best practice" file closing letter to Mrs Bascoe and disposal instructions. A file such as this should help avoid some of the disputes which arise in probate and suchlike claims or, as here, give the court confidence in the evidence and professional abilities of the witness concerned."

In *Coles v Reynolds* (2020) Paul Matthews J said that he was "*entirely satisfied on the basis of this material that the deceased had capacity to make it, and that it was duly executed.*" In addition to a detailed attendance note on the meeting at which the instructions for the will, the firm had standard checklists which had space for comments on amongst other things the client's demeanour and reasons for making the will. The checklists were used both at the initial interview and when the client came into the office to execute the will. At execution, a different fee earner saw the client, went through the will with her and completed the check list.

The solicitor must take instructions in the absence of anyone who stands to benefit or is in a position to exert influence

13-007 When discussing the importance of the "Golden Rule" (set out at para.13-006). Templeman J added two other precautions which he considered should be taken. First:

> "If the testator has made an earlier will, this should be considered by the legal and medical advisers of the testator and, if appropriate, discussed with the testator.
>
> The instructions of the testator should be taken in the absence of anyone who may stand to benefit, or who may have influence over the testator.
>
> These are not counsels of perfection. If proper precautions are not taken injustice may result or be imagined, and great expense and misery may be unnecessarily caused."

It is obviously a sensible precaution. In *Hawes v Burgess* (2013) the court commented on how much more difficult it is to assess capacity when someone else is present and speaking on behalf of the client. The same point was made in *Re Ashkettle* (2013). In both these cases one of several siblings had taken their parent to see a solicitor and remained while instructions for the will were given.

Clients with borderline testamentary capacity are often vulnerable to undue influence which is another reason for seeing them alone. In *Killick v Pountney* (2000) an important factor in the court's decision that there had been undue influence was the fact that the beneficiary had been present for some of the time at the interview.

The House of Lords in *Barclays Bank v Etridge* (2001) reviewed the law on undue influence in the context of charging one spouse's interest in the matrimonial home as security for the debts of the other. One practical recommendation it made was that the interview with the client must be in the absence of the person benefiting from the transaction. There must be a clear explanation of the nature and consequences of the act. It is then for adult persons of competent mind to decide whether they will do an act. The solicitor does not need to approve of the client's decision. Independent and competent advice does not mean independent and competent approval.

In exceptional cases where it is glaringly obvious that the spouse is being grievously wronged, Lord Nichols said that the solicitor should decline to act further. Many practitioners are concerned that the effect of not acting is merely that the client will be coached better and taken elsewhere by the person exerting the influence. However, in *Powell v Powell* (1900) Farwell J said that a solicitor "ought not to go on, if he disapproves, simply because he thinks that someone else will do the work if he does not".

Earlier wills should be considered

13-008 This was the second additional precaution added by Templeman J when discussing the "Golden Rule". Again, it is a sensible precaution. Earlier wills may show a pattern. If the client is suddenly deviating from that pattern, it is important to explore the reason with the client. See, for example *Charles v Fraser* (2010) where examination of the earlier will would have alerted the will drafter to a number of problems including the existence of a mutual will agreement. It is good practice to obtain a copy of the previous will which may raise queries as to the reason for changes or throw light on what exactly the client wants. In *Bond v Webster* (2024), the will drafter had been instructed by one of the deceased's children not to approach the firm that had prepared the previous will to ask for a copy. The court was very critical of this.

The solicitor must try to establish what property the testator owns and in what capacity

Clients do not always remember how they own property. In *Chittock v Stevens* (2000) a house was believed to be in joint names but eight months after the death of the husband (partially intestate) it was discovered that it had been in his sole name. It is desirable either to check the basis of ownership or record that the will has been prepared on the basis of the information provided by the client. Resolve any ambiguities or uncertainties with the client. **13-009**

Joint property is particularly problematic. In *Carr-Glynn v Frearsons* (1998) the testatrix (aged 81) consulted a solicitor to make a will leaving her interest in a property "Homelands" to her niece. She owned the property with her nephew and was uncertain as to whether she owned it as beneficial joint tenant or tenant in common. Her solicitor advised her that the gift of "Homelands" could not take effect if she held it as a beneficial joint tenant. The solicitor asked if the testatrix wanted her to obtain and check the deeds. The testatrix said that she would do it herself but that in the meantime she wanted to get on with making her new will. The solicitor prepared the will but also wrote to the client setting out clearly that the will would be ineffective if she owned the property as beneficial joint tenants with her nephew. The client did not check the basis of ownership and, when she died, it was discovered that she had owned the property as beneficial joint tenant.

The Court of Appeal found that the solicitor was in breach of her duty which extended beyond the mere preparation of the will to steps necessary to give effect to the client's testamentary intentions. Many people consider the decision rather harsh but according to the Court of Appeal the solicitor's breach lay in not explaining to the client that she could have served a precautionary notice of severance without having to check the basis of ownership. Had the solicitor given this explanation, there would have been no liability had the client declined to serve the notice.

A beneficial joint tenancy also caused a problem in *Re Woolnough* (2002). The firm of solicitors overlooked the fact that serving a notice of severance is just one way of severing a joint tenancy (see para.21-019) and did not realise that severance had occurred before death.

There may also be cases where property held in joint names is actually held on a resulting trust for the party who provided the funds. See *Sillett v Meek* (2007); *Aroso v Coutts* (2002) and *Goodman v Carlton* (2002) for examples of argument over the basis of ownership after the death of one party. In *Sillett v Meek* the solicitor who had taken instructions for a will knowing of the existence of a joint bank account containing substantial funds was criticised for failing to establish the basis of ownership. It is important to explore the nature of ownership while the client is alive and it is possible to clarify and record it. If possible, clarify and record the basis of ownership of joint funds.

Arguments over the beneficial ownership of land are particularly common. Note, however, that the House of Lords held in *Stack v Dowden* (2007) that in a domestic consumer context the presumption should be that beneficial ownership follows legal ownership irrespective of the level of contribution. The effect is that the person alleging an interest which is different from the legal title has to prove it. Domestic consumer context is not limited to cohabiting couples. It has been held to extend to friends buying a property together (*Gallarotti v Sebastianelli* (2012)) and to purchases by parent and child (*Adekunle v Ritchie* (2007)) although in *Laskar v Laskar* the court held that the principle did not apply to a purchase by mother and daughter because the purchase was intended to be an investment and there was no mutual commitment to each other for the future. The Privy Council said in *Marr v Collie* (2017) that a purchase as an investment by a cohabiting couple would not inevitably require the resulting trust solution:

> "In this, as in so many areas of law, context counts for, if not everything, a lot. Context here is set by the parties' common intention or by the lack of it."

The moral is that in a case where property is in the name of one party but another may have an interest (e.g. where one party has moved in with another and has made substantial contributions to the costs of the property), it is important to explore the parties' intentions and, if necessary, to suggest changes in the legal ownership so that the position is clear. Note, however, that *Stack v Dowden* principles have no application where the transfer deed contains an express declaration of trust. In *Pankhania v Chandegra* (2012) this point was overlooked at first instance. An express declaration of trust can be set aside on the ground of mistake, fraud or undue influence but in the absence of such factors the terms of the express declaration are conclusive in the absence of subsequent agreement or the effect of proprietary estoppel. In *Nilsson v Cynberg* (2024), the Court of Appeal held that "subsequent agreement" did not require a subsequent formal agreement complying with the requirements of the Law of Property (Miscellaneous Provisions) Act 1989. A subsequent informal common intention constructive trust could suffice.

Does a third party have an interest in property "owned" by the client as a result of proprietary estoppel?

13-010 In *Gillett v Holt* (1998) the Court of Appeal confirmed that a promise to leave property by will can give rise to a claim in proprietary estoppel. The necessary elements are a promise relied on by the promisor resulting in detriment to the promisee such that it would be unconscionable for equity not to provide a remedy. The promisee will not necessarily receive everything he or she feels entitled to. There are different approaches to the question of how to quantify the value of a claim.

One line of authority states that the essential aim is to give effect to the claimant's expectation unless it would be disproportionate to do so. The other takes the view that essential aim of the discretion is to ensure that the claimant's reliance interest is protected, so that she is compensated for such detriment as she has suffered. The two approaches can result in very different amounts.

In *Jennings v Rice* (2002) Robert Walker LJ drew a distinction between cases in which:

(1) the assurances and reliance have a consensual character not far short of a contract where the court is likely to give effect to the claimant's expectations;
(2) the claimant's expectations are uncertain or are too high given the assurances made where the court may regard the expectations as no more than a starting point.

In *Davies v Davies* (2016) Lewison LJ commented (at [41]) in relation to the second type of case that it was not entirely clear "what the court is to do with the expectation even if it is only a starting point". He described counsel's suggestion that the weight attached to expectation might vary depending on the clarity of the expectation, the degree of detriment and the length of time the expectation was reasonably held as "a useful working hypothesis".

The Supreme Court considered the conflicting lines of authority in *Guest v Guest* (2022). In a majority decision and found in favour of the expectation line. The aim of the equitable estoppel-based remedy is to prevent the unconscionable repudiation of promises or assurances about property (usually land) upon which the promisee had relied to his detriment. The normal and natural remedy is to hold the promisor to the promise, because that is the simplest way to prevent the unconscionability inherent in repudiating it. However, the remedy is always discretionary, and liable to be tempered by circumstances which might make strict enforcement of the promise disproportionate. Lord Briggs who delivered the leading judgment said: "*In my view the best summary of the proportionality test is that the remedy should not, without some good reason, be out of all proportion to the detriment, if that can readily be identified. If it cannot, then the proportionality test is unlikely to be of much use.*"

Does the client have a general power of appointment?

If so, it is important to clarify the client's wishes for the trust property. The property subject to the general power will pass as part of a general residuary gift where the power has not been expressly exercised (Wills Act 1837 s.27). However, it is preferable to exercise the power expressly to avoid later allegations that the client was not aware of the effect of the residuary gift: see *Gibbons v Nelsons (A Firm)* (2000). **13-011**

The solicitor's role in taking instructions

The solicitor should ensure that the client is not under some misapprehension as to the effect of the solicitor's instructions which if corrected might lead to different instructions. It is not possible to give an exhaustive list of all the points which should be drawn to a client's attention but the following are among the most important: **13-012**

(a) Jointly held property will pass to the surviving joint tenant even if the will says otherwise.
(b) If adequate financial provision is not made for dependants and certain relatives, family provision claims may be made.
(c) Gifts of specific items will be adeemed if the items are sold or changed in substance unless specific provision is made.
(d) Unless contrary provision is made most types of gift will lapse (and fall into residue or pass on intestacy) if the donee predeceases. A gift will, however, take effect if the beneficiary survives for even a very short time or is deemed to survive under s.184 of the Law of Property Act 1925. This may not correspond with the client's wishes so that a survivorship clause should be considered.
(e) Spouses and civil partners will often make wills in mirror form leaving everything to the other and if the other predeceases making a number of pecuniary and specific legacies to the same legatees and then leaving the residue to the same substitute residuary beneficiaries. It is important to ask whether the parties would want the legacies paid under each will if they died

in quick succession or only once. See *Jump v Lister* (2016) where the residuary beneficiaries were extremely unhappy because the way the wills were drafted meant that the legacies were paid twice as a result of which their entitlement is significantly reduced.

(f) Unless contrary provision is made in the will, a person taking a property charged with a debt takes it subject to that debt (s.35 of the Administration of Estates Act 1925). Check the testator's wishes in relation to a specific gift of an asset which is (or may be at the time of death) charged with a debt.

Be particularly careful where there is life assurance linked to the debt. Make sure that there is no ambiguity as to where the proceeds of the policy are going. Normally the testator will want the person who is responsible for the debt to take the benefit of the policy so as to have funds available. This may require careful drafting.

(g) Payments from pension funds and insurance policies may be payable to beneficiaries independently of the terms of the will. In the case of pension schemes where lump sums are payable at the discretion of the trustees of the scheme, it is usually possible for an employee to leave a statement of his wishes for the destination of the sum payable. Such a statement is not binding on the trustees but will be considered by them. A client who has the benefit of such a scheme should be advised to make a statement.

(h) Does the client want the solicitor to disclose the contents of the will to an attorney or deputy if they lose capacity? Attorneys and deputies may have to decide what assets to sell. Knowing what is in the will helps the attorney or deputy make an informed choice as to which assets to sell. For this reason many clients will make a copy of their will available to their attorney when they make a lasting power of attorney. Others prefer not to on the basis that they may wish to change their will and/or may die before the attorney needs to act on their behalf. Where attorneys or deputies acting for a person who has lost capacity are unaware of the contents of the will, in the past there was uncertainty as to whether solicitors could properly do this or whether they were bound by their duty of confidentiality. Joint guidance "*Access to and disclosure of an incapacitated person's will*" produced by the SRA, Court of Protection, Office of the Public Guardian, Legal Ombudsman, Law Society and Society of Trust and Estate Practitioners and discussed at para.16-022 makes it clear that an attorney or deputy is the agent of the client and is normally entitled to disclosure unless the client has instructed otherwise. It states that "it is advisable for the question of disclosure of the donor's will to be discussed and recorded at the time of making the will".

An explanation of the effect of the will should be provided

13-013 It is important that the client receives a clear explanation of the effect of the will before execution. Ideally the explanation will:

(a) Refer to beneficiaries by name rather than description to avoid problems such as confusion over whether the beneficiaries are to include relatives of the testator's spouse or civil partner (see *Wales v Dixon* (2020)).

(b) Explain what will happen if a gift or part of a gift fails. This is particularly important where a gift is to be divided amongst the testator's children: does the client want the statutory substitution provision contained in Wills Act

1837 s.33 to apply or to be excluded? It is preferable for the will to provide expressly for what is to happen to the share of a predeceased child. In the absence of such provision, there may be uncertainty as to whether or not the testator intended to exclude it (although it will apply unless clearly excluded, see *Hives v Machin* (2017)) or it may be overlooked as in *Naylor v Barlow* (2019).

(c) Give an indication of how much on current values will pass under residuary or formula gifts. See, for example, *Re Williams (Deceased)* (2021) where becausc of a misunderstanding as to what was to be included in specific gifts, the residue was valueless. The residue was to be divided between the testator's children in differing proportions but, as drafted, there was nothing left to divide. Such a problem can also arise where a client is less wealthy at death than when the will was made. The specific gifts, debts and liabilities may exhaust the estate so that nothing is left for the residuary beneficiary. It may be more satisfactory to leave the estate to be divided between the various beneficiaries without valuable specific or pecuniary legacies.

Similarly, where a client wants to leave an amount equal to the value of their unused nil rate band, it is important to explain that if the nil rate band is used up by lifetime gifts or other gifts made in the will, the legacy will be valueless. See, for example *Royal Commonwealth Society for the Blind v Beasant* (2021).

(d) Where a client wants to leave a specific asset to one beneficiary, give a warning of the possibility of ademption and of the danger that the value of that asset may rise or fall disproportionately. See *Skillett v Skillett* (2022) where a father's will gave one child an asset valued at £50,000 at the time the will was made and pecuniary legacies of £50,000 to the other three children. At the date of death, the value of the asset had increased to £110,000. The other three children were not happy. Again, it may be preferable to give shares of residue perhaps with an option or one child to purchase the asset at market value at the date of death.

4. DUTIES RELATING TO THE EXECUTION OF THE WILL

The solicitor must offer to oversee the execution of the will

The case of *Esterhuizen v Allied Dunbar* (1998) suggests that a solicitor must make the following offer: **13-014**

- the solicitor will attend the client at home and supervise execution;
- the client can come to the solicitor's office and have execution overseen; or
- if the client prefers he or she can execute the will at home without supervision.

If the client prefers to execute the will without supervision the solicitor should send a letter explaining exactly how to execute the will.

If the will is returned after execution, the solicitor must check it

In *Ross v Caunters* (1980) the solicitor sent the testator a letter with the will saying that attestation was required by "two independent witnesses". When the will was returned to the solicitor, one of the witnesses had the same surname as one of the **13-015** beneficiaries. The solicitors did not query this. The witness was married to the beneficiary who, therefore, lost her entitlement. Megarry VC found that the solicitor had been negligent because he had failed:

- to warn the testator that a spouse of a beneficiary should not witness;
- to check whether the will was properly attested;
- to observe that the attesting witness was the spouse of a beneficiary; and
- to draw this to the attention of the testator.

In *Gray v Richards Butler (A Firm)* (2000) the judge accepted that a solicitor owes a duty to a testator, at execution and also when the will is returned after execution.

In *Humblestone v Martin Tolhurst Partnership (a firm)* (2004) the defendants were instructed to draft a will. The client returned it to them for safe keeping. Although the will was checked when it was returned, the solicitors failed to notice that the client had not signed it. This was not noticed until after the client died. The claimant successfully sued for the legacy he would have received if the will had been valid. The court held that the duty to check the validity of the will extended to the potential beneficiaries as well as to the testatrix.

If instructed to attend a client, keep the appointment

13-016 In *Hooper v Fynmores (A Firm)* (2002) a solicitor prepared a will for an elderly client, in early September 1997, increasing the claimant's share in residue by £40,000. The solicitor who prepared the will wrote to the client asking if he would like him to bring it out for signature.

The client went into hospital and arranged that the solicitor would visit him on 13 October. However, the solicitor himself went into hospital and cancelled the appointment. He did not arrange a new appointment and did not discuss the -possibility of sending a substitute. The client died on 21 October without -executing the will. The Court of Appeal found that the solicitor had been negligent.

Solicitors have a duty to satisfy themselves that a delay in executing a will resulting from the cancellation of an appointment will not be disadvantageous to the client. If necessary, the solicitor should appoint a substitute. An appointment with an elderly client in hospital should not be cancelled unless the client is agreeable to it.

Sometimes clients are unwilling to execute a will. A solicitor is not required to ensure that a client executes a will. There may be circumstances where continuing to press a client could amount to undue influence. It will normally be appropriate to write to clients reminding them that the will has not been executed and asking if they want any alteration to be made.

Do not allow a client to execute a will conditionally

13-017 See *Corbett v Newey* (1996) where solicitors allowed the testatrix to sign the will but not date it. Her intention was that it should not come into operation until certain lifetime gifts had been completed. The will was not valid because it had not been executed unconditionally. The solicitors had to compensate the -disappointed beneficiaries.

5. Duties Relating to Records

It is particularly important to clarify in correspondence any limitations imposed on the extent of the service (see para.13-019) or on the extent of the solicitor's knowledge of the client's assets (see para.13-009 and following). **13-018**

Full attendance notes are a solicitor's protection against false allegations. In addition, the discipline of preparing them may also help to avoid a mistake. Courts place a great deal of weight on good contemporaneous notes but are unimpressed by those prepared after the event and particularly those prepared from memory in the knowledge of future litigation (see *Killick v Pountney* (2000)). When taking instructions for a will it is sensible to have a checklist so that important questions are not omitted.

A solicitor who is present at the execution of a will by a testator who is frail (whether mentally or physically) should always make a full and careful attendance note (see para.13-006.)

After execution solicitors should take a photocopy for their file if they are not keeping the original. Photocopies are admissible as proof of the terms of the will if the will is lost (see para.10-004).

There is no point in a client making a will if it cannot be found at death. Whether the client takes the original or makes other arrangements, explain the importance of informing close family members or friends where it can be found. Make sure that your filing system is arranged in such a way that original wills retained by you can be found when required, which may, of course, be many years in the future. The question of when a will can be safely destroyed troubles many solicitors. The Law Society's Practice Note "*File retention: wills and probate*" (1 November 2018) (available on the Law Society's website) says at section 3.1:

> "You should store the original will until after the death of the client, or until you are able to return the original to the client.
>
> Some firms keep wills indefinitely, while others have a policy of holding the original will for fifty years from the date of its creation. There is no absolute rule, but you should always err on the side of caution, even if you believe or know that a later will has been made."
>
> [*https://www.lawsociety.org.uk/topics/private-client/file-retention-wills-and-probate* ©The Law Society]

The SRA Ethics Guidance on Drafting and preparation of wills issued on 6 May 2014 (updated 25 November 2019) says in relation to storage of wills:

> "The Probate Service offers a low cost wills storage service. It may be in a client's best interests to use this service rather than pay your business or a bank for storage services. Even if your business does not charge clients to store the original copy of their will, it may be more convenient for some executors if a will is stored by a central official service.
>
> Some clients may prefer you or your business to store the original copy of their will, particularly where it can be retrieved easily and quickly by their executors or if they wish to make an alteration. You should advise your client about storage options that are available. The most important thing is to make sure your client understands the importance of their executor(s) knowing where to locate the original copy of the will following the client's death.
>
> - make sure that all their executors know where to find the original version of the will;
> - keep a copy of the will at their home with the relevant details;
> - keep you informed of any changes to their address or contact details, and

- review their will regularly to make sure it still reflects their wishes and circumstances."

HM Courts and Tribunal Service has issued guidance updated on 1 May 2024 (available on the Gov.UK website), *How to store a will with HM Courts and Tribunals Service*. There is a one-off charge of £22 payable by check or postal order to HM Courts and Tribunals Service.

You can charge for storage provided your retainer makes this clear. It is possible to register wills with commercial service providers or to deposit them at the Probate Registry. Either step increases the chances of the will being found.

It is preferable to attach nothing to an original will since the presence of pin holes or clip impressions may lead to an allegation of attempted revocation in which case evidence will be required (see NCPR, r.15).

Where a solicitor has prepared a will which is later disputed, the solicitor may be asked to provide information about the circumstances in which instructions were taken and the execution of the will. The duty of confidentiality owed to the client passes to their personal representatives so information can only be provided with their consent. However, failure to provide information which could have headed off a probate action is likely to incur a costs penalty as was the case in *Larke v Nugus* (2000) and Law Society's Practice Note "Disputed Wills" (5 September 2023) available at *https://www.lawsociety.org.uk/topics/private-client/disputed-wills*.

6. Duties Relating to General Advice

13-019 A solicitor who has agreed to prepare a will for a client is under an obligation to take any steps necessary to put the client's testamentary wishes into effect. The solicitor should, therefore, explain any problems, disadvantages and necessary steps. It is possible to limit the terms of the retainer (for example by offering to draft a will but not to offer detailed advice on tax planning without a separate charge) but as we have already seen the obligation is on the solicitor to clarify the terms of the retainer (*Gray v Buss Murton* (1999)).

Where a solicitor claims to have limited the retainer, they must have written evidence of the agreement to have any hope of success (see *Hurlingham Estates Ltd v Wilde & Partners* (1997)). Writing is required, not merely as -evidence of what has been agreed, but so that the client can consider (and discuss with others) the implications and wisdom of the limitation independently of the solicitor. Furthermore, even if the client consents, the solicitor will not be able to rely on the consent unless it is informed. In particular the client must understand whether the limitation is one which is reasonable and whether it is necessary for the client to seek advice elsewhere. Where clear oral assurances are given at the outset, the subsequent provision of letters of engagement will not necessarily limit the previous assurances. The terms of the retainer would have to be varied by agreement so as to include limitation: see *Halsall v Champion Consulting Ltd* (2017).

A solicitor cannot gain protection from liability by claiming to rely on counsel's opinion. In *Estill v Cowling, Swift & Kitchin* (2000), an estate suffered unnecessary inheritance tax because an inappropriate discretionary trust was established in the testatrix's lifetime. Arden J (as she then was) said that solicitors do not abdicate their professional responsibility when they seek the advice of counsel:

> "He must apply his mind to the advice received. But the more specialist the nature of the advice, the more reasonable is it likely to be for a solicitor to accept and act on it."

If the solicitor has accepted a general retainer to put the client's testamentary wishes into effect, it may also be appropriate to advise on other methods of disposal such as lifetime gifts and on the possible advantages of taking out insurance policies expressed to be for the benefit of third parties.

The solicitor cannot give investment advice unless authorised under the Financial Services and Markets Act 2000. If appropriate, the solicitor may advise the client to obtain expert investment advice.

It is important to warn clients that a will should never be regarded as permanent. Changed circumstances should lead to a review of the will (particularly changes in family circumstances such as marriage, separation, divorce, entering into or terminating a civil partnership, the birth of children and changes in financial circumstances such as inheritance of property or retirement). A solicitor who is acting for a client in relation to other matters (such as a divorce) should always suggest the making of a new will if it seems to be desirable. When advising a married client or client in a civil partnership who intends to make a will it is desirable to suggest that the spouse or civil partner also considers making a will so that the dispositions of the estates can be considered together. Although there is no obligation, it is helpful to warn clients who are disposing of a residence completely or moving to cheaper accommodation that they should keep records of the date of disposal, the value of the property at that date and the fact that the property was used as a residence. This information will be required if the client's personal representatives wish to claim a downsizing allowance after death: see para.4-025 and following.

There is no obligation for a solicitor to inform former clients of changes in the law which make it desirable for them to make new wills, although many would regard it as good marketing. It is important that the terms of the retainer establish that there is no continuing obligation to do this and there may be circumstances where an adviser who has taken a proactive stance in offering advice may be held to have varied the initial retainer to produce such an obligation. See the discussion in *Mehjoo v Harben Barker* (2013) and (2014).

7. SOLICITOR AS A BENEFICIARY

Where a person is a beneficiary of a will which he or she has prepared, positive **13-020**
evidence will be required of the testator's knowledge and approval of the contents of the will (see *Wintle v Nye* (1959)). Where the will is simple and short and the testator has had an opportunity to read it, the court may not require any additional evidence (see *Fuller v Strum* (2001)).

The SRA Standards and Regulations 2019 replacing the SRA Code of Conduct 2011 requires those regulated by the Financial Services Authority to act with honesty and integrity and in the best interests of the client (principles 4, 5 and 7). Firms should have a clear policy in place setting out what a member of the firm should do if requested to prepare a will in such cases.

The SRA Ethics Guidance: *Drafting and preparation of wills* issued on 6 May 2014 (updated 25 November 2019) says this:

> "*Gifts to you or someone in your business*
> If you draft a will where the client wishes to make a gift of significant value to you or a member of your family, or an employee of your business or their family, you should satisfy yourself that the client has first taken independent legal advice with regard to making the gift.
>
> This includes situations where the intended gift is of significant value in relation to the size of the client's overall estate, but also where the gift is of significant value in itself. Paragraph 6.1 of each of the Codes requires you not to act if there is an own interest conflict or a significant risk of an own interest conflict. In a situation like this, you will usually need to cease acting if the client does not agree to taking independent legal advice.
>
> There may be some exceptions where you can continue to draft the will even if the client has not received independent legal advice for example, if you draft wills for your parents and the surviving parent wishes to leave the residuary estate to you and your siblings in equal shares.
>
> However, whether it is appropriate to do so will depend upon the specific circumstances of each situation, and in each case you should consider whether your ability to advise, and be seen to advise, impartially is undermined by any financial interest or personal relationship which you have."

Solicitors are not prevented from preparing a will which appoints the solicitor or a partner as an executor even where the will contains a charging clause. However, the client must be clearly advised that it is not necessary to appoint a professional as an executor and must be given guidance on how the charges would be calculated. See Law Society Practice Note "*Appointment of a Professional Executor*" (22 May 2023) available on the Law Society website, and the SRA Ethics Guidance: *Drafting and preparation of wills* issued on 6 May 2014 (updated 25 November 2019) which includes the following:

> "*The appointment of executors*
> Your client might decide to appoint you, your business or other people in your business as executors in the will you are drafting for them.
>
> However, you must not exploit a client's lack of knowledge by leading them to believe that appointing a solicitor as an executor is essential or that it is the default position for someone making a will.
>
> Principle 7 of the Principles requires you to act in the best interests of each client. In this context this means not encouraging clients to appoint you or the business you work for as their executor unless it is clearly in their best interests to do so.
>
> In some cases it might be beneficial for a client to appoint a solicitor to act as an executor – for example, if their affairs are complex, or there are potential disputes in the family. However, in other cases there may be little or no advantage to the client – for example, if their estate is small or straightforward. A professional executor is likely to be more expensive than a lay person and the client should be advised about this.
>
> Before drafting a will which appoints you or your business (or someone else in the business) as the executor(s), you should be satisfied that the client has made their decision on a fully informed basis. This includes:
>
> - explaining the options available to the client regarding their choice of executor;
> - ensuring the client understands that an executor does not have to be a professional person or a business, that they could instead be a family member or a beneficiary under the will, and that lay executors can subsequently instruct a solicitor to act for them if this proves necessary (and can be indemnified out of the estate for the solicitors' fees);
> - recording advice that is given concerning the appointment of executors and the client's decision."

8. Duties of Solicitor Acting for Personal Representatives

Personal representatives will frequently retain a solicitor to act for them in the administration of an estate. The personal representatives are then the solicitor's clients. The beneficiaries or family of the deceased are not. If there is any dispute arising out of the administration the solicitor must be careful not to allow an actual or potential conflict of interest to arise by advising the beneficiaries or family of the deceased while he continues to act for the personal representatives. See *Re Exler deceased* (2017) for a particularly striking example of a solicitor failing to appreciate that a conflict of interests had arisen. **13-021**

It is particularly important that the solicitor reminds the personal representatives that they owe their duty to the estate and not to particular beneficiaries. They should remain neutral if there is a dispute between beneficiaries. Where personal representatives incur costs by acting to further the interests of one set of beneficiaries at the expense of another, they will be penalised by the court. See *Tod v Barton and Royal Society of Chemistry* (2002) and *Breadner v Granville-Grossman* (2001).

The duties of a solicitor in acting for personal representatives include giving advice and taking action in the administration on the clients' behalf. Immediately after the death the solicitor will be called upon to obtain any will of the deceased, advise on its validity and take steps to obtain a grant including the preparation of the appropriate oath and the inheritance tax account (if required). In some cases it will also be necessary to obtain evidence in support of the application (such as affidavits (or witness statements) of due execution).

Once the grant has been obtained the solicitor's duty is to advise the personal representatives on their duties. In particular the solicitor will be required to advise on the collection and realisation of the estate, the payment of debts and the distribution of the estate to the beneficiaries.

In *Cancer Research Campaign v Ernest Brown & Co (A Firm)* (1997) Harman J reviewed the authorities to decide whether or not executors had an obligation to inform legatees of a gift made to them in advance of distribution. He concluded that they had not on the basis that a legatee has no specific right in any asset in the estate. They have merely a chose in action to compel the proper administration of the estate. The estate may have such heavy debts that there is nothing left for legatees. Solicitors acting for executors could not be under any more extensive liability and so they had no obligation either. This was unfortunate for the legatees in question who would have varied their entitlement to achieve a tax saving had they been informed within the two-year time period.

However, there is no doubt that it is good practice to inform beneficiaries of their interest in an estate. Even the authorities relied upon by Harman J suggest this.

Difficulties can arise when a solicitor acts for the personal representatives of a disputed will. Simple steps need to be taken in the administration of the estate to secure the assets. If the personal representatives of the disputed will have already obtained a grant and the dispute relates to revocation of the will, they should agree with those seeking to have the grant revoked what steps can be taken. Where no grant has yet been obtained, the best course of action may be for both sides to agree to the appointment of a professional on an interim basis with authority limited to safeguarding the estate. See *Sifri v Clough & Willis* (2007).

Because personal representatives are neutral, there is no conflict of interests where a personal representative wishes to bring or defend a claim under the Inheritance (Provision for Family and Dependants) Act 1975 although they must take care to keep the roles (and legal fees) separate. See *Bowser v Smith* (2023) where a solicitor brought an unsuccessful action to remove his co-executor on the mistaken basis that her 1975 Act claim presented a conflict of interests. He suffered an adverse costs order for mistakenly bringing an action to remove the deceased's estranged wife as executor on the basis of a conflict of interests.

Missing beneficiaries cause problems for personal representatives. Solicitors must explain that the duty of the personal representatives is to distribute the estate to those entitled and advise on the possible ways of dealing with the situation arising from missing beneficiaries (see Ch.14).

Once the administration is complete the solicitor will prepare (or will -supervise the preparation of) the estate accounts prior to the distribution of residue.

Residuary beneficiaries can take complaints to the legal ombudsman. The Law Society's Practice Note "Complaints to the Legal Ombudsman" issued on 13 December 2012 recommends treating any complaint from a residuary beneficiary in the same way as a complaint from a client.

9. DUTIES IN RELATION TO ANTI-MONEY LAUNDERING LEGISLATION

Introduction

13-022 Solicitors are becoming subject to an increasing burden of regulation in relation to money laundering. The main body of UK law relating to money laundering is contained in the Proceeds of Crime Act 2002 and the Terrorism Act 2000.

What follows is a very brief outline of the relevant legislation. The Law Society has helpful guidance available on its website.

The principal offences

13-023 The Proceeds of Crime Act 2002 creates a single set of money laundering offences applicable throughout the UK to the proceeds of all crimes. It also creates a disclosure regime, which makes it an offence not to disclose knowledge or suspicion of money laundering, but also permits persons to be given consent in certain circumstances to carry out activities which would otherwise constitute money laundering. The Act applies to all solicitors, although some offences apply only to persons within the regulated sector, or nominated officers.

The principal offences are:

- *Section 327—concealing* A person commits an offence if he conceals, disguises, converts, or transfers criminal property, or removes criminal property from the UK. Criminal property is property which is, or represents, a person's benefit from criminal conduct, where the alleged offender knows or suspects that it is such.
- *Section 328—arrangements* A person commits an offence if he or she enters into, or becomes concerned in an arrangement which he or she knows or suspects facilitates the acquisition, retention, use or control of criminal property by or on behalf of another person.
- *Section 329—acquisition, use or possession* A person commits an offence if he or she acquires, uses, or has possession of criminal property otherwise

than for full valuable consideration.

A person will have a defence to a principal money laundering offence if he or she:

- makes an authorised disclosure prior to the offence being committed and gains appropriate consent (the consent defence); or
- intended to make an authorised disclosure but had a reasonable excuse for not doing so (the reasonable excuse defence). See Proceeds of Crime Act 2002 s.338.

Disclosure is made to the firm's nominated officer who will consider whether or not to make disclosure to the Serious Crimes Agency (SOCA).

In addition to the above a person commits the offence of non-disclosure under s.330 if:

- they know or suspect, or have reasonable grounds for knowing or suspecting, that another person is engaged in money laundering;
- the information on which their suspicion is based comes in the course of business in the regulated sector (businesses within the regulated sector are set out in Sch.9; firms of solicitors will normally be within the regulated sector);
- they can identify the person engaged in money laundering or the whereabouts of any of the laundered property, or they believe, or it is reasonable to expect them to believe, that the will may assist in identifying the person or the whereabouts of any of the laundered property; and
- they fail to disclose that knowledge or suspicion, or reasonable grounds for suspicion, as soon as practicable to a nominated officer or SOCA.

There are also "tipping off" offences contained in the Proceeds of Crime Act 2002, as amended. A further offence is created by the Terrorism Act 2000 s.18 which applies where a person enters into or becomes concerned in an -arrangement which facilitates the retention or control by or on behalf of another person of terrorist property by concealment, removal from the jurisdiction, transfer to nominees, or in any other way. It is a defence if the person proves that he did not know and had no reasonable cause to suspect that the arrangement related to terrorist property.

Regulatory requirements and the Anti-Money Laundering Directives

Introduction

Regulatory requirements were first introduced in relation to money laundering by the Money Laundering Regulations 2007 (SI 2007/2157). These were revoked by the Money Laundering, Terrorist Financing and Transfer of Funds (Information on the Payer) Regulations 2017 (SI 2017/692) (the 2017 Regulations) implementing the Fourth Anti-Money Laundering Directive. This was particularly significant for private client practitioners as it introduced the trusts register. **13-024**

The Fifth Anti-Money Laundering Directive introduced further amendments. The UK government was required to transpose the Fifth Directive into UK legislation by 10 January 2020. The Money Laundering and Terrorist Financing (Amendment) Regulations 2019 (SI 2019/1511) (the 2019 Regulations) introduce a number of the required amendments relating to the Trusts Register.

Relevant persons

13-025 The 2017 Regulations apply to all "relevant persons" as defined in regs.3 and 8. These include solicitors but extend to estate agents, banks and trust and company service providers. The 2019 Regulations extend the definition further to include, for example, letting agents, art dealers, cryptoasset exchange providers and custodian wallet providers.

Need for identity checks on customer and beneficial owner

13-026 Relevant persons are required by reg.27 to carry out "customer due diligence" as defined in reg.28. The relevant person must:

(a) identify the customer unless the identity of that customer is known to, and has been verified by, the relevant person;
(b) verify the customer's identity unless the customer's identity has already been verified by the relevant person; and
(c) assess, and where appropriate obtain information on, the purpose and intended nature of the business relationship or occasional transaction.

Regulation 28(3) imposes obligations where the customer is a body corporate. So, for example, the relevant person must obtain and verify its name, company number, the address of its registered office and, if different, its principal place of business.

Regulation 3A (inserted by the 2019 Regulations) imposes an obligation on the relevant person, where the customer is a legal person, trust, company, foundation or similar legal arrangement, to take reasonable measures to understand the ownership and control structure of that legal person, trust, company, foundation or similar legal arrangement.

Regulation 28(4) imposes obligations where the customer is beneficially owned by another. So, for example, the relevant person must identify the beneficial owner, take reasonable measures to verify the identity of the beneficial owner and, if the beneficial owner is a legal person, trust, company, foundation or similar legal arrangement take reasonable measures to understand the ownership and control structure of that legal person, trust, company, foundation or similar legal arrangement.

The 2019 Regulations insert a new reg.28(19) which confirms that electronic ID verification can be considered as a reliable source of evidence, where the electronic process is free from fraud and provides sufficient assurance of the identity of the individual

The 2019 Regulations introduce a new reg.30A which requires a relevant person to check that a new client has filed details of the persons with significant control with the registrar (i.e. Companies House) and to report any discrepancies identified.

Regulation 27 provides that due diligence has to be carried out when the relevant person:

(a) establishes a business relationship;
(b) carries out an occasional transaction exceeding specified figures;
(c) suspects money laundering or terrorist financing; and

(d) doubts the veracity or adequacy of documents, data or information previously obtained for the purposes of identification or verification.

Who is the beneficial owner?

Solicitors are used to performing identity checks on new clients but the 2007 Regulations introduced the concept of the "beneficial owner" for the first time. "Beneficial owner" is now defined in relation to a trust in reg.6 of the 2017 Regulations as follows: **13-027**

(a) the settlor;
(b) the trustees;
(c) the beneficiaries;
(d) where the individuals (or some of the individuals) benefiting from the trust have not been determined, the class of persons in whose main interest the trust is set up, or operates;
(e) any individual who has control over the trust.

Paragraph 2 of reg.6 defines "control" in (e) above as "a power (whether exercisable alone, jointly with another person or with the consent of another person) under the trust instrument or by law to:

(a) dispose of, advance, lend, invest, pay or apply trust property;
(b) vary or terminate the trust;
(c) add or remove a person as a beneficiary or to or from a class of beneficiaries;
(d) appoint or remove trustees or give another individual control over the trust;
(e) direct, withhold consent to or veto the exercise of a power mentioned in sub-paras (a)–(d).

Regulation 6(4)(a) provides that where an individual is the beneficial owner of a body corporate which is entitled to a vested interest which is:

(a) in possession or in remainder or reversion, and
(b) defeasible or indefeasible,

in the capital of the trust property or which has control over the trust, the individual is to be regarded as entitled to the interest or having control over the trust.

The definition of control is wide. However reg.6(4)(b) provides that an individual does not have control merely as a result of certain statutory provisions including Trustee Act 1925 s.32 (consent of person with a prior interest to an advancement of capital) and Trusts of Land and Appointment of Trustees Act 1996 s.19(2) (appointment and retirement of trustees at instance of the -beneficiaries), nor as a result of the rule in *Saunders v Vautier*. This is -obviously a helpful provision but it is limited in effect. It will not apply where the trust instrument has replaced the statutory provision with an express one.

In relation to an estate of a deceased person in the course of administration reg.6(7) defines the beneficial owner as the executor or administrator for the time being. This is helpful as it means that customer due diligence is not required on the beneficiaries of the estate. However, if a continuing trust arises, customer due diligence will be required on the "beneficial owner" at the point when assets are transferred to the trust.

What is a relevant trust and why does it matter?

13-028 The 2017 Regulations implemented the Fourth Money Laundering Directive, the objective of which was to prevent anonymous structures, such as companies and trusts, from being used to finance terrorism and laundering money. A major part of the Directive was the requirement that Member States should impose record keeping requirements on trustees of relevant trusts and introduce a register of express taxable relevant trusts. The registration requirement was extended by reg.45ZA of the 2017 Regulations as from 6 October 2020 to non-taxable trusts unless they are excluded from registration under Sch.3A of the 2017 Regulations.

Relevant trusts are defined in reg.42(1)(b) as follows:

> "(i) a UK trust which is an express trust;
> (ii) a non-UK trust which is an express trust; and
> (aa) receives income from a source in the United Kingdom; or
> (bb) has assets in the United Kingdom,
> on which it has incurred a tax liability.; or
> (iii) any other non-UK trust which is an express trust, is not a trust listed in Schedule 3A (excluded trusts) and whose trustees (in their capacity as such):
> (aa) acquire an interest in land in the United Kingdom; or
> (bb) enter into a business relationship with a relevant person, where at least one of those trustees is resident in the United Kingdom and the trust is not an EEA registered trust."

A trust has a tax liability if in the relevant tax year, it has a liability to pay income tax, capital gains tax, inheritance tax, stamp duty land tax, land and buildings transaction tax or stamp duty reserve tax. A trust disposing of a capital asset triggering a gain which escapes tax because the gain is covered by the annual exemption or by brought forward losses has no liability to capital gains tax so, unless it has other tax liabilities, it is not taxable. A discretionary trust which owns a residence in which one of the beneficiaries is permitted to live will have no inheritance tax liability until a 10-year anniversary arrives. Trustees who have mandated income to beneficiaries have no income tax liability and therefore the trust will not be taxable unless it has a liability for another tax.

A trust is a non-UK trust If all the trustees are resident outside the UK. If there is a mixture of UK resident and non-resident trustees, the trust is a UK trust if the settlor of the trust was resident and domiciled in the UK at the time the trust was set up or when the settlor added funds to the trust. Otherwise, the trust is a non-UK trust. See reg.42(c)–(e).

The directives are concerned only with express trusts and not with those arising as a matter of law, nor are they concerned with estates. However, when HMRC introduced the trust register, they decided to use it as the means of accessing self-assessment tax returns. As a result, trustees of non-express trusts and personal representatives of estates which require a self-assessment tax return (so-called "complex" estates) are required to register details. They are not, however, required to keep the information up-to-date.

Information keeping requirements

13-029 Regulation 44(1) provides that trustees of a relevant trust must maintain accurate and up-to-date records in writing of all the "beneficial owners" (as defined in reg.6) of the trust, and of any "potential beneficiaries". "Potential beneficiaries" are defined in reg 44(5) as "any other individual referred to as a potential beneficiary in a document from the settlor relating to the trust such as a letter of wishes".

Except where the beneficial owners include a class of beneficiaries, not all of whom have been determined, the following is required.

In the case of individuals:

(a) full name;
(b) national insurance number or unique taxpayer reference, if any;
(c) if the individual does not have a national insurance number or unique taxpayer reference, their usual residential address;
(d) if the address provided under sub-paragraph (c) is not in the UK:
    (i) passport number or identification card number, with the country of issue and the expiry date of the passport or identification card; or
    (ii) if the individual does not have a passport or identification card, the number, country of issue and expiry date of any equivalent form of identification;
(e) date of birth;
(f) the nature of the individual's role in relation to the trust
(g) a contact address for the trustees;
(h) the full name of any advisers who are being paid to provide legal, financial or tax advice to the trustees in relation to the trust.

Where a legal entity is a beneficial owner:

(a) corporate or firm name;
(b) unique taxpayer reference, if any;
(c) registered or principal office;
(d) the legal form of the legal entity and the law by which it is governed;
(e) if applicable, the name of the register of companies in which the legal entity is entered (including details of the EEA state or third country in which it is registered), and its registration number in that register;
(f) the nature of the entity's role in relation to the trust.

Where the beneficial owners include a class of beneficiaries, not all of whom have been determined, a description of the class of persons who are beneficiaries or potential beneficiaries under the trust is sufficient.

The information must, on request, be provided to any law enforcement authority (reg.44(5)) and to those required to carry out due diligence. Law enforcement authority is defined in reg.44(10).

The trust register and taxable relevant trusts

If the trust is liable to pay tax, the required information must be placed on a central register which under the 2017 Regulations is accessible only by competent authorities, including government agencies. The information must be provided within 90 days of the trust incurring a tax liability. If trustees becomes aware that any of the information provided (other than information relating to the value of the trust assets) has changed, they must update the register on or before 31 January after the tax year in which the change occurred; or if they are not liable to pay any UK taxes in that year, on or before 31 January after the tax year in which they are liable to pay any UK taxes. If the trustees are not aware of any changes, they must confirm that fact on or before 31 January after the tax year in which they are liable to pay any UK taxes (reg.45(9)). Regulation 45(2) requires trustees of taxable **13-030** relevant to register the information set out at para.13-029, together with the following additional information about the trust.

(a) the full name of the trust;
(b) the date on which the trust was set up;
(c) a statement of accounts for the trust, describing the trust assets and identifying the value of each category of the trust assets at the date on which the information is first provided to the Commissioners (including the address of any property held by the trust);
(d) the country where the trust is considered to be resident for tax purposes;
(e) the place where the trust is administered.

The trust register and personal representatives

13-031 Personal representatives only have to register if the estate is "complex". An estate is considered complex if:

- the value of the estate exceeds £2.5 million;
- tax due for the whole of the administration period exceeds £10,000;
- value of assets sold in any tax year for date of deaths up to April 2016 exceeds £250,000 or £500,000 for date of deaths after April 2016.

The information required for estates consists of:

- name of deceased;
- date of birth of deceased;
- NI number if deceased was UK resident unless a minor; and
- an address and passport for deceased (or ID number for non-UK residents, if there is no NI number).

Information as to assets and beneficiaries is not required.

The trust register and non-taxable trusts

13-032 **Introduction** The Fifth Anti-Money Laundering Directive significantly extends the requirements of the Fourth Directive by requiring trustees of express trusts to register even if they have no tax liability.

Regulation 45ZA of the 2017 Regulations requires the following trusts to register details of beneficial owners even though they have no tax liability unless they are excluded from the need to register by Sch.3A or are already registered in the EEA.

- UK express trusts;
- Non-UK express trusts which have at least one UK resident trustee and: (i) enter into a business relationship with a relevant person; or (ii) acquire an interest in UK land;
- Non-UK express trusts where none of the trustees are UK resident which acquire an interest in UK land.

13-033 **The main exclusions** The most relevant exclusions for private client purposes are set out below.

(1) (Paragraph 1) Legislative Trusts, for example the statutory trust imposed on intestacy).
(2) (Paragraph 2) Trusts created by court order, for example on divorce.
(3) (Paragraph 4) Trusts of:

(a) a life policy paying out only on the death, terminal or critical illness, or permanent or temporary disablement of the person assured; or to meet the cost of healthcare services provided to the person assured;

> Example 1 (taken from TRSM23030)
>
> Karl takes out a 40-year term life insurance policy, which is written into trust at commencement. The policy will only pay out on the event of Karl's death within the 40-year term, and the policy is not able to be surrendered during that term. As this meets the conditions, the trust holding the policy is excluded from registration.

TRSM23030 sets out HMRCs' view that the exclusion applies to policies which have or can acquire surrender values.

> "The general position is that trusts holding policies with surrender values can remain excluded from registration under Sch3A(4) until such time as the policy is actually surrendered. If a policy is surrendered and the cash sum is retained in the trust, the trust would be required to register from that point."

However, HMRC considers that the exclusion does not extend to policies such as Insurance Bonds which principally have an investment motive.

> "However, some policies (such as investment bonds) are designed to provide regular or periodic payments to the policyholder in the form of surrenders or part-surrenders during the term of the policy, with a small life assurance element payable on death which is incidental to the benefits provided through the surrenders. In those cases, HMRC's view is that the withdrawals of cash in the event of a part or full surrender does constitute a pay out from the policy, because those withdrawals are intended from the outset as expected payments of funds from the policy. As this occurs on an occasion other than those listed at Sch3A(4), the exclusion does not apply to trusts holding these policies."

(b) an insurance policy paying out only on the temporary disablement of the person assured, applied for at the same time as a life policy under (a), or to meet the cost of healthcare services.

(c) the prospective death benefits payable on the death of the person assured under a retirement policy.

(4) (Paragraph 5) Charitable Trusts whether registered as charities or exempt from registration.

(5) (Paragraph 6) Pilot Trusts holding property with a value not exceeding £100, and created before the regulations comes into force (6 October 2020). Note that pilot trusts created on or after that date are not excluded.

(6) (Paragraph 6A) Bank accounts held for a minor or person lacking capacity within the meaning of Mental Capacity Act 2005 s.2. See TRSM23160. The exclusion extends to deposit accounts. Other assets, e.g. shares, held on a bare trust are not excluded. Child Trust Funds and Junior ISAs are excluded because HMRC says they are not trusts (really?). See TRSM 10030 and 23160. A National Savings Certificate (NSC) purchased in the name of a minor does not itself create an express trust. However, an NSC may be purchased by trustees and held on trust for a minor child. If so, this

would be an express trust which would be registerable on TRS unless any other exclusion from registration applies. Premium bonds are not registerable on TRS because a premium bond purchased in the name of a minor does not create an express trust. Premium bonds cannot be held jointly or in trust. See TRSM23160.

(7) (Paragraph 7) Trusts effected by will where:

(a) the trust is holding only the property comprised in a person's estate on death, and

(b) less than two years has passed since that person's death.

The exclusion for will trusts is very welcome but note that it is limited to a maximum of two years so, unless the trust is wound up within two years of death, it will have to be registered at the end of that period—or earlier, if at any date beforehand the trust accepts an addition of property from outside the estate, it will then need to register within 90 days from that date.

The exclusion is limited to trusts effected by will. If a testator leaves property by will to a trust created in his lifetime (e.g. a pilot trust), the exclusion from registration does not apply. The pilot trust will be already registered unless it was created before 6 October 2020. See TRSM23020.

Similarly, a trust created by post-death variation is not created by will and so does not benefit from this exclusion. The trust is treated as created by the person varying. See TRSM23020.

HMRC take the view that a standard trust of residue "I give my estate on trust to my executors to pay debts, funeral expenses and to hold the balance for my husband absolutely" creates a trust which must be registered if the administration continues for more than two years. However, there are according to HMRC some subtle distinctions. See below.

(8) (Paragraph 8) A trust holding only death benefits received under a policy within para.4, where less than two years has passed since that person's death.

Example 2 (taken from TRSM23030)

Grace takes out a whole of life insurance policy which is written into trust and qualifies for exclusion from registration.

On Grace's death, the trust receives the pay-out from the policy. The trust remains excluded from registration for up to two years from the date of death, giving time for the trustees to direct the pay-out to the beneficiaries of the trust.

(9) (Paragraph 9) Trusts of jointly held property but only where the trustees and the beneficiaries are the same persons. See para.13-035 below.

(10) Trusts meeting certain legislative requirements are excluded:

- (Paragraph 16) Trusts for bereaved minors or bereaved young persons.
- (Paragraph 22) Trusts for a disabled beneficiary.
- (Paragraph 17) Heritage funds.
- (Paragraph 18) Personal injury trusts.
- (Paragraph 19) Trusts for tenants' service charges.

13-034 **Bare trusts** Bare trusts are not taxable trusts as income and gains are treated as belonging to the beneficiary.

A number of responses to the Consultation suggested that bare trusts should be excluded from the new registration requirement. However, HMRC did not agree. TRSM10030 says:

> "There is no specific exclusion from registration for bare trusts. In general, if a bare trust is an express trust it should register on TRS".

But the bare trust may fall within an exclusion, or it may not be an express trust.

- *Bare trusts arising on transfers of land to minors?* These are not express trusts and so are not required to register. TRSM23050 says:

  > "Where property is conveyed to one or more persons under the age of 18 alone, Schedule 1(1) of the Trusts of Land and Appointment of Trustees Act 1996 provides that the land is to be held in trust for the benefit of those persons. Likewise, where property is conveyed to one or more persons under the age of 18 and other persons over the age of 18, Schedule 1(2) of that Act provides that the land is held in trust by the persons over the age of 18 for the benefit of themselves and the person or persons under the age of 18. Trusts created in this way are excluded from registration as trusts imposed by legislation."

  TRSM23050 has an example of a transfer of land to a mixture of adults and minors:

  > Example 3
  > "F transfers the legal and beneficial interest in a property to his 3 children, A, S and D, to hold equally as joint tenants. D is under 18 and unable to hold the legal title to the land so A and S are treated as holding the property on bare trust for the benefit of themselves and D, until D reaches 18. As a trust imposed by legislation, this trust is not required to register."

- *Bare trusts arising on transfers of land to more than four people?* TRSM23050 also deals with the position where land is conveyed to more than four people. Section 34(2) of the Law of Property Act 1925 provides that the land is to be held in trust by the first four for the benefit of all the persons who have a beneficial entitlement to the land. This is a statutory trust, not an express one, and therefore excluded from the need to register.
- *Bare trusts and partnership property?* Where property is purchased using partnership money but is held in one partner's name, there is a general presumption under Partnership Act 1890 s.20, s.21 that the property belongs to the partnership as a whole. A partner holding property on behalf of the partnership in this way is not holding on an express trust so there is no registration requirement.

However, in many cases there will be an express declaration in a partnership deed that property is being held on trust for the partnership. If so, this is an express trust which would have to be registered. See TRSM23050.

- *Bare trust where PRs appropriate asset to a legatee before sale?* HMRC confirmed on their Agent Forum (*https://community.hmrc.gov.uk*) 17, that appropriations to a beneficiary for the purpose of sale fall within para.14 of Sch.3A do not need to be registered on the Trust Register.

  They said:

  > "Where personal representatives appropriate property on bare trust for the benefit

of the beneficiaries to facilitate a sale of that property, Sch 3A(14) would exclude such an appropriation from registration."

Paragraph 14 is headed "Commercial transactions" and excludes:

"A trust created for the purpose of—
(a) enabling or facilitating a transaction effected for genuine commercial reasons; or
(b) protecting or enforcing rights relating to such a transaction, where the use of the trust is incidental to the principal purpose of the transaction."

13-035 **Co-ownership of land** TRSM23050 confirms that the proportions in which co-owned property is held as tenants in common are not relevant for registration purposes nor are changes from joint tenancy to tenancy in common. It has a number of useful examples.

It is important to note that the exclusion applies only while legal and beneficial ownership are the same.

Example 4

Alice and Bob own a property with a declaration of trust confirming they own as tenants in common. This trust is excluded from registration as an exempt co-ownership trust. However, if Alice dies and leaves her share to her daughter, Catherine, Bob now holds the legal title for himself and Catherine. The exclusion no longer applies. The trust will have to be registered within 90 days unless Bob appoints Catherine as a co-trustee in which case the exclusion will become available (see TRSM23020).

Will Trusts only have to be registered if they are in existence two years after death. The date may seem obvious but there can be cases where the trust does not come into existence until more than two years after the death. A trust cannot be registered until it comes into existence.

13-036 **Will trusts** Will Trusts only have to be registered if they are in existence two years after death. The date may seem obvious but there can be cases where the trust does not come into existence until more than two years after the death. A trust cannot be registered until it comes into existence. According to HMRC (see TRSM23020) a trust of a specific asset or pecuniary legacy starts at death so has to be registered before the two year anniversary unless it has come to an end before that date.

Example 5

I give £100,000 on trust for my son.

This trust is treated as coming into effect on death and therefore, if it continues after two years from date of death it must be registered on TRS.

HMRC say trusts of residue may commence at death or later, depending on the wording of the will. There are some fairly baffling distinctions dealt with at TRSM23020. HMRC say "*A careful examination of the wording of the will is needed to understand what type of trust it creates and when it arises*." The following examples are taken from TRSM23020.

(1) No express trust of residue:

A trust is only required to register on TRS if it is an express trust, so if the will does not create a trust, then no registration is required.

Example 6

Paula's will appoints Ronald as her executor and directs him to pay all debts and funeral expenses and transfer her residuary estate to her daughter, Leona. HMRC say:

> "The executor is not appointed as a trustee and no trust is declared over the estate. Any trust which arises is through operation of law because of Ronald's duties as executor and so is not an express trust. No TRS registration is required regardless of the length of the administration period."

(2) Estate held on trust for administration purposes:

A will may expressly state that the executor holds the estate upon trust as part of the administration of the estate (HMRC call it an administration trust).

Example 7

I give my estate to my executors on trust with power at their discretion to sell all or any part of parts of such property when they think fit. My executors shall pay my funeral and testamentary expenses my debts and any legacies given by this will out of such property or its proceeds of sale and hold the balance upon trust for such of Donald, Harold and Michaela as are living at my death and if more than one in equal shares.

HMRC say: "Whilst there may be overlap between the duties of an executor and a trustee, there is clearly an express trust which covers the administration period and therefore starts from the date of death. So, if the administration of the estate continues after 2 years from date of death it must be registered on TRS as a will trust rather than as an estate. This trust would continue until all of the assets are paid outright to Donald, Harold and Michaela. Note this is a separate consideration from whether the estate needs to register for tax purposes as a complex estate".

(3) Executors to hold residue on trust for a beneficiary absolutely:

For example, a will may appoint executors without creating a trust but leave the residuary estate on trust:

Example 8

"I appoint Sophie as my executor to pay my debts, funeral expenses and to hold the balance upon trust for Gisele absolutely".

HMRCs' view is that the trust does not arise until either assets are vested in the trustees or the residue is ascertained at which point they hold as bare trustees for Giselle. They say:

> "Here, the trust technically comes into existence when assets are appropriated to the trustees or the administration period ends and Sophie switches role from executor to trustee. It may be difficult to ascertain when this occurs. If the assets have not been transferred to Gisele within 2 years of death than the trust needs to be registered at that point if the administration period has ended or at the date when the administration period ends if later."

A trust created by Will may interact with an existing co-ownership trust.

Example 9

Alice and Bob own a property with a declaration of trust confirming they own as tenants in common. This trust is excluded from registration during Alice's lifetime as an exempt co-ownership trust (see TRSM23050).

Alice dies and by the terms of her will leaves her share of the property on trust to Bob to occupy for the remainder of his life, and thereafter to her daughter Clara. Alice's son David is appointed as executor and trustee of the will and also appointed as a second trustee of the property with Bob.

There are two trusts: 1) the new trust created by Alice's will; and 2) the ongoing trust of the property.

The trust created by Alice's will is excluded from the requirement to register for two years following Alice's death. If the trust is still in existence two years after Alice's death, the trust is required to register from that point.

The ongoing trust of the co-ownership property is no longer an exempt co-ownership trust, as explained above. Bob is holding the legal title for the benefit of himself and Clara.

Consultation and proposals for amendment of rules on registration

13-037 In 2023 HM Treasury began a new consultation on the Money Laundering, Terrorist Financing and Transfer of Funds (Information on the Payer) Regulations 2017, part of which relates to the trust register.

It considered that the rules on co-ownership property trusts and trusts created by variation should be aligned with the rules on trusts effected by will by introducing a common registration deadline of two years from the date of death. This would undoubtedly be very helpful for those dealing with estates.

It is also proposed a "de minimis" exemption for registration for small, low value trusts which would be made exempt from registration on the basis that they are low risk. The proposal is to exclude from registration a trust that meets all of the following tests:

- the trust is not liable for relevant UK taxes;
- the trust does not own or have an interest, in whole or in part, in UK land/real property;
- the trust does not hold more than £5,000 in assets;
- the trust does not distribute more than £2,000 in assets and expenses (combined) in any 12-month period.

Once a trust exceeds any of the threshold amounts, the trust would require registration. Should the value of a trust's assets to be above £5,000 and then fall below this amount, the trust would remain registerable.

From tax year 2024–2025 a new tax rule will take trusts out of income tax where their income is less than £500, allowing more trusts to meet the first test. However, the requirements are so stringent that very few trusts will come within the exception.

Professional bodies have pointed out that unless the final requirement is varied for the last year of a trust's life, when all remaining funds are distributed, virtually no trusts will qualify.

Access to the information on the Register

13-038 HMRC must make information available to a person who requests it if that person demonstrates a "legitimate interest". The Directive does not define legitimate interest, so it is for individual states to determine their own definition. The EU suggests that there is a benefit to having transparency in the ownership of corporate entities and trusts which raised the spectre of general public access.

However, the UK announced in the 2019 Consultation that it was taking a narrower approach and would only allow access to those involved in fighting money laundering and terrorist financing. Information is not provided on trusts which are not express and registered merely to obtain a tax return nor where an exemption applies such as a risk of harm (see below).

In order to demonstrate a "legitimate interest" TRSM60020 states that requesters must show:

- they are involved in an investigation into money laundering or terrorist financing, and
- they are requesting the information in order to further an investigation into a specified suspected instance of money laundering or terrorist financing.

Requesters are expected to provide a rational basis which objectively explains why they think the trust might be involved in money laundering or terrorist financing. Additionally, HMRC must conclude that:

- the information provided by the requester to support their request shows the requester has reasonable grounds to suspect the trust is being used for money laundering or terrorist financing, and
- releasing the information would not prejudice any existing or potential investigation (criminal investigation or proceedings or any other investigation mentioned in s.342(1) of Proceeds of Crime Act 2002).

Requesters can obtain access to Relevant Registered Trust information where a trust has a controlling interest in an offshore company or other entity that is not a UK or EEA entity. For these purposes, a Relevant Registered Trust has a controlling interest in an offshore company where it holds more than 50 per cent of shares or voting rights in that entity. For both types of requests, the information requested must be about a specific trust which can be identified with certainty from the information provided, and not about persons. Requesters must specify in their submission which type of Trust Data Request they are making. Even where all the requirements are met, the trust information may not be released to the requester if an exemption applies, for example, there is a risk of harm.

Regulation 45ZB(5) provides information will not be provided where HMRC consider that the information should be exempt because—

> "(a) they consider that making the information available would expose the beneficial owner to a disproportionate risk of fraud, kidnapping, blackmail, extortion, harassment, violence or intimidation;
> (b) the beneficial owner is under the age of 18; or
> (c) the beneficial owner—
> (i) lacks capacity within the meaning of section 2 of the Mental Capacity Act 2005;
> (ii) is incapable within the meaning of section 1 of the Adults with Incapacity (Scotland) Act 2000; or
> (iii) is incapable by reason of mental disorder within the meaning of Article 3(1) of the Mental Health (Northern Ireland) Order 1986,
>
> References to the beneficial owner include references to any other individual referred to as a potential beneficiary in a document from the settlor relating to the trust such as a letter of wishes."

Where trustees consider there is a risk of fraud, kidnapping etc under (a) above the trustees must notify HMRC in writing if they believe the risk of harm exemption may apply to one or more of their trust's beneficial owners.

The disproportionate risk, where it does occur, must arise directly from the release of the relevant TRS information.

Trustees should send an e-mail, putting "Beneficial owners at risk of harm" in the subject line to:

trs.riskofharm@hmrc.gov.uk and include the information set out at TRSM60040.

Discrepancy reporting

13-039 Solicitors are "Relevant Persons" within the 2017 Regulations and, as such, have certain obligations when either establishing, or maintaining an existing Business Relationship (see TRSM24010) with a registrable trust.

(1) Prior to establishing a Business Relationship, Relevant Persons are required to check that the trust is registered (if applicable), and the information is up-to-date;
(2) In line with their obligations to carry out ongoing monitoring, Relevant Persons must carry out discrepancy checks in accordance with their internal organisational risk assessments, policies, and procedures.

They can discharge their obligations by:

- requiring the trustee or agent to provide an up-to-date excerpt from the register, if the trust is required to be registered (see TRSM20000).
- checking for any material discrepancies (see TRSM70050) between information contained in the excerpt and any information which otherwise becomes available to Relevant Persons in the course of carrying out their duties under the Money Laundering Regulations.

TRSM70020 defines a "Business Relationship" as a business, professional or commercial relationship between Relevant Persons (see TRSM24020) and a customer, which arises out of the business of Relevant Persons, and is expected by Relevant Persons, at the time when contact is established, to have an element of duration. A one-off transaction does not create a "Business relationship".

Solicitors and the General Data Protection Regulation (GDPR)

13-040 We looked at the implications of the GDPR for personal representatives and trustees in Ch.13. There are also implications for solicitors. Obviously, firms will comply with the requirements for all clients. However there are particular issues for private client departments. Obviously, the department will hold data relating to beneficiaries of wills and trusts and family members of clients. Fortunately there are a number of exceptions which provide help.

When preparing wills or trusts, the client will provide details of the various beneficiaries which the firm will record and store. Does the GDPR require privacy notices to be sent to the potential beneficiaries? Fortunately, the answer is no. Article 14(5) applies a proportionality filter to privacy notices so that it is not necessary to provide information in various circumstances including where providing the information would breach confidentiality obligations. Following the death of the client the duty of confidentiality is owed to the personal representatives. They may themselves have a duty to give notice to the beneficiaries which the solicitor will normally undertake on their behalf.

Another exception to the requirement to provide privacy notices contained in art.14 is where compliance would involve a disproportionate effort. This may well exclude the need to communicate with members of a secondary class of discretionary beneficiaries who are only included in case the whole class of primary beneficiaries is wiped out and on whom a firm is holding very limited information. This exception might also apply where a deputy or attorney acting under a lasting possession has possession of the address book of the person who has lost capacity.

The UK in reliance on art.23 (right to restrict by way of a legislative measure the scope of the obligations and rights) provided an exception for legal professional privilege in the Data Protection Act 2018 Sch.2 Pt 4.19. (There was a corresponding restriction in the Data Protection Act 1998.)

Legal advice privilege is likely to mean, for example, that solicitors do not have to provide privacy notices to family members excluded from benefit.

Whenever a firm takes the view that communication is not required, it is helpful to document the decision in case a complaint is made to the Information Commissioner's Office (ICO). The ICO has draconian powers to impose penalties but is unlikely to exercise such powers where a firm has considered a problem, come to a decision on the basis of the available information and recorded the decision and its reasons.

The question of legal advice privilege arose under the Data Protection Act 1998 in *Dawson-Demer v Taylor Wessing* (2017). The Court of Appeal reversed the first instance decision dismissing a request from trust beneficiaries. The beneficiaries of an offshore trust were unhappy because the trustee (a trust corporation based in the Bahamas) had excluded them from the class of beneficiaries. They made a subject access request to the solicitors acting for the trustee, Taylor-Wessing, asking to see all the information held relating to them.

Taylor-Wessing argued that they should not have to comply with the request for the following reasons:

(i) the request was made for the collateral purpose of assisting in litigation in the Bahamas;
(ii) the exception for legal professional privilege contained in the 1998 Act would here be Bahamian legal professional privilege (since the trustees were Bahamian) and it would be disproportionate to expect UK solicitors to get to grips with the niceties of the Bahamian system;
(iii) legal professional privilege is extended in relation to trusts by the "*Londonderry*" principle which states that trustees do not have to disclose information if it would reveal the reasons for the exercise of their discretions.

The Court of Appeal rejected all the arguments. The reason behind a request is irrelevant. Legal professional privilege is UK legal professional privilege so there was nothing disproportionate in complying with the request. The exception for legal professional privilege is not extended by the "*Londonderry*" principle.

Obviously the case was troubling for trustees. Disgruntled beneficiaries are sadly common and much trouble for trustees and advisers could be caused by a subject access request. Firms competing for offshore work were particularly concerned as it made UK firms less attractive than those working in jurisdictions not subject to such rules.

When the Data Protection Bill was being discussed in parliament an amendment was proposed (amendment 48 on 13 December 2017) which would have enacted the so-called "*Londonderry*" principle that trustees do not have to disclose the reasons for the exercise of their discretion. The amendment was withdrawn following this statement from Lord Keen of Elie who made the point that the GDPR itself contained an exception in art.15(4) to the right to see data where the exercise of the right would "adversely affect the rights and freedoms of others". He said:

"Article 15 of the GDPR confers a general right for a data subject to seek access to personal data held by a controller, but there are a number of exemptions, set out directly in both article 15 and in Schedule 2 to the Bill. ...The Government's position remains that article 15(4) of the GDPR already prevents the disclosure of the material the noble Lord's amendment is concerned with. This is because the Government consider that the, 'rights and freedoms of others', referred to in article 15(4) includes the rights of both trustees and other beneficiaries. Where disclosure under data protection law would reveal information about a trustee's deliberations or reasons for their decisions that would otherwise be protected from disclosure under trust law, the Government's view is that disclosure would adversely affect the rights and -freedoms of trustees and beneficiaries in the trustees' ability to make independent decisions in the best interests of the trust without fear of -disagreement with beneficiaries." (Hansard, 13 December 2017: amendment 48)

Other regulatory requirements

13-041 Firms who deal with ongoing trust administration must comply with the automatic exchange of information regimes. The first was the Foreign Account Tax Compliance Act (FATCA). This is an inter-governmental agreement between the UK and the US. It was closely followed by the Common Reporting Standard (CRS) which was signed on 29 October 2014 by 51 jurisdictions including the UK. The UK committed to implementation by September 2017. The drafters of the CRS used FATCA as a model on which to base the CRs so there are many similarities between the two. The requirements of the two schemes are beyond the scope of this book.

For contracts entered into on or after 13 June 2014 it is necessary to comply with the requirements of the Consumer Contracts (Information, Cancellation and Additional Charges) Regulations 2013 (SI 2013/3134). The regulations apply to all contracts made with clients as they apply to contracts made:

- by distance selling,
- on-premises, and
- off-premises.

They require certain standard information to be provided relating to the nature of the services, charges and complaints handling. As with the earlier regulations there is a requirement for a cooling-off period where contracts are made other than at the solicitor's place of business. The client must be provided with information regarding the cooling off period. Failure to provide this results in the extension of the cancellation period beyond the usual 14-day period. The contract cannot be enforced until 14 days have elapsed from the end of the cooling off period. See reg.31.

Chapter Fourteen

PROTECTION OF PERSONAL REPRESENTATIVES

1. Introduction

Personal representatives are personally liable for any loss arising from a failure to carry out their duties. If they have incurred personal liability they may be able to obtain relief in a number of ways. **14-001**

(a) *The will may contain a relieving provision.* Many wills include a clause limiting the liability of personal representatives to liability for wilful fraud or wrongdoing and giving protection from liability for mistakes made in good faith. In *Armitage v Nurse* (1998) Millett LJ held that a clause purporting to exclude liability for everything except actual fraud was not repugnant or contrary to public policy. There is a core of obligations that beneficiaries must be able to enforce against trustees in order to give effect to the trust, but these obligations do not include the duties of skill, care, prudence and diligence. However, despite the decision, there was an increasing feeling that such clauses are not normally appropriate for professional trustees who are paid and can insure against the risk of liability. The Law Commission published a report (No.301) "*Trustee Exemption Clauses*" (19 July 2006) recommending that professional bodies should introduce practice rules to deal with the problem. The Solicitors' Code of Conduct 2007 r.2.07 stated that a limitation on liability must be in writing and brought to the attention of the client. There are no express references to exoneration clauses in the SRA Code of Conduct 2011 or in SRA Standards and Regulations 2019 replacing the Code. However, principles 4, 5 and 7 of the Standards require those regulated to act with honesty, integrity and in the best interests of the client.

    Where a clause relieves a personal representative from liability for everything except "wilful and individual fraud or wrongdoing", protection is available unless there is "conscious and wilful misconduct", what Millett LJ referred to in *Armitage v Nurse* (1998) as "knowing and deliberate breach of duty or reckless indifference" to the possibility of such breach. See also *Barnsley v Noble* (2016).

(b) *The court may grant relief under Trustee Act 1925 s.61.* The court has discretion to grant relief where a trustee "has acted honestly and reasonably and ought fairly to be excused".

    For example, this discretion was exercised in *Re Kay* (1897), under a forerunner of s.61, where a personal representative paid a legacy which appeared small in comparison to the estate at a time when he was unaware of liabilities which exceeded the total value of the estate. In *Daniel v Tees*

(2016), the judge concluded that disappointed beneficiaries had not demonstrated that they had suffered loss as a result of breaches of the trustees duties in relation to investment policy. However, he went on to consider, in case he was wrong, whether relief would have been available under s.61. He considered that it would. The trustees had not been "cavalier, self-interested or unthinking". On the contrary, "they worked hard and consistently and over a long period of time, to the best of their abilities and in reliance on what they reasonably believed to be competent professional advice, to achieve the best results that they could for the Trust".

(c) *The beneficiaries may grant a release.* The personal representatives can obtain a release from personal liability from all the beneficiaries affected by the breach. Such a release is only effective where the beneficiaries induced the personal representatives to perform the wrongful act (*Trafford v Boehm* (1746)) or if the beneficiaries are sui juris and fully aware of the breach.

(d) *Limitation.* Where personal representatives have incurred personal liability, they may be able to plead the defence of limitation. Creditors cannot bring an action against personal representatives for non-payment of debts after a period of six years has elapsed from date of distribution of the estate (Limitation Act 1980 s.1). Beneficiaries cannot bring an action against the personal representatives to recover land or personalty after the expiration of 12 years from the date on which the right of action accrued (Limitation Act 1980 ss.13 and 15(1)). However, no limitation period applies where a personal representative is fraudulent or where the personal representative is in possession of trust property or the proceeds thereof. The limitation period will not start to run against a beneficiary who is under a disability or where there has been fraud, concealment or mistake (Limitation Act 1980 ss.18, 38 and 32). If the administration is completed and the personal representatives continue to hold assets as trustees, any subsequent breaches of trust will be subject to the limitation periods applying to trustees (normally six years under Limitation Act 1980 s.21(3)). See *Davies v Sharples* (2006).

Personal representatives will obviously be anxious to avoid incurring personal liability. Complying with certain statutory provisions offers protection. These methods of obtaining protection are considered in this chapter.

2. STATUTORY ADVERTISEMENTS (TRUSTEE ACT 1925 S.27)

Protection from personal liability

14-002 Personal representatives who have distributed the assets of the deceased are personally liable to any beneficiaries or creditors for any unpaid debts and liabilities even though they were unaware of them at the time of distribution (*Knatchbull v Fearnhead* (1837)). They can protect themselves from such liability by advertising for claimants under Trustee Act 1925 s.27.

Note however that personal representatives may find themselves in a situation where they are fairly certain that claims exist but have not been able to identify the potential claimants. Trustee Act 1925 s.27 may not afford protection in such cases. In *Re Studdert (Deceased)* (2020) Chief Master Marsh said:

> *"the protection afforded by section 27 is, or at least may be, limited. It provides in subsection (2) that the personal representatives '... shall not ... be liable to any person of whose*

claim the ... personal representatives have not had notice ... provided they have advertised in the form required by the Act. ' It is unclear whether they would be treated as having notice of a class of claims which they believe may exist in relation to which the identity of the possible claimants is unknown. Indeed, there remains the possibility that the estate is insolvent."

In *Studdert* the deceased had been convicted of possessing pornographic images of children and there were strong grounds for suspecting that he had committed sexual offences in Poland which might give rise to claims for historic sexual abuse.

Because of the strong possibility that legitimate claims existed Chief Master Marsh ordered that no distributions of (the substantial) residue of the estate should take place until further attempts had been made to locate claimants and he gave directions as to what steps should be taken. He accepted that "*a complete bar on the distribution of the estate should not remain in place indefinitely*".

The advertisements

Under s.27, the personal representatives may give notice of their intention to distribute the assets of the estate, requiring any person interested to send in particulars of their claim (whether as a creditor or as a beneficiary: *Re Aldhous* (1955)) to the personal representatives within a stated time, not being less than two months from the date of the notice. This notice must be brought to the attention of the general public by: **14-003**

(a) placing an advertisement in the *London Gazette*;
(b) placing an advertisement in a newspaper circulating in the district in which land to be distributed (if any) is situated; and
(c) giving "such other like notices, including notices elsewhere than in England and Wales, as would, in any special case, have been directed by a court of competent jurisdiction in an action for administration" (in an action for administration the court would order the advertisement to be placed in such local or national newspapers as might be appropriate having regard to the circumstances of the case. In cases of doubt, personal representatives should apply to the court for directions as to where to place the advertisements since failure to comply with all the requirements denies them the protection of the section).

Searches

Section 27(2) provides that personal representatives are not freed **14-004**

> "from any obligation to make searches or obtain official certificates of search similar to those which an intending purchaser would be advised to make or obtain".

Although this subsection does not list the searches that have to be made, the prudent personal representative will make the same searches as a purchaser of land would make in the Land Registry or Land Charges Register, as appropriate, and the Local Land Charges Register, as well as searching in bankruptcy against the deceased and any beneficiary receiving assets.

Distributing the estate

Once the time limit on the notices has expired the personal representatives can distribute the estate having regard only to the claims of which they have notice. If **14-005** a claim is made after distribution by someone of whom they had no notice, the personal representatives are not personally liable. In these circumstances the disappointed claimant must recover the assets from the persons who received them from the personal representatives. So as to avoid delay in the distribution of the estate, these searches and advertisements should be made as early in the administration as possible.

The section does not relieve personal representatives from liability if they have notice of a claim. For example, if they know of a debt, they are under an obligation to pay it even though the creditor does not respond to the advertisement. In *MCP Pension Trustees Ltd v AON Pension Trustees Ltd* (2010) trustees had received notice of certain claims but had genuinely forgotten all about them. The trustees claimed that forgetting meant they ceased to have knowledge; and that at that point they ceased to have notice. The section includes no definition of what constitutes notice but the Court of Appeal held that s.27 is only concerned with whether the notice had been received by the time funds were distributed. Once actual notice is given, then in general it will persist and remain notice at the time of distribution. Trustees should, therefore, take particular care to maintain clear trust records so that no claims are overlooked.

A problem with s.27 is that having decided what are the appropriate newspapers, it may prove difficult to actually place the advertisement. For example, in *Re Gess* (1942), the deceased was Polish and died in England in 1939. Due to the war, no advertisements could be placed in Polish newspapers. Section 27 was of no assistance to the personal representatives who had to seek a different form of protection (they obtained a *Benjamin Order*—see para.14-009 and following).

Contingent liabilities

14-006 Although s.27 gives protection against claims of which the personal representatives have no notice; it gives no protection where personal representatives have distributed the estate with knowledge of a future or contingent liability.

If the personal representatives know that a debt will fall due at some time in the future, they will simply set aside a fund to meet that future liability when the time comes.

Contingent liabilities are less easy to deal with. For example, the deceased may have guaranteed a debt from a third party; the personal representatives cannot know whether or not the estate will be called upon to honour the guarantee. Similarly, there may be a threat of legal proceedings against the estate; while the personal representatives may suspect that the claimant will not take the matter further, they cannot be certain of this. The personal representatives must decide what to do in such a case and there are four courses of action open to them.

First, they can set aside assets from the estate sufficient to meet the contingent liability should it actually arise. This course of action will be unpopular with the beneficiaries since they will only receive the assets once the personal representatives decide the contingent liability can no longer arise (for example when the loan guaranteed by the deceased is paid off or the claimant in the proposed action abandons their claim). It does, however, give the personal representatives total protection provided they have set aside sufficient assets.

Secondly, they can distribute all the assets to the beneficiaries but obtain the beneficiaries' agreement to indemnify the personal representatives if the liability ever crystallises. This will be more popular with the beneficiaries, but the personal representatives should be wary since an indemnity is only as financially sound as the beneficiary who gives it. Thus, if the personal representatives distribute assets to a beneficiary who spends the money received on a holiday, an indemnity from that beneficiary will be worthless if they have no other assets. Furthermore, it may not be possible to obtain an indemnity; for example, where a beneficiary is a minor, lacks capacity to make the decision or simply refuses to give one. Even where an indemnity has been obtained from a beneficiary who is financially sound, the inheritance may have been invested in assets which are not easily realisable, for example, a house. In this case calling in the indemnity could cause severe financial hardship, since the beneficiary would have to sell their house to meet their obligation.

Thirdly, the personal representatives can insure against the liability arising. If cover can be obtained (and it depends very much on the risk involved) the only expense will be the premium on the policy; the assets will pass to the beneficiaries free of any liability as far as they are concerned. Provided the premium is not too high, the beneficiaries are likely to find this the most attractive solution.

Finally, as a last resort the personal representatives can apply to the court for directions. This is obviously an expensive option and personal representatives may wonder if the cost can be justified. However, they should apply where the potential liability is large and insurance cover is not available. In the case of *Re Yorke (Deceased), Stone v Chataway* (1997) Lindsay J gave guidance on this subject in the context of possible liability in the estates of deceased Lloyd's Names. He said that, as only a court order can give complete protection, it cannot be wrong for executors of Lloyd's Names to insist upon the protection of a court order.

In *Re K deceased* (2007) the court held that the same approach should be taken in relation to "stale" claims against the estate where it was unclear whether or not the claims were statute barred. The only way in which the personal representatives could obtain complete protection was to apply to the court for directions. For a fuller discussion see para.14-006 and following.

The IHTA 1984 creates several problems for personal representatives. Where a person dies within seven years of making a potentially exempt transfer, the lifetime transfer becomes chargeable. The transferee is primarily liable for the tax, but the personal representatives of the transferor become liable if the tax remains unpaid for 12 months. There is no obligation to report potentially exempt transfers and such transfers may remain undiscovered until after the personal representatives have distributed the assets. Moreover, the discovery of hitherto unknown lifetime transfers will increase the cumulative total of the transferor at the date of death; this may result in the withdrawal of the nil-rate band from all or part of the death estate with a consequent increase in the amount of inheritance tax due.

HMRC identifies undiscovered lifetime gifts as one of the key risk areas for personal representatives. In the IHT Toolkit (Guidance for tax agents and advisers on Inheritance Tax and completing form IHT400 in tax returns) published by HMRC to assist professionals complete the IHT400 identifies the omissions of gifts made as a common risk area for personal representatives and advises making careful enquiries. It says:

> "It is strongly recommended that you check all bank and building society statements for the seven years prior to death to see what transactions have taken place which may be regarded as 'gifting'. We would suggest initially checking at least the previous three years statements; this will provide you with a good indication of the gifting history of the deceased. If you find any withdrawals and transfers which seem unusual in their amount or regularity then you should consider a review of the bank statements for the full seven years.

> Ensure that associates of the deceased, particularly the family, are asked whether they have received anything from the deceased, including gifts for birthdays, Christmas or other religious festivals, and on marriage.
>
> Also check whether the deceased paid for anything on someone else's behalf, for example holidays, bills, or loaned them money which has been waived.
>
> Check whether the deceased owned any property jointly with anybody else. If they did, check whether the contributions to the purchase and other costs matched their respective interests in the property. You will also need to check how the joint owners funded their shares of the purchase price. It is quite common, for example for parents to give their children money to fund the children's shares, and that money is often not declared as a gift.
>
> You need to consider any ancillary costs of the purchase of a joint asset, for example, fees and Stamp Duty. If they were not paid in the same shares, then a gift will have been made.
>
> Check whether the deceased disposed of any property or assets within seven years of their death. If they did, check whether or not they were sold for full market value and the sale proceeds were received by the deceased. If they were not, then the disposal by the deceased may have included some element of gift which you need to tell us about."

It is important to take this guidance seriously as HMRC is very quick to impose penalties on personal representatives who put in inaccurate accounts without due care and, as a result, underpay tax.

Personal representatives who are solicitors acting in the course of their practice may be protected by their insurance. Non-solicitor personal representatives and solicitors who are not acting in the course of their practice have no such protection although it is possible to insure against specific risks.

The Revenue issued the following statement published in *The Law Society's Gazette*, 13 March 1991, the substance is now contained in IHTM 30044:

> "It may be helpful if I say that the capital taxes offices will not usually pursue for inheritance tax personal representatives who:
>
> - after making the fullest enquiries that are reasonably practicable in the circumstances to discover lifetime transfers, and so
> - having done all in their power to make full disclosure of them to the board of Inland Revenue have obtained a certificate of discharge and distributed the estate before a chargeable lifetime transfer comes to light.
>
> This statement of the board's position is made without prejudice to the application in an appropriate case of s.199(2) of the Inheritance Tax Act 1984.
>
> I am writing in similar terms to the Law Society of Scotland.
>
> DY Pitts
>
> Director Capital and Valuation Division, Inland Revenue."

It is clearly important that personal representatives do make adequate enquiries as the above statement only applies where the personal -representatives have made "the fullest enquiries that are reasonably practicable in the circumstances".

Deceased Lloyd's Names

14-007 The well-publicised problems at Lloyd's in the 1980s meant that many Names were faced with unquantifiable losses. To solve the problems Equitas was created. Names waived their claims against Lloyd's and in return received debt and litigation credits and reinsurance of outstanding open years into Equitas. All business for

1992 and prior years of account was reinsured to close with Equitas upon payment of the appropriate premium.

If the resources of Equitas proved inadequate to meet claims, they could be made against the Names (or their estates). This presented a problem for personal representatives who faced the possibility of personal liability if they distributed the estate without providing for this contingent liability.

The Society of Trust and Estates Practitioners brought the test case *Re Yorke (Deceased), Stone v Chataway* (1997) (referred to in para.14-006), hoping that the judgment would remove the need for individual applications to be made for all estates in a similar position. The judgment did not achieve this. It approved the use of Equitas but said that personal representatives would face different levels of risk depending on the circumstances of the case and that they could only obtain full indemnity by applying to court for directions. It was accepted that in appropriate cases, judged to be low risk, personal representatives could take indemnities or rely on insurance.

There is a streamlined form of application available which will be heard by a Master rather than a judge. This is dealt with in Practice Statement, *Chancery Division: Estates of Deceased Lloyd's Names* (2001) which replaced the 1998 Practice Direction.

The Practice Direction contains a specimen witness statement to support the claim form and a specimen draft order although both are likely to need adapting to suit the circumstances of the case.

The risk of liability falling on an estate has been much reduced by two events.

(1) There was a substantial increase in reinsurance cover to Equitas as from 31 March 2006, significantly lowering the risk of default by Equitas.
(2) As from 30 June 2009, all 1992 and prior year non-life business underwritten at Lloyd's by open and closed year Names together with the benefit of substantial reinsurance was transferred to a new company. The transfer binds all policyholders as a matter of UK law meaning that Names, and the personal representatives of deceased Names, no longer have any liability for 1992 and earlier years of account within the European Economic Area (EEA). However the extent to which the Pt VII transfer will be recognised by courts of other overseas jurisdictions in the event that a claim is brought against a Name in that jurisdiction after the transfer takes effect is uncertain. Therefore personal representatives may still wish to make an application to court.

Bankrupt beneficiaries

There is a risk of personal liability for a personal representative who pays a legacy direct to a bankrupt beneficiary rather than the trustee in bankruptcy. **14-008**

When a trustee in bankruptcy is appointed, all property (which is defined very widely in s.436 of the Insolvency Act 1986) belonging to the bankrupt automatically vests in the trustee in bankruptcy. The statutory definition of "property" includes "things in action".

A beneficiary of an estate who is declared bankrupt at a time when the estate is in the process of distribution is entitled to a thing in action—the right to compel due administration of the estate. The benefit of this asset vests in the trustee in the same way as do other assets of the bankrupt. The decision in *Raymond Saul & Co v Holden* (2008) confirmed that the trustee in bankruptcy is entitled to have the assets comprised in the estate distributed to him even if distribution takes place after the beneficiary is discharged from bankruptcy. Personal representatives should, therefore, consider making a bankruptcy search before distribution.

If the beneficiary is already bankrupt at the time of the death the thing in action is "after acquired property". The Insolvency Act 1986 s.333(2) requires a bankrupt to give notice to the trustee in bankruptcy of any after-acquired property. The trustee in bankruptcy may then claim such property by serving notice on the bankrupt.

Where personal representatives are aware that a beneficiary became bankrupt before the time of the deceased's death, they should insist on seeing the bankrupt's notice to the trustee in bankruptcy. They will then need to confirm whether the trustee in bankruptcy has served or intends to serve notice on the bankrupt. The trustee will normally do so in which case the personal representatives must distribute the property to the trustee.

Where personal representatives are not aware that a beneficiary was bankrupt at the date of the testator's death, the position in relation to after-acquired property is not entirely clear. Nineteenth century cases state that someone dealing in good faith with a bankrupt and without notice of the bankruptcy cannot be sued by the trustee in bankruptcy to recover the value of after-acquired property. Section 307(4) of the Insolvency Act 1986 gives protection to persons acquiring property in good faith, for value and without notice of the bankruptcy, but this does not protect personal representatives, as they have not "acquired" the relevant property but have transferred it to the beneficiary. If s.307(4) cannot be relied upon by the personal representatives, they will not obtain a good receipt from the beneficiary and will risk a claim for compensation by the trustee in bankruptcy.

The prudent course is to carry out a bankruptcy-only search in Form K16 at the Land Charges Department of Her Majesty's Land Registry against the name of each beneficiary to whom it is proposed to make a distribution. Registration in the Land Charges Department remains effective for a period of five years. A search should be made immediately before making a distribution to a beneficiary, since a search made at an earlier date would not reveal a bankruptcy order made between the date of the search and the date of the distribution.

Where a beneficiary is resident in another jurisdiction, it may be prudent (depending on the circumstances) to take local advice on the need for the equivalent of bankruptcy searches.

3. Benjamin Orders And Alternatives

14-009 The personal representatives will not be protected by Trustee Act s.27 if they are aware of the rights of a claimant but simply cannot find him. In these circumstances the personal representatives can apply to the court for a *Benjamin Order* permitting them to distribute the estate on the basis of a particular assumption.

For example, in the case from which the order took its name (*Re Benjamin* (1902)), the deceased by his will left a beneficiary a residuary gift. The beneficiary disappeared some nine months before the testator died and despite advertisements the beneficiary did not claim his share of the estate. In the circumstances the court permitted the assets to be distributed as if the beneficiary had predeceased the testator.

The order may allow the estate to be distributed on some other footing. Thus in an unreported case the estate was distributed on the basis that a child who predeceased the testatrix left no child surviving the testatrix. In *Re Gess, Gess v Royal Exchange Assurance* (1942), the administrators of a Polish national, who died domiciled in England, were unable to advertise for Polish claimants against the estate because of the outbreak of war. They knew of some debts and applied for permission to distribute the estate. The court held that they could distribute the estate, after setting aside a fund to meet the known Polish liabilities, without making further inquiries or advertisements on the basis that all the debts and liabilities of the estate had been ascertained.

Naturally there must be some factual basis for the assumption set out in the order so that full inquiries must be made by the personal representatives before the court will grant the order. The court will obviously require evidence. An order may be made without the court inquiring further into the circumstances if it is satisfied that the statutory advertisements have proved unsuccessful in tracing the missing person. The making of the order is not conditional on the personal representatives having complied with the requirements of s.27 as to advertisement and searches; the court will decide what, if any, advertisements ought to be made.

If the assumption on which the order was made proves to be wrong, because the supposedly dead beneficiary is shown to be alive, the beneficiary can claim their share of the assets from the other beneficiaries. However, the personal representatives are relieved of personal liability in these circumstances. Once an order is obtained, the personal representatives need take no further steps to protect themselves.

The drawback to applying for a *Benjamin Order* is that it is an expensive procedure. In *Evans v Westcombe* (1999) the court approved the purchase of an insurance policy to cover the possibility of a missing beneficiary returning as an alternative to seeking a *Benjamin Order*. It said that personal representatives, particularly of small estates, should not be discouraged from seeking practical solutions to difficult administration problems without the expense of resort to the court. The court also said that it did not wish to restrict the use of insurance to cases where the personal representative was not beneficially entitled.

Unfortunately the case also demonstrates the weakness of insurance. It may be difficult to quantify the amount to be insured. In *Evans* the missing beneficiary was entitled to half of the residue. The personal representative, therefore, obtained a policy for just over half the value of the estate. She was not advised to consider the possibility of interest. When the missing beneficiary returned, he demanded interest from the date of distribution of the estate. The court agreed that he was entitled to interest but there were no funds available to pay him. On the facts, the court was willing to relieve the personal representative from liability under the Trustee Act 1925 s.61. She had sought legal advice and shown herself willing to follow it and had been unaware of the possibility of interest.

It would have been preferable for the personal representative in *Evans* to have employed genealogists to trace the missing beneficiary. There have been huge improvements in the techniques used by genealogists and it is unusual for them to be unable to trace a missing beneficiary. In any event most insurance companies will now require evidence from genealogists before they will consider insurance.

It is normally better practice to use a firm which charges an hourly rate rather than one which takes a contingency fee (typically 30 per cent) from the entitlement of the beneficiary. This is because it is the responsibility of personal representatives to identify and then trace the persons entitled to share in the estate. They have no power to authorise third parties to demand part of a beneficiary's entitlement.

The question then arises of whether the costs of the genealogist should fall on the estate generally or on the missing person's share. There is nineteenth century authority that the estate should bear expenses "incidental to the proper performance of duties of personal representatives as personal representatives" (*Sharp v Lush* (1879)) and in *Evans v Westcombe* the court approved the cost of insurance falling on the general estate. RSC Ord.65 r.14B provided that the costs of inquiries to ascertain the person entitled to a share of the estate should fall on that share unless the court directed otherwise. Order 65 was repealed but a modern court would not necessarily find that the position has reverted to *Sharp*. The just result may be that the costs of locating the beneficiaries entitled to a distinct asset or share of the estate should fall on that asset or share. There is probably a difference between ascertaining how many distinct shares there are (cost to fall on the general estate) and then locating the claimants to a share (cost may properly fall on that share).

The safest (but expensive) course is to ask the court for directions. The court may make a *Benjamin Order* (see para.14-009). Alternatively, the court may order that known beneficiaries are entitled to their share of the estate immediately. The practical effect is that the cost of further investigations falls on those who have yet to be traced (see CPR PD40A (Accounts and inquiries) para.7).

4. Put Up or Shut Up Orders

14-010 Personal representatives may encounter a problem if after they have obtained a grant in common form, potential challengers either threaten to bring an action but take no steps or say that they require the personal representatives to re-prove the will in solemn form to establish its validity. They are protected under the Administration of Estates Act 1925 s.27 if they act in good faith. However, if they distribute knowing of allegations that the will is invalid, they leave themselves open to the charge that they are not acting in good faith. In such circumstances the courts have, following *Sherman v Fitzhugh Gates (A Firm)* (2003), developed a practice of making orders similar to *Benjamin* Orders which allow the personal representative to distribute the estate without liability unless the challenger issues proceedings within a stated period. These orders are often referred to as "put up or shut up" orders.

If an order is made the challenger can still bring a claim to revoke the grant and will be entitled to recover assets from the beneficiaries as having wrongly been paid. However, the personal representative will be protected. For an example of such an order being made, see *Cobden-Ramsay v Sutton* (2009). See also, *Re Thomas (Deceased)* (2021), the executor's brother (Gareth) had threatened to bring proceedings for revocation of the grant of probate (on the grounds that the deceased lacked capacity, or for some other unspecified reason) or for provision for minor grandchildren under the Inheritance (Provision for Family and Dependants) Act 1975. Judge Keyser KC directed that, the executor should be free to distribute the estate unless "Gareth shall have brought a claim for revocation of the grant or for relief under the 1975 Act within 28 days".

5. Illegitimate and Adopted Beneficiaries—Children of Unmarried Parents

14-011 The Family Law Reform Act 1987 abolished the concept of illegitimacy. This means that in the case of deaths on or after 4 April 1988 a person may take on the intestacy of a relative even though they, the relative or some person through whom they are related, were born of parents who were not married to each other at any time. In the case of deaths before that date the Family Law Reform Act 1969 gave more limited inheritance rights.

Similarly, references to relationships in wills made after 4 April 1988 are, unless a contrary intention appears, construed as including persons whose parents never married or who are related through such persons.

The statutory protection previously given to personal representatives who distribute an estate in ignorance of such potential beneficiaries has been withdrawn. However, with respect to intestacy only, s.18(2) of the Family Law Reform Act 1987 provides that a person whose father and mother were not married to each other at the time of their birth is presumed not to have been survived by their father or by any person related to them only through their father unless the contrary is shown. In the case of a person who has a second female parent by virtue of s.43 of the Human Fertilisation and Embryology Act, the presumption of predecease is extended to the second female parent or any person related only through the second female parent.

The Children Act 1989 has been amended to provide automatic parental responsibility for an unmarried father or second female parent provided they are named on the birth certificate. They did not previously have parental responsibility. The Inheritance and Trustees' Powers Act 2014 inserted a new sub-s.18(2ZA) into the Family Law Reform Act 1987 which disapplies the s.18(2) presumption where the father or other female parent is registered as the child's parent.

Personal representatives are protected if they distribute an estate in ignorance of an adoption of which they do not have notice. Disappointed beneficiaries can claim their share of the estate from the other beneficiaries but not from the personal representatives. The personal representatives, therefore, need take no special steps to protect themselves. See Adoption and Children Act 2002 s.72.

For a discussion of the implications of the Human Rights Act 1998 and the decision in *Hand v George* (2017) on the rights of adopted and illegitimate children under wills and trusts instruments pre-dating the coming into force of the relevant legislation see para.17-023.

6. THE PERSONAL REPRESENTATIVES' LIABILITY IN RESPECT OF THE DECEASED'S LEASEHOLDS

General

On death, a leasehold interest held by the deceased devolves on their personal representatives by operation of law, whether or not they enter into possession of the premises. The nature of their liability for rent or breach of covenants depends on whether their liability is: **14-012**

(a) representative, that is deriving from their office; or
(b) personal, that is arising when they enter into possession of the premises as assignees of the deceased's interest.

Representative liability

The personal representatives are liable as the deceased's personal representatives for rent due, and any breach committed prior to the death as well as for rent due and breaches committed from death to the expiry, or assignment of the lease (unless the deceased was the original lessee in which case the personal representatives are liable until the expiry of the lease irrespective of any assignment). **14-013**

In their representative capacity the personal representatives are liable to discharge any liability on a lease to the extent of the assets of the deceased which they have received. If the deceased was an assignee of the lease, the personal representatives can end their liability by surrendering or assigning the lease. If the deceased was the original lessee, assignment will not end their liability.

The Trustee Act 1925 s.26, however, protects the personal representatives from further liability once they have assigned (this protection cannot be excluded by the terms of the will). Section 26 as amended provides that the personal representatives will not be liable for a future claim if they do three things:

(a) satisfy all existing liabilities under the lease which may have accrued and been claimed up to the date of the conveyance to a purchaser or beneficiary;
(b) where necessary, set apart a fund to meet any future claims that may be made in respect of any fixed and ascertained sum which the lessee agreed to lay out on the demised premises, although the period for so doing may not have arrived; and
(c) assign the lease to a purchaser, legatee, devisee, or other person entitled to call for a conveyance.

Thereafter the personal representatives may distribute the deceased's residuary real and personal estate to or amongst the persons entitled thereto without setting aside a fund to meet any future liability under the lease and the personal representatives will not be personally liable in respect of any subsequent claim under the lease.

The lessor can follow the assets of the estate into the hands of the beneficiaries and claim payment from the assets or their proceeds (s.26(2)).

Personal liability

14-014 Personal liability arises when the personal representatives enter into possession, whether physically or constructively (for example, by receiving rent from a sub-tenant). The personal representatives are then personally liable for the rent and for any breaches of covenant arising while the lease is vested in them as assignees of the deceased's interest. As the personal representatives are not the original lessees, liability ceases once the personal representatives assign their interest.

Oddly, there are different limits on the extent of the personal representatives' personal liability. For rent, the liability is limited to the amount actually received (or that which with reasonable diligence might have been received) during their period as assignees (*Rendall v Andreae* (1892)). For breaches of other covenants the personal representatives are liable without limit.

The personal representatives have no protection under s.26 against *personal* liability; they should either obtain an indemnity from the beneficiaries or create an indemnity fund from the estate. This fund will be distributed to the beneficiaries once the personal representatives cease to be personally liable, for example, as a result of assigning the lease or termination. Such a fund may be unpopular with the beneficiaries who are likely to prefer an immediate distribution of property. It is, therefore, modern practice to insure against this liability, thus reducing the drain on the estate's assets.

7. LIABILITY FOR ACTS OF AGENTS

14-015 The Trustee Act 2000 s.11 gives trustees and personal representatives wide powers to appoint agents (and nominees and custodians under ss.16 and 17). The appointment can be on such terms as they see fit subject to the limitations contained in ss.14(3) and 20(3). They have to comply with the requirements of s.15 if they wish to delegate their asset management functions.

Section 23 provides that they are not liable for any act or default of the agents, nominees or custodians unless they failed to comply with the statutory duty of care:

(a) when making the appointment; or
(b) when reviewing the appointment as required by s.22.

8. The Six-Month Time Limit

The Inheritance (Provision for Family and Dependants) Act 1975 s.20 (see paras 20-003 and 20-004) gives personal representatives protection provided they wait until the expiry of six months from the grant of representation before distributing the estate, if the court then permits an out-of-time application to be made. **14-016**

Similarly, if the personal representatives wait for the same period before distributing the estate, they suffer no personal liability if the court then makes an order permitting an out-of-time application to have the deceased's will rectified under s.20 of the Administration of Justice Act 1982. However in neither case are the successful applicants denied the right to recover assets from the beneficiaries who received them from the personal representatives.

Personal representatives are, therefore, wise to wait six months from the grant before distributing the estate.

Where a claim form is issued under the Inheritance (Provision for Family and Dependants) Act 1975 within six months of the date of the grant, claimants have four months under the Civil Procedure Rules in which to serve the form. It is, therefore, arguable that personal representatives should wait ten months from the date of the grant before distributing as the protection of s.20 is only available where the court gives permission for an out-of-time application. It will be rare for claimants not to communicate *at all* with personal representatives before serving the claim form but it is possible. Personal representatives should, therefore, consider all the circumstances before deciding whether or not to delay distribution.

9. Administration Proceedings for Specific Relief

As we have seen, if the personal representatives distribute the estate to the wrong person or become liable for some expense that was not properly incurred for the benefit of the estate, they are (unless specifically protected) personally liable to make good any loss. **14-017**

In cases of doubt, prudent personal representatives will apply to the court (Chancery Division or county court where the net estate does not exceed in amount or value the county court limit, at present £350,000). Applications are made under CPR r.64.2.

It is possible to apply for a general "administration order". This means that the whole administration is carried out under the direction of the court. This is an expensive and time-consuming process and the court will only make such an order if it considers that the issues between the parties cannot properly be resolved in any other way.

It is much more common to ask the court to determine a specific question. CPR PD64A (Estates, Trusts and Charities) gives the following examples of claims which may be made:

"(1) *a claim for the determination of any of the following questions—*
  (a) any question as to who is included in any class of persons having:
    (i) a claim against the estate of a deceased person;
    (ii) a beneficial interest in the estate of such a person; or
    (iii) beneficial interest in any property subject to a trust;
  (b) any question as to the rights or interests of any person claiming:
    (i) to be a creditor of the estate of a deceased person;
    (ii) to be entitled under a will or on the intestacy of a deceased person; or
    (iii) to be beneficially entitled under a trust;
(2) *a claim for any of the following remedies—*
  (a) an order requiring a trustee—
    (i) to provide and, if necessary, verify accounts;
    (ii) to pay into court money which he holds in that capacity; or
    (iii) to do or not to do any particular act;
  (b) an order approving any sale, purchase, compromise or other -transaction by a trustee; or
  (c) an order directing any act to be done which the court could order to be done if the estate or trust in question were being administered or executed under the direction of the court."

Actions are brought in the Chancery Division by issuing a Pt 8 claim form. All the personal representatives must be made parties and any persons with an interest in or claim against the estate can be made a party if it is appropriate, having regard to the nature of the order sought. The trustees will be expected to have canvassed all the adult beneficiaries about the proposed or possible courses of action before applying for directions and to set out the details of the consultation undertaken in their witness statements.

The costs incurred by *all* the parties involved in the action for specific relief are usually paid from the estate or trust fund provided it can be shown that there was a problem which justified the application being made. The trustees or the party concerned may apply to the court at any stage of proceedings for an order that the costs of any party (including the costs of the trustees) shall be paid out of the fund (a "prospective costs order").

10. Administration of Justice Act 1985 s.48

14-018 Where there is doubt as to the construction of a will, s.48 allows the High Court, without hearing any argument, to authorise personal representatives or trustees to act in reliance on a written opinion of a barrister of at least 10-years' standing. The court will not make such an order if there is any dispute as to the construction since it would then be inappropriate to make an order without hearing argument. This provision allows a speedy resolution of difficulties of administration. The order will protect the personal representatives from any action for breach of duty.

The court order permits trustees or personal representatives to proceed on the basis of the accepted construction of the trust deed. It protects them against a claim that they have been wrongly administering the trust or estate, but it does not bind the beneficiaries, who are free to contend that a different construction was the right one (see *Re BCA Pension Trustees Ltd* (2015)).

The will or trust instrument may authorise the personal representatives or trustees to proceed on the opinion of a more junior barrister and/or without making an application to court. This is a sensible provision to include in a will as it may secure a significant costs saving. The STEP Standard Provisions 2nd and 3rd edition relieve trustees from liability if they act in accordance with the advice of counsel, of at least five years' standing, and provides that they may conduct legal proceedings in accordance with such advice without obtaining a court order.

CHAPTER FIFTEEN

THE PAYMENT OF DEBTS

1. INTRODUCTION

Personal representatives have a duty to pay the debts of the deceased and must do so with due diligence (*Re Tankard* (1942)). Different rules as to the payment of debts apply depending on whether an estate is solvent or insolvent. **15-001**

2. THE SOLVENT ESTATE

What is a solvent estate?

An estate is solvent when the assets are sufficient to pay funeral, testamentary and administration expenses and debts and other liabilities in full. Provided these can be paid, it is irrelevant that legacies cannot be paid in full. The beneficiaries of the estate will be concerned to know which assets of the estate will be used in payment of the debts and which will be available for distribution. **15-002**

Section 34(3) of the Administration of Estates Act 1925 provides that assets shall be taken in the order set out in Pt II of the First Schedule to the Act. However, special rules apply where property of the deceased was charged during the deceased's lifetime with payment of a debt. This situation will be considered first.

Debts charged on property

Introduction

Where a debt has been charged on property of the deceased *during the lifetime of the deceased* (for example, a mortgage debt charged on the deceased's house) Administration of Estates Act 1925 s.35 provides that such property will be primarily liable for payment of that debt. Thus, a beneficiary who accepts the property must accept it subject to the mortgage. The deceased may exclude s.35 by showing a contrary intention in the will, a deed or other document. A charge is usually expressly created by the deceased but may also arise by operation of law; for example an HMRC charge for unpaid tax or a charge imposed by the court on land belonging to a judgment debtor. **15-003**

The case of *Re Birmingham* (1959) illustrates the difference between a simple debt and a debt charged on property. T agreed to buy Blackacre from V for £3,500; contracts were exchanged and T paid a deposit of £350. T died before completion. In her will T left Blackacre to her daughter, D, and the residue to R. T's solicitors completed the purchase of Blackacre. The court held that D took Blackacre subject to an unpaid vendor's lien for the balance of the purchase price. However, the solicitor's costs were to be paid from the general estate since at the time of T's death they were not charged on Blackacre.

Several properties charged with one debt

15-004 If several properties are charged as security for one debt, each property bears a proportionate part of the debt (s.35(1)) and thus, if each property is given to a different beneficiary, each beneficiary will take his property subject to a charge for a proportionate part of the debt. This is so even if some of the properties are specifically given by the will while some merely pass as part of the residue. In *Re Neeld* (1962) the Court of Appeal said that in such a case the testator is not to be presumed to have thrown the whole debt on to the properties comprised in the residue.

Separate debts

15-005 Where separate properties are charged with separate debts and the debt charged on one property exceeds the value of that property the amount of the deficit will be made up from the deceased's general estate and not from the other charged properties. This will be so even if all the charged properties are given to one beneficiary (*Re Holt, Holt v Holt* (1916)). The only exception is where the testator makes it clear that a gift of several different properties is one gift the whole of which is to be treated as charged with several different debts. In that case the deficit will be made up from the other charged properties (*Re Kensington* (1902)).

The rights of creditors

15-006 Section 35 is only concerned with competition amongst beneficiaries as to the property to be used to pay debts. It does not affect the rights of creditors. A secured creditor may be paid by the personal representatives from the general estate instead of from the charged property; if this happens the doctrine of marshalling will apply as between the beneficiaries so that ultimately the debt falls on the charged property (see para.15-022).

Options to purchase

15-007 A testator may give an option to purchase a property in the will. The option may be at an undervalue but even so the person exercising it will be treated as taking the property as a purchaser not as a beneficiary. A purchaser is entitled to have any debt charged on the property paid off from the general estate (*Re Fison's Will Trusts* (1950)) so that they will take the property free from any debt charged on the property. This case also summarises case law on the principles applying where property subject to an option to purchase changes its nature between death and the date for exercise, for example where a company is taken over or liquidated. Broadly speaking where the option is at a stated price as opposed to a mere pre-emption right, there is an element of bounty and the option can be exercised at the stated price against the substituted property.

Contrary intention

Methods of showing contrary intention

Section 35 may be varied if the testator shows a contrary intention. Contrary intention is not shown by a simple direction in the will (or any other document) that debts be paid from *residue*; such a direction is to be construed as relating only to debts other than those charged on particular items (s.35(2)(a) and (b)). An additional indication of intention is required. Thus a gift of specific property *free from the debt* charged on it will suffice; as will an express direction that a mortgage or other charge be paid from residue. Less obviously, if a testator directs that debts be paid from a special fund (*other than residue*) the direction will be construed as extending to all debts including those charged on specific items of property. **15-008**

For example, if a testator has a mortgage debt charged on Blackacre and in their will directs that:

> "[M]y debts be paid from the proceeds of sale of my shares in X company and the residue of my estate be held for A",

all the testator's debts including the mortgage debt will be paid from the proceeds of sale. If the special fund is insufficient to pay off all debts, any unsatisfied balance of a charged debt will remain charged on the property and will not be paid from the general estate (*Re Fegan* (1928)).

A contrary intention need not be expressed in the will. In *Re Ross* (2005) the deceased made a homemade will which included a gift in the following terms "I leave devise and bequeath my apartment and contents thereof to my friend Irene Perrin-Hughes ...". At the date of the will the apartment was subject to a mortgage. The deceased was also paying premiums on an endowment policy taken out at the same time as the mortgage was arranged and for the same amount as the mortgage. Towards the end of his life, the deceased had increased his monthly payments under the policy so as to ensure that there would be sufficient funds to discharge the mortgage debt. On these facts the judge found that the deceased intended at the time when he made the will that the gift should be free of mortgage even though this was not expressly referred to in the will. Consequently s.35 applied.

For a recent example of the application of s.35 see *Petterson v Ross* (2013) where a beneficiary was given a property charged with a debt which was expressed to be free of mortgage. The residuary beneficiaries wanted the-mortgage to be discharged from the charged property. Unsurprisingly the court did not agree.

Taking instructions

When drafting a will for a client, always inquire whether there are any debts charged on property. If there are, ask whether or not the client wishes such debts to be paid from the general residue and draft the will accordingly. **15-009**

It is important to draft the will appropriately. In *Pierce v Barton* (2023) the deceased had bought a leasehold flat for his adult son, Paul, to live in the property was registered in Paul's name but with a charge in the father's favour for the purchase price of £87,727.52. This was because Paul had issues with alcohol and substance abuse, and the father wanted to prevent him from either selling or mortgaging the property to raise funds for these purposes.

The father wanted his will to release the charge on the property but the will was drafted to leave "Flat 2, , Weston-super-Mare North Somerset BS23 2DX free of all taxes".

The wording of the will was not appropriate. The problem was that the clause gave the flat to Paul, but Paul was already the registered proprietor of the leasehold interest while the deceased was the registered proprietor of the charge over the flat. Because the clause was ambiguous in the light of surrounding circumstances it was possible to admit extrinsic evidence, including evidence of the testator's intention, to assist in its interpretation: Administration of Justice Act 1982 s.21. For admissibility of extrinsic evidence generally see Ch.17.

Mortgage protection policies

15-010 The most common example of a debt charged on property during the deceased's lifetime is a mortgage. A client who wishes to make a will should be asked about their mortgage arrangements so that they can consider from what source the mortgage debt is to be paid. It is, however, common for mortgagors to take out a life policy to meet their mortgage borrowing. This is a life assurance policy which, on the mortgagor's death, pays either a fixed amount (equal to the original loan) or an amount sufficient to pay off the amount of the loan outstanding at the date of death (i.e. a reducing amount). If the proceeds are to be paid to the estate of the mortgagor they will increase the size of the estate for inheritance tax purposes. The policy may, however, be written in trust for a named beneficiary or assigned to the lender, in which case the proceeds will be paid to that person and will not increase the size of the deceased's estate for inheritance tax purposes.

If two people are buying property jointly they normally each take out such a policy. The terms of the policy may state that the proceeds are to be paid to the surviving joint tenant to the exclusion of the estate of the deceased; if no such statement is included the parties may write each policy in trust for the other. A solicitor, drafting a will, should inquire whether such a policy exists and, if one does, should make sure that the client takes it into account when deciding what directions to leave as to the payment of the mortgage debt.

If the client has bought a house in his or her sole name and has a mortgage protection policy which has not been assigned to the lender, it is clearly desirable for the client to leave the proceeds of the policy to the person who is taking the property subject to the mortgage, so that there will be funds available to that beneficiary for the discharge of the mortgage debt.

The statutory order for unsecured debts

Introduction

15-011 The deceased may make express provision for the payment of debts. In the absence of such provision the statutory order of application of assets applies and is set out in Pt II of the First Schedule to the Administration of Estates Act. It is as follows:

(1) Property of the deceased undisposed of by will, subject to the retention thereout of a fund sufficient to meet any pecuniary legacies.
(2) Property of the deceased not specifically devised or bequeathed but included (either by a specific or general description) in a residuary gift, subject to the

retention thereout of a fund sufficient to meet any pecuniary legacies, so far as not already provided for.

(3) Property of the deceased given for the payment of debts.
(4) Property of the deceased charged with the payment of debts.
(5) The fund, if any, retained to meet pecuniary legacies.
(6) Property specifically devised or bequeathed, rateably according to value.
(7) Property appointed by will under a general power (including the statutory power to dispose of entailed interests) rateably according to value.

Undisposed of property

Such property may arise where a will does not deal with all the assets of the deceased (i.e. where there is no residuary gift); it may also arise where a residuary gift fails wholly (i.e. where the residuary beneficiary predeceases the testator) or partly (i.e. where residue is given to two or more beneficiaries in *equal shares or equally* and one or more of the beneficiaries predeceases the testator, the share of the predeceased beneficiary lapses and passes to the testator's next-of-kin). Before debts are paid from the undisposed of property a fund is set on one side for payment of any pecuniary legacies. **15-012**

Residue

Any general gift of property, not comprised in a specific bequest or devise, will be a residuary gift. Thus in *Re Wilson* (1967) T made some specific and pecuniary legacies and then gave "all my real estate and the residue of my personal estate". Pennycuick J held that T's devise of realty fell within para.(2) despite the fact that there was no prior specific devise. Before any debts are paid from residue, a fund is set on one side for payment of pecuniary legacies to the extent that sufficient property was not set aside from any undisposed-of property. **15-013**

Property specifically given for or charged with payment of debts

Property is specifically *given* for payment of debts where a testator *directs in the will* that it be used for this purpose and leaves no directions as to what is to happen to any balance left over after the debts are paid, for example, "my debts are to be paid from the proceeds of my premium bonds". **15-014**

Property is *charged* with payment of debts when a testator *directs in the will* that it be used for this purpose and directs that any balance left over after the debts are paid be given to a particular beneficiary; for example "my debts are to be paid from the proceeds of sale of my shares in A Co and any balance is to go to X" or "I give X the proceeds of sale of my shares in A Co subject to payment of debts". This is quite different from the "charge" referred to in s.35 which deals with debts charged during the deceased's lifetime on particular assets. In the case of s.34 the assets were unencumbered *during the deceased's lifetime* and the charge is imposed by the will.

The retained pecuniary legacy fund

A fund will have been set on one side from the undisposed of property and/or residue to meet pecuniary legacies; if necessary that fund (or part of it) is taken to pay debts. Pecuniary legacies abate proportionally unless the deceased directed that certain legacies be paid in priority to the others. **15-015**

"Pecuniary legacy" is defined widely in s.55(1)(ix) of the Administration of Estates Act 1925 to include an annuity, a general legacy and a demonstrative legacy in so far as not discharged out of designated property (for classification of legacies see paras 16-002–16-008).

Property specifically devised or bequeathed rateably according to value

15-016 The order makes no distinction between devises (gifts of land) and bequests (gifts of personalty); both are equally available.

(a) *Value means value to the testator.* Thus a mortgage charged on the property would be deducted when calculating the value of the property but a legacy charged on the property by the testator in the will would not (*Re John* (1933)).

Example 1

Tim owns Blackacre, value £10,000 but subject to a mortgage of £4,000. Tim owns Whiteacre, value £10,000. Tim's will gives Blackacre to Bob and Whiteacre to Will but charges Whiteacre with payment to Lucia of a legacy of £6,000. There are debts to pay of £2,000 (apart from the mortgage) and no other assets. Blackacre had a value to Tim of £6,000 (£10,000 – £4,000). Whiteacre had a value to Tim of £10,000. Therefore:

Blackacre bears 6,000/16,000 £2,000 = £750 of the debts
Whiteacre bears 10,000/16,000 £2,000 = £1,250 of the debts

In addition Blackacre is charged with payment of the mortgage (unless the will directed otherwise) and Whiteacre with payment of the legacy.

(b) *Option to purchase.* A will may give a person an option to purchase property at a stated price. This price may well be at an undervalue in which case the will gives the "purchaser" a benefit. The personal representatives may wonder whether such property is available for payment of debts as if it were a specific gift.

In *Re Eve* (1956) Roxburgh J directed that when personal representatives were calculating what property to use for payment of debts they should not regard property subject to an option to purchase as equivalent to a specific gift of that property. They should first calculate whether once the purchase price for the property was paid there would be sufficient assets to meet all the debts of the testator. If there would, the purchaser is free to exercise the option and will purchase the property subject to the option. If there would not, the option cannot be exercised and the personal representatives must take the property and use it for payment of debts. Roxburgh J concluded that:

> "the property subject to an option is the last to be available for the payment of debts. For, indeed, in so far as the property subject to the option is required for the payment of debts, the option over the property cannot be exercised at all and the benefit of it is totally destroyed by the operation of law".

Property appointed under a general power of appointment

15-017 Where the testator has a general power of appointment (that is, a power to appoint property to anyone the testator pleases) and exercises the power expressly in the will, such property is taken last for payment of debts.

Section 27 of the Wills Act 1837 provides that where a testator has a general power of appointment which is not exercised expressly in the will it is deemed (subject to a contrary intention in the will) to have been exercised by any general gift contained in the will. Thus, for example, if X has a general power of appointment over Blackacre but makes no mention of the power or of Blackacre in the will a general gift of "all the rest of my property" or "all my realty" would be sufficient to dispose of Blackacre. However, if (as a result of s.27) property is included in a general gift it will be treated as available for payment of debts as part of residue not as property subject to a general power.

Property outside the statutory order

Property subject to a *donatio mortis causa* or to a statutory nomination is available for payment of debts but is not mentioned in the statutory order. It would, therefore, be taken after all the other assets were exhausted. According to *Re Eve*, if a testator gives a person an option to purchase property at an undervalue the property subject to the option is taken to pay debts when it is necessary to do so because all other assets are exhausted, and not otherwise. It is, however, impossible to say in what order assets subject to an option to purchase, *donatio mortis causa* or nomination would be taken as between themselves. **15-018**

Variation of the statutory order

A gift of residue "subject to" or "after" payment of debts

A testator has a right to vary the statutory order. There are two ways in which this is commonly done. **15-019**

If residue is given to several beneficiaries in equal shares and one of those beneficiaries predeceases the testator that share of residue lapses and becomes undisposed of property. Undisposed of property is normally taken first for payment of debts and any balance will then be available to the testator's next-of-kin. If, however, the testator directs that residue be taken *after* payment of debts (or gives the residue *subject* to payment of debts) that is construed as an express direction that debts be paid from the whole residue before it is divided into shares. Thus, the living beneficiaries and the testator's next-of-kin will bear a proportionate part of the debt and will, therefore, receive a proportionate share in the balance.

Example 2

(a) *No contrary intention.* Tuli gives certain specific bequests and leaves the residue to Aaron and Bill in equal shares. Bill predeceases Tuli. The estate, after setting aside the specific bequests but before paying debts and other liabilities, amounts to £20,000. Debts amount to £8,000. Bill's lapsed share amounts to £10,000. The debts will be paid from that lapsed share leaving a balance of £2,000 available to Tuli's next-of-kin. Aaron will take £10,000.

(b) *Contrary intention.* The same situation but Tuli leaves the residue *after payment of debts* to Aaron and Bill in equal shares. The debts must be paid from the £20,000 before it is divided into shares. £12,000 will be left after payment of debts and this will be divided equally between Aaron and Tuli's next-of-kin. Aaron will, therefore, take £6,000 and Tuli's next-of-kin will take £6,000.

Property "given for" or "charged with" payment of debts—intention to exonerate residue

15-020 If a testator merely gives property for or charges property with payment of debts this will not in itself be sufficient to vary the statutory order. Such property will merely fall within paras (3) or (4) of the statutory order (i.e. property specifically given or charged with payment of debts) and will, prima facie, be taken after property within paras (1) and (2) of the statutory order (i.e. undisposed of property and residue) is exhausted. However, if the will shows an intention to exonerate the property which would otherwise be taken first, this will vary the statutory order. It has been held that where a will contains a gift of residue to a beneficiary together with a direction that debts be paid from a specified fund this shows an intention to exonerate the residue and the statutory order will be varied.

In *Re James* (1947), for example, the testator charged certain specific property with payment of debts and gave the residue to his wife. Roxburgh J held that the will showed a clear intention to exonerate the residue and therefore the debts would be paid from the charged property.

Conversely in *Re Gordon* (1940) a testatrix directed that her debts be paid from a sum of £50 and any balance remaining be paid to a named charity. There was no gift of residue. It was held that the statutory order was not varied as there was no indication of an intention to exonerate other property; therefore, the debts were to be paid from the undisposed of property and the £50 was to be paid in full to the charity.

Presumably any form of words could be used in a will to show an intention to exonerate other property. Thus in *Re Gordon* had T expressly declared that debts were to be paid from the £50 "in exoneration of any undisposed of property" the result would have been different.

Desirability of making express provision for payment of debts

15-021 When drafting a will it is desirable to discuss with the testator the possibility of making express provision for the payment of debts since this will allow a testator to consider the question of debts and to make his own decision as to the property to be used.

The doctrine of marshalling

15-022 If a personal representative takes assets falling within one of the later paragraphs in the statutory order to pay debts before assets falling within the earlier paragraphs are exhausted, the creditors will be entirely unconcerned. Creditors merely want payment; the source of the payment is irrelevant to them. A beneficiary, on the other hand, will be very concerned if property which that beneficiary hopes to take is wrongly used to pay debts. Marshalling is a way of adjusting the assets so as to compensate a disappointed beneficiary where a payment has been made from the wrong assets.

Example 3

Eda is administering the estate of Thea. Thea's will left her shares in ABC Ltd (value £2,000) to Spiro and the residue of the estate to Ravi (the residue consists of land worth £20,000). There is a debt of £2,000 to pay. The debt should be paid from residue. If Eda uses the shares to pay the creditor, Spiro will be disappointed.

However, Spiro can be compensated from property falling within any of the earlier paragraphs. Spiro is therefore entitled to £2,000 from the residuary assets.

For a recent example of marshalling see *Petterson v Ross* (2013). As explained at para.15-008, a property charged with a mortgage was specifically given free of mortgage. The mortgage company repossessed the property and discharged the debt from the proceeds of sale. The court held that the specific beneficiary was entitled to compensate herself from the property that ought to have been used, the residue.

3. INSOLVENT ESTATES

Introduction

An estate is insolvent if the assets are insufficient to pay all the funeral, testamentary and administration expenses, debts and liabilities. The beneficiaries of the deceased's will or the deceased's next-of-kin under the intestacy rules will receive nothing and the creditors of the estate will not all be paid in full. **15-023**

The administration of insolvent estates is governed by the Administration of Insolvent Estates of Deceased Person Order 1986 (SI 1986/1999) (the 1986 Order). The 1986 Order creates some difficulties because, instead of containing a complete code applicable to insolvent estates of deceased persons, it contains numerous paragraphs that "modify" the provisions of the Insolvency Act 1986 that apply to living debtors. Thus, in order to access the law in relation to insolvent deceased estates, it is necessary to look at two sources of legislation. Unfortunately it is often not clear how the modifications take effect.

See, for example *Re Vos* (2006) (discussed at para.15-028) where the court had to decide how the relating back rule applies where a trustee in bankruptcy is appointed to deal with an insolvent estate after a grant has been taken out. The court decided that the appointment relates back to the date of death meaning that all the actions of the personal representative are void unless ratified by the court as being in the best interests of the estate.

Another example is *Re Estate of Platon Elenin (Boris Abramovich Berezovsky)* (2015) which considered the correct interpretation of the 1986 Order in a £40 million bankruptcy where there was disagreement as to the date on which debts were valued. The court confirmed that assets and liabilities are identified and quantified at the date of death not the date the insolvency administration order was made.

Berry v Child Support Agency (2016) revealed a further problem. The 1986 Order does not appear to make provision for the payment of liabilities such as arrears of child support which are not provable in a bankruptcy because they survive the discharge of the bankrupt. However, having described the legislation as "something of a conundrum" Judge McCahill QC interpreted art.4(1) of the 1986 Order in such a way that the estate had to meet the liability.

Methods of administering an insolvent estate

Introduction

There are three methods of administering an insolvent estate: **15-024**

1. The most economic and straightforward method is for the deceased's personal representatives to do so under a normal grant of representation. Creditors are entitled to take a grant. If a creditor wants to administer and those entitled in priority will neither renounce nor get on with the job, the creditor can use the citation process to try and clear them off or apply to the registrar to pass them over under the Senior Courts Act 1981 s.116. There is no need for the person appointed to be a qualified insolvency practitioner (1986 Order art.4(3)).
2. It is possible for the court to take over the administration by making an administration order under CPR Pt 64. This means that the personal representatives act under the direction of the court. The courts are not anxious to undertake such a role and professional advisers rarely consider this route.
3. The other alternative is for the estate to be administered by a trustee in bankruptcy following an insolvency administration order made by the bankruptcy court. Creditors or personal representatives can petition and in either case the order vests the estate in the Official Receiver. Subsequently a trustee in bankruptcy will be appointed. The creditors will normally appoint the trustee in bankruptcy and the creditors' committee.

In general, it does not matter whether the estate is administered by a trustee in bankruptcy or by the deceased's personal representatives. The 1986 Order art.4(1) provides that, whether the estate is administered by a trustee in bankruptcy or by the deceased's personal representatives, the same rules apply to:

(a) the respective rights of creditors;
(b) provable debts;
(c) the valuation of future and contingent liabilities; and
(d) the priority of debts.

However, there are certain situations where a trustee in bankruptcy has advantages. Where the personal representatives start the administration, an application can be made for a trustee in bankruptcy take over. A trustee in bankruptcy has the following additional powers.

Challenging lifetime transactions for the benefit of the estate

15-025 A trustee can challenge transactions:

(a) under the Insolvency Act 1986 s.339 if made at an undervalue within "the relevant time" (two years ending with death or five years if the deceased was insolvent at the time or became so as a result of the transaction: Insolvency Act 1986 s.341 as modified by the 1986 Order);
(b) under the Insolvency Act 1986 s.423 if made at an undervalue for the purpose of putting assets beyond the reach of creditors; and
(c) under the Insolvency Act 1986 ss.340–342 which have preferred some creditors at the expense of others.

Personal representatives are not entitled to bring proceedings to set aside any preference or transaction at an undervalue; if there are grounds for taking such action, that would be a reason for presenting an insolvency administration petition to allow a trustee in bankruptcy to be appointed and pursue such claims.

Disclaiming onerous property

A trustee can disclaim onerous property even if he/she has gone into possession, attempted to sell it or in some other way exercised rights of ownership (Insolvency Act 1986 s.315). Onerous property is defined in s.315 as any: **15-026**

(a) unprofitable contract; and
(b) property in the deceased's estate which is unsaleable or not readily saleable, or is such that it may give rise to a liability to pay money or perform any other onerous act.

For example, therefore, any lease which contains covenants on the part of the tenant can be disclaimed.

Dealing with the deceased's dwelling house

Other people may have an interest in assets of the deceased (typically a spouse in the matrimonial home). Personal representatives and trustees in bankruptcy can apply to the court for an order for sale. Where the application is first made by the trustee in bankruptcy more than 12 months after the deceased's property vested in them, the court will assume, unless there are exceptional circumstances, that the interests of the creditors outweigh all other considerations (Insolvency Act 1986 s.335A(3)). Where the application is made by personal representatives, there is no such assumption so they may have more difficulty. There is a limit of three years on the period during which the trustee in bankruptcy can deal with a bankrupt's interest in a dwelling house which is the sole or principal dwelling house of the bankrupt, the bankrupt's spouse, civil partner or a former spouse or civil partner (Insolvency Act 1986 s.283A). **15-027**

It is possible for personal representatives to apply for the appointment of a trustee in bankruptcy if it becomes apparent that there are reasons justifying it at any stage of the administration.

Dangers for professionals when estate insolvent

It is important to consider the position as to payment of professional charges where an estate is insolvent. The rules for ordinary personal representatives have changed as a result of the Trustee Act 2000 s.35(3)(b). A solicitor's charges whether made under an express charging clause or under the statutory power contained in s.28 are no longer regarded as a legacy but as "administration expenses". As such they have priority over the preferential debts listed in the Insolvency Act 1986. **15-028**

A trustee in bankruptcy can charge for his or her services and again the charges will be administration expenses and have priority over preferential debts.

Professionals appointed as executor should bear in mind that, although administration expenses have priority, the estate may be too small to cover them. Therefore, if there is a chance that an estate will be insolvent, it is important to assess the risk before committing a substantial amount of time to the estate. Professional executors and, indeed, other executors, may want to renounce. It is important not to intermeddle in an estate which may be insolvent.

There is also a danger that if a trustee in bankruptcy is appointed, during the administration, the professional's charges may not be ratified by the court: see para.15-028.

Where personal representatives are administering an estate which is (or may turn out to be) insolvent it is important that they observe the correct order for payment of creditors. This is:

(a) funeral, testamentary and administration expenses; and then
(b) the bankruptcy order.

This order cannot be varied by the testator. If the personal representatives do not follow the statutory order they will incur personal liability for "superior" debts which have been left unpaid. Therefore, if there is any possibility that an estate may be insolvent the personal representatives should observe the statutory order when paying debts.

Where a trustee in bankruptcy is appointed under an insolvency order, the appointment relates back to the date of death. Hence, payments made between death and the order are void unless ratified by the court (Insolvency Act 1986 s.284, as modified by the 1986 Order). Solicitors acting in relation to the administration should be careful about running up legal expenses unless they are clearly for the benefit of the estate as the court will not ratify unnecessary expenses. See *Re Vos; Dick v Kendall Freeman* (2006), where the court disallowed a significant portion of the solicitor's costs incurred in litigation which the court considered was clearly not for the benefit of the estate.

Assets and liabilities

Introduction

15-029 When a living person is declared bankrupt there are special rules of bankruptcy which swell the bankrupt's assets. These rules also apply to an insolvent estate by virtue of the 1986 Order. The same Order provides that where a bankruptcy petition is presented and then the debtor dies, the bankruptcy proceedings may continue despite the death of the debtor.

All debts and liabilities, present or future, certain and contingent, liquidated or unliquidated are provable against an insolvent estate. If the value of a liability is uncertain (because it is contingent or for any other reason) its value must be estimated (Insolvency Act 1986). A debt which is statute-barred is not provable where the estate is insolvent.

Availability of joint property

15-030 A Court of Appeal decision (*Re Palmer (Deceased) (A Debtor)* (1994)) held that jointly held property passed to the co-owner on death as usual and was not available to the administrator of the estate.

The effect of this decision was reversed by a new s.421A inserted into the Insolvency Act 1986 by the Insolvency Act 2000 s.12. The trustee in bankruptcy of a deceased insolvent can now apply to the court to recover the value of the deceased's former interest in joint property from the survivor for the benefit of the estate. The trustee in bankruptcy can only make the application where the petition for the insolvency order is presented after 2 April 2001 and within five years from the date of death. When deciding whether or not to make the order the court must have regard to all the circumstances of the case including the interests of the creditors and the surviving joint tenant. Unless the circumstances are exceptional, the court must assume that the interests of the creditors outweigh all other considerations.

Note that the application must be made by a trustee in bankruptcy so, where the deceased was a joint tenant, this will be a reason for creditors to petition for an insolvency administration order appointing a trustee.

Secured creditors

A creditor may have security for a debt; for example a bank may have given a loan to the deceased and taken a charge over the deceased's house or other assets as security. Such a creditor has a choice. **15-031**

(a) The creditor may rely on their security and not prove for their debt at all. This is a safe course provided the security is sufficient to cover the debt.
(b) The creditor may realise the security and if the security is inadequate prove for any balance as an unsecured creditor.
(c) The creditor may value the security and prove for any balance as an unsecured creditor. Care must be taken in such a valuation. If the creditor puts too low a value on the security the personal representatives can insist on redeeming it at that value leaving him to prove as an unsecured creditor for the balance. If they put too high a value on it and prove as an-unsecured creditor for the balance, they will prove for an insufficient amount.
(d) The creditor may surrender their security and prove for the whole debt as an unsecured creditor.

In so far as the secured creditor obtains payment by realising the security, they have priority over all unsecured creditors of the estate and receive payment in priority to the funeral, testamentary and administration expenses.

Funeral, testamentary and administration expenses

These are paid in priority to all unsecured debts and liabilities of the deceased and are paid in priority to preferred creditors. Where an estate is insolvent "reasonable" funeral expenses are likely to be on a lower scale than would be the case with a solvent estate. Personal representatives' charges now rank as administration expenses (Trustee Act 2000 s.35). **15-032**

Other debts and liabilities

The bankruptcy order

The 1986 Order provides that the bankruptcy order is to apply to the payment of all other debts and liabilities. **15-033**

The bankruptcy order is set out in Insolvency Act 1986 ss.328 and 329 and is as follows (after the payment of the expenses of the bankruptcy):

(a) preferred debts;
(b) ordinary debts;
(c) deferred debts.

With the exception of preferred debts (see para.15-034), within each category the debts rank equally and if the assets are insufficient to meet the debts of one category in full, all debts in that category abate proportionally.

Creditors can claim for debts which are contingent, future or the value of which can only be estimated (Insolvency Act 1986 s.382(3)).

Where a trustee in bankruptcy is administering the estate, the trustee must estimate the value of any debt which is uncertain. This is subject to the court's overall supervision. Once estimated by the trustee or by the court, this is the amount which is treated as due (Insolvency Act 1986 s.322(4)).

Where personal representatives are administering the estate, they must estimate the value of the debt. If the other creditors do not accept the valuation, the personal representatives should apply to the court for directions under CPR Pt 64.

Preferred debts

15-034 As from 1 January 2015 preferred debts are divided into two categories: (1) ordinary preferential debts which rank equally among themselves after the expenses of the bankruptcy; and (2) secondary preferential debts which rank equally among themselves after the ordinary preferential debts. See Insolvency Act 1986 s.386 as amended by Banks and Building Societies (Depositor Preference and Priorities) Order 2014 (SI 2014/3486) Pt 2.

Ordinary preferred debts are set out in Insolvency Act 1986 Sch.6, paras 8–15B (e.g. contributions to occupational pension schemes; remuneration of employees for the four months before death—such amount not to exceed the limit prescribed by the Secretary of State (currently £800); levies on coal and steel production; deposits covered by Financial Services Compensation Scheme).

Secondary preferential debts are listed in Sch.6 paras 15BA, 15BB and 15D and are amounts owing to one or more eligible persons in respect of an eligible deposit in excess of any compensation payable under the Financial Services Compensation Scheme, certain deposits made through an authorised non-UK branch of a credit institution and amounts owing to HMRC for VAT or deductions from a payment made to another person.

Before 6 April 2014 all landlords had a power to distrain for rent. If a landlord carried out a distraint on the deceased's goods within three months of death the preferred creditors had a first claim on the goods (or the proceeds of sale). This was to prevent a landlord making use of the special remedy of distraint to obtain payment from the assets of the estate before the preferential creditors. If the landlord recovered an amount in excess of six months' rent accrued due before death any excess had to be held for the estate.

The Tribunals, Courts and Enforcement Act 2007 s.71 abolished the common law right to distrain for arrears of rent. A landlord under a lease of commercial premises is able under s.72(1) of that Act to exercise a new (and more limited) statutory right, called commercial rent arrears recovery (CRAR), to enter let premises, take control of goods belonging to the tenant, sell them and recover rent arrears from the proceeds of sale.

Effectively, the same limitations apply to CRAR in relation to bankrupts as applied to distraint. Thus, a landlord is specifically given a right to exercise CRAR over property of the bankrupt limited to six months' rent due prior to the commencement of the bankruptcy, with a right to prove in the bankruptcy for the balance (IA 1986 s.347(1)).

If CRAR has been exercised within three months prior to the bankruptcy order, the goods or proceeds of sale of the goods are charged for the benefit of the bankrupt's estate with payment of any preferential debts to the extent that these cannot be paid out of the bankrupt's estate (Insolvency Act 1986 s.347(3A)). In these circumstances, the landlord will rank as a preferential creditor.

Similarly, any amounts deducted by HMRC under Pt 1 of Sch.8 to the Finance

Act (No.2) 2015, within three months prior to the bankruptcy are charged with the-preferential debts of the bankruptcy to the extent that his estate is insufficient to meet them. See Insolvency Act 1986 s.347(3).

Ordinary debts

These are all other debts which are not deferred. **15-035**

Interest

Any surplus remaining after the payment of preferred and ordinary debts shall **15-036** be used to pay interest on preferential and ordinary debts from death till payment (ordinary debts ranking equally with preferential debts for this purpose). The rate of interest payable is whichever is the greater of:

(a) the rate specified in s.17 of the Judgments Act 1838 at death; and
(b) the rate otherwise applicable to that debt.

Deferred debts

Deferred debts are debts owed in respect of credit provided by a person who **15-037** (whether or not the deceased's spouse at the time the credit was provided) was the deceased's spouse at the date of death. Such debts are payable after the payment of preferred and ordinary debts and the interest thereon.

Liability for unpaid debts

Personal liability of personal representatives

If a personal representative pays an inferior debt knowing of the existence of a **15-038** superior debt, the payment is taken as an admission by the personal representative that they have sufficient assets to pay all debts of which they have notice which rank in priority to the inferior debt. The personal representative will, therefore, be personally liable to pay all such debts.

However, they are not personally liable if, without undue haste, they pay an inferior debt without notice of a superior one. This is unlike the position of a personal representative who pays a *beneficiary* without notice of the existence of a debt of the deceased.

Limited protection

A personal representative is under a duty to pay all debts in the same category **15-039** pari passu (i.e. proportionately) and has no right to prefer one creditor above others in the same class. However, under s.10(2) of the Administration of Estates Act 1971 there is limited protection for a personal representative who pays a debt in full at a time when he has no reason to believe the estate is insolvent. A personal representative who makes a payment in such circumstances to a creditor (including himself, unless he took a grant of representation in the capacity of creditor) is not liable to account to other creditors of the same class as the creditor who has been paid, if it subsequently appears that the estate is insolvent.

The section does not protect a personal representative against creditors in a superior category nor does it protect a personal representative who had any reason to believe that the estate was insolvent.

The problem of bankrupt beneficiaries

15-040 A personal representative who pays a legacy direct to a beneficiary who is bankrupt rather than to the trustee in bankruptcy runs the risk of personal liability (see further Law Society's Practice Note "*Bankrupt Beneficiaries*" (15 September 2011) (available on the Law Society's website)). When a trustee in bankruptcy is appointed, all property (which is defined very widely in s.436 of the Insolvency Act 1986) belonging to the bankrupt automatically vests in the trustee in bankruptcy: s.306 of the Insolvency Act 1986. A beneficiary of an estate has a chose in action—the right to compel the due administration of the estate. If, therefore, a beneficiary is declared bankrupt during the administration of the estate, the chose in action will vest in the trustee in bankruptcy in the same way as other assets.

The beneficiary may have been automatically discharged from bankruptcy before the personal representatives are ready to distribute but, despite the discharge, the personal representatives must distribute the assets to the trustee not the beneficiary: see *Re Bertha Hemming Deceased, Raymond Saul & Co v Holden* (2008) which confirms this. Only in cases in which the bankrupt has already been discharged from bankruptcy at the time of the death of the testator or the intestate under whose estate the former bankrupt benefits does the trustee in bankruptcy have no claim.

If the beneficiary is already bankrupt when the death occurs, the chose in action is "after-acquired property". Section 333(2) of the Insolvency Act 1986 requires the bankrupt to give notice to the trustee in bankruptcy of any property devolving on him. The trustee in bankruptcy is then entitled to claim it by serving notice under Insolvency Act 1986 s.307 on the bankrupt. The personal representatives would then be required to transfer the estate assets to the trustee.

There is no specific protection for personal representatives who distribute in ignorance of a bankruptcy. The safe course is, therefore, to carry out a bankruptcy-only search at the Land Charges Department of HM Land Registry before making a distribution. See also para.14-008.

Chapter Sixteen

LEGACIES AND DEVISES

1. Legacies and Devises

legacy is a gift in a will of personalty; a devise is a gift in a will of realty. 16-001

2. Classification of Legacies

Four types of legacy

A Legacies may be classified as specific, general, demonstrative, pecuniary or residuary. The classification is important because different types of legacy have different characteristics. 16-002

Specific legacies

A specific legacy is a gift of a particular item of property owned by the deceased at the time of death and distinguished from all other property owned by the deceased of a similar type. 16-003

Examples of specific legacies are:

"I give the gold ring I bought in Manchester to X."

"I give my shares in ABC Ltd to Y."

Specific legacies suffer from the disadvantage that they may fail as a result of the doctrine of ademption. Ademption means that a specific legacy fails if the subject matter has ceased to form part of the deceased's estate at death. This may be because the property has been sold or has completely changed its substance. The disappointed beneficiary will receive no compensation from the rest of the estate. Only specific legacies suffer ademption; therefore when construing a will the court tends to construe a legacy as general rather than specific where possible (*Re Rose* (1949); and for a fuller discussion of ademption, see paras 16-016–16-022).

As we saw at para.15-014, specific legacies (and devises) are available for payment of debts, but only after such items as undisposed of property, residue and any retained pecuniary legacy fund have been exhausted.

General legacies

A general legacy is a gift in a will of an item of property which is not distinguished from property of a similar type. If the deceased does not own property at the date of death corresponding to the description in the will, the personal 16-004 representatives must purchase suitable property using funds from the estate unless the legatee is willing to accept the cash equivalent. In determining from which part of the estate such funds are to be provided a general legacy is treated as a pecuniary legacy so that the same rules which apply to the incidence of pecuniary legacies—see paras 16-050–16-054—apply to the incidence of general legacies. Similarly the same rules apply in relation to availability for payment of debts. See para.15-015.

An example of a general legacy is:

"I give 100 shares in ABC Ltd to Y."

This is a gift of *any* 100 shares in ABC Ltd. The mere fact that at the time of making the will the testator owned exactly 100 shares in the company is not sufficient to turn the legacy into a specific legacy (*Re Willcocks* (1921)). If a legacy is to be construed as specific there must be a clear indication in the will itself that the testator is referring to particular property owned at the time of the will. A general legacy is not liable to ademption but will be taken for payment of debts before specific legacies: see para.16-009.

Demonstrative legacies

16-005 A demonstrative legacy is "in its nature a general legacy but there is a particular fund pointed out to satisfy it" (per Lord Thurlow, *Ashburner v MacGuire* (1786)).

Examples of a demonstrative legacy are:

"I give £100 to X to be paid from my current bank account."

"I give £100 to Y to be paid out of my National Savings Certificates."

A demonstrative legacy combines the attributes of general and specific legacies. It is treated as a specific legacy to the extent that the particular fund is in existence at the date of death and is therefore taken for payment of debts after general legacies. If, however, the particular fund is not in existence at the date of death the legacy is not adeemed (as a specific legacy would be). Instead it is treated as a general legacy and paid from any other property available in the estate.

Pecuniary legacies

Description

16-006 A pecuniary legacy is a gift in a will of money. Most commonly a pecuniary legacy is general (for example, "I give £100 to X") but it may be specific (for example, "I give the £100 I keep in a box under the bed to Y") or demonstrative (for example, "I give £100 to Y to be paid from my current bank account)".

Annuities

16-007 An annuity is a pecuniary legacy payable by instalments.

Administration of Estates Act 1925 s.55(1)(x)

16-008 Section 55(1)(x) defines a "pecuniary legacy" for the purposes of the Act. The expression:

> "[I]ncludes an annuity, a general legacy, a demonstrative legacy so far as it is not discharged out of the designated property, and any other general direction by a testator for the payment of money, including all death duties free from which any devise, bequest or payment is made to take effect."

Thus, a gift of "the £100 I keep in a box under my bed" being a specific legacy is not treated as a pecuniary legacy for the purposes of the Administration of Estates Act; the £100 would, therefore, rank with the other specific legacies for payment of debts.

Availability for payment of debts

In the order of availability of property for payment of debts set out in the **16-009**
Administration of Estates Act 1925 (see para.15-011), the fund set on one side for payment of general pecuniary legacies is taken fifth, whereas specific legacies (and devises) are taken sixth after the retained fund has been exhausted. If only part of the retained fund is required for payment of debts the various pecuniary legacies will abate proportionally (unless the testator indicated that one legacy was to be paid in priority to the others in which case the indication is binding on the personal representatives).

Residuary legacies

A residuary gift in a will passes the property of the deceased not otherwise **16-010**
disposed of. It may be a gift of the entire net estate if no other dispositions have been made or it may be a gift of what is left after payment of specific and general gifts.

3. DEVISES

A devise is a gift of realty and can be either specific or residuary. If specific it is **16-011**
subject to the rules on ademption.

4. FAILURE OF LEGACIES AND DEVISES

Introduction

A gift made in a valid will can fail for a number of reasons. Some of the more **16-012**
important are listed below:

(a) disclaimer;
(b) ademption;
(c) the beneficiary predeceases the testator;
(d) divorce or the termination of a civil partnership;
(e) uncertainty;
(f) the beneficiary witnesses the will;
(g) the gift is contrary to public policy or for an illegal or immoral purpose;
(h) the gift is conditional and the condition is not fulfilled;
(i) the doctrine of satisfaction;
(j) the gift is induced by force, fear, fraud or undue influence (this has already been considered at para.2-039 and following); and
(k) the gift infringes the rules against perpetuity or accumulations (a full

consideration of the history and previous versions of these rules and their consequences is beyond the scope of this book).

Effect of failure

16-013 Any legacy or specific devise which fails will fall into residue unless the testator has included a substitutional gift. If a residuary gift fails, the property is undisposed of and passes under the intestacy rules to the testator's next-of-kin.

Disclaimer

16-014 No one can force another to accept a benefit under the will. Beneficiaries are free to disclaim any property given by will. However, it is not normally possible to pick and choose parts of a single gift. Unless the will provides to the contrary, the whole of a gift must be disclaimed or the whole must be accepted; if, however, two entirely separate gifts are made one may be accepted and the other disclaimed (in other jurisdictions partial disclaimers are possible). Once a person has accepted any benefit from a gifted property (for example, income from or interest on it) it is too late to disclaim, it may, however, be possible to vary the terms of the deceased's disposition by a variation agreement. A fuller discussion of the practical considerations involved in disclaimers and variations will be found in Ch.19.

A voluntary disclaimer made during the lifetime of a testator is ineffective (see *Smith v Smith* (2001)). This is because, until the death of the testator, a beneficiary has no interest to accept or disclaim; there is a mere expectation of an interest.

Estates of Deceased Persons (Forfeiture Rule and Law of Succession) Act 2011

16-015 Before the provisions of this Act came into force a disclaimer gave rise to problems of succession because the person who had disclaimed was not be treated as having predeceased. The Act makes two changes:

(1) Section 1 inserts a new s.46A into the Administration of Estates Act 1925 which provides that a person who disclaims an interest in an intestate's estate is to be treated as having predeceased the intestate. This allows their issue to replace them under the statutory trusts. See para.3-015.
(2) Section 2 of the Act inserts a new s.33A into the Wills Act 1837 which allows the issue of a child of a disclaiming testator to replace him. See para.16-032.

Ademption

Introduction

16-016 As we saw in para.16-003 a specific legacy or devise will fail if the subject matter does not form part of the testator's estate at death. Ademption may occur as a result of sale or destruction of the asset or a change in substance. A disappointed beneficiary has no right to receive the proceeds of sale where property has been sold, nor any right to the proceeds of any insurance policy where property has been destroyed. There are a number of aspects of the doctrine of ademption which warrant fuller consideration.

A change in substance

16-017 A change in substance will cause ademption to take place but a mere change in form will not. It is sometimes difficult to decide whether a change is one of substance or of form. In *Re Clifford* (1912), T gave 23 "of the shares belonging to me" in a named company. After the date of the will the company changed its name and subdivided each share into four. Swinfen Eady J held that the legacy was not adeemed since the subject matter remained exactly the same although changed in name and form. The beneficiary, therefore, took 92 of the new shares. In *Re Slater* (1907), a testator made a gift of shares in Lambeth Waterworks Company. After the date of the will the company was taken over and amalgamated with other waterworks companies into the Metropolitan Water Board which issued stock to replace shares held in the old companies. The Court of Appeal held that the legacy was adeemed since the new stock was in an entirely different organisation.

In *Re Dorman, Smith v National Childrens Home* (1994) the deceased left the sums contained in a named deposit account to the trustees of a settlement in which she had enjoyed a life interest. These sums represented income of the trust fund which she had received but not spent. After the date of the will her attorney, acting under an enduring power of attorney, closed the accounts on her behalf and transferred the amounts held to an account bearing a higher rate of interest. The court held that because the accounts were so similar and were funded in the same way there was no change of substance and no ademption.

Problems often arise where an attorney has to sell property that has been specifically given. See para.16-022.

Effect of republication

16-018 If a legacy has been adeemed and the testator afterwards makes a codicil which republishes the will, it normally has no effect on the ademption. For example, if T left Blackacre to B, sold Blackacre, then made a codicil republishing the will, B would still have no rights to the traceable proceeds of sale even if they were identifiable.

However, as a result of the republication the will may be construed in such a way that a gift which would otherwise have been adeemed will be saved. For example, a testator (T) gives "the house in which I now reside to X". Such a gift is a specific devise and if T sells the house after the date of the will it will be adeemed; if T buys another house X is not entitled to the replacement. However, if T makes a codicil to the will after the purchase of the replacement house, the will is republished as at the date of the codicil and, since the wording used in the gift is wide enough to cover *any* house in which T is residing at the appropriate time, X will be entitled to the replacement house.

A codicil republishing a will can only have the effect of passing a replacement asset if the wording used in the original will is sufficiently wide. If, for example, T gave "the three-stone diamond ring I bought in London in 1971 to X" and the ring was stolen the gift would be adeemed; if the ring was insured T might use the insurance money to buy an identical three-stone ring but even if T made a codicil republishing the will the wording would be too specific to cover the replacement and X would get nothing.

The effect of the doctrine of conversion

16-019 When a vendor enters into a binding contract to sell realty the equitable doctrine of conversion applies so that the vendor is treated from the date of the contract as having an interest in the proceeds of sale rather than in the realty. If T makes a will leaving freehold property, Blackacre, to B and then enters into a binding contract to sell Blackacre, the devise is adeemed from the date of the contract. If T dies between contract and completion B is entitled to any rent or other income Blackacre may produce until completion but B is not entitled to the proceeds of sale, which will fall into residue.

The anomalous rule in *Lawes v Bennett* (1785) can in certain circumstances convert property retrospectively; this may lead to ademption. If T makes a will leaving Blackacre to B and residue to R, later grants an option to purchase Blackacre to O and dies before the option has been exercised, Blackacre passes to B. However, if O subsequently decides to exercise the option this effects a retrospective conversion so that Blackacre is deemed to have been converted into proceeds of sale from the date of T's death. The sale proceeds are therefore paid to R and not to B. B is not, however, required to repay any rents or income received since the date of death.

The rule in *Lawes v Bennett* was extended to a gift of shares subject to an option to purchase in *Re Carrington* (1932). The result was that, when the option to purchase the shares was exercised, the shares were deemed to have been sold as at the date of the testator's death. The gift of shares was treated as adeemed and the proceeds of sale fell into residue.

If the will is made or republished after the date of the grant of the option the testator is deemed to have intended to pass to the beneficiary the property or the proceeds of sale so that no ademption will take place even if the option is exercised. The beneficiary will be entitled to the proceeds of sale (*Drant v Vause* (1842)).

Certain statutes disapply the effect of conversion for the purposes of succession. For example, under the Mental Capacity Act 2005 ss.16 and 18 the Court of Protection has wide powers to dispose of property on behalf of a person who lacks capacity to deal with their own property. Schedule 2 para.8(3) provides that if the property disposed of was real property, any property representing it is to be treated, so long as it remains part of P's estate, as if it were real property. Schedule 2 para.8(4) provides that where the court directs a disposal of the personal property of a person who lacks capacity, on which disposal there would be a conversion of that property into real property, the court may direct that the property representing the property disposed of is to be treated (so long as it remains the person's property or part of their estate) as if it were personal property. Another example of statutory disapplication can be found in the Settled Land Act 1925 s.75(5) which provides that capital money arising under the Act is to be "treated as land" for all purposes of disposition, transmission and devolution.

Property to be ascertained at date of death

16-020 A testator may make a gift of assets to be ascertained at the date of death, for example a gift of "all the shares in ABC Co which I own at my death". Such a gift is not subject to the doctrine of ademption as such, although it will fail if the testator owns no assets corresponding to the description at the date of death.

Problems when drafting a will

The effect of the doctrine of ademption should always be explained to a client who wishes to make a bequest or devise of a specific item. It is possible to include words of substitution so that a testator might give "my shares in ABC Co or any shares representing that investment at the time of my death". However, such a gift may well create problems for the personal representatives in identifying such shares, particularly if the death occurs some time after the will is made. It may, therefore, be preferable simply to point out to the client the importance of reviewing the will periodically so that it can be changed if an asset specifically given is sold, destroyed or substantially changed. **16-021**

It may be possible to word the gift so that the precise property is to be ascertained at the date of death (as suggested in para.16-020) or to give a pecuniary legacy in substitution for a legacy failing by reason of ademption. In cases where a testator is not irretrievably wedded to making specific gifts, it may be more satisfactory to give shares of residue.

Sales on behalf of donors who lack capacity to manage their property and financial affairs

The Mental Capacity Act 2005 ss.16 and 18 give the Court of Protection (and deputies appointed by it) wide powers to deal with the affairs of persons who do not have capacity to manage their own property. There is a danger that assets will be dealt with in a way inconsistent with the terms of a will made before the loss of capacity. Schedule 2 to the Mental Capacity Act 2005 contains provision to ensure as far as possible that ademption of gifts in such a will does not occur. The schedule provides that (in so far as circumstances allow) testamentary beneficiaries shall take the same interest in substituted property as they would have taken in the original property. This makes it unnecessary for a new will to be made by the court. There may be problems identifying the "same interest in substituted property". See for example *Hives v Machin* (2017) where the proceeds of an investment bond were paid into a current account from which debts were paid and the net amount was then transferred to an interest-bearing account. **16-022**

There is no corresponding provision to prevent ademption resulting from actions of an attorney acting under an enduring or lasting power of attorney. Hence a sale will result in ademption. The dangers of such ademption were illustrated in *Re Dorman, Smith National Childrens Home* (1994), although on the particular facts of the case the court was able to find that ademption had not taken place because the asset was replaced by another so similar that there was merely a change of form not substance. In *Banks v National Westminster Bank* (2005), however, the gift of a house sold by the attorney was adeemed following its sale.

The Court of Protection has made it clear that in property and financial affairs both attorneys and deputies owe a duty when making financial decisions, so far as is reasonably possible, not to interfere with the succession plans made by the person for whom they act. See *Treadwell v Lutz* (2013). If the attorney is aware of the terms of the will, and if estate is large enough to justify the cost, an attorney who is forced to sell an asset which has been specifically given by will should make an application to the Court of Protection for a statutory will to provide for the disappointed beneficiary.

Solicitors in possession of the will of a client have been uncertain as to whether the duty of confidentiality prevented them disclosing the contents of a will to that person's attorney. A very useful joint guidance note, "Access to and disclosure of an incapacitated person's will" (17 March 2017), has been produced by the SRA, Court of Protection, Office of the Public Guardian, Legal Ombudsman, Law Society and Society of Trust and Estate Practitioners. This states that a solicitor can accept instructions to disclose the contents of a will given by a person who has the testator's authority. A person appointed under a power of attorney and a deputy appointed by the Court of Protection has that authority (unless it has been restricted). It is recommended in the guidance that the question of disclosure is discussed with client at the time a will is made and, if later, at the time a lasting power of attorney is made.

Beneficiary predeceases testator

Introduction

16-023 In order to take a gift under a will a beneficiary must survive the testator. If the beneficiary predeceases the testator a legacy will lapse and fall into residue or if it is a residuary gift will pass under the intestacy rules. A beneficiary need only survive for a very short period—a minute or a second will suffice.

If a gift is to joint tenants or is a class gift, it will not lapse unless all the joint tenants or members of the class predecease the testator; if one joint tenant or class member survives the testator, that one person takes the whole gift. If a gift is to tenants in common, the share of any tenant who predeceases the testator will lapse.

A testator cannot exclude the doctrine of lapse by declaring that it is not to apply. A testator can, however, include a substitutional gift providing that if the beneficiary predeceases the property is to pass to another person.

Will drafters should always point out to clients the possibility that a beneficiary may predecease so that the client can consider including a substitutional clause.

It is also common to include a survivorship clause in a will. A survivorship clause states that a beneficiary is only to take a benefit under the will if the beneficiary survives the testator for a stated period (usually 28 days). The effect is to prevent a beneficiary who only survives the testator by a very short period from benefiting under the will. The importance of such a clause is obvious when it is remembered that a beneficiary may be *deemed* to survive under the Law of Property Act 1925 s.184 (see para.16-024). Without a survivorship clause, the testator's property would pass under the terms of the beneficiary's will or to the beneficiary's next of kin under the intestacy rules. Such a devolution of property might be contrary to the testator's wishes.

Substitutional and survivorship clauses may alter the inheritance tax payable on an estate by substituting a non-exempt for an exempt beneficiary, or vice versa. Since the introduction of the transferable nil-rate band, it is not always advisable to include them in wills made by married couples or civil partners. For a fuller discussion of this topic see para.22-043 and following.

There may also be reasons for not including a survivorship clause in mirror wills where, in the event of the primary beneficiary predeceasing, significant pecuniary and specific legacies are to be paid. Including a survivorship clause will result in the legacies being paid twice unless the will is worded appropriately. See para.17-002.

Where the order of deaths is uncertain

It can sometimes happen that there is no evidence as to the order in which people **16-024**
have died, for example where two people die in a car accident or one person dies in a road accident and the other dies at home at an uncertain time. In such a case, s.184 of the Law of Property Act 1925 provides that for the purposes of succession to property the deaths are presumed to have occurred in order of seniority so that the elder is presumed to die first. The section applies equally on intestacy.

Example 1

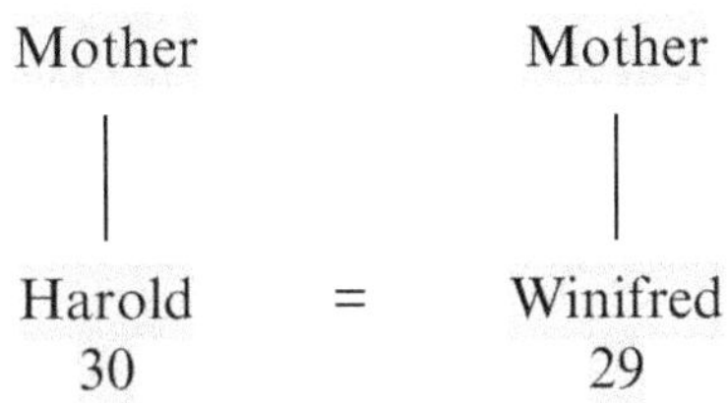

Harold and Winifred both die in a car accident; the order of their deaths is uncertain. They have each made wills leaving all their property to the other. They have no children. Each has a mother who survives.

Harold, being the elder, is presumed to die first. His property therefore passes under the terms of his will to Winifred who is presumed to have survived him. His property forms part of her estate. The gift in Winifred's will to Harold lapses and her estate (which now includes Harold's property) passes to her mother under the intestacy rules. It is unlikely that Harold would have wished his property to pass to Winifred's mother in preference to his own; had he included a survivorship clause in his will his property would not have passed to Winifred and so would not have gone to her mother.

For a modern example of the presumption in action, see *Scarle v Scarle* [2019].

Exceptional cases where legacies do not lapse

There are two situations where, despite the fact that a beneficiary has predeceased **16-025**
a testator, a gift will not fail:

(a) gifts in discharge of a moral obligation;
(b) section 33 of the Wills Act 1837.

Point (a), is of comparatively minor importance and can be dealt with briefly; (b), however, warrants a more detailed examination.

Gifts in discharge of a moral obligation

If a testator makes a gift to beneficiary in order to discharge a moral obligation **16-026**
and the beneficiary predeceases the testator the gift will not lapse but will form part of the beneficiary's estate. Examples of gifts which have been held to be in discharge of a moral obligation are a direction to pay a statute-barred debt (*Williamson v Naylor* (1838)) and a mother's direction that the creditors of her deceased son be paid (*Re Leach's Will Trusts* (1948)).

The precise limits of the rule are uncertain and it may be that it applies only to directions to pay debts and not to ordinary gifts (*Stevens v King* (1904)).

Section 33 of the Wills Act 1837

16-027 **The section** Section 33(1) (as substituted by the Administration of Justice Act 1982) applies where a testator dies after 31 December 1982. The substituted s.33 provides that where:

(a) a will contains a devise or bequest to a child or remoter descendant of the testator; *and*
(b) the intended beneficiary dies before the testator, leaving issue; *and*
(c) issue of the intended beneficiary are living at the testator's death,

then, unless the will contains a contrary intention, the devise or bequest shall take effect as a devise or bequest *to the issue* living at the testator's death.

Section 33(3) provides that such issue take "according to their stock, in equal shares if more than one, any gift or share which their parent would have taken".

Example 2

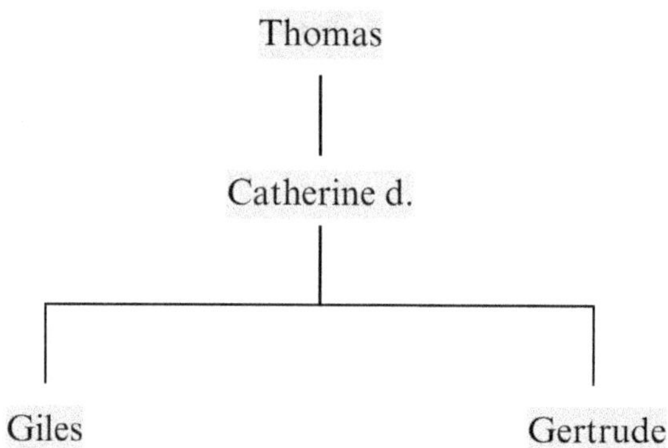

Thomas leaves Catherine a legacy of £20,000 in his will but Catherine predeceases Thomas. Normally the gift to Catherine would fail; however, as a result of s.33 the gift does not fail but passes equally to Giles and Gertrude who take £10,000 each.

Section 33 goes on to provide that no issue shall take whose parent is living at the testator's death and so capable of taking.

Example 3

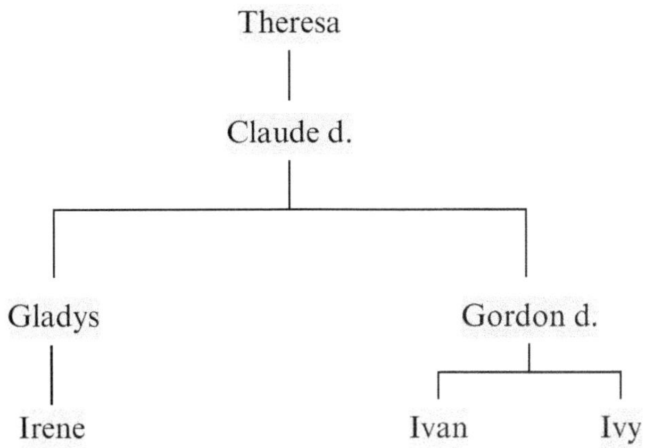

Theresa leaves Claude a legacy of £20,000. Claude and Gordon predecease Theresa. The gift to Claude does not lapse but passes to his issue. Gladys receives one-half (her issue are entitled to nothing as she is still alive); Gordon has predeceased Theresa and therefore his share of £10,000 is divided equally between his issue, Ivan and Ivy, who take £5,000 each.

The section does not make it clear whether, where a gift is contingent, substituted beneficiaries must satisfy the same contingency as primary beneficiaries. Etherton J in *Ling v Ling* (2002) said that they must. The same view was taken in *Naylor v Barlow* (2019).

Class gifts Sometimes gifts are made to a class of beneficiaries. Section 33(2) provides that where: **16-028**

(a) a will contains a devise or bequest to a class of persons consisting of children or remoter descendants of the testator; and
(b) a member of the class dies before the testator, leaving issue; and
(c) issue of that member are living at the testator's death.

then, unless a contrary intention appears in the will, the devise or bequest shall take effect as if the class included the issue of its deceased member living at the testator's death. Under s.33(3) the issue take *per stirpes* according to their stocks, in equal shares if more than one, the share which their parent would have taken and, subject to s.33A (see para.16-032) no issue whose parent is living at the time of the testator's death shall take.

Example 4

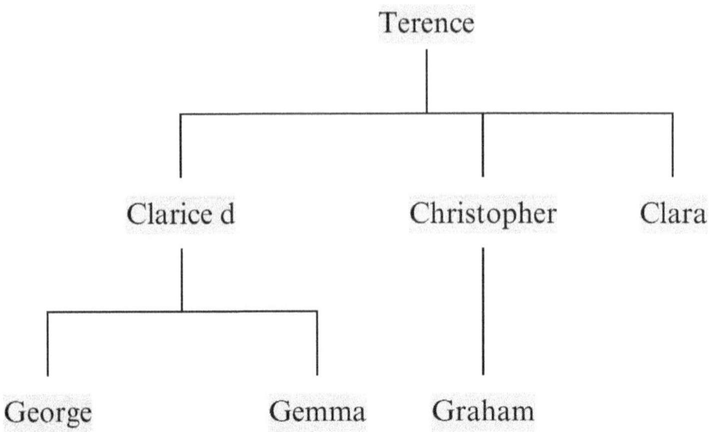

Terence leaves £30,000 to be divided "amongst all my children". Clarice predeceases Terence. Her one-third share (£10,000) will be divided *per stirpes* amongst such of her issue, George and Gemma, as survive Terence. Section 33(3) will apply so that no issue shall take whose parent is living at the testator's death. Therefore Graham will take nothing.

16-029 **Contrary intention** Both s.33(1) and 33(2) are expressed to be subject to contrary intention. There is, however, some uncertainty as to precisely what constitutes "contrary intention" for this purpose. The original s.33 of Wills Act 1837 stated that it was not to apply when an interest was determinable at or before death. Thus, that section did not save a life interest to a child of the testator who predeceased, nor a gift to a child of the testator as a joint tenant or as a member of a class who predeceased leaving surviving joint tenants or class members; nor did it apply to a gift contingent on an event which had not occurred when the child predeceased. The substituted s.33 does not contain such exclusions and it is not clear whether or not a testator making gifts on such terms thereby demonstrates a contrary intention. If a testator does not wish the issue of a deceased child (or remoter descendant) to take a benefit the safest course is to include a provision stating what is to happen in the event of such predecease (see the discussion of the substituted s.33 and will drafting at para.16-031).

In *Ling v Ling* (2002) the court had to consider whether or not a will which gave property to children "living at my death" expressed contrary intention. The court held that those words added nothing. They merely stated expressly what would otherwise be implicit, that a class is normally composed of those members, if any, in existence at the death of the testator. To exclude s.33 there would have to be words making it clear that issue were not to be substituted.

In *Rainbird v Smith* (2012) where the gift was to "such of them, my daughters, as shall survive me" and "if more than one, in equal shares" the court considered that it was plain that the testator's intention had been to leave the estate only to those daughters who survived her. Had the intention not been so limited, the words "such of them ... as shall survive me" would not have been included. Importantly, the use of the language "and if more than one, in equal shares" showed that the amount each of them might get had been intended to increase if any of the other daughters predeceased the testator. It was probably significant that, although the court did not admit extrinsic evidence under the Administration of Justice Act 1982 s.21 because it considered that the meaning was clear without it, there was strikingly clear extrinsic evidence that the -testator had only wanted to leave her estate to those children living at her death.

In *Hives v Machin* (2017) the testatrix had left her residuary estate to such of her three sons who were "living at my death". Timothy Fancourt QC sitting as a deputy judge considered the two earlier cases. While it was necessary to construe the words in the context of the particular will, he had no hesitation in taking the same view that Etherton J had taken in *Ling v Ling*. The words "living at my death" gave no indication of an intention that the deceased beneficiary's issue (as distinct from the deceased beneficiary) should be excluded from taking under s.33. The decision makes clear that the "default" setting is that the section applies unless there is evidence of an intention that it should not. It follows that where a testator does not want a child's issue to be substituted, it is important to state expressly what is to happen to a lapsed share.

Children whose parents were not married and children en ventre sa mere Section 33(4) provides that for the purposes of s.33 the illegitimacy of any person is to be disregarded. Thus, a child whose parents were not married can take in the same way as a child whose parents were married. The subsection also provides that a child *en ventre sa mere* is living for the purposes of the section. **16-030**

The effect of the substituted s.33 on will drafting As explained at para.16-029 if a testator does *not* want s.33 to apply it is desirable for the avoidance of doubt to state in the will what is to happen where a child predeceases. However, even in those cases where a gift to a testator's deceased child (or remoter descendant) *is* to pass to the child's issue, it is desirable to include an express provision to this effect rather than to rely on the section for the following reasons: **16-031**

(a) If the substitution is set out in the will, a solicitor can be certain that the effect of the statutory provision is brought to the attention of the client; this gives the client the opportunity to request an alternative if the -statutory provision does not correspond with their wishes.
(b) If the gift to the testator's child (or remoter descendant) is contingent it is desirable to provide expressly for the possibility that the child might survive the testator but die without fulfilling the contingency.
(c) If the gift to the testator's child (or remoter descendant) is contingent it is desirable to state expressly whether or not a substituted beneficiary is to take subject to the same contingency.
(d) It avoids the risk that those administering the estate will overlook the effect of s.33. See, for example *Naylor v Barlow* (2019) where two separate firms of solicitor failed to identify that the testator's grandchildren were entitled to their deceased father's share until more than two years had elapsed. The failure was particularly unfortunate as the father's gift was subject to a condition which had to be complied with within nine months of the grandfather's death. The daughters had not complied with the condition (knowing nothing about it) and lost the benefit of the legacy. See para.16-048 below.

In cases where a gift is made to anyone other than a child (or remoter descendant) of the testator (for example "to the children of my brother") an express substitutional gift to issue *must* be included if the testator wants the gift to pass to issue in substitution for a beneficiary who predeceases. Section 33 applies only to gifts to the testator's children (or remoter descendants).

16-032 **Section 33A** Section 33 of the Wills Act 1837 applies only where children or issue *predecease* the testator. It has no application where a gift fails for any other reason, for example because of disclaimer or the effect of the forfeiture rule. (For forfeiture rule see para.16-045 and following.)

Example 5

Tessa leaves £100,000 to her son, Sam. Sam has two children, Gerry and Gemma. In 2010 Sam murders his mother in a fit of rage and so forfeits his entitlement under his mother's will. Gerry and Gemma do not replace Sam under s.33 because Sam did not predecease his mother.

The Law Commission recommended in "The Forfeiture Rule and the Law of Succession" (Law Com. No.295) that the harshness of this aspect of the rule should be mitigated. The Estates of Deceased Persons (Forfeiture Rule and Law of Succession) Act 2011 came into effect on 1 February 2011 and inserted a new s.33A into the Wills Act. It provides that, subject to contrary intention in the will, a person who disclaims or forfeits an entitlement under a will is to be treated for the purposes of this Act as having died immediately before the testator. If the facts of the above example occurred after s.33A came into force, there would be a different result.

Example 6

Tessa leaves £100,000 to her son, Sam. Sam has two children, Gerry and Gemma. In 2014 Sam murders his mother in a fit of rage and so forfeits his entitlement under his mother's will. As a result of s.33A Sam is now treated as having predeceased his mother and Gerry and Gemma do replace Sam.

The Law Commission recommendation was that the rule that a person killing the deceased should be deemed to have predeceased would be of general application. The wording of s.33A is, however, limited to "the purposes of this Act". The only provision in the Wills Act dealing with substitution is s.33 which is limited to gifts to children and issue of the testator. There is, therefore, doubt as to whether the deeming provision applies to all gifts or only those to the testator's children. In *Macmillan Cancer Support v Hayes* (2017) Mark Raeside QC sitting as a deputy judge was asked to decide whether the deeming provision would apply to an unlawful killing by the testatrix's husband. He had already agreed to relieve the husband's estate from the effects of the forfeiture rule which made it unnecessary for him to express an opinion and he declined to do so.

Divorce

Wills Act 1837 s.18A as amended by the Law Reform (Succession) Act 1995

16-033 As we saw at para.2-054 and following, in cases where a marriage is dissolved or annulled or a civil partnership is terminated the former spouse is to be treated as having died on the date of dissolution or annulment. Thus, any gifts made by will to a spouse and appointments of a spouse as executor will fail.

The effect of the s.18A amendment on will drafting

16-034 The fact that the former spouse is to be treated as *dying* on the date of dissolution or annulment means that a substitutional gift expressed to take effect "if my spouse predeceases or does not survive me for [a specified period]" will now take effect if the primary gift to the spouse fails as a result of s.18A.

It is no longer necessary to include the words "or fails for any other reason".

It is, of course, always desirable to suggest that clients who are contemplating divorce should review their wills and that they should do so as early as possible since the mere fact of separation (or even a decree of judicial separation) will not revoke testamentary dispositions.

Uncertainty

Introduction

If it is impossible to identify either the subject matter or the objects of a gift, it will fail for uncertainty. **16-035**

Uncertainty of subject matter

Gifts of "some of my best table linen" (*Peck v Halsey* (1726)) or of "a handsome gratuity" (*Jubber v Jubber* (1839)) have been held to be void for uncertainty. In some cases such gifts may now be saved by the Administration of Justice Act 1982 s.21. **16-036**

A gift may prima facie be of an uncertain amount and yet be capable of assessment in which case it will not fail. For example, a clause giving a beneficiary a power to select such items as he wishes is valid; so also is a direction that a beneficiary enjoy "a reasonable income" from the testator's properties (*Re Golay* (1965)) since the court can, if necessary, determine what amounts to a reasonable income.

Uncertainty of objects

If the beneficiaries are not clearly identified the gift will fail. Thus, a gift to "the son of A" where A had several sons fails for uncertainty (*Dowset v Sweet* (1753)). It is, therefore, important when drafting a will to take care to check the names of individuals and institutions intended to benefit. **16-037**

The only case where a gift will not fail for uncertainty of objects is where a testator wishes to make a charitable gift and does not sufficiently identify the charity which is to benefit. The gift will not fail so long as it is clear that the gift is for exclusively charitable purposes. The court will direct a scheme to give effect to the gift. Where there is an error in the name of a charity a cheaper procedure is to apply to the Attorney General for directions under the *Royal Sign Manual*.

The beneficiary witnesses the will

The general rule

Section 15 of the Wills Act provides that a gift made to a beneficiary fails if: **16-038**

(a) the beneficiary witnesses the will; or
(b) the spouse or civil partner of the beneficiary witnesses the will.

The validity of the will itself is not affected. The rule exists to ensure that wills are reliably witnessed by independent persons. Notice that the section only causes loss of entitlement if a beneficiary witnesses a will. It says nothing about beneficiaries signing a will on behalf of the testator as permitted by s.9(a) of the Wills Act 1837. In *Barrett v Bem* (2012) the Court of Appeal confirmed that a beneficiary who signed on behalf of the testator would not forfeit entitlement although knowledge and approval of the will would have to be proved. The court did consider that the circumstances surrounding the signature raised doubts as to the testator's knowledge and approval of the will.

Beneficial gifts only

16-039 Section 15 applies only to beneficial gifts. Thus, if a gift is made "to X as trustee to hold for Y" and X or X's spouse or civil partner witnesses the will the gift does not fail. The gift would fail if Y or Y's spouse or civil partner witnessed the will.

Subsequent events irrelevant

16-040 It is the time of execution which is important. Subsequent events are irrelevant. Thus, where a witness married a beneficiary *after* the date of execution of the will the gift remained effective (*Thorpe v Bestwick* (1881)). Similarly, if a gift is to the holder of an office or to a person fulfilling a description the gift will remain effective even though a witness later takes up the office or comes to fulfil the description (*Re Ray's Will Trusts, Public Trustee v Barry* (1936)).

Gift made or confirmed by independently witnessed will or codicil

16-041 A gift will not fail if there is a codicil or will which can be said to confirm the will and which is not witnessed by the beneficiary (or the beneficiary's spouse or civil partner). It is not necessary to find any express reference to the gift in the independently witnessed will or codicil. In *Re Trotter* (1899) T made a gift by will to B, a witness; there were two later codicils to the will; B did not witness the first but did witness the second. The court held that, as there was one independently witnessed codicil, the gift to B did not fail.

Secret trusts

16-042 If T creates a secret (or half secret) trust in favour of X and X or X's spouse or civil partner witnesses the will, X does not lose his entitlement. This is because X takes under the trust and not under the will (*Re Young* (1951)).

Superfluous attesting witnesses

16-043 In the case of a testator dying after 29 May 1968, the Wills Act 1968 provides that the attestation of a will by any beneficiaries or their spouses or civil partners is to be disregarded if without them the will is duly executed. Thus, if a will is witnessed by three people, one of whom is a beneficiary (or spouse of a beneficiary) that person may take a gift in the will; however, if two of the three witnesses (or their spouses) are beneficiaries their signatures cannot be disregarded and neither can take.

If a person (other than the testator) has signed a will, it is presumed that the signature is as a witness. The presumption can be rebutted, for example, by evidence that the signature was to indicate approval of the testator's disposition. If a beneficiary (or spouse or civil partner of a beneficiary) is able to show that a signature was in such a capacity, there is no question of loss of entitlement.

Charging clause no longer treated as a legacy

A charging clause used to be regarded as a pecuniary legacy. However, the Trustee Act 2000 s.28 provides that a charging clause is no longer a legacy for the purposes of the Wills Act 1837 s.15 or for the purposes of abatement of legacies. This means a solicitor can witness a will containing a charging clause even though the solicitor (or the firm in which the solicitor is a partner) is appointed executor. The right to charge will not be forfeited. **16-044**

Because a charging clause was regarded as a legacy, it used to be necessary to provide that a solicitor's charges be paid "in priority to other pecuniary legacies". This was to prevent them abating with the other pecuniary legacies where the estate was too small to pay all pecuniary legacies in full. As the Trustee Act 2000 s.18 provides that such clauses are no longer legacies, there is no question of abatement and such clauses are unnecessary.

The gift is for an illegal or immoral purpose or contrary to public policy

Introduction

Such a gift cannot take effect. The principles to be applied in deciding whether a gift is illegal, immoral or contrary to public policy are the same as in the law of trusts. The law relating to public policy is not fixed but changes with the passage of time. **16-045**

In *Gray v Barr* (1971) a broad principle of public policy was expressed as being "that no man should be allowed to profit at another person's expense from his own conscious and deliberate crime". Thus, if one person, B, is found guilty of unlawfully killing another, T, B cannot take any benefit under the will of T or under the intestacy rules if T dies intestate; nor can they take an interest in joint property passing by survivorship.

The rule of public policy will not apply if the killing was carried out while B was insane within the *McNaghten* rules because the verdict is one of not guilty by reason of insanity.

There was some doubt as to whether the forfeiture rule applied to all or only some types of manslaughter.

Re H (Deceased) (1990) had suggested that the rule of public policy applied to prevent B taking any benefit if the person has been found guilty of deliberate, intentional and unlawful violence but not otherwise.

However, the majority in *Dunbar v Plant* (1998) held that the forfeiture rule applied to all cases of manslaughter. The harshness of applying the forfeiture rule inflexibly to all classes of manslaughter in all circumstances was mitigated by the Forfeiture Act 1982 (see para.16-046) which allows relief from forfeiture in certain circumstances. Phillips LJ said:

> "I can see no reason now for the court to attempt to modify the forfeiture rule. The appropriate course where the application of the rule appears to conflict with the ends of justice is to exercise the powers given by the Act."

In *Dalton v Latham* (2003) (where the claimant was acquitted of murder on the grounds of diminished responsibility but pleaded guilty to manslaughter) Patten J held that *Dunbar v Plant*:

> "[M]ust now be taken to be a binding statement of the law as to the application of the rule of public policy. It applies to all cases of unlawful killing, including manslaughter by reason of diminished responsibility or by reason of provocation. The only possible exception is where the defendant is found to be criminally insane, which leads to an acquittal."

In *Amos v Mancini* (2020) the forfeiture rule was held to apply to a case of causing death by careless driving.

The forfeiture rule was applied in a case of negligent manslaughter in *Land v Land* (2007) despite the fact that an application under the Forfeiture Act 1982 was impossible because it was out of time. However, the court allowed the deceased's son to make an application under the Inheritance (Provision for Family and Dependants) Act 1975 on the basis that reasonable financial provision had not been made for his maintenance.

"Unlawful killing" includes aiding, abetting, counselling or procuring the death of another person, for instance by assisting with their suicide, a crime under s.2 of the Suicide Act 1961. A criminal conviction is not necessary. In *Dunbar v Plant* (1997), the rule was applied to the survivor of a suicide pact.

In *Ninian v Findlay* (2019), Chief Master Marsh held that by travelling with her terminally ill husband to the Dignitas Centre in Zurich at a time when he was unable to make the journey unaided, Mrs Ninian had provided assistance and involvement which did amount to acts which were capable of assisting her husband's suicide. She was, therefore, subject to the forfeiture rule. However, relief from forfeiture was granted under the Forfeiture Act 1982 (see para.16-046 below).

Until the Estates of Deceased Persons (Forfeiture Rule and Law of Succession) Act 2011 came into force B's issue were unable to replace him under the statutory trusts arising on an intestacy because B had not predeceased the intestate. However, the position is now different (see para.16-047). Similarly issue of a child whose interest was forfeit could not take under Wills Act 1837 s.33.

Relief under Forfeiture Act 1982

16-046 The Forfeiture Act 1982 allows the court to offer relief from the harshness of the forfeiture rule. It does not apply where a person has been convicted of murder but applies in any other case where one person has unlawfully killed another (for example, manslaughter) and is precluded by reasons of public policy from taking an interest in property. An offender may apply to the court within three months of the date of conviction (s.2) for an order modifying the forfeiture rule in respect of any beneficial interest which the offender would have acquired from the deceased (but for the forfeiture rule) inter alia:

(a) under the deceased's will or on intestacy;
(b) on a nomination by the deceased; and
(c) as a *donatio mortis causa* (s.2(4)(a)).

An application may also be made where property had been held on trust for any person and as a result of the deceased's death but for the forfeiture rule the offender *would have* acquired an interest in the trust property (s.2(4)(b)).

No application may be made after the expiry of the three-month period (s.2(3)). This time limit is strict and the court has no discretion to extend it. See *Land v Land (Deceased)* (2007).

In *Challen v Challen* (2020) a woman was initially convicted of murdering her coercive husband, was given leave to appeal and was subsequently convicted of manslaughter. Paul Matthews J held that in such a case, it is the subsequent conviction which is the relevant one for the purposes of s.2(3) of the Act and the time-limit provided for. He went on to say that in his opinion it is only at the point of sentence and not, if this is earlier, when the court accepts the plea, that there is a "conviction" within s.2(3) of the 1982 Act.

Section 4(5) of the Act *appears* to provide that where there is more than one interest in property to which the forfeiture rule applies the court may exclude the rule in respect of any *but not all* and where there is one such interest the court may exclude the rule in respect of *part only* of that interest. However, in one of the first applications to come before the court (*Re K* (1985)) Vinelott J stated that the Act was a private members bill and is not couched in technical language but is intended to be understood by persons other than lawyers specialising in property and trust matters. He said that in his view s.4(5) was intended to enlarge the power of the court by making it abundantly clear that the court is not bound to relieve against the forfeiture rule entirely or not at all but that the court is free if it chooses to modify the effect of the rule to a limited extent. His first instance judgment was approved by the Court of Appeal.

The court must not make an order unless satisfied that the justice of the case requires the forfeiture rule to be modified having regard to the conduct of the offender and of the deceased and to such other circumstances as appear to the court to be material (s.2(2)). In *Dunbar v Plant* (1998) the Court of Appeal allowed relief from forfeiture to the survivor of a suicide pact in relation to the proceeds of an insurance policy taken out by the survivor's fiancé (he had died as a result of the pact). The court held that the survivor had committed the criminal offence of aiding and abetting her fiancé's suicide and, therefore, the forfeiture rule applied. However, the Forfeiture Act 1982 s.1(2) allows courts flexibility in applying the rule in cases where public policy demands a more sympathetic approach. Accordingly, she was granted full relief from forfeiture.

Similarly in *Ninian v Findlay* (2019) where a terminally ill husband had decided to go to Dignitas to end his life and was assisted by his devoted wife, the court decided that while the wife, by assisting in the suicide, had made herself subject to the forfeiture rule, it was appropriate to grant relief.

An application can be made by personal representatives of the killer as occurred in *Macmillan Cancer Support v Hayes* (2017). The testatrix's husband had killed her and then committed suicide.

In *Chadwick v Collinson* (2014) the court refused to grant relief. The level of the applicant's culpability was reduced, perhaps even significantly, by the impact of the mental disorder from which he was suffering at the time of the killing. However, it was not reduced to a level where it could properly be said to be so low that to give effect to the forfeiture rule would be contrary to the public interest.

A personal representative, who is administering an estate where the deceased was unlawfully killed by another person who would, but for the forfeiture rule, have received property under the deceased's will or on intestacy; under a a nomination by the deceased; or as a *donatio mortis causa*, should wait for the expiry of the three months from conviction before distributing such property to others. Those acting for a person charged with an unlawful killing offence, who would otherwise inherit, should have the time limit firmly in mind.

Section 3 of the Act provides that the forfeiture rule is not to be taken to preclude any person from making an application under the Inheritance (Provision for Family and Dependants) Act 1975. Such an application can be made if the requirements of that Act are complied with. Thus, an applicant must be able to show that the disposition of the deceased's estate effected by the will or by the intestacy rules did not make reasonable financial provision for the applicant (*Re Royse* (1984)). See *Land v Land* (2007).

The forfeiture rule does not apply to interests arising under lifetime trusts where interests crystallised when the trusts were executed. In *Henderson v Wilcox* (2016) a son, suffering from a serious mental disorder and autism, killed his mother in a severe assault. She had made a will leaving her entire estate to him. The court refused relief from the forfeiture rule. The attack was the culmination of a number of attacks and he had known that they were wrong. Justice did not require modification of the rule. However, his mother had settled her half interest in the family home on discretionary trusts with professional trustees, the beneficiaries being her, a nephew and the claimant. The court granted a declaration that the forfeiture rule did not apply to the trust. The claimant's status as a discretionary beneficiary of the trust was neither created nor enlarged by his mother's death. Anything which he received would be as a result of the trustees' decision and not by virtue of the death itself. The forfeiture rule did not prevent the trustees exercising their discretion in the claimant's favour.

A person who forfeits can now be treated as having predeceased the victim for the purposes of the intestacy rules

16-047 *Re Jones (Deceased)* (1997) and *Re DWS* (2000) made it clear that a person whose interest has been forfeited was not to be treated as having predeceased. Hence, in the case of an intestacy, the statutory trusts would not apply to allow -substitution of issue as issue cannot take if their parent is "living". In *Re DWS* (2001) a son killed his parents and as a result forfeited his entitlement under the intestacy rules. The Court of Appeal held that the effect of s.47(1)(i) of the Administration of Estates Act 1925 was that the issue of a child of the intestate could take only if their parent had in fact predeceased the intestate. A child of surviving issue could not take in preference to their parent. If a surviving parent was prevented from taking by disclaimer or disqualification, the intestate's estate should pass, not to their child, but to those entitled if the deceased had died without issue.

However, with effect from 1 February 2011 the position has changed. The Estates of Deceased Persons (Forfeiture Rule and Law of Succession) Act 2011 inserted a new s.46A into the Administration of Estates Act 1925 which provides that where a person who would have been entitled to an interest in the residuary estate of an intestate forfeits (or disclaims) his entitlement, he is to be treated for the purposes of the Wills Act 1837 as having predeceased the intestate. The result is that any issue of the person forfeiting or disclaiming can replace him under the statutory trusts. There is doubt as to whether the provision extends to persons who are not issue of the deceased: see para.16-032.

The court retains power to modify the effects of the forfeiture rule (s.46A(3)).

Failure of a condition

16-048 If a legacy is conditional on an event or circumstance which at the date of death is impossible or not present, the legacy will fail. However, the court may be able to construe the will in such a way that the legacy is found not to be conditional on the event or circumstance.

In *Watson v National Children's Home* (1995) a testator left half of his estate to one charity and the other half to a second charity conditional on the latter caring for his domestic pets. If the second charity did not agree to do so the residue was to pass entirely to the first charity.

At the time of his death the deceased had no pets. The first charity argued that the gift to the second charity failed because the second charity could not fulfil the condition. The court held that the condition was impossible to fulfil and should be regarded as spent. As such the second charity took the gift absolutely. The clause had to be construed as requiring the charity to care for any of the deceased's pets but if there were none the gift should still pass. If thc gift was not construed in this way, it would be deemed ambiguous and extrinsic evidence would be admitted under s.21 of the Administration of Justice Act 1982. The deceased had clearly stated that only if the charity refused to look after his pets should the gift fail.

It may be that a condition attaching to a legacy is void. In *Nathan v Leonard and National Association For Mental Health* (2002) the deceased directed that, if any one of the beneficiaries wished "*to contest or disagree with my will*", the entire estate was to go to a married couple who were taking two-thirds of the residue and who she was anxious to provide for adequately. One of the other residuary beneficiaries made a claim under the Inheritance (Provision for Family and Dependants) Act 1975 for further provision to be made for him from the estate. The married couple contended that this brought the forfeiture clause into effect. The court agreed that making an Inheritance Act claim would amount to contesting the will for this purpose (although strictly speaking a claim under the Act does not challenge the validity of the will; it simply asks the court to vary the way in which property is left: see Ch.20) and would breach the clause. However, there were three issues to consider:

(a) Was the forfeiture clause void either for repugnancy or because it was contrary to public policy?
(b) If it was valid, had it been breached?
(c) If breached, was the gift over to the married couple effective?

The court held that the clause imposing forfeiture was not repugnant. A condition is only repugnant if it is inconsistent with ownership. There is nothing inconsistent about a gift subject to divesting. Inconsistency only arises if the gift purports to limit the incidents of ownership, such as the ability to sell.

Equally, although the condition might well have a strong deterrent effect on a beneficiary who was contemplating making a claim under the Act, that did not in itself make the condition contrary to public policy.

However, it was clear that some words had been mistakenly omitted from the final sentence of the codicil. Since it was impossible for the court to say what the omitted words were, the condition failed for uncertainty. The legacies were, therefore, void on the basis of uncertainty.

That meant that the second and third issues did not have to be decided. The judge said that if he had been required to decide, he would have found that the condition had been breached and that the gift over took effect.

Where compliance with a condition is impossible, a gift can take effect free of the condition. See, for example:

- *Re Greenwood* (1903) where the beneficiary died before he was required to comply with the condition and was therefore excused from performance by the act of God.
- *Re Berens* (1926) where performance of the condition that the beneficiary

obtain a particular coat of arms was "impossible of fulfilment" because the arms in question had already been granted to another.

- *Re Jones* (1947) where a condition subsequent requiring a village hall to be completed within a certain period of time was not complied with because assets had not been saleable due to war conditions, making it impossible to build the hall.

In *Naylor v Barlow* (2019) the testator had left a share of his estate to one of his sons conditional on payment of a stated sum to two of his siblings within nine months of death. The son predeceased but left two daughters who were entitled to replace him under Wills Act 1837 but subject to the same condition. Those dealing with the administration did not identify the daughters' rights and so did not inform them of the condition. The failure to comply with the condition was not a case of impossibility. There is a distinction between the situation where a beneficiary fails to fulfil a condition (otherwise capable of fulfilment) simply because he does not know about it in sufficient time to do so and the different situation where it is physically impossible for him to fulfil the condition, as where the College of Arms will not award him the stipulated arms. In the latter situation, neither the testator nor the beneficiary has any control over whether or not the condition can be fulfilled whilst in the former situation the condition could have been made contingent on notification.

The doctrine of satisfaction

16-049 The equitable presumption of satisfaction is based on the assumption that a parent would wish to treat their children fairly and would not wish to make -provision for one of their children twice over at the expense of their other children. In appropriate circumstances equity will presume that the second gift satisfies the first. It is merely a presumption and can be rebutted by evidence of the testator's intention.

The presumption of satisfaction has various aspects. We are here concerned with the ademption of a legacy as a result of a subsequent portion. The topic may sound rather outdated but there have been a number of recent cases confirming that the presumption is still active.

A "portion is ... very broadly speaking, a gift intended to set up a child in life or to make substantial provision for him or her ..." per Lindsay J in *Re Cameron (Deceased)* (1999).

It is only lifetime gifts which are classified as "portions" that cause problems in this context. A mere gift is not a portion. There must be an idea of making a permanent provision for the child.

In *Taylor v Taylor* (1875) it was held that paying for the son's entry into Middle Temple, buying him an army commission (after he had given up the idea of law) and buying him a mining business (after he had given up the idea of the army) were all portions. However, other lesser payments including paying his gambling debts were not.

In *Re Cameron* (1999) it was held that it was irrelevant whether the gift was made by the father or the mother (or someone else in loco parentis). The gift in *Re Cameron* was actually made *on behalf* of the mother under an enduring power of attorney. Moreover, it was made not to the legatee but to the child of the legatee to cover school fees.

In *Race v Race* (2002) Behrens J concluded that the rule against double portions can now apply to gifts of land (previously there was some suggestion that it applied only to personalty).

In *Casimir v Alexander* (2002) Hart J held that the age of the child was irrelevant. The child in question was an old-age pensioner. The gift was a house and thus not a means of assisting her to earn her own livelihood. The gift was capable of being a portion as the key element is the permanent nature of the provision rather than the age or status in life of the donee. However, on the facts, there was sufficient evidence to rebut the presumption. The deceased regarded his daughter as having "earned" the gift through her long years of caring for him and his wife. Moreover, it was a condition of the gift purchase that she would continue caring for her father in the new house. This meant that there was a motive for the lifetime gift which differentiated it from the testamentary gift.

Kloosman v Aylen and Frost (2013) was a similar example where it was clear that the deceased had not intended lifetime gifts to his two daughters to be in satisfaction of their entitlement under the will. He regarded his two daughters as having earned the gifts by taking care of him during a long illness.

When deciding whether or not a legacy has failed as a result of the doctrine of satisfaction, it is the donor's intention at the time of the later gift that is important not the intention at the time of the will. Obviously, if it is apparent at the time a will is made that a testator is intending to make a subsequent gift to one child, it will be sensible for the testator to make a written statement as to his present intention and place it with the will.

5. INCIDENCE OF PECUNIARY LEGACIES

Introduction

Throughout this section the term "pecuniary legacy" is used in the Administration of Estates Act sense to cover a general legacy, an annuity or a demonstrative legacy so far as it is not discharged from the designated property. **16-050**

If a will gives a pecuniary legacy to a beneficiary, the personal representatives will need to know from which part of the estate they are entitled to take assets to pay the legacy. We saw in Ch.15 that personal representatives have a similar problem when deciding which assets are to be used for payment of debts and that there are statutory rules which govern availability of assets for payment of debts. The position with regard to pecuniary legacies is, however, much less certain. This area of the law has been described as "tortuous" and "notoriously obscure" (*Re Taylor's Estate* (1969) per Salt QC). It is most desirable that anyone drafting a will should avoid any problems of statutory interpretation by stating expressly what property is to be taken for payment of pecuniary legacies.

However, in the opinion of the writers this tortuous area has been simplified by the Law Reform (Succession) Act 1995.

No undisposed of property

The pre-1926 rules still apply, which means that pecuniary legacies are payable from residue. Under the rule in *Greville v Brown*, where a testator gives residue (both real and personal) in one mass to a beneficiary the realty is available to pay pecuniary legacies *but only* in so far as the personalty is exhausted. The precise wording of the gift is irrelevant so long as the testator makes it clear that there is one single gift consisting of both realty and personalty. An example of such wording is "I give all my residue, both real and personal, to X". **16-051**

Under the rule in *Roberts v Walker* where a testator directs that pecuniary legacies be paid from a mixed fund of realty and personalty, the legacies are payable *proportionately* from both realty and personalty. An example of such wording would be:

> "I give my residue, real and personal, on trust for sale to my trustees to use the proceeds to pay my legacies and hold any balance for X."

The question of the extent to which realty is available will only rarely be of any importance. For example, if residuary realty is given to one person, R, and residuary personalty to another person, P; R will obviously want to insist that legacies be paid exclusively from personalty and P will be equally anxious that realty be made available.

Undisposed of property

16-052 The Trusts of Land and Appointment of Trustees Act 1996 amends the Administration of Estates Act 1925 s.33 to read as follows:

> "(1) On the death of a person intestate as to any real or personal estate, that estate shall be held in trust by his personal representatives with the power to sell it.
> (2) The personal representatives shall pay out of—
> (a) the ready money of the deceased (so far as not disposed by his will, if any); and
> (b) any net money arising from disposing of any other part of his estate (after payment of costs),
> all such funeral, testamentary and administration expenses, debts and other liabilities ... and out of the residue of the said money the --personal -representative shall set aside a fund sufficient to provide for any pecuniary legacies bequeathed by the will (if any) of the deceased."

The effect of the amended s.33(2) is, therefore, to make undisposed-of property primarily liable for payment of pecuniary legacies. Ready money will be used first but thereafter it is irrelevant whether the undisposed of property is realty or personalty.

Example 7

T's will leaves a pecuniary legacy of £6,000 to L and the residue to A and B in equal shares. A predeceases T and the gift to him lapses. The estate amounts to £20,000. There are no debts. Since s.33(2) expressly directs that pecuniary legacies be paid from money arising from disposing of *any* part of the estate as to which the deceased was intestate, the pecuniary legacy will be paid from the lapsed share of residue irrespective of whether it is realty or personalty. Therefore B gets £10,000 and A's lapsed share of £10,000 is used to pay L's legacy of £6,000. The balance of £4,000 left after payment of the pecuniary legacy will pass under the intestacy rules to T's next-of-kin.

Are there any circumstances in which s.33(2) does not apply?

16-053 Before s.33 was amended by the Trusts of Land and Appointment of Trustees Act 1996 it was clear that the direction to pay pecuniary legacies contained in s.33(2) related only to the proceeds of the *statutory* trust for sale imposed by s.33(1). The statutory trust for sale could not apply if a will imposed an *express* trust for sale because there cannot be two trusts for sale, one statutory and one express, applying to the same property (*Re McKee* (1931)). The express trust took precedence over the statutory trust imposed by s.33(1). If s.33(1) did not apply then neither did s.33(2) which deals with the proceeds of sale arising under the statutory trust.

Example 8

A testator died before 1 January 1996 leaving a pecuniary legacy of £6,000 to L and directing that the residue was to be held *on trust for sale* for A and B in equal shares. A predeceased T and the gift to him lapsed. The estate amounted to £20,000.

Since the testator had imposed an express trust for sale on the residue there was no room for a statutory trust for sale to apply to the residue. If s.33(1) did not apply to the undisposed-of property, neither did s.33(2). The question then arose of what property was to be used to provide for the payment of the legacy to L. Unfortunately the answer was by no means certain.

There were several conflicting cases—*Re Midgley* (1955); *Re Beaumont's Will Trusts* (1950); and *Re Taylor's Estate* (1969). The better view was that when s.33(2) did not apply, the payment of legacies was still governed by the pre-1926 rules. The result was that legacies were not payable primarily from undisposed of property.

However, since the Trusts of Land and Appointment of Trustees Act 1996, it seems to the writers that in the amended s.33 the link between the two subsections is broken. Pecuniary legacies are to be paid from cash in the estate at death or produced by the sale of *any* part of the estate and, therefore, it is irrelevant whether the undisposed-of property is held on a statutory or an express trust.

If this interpretation of the new section is correct it removes an area of unnecessary complexity and uncertainty from the administration of estates. Where the will makes no special provision for the payment of pecuniary legacies, they will always be paid from cash either contained in the estate at death or resulting from the disposal of any part of the estate as to which the deceased was intestate.

Will drafting

Despite the probable simplification of the law it is clearly desirable when drafting wills to state expressly what property is to be used for payment of pecuniary legacies. For example, a testator may leave residue "subject to payment of legacies". It is common for trusts for sale to direct that legacies be paid from residue before division into shares. 16-054

6. INCOME FROM AND INTEREST ON LEGACIES AND DEVISES

Introduction

A personal representative cannot be compelled to pay legacies and distribute the estates before the expiry of one year from the death (Administration of Estates Act 1925 s.44). Even in a very simple administration there will inevitably be delay between the death and the distribution. Beneficiaries will want to know what rights they have to income or interest in that period. 16-055

This part of the chapter is concerned with the rights of a beneficiary:

(a) to receive *income* which has been produced by assets in the period between the death of the testator and the vesting of the assets in the beneficiary; and
(b) to receive *interest* paid from the estate on the value of a pecuniary (or

general) legacy in the period between the death of the testator and the payment of the legacy to the beneficiary.

Income

Introduction

16-056 Some assets by their very nature are incapable of producing income (for example, a painting, a ring, a piece of furniture) in which case the question of a beneficiary's right to income is irrelevant. Other assets do, however, produce income (for example, a house which is rented to a tenant, company shares, government stock). We are concerned with the rights of beneficiaries to receive this income. It is necessary to distinguish the following types of gift:

(a) immediate specific gifts;
(b) contingent and deferred specific gifts;
(c) contingent pecuniary legacies;
(d) immediate residuary gifts; and
(e) contingent and deferred residuary gifts.

Immediate specific gifts

16-057 A specific legacy or devise which is to take immediate effect carries with it the right to any income accruing to the property in the period between the death of the testator and vesting. The beneficiary is not, however, entitled to receive the income *as it arises*; instead, the beneficiary must wait until the personal representatives vest the property in the beneficiary by means of an assent. The assent operates retrospectively to give the beneficiary the right to receive the income which has accrued since the date of death.

An assent can be oral in the case of all assets other than land, for which a written assent is required. An assent indicates that the asset is not required for payment of debts and is available to the beneficiary. (See para.18-003 and following.) A specific beneficiary must bear all liabilities relating to the asset after the assent and thus must bear any costs of transporting, insuring or transferring the asset unless there is a direction to the contrary in the will. It is common for a clause to be included in a professionally drawn will directing that such expenses be paid from residue.

Contingent and deferred specific gifts

16-058 An example of a contingent specific gift is "to X if X becomes a solicitor" and an example of a deferred specific gift is "to X after the expiry of five years". Prior to 1925 neither type of gift carried with it the right to receive income. However, s.175 of the Law of Property Act 1925 provides that such gifts do carry with them the right to income (unless the testator has indicated otherwise). Such income will, therefore, be added to the capital and will devolve with it. In the case of will trusts arising under wills executed before 6 April 2010 (the date on which the Perpetuities and Accumulations Act 2009 came into force) or lifetime trusts created before that date, income can only be accumulated for so long as the statutory rule against accumulations permits (Law of Property Act 1925 ss.164–166 as amended by the Perpetuities and Accumulations Act 1964 s.13). Thereafter the income will either fall into residue or pass under the intestacy rules. In the case of trusts subject to the

2009 Act there are no statutory restrictions so, unless the will or trust instrument contain restrictions, income can be accumulated throughout the life of the trust.

Contingent pecuniary legacies

In the absence of an express direction contingent pecuniary legacies do not normally carry interest. Interest is payable from the date of the death in the four situations set out in para.16-066. **16-059**

If, for example, a testator leaves "£100,000 to my great-granddaughter contingent on her reaching 25" any interest or income produced by the £100,000 will be paid to the residuary beneficiary. This is unlikely to be what the testator would wish so it is preferable to either include an express direction to pay interest or, probably more satisfactory, to provide that the legacy is to be held on trust with appropriate trustee powers for appointment of income and capital.

Immediate residuary gifts

An immediate residuary gift whether of realty or personalty carries with it the right to income accruing after the testator's death. **16-060**

Contingent and deferred residuary gifts

Contingent residuary bequests have always carried the right to income, contingent residuary devises carry the right to such income as a result of the Law of Property Act s.175. In the absence of contrary direction such income will be added to capital (subject to the rule against accumulations) and will devolve with it. **16-061**

Section 175 does not mention *deferred* (or deferred, contingent) bequests which are, therefore, subject to the pre-1926 rules and do not carry the right to income. In the absence of a direction to the contrary income will pass to the person entitled to undisposed-of property.

There is some uncertainty as to whether a *deferred* residuary devise carries the right to income. The better view appears to be that it does with the result that income will be added to capital.

The effect is that probably all residuary gifts carry the right to income apart from deferred (or deferred, contingent) residuary bequests. Examples of such gifts would be "my personalty to X after the death of A" or "my personalty to X after the death of A if X becomes a solicitor".

Apportioning income

In the case of wills and trusts created or arising before 1 October 2013, the Apportionment Act 1870 requires income to be apportioned on a daily basis unless, as was normally the case, it was excluded. **16-062**

In the absence of any direction to the contrary in the will s.1 of the Apportionment Act 1870 provides that:

> "All rents, annuities, dividends and other periodical payments in the nature of income ... shall, like interest on money lent, be considered as accruing from day to day and shall be apportionable in respect of time accordingly."

Interest is required at common law to be apportioned on a daily basis.
Where the Act is not excluded apportionment calculations are required.

Example 9

T leaves shares in ABC Ltd to X and residue to R. A dividend of £365 is declared for a period, 100 days of which precede the death and 265 days of which follow the death. The Apportionment Act is not excluded. The dividend must be apportioned between X and R. R will get the pre-death income attributable to the 100-day period and X will get the post-death income attributable to the 265-day period.

R will get 100/365 × £365 = £100

X will get 265/365 × £365 = £265

The Law Commission recommended in "Capital and Income in Trusts: Classification and Apportionment" (Report No.315) that the rules requiring apportionment be abolished. The Trusts (Capital and Income) Act 2013 does so for trusts created or arising on or after 1 October 2013.

As well as disapplying the Apportionment Act, it also disapplies the equitable apportionment rules known as the rule in *Howe v Lord Dartmouth* (1802), the rule in *Re Earl of Chesterfield's Trusts* (1833) (see para.18-018 and following) and the rule in *Allhusen v Whittell* (1867) which were designed to achieve fairness between income and capital beneficiaries but which were regarded as more trouble than they were worth.

The Apportionment Act 1870 and the Trusts (Capital and Income) Act 2013 (and the disapplication of either of them) concern the allocation of income between income and capital beneficiaries. They have no application to the computation of inheritance tax on capital, which, according to inheritance tax valuation rules, must reflect accrued income (see para.4-047). Neither do they have any application as regards income tax which is charged when income is payable or paid (i.e. when it arises) and not as it accrues (i.e. is in the process of arising) from day to day (see para.6-016).

Entitlement to interest

Introduction

16-063 Interest is paid to a pecuniary legatee (or general legatee or demonstrative legatee if the designated fund has been exhausted) from the time at which the legacy is payable. The interest is to compensate the legatee where payment of the legacy is delayed. The interest is paid from residue and is treated as an administration expense. The testator may make express provision for the payment of interest and order that more or less interest be paid.

Rate of interest

16-064 Where disputes arise as to the administration of an estate, the court has power to order personal representatives to account under CPR Pt 64 and can order the payment of interest. Under CPR PD40 (Judgments, orders, sale of land, etc.) para.15:

> "interest shall be allowed on each legacy at the basic rate payable for the time being on funds in court or at such other rate as the court shall direct, beginning one year after the testator's death".

It therefore appears that in the absence of any express provision in the will this is the rate at which personal representatives should allow interest. From 23 August 2023, the rate increased from 3.375 per cent to 5.00 per cent reducing to 3.94 per cent from 12 June 2024.

Time for payment In the absence of any direction to the contrary from the testator, the general rule is that a legacy is payable one year from the testator's death (this period is sometimes referred to as the executor's year). It may well be impossible to pay a legacy at the end of the year because of problems with the administration. If the legacy is not paid by the end of that period the legatee becomes entitled to interest from that date. **16-065**

A testator may specify that a legacy is to be paid at a particular date; for example "£2,000 to X to be paid immediately after my death" in which case interest will be payable from the date specified. Similarly, if a testator directs that a legacy is contingent on the happening of an event or is deferred until a future date interest will be payable not from the end of the executor's year but from the date of the specified event or the future date. However, if a testator directs that a contingent or deferred legacy be severed from the rest of the estate and set aside for the benefit of the legatee it will carry interest from the end of the executor's year.

Four special cases when interest is paid from death

There are four exceptional cases when a pecuniary legacy (or general legacy or demonstrative legacy if the designated fund has been exhausted) carries interest from the date of death: **16-066**

(1) *Satisfaction of a debt.* A legacy to a creditor which is to satisfy a debt carries interest from the date of the death unless the will fixes a later date for payment.
(2) *Legacy charged on realty.* For historical reasons a vested legacy charged on realty carries interest from the date of death, unless the testator fixed a later date for payment.
(3) *Legacy to a testator's minor child.* If a testator gives a legacy to their minor child or to a minor to whom they are in loco parentis the legacy carries interest from the date of death. The rule is an old one designed to provide maintenance for the child; if, therefore, any other fund is designated for its maintenance, the legacy will not carry interest.

    Moreover, the rule only applies where the legacy is given to the child directly; interest is not payable from death if the legacy is given to trustees to hold for the child (*Re Pollock* (1943)).

    Interest is payable from death if the legacy is contingent on the child reaching full age or marrying earlier but it is probably not so payable if the contingency has no reference to the child's minority (for example reaching an age greater than majority).
(4) *Legacy to a minor with intention to provide maintenance.* If a testator gives a legacy to any minor (not necessarily the testator's own child or a person to whom the testator is in loco parentis) and shows an intention to provide for the minor's maintenance, it carries interest from death unless the will

designates some other fund for maintenance. Unlike the previous rule interest will be carried from death by a legacy contingent on reaching an age greater than majority.

Will drafting

16-067 A person who is drafting a will may prefer to make express provision for the payment of interest rather than leaving personal representatives and beneficiaries to rely on these rather technical rules.

Options to purchase

16-068 A will may give someone the right to purchase an asset of the estate. If the will is silent, the asset is valued at market value at the date of death: see *Re Bliss* (2001). An open market valuation differs from a probate valuation in that it takes into account matters such as a right of occupation granted by will which a probate valuation would ignore. *Re Bliss* also decided that the valuation should not take into account events subsequent to death unless the will directed otherwise. In *Re Bliss* the option to purchase was subject to the right of the deceased's husband to occupy part of the property. A few months after the death and before the option had been exercised, the husband moved out and indicated that he would not return. The valuation was still to be carried out subject to his right to occupy.

Re Bowles (2003) held that time for the exercise of an option will not be of the essence where the will contains no prescribed consequences for failure to act in time. The testator's will gave a beneficiary the right to buy part of a farm at the value agreed between the executors and HMRC. He had to be informed of this right within six months of the testator's death and then had three months to decide whether he wanted to exercise the option. Almost three years after the death agreement had still not been reached with HMRC. The court held that the time limits were directory in nature and that the beneficiary was entitled to wait until the price was ascertainable. From then he would have a reasonable time to exercise the option. To have found that the time limits were mandatory might have defeated the testator's intention.

Chapter Seventeen

CONSTRUCTION OF WILLS

1. Introduction and Modern Approach

Questions of construction are dealt with by the Chancery Division and not the Probate court. **17-001**

Entire books have been written on the principles governing the construction of wills. One chapter can do no more than give a very brief introduction to some of the more important principles involved. Construction is not a matter of applying a series of rules in a rigid and pre-determined way. The courts are moving towards a more natural and inclusive approach to construction, generally. In *Charles v Barzey* (2002) in the Privy Council, Lord Hoffman said that

> "the interpretation of a Will is in principle no different from that of any other communication. The question is what a reasonable person, possessed of all the background knowledge which the testatrix might reasonably have been expected to have, would have understood the testatrix to have meant by the words which were used."

In *RSPCA v Sharp* (2010) the Court of Appeal (per Lord Lloyd at [115]) said that the approach to the construction of wills should accord with the approach to the construction of contracts taken by the House of Lords in *Investors Compensation Scheme Ltd v West Bromwich Building Society* (1998):

> "The principle that words should be given their 'natural and ordinary meaning' reflects the commonsense proposition that we do not easily accept that people have made linguistic mistakes, particularly in formal documents. On the other hand, if one would nevertheless conclude from the background that something must have gone wrong with the language, the law does not require judges to attribute to the parties an intention which they plainly could not have had."

Lord Neuberger said in *Marley v Rawlings* (2014) (at [18]):

> "During the past forty years, the House of Lords and Supreme Court have laid down the correct approach to the interpretation, or construction, of commercial contracts in a number of cases … When interpreting a contract, the court is concerned to find the intention of the party or parties, and it does this by identifying the meaning of the relevant words:
>
> (a) in the light of:
> (i) the natural and ordinary meaning of those words,
> (ii) the overall purpose of the document,
> (iii) any other provisions of the document,
> (iv) the facts known or assumed by the parties at the time that the document was executed, and
> (v) common sense, but

(b) ignoring subjective evidence of any party's intentions."

He went on to say at [20]:

> "When it comes to interpreting wills, it seems to me that the approach should be the same. Whether the document in question is a commercial contract or a will, the aim is to identify the intention of the party or parties to the document by interpreting the words used in their documentary, factual and commercial context."

At [23] he referred to the well-known suggestion of James LJ in *Boyes v Cook* (1880) (see para.17-009) that, when interpreting a will, the court should "place [itself] in [the testator's] arm-chair" and said that this was consistent with the approach of interpretation by reference to the factual context.

However, at [24] he made the point that in relation to wills, as opposed to contracts, there is a highly relevant statutory provision, Administration of Justice Act 1982 s.21 which allows extrinsic evidence, including evidence of the testator's intention to be admitted in certain circumstances (see para.17-012).

Accordingly, in his view, a will is to be interpreted in the same way as any other document, but with the admission of extrinsic evidence under s.21 in appropriate circumstances.

Lord Neuberger's dicta have become the starting point for questions of construction. The focus on establishing the intention of the testator as expressed in the will means that there is less reliance on precedent and what other courts decided about similar wording used by other testators. The Privy Council emphasised the danger of adopting prima facie principles of construction in *Sammut v Manzi* (2008). Thus, Lord Phillips of Worth Matravers said:

> "The starting point when construing any will is to attempt to deduce the intention of the testator by giving the words of the will the meaning that they naturally bear, having regard to the contents of the will as a whole.
>
> There were placed before their Lordships no less than 17 decided cases, some of which involved decisions on wording that bore some similarity with that used in the present case. Little assistance in construing a will is likely to be gained by consideration of how other judges have interpreted similar wording in other cases. Counsel rightly recognised that the starting point must be to look at the natural meaning of the wording of the will to be construed without reference to other decisions or to prima facie principles of construction."

Following Lord Neuberger's comments in *Marley v Rawlings*, a number of cases managed to interpret words in a way which was not entirely obvious because of the general context. See, for example, *Reading v Reading* (2015), where Asplin J felt able to construe the expression "issue" as including step-children where there were indications in the will as a whole and the factual background that this was the testator's intention. Had it been necessary, she would have admitted extrinsic evidence of the testator's intention in the form of the solicitor's attendance note under Administration of Justice Act 1982 s.21.

2. THE OBJECT OF THE COURT IS TO ASCERTAIN THE TESTATOR'S EXPRESSED INTENTION

Starting point is natural and ordinary meaning of words used

The object of the court is to ascertain the testator's intention *as expressed in the will*, as Patten J said in *RSPCA v Sharp*. In other words, the court is simply concerned to determine the meaning of the words written; it will not speculate or conjecture as to what the testator's "real" intention may have been. If the will makes sense and is not ambiguous on its face, there is no scope for interpreting the words used a different meaning. (It may sometimes be possible to admit extrinsic evidence to show that the words were intended to mean something different or to rectify the will where it does not carry out the testator's wishes.) **17-002**

Thus, in *Jump v Lister* (2016) a childless couple made mirror wills. Each provided that if the other predeceased a number of pecuniary legacies were to be paid and the residue to the husband's two nieces. The couple were found dead in circumstances in which the order of deaths was uncertain. The wife was older and so was deemed to die first (under LPA 1925 s.184: see para.16-024). The gift to her, therefore, failed and the substitutional gifts took effect.

The husband was deemed to have survived his wife but her will, like his, contained a general survivorship clause providing that "My estate is to be divided as if any person who dies within 28 days of my death had predeceased me." Hence, the wife's gift to her husband failed and the same pecuniary legacies were payable. The residuary legatees were unhappy at the reduction in size of their entitlement and threatened to sue the solicitors in negligence. As a preliminary an application was made asking for the wife's will to be construed as if the general survivorship clause did not apply to the gift to her husband. The application was refused. The wording of the survivorship clause was clear and unambiguous. There was nothing in any part of either will to suggest that the "omnibus" survivorship clause did not apply to the entire will. Neither the admissible factual background (or matrix), nor common sense, could in the opinion of the judge be permitted to contradict what he considered to be the clear and unrestricted wording of the will. The legacies had to be paid twice.

The same result occurred in *Gledhill v Arnold* (2015), where a testator left his interest in the house he shared with his sister-in-law to her for life, or until she moved out and then on the trusts of residue. The residue was left to the sister-in-law absolutely with a substitutional gift to her children should she predecease. The deceased's earlier will had specifically left the interest in the house to the children after the sister-in-law's interest came to an end and the instructing solicitor gave evidence that the intention had been to do the same in the final will. Sonia Proudman J refused to interpret the will to give effect to the testator's intention in this way on the basis that there was no ambiguity in the will to justify departing from the normal meaning. (However, she did agree to rectify it under Administration of Justice Act 1982 s.20. See para.2-034 and following and para.17-007.)

Other matters are relevant

In *Reading v Reading* (2015) the testator and his wife had five children between them from previous marriages. They made mirror wills with the intention of treating the five children equally, provision being made for the grandchildren as well. **17-003**

Clause 3 of the testator's will established a nil-rate band trust, the beneficiaries of which were expressed to be "my wife ... and any issue of mine who are alive at the start of or born during the trust period". If his wife failed to survive him by 28 days, clause 4 directed that the estate was to be divided between his named children and stepchildren. The testator also wrote a letter of wishes stating that, subject to his wife's needs, the capital should be divided between his children and stepchildren equally. The solicitor who drafted the will gave evidence that the testator and his wife clearly wanted all five children and stepchildren, plus the children of those five, to be potential beneficiaries of the trust. However, he admitted that in drafting the will he had overlooked the fact that the word "issue" would not normally include the testator's stepchildren or their children. Asplin J said—applying Lord Neuberger's approach as set out at para.17-001—that it was clear that the natural and ordinary meaning of "issue" did not include stepchildren. However, it was also necessary to consider the context of the words or phrase used in the sense of the overall purpose of the will as a whole and the other provisions contained in it. Had the wife predeceased, the estate would have been held for the named children and stepchildren equally. With that in mind it would be odd if the intention was to exclude stepchildren from the nil-rate band trust if she survived. It was also relevant that the testator appointed a child and stepchild as co-executors. As part of the relevant factual matrix it was appropriate to consider the letter of wishes which referred to stepchildren benefiting under the discretionary trust. Overall, taking those factors into consideration, and applying common sense, Asplin J concluded that the words "issue of mine" and "such of my issue" respectively included both children and stepchildren and their children. She would also have admitted extrinsic evidence of the testator's intention under Administration of Justice Act 1982 s.21(1)(c) (see para.17-012 and following) had it been necessary but would have refused rectification under Administration of Justice Act 1982 s.20 (see para.2-034 and following) on the basis that the "error" was a professional misjudgement rather than a clerical error as required by the statute.

In *Bracey v Curley* (2022) Philip Mott QC sitting as a Deputy Judge doubted that this was correct but said that he did not need to depart from that decision, or to decline to follow it as the circumstances of the two cases differed. *Reading v Reading* involved a positive choice of a word which had an established legal meaning, whereas *Bracey v Curley* involved the omission of words intended to make clear the conditions applying to a disposition.

In *Robinson v The Royal Society* (2015) a will was expressed to apply "only to property of mine which is situated at my death in the United Kingdom". The normal meaning of "United Kingdom" does not extend to the Channel Islands or Isle of Man. It is limited to England and Wales, Scotland and Northern Ireland. In fact, the testator who was resident and working in Switzerland at the time the will was made owned virtually nothing in the UK. His major assets were bank accounts in Jersey and the Isle of Man. This was still true at the date of his death so that the bulk of his estate would have passed on intestacy rather than to the residuary legatee, the Royal Society. The judge took into account the facts at the date the will was made and concluded that it was permissible to give the expression "United Kingdom" an extended meaning. He did say however, that had he been unable to admit extrinsic evidence of the testator's intention (which was overwhelming) he would have found it much more difficult to reach that conclusion. See also *Partington v Rossiter* (2021) where exactly the same mistake was made, and the court was able to give an extended meaning to the term.

A term may be implied if it is necessary

In *Scarfe v Matthews* (2012) Nicholas Strauss QC, sitting as a deputy judge, said that in relation to the construction of contracts: **17-004**

> "it is now recognised that consideration of whether terms should be implied into a contract are an integral part of the exercise of construing it. A term is to be implied if that is what the reasonable observer, with knowledge of the relevant background, would understand the contract to mean. This may arise because the parties have not 'thought through' the issue which has now arisen."

In other words, a term is implied where, having regard to the terms of the contract and the evidence as to its background, the court is sure that this is what the parties would have provided expressly if they had thought the issue through. The judge said that the same approach applies to the construction of a will. He, therefore, felt able to imply a limitation on a clause which directed that inheritance tax resulting from his death was payable from residue to prevent the clause applying to the tax payable by any of his children who, contrary to his wishes, exercised their inheritance rights over French property comprised in the estate. The tax provision was to protect the beneficiaries under the will. The judge held that a reasonable observer would have taken the testator to have intended the clause to be limited in this way.

Where the wording of a gift is too vague to be given a specific meaning the court cannot rewrite the gift which, therefore, fails for uncertainty (see paras 16-035–16-037).

Some words have several meanings

If the words used in the will are clear and unambiguous, it is not possible for the court to attribute to them meanings they do not normally bear in order to produce a result which is thought to be more in accordance with the testator's intentions: see para.17-002. However, some words have several meanings in which case the court must try and determine in what sense the testator used the word. "Money" is a good example of such a word since it can mean merely notes or coins, can include money "in the bank" or can be used loosely to cover assets in general. The House of Lords in *Perrin v Morgan* (1943) took the view that the word was capable of having a very wide meaning indeed and that courts should carefully consider the context before attributing a narrow meaning to the word (particularly if the result of such an interpretation would be to leave a large part of the estate undisposed). **17-005**

The dictionary principle

A testator is free to show that words used in the will are used in an unusual way. This may be done expressly, by including a definition clause; for example, a testator may say that wherever they refer to "my monkey" they mean "my son". It is more likely, however, that the will as a whole may suggest that an unusual meaning is attached to one word. Thus, in *Re Lowe* (1890) a testator made a gift "to all my children, apart from X". (X was illegitimate.) At that time the word "children" did not include illegitimate children unless the testator indicated that he wanted it to do so. It was held that the specific exclusion of X indicated that the testator regarded the word "children" as including illegitimate ones, so that all the testator's illegitimate children, apart from X, could take. **17-006**

Rectification of a will

17-007 Section 20 of the Administration of Justice Act 1982 provides that

> "if a court is satisfied that a will is so expressed that it fails to carry out the testator's intentions, in consequence:
>
> (a) of a clerical error; or
> (b) of a failure to understand his instructions,
>
> it may order that the will shall be rectified so as to carry out his intentions".

A fuller discussion of this provision is contained in para.2-034 and following.

3. Extrinsic Evidence

The general rule

17-008 The general rule is that the court construes the words written in the will and will not admit extrinsic evidence of the testator's intention. However, there are certain circumstances where extrinsic evidence is admissible.

The first three are long established; the others were introduced by the Administration of Justice Act 1982.

Where the words used are not apt to fit the surrounding circumstances

17-009 This is sometimes referred to as "the armchair principle". Per James LJ, *Boyes v Cook* (1880):

> "You may place yourself, so to speak, in [the testator's] armchair, and consider the circumstances by which he was surrounded when he made his will to assist you in arriving at his intention."

An illustration of this rule is *Thorn v Dickens* (1906) where the testator left "all to mother" but did not have a mother living at the time he made his will; extrinsic evidence of the testator's circumstances was admitted to show that he was in the habit of calling his wife "mother" with the result that she was able to take. Similarly, in *Re Fish* (1893) the testator left property to "my niece, Eliza Waterhouse" but did not have a niece of that name; extrinsic evidence was admitted to show that his wife had a great-niece of that name and it was found that the testator had used the word "niece" in a wide sense so that the great-niece was able to take the gift. In both these cases there was no-one who fitted the description used in the will. If there had been (for example, if in *Thorn v Dickens* the testator's mother had been alive at the time the will was made) then no extrinsic evidence could have been admitted and the apparent beneficiary would have taken. Declarations made by the testator as to their intention are not admissible; only evidence *of the surrounding circumstances* is admissible.

Where there is a latent ambiguity

17-010 A latent ambiguity is one which does not become apparent until an attempt is made to give effect to the dispositions in the will. Thus, if a testator makes a gift of "my motor car" and it turns out that, at the time of the will, he owned six cars or, if a testator makes a gift to "my nephew, John Jones" and it turns out that he had several so named, extrinsic evidence *including evidence of declarations made by the testator* as to his intention will be admitted to show which car was intended to be the subject matter of the gift or which nephew was intended to benefit. If there is no evidence available, the whole gift will fail for uncertainty.

An example of a latent ambiguity is *Re Jackson* (1933). The testator made a gift "to my nephew, Arthur Murphy"; he had one illegitimate nephew and two legitimate nephews of that name. At that time illegitimate relationships were ignored unless the will showed a contrary intention. Therefore, had there been only one legitimate nephew that nephew would have fitted the description and would have taken the gift (even if there had been evidence that the testator's intention was that that person should not take). However, as there were two such nephews there was a latent ambiguity and extrinsic evidence, including evidence of the testator's *intention*, was admitted. This evidence showed that, in fact, the testator had intended to refer to the illegitimate nephew and he, therefore, took the gift. In *Pinnel v Anison* (2006) the wording of the will made a gift to "my sister Doreen Hall of [address given]". The deceased had lost contact with his family. He had a sister whose name was Doreen Anison. A woman called Doreen Hall lived at the address given in the will which was in the area where the deceased had spent his childhood. She was, however, not related to the deceased. The gift was clearly ambiguous. Extrinsic evidence showed that the deceased had made amateurish attempts to find his family before making the will. From this the court was able to conclude that he had intended the gift to go to his sister not to Doreen Hall and the will was construed accordingly.

To rebut a presumption of equity

In certain circumstances equity raises presumptions; for example, that a legacy from a father (or person in loco parentis) to his child will be adeemed if the father (or person in loco parentis) after the date of the will gives the child an inter vivos portion. These presumptions may be rebutted by extrinsic evidence (including evidence of declarations made by the testator as to their intention). **17-011**

Administration of Justice Act 1982

In the case of deaths occurring after 31 December 1982, s.21(1) of the Administration of Justice Act 1982 provides that extrinsic evidence, *including evidence of declarations as to the testator's intention*, may be admitted to assist in the interpretation of a will in so far as: **17-012**

(a) any part of it is meaningless,
(b) the language used in any part of it is ambiguous on the face of it, and
(c) evidence other than evidence of the testator's intention shows that the language used in any part of it is ambiguous in the light of the surrounding circumstances.

An example of paragraph (b) is a gift of "my money" or "my effects".

Paragraph (c) appears to have extended the existing rules on extrinsic evidence in two ways.

(1) Evidence of surrounding circumstances (though not direct evidence of the testator's intention) can now be admitted to *raise the possibility* that an

ambiguity exists, whereas, prior to the 1982 Act, evidence could only be admitted where the words did not fit the surrounding circumstances. Thus, where a testator makes a gift to "my niece, Ann" it would now be possible to admit evidence to show that, although the testator had only one niece called Ann, there was a niece of his spouse also called Ann.

(2) It is now possible to admit direct evidence of the testator's intention in cases other than latent ambiguity.

In a helpful judgment (*Re Williams, Deceased* (1985)), Nicholls J stated the principles to be applied when considering the admissibility of extrinsic evidence. He reminded practitioners that the section is merely *an aid* to construction. Thus, evidence may be admitted to show which of several possible meanings a testator was applying to a particular word or phrase (for example "my money", "my effects"). The meaning may be one which without the evidence would not have been at all apparent but so long as the word or phrase is *capable* of bearing that meaning in its context this does not matter. However, it may be that the extrinsic evidence reveals a meaning attached by the testator to a word or phrase which no matter how liberal the approach of the court, the word or phrase cannot bear. The court will not allow extrinsic evidence to vary or contradict the language used in the will since this would amount to rewriting the will for the testator and this can only be done, if at all, under the rectification provisions. However, the more relaxed approach taken by the courts to questions of interpretation following the statements of Lord Neuberger in *Marley v Rawlings* (2014) quoted at paras 17-001 and 17-002 means that they are much more willing to rewrite wills without having recourse to the remedy of rectification provided it is clear what was intended. For two examples see *Brooke v Purton* (2014) and *Burnard v Burnard* (2014).

A recent example of s.21 in action is *Harris v The Beneficiaries of the Estate of Margaret Alice Cooper (Deceased)* (2010). The deceased in a homemade will left her house to an old friend (who she also appointed as her executor) and her "money" to "my surviving relatives". Norris J held that she was clearly using money in a very general sense to cover everything except the house. The next question was who were the surviving relatives? She had never married and had no surviving parent or siblings. Her relatives were, therefore, the offspring of her dead uncles and aunts: their children (who were her first cousins) and then the children and issue of the first cousins (first cousins once and twice removed). There were 29 first cousins once removed but only three surviving first cousins who between them had seven children. The executor who had known the deceased for 64 years before her death said that the only members of her family she talked about were the three known surviving first cousins and that he had always assumed that they were the people the deceased intended to benefit. Norris J described this evidence as "powerful" and agreed that the first cousins were intended to benefit. He concluded that the reference to "surviving" was intended to provide for the substitution of the children of any deceased first cousin. However, as all the first cousins survived, they took equally.

In *Spurling v Broadhurst* (2012) a will left the residue "to Veronica Broadhurst, Ann Foden, the living grandchildren of Veronica Broadhurst, and David Spurling in equal shares". It was agreed that the gift which was wholly ambiguous and that there were four different ways to construe the gift. Extrinsic evidence was admitted to show that the deceased had been a fair man who was particularly concerned to benefit the younger generation. The clause was therefore construed to give an equal share to Veronica, Anne and each of the seven Broadhurst grandchildren and the four Spurling grandchildren 13 shares in all.

In *Reading v Reading* (2015) (see para.17-003) extrinsic evidence would have been admitted under s.21(1)(c) had it been necessary and in *Robinson v The Royal Society* (2015) (see para.17-003) extrinsic evidence was admitted under s.21(1)(c).

4. The Will Speaks from Death

Section 24 of the Wills Act 1837

Section 24 provides that as regards property every will shall be construed "to speak and take effect as if it had been executed immediately before the death of the testator, unless a contrary intention shall appear by the will". Thus, a gift of "the contents of my house" will pass the contents owned at the date of death, not merely those owned at the date of the will. **17-013**

Contrary intention

Introduction

A will may expressly state that the testator is giving an asset owned at the date of the will. In the absence of an express statement, certain words and expressions are commonly found to show contrary intention. **17-014**

"My"

If the testator couples the word "my" with a gift of a specific item (for example, "my piano") it is possible that the court will construe the gift as a gift of the particular piano owned at the date of the will. Therefore, if the piano is sold or destroyed after the date of the will the gift is adeemed and cannot pass a piano purchased later and owned at the date of the death. However, if the word "my" is coupled with a description of property capable of increase or decrease (for example, "all my shares") there is no contrary intention and the gift will pass any shares owned at the time of death. **17-015**

"Now" or "at present"

The use of such words will be taken as showing a contrary intention (that is, as referring to the date the will is made) if they are an essential part of the description. Thus, in *Re Edwards* (1890) the testator made a gift of "my house and premises where I now reside". After the date of the will he let a part of the property. The court held that the word "now" indicated a contrary intention so that the whole of the property occupied at the time the will was made (including the part subsequently let) passed to the beneficiary, not merely the part occupied at the date of the death. **17-016**

If, however, the words are regarded as mere additional or superfluous description which has simply become inaccurate by the date of the will the court is unlikely to find that they show a contrary intention. In *Re Willis* (1911) a testator gave "all my freehold house and premises situated at X and known as Y and in which I now reside". After the date of the will he acquired two further plots of land which he enjoyed with the original house. The court held that there was no contrary intention so that the gift was to be construed at the date of death; thus the additional plots were included.

Section 24 has no application to people

17-017 Section 24 only applies to property; as regards people a will is construed at the date it is made (unless there is a contrary intention). A gift made "to the eldest son of A" is construed as a gift to the person fulfilling that description at the date the will is made. If that person predeceases the testator the gift fails and does not pass to the eldest surviving son.

It is important to remember that where a will is republished it is construed as if made at the date of the republication.

If a testator makes a gift to a beneficiary who fulfils a particular description (for example, "the wife of X") and to the testator's knowledge no-one fulfils that description at the date of the will the court will construe the gift as one made to the first person to fulfil the description. Once a person has fulfilled the description the gift is construed as a gift to that person even if the description later becomes inaccurate; thus, if in the previous example X and his wife were divorced after the date of the will she would still be entitled to the gift on the testator's death, even if X had remarried.

In *Thomas v Kent* (2007) a will contained a gift to the testator's "brothers and sisters in equal shares, the share of any deceased brother or sister to be taken by his or her children in equal shares". At the date of the will the testator had one surviving brother and three surviving sisters. The question arose as to whether the children of a brother who died before the will was made could take under this gift. The Court of Appeal held that they could. As the testator referred to "brothers" (plural) when only one brother was alive showed that he intended the gift to be available to the children of all his siblings whether alive at the time of the will or not (a further question of whether the children of brothers and sisters could take under the substitutional gift only if alive at the date of the will was remitted to the High Court for further argument).

Gender Recognition Act 2004

Introduction

17-018 Section 9 of the Gender Recognition Act 2004 provides that where a gender recognition panel issues full gender recognition certificate to a person, the person's gender becomes for all purposes the acquired gender.

Before issuing a certificate, the panel must be satisfied that the applicant:

- has, or has had, gender dysphoria;
- has lived in the acquired gender throughout the preceding two years; and
- intends to continue to live in the acquired gender until death.

Where a will is made before the Act came into force (4 April 2005) the gender recognition certificate has no effect. In wills made after that date a gift made by reference to gender will include a person who has acquired a full certificate in the specified gender.

Example 1

A testatrix leaves her estate to her nieces. The will is made in 2006. In 2010 her nephew, John, obtains a full female gender recognition certificate. "John" is entitled to share in the gift.

The Act is rarely relevant to the administration of estates as most gifts are not conditional on gender. A gift to a person by name is a gift to the person with that name at the date the gift is made.

Protection for trustees and personal representatives

Under s.17 trustees or personal representatives are relieved from any fiduciary duty to inquire whether a gender recognition certificate has been issued to any person or revoked, even if that fact could affect entitlement to property which they are responsible for distributing. The beneficiary will nevertheless retain their claim to the property and may enforce this claim, e.g. by -following the property into the hands of another person who has received it instead. **17-019**

Powers of the court

Under s.18 the court has power to make orders to deal with the situation where the devolution of property under a will or other instrument is different from what it would be but for the change of gender. A person who is adversely affected by the different disposition can apply to the court. The court, if satisfied that it is just to do so, may make such order as it considers appropriate in relation to the person benefiting from the different disposition of the property. **17-020**

If, for example, a will left property to the "*eldest daughter*" of X, and there is an older brother who obtains a full female gender recognition certificate, then the person who was previously the "*eldest daughter*" will cease to enjoy that position. She could apply to court.

5. Property Subject to a General Power of Appointment

General and special powers of appointment

Instead of making an outright gift of property to a named beneficiary, a testator may give one person a power to appoint property to others. The power may be entirely unlimited, so that the appointer can appoint to anyone, in which case it is referred to as a "general" power, or the power may be limited, so that the appointer can appoint only amongst certain specific people (for example the children of X), in which case it is referred to as a "special" power of appointment. **17-021**

A person with a general power of appointment is free to deal with the property exactly as they please and is therefore for many purposes treated as the owner of the property subject to the general power of appointment. For example, if a person exercises such a power by will, the property subject to the power is available for payment of the deceased's debts (see para.15-017).

Method of exercising a general power of appointment

A testator may make an express appointment by will but this is not essential. Section 27 of the Wills Act provides that, where a testator has a general power of appointment exercisable by will, it can be exercised by any general devise or bequest without the necessity for an express reference to the power. **17-022**

A general devise or bequest is one where the subject matter is described in a general manner, for example "all my leasehold land", "all my land in Hampshire" or "all my shares". If property subject to a general power is to pass under the terms of such a gift, it must correspond to the general description.

Section 27 is subject to contrary intention. However, the court will not readily find such an intention. Thus in *Re Jarrett* (1919) the fact that the testator had made an express appointment in the will which failed was found not to show a contrary intention and the subject matter of the power passed as part of the residue.

It is preferable when preparing a will for someone with a general power of appointment to refer expressly to the property subject to the power. This ensures that the person with the power actively considers whether the disposition of the property is satisfactory and the person entitled in default of appointment does not suspect that the testator simply forgot that the property would pass as part of the residue. For an unfortunate example where this was not done see *Gibbons v Nelsons (a firm)* (2000).

The section does not apply if the terms of a general power of appointment require an express reference to the power or the property. Special powers of appointment are not covered by the section and therefore need to be expressly exercised (unless the terms of the power provide otherwise).

6. SPECIAL RULES RELATING TO CHILDREN

Adopted children

17-023 The Adoption and Children Act 2002 s.67, replacing the Adoption Act 1976 s.39, applies to any adoption order made by a court in the UK, the Isle of Man or the Channel Islands and to certain foreign adoptions. It provides that:

(a) an adopted child is to be treated as the legitimate child of the married couple who adopt it or, if the adoption is by one person, as the legitimate child of that one person (but not as a child of any actual marriage of that person); and
(b) an adopted child is to be treated as if it were not the child of any person other than the adopting parent(s).

Thus adopted children are treated as the children of the adopting parents but only in relation to wills of persons dying on or after 1 January 1976. They are also treated as the child of the adopting parents in relation to deaths intestate on or after 1 January 1976. There was an earlier statute (Adoption of Children Act 1949 s.9) which gave adopted children inheritance rights from their -adopting parents but this was also limited and applied only to wills made on or after 1 January 1950.

It is immaterial whether the adoption order is made before or after the testator's death. For example, if T gives property "to A for life, remainder to the children of A" any child adopted by A, whether before or after T's death, will be entitled to share in the gift, unless there is any contrary intention shown.

There have been challenges to the rule that adopted children cannot take under wills and trust instruments made before the date of the amending legislation based on alleged breaches of the European Convention of Human Rights art.8 (respect for private and family life) and art.14 (no discrimination on any ground including birth). For claimants to succeed in a UK court they must show not only that they are victims of an infringement of the Convention but also that the Human Rights Act 1998 confers on them a right to seek a remedy for that infringement in the domestic court. Human Rights Act 1998 s.2 requires domestic courts to take into account any relevant decision of the European Court of Human Rights and s.3 of the Human Rights Act 1998 requires domestic legislation to be given effect to, so far as possible, in a way which is compatible with the Convention rights.

A challenge was unsuccessful in *Upton v National Westminster Bank Plc* (2004) on the basis that the current legislation is not discriminatory and there are sound reasons (such as certainty) for not making such legislation retrospective. In *Gregg v Pigott*, Re Erskine 1948 Trust (2012) the challengers had limited success. Mark Herbert QC, sitting as a deputy judge, found that, while s.3 of the 1998 Act is not generally retrospective, it can be in cases where that is achieved without unfairness. He concluded that because of a number of special features, without any one of which he would have reached a different conclusion, the trust should be construed in such a way as to eliminate the discrimination against adopted children.

In *Hand v George* (2017) the claimants succeeded. Rose J declined to follow the approach of Mark Herbert QC. Instead she concluded that, given the substantial number of decisions of the European Court making it clear that discrimination against adopted and illegitimate people was unacceptable, she should read the statutory provision disapplying the new rules on adoption in relation to instruments made before the commencement of the statute in such a way as to make it comply with the claimants' Convention rights. To prevent an unfair interference with pre-existing rights and inappropriate retrospectivity, she suggested that the disapplication of the new rules for instruments already in existence should be limited to cases where the beneficiary of the disposition has done something to avail himself or herself of the property right in question before the coming into force of the Human Rights Act 1998. Beneficiaries of a will or trust will normally have done nothing to avail themselves of inheritance rights so adopted children would appear to be generally able to inherit under instruments pre-dating the relevant legislation. The same reasoning will apply to illegitimate children: see para.17-024.

Note, however, that in *PQ v RS* (2019), Chief Master Marsh, while expressing no view as to whether *Hand v George* (2017) was correctly decided, did agree with counsel that there was a doubt about whether it would be followed. The case involved a very large settlement pre-dating the relevant statutes, where trustees were understandably unwilling to run any risk of suggestions that they had wrongly exercised their powers in favour to a legitimated child of one of the life tenants. They, therefore, made an application to court asking for approval of their proposed actions.

However, in *Re JC Druce Settlement* (2019) (an application in relation to illegitimate descendants) Judge Keyser QC saw no proper basis for declining to follow the *Hand v George* approach. In *Goodrich v AB* (2022) Chief Master Schuman followed the same approach when considering whether a reference to "spouses" in a deed of settlement dated 11 April 1990 should be construed to include civil partners and same sex spouses.

Where a disposition by will depends on the date of birth of a child or children, the Adoption and Children Act 2002 s.69(2) provides that the disposition is to be construed, in the absence of contrary intention, as if:

(a) the adopted child had been born on the date of the adoption; and
(b) two or more children adopted on the same date had been born on that date in the order of their actual births.

But this does not affect any reference to a person's age.

Example 2

T makes one gift "to the children of A living at my death" and one gift "to the children of A born after my death". T dies in 2006 and after T's death A adopts a child who was born in 2004. This child is treated as born on the date of the adoption and is therefore not a child living at T's death and cannot take under the first gift. However, it is a child born after T's death and can take under the second gift.

Section 69(2) does not affect any reference to the *age* of a child. Thus, if T gives property "to the first child of A to reach age 25" and A gives birth to a child in 1978 and in 1980 adopts a child who is aged 12, it is the adopted child who will reach age 25 first and be entitled to the gift. A gift to "the eldest child of A" would probably not be construed as containing a reference to an age so that the general rule would be applied; thus, the adopted child would be treated as born on the date of the adoption and therefore as being younger than the natural child.

Section 70 of the Adoption and Children Act 2002 makes specific provision for the adoption of illegitimate children by a parent. Adoption and Children Act 2002 s.70(1) provides that where a disposition depends on the date of birth of a person who was born illegitimate and who is adopted by one of the natural parents as sole adoptive parent, s.69(2) does not affect entitlement to property.

So, for example, if a testator dies in 2001 bequeathing a legacy to his eldest grandchild living at a specified time, and

- his unmarried daughter has a daughter, Blossom, in 2002 who is the first grandchild,
- his married son has a son, Tyger, in 2003,
- subsequently his unmarried daughter adopts Blossom as sole adoptive parent.

the status of Blossom remains unchanged. She, not Tyger, is the eldest grandchild.

Although s.33(1) of the Human Fertilisation and Embryology Act 2008 provides that the woman who carries a child as a result of the placing in her of an embryo or of sperm and eggs is to be treated as the mother of the child, sub-s.(2) provides that this is not the case where the child is adopted by another person. An adoption order will also prevent a man being treated as the father under s.35 or s.36 and a woman being treated as the child's other female parent under s.42 or s.43.

Where a child is born as a result of a surrogacy arrangement, the woman who carries the child is the mother unless a parental order is obtained under Human Fertilisation and Embryology Act 2008 s.54. The effect of such an order is broadly the same as an adoption order. For more detail on when a man or woman is treated as a child's father or other female parent, see para.3-006.

Children whose parents were not married

17-024 In any will or codicil made after 4 April 1988, under Family Law Reform Act 1987 s.1(1) references to relationships are construed without regard to

> "whether or not the father and mother of either [person], or the father and mother of any person through whom the relationship is deduced, have or had been married to each other at any time".

Thus a gift "to my children" includes both legitimate and illegitimate children. A gift "to my grandchildren" includes all the testator's children's children regardless of whether the testator was married at any time and regardless of whether their children were married at any time. The will may show a contrary intention should the testator so wish.

In the case of wills and codicils made after 31 December 1969 and before 4 April

1988, the Family Law Reform Act 1969 s.15 applies. This makes provision the effect of which is similar, in most respects, to the 1987 Act.

As we saw in relation to adopted children, there are strong arguments that the exclusion of illegitimate children in cases where the will or trust instrument predates the relevant statute is discriminatory. In *Re JC Druce Settlement* (2019) it was accepted that the approach taken by Rose J in *Hand v George* should be followed. As a result, illegitimate descendants were included in the class of beneficiaries created by a 1959 settlement.

7. Class Gifts

The class closing rules

Necessity for such rules

A class gift is a gift of property to be divided amongst persons fulfilling a general description (for example "the children of A", "the children of A who reach 18"). The size of any individual's share will depend upon the number of persons who fulfil the description. This makes distributing the property difficult since until A dies it is always possible that the number of persons fulfilling the description will increase. Personal representatives would, therefore, have to wait till A's death before giving any child a share in the property. **17-025**

To avoid this inconvenient result, certain rules of construction known as "the class closing rules" have been developed; the effect of the rules is to close a class at an artificially early date in order to allow earlier distribution. Beneficiaries who are born after the class has closed lose their entitlement; the unfairness that this may cause is thought to be outweighed by the convenience of allowing early distribution. However, if a testator does not want the class to close early, the rules can always be expressly excluded (subject to the rules against perpetuity). Clear words should be used to exclude the rules. An example of sufficiently clear wording is "to the children of A *whenever born*".

The precise details of the rules vary according to the type of gift (immediate, deferred or contingent) but the principle is that the class closes as soon as there is one beneficiary entitled to immediate distribution.

Throughout this section the word "living" includes a child *en ventre sa mere*.

Immediate class gifts

An example of such a gift is "to the children of A". If there is any child of A living at the date of the testator's death the class closes and the personal representatives distribute to the class members then in existence (*Viner v Francis* (1789)). No child born after the class has closed can take any interest. If there are no children living at that date, there is no class closing rule applicable and the class will remain open until A dies. **17-026**

Deferred class gift

An example of such a gift is "to X for life remainder to the children of A". In this case the property cannot be distributed while X is alive and the class, therefore, remains open until X dies. It will include any children living at the testator's death and any children born thereafter and before the death of X. If any such child dies **17-027** before the property is actually distributed, their share will be paid to their estate. No child born after the class has closed can take any interest. If there were no children living at the testator's death and none born before X's death, there is no class closing rule applicable and the class will remain open until the death of A.

Contingent class gift

17-028 An example of such a gift is "to the children of A who reach 18". If any child has reached 18 when the testator dies, the class closes at that date and will include any child living at that date who reaches the age of 18. If a child dies without fulfilling the contingency their "share" is divided amongst the other members of the class who fulfil the contingency. If no child has reached 18 at the date of the testator's death, the class remains open until a child reaches 18 and will include any child living at that date who reaches 18. Again if any child dies without fulfilling the contingency their "share" is divided amongst any others who do fulfil the contingency. No child born after the class has closed can take any interest.

Deferred and contingent class gifts

17-029 An example of such a gift would be "to X for life, remainder to the children of A who reach 18". In this case the property cannot be distributed whilst X is alive and the class, therefore, remains open until X's death. It will close at X's death if any child living at the testator's death has reached 18 and will include any children living at the testator's death or born since who reach 18. If any child, living at the testator's death, reaches 18 but dies before distribution the class closes on X's death and the share of the deceased child is paid to his estate. If no member of the class has reached 18 at the time of X's death the class remains open until the first child reaches 18. No child born after the class has closed can take any interest.

Acceleration of the date for closing a class

17-030 If there is a postponed class gift (for example, "to X for life, remainder to the children of Y") it may happen that the prior interest fails, perhaps because the life tenant predeceases the testator or because the gift to the life tenant is void. In such a case the gift to the class is accelerated so that it is treated as an immediate class gift. The class will, therefore, close at the testator's death (if there are any members then living) and any later born children will be excluded (*Re Johnson* (1893)).

A life tenant may wish to disclaim or surrender the life tenancy and the question then arises of whether one person can by voluntarily dealing with their own interest affect the membership of the class. In *Re Davies* (1957) Vaisey J held that where a life tenant disclaimed, the gift to the class would be accelerated and would close immediately thereby excluding any later born members. However, the decision has been criticised as not reflecting the probable wishes of a testator; Goff J refused to follow it in *Re Harker's Will Trusts* (1969) and held that where a life tenant surrendered her life interest the class would remain open until her death.

Gifts of a specified amount to persons fulfilling a description

17-031 If a testator gives "£1,000 to each of the children of A", it is not a class gift since the amount each child is to receive does not vary according to the number of persons fulfilling the description. However, problems arise in distributing such a gift and these problems are similar to the problems which arise in connection with class gifts. The number of persons fulfilling the description may increase at any time before A's death and so the personal representatives cannot know how much money they should retain to cover the possibility of future children being born. In order that the personal representatives should be able to complete the distribution without difficulty, there is a rule of construction which provides, in the absence of a contrary intention, that only persons who are alive at the testator's death can take; if there is no-one alive at that date fulfilling the description, the entire gift fails. This is a drastic rule but it enables the personal representatives to distribute the estate without having to worry about retaining assets to cover a possible future liability.

Class gifts to children of the testator who predecease

Normally a person who predeceases the testator can take no benefit under a class gift. Section 33 of the Wills Act 1837 as substituted by Administration of Justice Act 1982 s.19 provides that, in the absence of contrary intention, where a class gift is made to children or remoter issue *of the testator* and a member of the class predeceases the testator leaving issue who survive the testator, the issue take *per stirpes* the share which their parent would have taken (see para.16-027). Section 33A extends this rule to children treated as predeceasing because they disclaimed or forfeited their entitlement. **17-032**

8. Gifts to Spouses

Same sex marriage

Section 1 of the Marriage (Same Sex Couples) Act 2013 makes marriage between same sex couples lawful. Section 11 provides that marriage has the same effect in relation to same sex couples as it has in relation to opposite sex couples. **17-033**

Schedule 4 provides that s.11 does not alter the effect of any private legal instrument made before 13 March 2014 (the date the section came into force).

However, in private legal instruments made on or after that date references to "*husband*", "*wife*", "*spouse*", "*widow*", "*widower*" and "*marriage*" will include same sex marriages unless the instrument says otherwise.

The limitation imposed by Sch.4 was considered by Chief Master Schuman in *Goodrich v AB* (2022). She adopted the approach of Rose J in *Hand v George* and concluded that the effect of the schedule is discriminatory in that, post the Human Rights Act 1998, it seeks to continue to make a distinction between same-sex and opposite-sex spouses in instruments. She directed that the schedule should be read as only excluding same sex spouses from taking a benefit under private legal instruments made before 13 March 2014 in cases where a beneficiary of the instrument "*has done something to avail himself or herself of the property right in question before the coming into force of the Human Rights Act 1998*". Effectively, therefore, same sex spouses will be able to benefit whatever the date of the instrument.

Civil partner not a spouse

In *Goodrich v AB* (2022) Chief Master Shuman was asked to consider whether the term "spouse" could be interpreted as including civil partners. She held that the particular trust instrument could be interpreted in that way for various fact specific reasons. However, she was also asked to consider the position generally. She held **17-034** that, while it was clearly discriminatory to distinguish between civil partners and spouses, she had difficulty in reading down the Civil Partnership Act 2004 in a way that would make it compliant with the European Convention. Parliament had introduced a new legal relationship, and eliding spouses and civil partners would, she considered go beyond what the court should do. To paraphrase Lord Rodger in *Ghaidan v Godin-Mendoza* it would fall the wrong side of the line into judicial vandalism rather than judicial interpretation.

The result is that a gift expressed to be made to a "spouse" cannot take effect as a gift to a civil partner. A civil partner is not a spouse. If civil partners are to be included the will or settlement must either say so expressly or define spouse to include civil partner as defined in s.1 of the Civil Partnership Act 2004 and references to marriage to include civil partnership.

The point is of even more importance since the amendments to the Civil Partnership Act 2004 made by the Civil Partnerships, Marriages and Deaths (Registration etc) Act 2019 and the Civil Partnership (Opposite-Sex Couples) Regulations 2019 (SI 2019/1458) which allow opposite sex partners to enter into civil partnerships.

If the intention is to include civil partners, there must be an express provision doing so. It is important to define the term as different jurisdictions have different forms. It is usually desirable to define it by reference to Civil Partnership Act 2004 s.1 as amended.

9. DECIDING WHETHER A GIFT IS ABSOLUTE OR LIMITED

Section 22 of the Administration of Justice Act 1982

17-035 Testators who draft wills without professional advice sometimes give property to X and then direct that on X's death what remains should pass to Y. This is because non-lawyers often think that it is possible to give the rights of an absolute owner to persons in succession. The effect of such an attempt depends on the precise words used in the will but may be construed in any of the following ways:

(a) an absolute gift to X, the gift over to Y failing, either as a trust which is void for uncertainty, or because it is repugnant to X's absolute interest;
(b) a life interest to X, with remainder to Y absolutely; and
(c) a life interest to X, with remainder to Y absolutely but subject to X's power to dispose of the capital by lifetime transfer.

Section 22 of the Administration of Justice Act 1982 introduces a presumption where a testator gives property to his spouse in terms which would in themselves give an absolute interest but by the same instrument purports to give *his issue* an interest in the same property, the gift to the spouse is presumed to be absolute despite the purported gift to issue. The presumption applies in the case of deaths occurring after 31 December 1982.

This section is designed to solve the problem of unintended life interests. However, it has no application to gifts other than gifts to spouses and civil partners.

The case of *Harrison v Gibson* (2006) shows that even in the case of gifts to spouses there may still be narrow distinctions depending on the exact wording of the will. In that case the wording was:

> "The Bungalow I leave in trust to my wife. On her death the bungalow is to be sold and cash raised is to be equally divided between my children [the names of the children are given]."

After the signature the following words were added "no doubt if mum runs into money problems you can sort something out like selling bungalow". The judge held that on this wording the terms of the will did not in themselves give an absolute interest to the spouse so s.22 had no application. He also held that if he was wrong in that conclusion the wording clearly showed a contrary intention so that either way a life interest had been created.

The rule in Lassence v Tierney

This rule attempts to reconcile inconsistent provisions in a will. In *Hancock v* **17-036**
Watson (1902) it was said:

> "If you find an absolute gift to a legatee in the first instance and trusts are engrafted or imposed on the absolute interest which fail either from lapse or invalidity or any other reason, then the absolute gift takes effect so far as the trusts have failed, to the exclusion of the residuary legatee or next of kin, as the case may be."

The rule imputes to T an intention that the absolute gift be modified only so far as is necessary to give effect to the trusts.

Example 3

T gives property to A absolutely and later in the will directs that the property given to A absolutely is to pass, after A's death, to the children of B. If B dies without children, A (or A's estate) will be entitled to the capital.

The difficulty in such cases is deciding whether or not there was an absolute initial gift. It is comparatively simple to find such a gift where the testator makes the absolute gift in the will and engrafts the trust in a later codicil or where, as in the previous example, there is an absolute gift followed by a later clause engrafting the trust. But difficult questions of construction will arise where a series of gifts is made in one continuous sentence.

CHAPTER EIGHTEEN

COMPLETING THE ADMINISTRATION

1. ASSENTS

Introduction

Once the personal representatives have paid all the debts and liabilities of the estate they must vest the available assets in the beneficiaries who are entitled to them which will normally require an assent. They must prepare an account to show the amount of residue available to the residuary beneficiaries. **18-001**

Position of beneficiaries before assent

As we saw in paras 11-027–11-029, a beneficiary (with the possible exception of a specific beneficiary) under a will or a person entitled under the intestacy rules has no legal or equitable proprietary interest in any asset comprised in the estate. They merely have a chose in action in the estate (i.e. the right to have the deceased's estate properly administered) and they only obtain rights to assets when the personal representatives indicate by means of an assent that these assets are not required for the purposes of the administration. **18-002**

Assents in respect of pure personalty

Assents by executors

An executor (and probably an administrator with the will annexed) passes title to pure personalty by means of an assent. An assent is an indication from the personal representative that a particular asset is not required for the purposes of the administration. It is not required to be in any particular form; it can be oral (for example, where a personal representative tells a beneficiary that their legacy is ready for collection) or implied from conduct (for example, where a personal representative allows a beneficiary to take possession of an asset). The beneficiary actually derives title from the will not from the assent; the effect of the assent is merely to activate the gift in the will. **18-003**

If particular formalities are required to transfer the legal title to an asset, the assent cannot itself pass the legal title. In such a case once the assent has been made the personal representative holds the asset as bare trustee for the-beneficiary until the appropriate formal requirements have been complied with.

Most choses (or things) in action require special formalities; money in a Post Office Savings Bank, Trustee Savings Bank or National Savings Certificates require withdrawal or transfer forms; company shares require a share transfer. Although the personal representatives may have themselves registered as members of a company, s.773 of the Companies Act 2006 provides that a personal representative may transfer stocks and shares without being first registered. There are no formalities required by law to transfer money from a bank account; a letter of instruction should be sent to the bank together with an office copy of the grant of representation, although many banks will release limited funds without sight of the grant.

In the case of a specific legacy (but not a residuary or general legacy) the assent is retrospective to the date of death so that the legatee becomes entitled to income produced by the subject matter of the gift since the testator's death.

Thus, in *IRC v Hawley* (1928) the personal representatives did not make an assent of company shares in favour of a specific legatee for nearly three years after the testator's death. It was held that, because an assent to a specific legacy is retrospective, once the assent had been made the Revenue were entitled to assess the beneficiary to income tax on dividends which had been declared in the intervening years.

Similarly, an assent is retrospective in relation to expenses, so a specific legatee becomes responsible for the costs of transferring and maintaining the property: see *Re Pearce* [1909]. This includes costs of packing, delivering and insuring bulky or delicate chattels and the costs of obtaining a share transfer for company shares.

Many testators would prefer such costs to be paid from residue and it is, therefore, common for an express direction to this effect to be included in a will.

In *Re Clough-Taylor, Coutts & Co v Banks* (2003) an asset specifically bequeathed had been taken by a third party who alleged that the deceased had given it to him during her lifetime. The court held that the executor has no duty to take anything other than normal or routine steps to collect in assets and deliver them to specific legatees. The specific legatee would have to bear the cost of any litigation to recover the asset. The court said it would be helpful—though not strictly necessary—for the executor to assign to the legatee any cause of action it had in relation to the chattel.

In *Re Aspinall (Deceased)* (2017) a specific devisee of land, part of which had been made subject to a compulsory purchase order some years before the will was made, was held not to be entitled to the final instalment of compensation. The payment, therefore, fell into residue.

Assents by administrators

At common law an administrator had no power to assent in the case of an intestacy (see, W.J. Williams, *Law Relating to Assents* (London: Butterworth & Co, 1947), p.96).

Section 36(1) of the Administration of Estates Act 1925 gives administrators as well as executors the power to make title to land (freehold or leasehold) by means of a written assent but it does not mention other property. Administrators must therefore pass title to other property by the method appropriate to the nature of the subject matter. Chattels, money and bearer securities pass by delivery, shares, stock and debentures by transfer and most other choses in action by assignment.

Assents in respect of land

Administration of Estates Act 1925 s.36

18-004 In general, a document which is to convey or create a legal estate in land must be a *deed* (Law of Property Act 1925 s.52(1)). However, as an exception to this rule, s.36(1) of the Administration of Estates Act gives personal representatives (both executors and administrators) power to *assent* to the vesting of any estate or interest in land (whether freehold or leasehold) in any person entitled (whether beneficially, as trustee or as personal representative of a deceased beneficiary who is entitled to property) *whether by devise, bequest, devolution, appropriation or otherwise*. An assent is a form of conveyance and becomes an essential link in the title of the assentee.

"*Devolution*" covers a person taking under the intestacy rules. The meaning of "*or otherwise*" presents some problems. The other words in the section all refer to transactions which a personal representative would be called upon to effect in the course of the administration of the estate. Probably therefore the words "or otherwise" should be construed ejusdem generis and should not be taken to cover any transaction which is not part of the administration; thus, if a personal representative is selling property or is asked by a beneficiary to transfer the property to a purchaser from the beneficiary the personal representative should not risk using an assent but should use a conveyance or transfer.

Form of assent

Section 36(4) of the Administration of Estates Act provides that **18-005**

> "an assent shall be in writing, signed by the personal representative and shall name the person in whose favour it is given and shall operate to vest in that person the legal title to which it relates; and an assent which is not in writing or not in favour of a named person shall not be effectual to pass the legal estate".

It is clear that an assent of land by a personal representative in favour of another person must comply with the requirements of s.36(4) if it is to pass the legal estate. According to Pennycuick J in *Re King's Will Trusts* (1964) the same requirements must be complied with where a personal representative wishes to vest land in themselves (whether beneficially or as trustee or as personal representative of another deceased). The reasoning of Pennycuick J has been criticised by various writers (see R.R.A. Walker, "Personal Representatives Assenting to Themselves" (1964) 80 L.Q.R. 328) but even if the criticisms are justified the provision of a signed, written assent by a personal representative in their own favour is hardly an onerous task and has the merit of avoiding any possible doubt or uncertainty.

It is important to remember that a personal representative is always free to convey land by means of a deed and will often choose to do so (for example, where indemnity covenants are required from the beneficiary).

In the case of registered land the personal representatives have three choices. They can:

(1) become the registered owners in their capacity as personal representatives—this option might be used if, say, the beneficiary of the will is under age;
(2) transfer the property to the beneficiary, or to the executor as trustee, by a deed called an assent (they can do this without being registered as owners first);
(3) transfer the property to a purchaser in their capacity as personal representatives.

The effect of an assent

18-006 Section 36(2) of the Administration of Estates Act provides that an assent relates back to the date of death of the deceased unless a contrary intention appears. This is unlike the position in respect of assents of personalty where only an assent to a specific legacy relates back. Thus, a specific or residuary devisee would be entitled to any rents or profits produced by land from the date of death of the deceased.

Protection of purchasers and beneficiaries

18-007 A person in whose favour an assent or conveyance is made may require that notice of the assent is endorsed on the grant of representation at the cost of the estate under s.36(5). A purchaser will insist that a conveyance from personal representatives contains a statement that the personal representatives have not previously given or made any conveyance or assent in respect of the legal estate. If this statement is incorrect, it cannot prejudice the title of any previous *purchaser;* but if there was a previous assent in favour of a *beneficiary* the purchaser will take the legal title in preference to that beneficiary if, and only if, there was no notice of the previous assent endorsed on the grant of representation *and* the purchaser accepted the conveyance on the faith of the statement in the conveyance (s.36(6)).

There is no point in such a statement being included in an assent in favour of a beneficiary since s.36(6)) only protects *purchasers.*

A purchaser has no right to examine a will to ascertain that land was assented to the person actually entitled. However, s.36(7) protects such a person by providing that in favour of a purchaser, unless notice of a previous assent or conveyance has been endorsed on the grant of representation, an assent or conveyance made by a personal representative is "sufficient evidence that the person in whose favour [it] is given is the person entitled to have the legal estate conveyed to him". The section only says that an assent is "sufficient" evidence not "conclusive" evidence; thus, if facts have come to the purchaser's knowledge before completion which indicate that the assent was in fact made in favour of the wrong person, the purchaser cannot rely on the assent (*Re Duce and Boots Cash Chemists (Southern) Ltd's Contract* (1937)).

Protection of personal representatives

18-008 A personal representative will not want to distribute assets until satisfied that all liabilities have been dealt with. Section 36(10) provides that personal representatives may, as a condition of giving an assent or making a conveyance, require security for the discharge of any duties, debts or liabilities to which the property is subject (for example, a mortgage debt or charge for inheritance tax). If reasonable arrangements have been made for discharging such liabilities, however, the personal representative cannot refuse to make the assent to a beneficiary entitled to the property.

If the personal representative is uncertain whether or not land will be required for the payment of liabilities, they may under s.43 of the Administration of Estates Act allow a beneficiary to take possession of the land prior to the making of a formal assent. The personal representative can subsequently retake possession of the property and dispose of it if it becomes necessary in the course of the administration.

If the deceased owned land which was subject to covenants for breach of which the personal representatives will remain liable (for example where the deceased was an original lessee or where there have been indemnity covenants) the personal representatives will wish to protect themselves by obtaining an indemnity covenant from the beneficiary. They will therefore have to use a deed when transferring the property to the beneficiary instead of merely an assent.

2. PERSONAL REPRESENTATIVE OR TRUSTEE

Personal representative for life

A personal representative retains office for life and is not discharged from office even when all the debts and liabilities have been paid and all the assets distributed. If there are any subsequent accretions to the estate (for example, if a debt which had been regarded as irrecoverable is paid to the estate or if someone dies leaving a legacy to the deceased which is saved from lapse by one of the exceptions to the doctrine of lapse) the personal representative must distribute such accretions and conversely if legal proceedings are brought or claims made against the estate the personal representatives must deal with them on behalf of the estate. **18-009**

Comparison with trustees

A personal representative may be a trustee of property left by will or passing under the intestacy rules. This may be because: **18-010**

(a) the testator expressly appointed the personal representative as trustee; or
(b) the testator left property on trust but did not expressly appoint trustees; or
(c) a trust arises under the intestacy rules (although there is some doubt as to whether administrators become trustees in such a case).

Even where a personal representative is not appointed as a trustee there are certain similarities between personal representatives and trustees:

(a) Personal representatives, like trustees, are in a fiduciary position. They must act with the utmost good faith and must not profit from their position.
(b) The provisions of the Trustee Act 1925 apply equally to personal representatives where the context admits.

However, there are also important differences:

(a) The function of a personal representative is to wind up the estate and distribute the assets, whereas the function of a trustee is to hold assets for the beneficiaries.
(b) Executors (and probably administrators) have joint and several authority to deal with *personalty* (they must act jointly if they are to convey *land* although one personal representative can enter into a contract for sale binding on any other personal representatives: *Fountain Forestry Ltd v Edwards* (1975)). Trustees must always act jointly.
(c) A sole personal representative may give a good receipt for money for the sale of land whereas at least two trustees (or a trust corporation) are required.
(d) The period of limitation is 12 years against a personal representative but only six years against a trustee.

(e) If a sole personal representative dies without having completed the administration there will either be transmission of office under the chain of executorship or a grant *de bonis non administratis* must be taken out by the person entitled under the Non-Contentious Probate Rules 1987 (SI 1987/2024). If, however, a sole or last surviving trustee dies the trust property devolves on the trustee's personal representatives.

(f) A trustee has power to appoint additional or substitutional trustees. A personal representative has normally no power to appoint additional or substitutional personal representatives (although a person entitled to administration may nominate another administrator in certain cases where two administrators are needed because of a minority or life interest).

(g) Personal representatives owe their duty to the estate as a whole, trustees to the individual beneficiaries (*Re Hayes Will Trusts* (1971)).

(h) When personal representatives transfer assets to a "legatee" there is no gain or loss for capital gains tax purposes. The legatee takes over the acquisition value of the personal representatives (together with any expenses of transfer). When a beneficiary of a trust becomes absolutely entitled as against the trustee there is a deemed disposal which may trigger a charge to CGT. Where the will directs that the personal representatives are to hold on trust, the beneficiary may become absolutely entitled before the personal representatives have assented the assets to themselves as trustees. In such a case the beneficiary takes as legatee and not as a trust beneficiary.

In view of the differences it is obviously important to ascertain at what point the personal representative ceases to hold assets as personal representative and starts to hold them as trustee.

Transition from personal representative to trustee

Intestacy

18-011 Under the Administration of Estates Act 1925 undisposed of property may have to be held on trust either for a spouse for life (where death occurred before 1 October 2014) or on the statutory trusts until a beneficiary achieves a vested interest. There is some doubt as to whether administrators on intestacy ever become trustees in the true sense or whether they continue to hold property as administrators. The better view would seem to be that they do not become trustees. However, Romer J in the case of *Re Yerburgh* (1928) stated that administrators become trustees as soon as all liabilities have been discharged and the amount of residue to be held on trust has been ascertained. Romer J went on to state that the administrators ought to mark the moment when residue was ascertained by making an assent to the property vesting in themselves as trustees. It is unclear whether the judge meant that the assent was essential in order to vest the property in the administrators in their capacity as trustees or whether he meant that the assent was merely desirable in practice in order to indicate that the change in capacity had occurred, the change occurring automatically once the residue was ascertained.

Where the personal representative is not appointed as trustee

18-012 In the case of a specific legacy, once personal representatives have indicated by means of an assent that an asset is not required for payment of debts the asset is held on trust for the specific beneficiary (*Re Grosvenor* (1916)).

In the case of residue the position is rather unclear but the better view appears to be that a person continues as a personal representative even if they may acquire some aspects of trusteeship.

In *Harvell v Foster* (1954) the Court of Appeal stated that the personal representatives remain liable in their capacity as such for the residue of the estate until it is vested in the beneficiary entitled. If the vesting is delayed (as it may be for example where the beneficiary is a minor and cannot give a good receipt) liability as a personal representative will continue. This was a convenient result as it allowed the court to order the surety's for the administration bond to make payment where the administrator had absconded with the bulk of the estate after payment to him. Had the court found that the administration had been completed when the residue was ascertained, the beneficiary would have been left uncompensated.

The Court of Appeal considered the earlier decision of *Re Ponder* (1921). Sargant J had found that an administrator who had completed the administration was a trustee of the residue within the terms of the Trustee Act 1893 for the purposes of allowing the court to appoint additional trustees to act with her.

Lord Evershed described the decision that an administrator of an intestate's estate could, in time, assume the character and functions of a trustee in the same way as one appointed by will executor and trustee as "novel". He said that the Court of Appeal was unable to accept the view, which Sargant J's language read without qualification would seem to support, that because a personal representative who has cleared the estate becomes a trustee of the net residue for the persons beneficially interested, the clearing of the estate necessarily and automatically discharges him from his obligations as personal representative and, in particular, from the obligation of any bond he may have entered into for the due administration of the estate:

> "[I]n our view, the duty of an administrator, as such, must at least extend to paying the funeral and testamentary expenses and debts and legacies (if any) and where, as here, immediate distribution is impossible owing to the infancy of the person beneficially entitled, retaining the net residue in trust for the infant. At least until the administrator can show that he has done this, it cannot, in our judgment, be said of him that he has duly administered the estate according to law."

For capital gains tax purposes HMRC consider that once the residue is ascertained, personal representatives hold any undistributed assets as a bare trustee for those entitled. Thus, a sale will automatically be on behalf of the beneficiary so any capital gains tax liability will be assessed at their rates. It can be difficult to determine exactly when residue is ascertained so if personal representatives are going to sell, it is sensible to appropriate the asset to the residuary beneficiary before sale to avoid any doubt. See para.CG30810 which says:

> "Residue is only ascertained when the personal representatives have both established the net worth of the estate and provided the liquid funds to pay liabilities and pecuniary legacies. Once that point is reached residue is ascertained and it is irrelevant that the assets have not been distributed."

Where the will appoints the personal representative as trustee

If personal representatives are directed to hold residue on trust there is some authority for saying that as soon as liabilities are discharged and the residue ascertained the personal representatives automatically start to hold the property in their capacity as trustees (*Re Cockburn's Will Trusts* (1957)). However, the posi- **18-013** tion is far from clear and there are dicta in *Attenborough v Solomon* (1913) which suggest that the change does not take place automatically but only when the personal representatives assent the property to themselves in their capacity as trustees. An assent is certainly desirable since it will avoid any doubt as to whether or not a change in capacity has occurred.

Revenue's view

18-014 There are a number of situations where it is important to know whether personal representatives are still holding assets as part of the administration or whether they are holding them as trustee for beneficiaries. For example:

- the legatees would be liable at a lower rate of capital gains tax than the personal representatives on the disposal of assets in the estate;
- the legatees have unused annual exemption or losses available that could be used to cover the gains;
- the legatee is a charity and any gain on the disposal would be exempt.

As explained above, HMRC consider that assets remain vested in the personal representatives until residue has been ascertained unless specific steps have been taken to vest the assets in advance of ascertainment of residue: see para.CG30781 of the *CGT Manual*.

3. RECEIPTS AND DISCHARGES

Introduction

18-015 A beneficiary discharges a personal representative from liability by means of a receipt signed by the beneficiary. A residuary beneficiary normally signs the estate accounts.

Pecuniary legacies

18-016 It used to be common for solicitors to ask pecuniary legatees, who wished to receive their legacies in the form of a cheque sent through the post, to sign a receipt in advance. The Law Society's Land Law and Succession Committee considered this practice and on 14 October 1992 stated in the *Gazette* that it considered that

> "it is no longer reasonable or necessary for legatees and beneficiaries to be asked to sign receipts in advance of payment being made and that such a practice is bound to generate additional correspondence and thus to add unnecessarily to the cost of the administration of the estate".

Precedents for simple forms of receipt for the payment of pecuniary, specific and residuary legacies are available. However, solicitors may find it more convenient to ask the legatee or beneficiary to acknowledge receipt by signing and returning a duplicate copy of the letter accompanying the cheque. In any case, s.3 of the Cheques Act 1957 provides that:

> "An unindorsed cheque which appears to have been paid by the banker on whom it is drawn is evidence of receipt by the payee of the sum payable by the cheque."

So far as residuary beneficiaries are concerned, the solicitor will normally send them copies of the estate accounts (already approved by the personal representatives). The Law Society's Committee recommended sending a cheque at the same time

> "with a request that the beneficiaries acknowledge payment by signing a receipt either endorsed on the accounts or supplied separately and with the receipt to include, if needed, a discharge to the personal representatives".

Obviously, there may be cases where there has been ill feeling during the administration and the solicitor anticipates that the residuary beneficiary may be difficult. In such a case, the Law Society's Land Law and Succession Committee recommended that

> "residuary beneficiaries should be sent in advance copies of the approved accounts and be asked to sign a form of receipt and discharge to the personal representatives on the basis that they will be sent a cheque immediately upon the solicitors receiving the form back signed".

The following form of receipt is a plain English redraft by Richard Oerton of the form originally produced by the Committee. It appeared in *Clarity*.

> "THE LATE ....
>
> The estate accounts show the final sum due to me as £..........
>
> I approve the accounts and will accept that sum in full satisfaction of all my claims against the estate.
>
> Please pay it by a crossed cheque in my favour and send it to me by post."

Although it is common to include a discharge to the personal representative in the form of a receipt, it could only be effective if the beneficiaries had been given full and accurate details of all dealings with the estate assets and liabilities.

Minors cannot give a good receipt for money

Unless the will provides otherwise, a minor cannot give a good receipt for money **18-017** (*Re Somech* (1957)). A married minor or minor in a civil partnership can give a good receipt for income but not for capital (Law of Property Act 1925 s.21). It is often said that the parent or guardian of a minor cannot give a good receipt on behalf of the minor without express provision in the will. However, the Children Act 1989 provides that all parents with parental responsibility have the same rights, powers and duties as guardians appointed under the Children Act. These rights are set out in s.3 and include

> "the right to receive or recover in his own name *for the benefit of the child*, property of whatever description and wherever situated, which the child is entitled to receive or recover".

There may be circumstances where the testator may not be happy to allow the parent or guardian to receive the legacy. It does not appear that the personal representatives would be entitled to withhold the legacy (although the minor's parent may have trouble extracting the money if the personal representative is unwilling to pay it over). The best course is to leave a substantial legacy to trustees to hold for the benefit of the minor and in the case of small amounts to state expressly whether or not the personal representative is to release funds to the parent or guardian.

Under the Administration of Estates Act 1925 s.42 personal representatives have power where a minor is absolutely entitled to a legacy to appoint a trust corporation or at least two individuals (and not more than four) to hold the property on trust until the minor reaches 18. The trustees can give the personal representatives a good receipt. However, s.42 does not apply where the infant's interest is contingent (for example on reaching 18).

4. The Equitable Rules of Apportionment

Introduction

18-018 These rules were developed to try to achieve fairness between tenants for life and remaindermen. However, they lead to extremely complicated calculations and professionally drawn wills have for many years excluded them as a matter of course. The Trusts (Capital and Income) Act 2013 disapplies the three equitable rules dealt with in paras 18-018–18-021 in all trusts created or arising on or after 1 October 2013 (unless the instrument provides otherwise).

Howe v Lord Dartmouth

18-019 If residuary personalty is left to persons in succession there is an obligation under the rule in *Howe v Lord Dartmouth* (1802) to sell wasting, hazardous, and unauthorised assets. Pending sale the tenant for life is not entitled to the income from such assets since otherwise they might obtain a benefit from the personal representatives' delay. Instead they are entitled to interest at four per cent per annum on the value of the assets. Any surplus income is treated as capital and invested in authorised investments. This rule exists to protect remaindermen.

Re Earl of Chesterfield's Trusts

18-020 The rule in *Re Earl of Chesterfield's Trusts* (1883) exists to protect the life tenant. There is an obligation to sell reversionary interests and other non-income producing assets. There will inevitably be some delay before such a sale can be effected and no income is earned during the period. Therefore the proceeds of sale of such assets are not treated as exclusively capital but are apportioned between capital and income.

Allhusen v Whittell

18-021 This rule provides that where residue is left to persons in succession, debts and other outgoings (such as legacies) are to be treated as paid partly from capital and partly from income accruing to that portion of capital during the period between the testator's death and the payment of the outgoings. The principle is that the life tenant is entitled to income from the net residue after payment of debts and other liabilities but not to income from those assets which are needed for the payment of debts and which, therefore, do not form part of the net residue.

5. The Legal Rules of Apportionment

18-022 As explained in para.16-062, income is treated as accruing on a daily basis under the common law rules of apportionment of interest and the Apportionment Act 1870. Thus, income received after death must be apportioned if it relates to a period part of which falls before, and part of which falls after death.

Most professionally drawn wills have for many years excluded the need for such apportionments.

If the will created a trust in favour of a life tenant, the need for-apportionments had to be expressly excluded on the life tenant's death as well as on the testator's death. The Trusts (Capital and Income) Act 2013 disapplies the Apportionment Act in all trusts created or arising on or after 1 October 2013 (unless the instrument provides otherwise).

Irrespective of whether the need for apportionments is excluded for *distribution* purposes, apportionments will still have to be made to calculate the value of the estate at death for *inheritance tax purposes* (see para.4-047).

When calculating the liability of the estate to *income tax* no apportionments are made no matter what the will says; any income which is payable after death is treated as income of the estate and not of the deceased even though part or all of the income may be attributable to a period falling before death (however, as we saw at para.6-016 there is an income tax relief available where income has been apportioned and charged to inheritance tax). The position is rather different on the death of a life tenant of a trust. For income tax purposes HMRC will follow the terms of the trust instrument. If that does not exclude the need for apportionment of income on the death of a life tenant the income tax liability will be apportioned between the life tenant's estate and the person next entitled; but if it does exclude the need for apportionment, tax on all income payable after death will be treated as the liability of the person next entitled.

6. ACCOUNTS

The purpose of accounts

The personal representatives will prepare a variety of accounts for different purposes. At an early stage of the administration they must complete an inheritance tax account (unless the estate is an "excepted estate" (see para.10-039 and following) in which case no account is required). They will also keep records of any income of the estate so that any income tax liability of the estate can be calculated. **18-023**

In addition, before the personal representatives can complete the administration they must produce estate accounts for the residuary beneficiaries. The purpose of such accounts is to list all the assets of the estate, all the debts, liabilities and expenses that have been paid, all the legacies that have been paid and then to show the balance which is available for distribution to the residuary beneficiaries. The personal representatives will also show how the entitlement of each residuary beneficiary is to be paid. Thus, if the personal representatives propose to pay part of the entitlement in cash and to transfer assets *in specie* to make up the balance this must be explained. The residuary beneficiaries signify their approval of the accounts by signing them and acknowledging receipt of any amount due. This discharges the personal representatives from liability (see para.18-015).

The form of the accounts

There are no rules as to the form of estate accounts. However, they *must* be clear and easy to understand since their purpose is to convey information to the residuary beneficiaries. An account may be prepared vertically showing assets less liabilities or as a double-sided account showing receipts on one side and payments on the other. **18-024**

An account normally commences with a narrative which sets out such matters as the date of death of the deceased, the date of the grant of representation, a summary of the dispositions made in the will (or of the effect of the intestacy rules), the value of the gross and net estate and any other information relevant to the administration (for example, whether any interim payments have already been made to the residuary beneficiaries, whether it is proposed to transfer assets *in specie* to the residuary beneficiaries). The purpose of such a narrative is to make the account more intelligible to the beneficiaries. In order to cut down the amount included on the account, details of investments may be relegated to separate schedules.

It is usual, except in the case of very small estates, to divide the account into a capital account and an income account. Such a division is essential if a life interest has been created in the residue since one person will be entitled to capital and another to income.

If separate capital and income accounts are prepared it will be necessary, unless the need to apportion has been excluded, to make apportionments of any income received after death which is attributable partly to the period before and partly to the period after death. The former will be shown on the capital account as part of the residuary cash. The latter will be shown on the income account; if the income-producing asset was specifically bequeathed the income will pass to the specific beneficiary, if it was not it will pass as part of the residuary income.

A simple estate account is set out below.

"Mrs Amy Sharpe Deceased

Mrs Amy Sharpe of the Seaview Nursing Home, Bognor Regis, died on 4 January 2022 at the age of 96.

Probate of her will was granted on 6 April 2022 to her daughter, Miss Catherine Sharpe.

By her will Mrs Sharpe left £2,500 to each of her two grandchildren, Mr David Kay and Mrs Elizabeth Forbes. The residue was given after payment of debts, funeral, testamentary and other expenses and legacies to Mrs Briony Kay and Miss Catherine Sharpe. The will excluded the need to apportion income. The personal effects have been taken by Miss Catherine Sharpe in partial satisfaction of her entitlement at an agreed valuation of £410. Mrs Sharpe had made chargeable lifetime transfers in the seven years before her death.

Capital Account

	£	£
Hinckley Building Society account		181,500
Northern Crest Unit Trust		188,520
Current account		680
Cash in hand		70
Personal effects—estimated value		410
GROSS ESTATE		371,180
Less debts and other expenses		
Funeral expenses	1,450	
Solicitors' fees	520	
Arrears at nursing home	760	
Inheritance tax	8,000	

Capital Account

	£	£
		(10,730)
NET ESTATE		360,450
Less legacies		
Mr D. Kay	2,500	
Mrs E. Forbes	2,500	
		(5,000)
Residue available to beneficiaries		355,450
1/2 Mrs B. Kay	177,725	
1/2 Miss C. Sharpe	177,725	
		355,450

Income Account

	£	£	£
Income received since death			
Hinckley Building Society		700	
Northern Crest Unit Trust		1,800	
			2,500
Less: Interest on bank loan taken out to pay inheritance tax			
			(100)
Income available to beneficiaries			2,400
1/2 Mrs B. Kay	1,200		
1/2 Miss C. Sharpe	1,200		
			2,400

Having calculated the entitlement of the two residuary beneficiaries to capital and income it would then, strictly speaking, be necessary to produce an account for each showing how their entitlement is to be made up. However, on these facts each will receive her entitlement in cash (apart from the personal effects valued at £410 which are to go to Catherine Sharpe) so that the preparation of additional accounts is not essential.

Signature of the accounts

A residuary beneficiary normally gives a receipt is by signing the accounts. Such a receipt normally includes an indemnity, for example, "I agree to accept the assets shown in full satisfaction of my entitlement and hereby discharge X as executor and indemnify him against all claims and demands." However, such a release and indemnity is only effective if the beneficiary had full knowledge of all the assets, accounts and dealings. **18-025**

If a beneficiary persists in a refusal to approve accounts they may commence an administration action for examination of the accounts. If they do not, the personal representatives may, in theory, pay the outstanding funds into court under the Trustee Act 1925 s.63 as amended by s.36(4) of and Sch.III to the Administration of Justice Act 1965. However, the court is normally extremely unwilling to accept such payments and, in any event, it involves the estate in extra expense and should not be attempted unless there is no satisfactory alternative. If the reason that approval is not forthcoming is that a beneficiary is missing, the personal representatives may have taken steps earlier in the administration to obtain a *Benjamin Order*; if they have not they should consider either obtaining an indemnity from the other beneficiaries or obtaining insurance cover or retaining assets.

In *Mussell v Patience* (2018) the executors took a different course. They asked the court to go through the accounts and approve them in place of the recalcitrant beneficiaries. The administration of the estate had been very protracted. The testatrix had died in 1997 leaving her estate to be divided between her four children. There were various disputes between the beneficiaries and legal expenses were incurred by the executors (one of the children and a former partner in the firm that drafted the will). Two residuary beneficiaries refused to approve the estate accounts.

They objected to certain invoices for legal fees charged by the executors' solicitors and contended that, as beneficiaries, they were entitled to have sufficient information in order for them to determine whether those charges were reasonable.

Matthews J agreed that, as preliminary, he had to decide the legal test the court should apply in deciding whether to strike out an entry from the executors' accounts.

He said that the rules on detailed assessment of legal costs under the Solicitors Act 1974 are not applicable to settling an account between executor and beneficiary, because the court is not conducting a detailed assessment of the legal costs. An executor has only to show (1) that the sum concerned was spent, and (2) that it was spent in the fair execution of the estate administration. In particular, the executor is not required at the outset to prove by his or her voucher(s) that the charge made is reasonably incurred or reasonable in amount. That is what the system of assessment of solicitors' costs is for.

Residuary beneficiaries may apply for assessment of legal fees under Solicitors Act 1974 s.71(3). The sub-section provides as follows:

> "Where a trustee, executor or administrator has become liable to pay a bill of a solicitor, then, on the application of any person interested in any property out of which the trustee, executor or administrator has paid, or is entitled to pay, the bill, the court may order—
>
> (a) that the bill be [assessed] on such terms, if any, as it thinks fit; and
> (b) that such payments, in respect of the amount found to be due to or by the solicitor and in respect of the costs of the [assessment], be made to or by the applicant, to or by the solicitor, or to or by the executor, administrator or trustee, as it thinks fit."

The Court of Appeal considered the sub-section in *Kenig v Thomson Snell and Passmore LLP* (2024) and confirmed the decision of Costs Judge Brown. The issue was whether beneficiaries can challenge a charge-out rate agreed by the executor with the firm or, as is the case under s.71(1) where third parties have agreed to pay another's costs, they are limited to challenging items which should not appear in the bill.

The Court of Appeal agreed with the costs judge that there are significant differences between s.71(1) and s.71(3).

- In s.71(1) cases the court can only make "the same order (if any) as it might have made if the application had been made by the client".
- In s.71(3) cases the court can order that the bill be assessed "on such terms, if any, as it thinks fit".

The solicitors had argued that the Court of Appeal decision in *Tim Martin Interiors Ltd v Akin Gump LLP* (2011) (a mortgagor complaining that the bank had used a firm which charged unnecessarily high rates) prevented the beneficiaries challenging the level of charges. The Court of Appeal had held in *Tim Martin* that applicants under s.71 could only challenge items which should not have been included at all as opposed to challenging the level of charging. The Court of Appeal had drawn no distinction between s.71(1) cases and s.71(3) cases.

However, Lord Justice Stuart-Smith, who delivered the judgment of the court in *Kenig*, held that *Tim Martin* was concerned only with s.71(1) so anything said about s.71(3) was obiter. The Costs Judge was correct to find that *Tim Martin* was distinguishable. An application under s.71(3) is materially distinct from an application under s.71(1) for the following reasons:

(1) Section 71(1) expressly provides that the third party may apply to the court "as if he were the party chargeable with it" and the court may make the same order (if any) "as it might have made if the application had been made by the party chargeable with the bill." Those restrictions do not appear in s.71(3).

(2) Where a solicitor is instructed by an executor to administer an estate, the interest of the estate was held in the earlier case of in *Re Brown* (1867) to be central to consideration of the reasonableness of the costs in a way that forms no part of the exercise undertaken by an assessment being conducted under s.71(1).

(3) Section 71(3) makes express provision for the court to make an order that "such payments, in respect of the amount found to be due to or by the solicitor ... be made to or by the applicant, to or by the solicitor, or to or by the executor, administrator or trustee, as it thinks fit." There is no equivalent provision attached to s.71(1): the orders that the court may make pursuant to a s.71(1) assessment are limited to "the same order (if any) as it might have made if the application had been made by the party chargeable with the bill".

A residuary beneficiary who lacks mental capacity will be unable to approve the accounts. A receiver or deputy may have been appointed by the Court of Protection to deal with that person's affairs. In this case the personal representatives should inform the receiver or deputy of the entitlement and act in accordance with their directions. Provided the personal representatives act in accordance with the court's directions they will obtain a good discharge. If no receiver has been appointed then an application should be made to the Court of Protection for the appointment of a deputy. Such an application is normally made by a close relative of the disabled beneficiary. The personal representatives will retain the assets pending the application.

Chapter Nineteen

POST-MORTEM ALTERATIONS

1. Introduction

19-001 The persons entitled to a deceased person's property under the terms of the will or under the intestacy rules may not need or want the property left to them. It is always possible to make a lifetime gift of the unwanted property but such a gift would normally have inheritance tax and capital gains tax consequences. It is sometimes possible for the disposition of a deceased person's estate to be rewritten after the death and treated for some tax purposes as if the deceased had left the property that way. An alteration may achieve a more satisfactory disposition of the property of the deceased and/or a saving of tax.

There are a number of ways in which alterations after death to the dispositions of a deceased person's property can be achieved. In this chapter we will consider the following methods:

(a) a "disclaimer";
(b) a "variation";
(c) an order made under the Inheritance (Provision for Family and Dependants) Act 1975;
(d) a "precatory trust";
(e) events occurring within two years of death affecting property settled by death where there has been no interest in possession.

In each case we will consider the effect on succession to property and on taxation.

2. Disclaimer

The succession effect of disclaimer

Introduction

19-002 It was said as long ago as 1819 that "the law certainly is not so absurd as to force a man to take an estate against his will" (per Abbot CJ in *Townson v Tickell* (1819)); the right of disclaimer is long established. A beneficiary is free to disclaim any property. A person entitled on intestacy is also apparently free to disclaim entitlement under the intestacy rules (*Re Scott* (1975)). A disclaimer is simply a refusal to accept property.

Limitations on the right to disclaim

19-003 The right to disclaim a gift is lost altogether once any benefit from it has been accepted by the beneficiary. This will be the case where, for example, the beneficiary has had the property vested in them or where they have received income from a specific legacy or interest on a pecuniary legacy.

Unless the will provides to the contrary, it is not possible to disclaim part only of a single gift; the entire gift must be given up. If a beneficiary is entitled to two separate gifts, they can disclaim one while accepting the other. Thus a beneficiary given two legacies, one of £1,000, the other of a clock, can disclaim the clock and still accept the money (or vice versa). Other jurisdictions have different rules which may allow partial disclaimer.

The effect of disclaiming

19-004 If a beneficiary disclaims a gift in the will or an entitlement under the intestacy rules, the property passes as if the gift to them had failed. The destination of the disclaimed property thereafter depends on the nature of the gift or entitlement that has been given up.

A will may provide expressly for what is to happen if a gift cannot take effect for any reason. In the absence of express provision the following rules apply. If a non-residuary gift in a will is disclaimed then the property will fall into residue. If a residuary gift is disclaimed, the property passes under the intestacy rules, unless the gift is a class gift in which case it passes to the other members of the class. If it is a gift to joint tenants, it passes to the other joint tenant.

If a gift in a will is disclaimed, this does not prevent the beneficiary receiving the property (in whole or in part) under the intestacy rules. Thus, if a deceased died leaving a spouse and children having by will given his entire substantial estate to his wife, she could disclaim her interest under the will and still share in the property with her children under the intestacy rules. If this distribution is unacceptable, a "variation" might be more appropriate (see para.19-013 and following).

Where one or more a members of a class disclaim their share of a gift, the disclaimer will either result in the property passing to the remaining members of the class or, if there are none, to the next category of relatives.

Where the disclaimer is made by a child (or issue) of the testator on or after 1 February 2012, the date on which the Estates of Deceased Persons (Forfeiture Rule and Law of Succession) Act 2011 came into force, the child is treated as having predeceased the testator with the result that any issue of the disclaiming child take their parent's share (Wills Act 1837 s.33A). See para.16-032.

A disadvantage of disclaimer is that the original beneficiary has no control over the ultimate destination of the property, which must pass under the terms of the deceased's will or the intestacy rules. This may be acceptable to the beneficiary who merely wants to give up their rights to certain property (perhaps because it carries with it onerous covenants or unacceptable conditions), but it will not be acceptable if they want to ensure that someone other than the residuary beneficiary or next-of-kin takes in their place. In the latter case a "variation" would ensure they achieve their wishes.

Method of disclaiming

19-005 There are no statutory provisions governing the method of disclaiming a gift in a will or an entitlement under the intestacy rules. It is sufficient for the beneficiary to indicate their intention to the deceased's personal representatives either orally or in writing. Disclaimer can be by informal acts but will not be readily presumed where it is to the advantage of the person to retain the gift. There is a presumption that a person will accept a legacy unless the contrary is proved (see *Cook v IRC* (2002) and the cases cited in *Re Strattons Disclaimer, Stratton v IRC* (1958)). Written notice is, therefore, advisable. A letter stating that the beneficiary does not want the property is sufficient.

The taxation effect of disclaimer

The inheritance tax rules

Requirements of IHTA 1984 s.142 Under general principles a beneficiary who refuses to accept an entitlement is treated as making a transfer of value for the purposes of inheritance tax. Thus, if the beneficiary were to die within seven years of disclaiming, tax would (subject to any exemptions and reliefs available) be payable. If certain statutory requirements are complied with, a disclaimer will not be treated as a transfer of value. Inheritance tax will, instead, be payable as if the deceased had left their property to the person entitled once the disclaimer takes effect. The requirements are set out in IHTA 1984 s.142: **19-006**

(a) the disclaimer must not be made for consideration in money or money's worth (other than the making of a disclaimer or variation in respect of another disposition) (s.142(3));
(b) the disclaimer must be in writing (s.142(1)); and
(c) the disclaimer must be made within two years of the death (s.142(1).

Provided these requirements are complied with, no further formalities are required. In particular, there is no requirement for a statement that s.142 is to apply; as we shall see at para.19-015, such a statement is required in the case of a post-death variation.

The property disclaimed will pass to the person next entitled under the terms of the deceased's will (or the intestacy rules). The original beneficiary will not be treated as making a transfer of value. If the change of entitlement results in a change in the amount of inheritance tax payable on the deceased's estate (for example, where the spouse exemption becomes available on more or on less of the estate) the personal representatives will recalculate the tax and submit a corrective account to HMRC.

In some cases the effect of a disclaimer may be to increase tax. For example, the spouse exemption will be lost if the spouse disclaims. In such cases a disclaimer which is not in writing or which is made more than two years after death should be considered. Section 142 will not then apply, the surviving spouse will be treated as making a transfer of value but, provided this is a potentially exempt transfer and the spouse does survive seven years, no tax will be payable.

A disclaimer is unilateral. The consent of the personal representatives of the deceased is not required to a disclaimer even if its effect is to increase the tax due.

Section 142(1) refers to the disclaimer of property comprised in the deceased's estate immediately before death "whether passing by will, intestacy *or otherwise*". As a result of the reference to property passing "otherwise" than by will or intestacy, it is possible to disclaim an interest in joint property passing by survivorship (property in which the deceased had merely an interest in possession is not treated as a part of the deceased's estate for the purposes of disclaimer (s.142(5))). **19-007**

The property must be comprised in the deceased's "estate" immediately before death. Normally for inheritance tax purposes the estate is defined by IHTA 1984 s.5 as everything in the beneficial entitlement of the deceased other than excluded property. For the purposes of s.142 (so, for variations as well as disclaimers), the definition is extended by s.142(5) to include excluded property but not any property in which the deceased had a qualifying interest in possession by virtue of section 49(1) or which is treated as part of the estate under the reservation of benefit rules contained in s.102 of the Finance Act 1986.

19-008 The implications of the changes to the definition of "estate" are as follows.

Excluded property The inclusion of this property is helpful to taxpayers.

Example 1

Unwin, a UK domiciled legatee, inherits foreign situs property under the will of Nonna, his non-UK domiciled grandmother. Unwin can disclaim foreign situs property or vary its destination under s.142. Without the extended definition of "estate" Unwin would be unable to do so.

Property in which deceased had an interest in possession The exclusion of such property means that a remainder beneficiary cannot vary the destination of the remainder interest under s.142.

Reservation of benefit Where property is treated as part of a person's estate under the reservation of benefit rules, it is of course actually owned by someone else. Unsurprisingly, s.142 is not available.

Example 2

Magda gives her holiday home to her son, Serge, but continues to use it extensively for holidays. Although it is treated as part of her estate for most inheritance tax purposes, it is not part of her estate for s.142.

19-009 **Disclaimer of interest in possession on behalf of deceased** As we will see at para.19-017 HMRC does not accept that it is possible to vary an interest in possession once the beneficiary has died but does accept that the interest can be disclaimed under IHTA 1984, s.93 on behalf of the beneficiary provided no benefit was taken from the settled property.

Quite apart from s.142 there is power for a person to disclaim any interest in settled property under s.93 of the IHTA 1984 which applies to interests under lifetime settlements as well as under wills and which imposes no time limit. Both life interests and reversionary interests can be disclaimed. Provided the disclaimer is not made for consideration in money or money's worth, inheritance tax is charged as if the person had never become entitled to the interest. In order to disclaim the beneficiary must have taken no benefit from the interest so lapse of time may make it difficult for the beneficiary to establish that they are still legally able to disclaim. The disclaimer must be made by both the personal representatives of the dead beneficiary and the beneficiaries of their estate. See *IHT Manual* para.IHTM35164.

If the deceased had an interest in possession and they had, *and had -exercised by will*, a general power of appointment over the property, HMRC regard that -property as part of the deceased's estate at death. Thus, any disclaimer must meet the conditions of s.142 rather than s.93. See *IHT Manual* para.IHTM35165.

The capital gains tax rules

19-010 Under general capital gains tax principles a disclaimer is a disposal by the original beneficiary for capital gains tax purposes. However, the Taxation of

Chargeable Gains Act 1992 s.62(6) provides that if certain conditions are complied with, a disclaimer will not be treated as a disposal. Instead the property will be treated as if left by the deceased to the person entitled once the disclaimer has taken effect. As death is not a disposal, no capital gains tax will be payable. The conditions are identical with those required for inheritance tax relief. No further formalities are required.

The income tax rules

There is no statutory provision which makes a disclaimer retrospective for income tax purposes. Therefore, the position with respect to income from the property disclaimed is governed by the general law. As a disclaimer operates by preventing a gift from taking effect at all, the disclaiming beneficiary has no entitlement to income from the disclaimed asset(s). The disclaimer, therefore, prevents the disclaiming beneficiary having any income tax liability. HMRC have apparently argued that the disclaiming beneficiary's interest remains intact up to the date of the disclaimer, but this seems contrary to principle. **19-011**

Certainly in relation to pecuniary legacies the position is clear. A pecuniary legacy carries with it, in certain circumstances, the right to receive interest (see para.16-063 and following). If interest is neither paid nor claimed, there is nothing for the legatee to be assessed to tax on (*Dewar v IRC* (1935)) unless a fund to meet the legacy has been set aside (*Spens v IRC* (1970)). A disclaimer can only be made where no income or interest has been accepted so a legatee who is able to disclaim will not have any income to be assessed.

Specific legatees and residuary beneficiaries should be treated in the same way as, again, the gifts never take effect.

A disclaimer is a refusal to accept an entitlement rather than a gift of the entitlement to a new beneficiary. This can have an important, and beneficial, income tax consequence for parents.

The anti-avoidance legislation contained in Pt 5 Ch.5 of the Income Tax (Trading and Other Income) Act 2005 provides that a settlor will remain liable for income tax on income from a settlement in which the settlor, spouse or civil partner retains an interest and will be liable for income tax on income applied for their minor children who have neither married nor formed a civil partnership. The definition of a settlement is wide enough to catch a post-death variation (see para.19-024) but HMRC will apparently normally accept that a disclaimer is not a settlement on the basis that the property has never been owned by the person disclaiming.

The stamp duty rules

There is no stamp duty on voluntary dispositions. Similarly, under para.1 Sch.3 to the Finance Act 2003 any land transaction is exempt from stamp duty land tax if made for no consideration. There will, therefore, normally be no stamp duty or stamp duty land tax on a disclaimer. **19-012**

3. Variations

The succession effect of variation

A variation is really a lifetime gift

19-013 A variation is a direction from a beneficiary to the personal representatives to transfer property to someone other than the original beneficiary. There are no special rules on the form of a variation for succession purposes since it is, in effect, an ordinary lifetime gift. In cases where one or more of the recipients of the property under the variation is providing no consideration, a deed is advisable as the personal representatives may be reluctant to act on the basis of an unenforceable agreement.

For succession purposes, a variation is similar to a disclaimer in that the original beneficiary gives up their rights to receive property under the terms of the will or the intestacy rules but a variation differs from a disclaimer in three material respects:

(a) A variation is possible even though the original beneficiary has accepted the property, whether by receiving income or by having the property vested in them. It is even possible to vary the deceased's dispositions once the administration of the estate is complete.
(b) The original beneficiary can make a partial variation of a gift by, for example, giving up part of a gift. (This is not possible in the case of a disclaimer unless the will makes specific provision.)
(c) The original beneficiary can control the ultimate destination of the property since it passes to whoever they specify. The property does not have to pass under the terms of the deceased's will or the intestacy rules.

Thus, a variation may provide a solution where a person has inherited property which they do not want but which they do not wish to pass to the person next entitled under the deceased's will or the intestacy rules.

Example 3

Ann dies leaving her residuary estate to her husband Brian. He has no need of it and wishes to give the property direct to his two grandchildren, rather than to his child, Charlotte. A disclaimer will not achieve his aim since if he were to disclaim his interest under the will and his entitlement under the intestacy rules, the property would pass to Charlotte.

In the above example Brian could achieve his aim by making an ordinary lifetime gift to the grandchildren without altering the disposition by the deceased at all. However, this would be a potentially exempt transfer for inheritance tax purposes and a disposal for capital gains purposes which might result in unnecessary payments of tax being made. If he complies with the requirements of the IHTA 1984 s.142 and Taxation of Chargeable Gains Act 1992 s.62(6), he can vary the terms of the will in favour of his grandchildren and can avoid the transaction being treated as his lifetime gift for capital tax purposes.

When choosing between a variation complying with the statutory requirements and an ordinary lifetime gift, tax considerations should be uppermost in the beneficiary's mind since variation is basically a tax concept.

It is important to remember that the reading back is only effective for the specified taxes. There is no general reading back. See the discussion in *Barrs Residential and Leisure Ltd v Pleass Thomson & Co* (2020) where a post-death variation passed the deceased's mobile home to his son. Under the Mobile Homes Act 2013, the benefit of a pitch agreement for a mobile home can pass to a person entitled to the home by virtue of the deceased's will or under the law relating to intestacy. The son was entitled under the variation and so did not acquire a right to the pitch agreement.

A person who varies to give up a legacy with the intention of preserving their rights to means-tested benefits or to limit their ability to pay care home fees is likely to fall foul of the rules on deliberate deprivation. The regulations governing means tested benefits provide that persons who have deliberately deprived themselves of assets with the intention of preserving their right to benefits, will be treated as still in possession of the assets. The assets are "notional capital" of the person. See, for example, the discussion in *FSS v LMS* (2020).

Binding agreement to vary

In *Crowden v Aldridge* (1993) the residuary beneficiaries signed a memorandum after the funeral agreeing that the will should be varied in favour of the deceased's housekeeper and stating that each would sign a deed to that effect. When the deed was prepared four of the beneficiaries refused to sign. The court held that the memorandum was a document showing intention to create legal effect and therefore it varied the distribution of the estate as soon as it was communicated to the executors. **19-014**

The taxation effect of variation

The inheritance tax rules

If an original beneficiary makes a lifetime gift of all or part of the property inherited, this is a transfer of value for inheritance tax purposes. Thus, if they die within seven years of the gift, inheritance tax will be payable (subject to any exemptions and reliefs which may be available). However, IHTA 1984 s.142(1) provides that if certain conditions are complied with, a variation will not be treated as a transfer of value. Instead, inheritance tax will be payable as if the deceased had left their property to the substituted beneficiary or beneficiaries. **19-015**

The first three conditions are the same as those applying to disclaimers. Conditions (d) and (e) apply only to variations. The conditions are:

(a) the variation must not be made for consideration in money or money's worth (other than the making of a disclaimer or variation in respect of another disposition) (s.142(3));
(b) the variation must be in writing (s.142(1));
(c) the variation must be made within two years of the death (s.142(1));
(d) the instrument in writing which makes the variation must contain a statement by the person or persons making the instrument (and, where the variation results in additional tax being payable also by the personal representatives) to the effect that they intend s.142(1) to apply to the variation. The personal representatives may only refuse to make the statement if no or no sufficient assets are held by them as personal representatives for discharging the additional tax (s.142(2)); and
(e) where additional tax becomes payable as a result of the instrument the person or persons making the instrument and the personal representatives are under a duty to deliver a copy to HMRC and notify them of the amount of the additional tax (s.142(2A)).

As in the case of a disclaimer, any property comprised in the deceased's estate immediately before death, whether passing by will, intestacy *or otherwise*, can be the subject of a variation (s.142(1)). It is, therefore, possible to vary the destination of property passing by survivorship.

Section 142(5) changes to the normal definition of "estate" applies to variations in the same way that it applies to disclaimers: see para.19-008.

Section 142(6) provides expressly that a variation agreement will be effective for inheritance tax purposes whether or not the administration is complete or the property concerned has already been distributed to the original beneficiary.

The variation is effective for all inheritance purposes so a person who has varied property will not be regarded as making a gift of that property for the purposes of the gift with reservation provisions. There is also protection in para.16 Sch.15 to the Finance Act 2004 to prevent the pre-owned assets rules applying to post-death variations. Because it is effective for all inheritance tax purposes a variation directing a residence or interest in a residence to lineal descendants of the deceased is capable of securing the residence nil-rate band for the estate (assuming the other requirements are satisfied).

HMRC take the view that a variation, once made, is irrevocable and that s.142 will not apply to an instrument redirecting any item that has already been redirected under an earlier instrument. *Russell v IRC* confirms HMRC's view that it is not possible to redirect any item or any part of an item which has already been redirected under an earlier instrument. It is, however, possible to combine reading back under a variation with a disclaimer and/or an event occurring within two years of death.

It is possible to have any number of variations in relation to the same estate so long as they each deal with different assets. A variation, once made, cannot be amended or corrected, unless the court rectifies the variation to correct mistakes in the way the transaction had been recorded. See *Martin v Nicholson* (2004); *Wills v Gibbs* (2007); *Ashcroft v Barnsdale* (2010); and *Giles v RNIB* (2014) for examples of successful applications for rectification.

HMRC has published guidelines setting out the requirements which an instrument must satisfy to qualify under s.142. They were contained in a letter published in the *Law Society Gazette* of 22 May 1985, p.1454 and are available at *IHT Manual* para.IHTM35021 (amended to take account of a change in practice made on 1 August 2002). The published requirements are that the instrument must:

- be in writing and must be made by the person or any of the persons who benefit or would benefit under the dispositions of the property comprised in the deceased's estate immediately before their death;
- be made within two years after the death; and
- clearly indicate the dispositions that are the subject of the instrument, and vary their destination as laid down by the deceased's will or under the law relating to intestate estates; or otherwise
- the instrument must contain a statement of intent that the disposition is to be treated as the deceased's;
- the instrument must be sent to HMRC within six months if it results in additional tax being payable. It must be accompanied by a calculation of the additional tax due.

The effect of the third bullet point is that the variation must refer to the original disposition. In HMRC's view a document such as a deed of assignment which merely transfers property in fact received by a legatee to a third party without mention of the will does not satisfy this requirement. The third bullet also requires that the destination of the property is varied. However, it is not fatal to a s.142 claim if the property ends up back in the same place that it started, so long as the initial destination of the property was varied. Such circular variations often arise in relation to deceased beneficiaries. See para.19-017.

Variation in favour of charities

The Finance Act 2012 amended s.142 by inserting new sub-ss.(3A) and (3B) which provide that a variation redirecting property to a charity is not effective for inheritance tax purposes unless there is evidence to show that the charity has been informed of the variation. If the property is to be held on trust for charitable purposes, it is the trustees who must be informed. **19-016**

No formalities are required so any sort of written confirmation from the charity will be sufficient evidence.

The change was introduced because it was previously possible for a taxpayer to vary an estate to give property to a charity, claim a reduction in inheritance tax on the basis of the charity exemption and then fail to give the property to the charity.

The provision does not apply to disclaimers.

Deceased beneficiaries

It is possible to make a variation on behalf of a person who has died redirecting that person's entitlement on an earlier death. Such a variation may result in the property returning to the original beneficiary via a different route but in a more tax-efficient manner. Paragraph IHTM35042 of the *IHT Manual* says that such a redirection on behalf of a deceased beneficiary does not infringe the requirement to change the destination of the property. **19-017**

Example 4

Jamil, who has made no lifetime transfers, dies leaving £100,000 to his brother, Tariq, and the rest of his estate to charity. Tariq dies six months later leaving his estate of £1 million to his sons. The sons can vary Jamil's will to leave the £100,000 directly to them instead of to their father.

Who should make the variation on behalf of a dead beneficiary? In the IHT Manual at IHTM35042 HMRC says: "*The executor of a person who has died may make a variation redirecting that person's entitlement on an earlier death*". However, it goes on to say: "*Where the variation reduces the entitlement of the beneficiaries of the second deceased then the beneficiaries should also agree to the variation. If the beneficiaries are not a party to the deed of variation then we should request other written evidence of their consent*".

HMRC does not consider that it is possible to redirect a life interest after the death of the life tenant. Once the life tenant dies, there is no property in existence that can be redirected. Many people thought this interpretation was wrong but it received judicial support in *Soutters Executry v IRC* (2002). It is possible to disclaim a life interest (see para.19-009).

It is possible to vary a will to direct property into the estate of a deceased beneficiary. For example, a wife dies with a full nil rate band is £325,000 available and leaving her estate of £525,000 (cash and investments) to her son. Inheritance tax will be paid on £200,000.

Her husband dies 18 months later (also with a full nil rate band of £325,000 available) leaving his estate of £125,000 (cash and investments) to the same son. No inheritance tax is payable but the husband has unused nil rate band.

The son can redirect £200,000 of his mother's estate to his father so utilising the whole of his father's nil rate band. There will then be an IHT saving on the redirected £200,000 (of £80,000).

Whether to have the transfer treated as the deceased's

19-018 A beneficiary (B) will often wish to have the transfer treated as the deceased's for inheritance tax purposes since this results in only one possible charge to tax, from the deceased to the new beneficiary; whereas if B makes a lifetime gift there is one charge from the estate to B and a risk of a second charge if B dies within seven years of the gift.

However, if B is the spouse of the deceased it may be beneficial not to have the transfer treated as the deceased's since the initial transfer to B is exempt; there is still the risk of a charge if B dies within seven years but this will be at B's rates and tapering relief will be available after three years.

Anti-avoidance

19-019 Section 142(3) provides that there is no reading back if a variation or disclaimer is made for any consideration in money or money's worth (other than the making, of another variation or disclaimer). This is designed to prevent non-exempt beneficiaries varying the disposition of the estate in favour of a spouse or civil partner in return for a promise to make potentially exempt transfers of a larger amount than the original entitlement to obtain the spouse exemption for the estate. HMRC is suspicious of such variations. Paragraph IHTM35093 of the *IHT Manual* states that HMRC will ask:

(i) whether there had been any discussion between the parties before the variation was made about how the benefit redirected to the spouse or civil partner should be dealt with; and
(ii) whether subsequent to the variation the spouse or civil partner has made any transfers to the original chargeable beneficiaries, or is contemplating making any such transfers.

Lau v RCC (2009) is a case where there was no reading back because the variations had been made in return for a binding promise from the surviving spouse to make lifetime gifts. *Vaughan-Jones v Vaughan-Jones* (2015) was a case where the taxpayers applied for rectification of a defective variation. HMRC declined to appear in the application stating that it was futile. HMRC took the view that the case was on all fours with Lau because the solicitor's attendance note recorded that the surviving spouse would, after the variation made by the deceased's sons in her favour, transfer as much to them as she could spare. The taxpayers' view was that the cases differed. In *Lau* there had been an enforceable agreement for transfer of a specified amount.

Rectification was granted in *Vaughan-Jones* and we do not know whether HMRC continued to argue that the variation was ineffective. However, given that HMRC will ask questions about agreements and discussions between the parties, it is clearly important that no promises are made or agreements entered into.

The lack of agreement or promise leaves the non-exempt beneficiaries in a vulnerable position. An attractive alternative is for the original beneficiaries' variation to create a fixed term or terminable life interest for the spouse, the property reverting to them once the life interest ends. In this case the *Manual* says that HMRC will ask whether the trustees have already exercised the power of appointment or whether an exercise of it is contemplated.

Where a variation creates a life interest, s.142(4) of the IHTA 1984 must be considered. This provides that where a variation results in property being held in trust for a person for less than two years after the death, the disposition of the property that takes effect at the end of the period is to be treated as if it had had effect at the date of the death. In other words the trust drops out. If, therefore, adult children vary the disposition of their father's estate to give their mother an interest in possession lasting 12 months and then to themselves absolutely, the children will be treated as if the gift to them took effect on their father's death. The mother's life interest is disregarded and the desired inheritance tax saving is lost.

If a surviving spouse with a terminable life interest dies within two years, it is the death and not the variation that results in the termination of the life interest and s.142(4) will not be in point.

If the trustees choose to terminate the life interest within two years, HMRC will probably take the view that it is the variation which results in the termination and so s.142(4) would apply.

It is unclear whether a life interest of exactly two years is or is not caught by s.142(4). In *Kevern v Ayres* (2014) HMRC argued that a life interest of exactly two years did fall foul of s.142(4) but the case was remitted for procedural reasons so we do not know what view the court would have taken. Clearly the safe course is either to specify two years plus one day or to make the interest terminable at the discretion of the trustees.

Variations and the residence nil-rate band (RNRB)

Because variations which comply with the requirements of s.142 are read back for all inheritance tax purposes, they can be used to obtain the benefit of the RNRB where the original disposition of the estate would not have done so. **19-020**

Example 5

Taj dies leaving a pecuniary legacy of £1 million to his son, residue of £1 million which includes his residence worth £800,000 to his cohabitee. No RNRB is currently available to the estate as the house is inherited by the cohabitee not by the lineal descendant.

There is no point in the personal representatives appropriating the residence to the son as HMRC regards an appropriation as an administrative act by the personal representatives and not as "inheriting" (see IHTM46033 which explains that inheriting requires a "disposition on death"). However, the son and cohabitee can vary the disposition of the estate to give the son an interest in the residence equal to the RNRB. This will be read back for all inheritance tax purposes. Although reading back is not available where a variation or disclaimer is made for any consideration in money or money's worth, consideration consisting of the making of a variation or disclaimer in the same estate is not included (see s.142(3) and para.19-019).

There is no requirement that the lineal descendant retains the residence after inheriting it so the son can sell the interest to the cohabitee if desired.

The capital gains tax rules

Under general principles a redirection of property inherited will amount to a disposal by the original beneficiaries for capital gains tax purposes. **19-021**

A legatee who does not want the redirection to be treated as a lifetime disposal can take advantage of s.62(6) of the Taxation of Chargeable Gains Act 1992, which provides that if certain conditions are complied with a variation will not be treated as a disposal. Instead, the property will be treated as if the deceased had left it to the substituted beneficiary or beneficiaries. The conditions are identical to those required for inheritance tax purposes.

It does not matter whether the variation is made while the assets are still vested in the personal representatives or after they have transferred them to the legatee (see *CGT Manual* para.CG31610). If the original legatee has sold the asset, a variation can pass the proceeds of sale. If the original legatee elects for reading back, the sale will be treated as made by the new benficiary for capital gains tax purposes (see para.CG31630).

The wording of s.142 of the IHTA 1984 and s.62(6) of the Taxation of Chargeable Gains Act 1992 differ in one important respect. Section 142(1) provides that, where the appropriate conditions are complied with, "*this Act* shall apply as if the variation had been effected by the deceased". Section 62(6)(b) provides that "this section shall apply as if the variation had been effected by the deceased". The result is that a variation is retrospective for the purposes of the charge to capital gains tax on death contained in s.62 but not for other purposes such as establishing a settlement.

The House of Lords' decision in *Marshall v Kerr* (1994) illustrated the importance of the difference. A UK domiciled beneficiary varied his entitlement under the will of a non-UK domiciled testator to create a settlement. He expected the settlement to be treated as created by the testator for capital gains tax purposes and therefore to be an offshore settlement. Sadly, this was not the case and the original beneficiary was treated as the settlor for the purposes of TCGA 1992 s.86. Section 68C of the Taxation of Chargeable Gains Act 1992 (inserted by the Finance Act 2006) provides expressly that where property becomes settled property in consequence of a variation, the person making the variation is to be treated as the settlor.

The extension of the rules on settlor interested trusts for the purposes of capital gains tax makes this an important point. A settlement is settlor interested if the beneficiaries include their spouse, civil partner or minor children of the settlor who have not married or formed a civil partnership (see TCGA 1992 s.169F). Where a settlement is settlor interested hold-over relief is not available when assets are transferred to the settlement. Hence a parent who varies an entitlement to produce a settlement for the benefit of a class which includes their own minor children will be treated as the settlor for capital gains tax purposes.

Whether to have the disposition treated as the deceased's

19-022 Although the inheritance tax and capital gains tax rules are basically the same, there is no need to have the disposition treated as the deceased's for both taxes. The original beneficiary is free to choose for each tax the method which is most beneficial in order to achieve their ends.

Each case depends on its own facts but, when deciding whether to elect that the disposition be treated as made on death for capital gains tax purposes, two points should be borne in mind:

(1) If a loss has arisen since the date of death the original beneficiary may wish to set the loss off against his or her own gains and so for capital gains tax purposes may choose to make a lifetime gift. If, as is often the case, the object of the variation is "connected" to the person varying, TCGA 1992

s.18 provides that the loss can only be set against gains arising on a disposal to the same person. TCGA 1992 s.286 provides that a person is "connected" to an individual if that person is the:

- individual's spouse or civil partner, or brother, sister, ancestor or lineal descendant, or
- the spouse or civil partner of a brother, sister, ancestor or lineal descendant, of the individual or of the individual's spouse or civil partner.)

Where the object of the variation is a connected person, it may be preferable to make a statement of intent that s.62(6) is to apply. The object of the variation will acquire the asset at its probate value and so will have an inbuilt loss which may be useful in the future.

(2) It is preferable to treat the gift as a lifetime disposition for capital gains tax purposes if the property has *increased* in value by an amount not exceeding the original beneficiary's available annual exemption from capital gains tax since the new beneficiary can take the benefit of the increased acquisition value at no cost to the original beneficiary.

Apart from these circumstances, it is usually preferable to have the disposition treated as the deceased's disposition for capital gains tax purposes since no capital gains tax liability arises when assets are transferred from an estate to a legatee.

The income tax rules

A variation raises problems with regard to income tax liability since (like disclaimer) there are no statutory provisions making the variation retrospective for income tax purposes. Thus, income arising between the date of death and the date of the variation will be taxed in accordance with the terms of the will (if any) and the rules on the taxation of the income of estates. **19-023**

Pecuniary legatees are entitled to interest in certain circumstances. However, if interest is neither paid nor claimed, there is nothing for the legatee to be assessed to tax on (*Dewar v IRC* (1935)) unless a fund to meet the legacy has been set aside (*Spens v IRC* (1970)). A specific legatee is entitled to income from the date of death. The legatee will, therefore, be assessed to tax on income arising after the death up to the date of the variation. Income arising after that date will be taxed as income of the new beneficiary unless the settlement provisions apply (see para.19-024). Since the original legatee will be assessed to tax on the income from death until the variation, it may be preferable for them to accept the income rather than passing it to the new beneficiary.

So far as residuary beneficiaries are concerned s.671 of the Income Tax (Trading and Other Income) Act 2005 provides that where different persons obtain absolute interests in residue in succession during the administration of the estate, the interest of the later beneficiary is treated as including the interest of the earlier beneficiary for the purpose of calculating their assumed income entitlement. Hence when determining how much has been paid out as income, the personal representatives will take into account all income payments made to the original beneficiaries as well as to the beneficiaries taking under the variation.

The settlement legislation

The anti-avoidance legislation contained in Pt 5 Ch.5 of the Income Tax (Trading and Other Income) Act 2005 provides that a settlor will remain liable for income **19-024** tax on income from a settlement in which the settlor, spouse or civil partner retains an interest in settlement property and will be liable for income tax on income applied for their minor children who have neither married nor formed a civil partnership. A post-death variation will normally amount to a -settlement. Parents should, therefore, be careful about making post-death variations in favour of minor children. Where feasible, a disclaimer will be preferable.

Stamp duty and variations

19-025 There is no stamp duty on voluntary dispositions. Under para.1 Sch.3 to the Finance Act 2003 any land transaction is exempt from stamp duty land tax if made for no consideration There will, therefore, normally be no stamp duty or stamp duty land tax on a variation.

The Trust Register and variations

19-026 The useful exclusion from registration for trusts effected by will does not apply to trusts created by post-death variation (see para.13-033). Such trusts must be registered within 90 days of creation. The settlor is the person varying not the deceased.

In February 2024 HM Treasury began a new consultation on the Money Laundering, Terrorist Financing and Transfer of Funds (Information on the Payer) Regulations 2017 ("Improving the Effectiveness of the Money Laundering Regulations"), part of which relates to the Trust Register. One of the proposals is to align the rules on registration of trusts created by variation with the rules on trusts effected by will. The result is that such trusts will not have to be registered for two years following the death.

4. Inheritance (Provision for Family and Dependants) Act 1975

19-027 There are two statutory provisions which are relevant for inheritance tax purposes where an order is made under s.2 of the 1975 Act.

- Section 19 of I(PFD)A 1975 provides that, where an order is made under s.2 then, for all purposes, including inheritance tax, the will or the law relating to intestacy shall have effect, and be deemed to have had effect as from the deceased's death, subject to the provisions of the order.
- Section 146(1) of IHTA 1984 provides that, without prejudice to I(PFD)A 1975 s.19, where an order is made under s.2 of I(PFD)A 1975 in relation to any property forming part of the net estate of a deceased person, the property is to be treated for inheritance tax purposes as if it had on his death devolved subject to the provisions of the order. The expression "net estate" is not defined in IHTA 1984 but presumably is as defined in I(PFD)A 1975 s.25(1).

Both s.19 of I(PFD)A 1975 and s.146(1) of IHTA 1984 operate automatically and the beneficiaries cannot decide to disapply them. The two sections have the same general effect for inheritance tax purposes: the estate is taxed in accordance with the order.

Example 6

A deceased left his whole net estate to his sister, and the court orders by way of reasonable financial provision that half of the net estate be paid to his widow. For inheritance tax purposes he will be treated as having left half to his sister and half to his widow, the half passing to his widow being entitled to the spouse exemption under IHTA1984 s.18.

However, there are differences between the two provisions:

(1) Section 19 of I(PFD)A 1975 only provides for the order to have retrospective effect in relation to the deceased's will and/or the law relating to intestacy. So it does not apply to the deceased's severable share of joint property. By contrast IHTA 1984 s.146 provides that any property forming part of the net estate of a deceased person shall be treated as if it had devolved subject to the provisions of the order.
(2) Section 19 of I(PFD)A 1975, is of general application and applies to other taxes such as income and capital gains tax.
(3) There are also difference in relation to Tomlin Orders.

Section 19 applies to court orders which includes a consent order in the strict sense: see *Thwaite v Thwaite* (1982).

Section 146 is wider. Section 146(8) provides that s.146 applies "where an order is made staying or dismissing proceedings under the 1975 Act on terms set out or scheduled to the order". Such an order is referred to as a Tomlin Order and the terms included in the schedule are not an order of the court as such; they are a contractual arrangement between the parties (see *Watson v Sadiq* (2013), at [50]).

Neither s.19 of I(PFD)A 1975 nor s.146 of IHTA 1984 will apply if an application is settled out of court and the terms are not embodied in a consent order or Tomlin Order.

If the tax has to be adjusted in consequence of the court order, the tax underpaid or overpaid does not carry interest from any date earlier than the date of the order (see *IHT Manual* para.IHTM35202).

There are no capital gains tax, stamp duty or income tax provisions corresponding to IHTA 1984 s.146. However, reading back under s.19 of I(PFD)A 1975 is of general application so will apply for all tax purposes. As explained above s.19 is limited to cases where there is an order of the court. It does not apply where an application under I(PFD)A 1975 is settled out of court, even if the terms are embodied in a Tomlin Order unless the order includes a positive requirement that the terms of the compromise be carried out: see para.31810 of the *Capital Gains Manual*.

The new beneficiary is liable to income tax on income arising after the date of death from property awarded to them.

5. PRECATORY WORDS

Where a testator expresses a wish that property left in their will to a beneficiary **19-028**
should be transferred by that beneficiary to someone else, and that beneficiary complies with the wish within two years of the death, IHTA 1984 s.143 provides that inheritance tax is payable as if the deceased had left the property to the eventual recipient. Such requests are made most commonly in relation to personal chattels.

The wish can be included in the will or communicated separately. The *IHT Manual* at para.IHTM35171 states that the request need not be in writing, but it should have been made in terms sufficiently certain for a court to have given effect to it had it been binding.

There are no special capital gains tax rules so the transfer will be treated as a disposal by the original beneficiary. It is likely that there will be no tax to pay as the asset may well not have increased in value by more than the level of the annual exemption. Also in the case of tangible moveable property there is an exception for a disposal of an item or set of items where the disposal consideration is £6,000 or less.

There are no special income tax rules, so income any receivable up to the date of transfer will be assessed to tax as part of the original beneficiary's income.

6. PROPERTY SETTLED ON DEATH WITHOUT AN INTEREST IN POSSESSION—EVENTS OCCURRING WITHIN TWO YEARS OF DEATH

19-029 Section 144(1) and (2) of the IHTA 1984 provide that:

- where property is settled by will, and
- within the period of two years after their death, and
- before an interest in possession arises, and
- an event occurs on which tax would otherwise be chargeable,

no tax shall be charged and the will shall be read as if it provided that on the testator's death the property should be held as it is held after the event.

It is an extremely useful section which allows reading back to occur where relevant property trusts are modified in the two years following death.

So, a testator may wish dispose of his estate in as tax-efficient manner as possible but obviously he does not know what the tax legislation will be when he dies or how rich he will be or what family he will have. He can leave his whole estate on discretionary trusts with a letter of wishes for his trustees explaining in general terms what he would like to happen to his property. His trustees can look at the circumstances existing at the date of death and make a distribution which is suitable in the light of those circumstances. The events that occur in the two years following death will be read back into the will and the estate will be treated as if it had been left in that way.

Example 7

Tariq leaves his entire estate of £1 million on discretionary trusts for the benefit of his spouse and children. One year after his death the trustees appoint £400,000 to one of the children and the residue to Tariq's spouse. Normally an appointment from a discretionary trust would attract an exit charge but here it does not. Instead the will is read as if it had left "£400,000 to a child and the residue to spouse".

Unlike a post-death variation, the reading back is automatic. There is no need for any election. This does mean though that trustees should be careful not to take any steps in the two years following death that they do not wish to be read back. For example, if they give a beneficiary a right to income within two years of death, they will retrospectively create an immediate post-death interest. This will result in the trust property becoming part of the beneficiary's inheritance tax estate which will probably be an unwanted outcome. See, for example, *Payne v Tyler* (2019) where the trustees had to apply to court for rescission of their appointment on the basis of mistake.

The section is useful where the terms of a settlement are not tax efficient at the date of death. The trustees can use their powers of appointment to amend the terms on which the property is held to achieve a more tax-efficient result.

Example 8

Gandalf leaves his entire estate on trust for such of his grandchildren that reach 25, equally if more than one. Included in the estate is his residence worth £500,000.

If the trust is left as it is, Gandalf's estate will not benefit from the residence nil-rate band because the trust is a relevant property trust. Although the beneficiaries of the trust are his lineal descendants, they will not be treated as inheriting because a relevant property trust is the "wrong" sort of trust (see para.4-019).

However, if, within two years of death, the trustees use their express or statutory powers to create retrospective immediate post-death interests in some or all of the residence, the residence nil-rate band will become available. This is because an immediate post-death interest is one of the limited number of settlements which qualify as inheriting for the purposes of the residence nil-rate band (see para.4-019).

Alternatively, an appointment of the residence or an interest in the residence could be made to one or more of the grandchildren absolutely. This would be read back to the date of death so again would secure the residence nil-rate band.

It is possible, but not necessary, for the terms of the trust to *require* the trustees to exercise their powers of appointment within two years of death. The section applies whenever events occur within two years of death.

There are no particular formalities required by s.144 but obviously the trustees must comply with any requirements of the trust instrument. The trust instrument will usually require powers of appointment to be exercised by deed or may require the consent of a named individual. If trustees fail to comply with a requirement for particular formalities, the purported exercise of the power will be void. For a recent example see *Smith v Stanley* (2019). The trust may also include a power to apply capital for the advancement or benefit of the beneficiaries which can usually be exercised without the need for a deed.

It is important that any deed of appointment is preserved and that any decision to advance capital is recorded in writing. This is because HMRC will require evidence that the terms of the original will trust were changed. The safest procedure in the case of a decision to advance capital informally is for the trustees to minute their decision and then execute a declaration that from the date of that decision they are holding the assets on a bare trust for the beneficiary. This crystallises the date on which the application was made which may be important for tax purposes.

Example 9

Hari leaves an amount equal to his available nil-rate band to a discretionary trust and the rest of his estate to his wife, Sahila. Within two years of death the trustees of the discretionary trust use their power to apply capital to give the nil rate sum to Sahila. They must preserve a record of their decision and of the transfer. When Sahila dies, her personal representatives will want to make a claim for the transfer of Hari's nil-rate band. HMRC will require evidence demonstrating that Hari's nil-rate band was not used. His will, of course, created a nil-rate band discretionary trust and it is, therefore, essential to have available documents to show that the dispositions in his will were altered.

The trustees do not have to wait until the executors have vested assets in them; they have a chose in action (the right to compel due administration of the estate) and so can appoint their rights under the will to the appointee.

There used to be a trap in the wording of the section. Reading back only occurs if the event is one "on which tax would be chargeable". No inheritance tax is charged on an appointment from a discretionary trust in the first three months following creation so an appointment made within the first three months after the death was not read back—see *Frankland v IRC* (1997) where an appointment of substantial assets to a surviving spouse was made within three months and as a result the spouse exemption was held not to be available.

However for deaths on or after 10 December 2014 the wording of the section has been amended to provide for reading back in the first three months.

The wording of the section had already been amended following the changes to the taxation of trusts introduced by Finance Act 2006. This Act created three new types of interest which can only be created on death and which receive privileged inheritance tax treatment. They are:

- immediate post-death interests,
- bereaved minor interests, and
- bereaved young person interests.

The terms of s.144 as originally drafted would not have allowed reading back where property originally held on relevant property trusts became held on one of the three privileged trusts within two years of death.

The Finance Act 2006 therefore amended s.144 to ensure that, reading back occurs where these new interests arise within two years of death: see IHTA 1984 s.144(3)–(6).

Example 10

Tamzin leaves her entire estate of £1 million on discretionary trusts for the benefit of her spouse and children. One year after her death the trustees appoint £300,000 to her son if he reaches 18 and the balance to her husband for life, remainder to her son. The appointments create a bereaved minor's interest under IHTA 1984 s.71A for her son and an immediate post-death interest for her husband. Both are read back into her will.

The event which causes reading back does not have to be an express appointment. Obtaining a right to income within two years of death can create an immediate post-death interest.

Example 11

Ted leaves his entire estate of £1 million to such of his children as reach 25, equally if more than one. They are to become entitled to income at 21. Ted believes that this will create a trust for a bereaved young person under IHTA 1984 s.71D.

When he dies, he has three children: Abe (22), Bea (20), and Chris (16). Abe has an immediate post-death interest which arises on Ted's death. Bea obtains an immediate post-death interest because she becomes entitled to income within two years of Ted's death and this is read back into the will. Only Chris has an interest in a bereaved young person's trust. This may not seem very important as all will become entitled to capital at 25 but the tax implications at 25 will be quite different. In the case of Abe and Bea there will be no charge to inheritance tax when they reach 25 as they are already treated as entitled to the trust capital. There will be a charge when Chris becomes entitled to capital based on the length of time the property has remained settled since his 18th birthday. There will be hold-over relief available when Chris becomes entitled to capital as it is a transfer from a trust for a bereaved young person. However, there will be no hold-over relief when Abe and Bea become entitled to capital as they do not have interests in a trust for a bereaved young person and neither is the transfer chargeable to inheritance tax.

There are no special capital gains tax rules applicable to s.144 appointments. The exercise of the trustees' discretion is a deemed disposal and re-acquisition by them (see para.7-051). The recipient acquires the asset at its market value when the discretion is exercised and not the value at death. As the appointment from the trust is not a transfer chargeable to inheritance tax no hold-over relief is available to the trustees.

However, it is often possible to avoid a charge to capital gains tax by making the appointment while the administration of the estate is still continuing. HMRC takes the view (see *CGT Manual* para.IHTM31430) that if the trustees exercise their power of appointment while the assets are still in the hands of the personal representatives and before the assets have vested in them as trustees, the assets should be treated as passing direct to the appointee under the terms of the will.

HMRC state in the Capital Gains Tax Manual at para.CG31430 that the assets appointed should be treated as never becoming subject to the trust. They are treated as though the deceased had passed the assets concerned directly to the legatee rather than into trust. The appointee then takes those assets as legatee and therefore acquires them at probate value like any other legatee.

From death until the event occurs, any income produced will be taxed first as part of the estate income (see para.6-018 and following) and then, if the property is transferred to trustees, the normal income tax rules for settlements where no beneficiary has a right to income will apply (see para.7-059 and following).

Section 144 was used extensively following the introduction of the transferable nil-rate band on 9 October 2007 (see para.4-015). Before that date, instead of leaving everything to the surviving spouse, the first spouse to die would often create a nil-rate band discretionary trust for the benefit of the surviving spouse and children so as to make use of the first spouse's nil-rate band. Now that it is possible to transfer the unused portion of the nil-rate band, many families take the view that the discretionary trust is unnecessary. If the trustees use their power of appointment within two years of death to appoint the funds to the surviving spouse:

(a) the appointment will be read back into the will with the result that the spouse exemption will be available on the whole of the estate of the first to die;
(b) the survivor's estate will have the benefit of two nil-rate bands.

Section 144 is used extensively in relation to the residence nil-rate band. We saw one illustration at Example 8 above (changing a settlement into one of the limited number of settlements that benefit from the residence nil-rate band). Other uses of s.144 will include:

- appointing a residence held on discretionary trusts to one or more lineal descendants (absolutely or on immediate post-death interests depending on circumstances);
- creating a nil-rate band discretionary trust for the surviving spouse and other family members where the assets inherited by the surviving spouse from the first to die will mean that the survivor's estate exceeds the taper threshold.

CHAPTER TWENTY

INHERITANCE (PROVISION FOR FAMILY AND DEPENDANTS) ACT 1975

1. INTRODUCTION

A testator is free to leave property in whatever way he or she pleases; no relative has a *right* to receive property under the will. However, this principle of testamentary freedom is to some extent eroded by the Inheritance (Provision for Family and Dependants) Act 1975. This Act gives the court limited powers to order financial provision to be made from the net estate of a deceased person for the benefit of certain categories of applicant. Applications under the Act can also be made where a person dies intestate. **20-001**

Significant amendments were made to the Act by the Inheritance and Trustees' Powers Act 2014 for deaths on or after 1 October 2014.

If an application is to be successful, the following matters must be established:

(a) the deceased died domiciled in England and Wales;
(b) he application is made within the time limit;
(c) the applicant falls into one of the five possible categories of applicant; and
(d) the will or intestacy rules have not made reasonable provision for the applicant.

If the necessary matters are established, the court must then decide whether and in what manner to order financial provision for the applicant from the net estate of the deceased (to help the court in its decision there are certain statutory guidelines to be taken into account).

The Act contains certain anti-avoidance provisions under which orders may, in limited circumstances, be made against people who have received property from the deceased before death (see para.20-047 and following).

Claims die with the applicant. Three High Court decisions have held that claims under the 1975 Act do not survive the death of the applicant: *Whyte v Ticehurst* (1986); *Re Bramwell (Deceased)* (1988); and *Roberts v Fresco* (2017).

All these decisions depended in part on the application of s.1 of the Law Reform (Miscellaneous Provisions) Act 1934 which provides that:-

> "(1) Subject to the provisions of this section, on the death of any person after the commencement of this Act all causes of action subsisting against or vested in him shall survive against, or, as the case may be, for the benefit of, his estate."

In each case, the judge held that an applicant's right to bring a claim under the 1975 Act was not in itself a cause of action, within the meaning of the 1934 Act, but a mere hope or contingency. That was because it was only after an order had been made in favour of an application for reasonable financial provision that any cause of action came into being and was vested in the applicant, so as to be capable of surviving his or death. In analysing a claim under the 1975 Act in this way, the judges followed, and applied by analogy, the reasoning of Denning LJ in *Sugden v Sugden* (1957), in which he had stated *obiter* (at p.134) that the right to bring a claim for financial relief on divorce under the Matrimonial Causes Act 1973 did not give rise to any cause of action until the court makes an order di-recting such relief.

This analysis of the right to bring a claim for financial relief under matrimonial legislation as a mere hope or con-tingency, rather than a cause of action, was swept away as a heresy by the Supreme Court in *Unger v Ul-Hasan* (2023). In his judgment at [116] Lord Leggatt said there could be no doubt that "*a financial order claim is not a mere hope or contingency. It is a cause of action and is therefore capable in principle of passing on death by op-eration of the 1934 Act.*"

However, the decisions in *Whyte*, *Bramwell* and *Roberts* had a second strand of reasoning which is unaffected by the Supreme Court decision in *Unger*. This was that the nature of a claim under the 1975 Act is, on a proper construction of the Act, intended to be purely personal. Booth J said in *Whyte*, at p.70A–E that to hold otherwise would:-

> "lead to the extraordinary result, as in this case, of a contest between the beneficiaries of two estates in the determination of which the court would have the well-nigh impossible task of assessing the matters to which the statute requires it to have regard, many of which are clearly based upon the fundamental assumption that one of the parties to the marriage survives at the date of the hearing."

In *Archibald's Estate v Stewart* (2023) these cases were considered. Deputy Master Francis refused to allow an application to be made on behalf of a deceased son, saying it was clear from those cases and comments made by the Supreme Court in *Unger* that applications could not be continued following the death of a spouse and that reasoning must apply, "a fortiori, *to claims by other classes of applicant whose right to relief is limited to such reasonable financial provision as is required for their maintenance. On a proper construction of the 1975 Act, such a claim is personal to the applicant and can only be pursued whilst the applicant is alive*".

This is an important practical point. However strong a claim may be (as it was in *Roberts v Fresco*), nothing will be awarded if the applicant dies before judgment.

2. Deceased Must have Died Domiciled in England and Wales

20-002 The Act applies only in the case of a deceased who dies domiciled in England and Wales after 31 March 1976 (s.1(1)); earlier legislation (which was narrower in its scope) applies to deaths before that date.

There is no equivalent statute applying to persons who die domiciled in Scotland. However, under Scots law, if a person dies domiciled in Scotland leaving a spouse and issue, the spouse is entitled to a one-third share in the whole of the moveable estate of the deceased and the children are entitled to another one-third share. If there is a spouse and no children the spouse's share is increased to one-half. The deceased is free to dispose only of the remaining portion.

Questions of domicile are becoming increasingly frequent. In *Schaffer v Cilento* (2004) the court had to decide whether the playwright Anthony Shaffer had abandoned his domicile of origin and acquired a domicile of choice in Queensland, Australia and, if so, whether he had then abandoned that domicile of choice and reacquired a domicile in England and Wales. Lewison J concluded that he had acquired a domicile of choice and had not abandoned it at the date of his death.

The following points were relevant. To acquire a domicile of choice it is not necessary to show that the intention to make a new home in the new country is irrevocable. The test is whether the person intends to make their home in the new country until the end of their days unless and until something happens to change their mind (*IRC v Bullock* (1976)). A domicile of choice can be lost in the same way that it is acquired. The person must have ceased to reside in the country and have no intention of returning there. The absence of intention must be unequivocal. A person in two minds does not have the necessary absence of intention. The abandonment of a domicile of choice is not to be lightly inferred.

In *Nathaneal, Cyganik v Agulian* (2006) the Court of Appeal emphasised the "adhesiveness" of the domicile of origin. The domicile of origin continues until it is proved that the person intended to make a home permanently or indefinitely in another country. "*Cogent and convincing*" evidence is required to establish a change of domicile and the burden is on the person alleging the change. See also *Holliday v Musa* (2006) where the Court of Appeal agreed that there was sufficient evidence to show that the deceased had made up his mind, consistent with his permanent home being in England, that England was where he wished to end his days and be buried.

3. TIME LIMITS

Application for provision under the Act must normally be made within six months of the date of the first effective grant of representation (s.4). If a grant is revoked because it was wrongly made, the application must be made within six months of the subsequent valid grant (*Re Freeman* (1984)). However, where a limited grant is made time runs only from the making of a full grant. This was decided in the case of *Re Paul Anthony Johnson (Deceased)* (1987) where a grant limited to pursuing negligence claims was made in 1983. The full grant of probate was made in 1987 and it was held that time ran from the date of the full grant. **20-003**

There can be uncertainty as to whether or not a grant is a full grant. The Inheritance and Trustees' Powers Act 2014 deals with this question for the purposes of various statutes including the Inheritance (Provision for Family and Dependants) Act 1975. It excludes grants which are limited to settled land or other trust property or which do not permit any of the estate to be distributed (for example, limited grants to allow the collection or protection of assets of the estate or representation of the estate in litigation).

The new provisions also require grants made outside the UK to be left out of account (unless it is a grant which is resealed under s.2 of the Colonial Probates Act 1892.

In *Re McBroom* (1992) Eastham J held that it is necessary for a grant of representation to have been taken out to the deceased's estate before an application can be made. However, the earlier case of *Re Searle* (1949) was not cited. In *Re Searle* Roxburghe J said that the time limit was concerned with applications being too late and not too early. The Inheritance and Trustees' Powers Act 2014 amends s.4 to provide that an application can be made before a grant of representation is taken out.

There are obvious practical difficulties involved in making an application before a grant has been taken out. These are dealt with in CPR 57.3A and 3B which states that:

"(3A) Where no grant has been obtained, the claimant may make a claim without naming a defendant and may apply for directions as to the representation of the estate. The written evidence must—

(a) explain the reasons why it has not been possible for a grant to be obtained;

(b) be accompanied by the original or a copy (if either is available) of the will or other testamentary document in respect of which probate or letters of administration are to be granted; and

(c) contain the following information, so far as known to the claimant—

(i) brief details of the property comprised in the estate, with an approximate estimate of its capital value and any income that is received from it;

(ii) brief details of the liabilities of the estate;

(iii) the names and addresses of the persons who are in possession of the documents relating to the estate; and

(iv) the names of the beneficiaries and their respective interests in the estate.

(3B) Where a claim is made in accordance with paragraph (3A), the court may give directions as to the parties to the claim and as to the -representation of the estate either on the claimant's application or on its own initiative."

4. Discretion to Allow Applications Out of Time

Unfettered discretion

20-004 The court has a discretion to allow applications outside the normal six-month time limit. This discretion is unfettered and the Act itself contains no guidance as to how the court should exercise it. However, in *Re Salmon (Deceased)* (1980) Megarry VC suggested six guidelines. These were concisely summarised in *Re Dennis* (1981) as follows:

> "First, the discretion of the court, though judicial, is unfettered. Second, the onus is on the applicant to show special reasons for taking the matter out of the general six month time limit; ... this is not a mere triviality but a substantial requirement. Third, the court has to consider how promptly and in what circumstances the application has been made after the time has expired; one has to look at all the circumstances surrounding the delay. Fourth, the court has to see whether negotiations has started within the six month period. Fifth, one has to consider whether or not the estate has been distributed before the claim has been notified. Sixth, the court has to consider whether refusal of leave to bring proceedings out of time will leave the applicant without recourse against anyone else ...."

(An example of a person against whom an applicant might have recourse would be a negligent solicitor.)

The list was not intended to be exhaustive and *Re Dennis* itself added a further guideline:

> "by analogy with applications for leave to defend in summary judgement proceedings, the applicant must show that he has an arguable case, a case fit to go to trial".

In *McNulty v McNulty* (2002) a widow brought a claim four years after death. The reason for the late application was that an asset of the estate which had been valued at £175,000 for probate purposes was subsequently sold to a building developer for £1,600,000. She had first discovered the increase in value in June 1998 but proceedings were not issued until April 1999. The court said that she could not be criticised for not bringing the claim before June 1998 but that "the matter was treated with inexcusable tardiness between June 1998 and April 1999". However, permission was given for the following reasons:

- she had a strong case on the merits; and
- the estate had not been distributed and as a result there would be no prejudice to the beneficiaries of the will in granting the application.

In *Berger v Berger* (2013) the Court of Appeal refused to allow a widow to apply out of time despite what it regarded as a strong arguable case because of the length of the delay (six and a half years from the date of the grant). In other cases of lengthy delay where applications had been allowed, there had been a change in circumstance to trigger the application—concealment of the true value of estate assets in *McNulty v McNulty* (2002) and a dramatic fall in interest rates in *Stock v Brown* (1994). Here there was no such trigger. The widow had simply come to the conclusion that the provision made for her was inadequate. However, in *Re Bhusate* (2019) Chief Master Marsh specifically rejected the need to find a "trigger event" in order to explain the delay. He said:

> "Where there is an obvious trigger, it is helpful to consider it, but I can see no basis in section 4 for a trigger factor being essential to engage the court's discretion. There is nothing in section 4 that requires such a gloss. As Sir Robert Megarry V.-C described section 4 in Salmon: "... the words ... could hardly be more neutral". There needs to be an explanation for the application for permission and the applicant must show sufficient grounds for granting the application. What those grounds may be is not constrained by the statute although it is evident that the longer the delay, the more compelling the grounds will have to be."

Cowan v Foreman (2019) attracted a great deal of interest because of trenchant comments made by Mostyn J at the first instance hearing. However the Court of Appeal did not agree with his view of the case and granted leave to apply out of time.

Mr Cowan was a very wealthy entrepreneur who had left his business assets (which qualified for business property relief) to a discretionary trust, the beneficiaries of which included his widow. The deceased's letter of wishes asked the trustees (who were solicitors) to regard his widow as the principal beneficiary of the discretionary trust fund. He left the rest of his assets to his widow on flexible life interest trusts under which the trustees had power to apply capital for the widow's benefit. In relation to the flexible life interest trust the deceased's letter of wishes said that income should be supplemented "by capital where required" and specifically asked for capital to be made available for medical purposes.

The trustees queried medical bills sent to them on behalf of Mrs Cowan. This led Mrs Cowan to complain that she felt "at the mercy of the trustees".

The six-month period expired on 16 June 2017 but no application was made until 12 November 2018. On 7 December 2017 Mrs Cowan's lawyers wrote to the trustees explaining her concerns, stating that she was considering a 1975 Act claim but hoped to be able to avoid litigation and asking the trustees to confirm that they would not seek to take advantage of any delay whilst Mrs Cowan obtained advice on her claim and explored resolution with the trustees. On 25 January 2018 the trustees confirmed that they would not take a point on the six-month deadline having passed pending receipt of a letter of claim. Unsuccessful attempts were made to negotiate a settlement, and finally, in November 2018, a claim and an application for leave to apply out of time were issued some 17 months after the expiry of the six-month period.

Mostyn J expressed astonishment when told that it was "common practice" for parties to agree stand-still agreements of this type and suggested that the practice should come to an immediate end as it was not for the parties to give away time that belongs to the court.

In relation to the application itself, he said that Mrs Cowan has to satisfy the court that:

(1) there were good reasons justifying the delay, and
(2) her claim was of sufficient merit to be allowed to proceed to trial.

He refused the application on the basis that (1) there was no good reason for the lengthy delay and (2) Mrs Cowan's case lacked sufficient merit. She had complained that the mere fact that she had no capital meant that reasonable financial provision had not been made for her. Mostyn J said that this argument was equivalent to a claim for forced spousal heirship in every case. He disagreed that she was at the mercy of the trustees referring to the letter of wishes. He said there was nothing to suggest that the trustees would blatantly defy the wishes of the deceased and, if they did, it "would likely amount to a breach of trust which would be actionable at the suit of the claimant". This last statement caused some surprise amongst private client practitioners.

The Court of Appeal made the following points when granting Mrs Cowan leave to apply out of time.

(1) Mostyn J had focussed only on two matters: delay and the strength of the case whereas many of the other matters listed in *Re Salmon* were relevant and should have been considered. For example:
   - negotiations had been ongoing throughout the period of delay;
   - although the estate had been distributed in the sense that assets had been transferred to the trustees, no individual would be required to refund funds if an order was made;
   - it was unlikely that there would be any possibility of obtaining redress against anybody.

(2) In relation to the delay, Mostyn J had taken an unduly disciplinary view of s.4. The time limit is not a triviality, but it should not be approached in the same way that time limits are treated under the CPR in relation to litigation which is being conducted. He had concluded that there must be not only an explanation but a "good reason" for the delay. This was not necessarily true. In *McNulty v McNulty* (2002) part of the delay was described as "inexcusable tardiness". Nevertheless, despite there being no good reason for that delay, having taken all the relevant factors into account the s.4 power had been exercised in the applicant's favour.

(3) The delay was not gross. It was under 18 months and for much of that time negotiations were continuing. In the view of the Court of Appeal, it was not until payments began to be made in April 2017 and the process of receiving income, seeking reimbursement in relation to additional expenditure and producing budgets for future needs and expenditure got underway in the subsequent months, that the reality of Mrs Cowan's situation became clear.

(4) In relation to the strength of the case, the Court of Appeal considered that Mostyn J failed to have proper regard to all the circumstances of the case, including the size of the estate, the length of the relationship, the fact that Mrs Cowan received only chattels of nominal value outright, she had no autonomy, no security and no direct interest in her home of 20 years which was owned through the discretionary trust.

(5) Mostyn J's view of the letter of wishes was misguided. He appeared to assume that the letter of wishes would be complied with in every respect, whatever the circumstances, whereas it is by its very nature unenforceable.

He also appeared to have relied incorrectly upon his conclusion that failure to comply with the letter of wishes would necessarily amount to an actionable breach of trust.

(6) In relation to standstill agreements the Court of Appeal agreed with Mostyn J that the final decision always rests with the court. However, it said that where there is a properly evidenced agreement to which no objection has been taken by the executors and beneficiaries, it was unlikely that in the ordinary way, a judge would dismiss an application for an extension of time.

King LJ stressed that if parties choose the "stand-still" route, there should be clear written agreement setting out the terms/duration of such an agreement and each of the potential parties should be included in the agreement. In the event that proceedings have, in due course to be issued, the court should be presented with a consent application for permission to be granted notwithstanding that six months has elapsed.

Shortly after this decision the Court of Appeal added further guidance in *Begum v Ahmed* (2019). It made the sensible point that it is necessary to consider any clear prejudice to the party seeking the extension if leave is withheld, and the prejudice to the other party if leave is granted. Prejudicial delay, such as delay during which the estate has been distributed, should normally be accorded more weight than delay which has caused no prejudice.

Floyd LJ (giving the judgment of the court) made the point that while an application will not be granted where the applicant does not have a real prospect of success on the merits of the claim, how far the merits may be taken into account depends on how clearly the facts emerge at the stage at which the discretion is being exercised. The court should not conduct a mini-trial at the interim stage. However, where the court is able to form a clear view of the merits as in *McNulty v McNulty* (2002) it is relevant and just to take that view into account.

Practical considerations for personal representatives

The reason for having such a short time limit is to enable personal representatives to distribute assets without fear of personal liability if a successful -application is later made. The Act provides therefore that a personal representative can distribute after the expiry of six months from the date of grant without -personal liability even if the court does later extend the time limit (s.20). Where an out-of-time application is allowed there is power to recover any part of the estate already distributed to the beneficiaries by the personal representatives. **20-005**

Obviously, a cautious personal representative would wait six months before distributing assets; a very cautious personal representative will wait even longer since a claimant, having issued a claim, has four months in which to serve it (CPR r.7.5). Yet in most cases such caution will be unnecessary and may even cause hardship if a beneficiary is in urgent need of finance. A personal representative must therefore carefully consider the circumstances before deciding how long to wait before distributing.

The following matters are relevant:

(a) Since an order for financial provision is made against the *net* estate of the deceased (see para.20-044) there can be no objection to paying funeral, testamentary and administration expenses, debts and liabilities before the expiry of the six-month period.

(b) It will normally be safe to pay a legacy to a beneficiary who is intending to make an application to obtain more (unless there is a risk of applications from other people).

(c) Since it is unlikely that the court would order provision to be financed out of a very small legacy when the estate is large such a legacy can safely be paid.

(d) Similarly it will often be safe to distribute assets to a beneficiary who has a strong moral claim, particularly if there is urgent need.

5. THE CATEGORIES OF APPLICANT

Section 1(1)

20-006 The following persons may apply to the court for an order in their favour on the ground that the deceased's will or the intestacy rules have not made reasonable provision for them.

Section 1(1)(a): The spouse or civil partner of the deceased

20-007 The applicant must show that there was a subsisting marriage or civil partnership at the time of the deceased's death. This category includes the wife of a polygamous marriage: *Re Sehota, Surjit Kaur v Gian Kaur* (1978). It also includes a party to a voidable marriage which has not been annulled prior to death.

A judicially separated spouse or a civil partner where a separation order is in place comes into this category but may be barred from making an application by a court order under ss.15, 15A, 15B or 15ZA of the Act. See further, para.20-008.

Unusually a person will be regarded as a surviving spouse or civil partner even though the marriage or civil partnership was *void*, provided the applicant entered into the marriage or civil partnership in good faith, unless in the lifetime of the deceased:

(i) the marriage or civil partnership has been dissolved or annulled; or
(ii) the applicant entered into a later marriage or civil partnership.

However, a ceremony which does not purport to be of the kind contemplated by the Marriage Acts, produces a non-marriage rather than a void marriage and the parties will not be eligible to make an application. See *AM v AM* (2001) and *Gandhi v Patel* (2002).

Section 1(1)(b): A former spouse or civil partner

20-008 A former spouse or civil partner is a person whose marriage or civil partnership with the deceased was dissolved or annulled during the deceased's lifetime by a decree made under the law of any part of the British Islands (the UK, Channel Islands and Isle of Man) or in any country or territory outside the British Islands by a divorce or annulment "which is entitled to be recognised as valid by the law of England and Wales" (s.25).

A former civil partner is a person whose civil partnership with the deceased was during the lifetime of the deceased either dissolved or annulled by an order made under the law of any part of the British Islands, or in any country or territory outside the British Islands by a dissolution or annulment which is entitled to be recognised as valid by the law of England and Wales.

The Act provides, however, in the interests of finality that a former spouse or civil partner may be barred from applying for financial provision by a court order on the granting of a decree of divorce, nullity, or judicial separation (s.15), or dissolution, nullity or separation order (s.15ZA). Sections 15A and 15B give the court the same power when making orders for financial provision following overseas divorce, dissolution of a civil partnership, nullity or separation orders. Such an order only prevents an application as a former spouse. It does not prevent an application made as a member of a different category; for example if the parties remarried or lived together in one household as husband and wife: see *Chekov v Fryer* (2015).

The Court of Appeal observed in *Re Fullard* (1981) that in view of the wide powers of the court to make financial arrangements on divorce, the number of cases in which it would be appropriate for a former spouse to apply under the family provision legislation would be small; an example of such a case might be where the deceased's estate receives the proceeds of a large insurance policy on the deceased's death or where the applicant had been provided for in the divorce proceedings by means of periodical payments rather than by a lump sum.

In *Barrass v Harding* (2001) and in *Cameron v Treasury Solicitor* (1996) the Court of Appeal emphasised that, where the parties regard themselves as having settled accounts with the divorce settlement, it will be inappropriate to make a family provision award unless there is some special circumstance. An example of special circumstance would be an assumption of responsibility by one party for the other after the divorce. The following have been held to be insufficient:

- the applicant's "parlous financial circumstances" and poor health in a case where the estate was bona vacantia (*Re Cameron*);
- the substantial value of the deceased's estate (*Barrass v Harding*); and
- the fact that the divorce was pre-1970 at a time when the court had much less extensive powers to redistribute property than it now has (*Barrass v Harding*).

Section 1A: A person who has lived in one household with deceased as spouse or civil partner

To be eligible the applicant must for the period of two years ending with the deceased's death have been living with the deceased: **20-009**

(a) in the same household as the deceased, and
(b) as if that person and the deceased were a married couple or civil partners.

The deceased must have died on or after 1 January 1996.

Notice that as a result of the wording of the subsection an application is bound to fail if there is any interruption in the two-year period of cohabitation prior to death—for example, where parties split up but then resume their relationship but fail to clock up a full two-year period before the death.

However, separations brought about by external circumstances, e.g. employment abroad, illness necessitating a stay in hospital or hospice care are irrelevant. In *Re Watson (Deceased)* (1999) exactly this situation arose. The deceased was hospitalised for three weeks prior to death. All parties accepted that the deceased had not ceased to be part of the household. In *Witkowska v Kaminski* (2006) the claimant had been away in Poland for the three months before the deceased's death in England, but this was not regarded as a bar to a claim under this section. In *Gully v Dix* (2004) the Court of Appeal held that the trial judge was correct in finding that a three-month absence caused by the deceased's "drinking binge", and consequent violent behaviour towards his partner, did not prevent the claimant being a person who had lived with the deceased as his wife for a period of two years ending with his death. It is necessary to look at the settled state of affairs that existed between the parties before the date of death and not the de facto separation between the couple.

Kaur v Singh Dhaliwal (2014) is a fairly extreme application of the principle. A couple had lived together in the deceased's flat for three months before, due to family difficulties, the deceased had to return to Pakistan. The female partner moved out. The deceased was away for a month and, after his return, there was a gap of eight or nine months during which the couple lived apart before they stayed together at the house of a friend of the claimant's for about two weeks and then moved into one of the deceased's flats for 21 months. They then purchased a flat together, in which they lived for a further two months up to the deceased's death. It was common ground that they had cohabited for one year and 49 weeks immediately prior to the deceased's death but there was a shortfall of about three weeks unless the earlier period was included.

The first instance judge found that the couple had lived together as husband and wife in one household during the initial three-month period; after that they were together whenever they could be, consistent with problems of accommodation and the needs of the deceased's family. They then lived together in one household for an unbroken period. Applying the principles of *Gully v Dix*, the separation, though lengthy, was not relevant as their relationship had subsisted throughout.

On appeal to the High Court Barling J held that the judge was entitled to reach this conclusion. Applying the principles from *Gully v Dix* it was clear that the parties' settled relationship continued during the disputed period. The interruption was for family reasons unconnected with the state of their relationship which subsisted in full measure throughout the period.

The case demonstrates that, although it is essential that to demonstrate that the household continued for the requisite period, it is not necessary to show that the parties lived together under the same roof for the whole of that period. The trial judge gave the useful analogy of one party being posted overseas for reasons connected with work.

It is often difficult to determine whether a couple are living together as husband and wife. In *Re Watson (Deceased)* (1999) the applicant and the deceased had known each other since 1964. She moved into the deceased's house in 1985. They had no sexual relationship after she had moved in although they had had one before. Mr Watson worked and provided most of the funds for the household. The applicant paid her share of the cost of utilities and would be responsible for shopping, cooking and gardening. Neuberger J, as he then was, held they had lived together as husband and wife. It is necessary to ask whether, in the opinion of a reasonable person with normal perceptions, it could be said that the two people in question were living together as husband and wife. However, "one should not ignore the multifarious nature of marital relationships". The fact that the couple had an agreement as to who paid for what and who did which jobs did not prevent the arrangement being a marital one. It was also irrelevant that the claimant had another property available to her.

Swetenham v Walkley (2014) might be regarded as an unusual decision. The claimant and deceased had met in the 1980s and started going out together. The deceased would often stay overnight at the claimant's house. He had his own bedroom and kept his clothes there, but slept more often at his own house. They attended social events as a couple, and the deceased integrated with the claimant's neighbours, grown-up children and their families. Once the deceased retired, they spent most of their days together, although each maintained their separate interests.

The claimant did the deceased's washing and ironing and he often paid for meals when they went out. They looked after each other when ill. The deceased's family argued that the pair had merely been close and mutually supportive friends. They relied on the fact that the deceased had not shared fundamental information with her, particularly the fact that he had retired, and an additional property he had bought.

The court found that the claimant was eligible under s.1(1A). The evidence, including the way in which the pair acted towards each other and the public face they displayed, indicated that the claimant's house had been a joint household. The fact that the deceased owned properties and still slept at one of them occasionally did not undermine that finding, nor did the fact that there was no communal pot of money. Most married couples would have discussed matters such as retirement and property purchases, but the fact that the deceased had not shared such information with the claimant did not negate their relationship. He was a private, somewhat eccentric man, but it was clear that he had been a true, supportive partner in a loving and committed relationship in which each had provided practical and emotional support throughout.

The deceased had not been living a life elsewhere, he had been living a life with the claimant. The existence of a sexual relationship was unimportant and not determinative. What counted was the tie between them: the cooking and laundry arrangements; the reminding each other of appointments and ensuring that such appointments were kept; the support provided to each other at times of illness; time spent together watching television or going out for food. Those were things which happened between friends. But one person doing all of those things all the time to the exclusion of all others for a period of approximately 30 years indicated something more deep-rooted and fundamental than mere companionship. The evidence pointed to the couple having lived as man and wife. There was no single determinative factor in that finding; it was a combination of all factors and behaviours including the duration of the relationship and, particularly, its exclusivity.

The element of public recognition in the relationship is important. A marriage and a civil partnership are publicly acknowledged relationships. It is not possible for two persons to live together as civil partners unless their relationship as a couple is an acknowledged one: see *Baynes v Hedger* (2008) and *Lindop v Agus* (2009).

Section 1(1)(c): A child of the deceased

This category includes a child of a non-marital relationship, a legitimated or adopted child and a child *en ventre sa mere*. A child who has been adopted is no longer eligible to make a claim as a child of the natural parent (*Re Collins (Deceased)* (1991)). **20-010**

There is no distinction between sons and daughters and neither age nor marriage are automatic disqualifications. However, in the case of an adult child, in necessitous circumstances it is difficult for a judge to form a view on what is reasonable. See para.20-029.

Section 1(1)(d): A person treated by the deceased as a child of the family

The definition contained in s.1(1)(d) was originally a person (not being a child of the deceased) who "in relation to any marriage or civil partnership to which the **20-011** deceased was at any time a party". The Inheritance and Trustees' Powers Act 2014 extended this category for deaths on or after 1 October 2014 by adding after "in relation to any marriage or civil partnership to which the deceased was at any time a party" the words "or otherwise in relation to any family in which the deceased at any time stood in the role of a parent".

There may be cases where it is difficult to decide whether or not the deceased was in a parental role. The 2014 Act also inserted a new s.1(2A) which provides that the reference to a "family" includes a family of which the deceased was the only member (apart from the applicant). Thus, a "single parent family" is included within the scope of s.1(1)(d) as amended.

The concept of "a child of the family" is imported from family law (Matrimonial Causes Act 1973 s.52(1)). In *Re Callaghan* (1984) and in *Re Leach (Deceased)* (1985) it was held that applicants were children of the family even though they were adult when the deceased married their parent. In *Archibald's Estate v Stewart* (2023) Master Francis held that a daughter-in-law had failed to establish that she had been treated as a child of the family. There was nothing to take relationship outside the usual relationship between parents and daughter-in-law. While the relationship was clearly one of mutual support and reciprocated kindness and hospitality, nothing suggested that she had been "taken under the wing" of the deceased and treated as a daughter in her own right, or that she herself assumed any responsibility to them as a child to one's parents.

Section 1(1)(e): A person maintained by the deceased

Introduction

20-012 Any person (not being a person included in the foregoing paragraphs) who immediately before the death of the deceased was being maintained wholly or partly by the deceased. There are a number of difficulties with this category, discussed below.

The meaning of "maintained"

The definition is contained in s.1(3) which provides that:

> "a person is to be treated as being maintained by the deceased (either wholly or partly, as the case may be) only if the deceased was making a substantial contribution in money or money's worth towards the reasonable needs of that person, other than a contribution made for full valuable consideration pursuant to an arrangement of a commercial nature".

A person is to be regarded as maintained by the deceased *only* if they can bring themselves within s.1(3) (*Re Beaumont* (1980); *Jelley v Iliffe* (1981)).

It is obviously difficult to state definitely what amounts to a "substantial contribution" but in *Jelley v Iliffe* the Court of Appeal regarded the provision of rent-free accommodation as substantial. In *Re Watson* (1999) the cohabitee applicant had also applied as a person maintained by the deceased on the basis that the deceased had provided her with rent free accommodation. She was not successful in this category. The court found that at the time she lived with the deceased, she had no housing "need" because she had a property of her own available to her. It was irrelevant that by the time of the application the property had become unsuitable for her ongoing needs because she was unable to manage stairs. The question of maintenance has to be determined by reference to the situation prevailing during the life of the deceased.

The original version of s.1(3) excluded anyone who had provided valuable consideration for the maintenance received. This meant that the court sometimes has to balance imponderables like companionship, care, support and other -services provided by an applicant against contributions of cash or accommodation provided by the deceased. The court accepted that such services are *capable* of amounting to full valuable consideration (*Re Wilkinson* (1978); *Re Beaumont*; *Jelley v Iliffe*). However, it was a question of fact in each case.

The Inheritance and Trustees' Powers Act 2014 amended the section for deaths on or after 1 October 2014 to introduce the narrower exception for consideration pursuant to an arrangement of a commercial nature. This means that contributions made between people in a domestic context of interdependency will not be weighed against one another for these purposes. The case law requirement that an assumption of responsibility must be present in order for an applicant to qualify to apply for family provision as a dependant is removed. See para.20-028.

The meaning of "immediately before the death"

Section 1(1)(e) expressly states that the applicant must have been maintained "immediately before the death" of the deceased. Problems have arisen in connection with this phrase. For example, in *Re Beaumont* the deceased had habitually maintained the applicant but had been unable to do so in the few weeks immediately before her death, when she was ill in hospital. Megarry VC accepted that the court must look at "the settled basis or ... general arrangement between the parties" not at "the actual, perhaps fluctuating, variation of it which exists immediately before ... death".

The transfer of a house is a one-off capital provision and does not amount to a continuing contribution even if the applicant is living in the house at the date of the deceased's death. Similarly, if capital is transferred to a trust for the benefit of the applicant, the ongoing contribution is made by the trust and not by the settlor so there is no on-going maintenance by the settlor: see *Baynes v Hedger* (2008).

6. Reasonable Provision

Two standards

Introduction

Section 1(2) of the Act sets out two standards for judging whether or not provision is reasonable, one to be applied in the case of a surviving spouse or civil partner (not including a judicially separated spouse or a civil partner where a separation order was in force) and one to be applied in other cases. **20-013**

The standard for surviving spouses and civil partners

This is such financial provision as it would be reasonable in all the circumstances for a spouse or civil partner to receive "whether or not that provision is required for his or her maintenance" (s.1(2)(a)). This standard was introduced so that the claim of a surviving spouse to matrimonial assets should be equal to that of a divorced spouse and the court's powers to order financial provision as extensive as in a divorce application. The fact that the provision is not limited to maintenance is significant. It means that the claimant's financial needs are not regarded as **20-014** determinative in arriving at the amount of an award. An elderly claimant in a case where the estate is large is entitled to a fair share even if the almost inevitable result is that there will be a remaining balance at death which will be inherited by those entitled to the estate: see *Berger v Berger* (2013).

The court has discretion to apply this standard where a decree of judicial separation, nullity or divorce has been made within 12 months of death and no order for financial provision has been made (or refused) in the matrimonial proceedings (s.14). The reason is that the applicant would otherwise have no opportunity to obtain a fair share of the matrimonial assets.

The standard for non-spouses and non-civil partners

20-015 This is "such financial provision as it would be reasonable in all the circumstances of the case for the applicant to receive for his *maintenance*" (s.1(2)(b)). It is -difficult to give a precise meaning to the word "maintenance" in this context. It does not mean just enough to enable a person to get by (i.e. mere subsistence) but on the other hand it does not extend to everything which may be regarded as reasonably desirable for their general benefit or welfare. Buckley LJ suggested in *Re Coventry* (1980) that it could be regarded as

> "such financial provision as would be reasonable in all the circumstances of the case to enable the applicant to maintain himself in a manner suitable to these circumstances".

The restriction of provision to that required for maintenance is often fatal to applications by non-spouses.

In *Ilott v The Blue Cross* (2017) the Supreme Court considered an application under the 1975 Act for the first time. Lord Hughes JSC described limitation to maintenance as a deliberate and important legislative choice. He said (at [14]) that, while the concept of maintenance is broad, the distinction between the two standards shows that,

> "it cannot extend to any or every thing which it would be desirable for the claimant to have. It must import provision to meet the everyday expenses of living. *In Re Jennings, decd* [1994] Ch 286 was an example of a case where no need for maintenance existed. The claimant was a married adult son living with his family in comfortable circumstances, on a good income from two businesses. The proposition that it would be reasonable provision for his maintenance to pay off his mortgage was, correctly, firmly rejected."

Lord Hughes went on to say that the level at which maintenance may be provided for is flexible and must be assessed on the facts of each case but is clearly not limited to subsistence level. Nor, although maintenance is by definition the provision of income rather than capital, need it necessarily be provided for by way of periodical payments, for example under a trust. It will very often be more appropriate, as well as cheaper and more convenient for other beneficiaries and for executors, if income is provided by way of a lump sum from which both income and capital can be drawn over the years.

Browne-Wilkinson J, as he then was, had suggested in *Re Dennis* (1981) that maintenance might extend to a lump sum to buy a house in which the applicant could be housed, thereby removing one expense from the applicant. Lord Hughes agreed that the provision of housing could be maintenance in some cases; but he suggested that this might be more appropriately dealt with via a life interest in a trust fund with a possible power to advance capital in case of need and referred with approval to such an arrangement by Munby J in *Re Myers* (2005).

The problem with a life interest is that it imposes a continuing relationship on the family and the applicant who are normally at daggers drawn following the litigation. Most people would find a clean break more satisfactory.

Interestingly in *Thompson v Raggett* (2018), the first case reported on a housing need, the judge made an outright award of the deceased's house to his cohabitee. However, there were unusual features:

- The estate was large and the chosen beneficiaries had had no expectation of inheriting. Providing sufficient funds to enable the applicant to secure a property still left a significant inheritance for the beneficiaries.
- The applicant was disabled and the property would have to be adapted to her needs. It was appropriate that she should be "in the driving seat" when it came to making decisions.

The decision in *Banfield v Campbell* (2018) is probably more typical. Master Teverson refused to make a capital award for housing to the disabled cohabitee, aged 66 at the time of the application. The estate was about £725,000, the major portion being the house which had been inherited from the deceased's husband. The contest was between the deceased's cohabitee and her son who was the residuary beneficiary of the will. The will left £5,000 to the cohabitee who was older than the deceased who had been expected to survive him.

It was accepted that reasonable financial provision had not been made for the applicant who was entitled to something. The question was, what? Master Teverson did not consider that the estate should be required to pay out as a lump sum an amount in the region of £350,000 to £450,000 to purchase suitable accommodation to be owned outright by the applicant. This was a clear case in which that would go beyond maintenance provision and be excessive capital provision. There was no reason why the estate should provide the applicant with a property to pass on to his relations.

Taking all the relevant factors into account, including, in particular, the applicant's resources and housing needs, the length of his relationship with the deceased and the size and nature of the net estate, he ordered:

(1) the property to be sold under the direction of the court,
(2) the applicant to be granted a life interest in one-half of the net proceeds of sale which were to be used in or towards providing alternative accommodation for him.

It would be open to the applicant to contribute capital of his own towards the purchase in which case it would need to be agreed and declared in what proportions the property was owned.

An objective standard

The court is to decide whether the provision made for an applicant *is* reasonable. **20-016**
This is an entirely objective question for the court to decide. It is not correct to ask whether or not the deceased acted reasonably. That is a different question.

A testator may act reasonably but still make a provision which is not -reasonable. See *Re Hancock* (1998) where the deceased had acted entirely reasonably in leaving his business land to those of his children who were active in the business, but after his death part of the land acquired a development value six times its probate assessment. That being the case, there was a failure to make reasonable provision for another daughter who was in straitened circumstances.

Conversely, the deceased may have acted unreasonably, indeed spitefully, towards a claimant, but the disposition made may be reasonable. See *Re Jennings* (1994), where the deceased had unreasonably failed, throughout the minority of his son, to discharge his maintenance obligations towards him. But by the time of his death many years later the son had made his own successful way in the world and stood in no need of maintenance; his claim accordingly failed, correctly, in the Court of Appeal.

Lord Hughes JSC said in *Ilott v The Blue Cross* (2017) that all cases which are limited to maintenance, and many others also, will turn largely upon the asserted needs of the claimant. It was important to put the matter of needs in its correct place. For current spouses and civil partners, need is not the measure of reasonable provision, but if it exists will clearly be very relevant. For all other claimants, need (for maintenance rather than for anything else, and judged not by subsistence levels but by the standard appropriate to the circumstances) is a necessary but not a sufficient condition for an order.

Before the Supreme Court decision in *Ilott v The Blue Cross* (2017) it had become conventional to treat the consideration of a claim under the 1975 Act as a two-stage process:

(1) has there been a failure to make reasonable financial provision and, if so,
(2) what order ought to be made?

In *Re Coventry* (1980) Goff LJ referred to these as distinct questions, and described the first as one of value judgment and the second as one of discretion.

However, in *Ilott v The Blue Cross* (2017) Lord Hughes said that in most cases there is a very large degree of overlap between the two stages. Although s.2 does not in terms enjoin the court, if it has determined that the will or intestacy does not make reasonable financial provision for the claimant, to tailor its order to what is in all the circumstances reasonable, this is clearly the objective. Section 3(1) of the Act, in introducing the factors to be considered by the court, makes them applicable equally to both stages. Thus the two questions will usually become:

(1) did the will/intestacy make reasonable financial provision for the claimant, and
(2) if not, what reasonable financial provision ought now to be made for him?

In many cases, the same considerations will be relevant to both questions. According to Lord Hughes there is nothing wrong with the judge simply setting out the facts as he finds them and then addressing both questions arising under the Act without repeating them. See further para.20-017.

Lord Hughes also made the point that both stages of the process are highly individual in every case. The order made by the judge ought to be upset only if he has erred in principle or in law. An appellate court must be very slow to interfere and should never do so simply on the grounds that its judge(s) would have been inclined, if sitting at first instance, to have reached a different conclusion. He described *Ilott v The Blue Cross* itself as an example of "much to be regretted prolongation, and presumably expensive prolongation, of the forensic process".

When are the facts to be assessed? Section 3(5) provides that they are assessed at the date of the hearing. Under s.3(5) the court will consider changes in the position of beneficiaries and applicants arising after the death of the deceased. In both *Re Hancock* (1999) and *McNulty v McNulty* (2000) the court took into account increases in the value of assets occurring after the death of the deceased. On an appeal, if the question is whether the trial judge made an error of principle the facts and evidence must be taken as they stood before him. If an appellate court, unusually, has to remake the decision on the merits, any request to adduce further evidence will have to be judged by the principles set out in *Ladd v Marshall* (1954).

According to *Ladd v Marshall* to justify the reception of fresh evidence, three conditions must be fulfilled:

(a) it must be shown that the evidence could not with reasonable diligence have been obtained for use at the trial;
(b) the evidence must be such that, if given, it would probably have an important influence on the result of the case, though it need not be decisive;
(c) the evidence must be such as presumably to be believed, or, in other words, it must be apparently credible, though it need not be incontrovertible.

7. THE COURT MUST DECIDE WHETHER AND IN WHAT MANNER TO MAKE AN ORDER (S.3)

This is a discretionary matter

The court is directed to consider various matters set out in s.3 when determining (1) whether the disposition of the deceased's estate makes reasonable provision for the applicant, and (2) if it considers that it does not whether and in what manner it should exercise its powers. **20-017**

The matters set out is s.3(1) are common to all categories of applicant and those in s.3(2)–(4) are specific to particular categories.

The Act sets this out as a two-stage process with the guidelines being considered at both stages. However, in *Ilott v Blue Cross* (2017) Lord Hughes suggested that this is not always required. He said at [24]:

> "There may be some cases in which it will be convenient to separate these questions, particularly if there is an issue whether there was any occasion for the deceased to make any provision for the claimant. But in many cases, exactly the same conclusions will both answer the question whether reasonable financial provision has been made for the claimant and identify what that financial provision should be. In particular, questions arising from the relationship between the deceased and the claimant, questions relating to the needs of the claimant, and issues concerning the competing claims of others, are all equally applicable to both matters. The Act plainly requires a broad brush approach from the judge to very variable personal and family circumstances. There can be nothing wrong, in such cases, with the judge simply setting out the facts as he finds them and then addressing both questions arising under the Act without repeating them."

The common guidelines (s.3(1))

Financial resources and needs

Under s.3(1) the court will in every application have regard to the following seven matters, set out as (a) to (g) in the sub-section: **20-018**

(a) *the financial resources and needs of the applicant;*
(b) *the financial resources and needs of any other applicant;*
(c) *the financial resources and needs of any beneficiary.*

The first three factors require the court to balance the resources and needs of all the persons with a claim on the estate.

In *Ilott v The Blue Cross* (2016) the Court of Appeal had said (at [61]):

"The claim of the appellant has to be balanced against that of the Charities but since they do not rely on any competing need they are not prejudiced by what may be a higher award than the court would otherwise need to make."

On appeal, the Supreme Court said (at [46]) that this statement should be treated with caution:

- Charities may not have conventional needs but they depend heavily on testamentary bequests for their work, which is by definition of public benefit.
- More fundamentally, the charities were the chosen beneficiaries of the deceased. They did not have to justify a claim on the basis of need under the 1975 Act, as the claimant necessarily had to do.
- It was wrong to say that the charities were not prejudiced by an increased award to the claimant; their benefit was reduced by any such award. An award under the Act is at the expense of those whom the testator intended to benefit.

Where a claimant is in receipt of means-tested benefits, it is difficult for the court to decide what level of award is appropriate. The Supreme Court in *Ilott v The Blue Cross* said that receipt of state support greater than the testator could sensibly provide may be an understandable reason why it was reasonable for the deceased not to make financial provision for the claimant: see for example *Re E, decd* (1966). More generally, benefits are part of the resources of the claimant, and it is relevant to consider whether they will continue to be received.

The court should take into account any needs which are reasonably likely to arise. Those needs do not need to be more likely than not, but the degree of probability should be taken into account. In *Challinor v Challinor* (2009) where the applicant was an adult suffering from Down's syndrome, her future increased needs for personal care and physiotherapy were taken into account. However, the court also said that "possibilities that are remote or speculative should not be found to be specific needs". In *Barron v Woodhead* (2009) provision of living accommodation for an applicant who would otherwise be homeless was considered particularly relevant. Similarly, in *Moore v Holdsworth* (2010) an award was increased to enable a chronically ill surviving spouse to return to the home she had shared with the deceased during their long marriage.

Poor financial circumstances do not guarantee an order. A much-cited dictum of Oliver J in *Re Coventry* (1980) is:

"It cannot be enough to say 'here is a son of the deceased; he is in necessitous circumstances; there is property of the deceased which could be made available to assist him but which is not available if the deceased's dispositions stand; therefore those dispositions do not make reasonable provision for the applicant'."

The problem of poor financial circumstances arises particularly frequently in cases involving adult children and was at the heart of the decision in *Ilott v The Blue Cross* (2017). This is discussed at para.20-029 and following.

In a number of cases judges have been asked to treat the fact that a successful claimant has incurred an obligation to pay a success fee under a conditional fee agreement (CFA) as an increased need. Such fees cannot be recovered by way of a costs order by virtue of s.58A(6) of the Courts and Legal Services Act 1990. In *SH v NH* (2020) the claimant was an estranged adult child with severe and debilitating mental illness. The estate (approximately £554,000) went to the deceased's widow. She was awarded £16,750 as a contribution towards her success fee. Cohen J considered two earlier conflicting decisions: *Clarke v Allen* (2019) which refused to take the liability into account and *Bullock v Denton* (unreported) which accepted an argument that a claimant's liabilities under a CFA should be considered as part of her financial needs. Cohen J followed *Bullock*, for what he said were "case specific reasons". He made an award which represented a contribution to the cost of the fee.

The decision was appealed but the Court of Appeal in *Hirachand v Hirachand* (2021) did not interfere with the award. Lady Justice King considered that a success fee is capable of being a debt, the satisfaction of which is in whole or part a "financial need" for which the court may in its discretion make provision in its needs based calculation.

It is clear that litigation costs other than those incurred under a CFA cannot be taken into account as financial needs when assessing an award. The correct approach is first to decide the substantive issue of the amount of the award (ignoring any contingent liability for costs) and then, subsequently and separately, to consider what order in relation to costs ought to be applied. This was the approach endorsed by Briggs J (as he then was) in *Lilleyman v Lilleyman* (2012). In his judgment, he made the point that in assessing the amount to award the deceased's widow he could not "make any assumptions as to the incidence or amount of any contingent costs liabilities arising from these proceedings, either for the estate or for Mrs Lilleyman, and would therefore have to leave them entirely out of account, however unrealistic in the real world that might prove to be". It proved unfortunate for Mrs Lilleyman as the award failed to beat a Pt 36 offer made by the defendants. The result would normally have been to make her responsible for the defendants' costs from the date of the offer, substantially reducing the benefit of her award. Briggs J slightly reduced the adverse impact on her by limiting her contribution to 80 per cent because of the aggressive way in which the defendants had conducted the litigation. The approach was confirmed in *Jassal v Shah* (2024).

Obligations and Responsibilities

Section 3(1)(d) requires the court to consider "*any obligations and responsibilities of the deceased towards the applicant or any beneficiary*". **20-019**

The Court of Appeal made it clear in *Re Jennings* (1994) that the obligations and responsibilities must still be operating on the deceased at the date of death. The deceased had abandoned his wife and son (the claimant) when the son was two. He had had no further contact with him and made no provision for him. When the father died, he left nothing to the son, the bulk of the estate going to charity. At first instance the judge construed s.3(1)(d) so as to include legal obligations and responsibilities which the deceased had, but had failed to discharge during the child's minority even though they were long spent and would have been incapable of founding a claim against him immediately before his death. The Court of Appeal said that was a wrong approach. The Act does not "revive defunct obligations and responsibilities". It was significant that the claimant had made a success of his life and was in a secure financial position. In *Myers v Myers* (2004) and *Gold v Curtis* (2005) the court accepted the idea of continuing obligations and responsibilities where applicants were in need.

Size and nature of estate

20-020 *Section 3(1)(e)* requires the court to consider the size and nature of the estate.

If an estate is large it is frequently relatively easy for the court to make adequate provision for applicants; where the estate is very small, however, it is often impossible to provide adequately for all beneficiaries and applicants. Costs do not normally come out of the estate. The losing party will in general be ordered to bear the costs. Solicitors should always bear in mind the question of costs when advising clients who wish to make a claim, especially one against a small estate. The impact of Part 36 offers must also be considered. In *Lilleyman v Lilleyman* (2012), as explained at para.20-018 above, the deceased's second wife obtained an award but failed to beat the Pt 36 offer made by the deceased's adult sons from his first marriage. The result was that she had to bear the costs of the sons from the date it was made and her benefit from the award was much reduced.

In *Hirachand v Hirachand* (2021) Lady Justice King referred at [64] to "the imperative of the full engagement in the Part 36 process and the importance of the parties making realistic offers in order to settle these difficult and distressing cases."

The source of the deceased's assets is often an important consideration. For example, the court is likely to be sympathetic to an application by a child when the deceased parent inherited a large part of their estate from the other parent (as in *Espinosa v Bourke* (1999) and *Banfield v Campbell* (2018)).

Disabilities

20-021 Section 3(1)(f) requires the court to consider "*any physical or mental disability of any applicant or any beneficiary*".

The availability of state aid, hospital accommodation and social security benefits may be considered (*Re Watkins* (1949)). In *Challinor v Challinor* (2009) an application was made on behalf of an adult daughter with Downs's syndrome. She had been cared for by Social Services for nearly 20 years. Her sister produced some rather alarming scenarios which, if they came to pass, would require private funding. Although the judge agreed that the applicant's deteriorating health meant that she had contingent needs which had not been reasonably provided for, "*possibilities that are remote or speculative should not be found to be specific needs*". He ordered that £85,000 in addition to the £15,000 already provided by the deceased be settled on discretionary trusts.

Any other relevant matter

20-022 Section 3(1)(g) requires the court to consider "*any other matter, including the conduct of the applicant or any other person which the court may consider relevant*".

This obviously gives the court a great deal of freedom. In *Re Snoek (Deceased)* (1983) an award to a spouse was set at a much lower amount than it would otherwise have been as a result of a history of assaults and other abuses in the years before the deceased's death.

However, *Barron v Woodhead* (2009) suggests that only quite extreme conduct by a surviving spouse should lead to a reduced award. In *Begum v Ahmed* (2019) EWCA Civ 1794, an application by a surviving spouse for leave to apply out of time, allegations were made that the spouse's conduct towards the deceased was such as to disentitle her to relief. The Court of Appeal allowed the application stating that it would be surprising if any such conduct would defeat her claim altogether.

In *Espinosa v Bourke* (1999) the applicant's conduct in abandoning her father while she went on extended holidays counted against her, as did the applicant's 15-year separation from her father in *Garland v Morris* (2007). In *Ilott v Mitson* (2016) the Court of Appeal had declined to put any weight on the lifelong estrangement between the deceased and her daughter on the basis that estrangement is not really a matter of fault on either side, but simply, in effect, a sad fact of family life. On appeal in *Illott v The Blue Cross* (2017) the Supreme Court considered that the fact of such a lengthy estrangement had to be taken into account although it counselled against making awards under the Act primarily rewards for good behaviour on the part of the claimant or penalties for bad on the part of the deceased.

In *Re Goodchild* (1997) the applicant's mother had died believing that there was an agreement between herself and her husband to leave their combined estates to their son after the death. The agreement was not enforceable but was regarded as relevant to the Inheritance Act application.

A testator should leave a record of reasons for excluding a close family member or dependant with the will. The Court of Appeal said in *Ilott v Mitson* (2011) that this final guideline is very wide and will draw in a range of factors amongst them potentially the views of the deceased. Goff LJ said in *Re Coventry* (1980) that a view expressed by a deceased person that he wishes a particular person to benefit will generally be of little significance, because the question is not subjective but objective, but that an express reason for rejecting the applicant is a different matter and may be very relevant. In *Ilott v Mitson* (2011), *Myers v Myers* (2004) and *Gold v Curtis* (2005) there were statements of the deceased's reasons for making no provision, but the court did not take the statements at face value. It is not advisable to include the reasons in the will itself as a will is a document of public record. In *Re Seagrave (Deceased)* (2007) the court accepted that a claimant's case is likely to be stronger in cases of intestacy than in cases where the deceased has shown an intention as to how the estate is to be divide by making a will. However, the case was decided on a preliminary issue and the existence or non-existence of a will is only one factor to be taken into account.

The guidelines applying to particular categories of applicant (s.3(2)–(4))

The surviving spouse or civil partner

Section 3(2)(a) provides that the court will consider: **20-023**

(a) the age of the applicant and the duration of the marriage;
(b) the contribution made by the applicant to the welfare of the family of the deceased, including any contribution made by looking after the home or caring for the family; and
(c) the provision the applicant might reasonably have expected to receive if on the day on which the deceased died the marriage (instead of being terminated by death) had been terminated by a decree of divorce. In *Re Besterman (Deceased)* (1984) the Court of Appeal held that this did not mean that the same provision should be made as if there were a divorce on the day of the death.

In *Moody v Stevenson* (1992) the Court of Appeal had seemed to suggest that the court should *only* consider the amount a spouse would have been entitled to on divorce. However, the Court of Appeal in *Re Krubert* (1996) stated that this approach was confusing when applied to a small estate. On divorce there were two parties to be considered whereas in a family provision case there was only one and, thus, it might well be reasonable to award the whole estate to a surviving spouse. In *P v G (family provision: relevance of divorce provision)* (2006) the court said:

> "The difference between divorce, where there are two surviving spouses to provide for, and death where there is only one, will not infrequently be reflected in greater provision under the Inheritance Act than would have been made on divorce even where the estate is large."

The Inheritance and Trustees' Powers Act 2014 amends s.3(2) of the Inheritance (Provision for Family and Dependants) Act 1975 to state that for deaths on or after 1 October 2014 the court is not required to regard the provision receivable on divorce as setting either an upper or lower limit on the provision which may be made in a family provision application.

Inevitably changes in divorce law affect the amount available to spouses under the Inheritance Act. The House of Lords decision in *White v White* (2001) resulted in a change of approach to applications by spouses. In *White* the House of Lords said there should be no bias in favour of the money earner and that a judge would always be well advised to "check his tentative views against the yardstick of equality of division". As a general guide, equality should be departed from only if, and to the extent that, there was good reason for doing so.

In *Re Adams* (2001) Behrens J said there was no reason to depart from the *White v White* principle of equality. In this case the deceased had been married to the claimant for 54 years and they had had 12 children. The deceased left her the household goods, his personal effects and a legacy of £10,000. The claimant contended that this was not reasonable and wanted to receive the family home. Three of her daughters opposed this. They accepted that the provision made was not reasonable but argued that the house was too large for her. The court held that the question of her needs was irrelevant. She was entitled to receive the family home.

In *Cunliffe v Fielden* (2005) Wall LJ said that in family provision applications caution was necessary when carrying out the *White* cross check with the provision available on divorce:

> "Divorce involves two living former spouses, to each of whom the provisions of section 25(2) of the Matrimonial Causes Act 1973 apply. In cases under the 1975 Act, a deceased spouse who leaves a widow is entitled to bequeath his estate to whomsoever he pleases: his only statutory obligation is to make -reasonable financial provision for his widow. In such a case, depending on the value of the estate, the concept of equality may bear little relation to such provision."

In *Berger v Berger* (2013) the trial judge had taken the view that a life interest for an elderly widow was reasonable, bearing in mind her age and health. The Court of Appeal disagreed. Since *White* the claimant's financial needs or reasonable requirements were not to be regarded as determinative in arriving at the amount of an award. It was clear that a divorce court would not have limited its ancillary relief order for the appellant to provision for her various financial needs for the rest of her life even if the almost inevitable result of giving her more was that there would remain a balance at her death which would simply be transmitted to the next generation as part of her estate. It was at least arguable that the starting point for an ancillary relief order in this case, given the very long period during which the appellant and the deceased had been together, would have been a 50:50 division of their assets.

Similarly, in *Cowan v Foreman* (2019) considered above in relation to applications for leave to apply out of time, the Court of Appeal differed from Mostyn J who at first instance had dismissed the application, in part, because the widow did not have a strong claim having been provided for through a discretionary and a life interest trust. Asplin LJ said:

> "when determining whether the substantive claim had a real rather than fanciful prospect of success, the Judge failed to have proper regard to all the circumstances of the case, including the size of the estate, the length of the relationship, the fact that Mrs Cowan received only the chattels outright, which it is accepted were of nominal value, she has no autonomy and no security and has no direct interest, even in the Montecito property which has been her home for more than 20 years".

In *Aston v Aston* (2007) the court accepted that in a case where a marriage had effectively come to an end before the deceased's death, the divorce fiction would play a large part in determining whether the provision already made for the widow was reasonable. She had already received more than she would have on divorce and so her application failed. The court took a similar approach in *Goenka v Goenka* (2014). The husband and wife had been involved in divorce negotiations when the husband committed suicide. The assets of the estate were increased by life assurance and the death benefit. But for the deceased's suicide, the wife would have stood to receive nothing more than a share of the pre-death assets. The judge considered that it was not right for the wife to receive more than that.

In *Hendry v Hendry and Others* (2019) an application for leave to apply out of time was dismissed partly because of a lack of explanation for the delay but also because the applicant surviving spouse had entered into a pre--nuptial -agreement severely limiting her entitlement if the marriage broke down. Master Shuman described the existence of the pre-nuptial agreement as significant:

> "Whilst the court retains jurisdiction to make a financial provision order on divorce the fact that the parties entered into a prior agreement which would determine the appropriate financial provision order should the marriage come to an end is something that must be given weight by the court."

The potential entitlement on divorce also worked against the surviving spouse in *Ramus v Holt* (2022) where the surviving wife had £1.6 million and her husband's estate had just over £1 million. She had already got more than she would have been expected to receive and, in addition, had the benefit of a terminable life interest in the residue of her husband's estate. She was not comfortable with the attitude of the trustees (two professionals and her daughter with whom she had a strained relationship) but the court held that reasonable provision had been made for her.

In *Cunliffe v Fielden* (2005) the court had to consider the effect on an award of a brief marriage. It said there is a clear distinction between brief marriages which end with divorce and those which end with death. A divorce involves a conscious decision by one or both of the spouses to bring the marriage to an end. The premature termination of the marriage caused by death is likely to be less important than it would be in the case of a divorce. However, this does not mean that the length of the marriage is irrelevant or that the widow is entitled to one-half of the estate. The brevity of the marriage is an argument against equality of division. It is particularly important in the context of assessing housing needs. There is a clear difference between a widow who has been married for many years and who had made an equal contribution to the family of the deceased and a person who has been married for only a short period and who has made little contribution to the family wealth. While a widow is entitled to have "a reasonable expectation that her life once again as a single woman need not revert to what it was before her marriage" (see *Miller v Miller* (2005)), it may well be inappropriate for her to continue living in the former matrimonial home.

In *Grattan v McNaughton* (2001) a husband left his whole estate to his two children subject to the right of his second wife to occupy the matrimonial home for as long as she remained a widow and did not cohabit. The court found that this was not reasonable provision. It widened the right of occupation by striking out the restrictions on cohabitation and remarriage and permitting her a right of occupation in any substitute property. She also took the residue absolutely subject to legacies of £5,000 to each of the children. In the light of this decision, it is probably necessary to warn a client who wants to include a restriction on cohabitation or remarriage that the restriction may well be removed in an Inheritance Act claim.

The former spouse or civil partner

20-024 Under s.3(2) guidelines (a) and (b) of the surviving spouse guidelines also apply in the case of an application by a former spouse. Guideline (c) does not apply unless the court has exercised its limited discretion to apply the surviving spouse standard (see para.20-014).

Unless there is some special reason, an application by a former spouse or civil partner who has already received financial provision on the termination of the marriage or civil partnership with a view to a "clean break" will rarely be successful (*Re Fullard* (1981)).

A person who has cohabited with the deceased for two years in one household

20-025 Section 3(2A) directs the court to consider:

(a) the age of the applicant and the length of the period during which the applicant lived in the same household as the deceased as a married couple or civil partners; and
(b) the contribution made by the applicant to the welfare of the family of the deceased, including any contribution made by looking after the home or caring for the family.

In *Negus v Bahouse* (2008) and *Webster v Webster* (2008) the court held that, a cohabitee is entitled to have the standard of living enjoyed with the deceased taken into account.

A child of the deceased

20-026 Section 3(3) requires the court to consider the manner in which the applicant was being or in which they might expect to be educated or trained. Evidence is important. In *Ubbi v Ubbi* (2018) the mother of the deceased's two (very young) children claimed that she and the deceased had intended to educate the children privately. Master Shuman did not accept this.

The children were so young that it was doubtful the question had been considered. They had not been put on the list for any private schools in the area. On the income and assets of the parties they would have been unable to fund private education for both boys to university level without a significant reduction in their living standards. He, therefore, refused to make any award under this head.

A person treated by the deceased as a child of the family

In addition to the education guideline set out above, s.3(3) requires the court to have regard: **20-027**

"(a) to whether the deceased maintained the applicant and, if so, to the length of time for which and basis on which the deceased did so, and to the extent of the contribution made by way of maintenance;

(aa) to whether and, if so, to what extent the deceased assumed responsibility for the maintenance of the applicant;

(b) to whether in [maintaining or assuming responsibility for maintaining the applicant] the deceased did so knowing that the applicant was not his own child;

(c) to the liability of any other person to maintain the applicant."

A person maintained by the deceased

Section 3 (4) requires the court to have regard: **20-028**

"(a) to the length of time for which and basis on which the deceased maintained the applicant, and to the extent of the contribution made by way of maintenance;

(b) to whether and, if so, to what extent the deceased assumed responsibility for the maintenance of the applicant".

The wording of s.3(3) and s.3(4) was harmonised by the Inheritance and Trustees' Powers Act 2014 for deaths on or after 1 October 2014. Previously the guideline for children of the family required the court to consider whether the deceased assumed responsibility, whereas the guideline for persons maintained required the court to consider the extent to which responsibility had been assumed.

8. APPLICATIONS BY ADULT CHILDREN

In *Ilott v The Blue Cross* (2017) Baroness Hale made the point that there is a wide range of public opinion about the circumstances in which adult descendants ought or ought not to be able to make a claim on an estate which would otherwise go elsewhere. That range of opinion may very well be shared by members of the judiciary who have to decide these claims. The problem with the present law is that it gives virtually no help in deciding how to evaluate the possible approaches or balance them with other claims on the estate. Nor did the Law Commission report which led to the 1975 Act. The Commission had considered limiting adult claims to children who were actually dependent on the deceased when he died, but their final recommendation was to remove all age limits "leaving the court to distinguish between the deserving and the undeserving". However, the Commission gave no further guidance as to who should be thought deserving and who should not. **20-029**

Approaches to claims by adult children have fluctuated since 1975. At one time the view was that adult able-bodied children had to show an additional "threshold" requirement of a special obligation owed to them by the deceased (see *Goodchild v Goodchild* (1997)). This derived from the dictum of Oliver J in *Re Coventry*

(1980) quoted at para.20-018, where, having said that necessitous circumstances were not enough, he continued:

> "There must, as it seems to me, be established some sort of moral claim by the applicant to be maintained by the deceased or at the expense of his estate beyond the mere fact of a blood relationship, some reason why it can be said that, in the circumstances, it is unreasonable that no or no greater provision was in fact made."

The Court of Appeal has however repeatedly made the point that adult children are in exactly the same position as any other maintenance applicant. There is no additional threshold requirement. See *Re Hancock* (1998); *Re Pearce* (1998); *Espinosa v Bourke* (1999) and *Ilott v Mitson* (2011).

The approach now is that the court will consider all the circumstances in reaching its decision and try to balance all factors. An adult able-bodied child who cannot produce any argument to buttress a claim beyond being badly off is still unlikely to be successful. In *Espinosa v Bourke* the applicant (the deceased's daughter) had behaved badly and had already received some benefit from the deceased during his lifetime. However, this did not outweigh the factors in her favour. These included:

- her poor financial position;
- the substantial size of the estate;
- the fact that the only beneficiary of the will was her son who was at university starting his career without compelling needs;
- the applicant had taken her father into her home and cared for him, at least to a degree, for seven years, thus providing some return for the financial provision he made for her during his lifetime; and
- the deceased had an obligation to the applicant in that he had promised her mother to pass on the mother's share of the paternal grandmother's portfolio of shares to her.

In both *Myers v Myers* (2004) and *Gold v Curtis* (2005) applications by adult children were successful and the court referred to the fact that parents have obligations and responsibilities to their children. However, in *Garland v Morris* (2007) an adult daughter's claim to provision from her father's estate failed despite her poor financial position. Counting against her were the following: the estate was not large, she had inherited from her mother and, to some extent, her misfortunes were of her own making. She had not been in contact with her father for many years before his death

In *Ilott v Blue Cross* (2017) Baroness Hale said she felt every sympathy for the difficult position in which the trial judge had found himself. He was faced with the complete disinheritance of an adult child in favour of charities in which the deceased had shown little or no interest while alive. The adult child was in straitened circumstances, living in rented accommodation which was almost entirely financed by benefits. The family lived within its modest means, but these were largely means-tested benefits. Mother and daughter had been estranged since the daughter left home to live with and then marry her husband, of whom the mother disapproved, three attempts at reconciliation having failed. The mother had left a letter explaining why she had disinherited her daughter, which the district judge did not find wholly "founded on truth". Respectable arguments could be mounted for giving the applicant nothing, or making the order the Court of Appeal made giving her enough to buy a house, thereby saving the state the cost of her housing benefits, or making the order he did make which was giving her a relatively small capital sum to allow her to replace worn-out domestic appliances. The Supreme

Court agreed and held that it was open to him to make the order he made and that it should not have been interfered with.

Despite all the fuss and lengthy litigation history of *Ilott*, the Supreme Court decision has not greatly changed anything. Lord Hughes emphasised the weight that should be given to the deceased's testamentary wishes which may make it a little harder for applicants to succeed. He also made the point that applicants other than surviving spouses and civil partners are entitled only to maintenance so where they have a housing need, it is likely to be appropriate to meet that need through a life interest trust rather than by an outright gift. Charities will be pleased that the Supreme Court emphasised the importance of the fact that an award which reduces their entitlement under a will impacts on their ability to carry out their work.

9. Types of Order

Under s.2(1) the court may make one or more of a number of orders. **20-030**

The types

Periodical payments

Such an order may provide for: **20-031**

- (i) payments of a specified amount (for example, £25 per week);
- (ii) payments equal to the whole or part of the income of the net estate (for example, one-third of the income from the net estate);
- (iii) payments equal to the whole of the income of such part of the net estate as the court may direct to be set aside or appropriated (e.g. the whole income from the deceased's shares in a named company); or
- (iv) payments to be determined in any other way the court thinks fit.

Section 2(3) provides that the order for periodical payments may direct that a specified part of the net estate shall be set aside or appropriated for making periodical payments from the income. However, no more may be set aside or appropriated than is sufficient to produce the income at the date of the order.

Periodical payments are for the term specified in the order. In the case of a former spouse the Act provides expressly that an order shall cease to have effect on the remarriage of the former spouse (s.19(2)). In any other case, however, the court must decide the date of termination when it makes the order. Orders for periodical payments may be varied (see para.20-043).

Periodical payments are unpopular because they are expensive to provide (requiring trust machinery to operate them) and lack finality. It is more common for the court to order a lump sum.

Lump sum payment

A lump sum may be made payable by instalments in which case the number, **20-032**
amounts and dates for payments of the instalments can be varied; apart from that a lump sum order cannot be varied (s.7). A lump sum is obviously appropriate in the case of an application by a surviving spouse, but it can also be ordered in the case of other applicants even though they are only entitled to maintenance. Where an

estate is very small a lump sum order is particularly useful; indeed it may be the only type of provision which can realistically be made.

Transfer of property

20-033 The court may order the transfer of a particular asset to an applicant. This may be advisable where a lump sum order would require an improvident sale of assets. Such an order once made cannot be varied.

Settlement of property

20-034 An order for settlement of property is particularly likely in the case of a minor or a person who is in need of protection. Such a settlement must be drafted with an eye to tax and trust law so that, for example, if possible a settlement should fulfil the requirements to create a bereaved minor's or bereaved young person's interest or an immediate post-death interest (see Ch.7). Such an order, once made, cannot be varied.

Acquisition of property for transfer or settlement

20-035 The court may order that assets from the net estate of the deceased be used to acquire a specified item (for example, a house) which will either be transferred to or settled on an applicant. Such an order, once made, cannot be varied.

Variation of marriage settlements

20-036 An ante- or post-nuptial settlement may be varied by the court for the benefit of the surviving spouse of the marriage or the children of the marriage or any person who was treated by the deceased as a child of that marriage. Such an order for variation, once made, cannot be varied.

A provision in a pension scheme allowing an employee to direct benefits to a spouse may be a settlement for this purpose: *Brooks v Brooks* (1996). Even where not directly available as a settlement, pension benefits may still be important as they may increase the resources of other people interested in the estate.

A "nuptial settlement" includes "all arrangements making continuing provision for one or both spouses qua spouse": See *Williams Mortimer & Sunnucks on Executors, Administrators and Probate*, 20th edn (London: Sweet & Maxwell, 2013) at para.59-27. A settlement which holds the matrimonial home is a nuptial settlement, regardless of whether the husband or wife or neither is a beneficiary, and regardless of where the purchase price came from: see *HN v AN* (2005). In *Roberts v Fresco* (2017) although the widower of the deceased had died before completing his claim, his daughter from his first marriage successfully applied for leave to bring an application to vary the nuptial settlement of a £9 million house in Bayswater in which the second wife had had a life interest on the basis that she had been treated by her father as a child of his second marriage.

Variation of civil partnership settlements

20-037 The court can vary for the benefit of the surviving civil partner, or any child of both the civil partners, or any person who was treated by the deceased as a child of the family in relation to that civil partnership any settlement made during the subsistence of or in anticipation of the formation of the civil partnership.

Variation of trusts on which deceased's estate held

This was introduced by the Inheritance and Trustees' Powers Act 2014 and allows the court to vary for the applicant's benefit the trusts on which the deceased's estate is held (whether arising under the will, or the law relating to intestacy, or both). This provides a more direct way of achieving a result that previously was likely to require the creation of a new trust or trusts to replace the existing trust or trusts under which the estate is held. **20-038**

The burden of an order

Any order made by the court may contain such consequential and supplemental provisions as the court thinks necessary or expedient for the purpose of securing that the order operates fairly as between one beneficiary of the estate and another. For example, if the court makes a periodical payments order or a lump sum order it may direct which part of the estate is to bear the burden; if the court orders that an asset which had been specifically left to a beneficiary is to be transferred to the applicant the court may vary the disposition of the estate to make alternative provision for the disappointed beneficiary. **20-039**

"Beneficiary" in this context includes the donee of a statutory nomination or a *donatio mortis causa* or a surviving joint tenant (see para.20-044).

Effect of order on inheritance tax

The court order alters the disposition of the estate of the deceased and is deemed to have done so from the date of death of the deceased for all purposes including the payment of inheritance tax (IHTA 1984 s.146). Thus, for example, if an order increases the amount passing to a surviving spouse the chargeable value of the estate for inheritance tax purposes will be reduced, whereas if less property passes to a surviving spouse the chargeable value will be increased. **20-040**

In *Re Goodchild* (1997) the court used its variation powers to order that the testator's will was to be treated as if it had always left £185,000 to trustees to pay the income to the deceased's second wife until her death or until 1 March 1996, whichever was the earlier, and subject thereto for the applicant absolutely. The purpose of the order was to get the benefit of the spouse exemption and avoid the inheritance tax which would have been payable had the property been left directly to the applicant. The parties took the risk of an inheritance tax liability arising on the death of the second wife if she died within seven years of the termination of the interest in possession.

The Court of Appeal expressed some reservations about the use of variation orders under s.1(4) to obtain a tax benefit. However, Morritt LJ admitted that

> "if the order made is properly within the jurisdiction of the court the fact that it was sought with the motive of seeking to achieve a better tax position is usually irrelevant".

He went on to say that in future, if such an order was sought

> "the grounds on which it is thought to be authorised by s.1(4) should be clearly demonstrated for the consents and wishes of the parties are not enough".

Other taxes

20-041 Section 146 applies only for the purposes of inheritance tax. IHTA 1975 s.19 provides that an order made under s.2 of the Act is read back to the date of death "for all purposes". The order will therefore produce reading back for capital gains and other tax purposes. As explained at para.19-027, there must be a court order, so the section does not apply if the matter is settled out of court, even if the terms are embodied in a Tomlin Order.

Interim payments

20-042 Under s.5 the court has power to make an interim order in favour of an applicant if it appears to the court that:

(a) the applicant is in immediate need of financial assistance but it is not yet possible to determine what order (if any) should be made; and
(b) property forming part of the net estate of the deceased is or can be made available to meet the needs of the applicant.

Clear evidence of immediate need is required. In *Smith v Smith* (2011) an application was refused. The Russian widow of the deceased (who had returned to Russia after his death) sought an order that she be allowed to occupy a house owned by the deceased, and that she be paid £25,000 under s.5 of the Act as she was "in immediate need". Her evidence of poverty was at odds with her ownership of a flat in Moscow, and her statement that she would use the funds to pay back loans did not amount to an immediate need under s.5, at least not in the absence of indications that her friends were seriously pressing for repayment.

Master Marsh disregarded a loan for the same reason in *Weisz v Weisz* (2019).

In *T v V* (2019), Lieven J described a s.5 order as "draconian" in a case where there was a real likelihood that, if the claimant lost, the money paid under s.5 would not be repaid. She said that it was, therefore, necessary to approach such an application with considerable caution, to scrutinise the claimant's evidence very carefully. Master Marsh in *Weisz*, while agreeing that the onus was on the claimant to provide evidence supporting the need for immediate assistance, made the point that a s.5 order is not draconian in circumstances in which it is agreed that an applicant is entitled to something and the dispute is simply as to quantum.

Variation of periodical payments order

20-043 The court has limited power under s.6 to vary a periodical payments order. It has no power to vary other orders (apart from the number, amounts and dates for payment of instalments of a lump sum). This is in the interest of certainty.

An application for variation can be made by the original recipient and also, inter alia, by the personal representatives of the deceased, a beneficiary of the estate or a former applicant (s.6(5)). It can be made during the currency of an order or, where the order was to terminate on the occurrence of a specified event, within six months of that event.

Only property already allocated for periodical payments (called "relevant property") can be affected by a variation order. The court cannot order that relevant property be increased (s.6(6)).

The court will consider all the circumstances of the case including any change in matters it considered when making the original order (s.6(7)). It has power to order that periodical payments continue after the occurrence of a terminating event specified in the original order (other than the remarriage of a former spouse where the termination occurs automatically under s.14 and cannot be varied). It can also direct payment of a lump sum or a transfer of property to the applicant from the relevant property. The variation order can be made in favour of any of the possible applicants. It is not limited to the original recipient (s.6(2)).

10. PROPERTY AVAILABLE FOR FINANCIAL PROVISION

The net estate

If the court decides to order provision to be made for an applicant such an order is made against the "net estate" of the deceased. The net estate is defined by s.25 as comprising: **20-044**

(a) "All property of which the deceased had power to dispose by his will (otherwise than by virtue of a special power of appointment) less the amount of his funeral, testamentary and administration expenses, debts and liabilities including any inheritance tax payable out of his estate on death."

This will obviously not include insurance policies where the proceeds are payable direct to a beneficiary rather than to the estate of the policyholder as the deceased has no power to dispose of such property (however, the writing of such a policy in trust may amount to a disposition for the purposes of s.10: see para.20-048).

(b) "Any property in respect of which the deceased held a general power of appointment (not being a power exercisable by will) which has not been exercised."

If the power was exercisable by will the property subject to the power falls into (a) above whether or not the deceased actually exercised it.

(c) Any property nominated by the deceased to any person under a statutory nomination (see para.20-048 and para.21-002) or received by any person as a result of a *donatio mortis causa* (see para.21-013 and following) less any inheritance tax payable in respect of such property and borne by the nominee or donee (s.8).

(d) The deceased's severable share of a joint tenancy, but only if the court so orders (see s.9 and para.20-046 and following and para.21-013.

(e) Any property which the court orders shall be available as a result of its anti-avoidance powers (see para.20-047 and following).

Lump sums payable under discretionary pension schemes and policies written in trust for others are not part of the net estate.

Nominated property

Any property nominated by the deceased to any person under a *statutory* enactment is included in the estate. *Howard v Cairnes* (1983) held that a nomination made in relation to a private employment scheme was not within the section: the term "enactment" was inapt to describe a mere trust deed which was the creature of a contract between employer and employee. **20-045**

Rathbone v Bundock (1962) held that whether the term "enactment" extended to secondary legislation depends on context.

In *Goenka v Goenka* (2014) Judge Hodge QC, sitting as a High Court judge, had to decide whether a nomination to his father by hospital consultant of a death in service benefit payable under the National Health Service Pension Scheme Regulations 1995 (SI 1995/300) (which were made under powers conferred by the Superannuation Act 1972) was made "in accordance with the provisions of an enactment". He said (at [57]) that there was no immediate statutory context within the 1975 Act, to lead the court to view the reference to any 'enactment' as limited to statutes.

While it would have been possible to give meaning to s.8 by construing the reference to any "enactment" as limited to primary legislation by way of Act of Parliament, he could see no good reason for so limiting it. He concluded that, since the nomination was made pursuant to rules made under a power conferred by a statute, the nomination should be regarded as made "in accordance with the provisions of any enactment" and within s.8. He therefore held that the lump sum death in service payment was to be treated as part of the deceased's "net estate".

The decision is important as it will extend to other pension schemes created by secondary legislation. Private pension schemes are not affected.

Joint property

20-046 As a result of the right of survivorship a deceased has no power to dispose of the interest under a joint tenancy by will. However, under s.9 where the deceased was a joint tenant of any property immediately before death the court may, for the purpose of facilitating the making of financial provision, order that the deceased's severable share of the property shall, to such extent as appears to the court to be just in all the circumstances (and after allowing for any inheritance tax payable), be treated as part of the net estate.

In the case of deaths occurring before 1 October 2014, the date on which the Inheritance and Trustees' Powers Act 2014 came into force, the discretion only exists in respect of applications made within six months from the date of the grant; there is no power to make such an order in connection with an out-of-time application. In the case of deaths occurring after that date, the limitation is removed and the deceased's share of joint property is available with all other assets.

If the application for a grant is delayed, an application under s.9 may in fact be made many years after the date of death. See *Dingmar v Dingmar* (2006) in which the Court of Appeal had to decide the value of the deceased's share of a house for the purposes of an application made many years after the death.

The application in *Dingmar* revealed an ambiguity in the section in relation to valuation. The section appeared to require the court to value the deceased's share at its value immediately before death. In *Dingmar* this would have significantly limited the amount available for the applicant wife. The Court of Appeal by a majority decision interpreted the section as referring to the extent of the deceased's interest at the date of death rather than its value at that time.

For deaths on or after 1 October 2014 the section has been amended to provide that the deceased's severable share of joint property is to be valued as at the date of the hearing of the application unless the court orders that the share is to be valued at a different date.

Section 9(4) expressly provides, for the avoidance of doubt, that for the purposes of this section there may be a joint tenancy of a chose in action, for example, the asset represented by a credit balance in a joint bank account.

In *Kourkgy v Lusher* (1981) Wood J said that the discretion to treat the interest as part of the net estate should be exercised before the court considers whether reasonable provision has been made so that the court can take its availability into account. That is sensible in practice but does not sit well with the limitation that the interest is only to be available if it will facilitate the making of the order.

Whether or not proceeds of life assurance policies taken out in relation to joint property form part of the deceased's estate or pass directly to third parties can be a difficult issue.

In *Powell v Osbourne* (1993) the deceased had separated from his wife and had begun to cohabit with the defendant, Miss Osbourne. The deceased and Miss Osbourne had purchased a property as joint tenants, with the assistance of a mortgage. The purchase price had been £91,000 and the mortgage was £85,000. The mortgage had been supported by an endowment policy, which would pay out after 15 years, or upon the earlier death of either party. The payment upon an earlier death was guaranteed to be at least £85,000. As at the date of death, there was no sale or surrender value attaching to the policy. After the deceased's death, Mrs Powell brought proceedings under the Act. Aside from any interest which the deceased had in the payment made under the policy and/or in the property, his estate was valueless. The Court of Appeal accepted Mrs Powell's argument that immediately before his death, the deceased could have severed the joint tenancy in respect of the property, which would have meant that he was entitled to a half-share of the property, but with the benefit of the half-share of the benefit of the policy monies. It could not be correct to regard, as the recorder in the court below had done, the policy as having only a negligible value, as to do that would be to evaluate it without any reference to his imminent death.

In *Murphy v Holland* (2004), however, the Court of Appeal held that a policy on joint lives was not available under s.9 at all. The deceased and his estranged wife had taken out a policy for a fixed term of 25 years which provided for the benefit to be paid out upon the death of the first of the lives assured, or upon the acceptance by the insurer that one of the assureds had contracted a terminal illness. Prior to his death, the deceased had formed a new relationship with Miss Holland; and, six days after his death, she had given birth to the claimant, who was therefore the daughter of the deceased and Miss Holland.

A claim was brought on behalf of the daughter under s.9, against what was alleged to be the deceased's severable share of the monies paid out to the deceased's estranged wife, pursuant to the terms of the policy. Both parties to the appeal had accepted that the terminal illness benefit had been held jointly. The claimant contended that it could not have been intended that the rights to the terminal illness benefit and the right to the death benefit should be treated differently so it followed that both benefits were held jointly.

Thomas LJ and Pill LJ did not agree with the claimant and saw no barrier to a policy providing for different interests arising in different circumstances. The death benefit was not held jointly. Mr and Mrs Murphy held separate rights to it so there was nothing to form part of the deceased's estate.

In *Lim v Walia* (2014) the deceased and her husband had taken out a life policy on themselves. Under the terms of the policy it would pay a fixed cash sum (£113,000), either:

- on death, if either life insured died within the policy period, or
- earlier if either life insured developed a terminal illness.

No death benefit was available if a terminal illness claim had been paid. The notes to the policy included a warning that the policy had no cash-in value at any time and made it clear that there was no return at the end of the period of insurance. The deceased died, intestate, within a month of receiving a diagnosis of cancer and without making a claim for terminal illness payment (or completing the execution of her will). The insurer paid a lump sum to the deceased's husband. The deceased's new partner made Inheritance Act claims on behalf of her minor son from the new relationship and her minor daughter from her marriage. The deceased had no assets other than the benefit of the policy.

At first instance Judge Hodge QC, sitting as a deputy judge, found that there was a joint asset.

(1) From the moment she became terminally ill, or perhaps from when she was first diagnosed with the illness, the deceased was entitled to pursue a claim under the policy for payment of the insured sum of £113,000 which, upon payment, would be owned by the policyholders, that is to say, the deceased and her husband, jointly.
(2) The right to pursue a claim for the payment was a chose in action and thus clearly fell within s.9, given the wording of s.9(4).
(3) As a result, immediately before her death the deceased was "beneficially entitled to a joint tenancy of property", the property being the chose in action consisting of the right to claim a terminal illness payment under the policy.

Sadly for the claimants the Court of Appeal disagreed, reversing the earlier decision 2:1. The trial judge had been correct in finding that the deceased had a severable share in the terminal illness policy. However, he had not correctly determined its value. The interest became valueless if the policyholder died without making a claim. This was what had happened and as a result the value of the deceased's severable share immediately before death was nil. Its value had evaporated. Where the value of an interest depends on death, as it does when the interest is a life policy, the value immediately before death is effectively the same as its value on death.

Anti-avoidance provisions

Introduction

20-047 A deceased might attempt to evade the Act either by:

- giving away property by lifetime transfer so that the net estate on death is substantially reduced, or
- entering into a binding contract to leave property by will; the effect of such a contract would be to give the other party to the contract a right to enforce it against the personal representatives, thus reducing the net estate available for family provision.

Sections 10 and 11 of the Act enable the court to prevent such evasion; they give power to order a person to satisfy a claim for family provision if they have benefited under a lifetime disposition or a contract to provide money or other property.

Lifetime gifts

20-048 A disposition is covered by s.10 if it was made:

(a) after 31 March 1976 and less than six years before the date of death of the deceased;
(b) with the intention of defeating an application under the Act; and

(c) for less than full valuable consideration.

A "disposition" for this purpose includes any payment of money (including insurance premiums) and any conveyance of property whether or not made by instrument. It does not, however, include any property subject to a statutory nomination or *donatio mortis causa* (as such property is made part of the net estate by I(PFD)A 1975 s.8) or any property appointed in the exercise of a special power of appointment, otherwise than by will.

Contracts

A contract is covered by s.11 of the Act if: **20-049**

(a) entered into after 31 March 1976;
(b) the deceased agreed to leave money or other property by will or agreed that money or other property would be paid or transferred to any person from this estate;
(c) the deceased made the contract with the intention of defeating an application under the Act; and
(d) when the contract was made full valuable consideration was not given or promised.

In the case of a contract there is no time limit as there is in the case of lifetime dispositions.

The intention of defeating an application

The deceased must have made a disposition or contract with the intention of defeating an application. Section 12 provides that this requirement is satisfied if the court is of the opinion on a balance of probabilities that the deceased's intention (though not necessarily the sole intention) in making the disposition or contract was to prevent an order for financial provision being made or to reduce the amount of the provision which might otherwise be ordered. **20-050**

In the case of a contract, s.12(2) provides that, if a contract is made for no valuable consideration at all (that is, by way of a deed), there will be a presumption that the deceased's intention was to defeat the application.

The facilitating of financial provision for the applicant

Even if a disposition is covered by s.10 or a contract is covered by s.11 the court will not use its anti-avoidance powers unless satisfied that to do so will facilitate the making of financial provision. **20-051**

The powers of the court are discretionary

If the court is satisfied of the above requirements it may make an order against a donee. However, this is a discretionary matter and in deciding what order (if any) to make the court is directed to consider the circumstances in which the disposition or contract was made, any valuable consideration that was given, the relationship (if any) of the donee to the deceased, the conduct and financial resources of the donee and all the other circumstances of the case (ss.10(6) and 11(4)). **20-052**

Orders against a donee of a disposition

20-053 The court may order a donee to provide such sum of money or other property as it may specify (s.10(2)). However, there are two limitations:

(a) if the donee was given money they cannot be ordered to provide more than the money paid to them by the deceased less any inheritance tax borne by the donee in respect of the payment (s.10(3)); and
(b) if the donee was given property they cannot be ordered to provide more than the value of the property at the date of death of the deceased less any inheritance tax borne by the donee in respect of the payment (s.10(4)) (if they have disposed of the property prior to the deceased's death the limit is the value of the property at the date of disposal).

Order against a "donee" under a contract

20-054 If the personal representatives of the deceased have not transferred money or other property to the donee in accordance with the provisions of the contract, before the date of the application, the court may order them not to make such payment or transfer, or to make no further payment or transfer or to make only a reduced payment or transfer (s.11(2)(ii)). The effect of such an order is to increase the net estate of the deceased available for financial provision.

If the personal representatives of the deceased have already transferred money or property to the donee before the date of the application in accordance with the provisions of the contract, the court may order the donee to provide such sum of money or other property as it may specify (s.11(2)(i)).

The court may only make such orders to the extent that the property transferred under the contract exceeds the value of any consideration given (the property to be valued at the date of the hearing) (s.11(3)).

Order against donee's personal representatives

20-055 If a donee has died, the court has the same powers against the donee's personal representatives under ss.10 and 11 as it would have had against the donee. However, once property has been distributed by the personal representatives the powers of the court cease with regard to that property. The personal representatives will not be liable if they distribute the donee's property without notice of the making of an application under ss.10 and 11 (s.12(4)).

Order against a trustee of the donee

20-056 If the deceased transferred property to a trustee or contracted to have property transferred to a trustee with the intention of defeating an application, the trustee can be ordered to provide property (s.13(1) and (3)). Section 13 also provides limits on the amount that the trustee can be ordered to repay.

Illustration of use of power

20-057 *Hanbury v Hanbury* (1999) is a good illustration of the court using its anti-avoidance powers. The deceased had had no contact with his mentally and physically disabled daughter from the date of the breakdown of his marriage to her mother save that he paid £900 per annum for her maintenance. After legal advice and with the intention of defeating any claim brought on behalf of the daughter, he transferred assets into either the joint names of himself and his wife or into her name alone. When he died he left his daughter £10,000 from his estate of £11,981 (apparently calculating that this would be sufficient to prevent a claim).

Sections 9 and 10 were used to recover more than £50,000 of assets from the second wife. Shares in investment trusts (worth £100,000 at the date of death) had been bought in the second wife's name from a joint bank account fed by both parties.

See *Re Dawkins (Deceased)* (1986) for another example of s.10 in operation.

Alternative action under Insolvency Act 1986

As an alternative to a s.10 claim, it is possible to bring an application under s.423 of the Insolvency Act 1986. This allows the court, if satisfied that a donor entered into a transaction at an undervalue for the purpose: **20-058**

(a) of putting assets beyond the reach of a person who is making, or may at some time make, a claim against him; or
(b) of otherwise prejudicing the interests of such a person in relation to the claim which he is making or may make,

to make such order as it sees fit to restore the position to what it would have been if the transaction had not been entered into, and to protect the interests of persons who are victims of the transaction.

In *B v IB* (2013) Parker J held that the Insolvency Act remedy is not confined to applications where the transferor is insolvent, nor need there be insolvency proceedings. The remedy is meant to be a wide-ranging anti-avoidance remedy. It is not the existence of insolvency but the existence of debt which triggers the remedy. The existence of a "tailor-made" remedy for family provision claims does not preclude reliance on s.423. The s.423 test is wider than the s.10 test and the remedy different. There are the following important distinctions between the two remedies:

(1) Under s.10 the applicant must prove that the disposition was made with the intention of defeating an application for financial provision.
(2) Under s.423 the applicant must prove that the purpose is to put assets beyond reach or prejudice interests, a more general purpose.
(3) Under s.10 the court can order the provision of "such sum of money or other property as may be specified in the order". Under s.423 the transaction is set aside.
(4) Under s.10 the court has to balance various factors such as the circumstances of the disposition made, any valuable consideration given, the relationship of the donee to the deceased, and the conduct and financial resources of the donee. Section 423 contains no such balancing requirement. It requires the court to make an order which, so far as is practicable, will restore the position to what it would have been if the transaction had not been entered into and will protect the interests of the victims of it, although there is some discretion in that s.423 states that the court "may" make an order.

11. The Choice of Court

The county court

20-059 As a result of the Courts and Legal Services Act 1990, the county court has unlimited jurisdiction (see the County Courts Act 1984 s.25).

Proceedings can issue in any county court. London-based practitioners may wish to have proceedings heard in the Central London County Court which has a Chancery Users list. The judges here have a great deal of expertise. However, it is necessary to ask expressly to be put in the Chancery Users list. The matter will not be allocated automatically just because of its nature.

The Family or Chancery Division of the High Court

20-060 An application for an order may be made either in the Chancery Division or in the Family Division. There are no rules limiting the applicant's freedom of choice and a practitioner is, therefore, free to choose whichever Division is more appropriate. Frequently they will be equally suitable so that the practitioner's choice may be governed by personal preference and experience. On occasion, however, one Division may have a particular advantage. For example, it is appropriate to use the Family Division in a case involving the determination of the award a spouse would have got on divorce. The Chancery Division is more suitable where there is a dispute as to the validity of a will which is alleged not to make reasonable financial provision for the applicant (in such a case the probate action can be heard immediately before the family provision application by the same judge with a consequent saving of time and expense), where the true meaning of the will must first be determined under a construction summons or where complicated accounts have to be taken.

12. Minimising the Chances of an Application Succeeding

Assess the risk when taking instructions

20-061 When taking instructions for a will, it is always necessary to ask about family members. It is worth having a standard question to establish whether the client is maintaining anyone.

Except in the case of a surviving spouse or civil partners, claims will not succeed unless reasonable financial provision *for maintenance* has not been made. A potential applicant who can meet his or her own income needs will not succeed. Even an applicant with unmet financial needs will not necessarily succeed since the court has to balance the competing needs of applicants and beneficiaries. However, there will be a risk of an application if the instructions involve any of the following.

- A second marriage with children from an earlier relationship where nothing is to be left to the children.
- An estranged child to whom nothing (or very little) is to be left.
- A cohabitee to whom nothing (or very little) is left. The issue will be whether they maintain themselves at the level enjoyed during the period of cohabitation?

- A surviving spouse or civil partner who is left no capital. On divorce or dissolution, the assets would be divided equally unless there was a reason to do otherwise. If most of the assets are owned by the client, a claim for capital by the survivor is likely to succeed.

What can be done to minimise the chances of a claim succeeding?

The testator should leave a statement of reasons

At the very least, testators should document their reasons for the disposition of the property. Since *Ilott v Blue Cross* (2017) the courts place increased weight on testamentary freedom. **20-062**

The beneficiaries named in the will have been chosen by the testator and the court will not lightly interfere. Although, often unpopular with clients, a discussion with family members of the contents of the will and reasons for it may help. See, for example, *Miles v Shearer* (2021) where a father who had made significant lifetime gifts to tis two daughters explained to them that his financial circumstances had changed, and he would not be in a position to make any further provision in his will. The discussion may itself prevent an application being made. Even if it does, the court is likely to attach some weight to the fact that the applicant was not "blindsided" by the content of the will.

Attach a forfeiture clauses to a legacy

Sometimes clients will leave a small amount to a potential applicant in the hope that it will reduce the risk of a challenge. It is possible to add a clause depriving a beneficiary of entitlement if the will is challenged. There used to be a fear that a forfeiture clause was contrary to public policy as trying to oust the jurisdiction of the court. **20-063**

In *Nathan v Leonard* (2002) the court upheld the principle that a condition providing that a beneficiary who challenges a will loses the benefit given in the will is valid and is not contrary to public policy. The condition does not prevent a claim being made. The claimant is free to bring the claim if prepared to take the risk of receiving nothing from the court and losing the entitlement under the will. On the facts the particular condition was held to be void for uncertainty as some words were clearly missing the will but that does not affect the principle.

Care needs to be taken when setting out the action that will trigger forfeiture. For example, a family provision claim is not a challenge to a will so the trigger must not be limited to a challenge to the will.

In *Sim v Pimlott* (2023) the High Court considered whether a deceased's wife was justified in pursuing a claim under the Act where the will provided for two cash gifts to her, subject to conditions, one of which was that she execute a deed of release of all rights she might claim against the estate under the Inheritance (Provision for Family and Dependants) Act 1975 or relating to any asset owned by the deceased at his death. The will also provided for a life interest for the wife which could be terminated by the exercise of a power of appointment.

Having regard to the factors set out in s.3 of the Inheritance (Provision for Family and Dependants) Act 1975, the judge found that the will, as drawn, constituted reasonable financial provision for the deceased's wife. In circumstances where the provision made by the will was objectively reasonable, it was also reasonable to include a provision intended to discourage the relevant beneficiary from commencing an unwarranted claim, with the attendant delay to the estate's administration and distribution of assets to beneficiaries, and the cost consequences of defending such a claim. He further held that it was wrong in principle for a person to pursue a claim knowing that in doing so, they would forego a certain benefit, and then to say that, because they have foregone that benefit, reasonable financial provision had not been made for them.

Use of discretionary trust

20-064 Where clients are concerned about leaving funds directly to a person with addiction (or similar) problems, a discretionary trust with a letter of wishes asking the trustees to use funds for the benefit of the individual but not to release cash while the problems continue is unlikely to be challenged successfully.

13. If a Claim is Made

Role of personal representatives

20-065 Personal representatives are required to administer the estate and transfer property to those entitled. Where a successful application is made, the applicant becomes a person entitled.

Personal representatives should remain neutral during proceedings and await the outcome. They should, of course, deal with any parts of the administration which do not depend on the outcome of the claim. For example, they should pay debts and make sure that assets are collected and secured.

They are joined as defendants because they are then required by CPR PD 57.16 to supply the following information.

- full details of the value of the deceased's net estate, as defined in s.25(1) of the Act;
- the person or classes of persons beneficially interested in the estate, and:
  - the names and (unless they are parties to the claim) addresses of all living beneficiaries; and
  - the value of their interests in the estate so far as they are known;
- whether any living beneficiary (and if so, naming him) is a child or a person who lacks capacity (within the meaning of MCA 2005); and
- any facts which might affect the exercise of the court's powers under the Act.

Practice Direction 57.15 provides that where a defendant who is a personal representative wishes to remain neutral in relation to the claim, and agrees to abide by any decision which the court may make, he or she should state this in Section A of the acknowledgment of service form. It is normally appropriate for the personal representative to do this leaving the beneficiaries (who are the interested parties) to fight it out with the claimant. See, for example, *Ilott v Blue Cross* (2017).

Personal representative who is also bringing a claim

20-066 A personal representative is in a fiduciary position and must not pursue a claim which is adverse to the estate. Making a 1975 Act claim is in no way inconsistent with the claimant's role as personal representative; they are not, by doing so, challenging the will, nor are they making a claim adverse to the estate, as they would be if (for example) they were claiming a beneficial interest in an asset which the deceased had purported to dispose of by their will. They are merely seeking a redistribution of the estate at the expense of the existing beneficiaries.

The question was considered by the court for the first time in *Bowser v Smith* (2023) where Sir Launcelot Henderson accepted that there is no principle of law which automatically requires a person who is bringing (or intending to bring) a claim under the 1975 Act, and who is also a personal representative of the deceased's estate, to cease acting in the latter capacity because of a conflict of interest. He did accept that it was necessary for care to be taken by a 1975 Act claimant who is also a personal representative to keep the two capacities distinct. So, for example the costs of the application must be kept separate from the costs of administering the estate.

The notes in the *White Book* to CPR r.57.16, which lays down the procedure for claims under s.1 of the 1975 Act, state at para.57.16.1 says:

> "An application under the Act does not impugn the validity of the grant or the will (if any). There is no need for a spouse or civil partner to renounce probate or the right to letters of administration if such a person wishes to claim under the Act. The personal representative may in that situation be the claimant. There is no need for the same person also to be joined as a defendant in their capacity as personal representative."

Personal representative who is also defending a claim

A personal representative will often be a beneficiary and may wish to defend a **20-067**
claim. There is nothing to prevent this, although, again, care should be taken to keep the costs of the two roles separate.

Chapter Twenty-One

DISPOSING OF PROPERTY OTHERWISE THAN BY WILL

1. Introduction

It is generally considered to be a "good thing" to make a will. In this chapter we will consider, first, to what extent it is possible to dispose of property on death without a will and, secondly, why solicitors advise clients to make wills. **21-001**

2. Disposition of Property Without a Will

Statutory nominations

Where a person is entitled to certain types of investments, they can nominate a third party to receive them on their death. In such cases the property will not vest in the nominator's personal representatives on death but will be paid directly to the nominee. The payer will, therefore, want to see the death certificate of the deceased but will not require production of the grant of representation. The nominated property does, however, form part of the deceased's estate for inheritance tax purposes. **21-002**

Nominations were originally designed to allow the poorer members of society to dispose of small amounts of money without the necessity of making a will or of their representatives obtaining a grant. They can be made in respect of deposits in certain Trustee Savings Banks, Friendly Societies and Industrial and Provident Societies up to a limit of £5,000 each. It used to be possible to nominate National Savings Certificates and deposits in National Savings Banks and Trustee Savings Banks but this power was withdrawn as from 1 May 1979 in respect of the latter and 1 May 1981 in respect of the two former (nominations of such property *made* before those dates remain effective).

To be valid, a nomination must be:

(a) in writing;
(b) made by a person who is 16 or over; and
(c) attested by one witness.

Since a will cannot be made by a person who is under the age of 18, a nomination is the only way in which a minor can dispose of property (unless they have privileged status) after death.

A nomination is revoked by subsequent marriage, a later nomination, or the death of the nominee before the nominator, but it is *not* revoked by a subsequent will. It is therefore important when drafting a will for a client to ascertain whether or not any nominations have previously been made. They are easily overlooked as the paying authority normally holds the nomination form.

Rights under pension schemes

An outline only

21-003 Pensions is an enormous subject and in a book of this length we can do no more than make a few comments on the most important aspects.

Death in service benefits and inheritance tax

21-004 Many employee pension schemes allow contributors to "nominate" a third party to receive benefits after the contributors' death either in the form of a lump sum or a pension. Where a lump sum is paid it is often the most substantial single asset passing on death and may be used to make a substantial gift to a beneficiary. However, such lump sums are normally only paid when the contributor dies in service and therefore the provision for the beneficiary may have to be reconsidered when the contributor ceases to contribute to the scheme (whether on retirement or as a result of changing jobs).

Such a "nomination" is not binding on the trustees of the pension fund being merely an indication of the deceased's wishes, although, naturally, they will usually abide by the expressed wishes of the deceased. This procedure is sometimes referred to as a "nomination" but it is obviously different from the type of nomination referred to in para.21-002, where the deceased has an absolute right to the property and is free to deal with it as they like whether after their death or during their lifetime. These benefits do not form part of the deceased's estate for inheritance tax purposes because the deceased had no control over the destination of the property.

Discretionary schemes must be distinguished from fixed schemes where, for example, the lump sum is paid to the estate of the employee and then under the terms of the employee's will or under the intestacy rules. Here the destination of the property is under the control of the employee and the payment will, therefore, be part of the estate for inheritance tax purposes.

Personal pension schemes

21-005 **Accessing pension benefits** Many people have paid significant amounts into personal pension schemes. Historically the funds had to be used to purchase an annuity. As annuity rates fell, this caused mounting dissatisfaction and a series of changes enhancing the rights of investors to access the funds contained in their pension schemes.

21-006 **Changes to rules on personal pension schemes introduced in 2014** Before the 2014 changes, different rules applied depending on whether the member died before or after 75 and whether benefits had already been taken. The rules were restrictive. Lump sum payments could be made to anyone at the discretion of the pension trustees who fell within the class named in the scheme rules, but income benefits could only be paid to a "dependant" of the scheme member. A dependant was a spouse, civil partner or child under 23. In some circumstances there was 55 per cent tax charge which was very unattractive.

Significant amendments to Finance Act 2004 were made by the Taxation of Pensions Act 2014 (TPA 2014). They took effect for pension fund death benefits payable on or after 6 April 2015. Not only did the changes allow much more flexibility in the way taxpayers can access their pension funds during their lifetime but, crucially, they allowed undrawn pension funds:

- to be passed on,
- more than once, and
- if taxpayers die below 75, completely tax free (at the time of writing).

Fairly obviously if taxpayers decide to withdraw cash from their pension fund, the withdrawn cash ceases to have any status as a pension. It is simply cash which the taxpayer can spend or invest. Unless the taxpayer has a particular reason for wanting a slab of cash, it is preferable to leave the funds invested in the pension wrapper, withdrawing only what is required for day-to-day expenses (income drawdown). The undrawn funds remaining in the pension scheme (the "pot") can then be passed on.

TPA 2014 made no changes to the legislation concerning inheritance tax. When a member of a scheme nominates a person to receive lump-sum death benefits, provided that nomination is not binding on the scheme trustees or provider, the lump sum is not part of the member's estate so no inheritance tax charge arises.

TPA 2014 effectively disposed of the 55 per cent charge (the death tax). Undrawn pension funds can generally be passed on free of tax. What is more, the person nominated by the member can pass any remaining pension pot to their own individual nominee who in turn can pass it on to a successor. Note that while the pension pot can be passed on many times (if large enough!), the original pension scheme member has no control over where it goes once it has left his or her hands. The only important matter is whether the death is before 75 or at 75 or more.

Death under 75 The pension pot can be paid to any individual free of tax either **21-007** as a lump sum or as income drawdown. Note, it makes no difference whether or not the deceased was drawing the pension before death.

Death at 75 or over If the pot is paid to an individual as a lump sum, it is taxed **21-008** at the beneficiary's marginal rate. Effectively if the fund is of any size this is likely to be 45 per cent since the receipt of a large sum in one tax year will almost inevitably push the recipient into the highest tax band. If the beneficiaries use drawdown to take the pension, they will pay income tax at their marginal rate on the withdrawals. Drawdown is likely to be more tax efficient as the beneficiary can manage withdrawals to stay in a lower tax band.

The lifetime allowance For those concerned with inheritance tax efficiency the **21-009** advice has always been to spend assets within the IHT estate rather than drawing on pension funds. Unfortunately, the amount saved into pensions was subject to the lifetime limit (in 2022 £1,073,100). If the lifetime allowance was exceeded, there was a charge to income tax at 75 or when funds were accessed. The charge was 55 per cent on lump sum payments or 25 per cent on income payments (which may also suffer an income tax charge when received, meaning a total charge of 55 per cent if the marginal rate is 40 per cent).

However, in an attempt to encourage retirees back into work, Jeremy Hunt announced in the Spring Budget 2023 the abolition of the lifetime allowance and an increase on the annual allowance (the maximum amount of pensions savings an individual can make each year with tax relief without incurring a tax charge) from £40,000 to £60,000. The result was to make the use of pensions as an inheritance tax planning tool very attractive.

However, at the time of writing HMRC have issued draft legislation which cap the amount of lump sums which can be paid tax free. Accompanying that draft legislation was a policy paper which indicated that they plan to tax income from inherited drawdown and annuities purchased from funds where the member died before age 75.

Decisions when planning how to pass on pension benefits

21-010 **Introduction** Owners of large pension pots in discretionary schemes, who also have other funds available, are better advised from a tax point of view to spend other assets and keep their pension funds. They can then pass on the undrawn funds free of inheritance tax.

Assuming there are undrawn funds available at death, the owner of the pot will have to decide whether to nominate an individual to take the undrawn funds as a pension pot or to leave the funds as a lump sum to a trust. At first sight leaving the undrawn funds in the pension wrapper as a pot to a legatee appears to have overwhelming tax advantages.

21-011 **Inheritance tax** *Outright gift of undrawn funds (the pot):* There is no inheritance tax on the first death provided the death benefit is not part of the deceased's estate. Similarly on the death of the nominee any remaining pension pot sits outside the estate of the nominee and can be passed on free of inheritance tax to a successor.

Undrawn funds transferred to a trust: there is no tax on the first death, as above. But there will be anniversary and exit charges. The anniversary will not fall 10 years after the death of the pension owner. This is because as a result of IHTA 1984 s.80 the funds are treated as still contained in the original pension trust which was created when the deceased joined the pension scheme. The 10-year anniversaries will be calculated on that basis and the first may fall very soon after the death. The anniversary and exit charges constitute a distinct tax disadvantage.

21-012 **Capital gains tax and income tax** *Outright gift of undrawn funds (the pot):* the beneficiaries pay at their own rates and may be lower rate taxpayers.

Undrawn funds transferred to a trust: The trustees pay capital gains tax and income tax at the higher trust rates. This looks like a disadvantage. *However*, the tax downsides of using a trust can be minimised if the trustees lend the trust assets to the beneficiary who will then pay income tax and capital gains tax at their own rates.

Using a trust has the following non-tax advantages:

- Protection for spendthrift beneficiaries: Trusts protect the funds. If the pot is simply passed on to the individual, the beneficiary can choose to withdraw the lot and spend it.
- Protection for successive generations: The use of a trust will prevent a surviving spouse who remarries from passing the pot on to the new spouse, rather than to the children (a particular concern if the children are from the deceased's previous marriage).
- The trust will be bespoke and the member can control the choice of trustees and beneficiaries (subject to the scheme rules).

A donatio mortis causa

21-013 **Introduction** A *donatio mortis causa* is a lifetime gift which is conditional on death. It has some of the attributes of a legacy and some of a lifetime gift. As many judges have observed, it is an anomaly. It enables a donor to transfer property on death without complying with any of the formalities of s.9 of the Wills Act 1837 or s.52 of the Law of Property Act 1925. Thus the doctrine may facilitate the abuses which those statutes are intended to prevent.

The Court of Appeal stressed in *Birch v Treasury Solicitor* (1951) that the courts must not allow the principle to be used as a device in order to validate ineffective wills. In *King v Dubrey* (2015) the Court of Appeal considered *donationes mortis causa* and made the point that there is scope for abuse and misunderstanding where gifts are made shortly before death, without formalities and without professional advice. Therefore the conditions should be strictly enforced and the courts should resist the temptation to extend the doctrine to an ever-wider range of situations.

There are four requirements which must be satisfied if a *donatio mortis causa* is to be valid. They are as follows:

The gift must be made in contemplation of death The death need not be immediate so it is, for example, sufficient that a person knows they have a serious illness and cannot live for long. It is irrelevant that death occurs from a supervening cause (such as an accident or a sudden second illness—*Wilkes v Allington* (1931)) but the gift fails if the donor recovers from the contemplated cause of death. The cause of death need not be an illness as such; contemplation of a dangerous operation is enough. The death which is anticipated need not be inevitable. The illness or event which the donor faces can be one which might be survived. In *Re Craven's Estate* (1937) the donor was about to undergo a serious operation which might have been successful. The gift was a valid *donatio mortis causa* (because the gift has to be conditional on death taking place (see para.21-015 below) the donor would have been entitled to recover the subject matter of the gift had he survived the operation and recovered). 21-014

In *King v Dubrey* (2015) the Court of Appeal said that the earlier case of *Vallee v Birchwood* (2013) was wrongly decided; in that case the donor had made a gift four months before his death at a time when there was no objective reason for him to have regarded his death as imminent, although it was clear that he was thinking about his possible death when he made the gift. The judge had held that there was a valid *donatio mortis causa*. The motive for the gift was that he subjectively contemplated the possibility of death in the near future and this was sufficient. The Court of Appeal said that death must be impending from a known cause. Old age or general frailty is not enough.

The gift must be conditional on death If the donor recovers from the contemplated cause of death, the gift will not take effect and the donor will be entitled to regain possession of the property. If, however, the donor dies then the gift to the donee becomes absolute. 21-015

In *Re Exler* (2017) Charles Hollander QC sitting as a deputy judge described a deathbed gift claim as "frankly hopeless". Leaving aside the conflicting versions of events the alleged donor had no reason to anticipate death. She had suffered a minor but not life-threatening heart attack and had recovered so, even if there had been a conditional gift, it would have lapsed. If there are formal requirements for transfer which need to be complied with in order to complete title, then the donee can compel the deceased's personal representatives to complete the transfer.

The donor must part with dominion over the property before death In *King v Dubrey* (2015) Jackson LJ said that it was not easy to understand what "dominion" 21-016 actually meant. Earlier judges had referred to the concept as "amphibious" and "slippery". From his review of the cases he concluded that "dominion" meant physical possession of (a) the subject matter or (b) some means of accessing the subject matter (such as the key to a box) or (c) documents evidencing entitlement to possession of the subject matter. In relation to bank and other financial accounts, HH Judge Paul Matthews held in *Rahman v Hassan* (2024) that giving possession of the papers containing details of logins and passwords to the claimant was sufficient. The donor was an elderly, sick man who had many accounts with financial institutions and could not possibly have memorised all these details. Accordingly, by handing over the papers to the claimant, he had put it out of his power to deal further with the accounts. Leave to appeal was given on this point.

Delivery must be made to the donee (or their agent) of the subject matter of the gift or the means of obtaining it. In the case of chattels it is usually readily apparent whether or not this has taken place, but in the case of choses in action it is a little more difficult. Since choses in action cannot be physically delivered, there must be delivery of the essential evidence of title which will entitle the possessor to the property given (for example, delivery of National Savings Certificates or bills of exchange).

In both *Sen v Headley* (1991) and *Woodard v Woodard* (1992) the deceased delivered a set of keys (in the first case of a house and in the second case of a car) but retained a set himself. In both cases the Court of Appeal held that the retention of the keys did not prevent the donor parting with dominion. In both cases, however, the donor was terminally ill in hospital and could not have made use of the second set of keys unless there had been an unexpected recovery which in any event would have revoked the gift. In *Woodard* it was also argued that the deceased should have handed over the registration document (and possibly the insurance certificate and servicing log book). The Court of Appeal rejected this argument. These items were not documents of title, nor was it essential to hand them over to give the defendant dominion over the car. The handing over would merely have been evidence of the intention to make a gift.

In *Vallee v Birchwood* (2013) the donor delivered keys to the house and the title deeds but continued in occupation of the property for four months until he died. The court held that the continued occupation did not prevent the gift being a *valid donatio mortis causa*. Continued enjoyment of his own property is not incompatible with an intention to make a gift effective on death. If the subject matter of the gift was a rental property, the donor would be entitled to enjoy the rent while he lived. That is no different in principle from the donor continuing to enjoy his own house by living in it. The delivery of the deeds put it out of his power to transfer.

In *King v Dubrey* (2015) the donor handed the title deeds to her house (which had unregistered title) to her nephew who was living with her. The Court of Appeal said that, on the authority of *Sen v Headley* (1991), this was sufficient to constitute delivering dominion over the property. The fact that the nephew kept the title deeds in his bedroom at his aunt's house, rather than depositing them at a bank or a solicitor's office, did not affect the position.

21-017 **The subject matter of the gift must be capable of passing as a valid donatio mortis causa** Most personalty is so capable (for example, chattels, bonds, insurance policies or National Savings Certificates). A cheque drawn by a third party can be the subject of a valid donation but a cheque drawn by the deceased cannot since it is merely an order to the deceased's bank to pay which will be automatically revoked by death: see *Curnock v IRC* (2003) and *Re Owen* (1949).

It has been suggested that shares cannot be the subject of a valid *donatio mortis causa* (*Re Weston* (1902)) but there seems to be no reason in principle why this should be so and indeed the possibility of a *donatio mortis causa* of company shares was accepted in *Staniland v Willott* (1852), although on the facts it was held to have been revoked by the donor's recovery from his illness.

It had been thought that land was not capable of passing by *donatio mortis causa* but the Court of Appeal held in *Sen v Headley* (1991) that this was not the case. The court held that unregistered land may be the subject-matter of such a gift if the title deeds to the property are handed over. In *Rahman v Hassan* (2024), HH Judge Paul Matthews, after an extensive review of the cases, held that there was no reason to distinguish registered and unregistered land. It was possible to have a valid *donatio mortis causa* of registered land despite the fact that there is no longer a role for the land certificate under the Land Registration Act 2002 as evidence to show delivery or dominion of title. Leave to appeal was given on this point.

Comparison with legacies

It is worth noting the more important similarities and differences between legacies and *donatio mortis causa*. **21-018**

(a) *Similarities*
   (i) *Lapse.* A *donatio mortis causa* lapses if the donee predeceases the donor. The subject matter will then form part of the donor's estate on death.
   (ii) *Tax.* Inheritance tax is payable on the property which is the subject matter of the *donatio mortis causa* as it is part of the donor's estate on death. A *donatio mortis causa* is, in effect, an incomplete gift so for inheritance tax purposes the property gifted remains part of the estate at death.
   (iii) *Liability for debts.* If the estate of the deceased proves insufficient to pay the deceased's debts then the subject matter of a *donatio mortis causa* may be taken.
(b) *Differences*
   (i) *No assent.* Normally the personal representatives of the deceased transfer title to beneficiaries by means of an assent. However, since death makes a *donatio mortis causa* absolute, the personal representatives need do nothing unless there are formal requirements which need to be complied with in order to complete the title.
   (ii) *Revocation.* A *donatio mortis causa* is revoked if the donor recovers from the contemplated cause of death or if the donor resumes possession and dominion of the property. It cannot be revoked by a subsequent will.

Joint tenancies

Joint tenancies are extremely important in practice since they are the most common way for property to be transferred without a will. Where the deceased was a joint tenant in equity of any property, on death the equitable interest will pass automatically to the surviving joint tenant(s). It will not devolve on the deceased's personal representatives and cannot pass under the terms of the will. This is because it is not possible to sever a joint tenancy by will. However, a joint tenant is free to sever the joint tenancy during his or her lifetime in which case the deceased and **21-019** the co-owners will hold as tenants-in-common in equity. Such an interest *will* devolve on the deceased's personal representatives and *will* pass under the deceased's will or on intestacy.

When preparing wills for clients it is important to explain that jointly-owned property will pass to the survivor no matter how short the period of survivorship may be, despite anything said in the will. For this reason it may be appropriate for a client to sever a joint tenancy. The client is then free to leave the beneficial tenancy-in-common to the survivor *provided the survivor survives* for a stated period.

In *Carr-Glynn v Frearsons* (1998) a client knew she was a co-owner of property but was uncertain whether she was a beneficial joint tenant or tenant in common. Her solicitor explained that the will would be ineffective if she was a beneficial joint tenant unless she severed the joint tenancy but did not explain that it was possible to serve a precautionary notice of severance. The Court of Appeal held that the solicitor was negligent for allowing the testatrix to execute the will not knowing whether or not it would be effective and without suggesting a precautionary notice of severance. Had the offer been made, there would have been no liability even if the testatrix had declined.

Joint tenancies can be severed without a notice of severance. Section 36(2) of the Law of Property Act 1925 introduced the notice of severance but expressly preserved all the existing methods of severing a beneficial joint tenancy. According to *Williams v Hensman* (1861) there are three methods:

(1) an act of anyone of the persons interested operating upon their own share may create a severance as to that share;
(2) mutual agreement; and
(3) any course of dealing sufficient to intimate that the interests of all were mutually treated as constituting a tenancy in common.

In *Re Woolnough*, Perkins v Borden (2002) a brother and sister, Len and Emmy, owned a property as beneficial joint tenants. They went together to see a solicitor and each made wills leaving the house to the survivor for life and then to their niece, Dorothy, with a substitutional gift to her children. In 1989 Dorothy died and Len made a new will selecting one of Dorothy's three children as his residuary beneficiary. Emmy left her will unchanged. After Emmy's death, Len made a new will leaving everything to charity.

The issue was whether or not the joint tenancy had been severed by mutual consent before Emmy's death. If it had, only half of the value of the house was in Len's estate. If it had not, he had the whole value of the house. The court found that the making of the two wills leaving the interest of the first to die to the survivor for life was inconsistent with the continuance of the joint tenancy and amounted to severance by agreement. It would not, of course, have amounted to severance had one joint tenant alone made a will dealing with the half share. This is because a will is ambulatory in form and has no effect until death. Clear evidence of mutual agreement will be required: see *Carr v Isard* (2007) where the evidence of mutual agreement was not sufficient and *Chadda v RCC* (2014) where it was.

Where, as in *Re Woolnough*, clients want to make wills which are inconsistent with a continuing joint tenancy, it is important that there is clarity as to when the severance takes place. Solicitors should consider preparing a signed agreement or notice of severance without delay.

The question of whether there has been a severance by mutual agreement may arise:

- when taking instructions for a will from a client who appears to hold the beneficial interest in the whole of an asset as a result of survivorship (like Len in *Re Woolnough*); or
- when administering an estate for a deceased who appears to be a sole surviving joint tenant.

Sometimes clients may want to make new wills because their spouse, civil partner or cohabitee has lost capacity and they want to leave their estate directly to their children instead of to the person who has lost capacity. It is important for the solicitor to check the basis of ownership of the matrimonial home. If it is owned as beneficial joint tenants, the joint tenancy must be severed if the will is to be fully effective. Serving notice is a unilateral act so notice can be served on a person who lacks capacity. It can also be served on their properly appointed attorney or deputy: *Quigley v Masterson* (2011). Conversely an attorney or deputy can sever on behalf of a person who lacks capacity.

Resulting and constructive trusts

There may be problems in determining the beneficial interests where two people have bought land without declaring the basis on which the beneficial interests are held. Previously the default position was that there would be a presumption of a resulting trust in proportion to the contributions made. However, in *Stack v Dowden* (2007) the House of Lords held that, in the domestic consumer context, beneficial entitlement is presumed to be the same as legal title. The correctness of this approach was confirmed in *Jones v Kernott* (2011) although it is worth noting that in both cases there was sufficient evidence to rebut the presumption. Hence, a conveyance into joint names indicates both legal and beneficial joint tenancy, unless and until the contrary is proved. **21-020**

In *Adekunle v Ritchie* (2007) John Behrens QC held that the *Stack v Dowden* approach was not limited to cohabiting couples living together in a platonic or sexual relationship. It applied in other domestic cases such as that of mother and son or friends buying together (see *Gallarotti v Sebastianelli* (2012)) but not where property is purchased as an investment (see *Laskar v Laskar* (2008)). Note, however, that the Privy Council said in *Marr v Collie* (2017) that a purchase as an investment by a cohabiting couple would not inevitably require the resulting trust solution. See para.13-009.

The presumption has no application where the beneficial entitlement is declared. The declaration is conclusive unless there is mistake, fraud or subsequent agreement or the effect of proprietary estoppel (see *Pankhania v Chandegra* (2012)).

Insurance policies

Where a life assurance policy has not been written in trust, the insurance company will pay the assured amount to the deceased's personal representatives. This sum will form part of the death estate and so can potentially attract inheritance tax. Inheritance tax will not be payable if the death estate falls within the nil-rate band or an exemption (such as the spouse exemption) applies. However, even if the property is to be paid to a spouse, the personal representatives will have to wait until a grant is obtained before the insurance company will hand over the money. This delay may be inconvenient at best or financially disastrous for the spouse, at worst. **21-021**

Rather than have the money channelled through the estate (which will be ill-advised for inheritance tax purposes if the sum is large and the intended beneficiary is not a spouse or a charity), it is better to have the money paid direct to the intended beneficiary. This can be achieved in one of two ways: (1) under the Married Woman's Property Act 1882 s.11 (MWPA), or (2) by express trust or assignment.

Under MWPA s.11, a policy of life assurance effected by a person on their own life can be expressed to be for the benefit of their spouse, civil partner, children (which includes children of a non-marital relationship) or any of them. This creates a trust in their favour and on death, the sum assured is paid direct to the trustees of the policy for the benefit of the named beneficiaries. No inheritance tax charge will arise in respect of the assured's estate where policies are written in trust in this way since the assured has no beneficial interest. However, provided the gift is not subject to a contingency, the named beneficiary receives an immediate absolute interest. Therefore, should the beneficiary predecease the assured, the beneficiary's estate suffers tax on the appropriate proportion of the value of the policy. Since the beneficiary has an immediate absolute interest in the policy, the assured is no longer free to surrender or assign the policy.

Since s.11 permits the assured to name their children as beneficiaries, it is advisable to appoint trustees to hold the money until the children reach a suitable age. If such trustees are not appointed, the assured's personal representatives will hold the money as trustees, on trust for the children. Should this situation arise, the sum is still not taxed as part of the assured's estate since the sum does not belong to the estate, it is merely administratively convenient for the personal representatives to hold the property in this way.

If the assured wants to benefit someone other than a spouse or children (such as a friend or grandchildren) the Married Woman's Property Act s.11 is of no use and the second method must be used. The policyholder writes the policy in trust for the desired beneficiaries. The trust has the same effect as one created under s.11. The same result will be achieved by assigning the benefit of the policy to the named beneficiary.

Where the benefit of a policy is written in trust or assigned, there is a transfer of value of the policy at market value or the total of premiums paid, whichever is the greater (IHTA 1984 s.167). If the transferor continues to pay the premiums, each payment will be a transfer of value although they are likely to be exempt under the annual exemption or normal expenditure out of income exemption.

In *Kempe v CIR* (2004) the deceased designated members of his family to take the benefit of a life assurance policy provided by his family. Under the terms of the policy he could change the designation at any time. If no beneficiaries were designated the sum assured passed to his estate. The Revenue successfully argued that the benefit of the policy remained part of his estate at death under IHTA 1984 s.5 because he had a "general power" over the policy which enabled him to dispose of the sum assured as he thought fit.

Lasting and enduring powers of attorney

21-022 A client who is making a will should consider making a lasting power of attorney under the Mental Capacity Act 2005. Any person may appoint an attorney to deal with their property. However, the power of attorney will automatically end if the person who made the appointment (the donor of the power) loses their mental capacity.

On or after 1 October 2007 it is possible to make lasting powers of attorney which will survive the incapacity of the donor. Lasting powers cannot be used until registered with the Public Guardian. There are two forms of lasting power of attorney: one authorises the attorney to make personal welfare decisions, the other authorises the attorney to make decisions about property.

The Enduring Power of Attorney Act 1985 similarly provided for the appointment of an attorney whose powers will survive the incapacity of the donor. No new enduring powers of attorney can be made on or after 1 October 2007, although existing enduring powers continue to be valid, whether or not registered before that date.

An attorney normally has power to sell the donor's property, and to a limited extent to give it away. A sale by an attorney of an asset which has been specifically given in the will causes ademption (see *Banks v National Westminster Bank* (2005) and *Re Dorman, Smith National Childrens Home* (1994)). It is sensible for a person making a lasting power to give the attorney a copy of the will or authorise anyone with custody of the will to show the attorney a copy so that the attorney can take the provisions into account so far as possible.

Recent joint guidance prepared by the SRA, Law Society, Court of Protection, Office of the Public Guardian, Legal Ombudsman and Society of Trusts and Estates Practitioners, and published on 13 March 2017, states that the will forms part of the financial affairs belonging to the donor and so unless the donor provides contrary instructions the attorney is entitled to a copy of the donor's will.

The guidance suggests the following procedure:

- discuss the question of disclosure of the donor's will at the time of making the will and record it;
- confirm the question when the lasting power of attorney is made having advised as to the consequences;
- incorporate the instructions on disclosure (and any limitations or restrictions) into the lasting power of attorney or include it in a side letter.

3. Lifetime Planning

Gifts

Introduction

As an alternative to leaving property to an intended beneficiary by will, a client can consider making a lifetime gift. Such a gift has the advantage of giving the beneficiary the immediate use of the asset but it has the corresponding disadvantage that the donor will lose the benefit of the property (unless, for example, the gift is to a spouse or civil partner). **21-023**

Therefore, it is important to ensure that the donor has no need of the property to be given away. A gift of money that will leave the donor with financial problems is a bad idea, as is the gift of an asset that the donor still wants to use. It is quite common for testators to want to leave books, jewellery, fishing tackle, golf clubs and similar items to friends or relatives but they would obviously not wish to make such gifts during their lifetime. While lifetime gifts should always be considered, they are usually only practicable where the donor is fairly wealthy. An additional advantage of lifetime gifts is that they may be useful in saving tax.

Tax considerations

21-024 Although tax should never be the first consideration, since lifetime transfers to individuals do not attract an immediate inheritance tax liability and become completely exempt after seven years, a lifetime gift will prima facie produce a saving. There is a danger that the donor will die within seven years of the -transfer in which case inheritance tax will be charged (subject to tapering relief). It may be wise to insure against the risk of death in this period. The advantage of saving inheritance tax may be outweighed by capital gains tax considerations.

Inheritance tax

21-025 Married couples or civil partners who wanted to provide for the survivor and children in a tax-efficient manner used to leave property by will to make use of the nil-rate band of the first to die typically by creating a nil-rate band discretionary trust for the benefit of the survivor and children. This would often require the transfer of assets between the couple to ensure that each party had sufficient assets to do this. Since the introduction of the transferable nil-rate band on 9 October 2007, this is no longer necessary. If the first to die has not made use of the nil-rate band, the proportion unused can be claimed by the personal representatives of the survivor (see para.4-015). However, couples who want the estate of the survivor to benefit from the residence nil-rate band may wish to create a -nil-rate band discretionary trust on the first death to avoid the estate of the survivor exceeding the taper threshold: see para.4-021 for taper threshold.

There are some inheritance tax exemptions which are only available for lifetime transfers so it makes sense to make use of these. For example:

(1) The annual exemption (IHTA 1984 s.19) and exemption for gifts made to parties marrying or forming a civil partnership (IHTA 1984 s.22) (see para.4-053).
(2) Single parents who want to make tax-efficient provision for their children, for example because they are terminally ill, are better advised to do so by lifetime transfer. Provided the gift complies with the requirements of IHTA 1984 s.11 (gifts for family maintenance) it falls outside the inheritance tax net completely (see para.4-057).
(3) Taxpayers who have surplus income can benefit from the normal expenditure out of income exemption contained in IHTA 1984 s.21 (see para.4-055).

Cohabiting couples with children should consider whether it is sensible for a richer partner to make gifts to the less rich partner to ensure that both have sufficient assets to make use of their nil-rate band. Then in the event of both parties dying at or about the same time they can each leave their estates to their children obtaining the benefit of two nil-rate bands. There will not be any tax saving if the couple equalise their estates but the first to die leaves their entire property to the other.

There is an advantage in making potentially exempt transfers of assets which are likely to increase in value over the next few years. Inheritance tax in the event of the transferor's death is calculated on the value of the property at the time the gift is made, not on its value at the time of death. Thus, the value of the property is effectively "frozen" and less inheritance tax will be payable. This value "freezing" will not occur if the donor continues to derive a benefit from the property given away. In such a case the reservation of benefit rules will apply and the property will be treated for inheritance tax purposes as part of the deceased's estate on death (see para.4-031 and following).

Grandparents who want to make provision for grandchildren may well consider doing so by lifetime gift in order to make funds available at an earlier date when they may be more useful and to reduce tax payable on their estates on death. Frequently they will prefer to transfer funds to a settlement for the benefit of the grandchildren rather than by outright gift. Such a transfer will be immediately chargeable to inheritance tax but, until the amount transferred exceeds the nil-rate band, the rate will be nil. However, there is the risk of dying within seven years in which case the loss of the nil-rate band will increase the tax payable on the death estate.

There are circumstances in which lifetime gifts are not advisable from an inheritance tax point of view.

(1) There is no advantage to making lifetime gifs if the donor is unlikely to survive seven years. It is sometimes suggested that there is an advantage if the donor survives three years as the rate of tax payable on the gift is reduced (taper relief) but this is only the case if the gift exceeds the nil-rate band. If the gift is within the nil-rate band, taper relief is of no benefit. Buying property eligible for business property relief such as shares quoted on the Alternative Investment Market (AIM) may be more attractive than making potentially exempt transfers as the assets only have to be owned for two years to obtain relief. Many companies offer schemes for taxpayers to invest in a variety of qualifying companies. Investment returns may be relatively modest given that the companies are, by definition, newer and smaller than those quoted on the Stock Exchange. However, for many people the inheritance tax benefits are the major concern.

(2) The residence nil-rate band (RNRB) is not normally available where a residence is given to lineal descendants by lifetime transfer although there is a downsizing allowance where property is disposed of on or after 8 July 2015. However, the allowance is limited to the value of assets left to lineal descendants.

Example 1

Jess gives her house (value £1 million) to her children in June 2017. She goes into care and her remaining assets are virtually exhausted on care home fees. She dies in May 2020 with an estate of £10,000 all of which she leaves to her children.

The transfer of the house is chargeable to inheritance tax at the full death rates because she died within three years of making it.

She is entitled to a downsizing allowance but it is limited to the £10,000 she leaves her children. Had she kept the house and left it to the children, she would have been entitled to RNRB of £175,000.

Capital gains tax

In view of the fact that capital gains tax is not paid on death and the donor acquires the property at its market value at death, lifetime gifts are apparently less advantageous. However, exemptions or reliefs may in many circumstances mean that no capital gains tax is actually payable, so that the gift can be made if other considerations make the disposition advisable. **21-026**

Where business asset disposal relief or investor's relief is available gifts of qualifying assets can be made at the attractive 10 per cent rate. See para.5-015 and following.

Hold-over relief is not available on potentially exempt transfers but is available under TCGA 1992 s.260 where a transfer is chargeable to inheritance tax. Hence lifetime transfers to relevant property settlements will attract hold-over relief (unless the settlement is settlor interested). See para.7-047.

Passing on a Business

21-027 The proprietor of a business should give careful consideration to what provision they wish to make for the continuation of the business after their death. It will often be preferable to do this by lifetime action rather than by will.

For example, if the business is run through a company, consideration should be given to the possible alteration of the articles so as to provide for the company purchasing its own shares and/or for rights of pre-emption in respect of these shares. If the client has at least 75 per cent of the votes, changes can be made unilaterally. If their share of the votes is lower, other shareholders will have to agree.

If the business is a partnership some provision should be made for succession to the deceased partner's interest by the remaining partners or by the deceased partner's relatives or for the realisation of the value of the interest when the partner dies or retires.

In making such arrangements taxation must be taken into account. It is important, however, that a tax-effective disposition should not be made if it conflicts with more general commercial considerations. Business property is favourably treated for tax purposes. A gift of a business or an interest in a business is eligible for inheritance tax business property relief (see para.4-072 and following) which may in itself produce a large saving in the tax payable. However, planning in advance may produce further savings.

Provision may be made in a partnership agreement for automatic accrual of goodwill. This means that when a partner dies their interest in the goodwill passes automatically to the other partners. Clearly this automatic accrual reduces the partner's interest in the goodwill and the value of the estate on death. To the extent that consideration in money or money's worth was given for the accrual clause, the entry into the clause will not be a transfer of value for inheritance tax purposes. There may be some difficulty in showing that consideration was given for such an accrual clause in the case of a family partnership. However, an estate duty case (*Attorney General v Boden* (1912)), which is generally considered still to be relevant, held that an agreement to work for the business is consideration in money or money's worth.

An option granted (for money or money's worth) to purchase goodwill at a fixed price may also give rise to a tax saving. The value of the goodwill to the partner on death is the price that the estate will be paid on the exercise of the option. An agreement that a partner's share *must* be purchased on death is not advisable as HMRC argues that this contract of sale may disentitle the deceased partner to the business property relief (see Statement of Practice 12/80, 13 October 1980).

HMRC accepts that automatic accruer clauses (where the share of a deceased partner passes automatically to the surviving partners in return for a payment either on valuation or in accordance with a formula) do not constitute binding contracts for sale and that neither do option arrangements (see *Law Society Gazette*, 4 September 1996, p.35).

Where a business is run as a company, there will frequently be pre-emption rights allowing the other shareholders a right to buy at a price fixed by, or to be fixed, in accordance with the company's articles of association. Such a pre-emption right is an option so that the same considerations apply as in the case of a partner's option to purchase goodwill.

4. WHY MAKE A WILL?

To avoid the application of the intestacy rules

As we explained in Ch.3, the property of a person who dies without making a will passes according to a strict legal order. A person who dies intestate, therefore, has no control over who are to be the recipients of their estate and so cannot benefit friends or charities without making a will. **21-028**

Persons who are married or in a civil partnership will usually want their property to pass to their spouse or civil partner, but it is only in the case of small estates that the whole of the estate will necessarily pass in this way under the intestacy rules. If the estate is larger and the deceased is survived by a spouse or civil partner and issue, the spouse or civil partner will take personal chattels, a statutory legacy of £70,000 (in the case of deaths on or after 6 February 2020) and only half the rest. A portion of the estate will go to the children, with a charge to inheritance tax if their share exceeds the available nil-rate band and the spouse may have insufficient funds to maintain an existing standard of living. While a variation may in some cases provide a solution, it is clearly more desirable to prevent the problem ever arising. A beneficiary who is under 18 cannot give up an interest in an estate; a parent or guardian cannot do so on behalf of a minor. Such a situation can be difficult to deal with. The surviving spouse often has to threaten a claim under the Inheritance (Provision for Family and Dependants) Act 1975 which can then be compromised.

Without a will clients cannot ensure that their wishes as to the disposition of their property will be respected; although, even with a will, there is the possibility of a relative or other dependant bringing a claim under the Inheritance (Provision for Family and Dependants) Act 1975.

Even though a client is satisfied with the general disposition of property under the intestacy rules, if they want to ensure that a particular item is to pass to one of the people specified in the intestacy rules, this can be only done by will. Furthermore, clients may wish to demonstrate expressly that they are happy for their property to pass to the persons who would be entitled under the intestacy rules by making a will in their favour. When making wills for cohabiting couples the solicitor should warn the couple that a subsequent marriage will revoke the will.

Appointment of personal representatives and trustees

In a will, a testator can make a choice of executors and trustees, whereas on intestacy the personal representatives are determined by r.22 of the Non-Contentious Probate Rules 1987 (SI 1987/2024) (see para.8-017). If a will is made, it is possible for the testator to choose persons who are suitable and who are likely to be willing to act. **21-029**

An executor's authority dates from death, whereas an administrator's dates only from the grant of representation; the appointment of an executor may, therefore, facilitate the administration of the estate.

Appointment of guardians

21-030 Testators are often concerned to provide appropriate care for their children particularly in the case of single, divorced or separated parents. Guardians can be appointed in the will. However, where, as is usually the case, the surviving spouse or civil partner has joint parental responsibility with the deceased, the appointment of the guardian will not take effect unless the surviving parent dies while the child is still at the minor. If that happens the guardian appointed by the first to die will act jointly with any guardian appointed by the survivor. This may not be desirable, so it is common to provide that an appointment is only to take effect if the other parent is already dead.

It is advisable to include an express appointment since this will ensure that the testator gives thought to whom to appoint. A client who proposes to appoint a guardian should consult the prospective guardian as to whether or not they are willing to act. The question of finance for the guardian should be considered. Guardians are dealt with more fully in para.22-022 and following.

It is not necessary to make a will to appoint a guardian. Guardians can also be appointed in any written document which is signed and dated. However, a will is a convenient place to do it.

Extension of statutory powers

21-031 If a will is made, additional powers can be conferred on personal representatives and trustees which will facilitate the administration. These powers are considered in para.22-046 and following.

Directions as to burial and disposal of body

Introduction

21-032 If the testator has special wishes as to burial or cremation these can be included in the will. However, as the will may not be looked at in time, it is much more sensible to communicate any particular wishes separately.

Various people had rights and duties in relation to a dead body. The deceased's personal representatives have the right to determine how and where the body should be disposed, even where other family members object.

Where personal representatives have not been appointed, the person with the best right to the grant takes precedence.

The court has the power, under the Senior Courts Act 1981 s.116, to appoint as administrator some person other than the person who would have the best right. Section 116 requires an answer to two questions: whether there are special circumstances which might displace the order of priority; and whether it is -necessary or expedient by reason of those special circumstances to displace the normal order of priority. The situations where it is appropriate to displace the order of priority for this purpose will be very rare: see *Buchanan v Milton* (1999).

The court also has an inherent jurisdiction to determine who is responsible for the burial. In *Anstey v Mundle* (2016) Klein J was asked to exercise the s.116 jurisdiction. However, he was concerned that the section was not appropriate because he was not being asked to pass over the person who would otherwise be entitled to a grant. Rather he was being asked to select, for the purposes of the limited grant to arrange the funeral, one of the people who would otherwise be entitled to a grant. He considered, and the parties agreed, that the court has, in appropriate circumstances, an inherent jurisdiction to determine who should be responsible for arranging the disposal of a body. He preferred to rest his decision on the court's inherent jurisdiction.

Although personal representatives will normally want to give effect to the deceased's wishes, they are not required to follow the deceased's wishes, as individuals have no property in their bodies after their death (*Williams v Williams* (1882)). In *Burrows v HM Coroner for Preston & McManus* (2008) Cranston J suggested that the proposition that the views of a deceased person can be ignored was no longer good law in the light of decisions of the European Courts of Human Rights that the views of a deceased person as to funeral arrangements and the disposal of his or her body must be taken into account. He suggested that this was easily accommodated within domestic law by regarding the deceased's wishes as a special circumstance in terms of s.116 of the Act. However, in *Ibuna v Arroyo* (2012) Peter Smith J expressly doubted this. The established law in England is that the executor has the primary duty to dispose of the body and is entitled to have regard to the expression made by the deceased but is not bound by them. Given that principle, there is no room for any post-mortem application of human rights in relation to a body as if it had some independent right to be heard.

It may not be possible to identify of the person with the best right to a grant without litigation. In *University Hospital Lewisham NHS Trust v Hamuth* (2006) there was a dispute over the validity of the will. The executor of the disputed will proposed to follow the instructions in the will and cremate the body while the family wanted a burial in the family plot. The body was in the mortuary of the NHS trust and Hart J held that, there being no way of resolving the dispute as to the validity of the will within an acceptable time period, the decision as to the appropriate arrangements for the disposal of the body had to be left to the NHS trust as the person currently in lawful possession of the body.

Alternative burials

Some people consider "alternative burials" in woods, fields or gardens. They **21-033**
must obtain the consent of the relevant local authority. One of the most popular alternatives to traditional burials and cremations are those in woodland or nature reserve burial grounds. There are a number of commercial sites opening around the country, promoting eco-friendly funerals and more informal ceremonies. At woodland burial grounds relatives may be able to plant a tree to mark the site either on or near the grave. At nature reserve burial grounds, which can be wild flower meadows or pastures, graves are either unmarked or may be marked by a small wooden plaque that will rot away naturally.

The burial of Princess Diana in the grounds at Althorp drew attention to the idea of being buried at home. However, an internment of this type requires a number of local authority permissions. Relatives will have to take advice from the Environment Agency which has a list of minimum distances from the site of a grave to water, cabling and wells or boreholes. It is not necessary to apply for planning permission to bury up to two people in a back garden although permission would be required to bury any more. There is a requirement to record the burial on the deeds to the property, in accordance with the Registration of Burials Act 1864. A location map must be attached to the deed to confirm the position of the grave and details of the name of the deceased, age, date and place of death should be recorded. This will reduce the potential -complication of the police being called if human remains are discovered during future garden maintenance or building work. There are obvious future problems, e.g. who would want to buy a property with a body in the garden? A certificate for burial issued by the Coroner or Registrar of Birth and Deaths (called the green disposal) will have to be obtained and any other procedural matters of the Registrar satisfied. The detachable section of this certificate needs to be completed and returned to the Registrar by the person who is arranging the burial.

There are a number of organisations which provide advice on secular funerals and "green" burials. See the British Humanist Association website which has publications on secular funerals and provides advice on non-religious funerals. See also the Natural Death Centre website which has a list of natural burial grounds.

Many people are happy that their organs should be taken after their death and used as transplants to help others. A rather smaller number are willing to donate their bodies to be used for anatomical examination and research.

The Human Tissue Act 2004 (HTA 2004) came fully into force on 1 September 2006 and replaces all previous legislation in this area. It introduces a new legislative framework making consent the fundamental principle underpinning the lawful storage and use of human bodies and the removal, storage and use of relevant material from the bodies of deceased persons. The type of consent and the requirements in relation to it vary according to the purpose for which the relevant material is used or stored. The possible purposes listed in HTA 2004 Sch.1 include, amongst others, anatomical examination, public display, research in connection with the functioning of the human body, transplantation, education or training relating to human health.

Consent for the donation of a body or relevant material for anatomical examination or public display differs from that required for transplantation. It can only be given by the individual who has chosen to donate. It cannot be given by anyone else on their behalf (HTA 2004 s.3). The consent must be in writing and is valid only if it is:

(a) signed by the person concerned in the presence of at least one witness who attests the signature;
(b) signed at the direction of the person concerned, in his presence and in the presence of at least one witness who attests the signature; or
(c) contained in a valid will of the person concerned.

Consent for other purposes, for example organ donation, does not have to be in writing although it is, of course, advisable for the avoidance of doubt. Donor cards are useful but the most effective method is registration on the NHS Organ Donor Register (see *https://www.organdonation.nhs.uk/register-to-donate/* [Accessed 6 March 2020]). As an alternative, a person can appoint a "nominated representative" under HTA 2004 s.4 to represent him after his death in relation to consent for any purpose other than anatomical examination. The nominated representative's consent cannot be overridden by other individuals including family members.

As from 1 December 2015 the Human Transplantation (Wales) Act 2013 provides that, in the absence of express provision in relation to consent, adults with capacity will, in most cases, be deemed to have given consent. Similarly in Northern Ireland from 1 June 2023 consent is deemed to have been given unless the person has registered a decision not to donate or is in an excluded group. These are minors and people lacking capacity to understand the change in law, visitors to Northern Ireland and temporary residents. Scotland has operated an opt-out system since 26 March 2021 with consent deemed to have been given, unless opt-out decision is registered on the NHS Organ Donor Register or the deceased was in an excluded group. These are adults without capacity to understand the deemed authorisation law, adults who have lived in Scotland for less than 12 months before their death and children under the age of 16.

Advance decisions or "living wills"

It is never lawful to take active steps to cause or accelerate death. Even where a person wishes to die, anyone offering assistance will be guilty of complicity in suicide under the Suicide Act 1961 s.2 (see *R. (on the application of Pretty) v DPP* (2002)). **21-034**

However, in certain circumstances it is lawful to withhold life-sustaining treatment such as artificial feeding and ventilation without which the patient will die (see *Airedale Trust v Bland* (1993)). A Practice Note was issued in 1996, *Official Solicitor: Vegetative State* (1996), which dealt with the procedure to be followed in applications for the withdrawal of artificial feeding and hydration. This Practice Note has been superseded by *Official Solicitor: Declaratory Proceedings: Medical And Welfare Decisions For Adults Who Lack Capacity* (2006). It combines the guidance given in earlier practice notes, and extends it to a wider range of medical and welfare disputes leading to litigation. It states that a directive given by the patient refusing or otherwise making decisions about treatment, if made and not revoked at a time when the patient had capacity, and if directed to the situation which in fact arises, is as binding a decision as it would have been if made at the time the question arises. However, where it is proposed to implement the terms of a directive in a manner which may lead to death or serious irreparable harm, the matter should be referred to the court.

It is becoming increasingly common for people to want to make advance decisions (sometimes referred to as "living wills") stating that in the event of a loss of mental capacity they do not wish to be given medical treatment for any life-threatening illness. Such a statement should not be incorporated into a will but should be kept separately. Close relatives should be informed of the existence and whereabouts of the statement.

Section 25 of the Mental Capacity Act 2005 recognised the validity of an advance decision for the first time. To be valid the advance decision must be applicable to the treatment proposed. The person making it can withdraw it any time (while they have capacity). An advance decision is not applicable to the treatment in question if, inter alia, any circumstances specified in the advance decision are absent, or there are reasonable grounds for believing that circumstances exist which the person making the advance decision did not anticipate at the time of the advance decision and which would have affected their decision had they anticipated them. This might include advances in medical treatment. If, as is usually the case, the decision relates to life-sustaining treatment, the following conditions must be satisfied. The decision must:

(a) be in writing:
  - (i) signed by the maker or by another person in their presence and by their direction;
  - (ii) the signature must be made or acknowledged in the presence of a witness;
  - (iii) the witness must sign to acknowledge in the presence of the maker; and

(b) state that it is to apply to that treatment even if life is at risk.

Many organisations have produced templates for living wills. A good example is that produced by Compassion in Dying. This allows individuals to tailor-make an advance decision refusing life-sustaining treatment if they are suffering from specified conditions.

It is necessary to be very specific in the terms of such a document. In *Re B: Consent to Treatment: Capacity* (2002) Ms B wrote a living will which stated that should the time come when she was unable to give instructions, she wished for treatment to be withdrawn if she was suffering from a life-threatening condition, permanent mental impairment or permanent unconsciousness. As a result of a ruptured blood vessel in her neck she was left paralysed from the neck down.

Her living will was not appropriate to the circumstances of her illness and the medical staff refused to withdraw treatment. She was able to give instructions that she did not wish treatment to continue but the medical staff questioned her mental capacity. The Court of Appeal found that Ms B possessed the requisite mental capacity to make decisions regarding her treatment and, thus, the administration of artificial respiration by the trust against her wishes amounted to an unlawful trespass. She was then able to withdraw consent to future treatment.

It is imperative that the requirements of s.25 are complied with. In *Re D (Withdrawal of Treatment)* (2012), D, faced with the prospect of surgery, which frightened him very much, had discussions with friends and family and, in particular, with his sister-in-law, G, to whom he gave a signed letter stating clearly that he refused any medical treatment of an invasive nature which would merely extend a reduced quality of life. He said that by "reduced quality of life" he meant one where his life would be one of a significantly reduced quality, with little or no hope of any meaningful recovery and where he would be in a nursing home/care home with little or no independence. Sadly, he suffered irreversible brain damage as a result of the operation and was left in an irreversible vegetative state. His letter was not valid under s.25 because it was not witnessed. As a result an application to court had to be made and D had to suffer several months of artificial nutrition and hydration.

In a lasting power of attorney dealing with health and welfare the donor can authorise the attorney to make decisions about refusing treatment even if the treatment is life sustaining. An advance decision will not be effective if the person making it later creates a lasting power of attorney which confers authority on the donee (or, if more than one, any of them) to give or refuse consent to the treatment to which the advance decision relates.

Tax considerations

21-035 The tax advantages to be gained from a carefully drafted will should be drawn to the testator's attention.

Private client practitioners have had a number of significant changes in legislation to deal with in recent years. It is important that they make clear to clients that any will prepared with a view to saving tax needs to be reviewed if there are major changes in tax legislation. It is also important to make clear that the solicitor is not taking on the responsibility of contacting the client. The solicitor may wish to contact the client as a matter of marketing, but it is normally undesirable to have an obligation to do so.

The normal retainer for drafting a will does not extend beyond the preparation of a draft will for the client to consider (see *Atkins v Dunn-Baker* (2004)) but, of course this may be varied by agreement.

CHAPTER TWENTY-TWO

PLANNING AND DRAFTING A WILL

1. INTRODUCTION

Taking instructions

When preparing a will for a client, a personal interview is usually desirable. The object of the interview is to obtain, in as short a time as possible, all the information needed to prepare the will. **22-001**

It is often helpful to have a checklist for taking instructions so that none of the information required is forgotten and no further correspondence or meetings are required. If the checklist is in the form of a questionnaire it may be possible for other members of the firm to use it to draft the will if necessary. An example of a simple checklist is included in the Appendix.

Checklists should include space for comment on the client's apparent capacity to make a will and their reasons for leaving the property in the way they have chosen. This is useful if questions are asked after the death about capacity, knowledge and approval of the contents and undue influence.

Clients may want advice on possible action that can be taken during their lifetime to arrange financial and business affairs sensibly. To advise properly, it is necessary to establish what property the client owns and whether there is any property (such as joint property or insurance policies) which will pass independently of the will.

If the testator is married or has a civil partner, it is advisable for the testator's spouse or civil partner to make a will at the same time. The reason for this is that thought can then be given to the ultimate destination of their respective estates.

When taking instructions from the client, record (on the questionnaire, if used) names and addresses for the testator, the executor(s), and the beneficiaries and, where relevant, any testamentary guardian(s) or trustee(s). Make sure that the details of the beneficiaries are correct—this is particularly important in the case of institutions, such as charities. Where specific items of property are dealt with in the will, a sufficient description is required so that they can be identified. It is important to avoid errors in description which may cause a gift to fail or necessitate applications to court to establish the correct meaning of a gift.

Types of disposition

Dispositions of property in a will are basically of three types—specific gifts, general legacies and gifts of residue. Testators should be encouraged to think carefully about the purpose of each intended gift. If they want a particular person to have a particular asset, then a specific gift is likely to be suitable (although they should **22-002** be warned that the gift will be adeemed if the property is sold or changed in nature). A substitutional gift can be included to deal with the possibility of ademption but fixing the value is difficult.

If testators want a particular person to have a fixed amount of money, then a general (pecuniary) legacy is suitable. A residuary gift is likely to be most suitable for the major beneficiary or beneficiaries of the estate. A residuary gift should always be included in a will so as to avoid the possibility of a partial intestacy. For the same reason, the testator should consider the possibility that the residuary beneficiary may predecease them and should consider whether they wish to include a substitutional beneficiary. Where a testator wants to benefit several people, it may be preferable to divide the estate proportionally rather than giving some specific or general legacies and some residue. Changes in the value or composition of the estate may mean that residuary beneficiaries take much less or much more than was originally intended.

The choice of dispositions will largely depend on the testator's family circumstances. Those with substantial estates may choose to leave the whole (or virtually the whole) of their estate to a discretionary trust with a wide class of beneficiaries on the basis that the trustees can review the needs of the potential beneficiaries and the tax legislation in force at the date of death and appoint the property appropriately. Provided appointments are made within two years of death s.144 of the IHTA 1984 will ensure that the appointments will be treated as taking effect on death for inheritance tax purposes (see para.19-029 and following).

Other testators may prefer more control over the disposition of their estates.

Options for married couples and civil partners with children

(a) All to spouse or civil partner

22-003 A will which leaves everything to the testator's spouse or civil partner will ensure that the survivor is provided for as far as possible. However, the testator has no control over the ultimate destination of the property and must trust the survivor to make appropriate dispositions. The combined estates are at risk of erosion through care home fees. There is a danger of accidental disinheritance of children where a surviving spouse remarries without realising that marriage automatically revokes an earlier will. If, because of the size of the estate, inheritance tax is a consideration the following points should be borne in mind:

- (i) no tax will be payable on the testator's death (since the spouse or civil partner exemption is available); and
- (ii) the surviving spouse or civil partner will take the benefit of any unused nil-rate band and residence nil rate band of the first to die: see para.4-015 and following;
- (iii) leaving everything to the survivor estate may mean that it exceeds the taper threshold of £2 million meaning that the residence nil-rate band is reduced or lost on the second death: see para.4-021.

(b) Spouse or civil partner for life remainder to children

With this type of disposition the testator retains control over the ultimate destination of the property. However, since the survivor is entitled only to the income from the property, they may have insufficient funds available; this problem can be alleviated if the trustees are given power to advance or lend capital to the survivor. It is usual to give the trustees overriding powers to terminate the life interest, accelerating the remainder interests. This is useful where the survivor no longer needs the income as if it is accumulated, it will simply increase the inheritance tax value of the estate. Many life interests are drafted with additional flexibility allowing the trustees to override both the life interests and the remainder interests and to appoint capital amongst a class of discretionary beneficiaries. This increases flexibility. The testator should leave a letter of wishes indicating his priorities; are the needs of the surviving spouse or civil partner to be of paramount concern or are the trustees to hold a balance between the different beneficiaries?

The inheritance tax consequences are virtually the same as in the case of an outright gift (since the survivor has an immediate post-death interest in possession in the settled property and the spouse exemption is therefore available).

There is a potential problem in relation to the residence nil-rate band where a residence or interest in a residence is left on life interest trusts in this way. The residence nil-rate band can only be set against the residence held on trust if lineal descendants of the beneficiary with the life interest are beneficially entitled to the residential property when the life tenant dies (see IHTA 1984 s.8J(5)). If the trustees have overriding powers which can be exercised after the life tenant's death to appoint the property away from the lineal descendants amongst a discretionary class, the lineal descendants are not "entitled" and the residence nil-rate band is not available.

Example 1

Wilma died in 2016 leaving her half of the matrimonial home to her husband, Harry, on flexible life interest trusts and then to their children absolutely. She left the rest of her estate to Harry absolutely. The trusts allow the trustees to apply capital for Harry's benefit and give them overriding powers which can be exercised at any time to appoint capital and income amongst a discretionary class of beneficiaries.

Harry dies in June 2024 when the former matrimonial home is valued at £600,000. His other assets are worth £1 million and all pass to his children absolutely.

Harry's estate benefits from Wilma's transferred nil-rate band. His own residence nil-rate band will be £175,000 and he has the benefit of Wilma's transferred residence nil-rate band which will also be £175,000.

He can set the combined residence nil-rate bands against his own half of the house (£300,000) but he cannot set any part against the half of the house held in the trust because his lineal descendants are not entitled at the date of his death. The result is that £50,000 of residence nil-rate band is lost.

Had the problem been appreciated before Harry's death the trustees could have released their overriding powers in relation to the residence completely or limited their possible exercise to Harry's lifetime. In either case the children would then be beneficially entitled to the residence on Harry's death.

If drafting a will containing a life interest of a residence or an interest in a residence where it is desired to obtain the benefit of the residence nil-rate band and to include overriding powers, either:

(1) limit the exercise of the overriding powers to the lifetime of the survivor (but this sacrifices flexibility); or
(2) create two life interest trusts, one for the residence or interest in a residence where the trustees cannot exercise overriding powers after the death of the

survivor and a second one for the rest of the estate where the overriding powers can be exercised after the survivor's death.

(c) Legacy to spouse or civil partner, residue to children

This type of disposition may be appropriate where the testator's spouse or civil partner is independently wealthy but should always be viewed with a certain amount of caution. Changed circumstances and/or inflation may make the provision for the survivor by means of a legacy quite inadequate in the future. The spouse or civil partner exemption for inheritance tax is lost, except to the extent of the legacy, but the children take a benefit from the estate at an earlier stage.

(d) Legacy to children, residue to spouse or civil partner

Like the gift discussed at (c) above, this type of disposition has the advantage of making some provision for the children immediately. The legacy should not, of course, be so large as to leave the surviving spouse with insufficient funds. Inflation and changed circumstances make it difficult to fix a "safe" amount.

There may be inheritance tax advantages with this type of gift. The spouse or civil partner exemption is lost to the extent of the legacy. However, there will be no tax payable until the nil-rate band is exhausted. Some provision can, thus, be made for the children immediately without an inheritance tax liability.

It is fairly common to give the children a legacy of "such amount as can pass at the date of my death without payment of inheritance tax". This is often referred to as a nil-rate band legacy. It is worded as it is so that, if the deceased has used up some of his nil-rate band by the time of death, only an amount equivalent to the unused portion will pass. The size of such a legacy obviously fluctuates in line with changes made to the value of the nil-rate band by successive governments. It may be increased where transferable nil-rate band and downsizing allowance is available and where property eligible for 100 per cent relief is included in the estate (see IHTA 1984 s.39A discussed below). Clients may not be comfortable with the idea of such a variable legacy.

If the deceased has the benefit of the whole or part of an unused nil-rate band of their predeceased spouse or civil partner, the size of their nil-rate band is increased by the amount transferred from the predeceased partner (see *Loring v Woodland Trust* (2014) which decided that this was the clear effect of the wording of IHTA 1984 s.8A). However, the additional nil-rate band is transferred only if it is claimed. The gift should therefore include a direction as to whether or not the personal representatives are required to claim it. Depending on the identity of the legatees and the executors, it may or may not be in their personal interest to claim the addition.

Example 2

Taliq leaves a legacy equal to the most that can pass without payment of inheritance tax to his children and the residue to his second wife. His estate is £1 million. His first wife died leaving Taliq everything so there is a full additional nil-rate band available for transfer.

If the children are the executors, they will want to claim the transferred nil-rate band. However, if the second wife is the executor, she is unlikely to want to do so as it will reduce the amount she takes.

A nil-rate band legacy of this type will not be increased as a result of the residence nil-rate band This is because the residence nil-rate band is only available where the lineal descendants are inheriting a residence or interest in a residence not where they are inheriting a cash sum. However, where a person disposes of a residence or interest in a residence on or after 8 July 2015 either completely or by moving to a cheaper property, their estate becomes entitled to a downsizing allowance equal to the lost relievable amount (IHTA 1984 ss.8FA, 8FE). Where an estate is entitled to a downsizing allowance a gift of the most that can be passed without payment of inheritance tax will be increased if a downsizing allowance is available and claimed (IHTA 1984 s.8L). Because it has to be claimed, it is sensible to include a direction as to whether or not the personal representatives are required to claim it.

The client should be warned that the amount payable under a nil-rate band legacy can fluctuate enormously. The nil-rate band may be frozen for long periods; at the time of writing the nil-rate band threshold has not been increased since 2009. Alternatively, it may be significantly increased as happened with the introduction of the transferrable nil-rate band in 2007. The amount passing under the legacy will be reduced to nothing if the testator has no nil-rate band available (for example, because there are chargeable lifetime transfers and/or other gifts by will to non-exempt beneficiaries). See *Royal Commonwealth Society for the Blind v Beasant* (2021) for an example of a legacy reduced to nothing.

Where an estate contains property which attracts 100 per cent business or agricultural property relief, very large amounts can potentially pass under such a gift. This occurs if the property eligible for relief is not specifically disposed of. In such a case the benefit of the relief is apportioned through the estate (IHTA 1984 s.39A). The effect will be to increase the size of a legacy worded as passing the most that can be passed without payment of inheritance tax. If half the estate was eligible for 100 per cent relief, the size of a nil-rate band legacy would be doubled. For this reason it is usually preferable to make a specific gift of property which is or may be eligible for relief. Alternatively it is possible to impose a maximum limit on the size of the gift. See the second clause below.

Where the testator wants to give the maximum amount possible without a payment of inheritance tax suitable wording is as follows:

> "I GIVE the maximum amount which will not give rise to a charge to inheritance tax by reason of my death taking into account the benefit of any transferrable nil-rate band and any downsizing allowance to which my estate may be entitled.
>
> For the avoidance of doubt I DIRECT my Trustees to claim any transferred nil-rate band available under IHTA 1984 s.8A and any downsizing allowance available under IHTA 1984 s.8FA or FB or any provisions replacing them."

A testator may want to limit the size of a nil-rate band legacy to the value of a single nil-rate band. If so, the gift should be worded as

> "an amount equal to the upper limit of the nil per cent rate band in the table of rates in IHTA 1984 Schedule 1 at the date of my death or the maximum I can pass without payment of inheritance tax whichever is the lesser".

It is necessary to include the second alternative because if the gift is simply an amount equal to the nil rate band as specified in the legislation, inheritance tax will be payable if the testator has used any of his nil rate band, for example by making lifetime gifts.

(e) Nil-rate band discretionary trust, residue to spouse or civil partner

Given the problems of fluctuating amounts passing under a nil-rate band legacy, it will usually be preferable to leave the legacy to a discretionary trust rather than to legatees absolutely. This option allows testators to build into their wills a large element of flexibility as funds can be made available to spouse/civil partner and issue as circumstances require. If the trustees appoint funds within two years of the death, the appointment will be read back into the will under IHTA 1984 s.144 (see para.19-029 and following). The beneficiaries will normally include the spouse and civil partner and issue of the testator. The trustees can take into account the respective needs of the various beneficiaries as well as the value passing under the gift. Holding assets in a trust outside the estate of the surviving spouse has the following further advantages:

(a) the assets are protected in the event that the surviving spouse remarries, becomes bankrupt or goes into care;
(b) the estate of the survivor is reduced for inheritance tax purposes which may be significant if the estate is near the taper threshold for the purposes of the residence nil-rate band.

Use of precedents

22-004 Precedents are an invaluable aid to good will drafting. Sometimes a precedent may be available which is almost exactly what is required, but this is unusual. In all but the simplest cases it is likely that the precedent will have to be substantially amended. Before a precedent can be adapted for use in a particular case it is important to understand what the precedent was intended to do. For example, if a precedent was designed for use where a complicated settlement is being created it is unlikely to be of much use in drafting a will which makes a straightforward absolute gift of residue.

Older precedents should be viewed with some caution since they may deal with problems which are no longer relevant (such as capital transfer tax rules) and may not deal with problems resulting from new law (such as those arising from amendments to the inheritance tax treatment of trusts in 2006). So that the terminology used in different parts of the will is consistent, it is best to use precedents from one particular source as far as possible and to take care when combining two or more precedents.

Wills were traditionally drafted without punctuation to avoid errors which might affect the meaning. However, almost invariably those preparing wills today use punctuation as an aid to understanding.

To make reading a little easier it is usual to divide the will into numbered clauses and to capitalise the words which explain what the clause is for (so that clauses making gifts usually contain words such as "I GIVE", clauses appointing an executor usually contains the words, "I APPOINT" and clauses containing trusts usually contain the words "UPON TRUST").

Definitions are helpful. For example, where several executors or executors and trustees are appointed the words "hereinafter together called 'my Executors'" (or "my Trustees") can be included so that references later in the will can be made to those persons without setting out their names again. If the client wants to make a gift of the house they are living in, it is much easier call it "the Property" and to define it at "as any property in which I am living at the date of my death". It may be necessary to extend that definition. For example, if the intention is to obtain the residence nil-rate band for an estate, the gift might continue "or any property which I own at the date of my death or have a beneficial interest in and which I have used as a residence at any time during my ownership". This would ensure that the gift could take effect if the deceased had gone into care before death and the former residence was commercially let at that point. It is necessary to give the executors a right to select if there is more than one such property in the estate at death. The definition does not deal with the possibility of the deceased dying without a residence at all. It is preferable to deal separately with entitlement to a downsizing allowance.

It is good practice to capitalise the first letter of the word defined so that the reader can see more readily that it is a defined term (for example, "my Trustee" not "my trustee"). All definitions should be grouped together. They can either appear at the start of the will or as a schedule at the end.

Structure of a will

A will usually includes the following: **22-005**

(1) words of commencement;
(2) revocation clause;
(3) appointment of executors (and trustees and guardians if appropriate);
(4) specific gifts (if any);
(5) general legacies (if any);
(6) a gift of residue;
(7) extension of executors' and trustees' powers and declarations; and
(8) attestation clause.

In the rest of this chapter we will consider the drafting of the various parts of the will.

2. The Formal Parts

Introduction

Every professionally drafted will should have the words of commencement, a revocation clause, a date clause and an attestation clause. For the sake of convenience these formal parts are dealt with together in this section. If the testator owns property in one of the EU States that are signatories of the EU Succession Regulation (see para.22-009) it is likely to be appropriate to include a choice of national law. **22-006**

Commencement

The commencement of the will is intended to identify the person making the will. The testator's full name and address should be included. If the testator is known to own property in a name which is different from the full name or to use a name which is not the true and proper name, it is advisable to refer to this fact in the opening words of the will. The reason for this is that after the testator's death it will be clear that the grant of representation should refer to both names. **22-007**

A commonly used form of wording for the commencement of the will is "This is the Last Will and Testament of me [AB] [(also known as [CD])] of [address] [occupation]". If the will is made in expectation of the testator's marriage or civil partnership, it is necessary to incorporate suitable words (see para.2-049 and following).

If the testator owns property abroad it is often appropriate to make separate wills to deal with property in each jurisdiction. A will can be expressed to deal with "my worldwide assets apart from those in [named jurisdiction]" or it can be limited to deal only with "my assets in [named jurisdiction]". In the latter case it is important to identify the jurisdiction correctly. Failure to do so can lead to a partial intestacy. See for example *Robinson v The Royal Society* (2016) where the testator, having made a Swiss will dealing with his Swiss assets, instructed an English firm of solicitors to prepare a will dealing with his remaining assets. The most significant of these were bank accounts in Jersey and the Isle of Man. The will was expressed to be limited to assets in the UK. Unfortunately, the UK consists only of England and Wales, Scotland and Northern Ireland. It does not include the Channel Islands or the Isle of Man.

Revocation clause

22-008 In para.2-059 and following we explained that a later will revokes an earlier will to the extent that it is inconsistent. If the later will deals with the testator's entire estate, all earlier wills and codicils are revoked. Nevertheless, for the avoidance of any possible doubt, a revocation clause should be included in all professionally drafted wills, even if the solicitor believes the present will to be the only will the testator has ever made.

The revocation clause can be included in the commencement of the will but it is often set out as a separate clause. An appropriate form of wording is "I REVOKE all former wills and testamentary dispositions made by me".

If the testator already has wills dealing with foreign assets the revocation clause should state that it does not revoke wills dealing with assets in that jurisdiction or that it is limited to this jurisdiction. Be careful if limiting the scope of the will. The UK does not include the Channel Islands or the Isle of Man so a will limited to the UK is not effective to pass assets in those jurisdictions. In two cases where this mistake was made applications to court were made successfully to admit extrinsic evidence to allow "United Kingdom" to be interpreted in an extended way: see *Royal Society v Robinson* (2015) and *Partington v Rossiter* (2021). Even where the court is willing, further applications will be necessary to establish that the local court is willing to accept that interpretation.

Choice of law of succession

Need for European Succession Regulation

22-009 On 4 July 2012 the EU adopted the Succession Regulation (EU) No 650/2012 (the SR) most of which did not take effect until 17 August 2015.

The UK Government exercised its right not to opt in to the SR. Despite the UK's opt-out (and despite Brexit), the SR is still significant for UK private client practitioners and anyone resident in the SR Zone (all EU Member States other than Denmark, Ireland and the UK). Signatory states will recognise a choice made by nationals of non-signatory states.

The Regulation was intended to deal with the problem that different EU States have different rules of private international law that apply where a person dies with assets in more than one country: some countries work on the basis of habitual residence, some on nationality and some on domicile.

Example 3

Freda, who is domiciled and lives in England, owns a holiday home in France. On her death France would apply its rules under which the law of her habitual residence applies. We would apply our rules under which succession to her moveable property is governed by the domestic law of her domicile (England and Wales) but succession to her land is governed by lex situs (the law of the country in which it is situate). France would accept that our rules require French law to apply (sometimes referred to as the "*renvoi*").

That is a simple example involving only two countries. Situations can be very much more complicated.

Effect of a choice of law

Article 21.1 of the SR introduces a general rule which EU States that have adopted the SR will apply. Under art.21 the law applicable to succession is that of the habitual residence at the time of death, unless, exceptionally, the individual was "*manifestly more closely connected with another state*". **22-010**

As an alternative, art.22 of the SR provides that a person may choose the law of their nationality as the law to govern their succession as a whole.

"Article 22: Choice of law

(1) A person may choose as the law to govern his succession as a whole the law of the State whose nationality he possesses at the time of making the choice or at the time of death.

A person possessing multiple nationalities may choose the law of any of the States whose nationality he possesses at the time of making the choice or at the time of death.

(2) The choice shall be made expressly in a declaration in the form of a disposition upon death or shall be demonstrated by the terms of such a disposition

(3) The substantive validity of the act whereby the choice of law was made shall be governed by the chosen law."

Choosing the law of their nationality allows testators to achieve certainty if, for example, there is doubt (or may be doubt in the future) about their habitual residence, or whether they are manifestly more closely connected with another state.

The law that applies, whether by choice or by default, can be the law of a state that is not a signatory (art.20).

"Article 20: Universal application

Any law specified by this Regulation shall be applied whether or not it is the law of a Member State."

Article 34 provides that states which have signed up will not accept a *renvoi* where a choice of national law has been made under art.22. Hence. a choice of national law may mean that a UK testator can escape the forced heirship rules which apply in many civil law jurisdictions (but see paras 22-010 and 22-012).

In the case of "third states" where no choice has been made the law that they will apply is its private international law including any *renvoi*. Third states are states which are not Member States.

Advice produced by the European Notaries Association (Règlement [UE] 650/2012 sur les successions transfrontalières: Livret pratique a l'usage des notaires) includes an example of applying private international law and accepting a renvoi in relation to the estate of Madame Brown, an English woman, resident in London. She dies with land and other property in England, Germany and Italy and has not chosen the law of her nationality to govern her succession. The guidance states that German and Italian notaries should accept the renvoi and apply German and Italian law to her German and Italian land.

The effect of the SR therefore seems to be that an English client resident in a part of the UK but owning a property in a signatory state, say Italy, can choose the law of England and Wales to apply to their succession and Italy will recognise that choice. However, if no choice has been made, Italy will accept the *renvoi*. Hence, making a choice is a good idea.

There is an argument that when an EU State applies the law chosen by a national of another country, it is the private international law that applies rather than its domestic law. If that is correct, a person choosing the law of England and Wales to apply to their succession who owns land in France and Italy would find that under our private international law, the law governing succession to land would be that of France and Italy respectively. There are reports of some notaries (particularly in France) taking that view but this is far from universal.

One choice for the whole succession

22-011 The relevant law chosen must apply to the whole of the succession. It is not possible to have different succession laws applying to one estate.

"*Succession*" is basically what passes under a will. It does not include property passing by survivorship or community of property regimes. If a couple holds assets in a country under a "community of property" regime, the assets pass automatically to the survivor (as with our beneficial joint tenancy) so do not form part of the *succession*. The SR does not affect tax or administrative matters. Any issues relating to tax, for example, are therefore excluded and are still governed by the existing rules.

The choice is made in a disposition on death. It can be made expressly or impliedly. An express choice is made in a disposition on death. An implied choice may be demonstrated by the terms of a disposition on death. For example, a choice may be implied if the disposition on death refers to specific provisions of the law of the state of the testator's nationality, or otherwise mentions that law. It is clearly preferable to have an express choice.

Some practitioners take the view that because the election must affect the whole succession, only one will is permitted. This does not seem to follow. Provided both wills refer to a choice of national law, there should be no problem. There are good reasons for having separate wills (and as advice will be needed on the effect of local tax law, there should be no additional expense).

(1) It is likely to speed up the administration if there are two wills which can be dealt with side by side rather than having to prove one here and then get it recognised in the other jurisdiction. Note that if the foreign will is made after the UK will, the Probate Registry may require sight of it to make sure that it does not revoke the UK will. It may be helpful, therefore, to re-execute the UK will if a foreign will is made later.

(2) It may make life easier when dealing with the foreign assets to have a will in a form familiar to the local jurisdiction.
(3) Tax consequences may flow from the distribution of the estate in accordance with the chosen law. For example, a foreign jurisdiction may tax assets that pass to the testator's children at a lower rate than assets that pass to other relatives or to non-relatives. This may lead to a higher tax burden if forced heirship provisions are displaced by the chosen law.
(4) Most civil law jurisdictions do not recognise the office of personal representative and so will regard a will giving assets to executors to distribute to beneficiaries as involving two transfers with, potentially, two charges to tax.
(5) Similarly most civil law jurisdictions do not recognise trusts so a simpler form of will is preferable.

European developments

Article 35 does permit a limit to the application of foreign law if the application of such law is *"manifestly incompatible"* with the public policy of the country in which the legal action is brought. In such a case, the application of such provisions of the foreign law may be refused by the court hearing the case. This happened in Germany—*German Federal Court Decision IV ZR 110/21*. **22-012**

The testator had British citizenship and had lived in Germany for over 50 years. He had elected that English law should govern the succession to his whole estate under art.22 of the European Succession Regulation EU 650/2012. The plaintiff, who was the adopted son of the testator, was excluded from the succession by the Will, so claimed his fixed compulsory portion under German law. This right to a share is irrespective of financial resources and needs.

The lack of an equivalent right to a fixed compulsory share for spouses and children under English law was sufficient for the German Federal Court to decide that the choice of law of the deceased's nationality would not be recognised in Germany because it was against German public policy.

The court decided that a pre-requisite for the non-application of foreign law was a close domestic connection to Germany. If family members, subject to the protection afforded by German public policy, were mainly in Germany, this would provide evidence of a German connection. In this case the habitual residence of the deceased and the claimant before and at the time of death, the location of the estate and the citizenship of the claimant were all German.

In France, Loi no. 2021-1109 du 24 aout 2021 confortant les principes de la République came into force on 1 November 2021 and amends arts 913 and 921 of the French Civil Code, by providing for an increased protection of the rights of protected heirs in situations where the deceased or one of the deceased's heirs is either from a member state of the EU or a habitual resident of a member state of the EU. French notaries are under an obligation before distributing the estate to inform those forced heirs whose rights may be affected by the provisions of the testator's Will of their entitlement under this law. This law conflicts not only with the EU Succession Regulation but also with the decision of the Cour de Cassation and so is likely to be challenged in the French Courts. Until then, however, it is unclear whether any elections for national law in wills of UK nationals who fall within the terms of arts 913 and 921 will be effective.

Choice of governing law

22-013 The UK will not recognise a choice of law governing succession but has always recognised a choice of governing law. Such a clause determines the law to be applied to the construction of a will and should be included where a testator has strong links with, and assets in, another jurisdiction. In the absence of a choice of governing law clause, the matter will depend on the testator's domicile. Where there may be doubt as to a testator's domicile, it is essential to include a choice of governing law. If there is any ambiguity as to how the will is to be construed, the question of domicile will have to be settled which is likely to be expensive. See, for example, *Perdoni v Curati* (2012) where the testator (who was Italian by birth but who had lived most of his life in London) had an English will. Shortly before he died, he made an Italian will which did not contain a revocation clause nor a governing law clause. If Italian law governed construction, the later will revoked the whole of the earlier will. If the law of England and Wales governed construction, only those parts of the earlier will which were inconsistent with the later will were revoked. The answer depended on the testator's domicile and required a trip to the Court of Appeal to establish what it was.

The date clause

22-014 The date can be included in the commencement of the will, or at the end immediately before the attestation clause. It is more common to include the date at the end.

The date clause may be important in identifying which of a number of wills was the last or in identifying the subject matter of a gift. The usual form of words is "IN WITNESS of which I have set my hand to this my will the day of 20."

The attestation clause

22-015 The presence of a correctly drafted attestation clause will in most cases satisfy the court that the requirements of Wills Act 1837 s.9 as amended (see para.10-053), are satisfied. The absence of an attestation clause will lead the registrar to require evidence to prove due execution under the Non-Contentious Probate Rules 1987 (SI 1987/2024) r.12.

The two most common forms of attestation are as follows:

(a) The short form.

> "Signed by the above named [AB] in our joint presence and then by us in [his/hers]."

(b) The long form.

> "Signed by the above-named [AB] as [his/her] last will in the presence of us both present at the same time who at [his/her] request in [his/her] presence and in the presence of each other have hereunto subscribed our names as witnesses."

These clauses, implying as they do that the witnesses signed in each other's presence as well as in the presence of the testator, go beyond the strict wording of s.9 as amended but may reduce the possibility of the attestation being challenged after the death.

Where the testator suffers from some disability which would cast doubt on the validity of the will due to the suspected absence of knowledge and approval of the wording of the will, the forms of attestation clause set out, above should be amended. The purpose of the amendment is to indicate that the testator did in fact know and approve of the contents of the will.

Thus, if the testator is blind, illiterate or seriously ill the attestation clause should state that the will was read over to the testator and that he or she appeared to thoroughly understand and approve its contents.

If someone signs on the testator's behalf (as permitted by Wills Act 1837 s.9(a)), this fact should be stated in the clause together with a confirmation that the will was signed in the presence of, and at the direction of, the testator. The person signing may sign in their own name or that of the testator. Although not advisable as it may raise suspicions, a beneficiary can sign on behalf of the testator without losing benefits given by the will: see *Barrettt v Bem* (2012).

Illustrations of such clauses appear below.

(i) *Attestation clause where someone signs on behalf of the testator.*

> "Signed by me [AB] with the name of the above-named [testator] as [his/her] last will in [his/her] presence and by [his/her] direction and by us as witnesses who in the presence of [AB] and the above-named [testator] and in the presence of each other so subscribed our names."

(ii) *Attestation clause where the testator is unable to sign (and someone signs on behalf of the testator).*

> "Signed by [AB] with the name of the above-named [testator] as [his/her] last will (the will having been first explained to [him/her] when the said [testator] appeared thoroughly to understand and approve the contents thereof) in [his/her] presence and by [his/her] direction in the presence of us present at the same time who at [his/her] request in [his/her] presence and in the presence of each other have written our names as witnesses."

(iii) *Attestation clause where the testator is unable to sign and signs with a mark.*

> "Signed by the above-named [testator] as [his/her] last will with [his/her] mark [he/she] being unable to sign his/her name because [of illness/injury] (the will having been first explained to [him/her] by [name] when the [testator] appeared thoroughly to understand and approve the contents of the will) in [his/her] presence and by [his/her] direction in the presence of us present at the same time who at [his/her] request in [his/her] presence and in the presence of each other have written our names as witnesses."

Whenever the circumstances are such that, after the testator's death, there may be doubt as to his or her capacity or as to his or her knowledge and approval of the contents of the will, the will drafter should try to be present at execution and should make a full and careful file note both of the interview where instructions were taken and of execution. It may be desirable to obtain a report on the testator's mental and physical state from a medical practitioner.

3. Executors and Trustees

Introduction

When taking instructions for the drafting of the will, the testator's wishes must **22-016** be ascertained as to the persons who will administer the estate (the executors) and who will act as trustees of any trust created under the will.

It is often administratively convenient to appoint the same people to hold both offices, a common form of wording being "I APPOINT [AB] of [address and occupation] and [CD] of [address and occupation] to be the executors and trustees of this my will ('my Trustees' which expression shall where the context so admits include the trustees for the time being)." The final words are required to make it clear that any powers conferred on the trustees are not personal to the original trustees.

Appointments should not be made contingent on surviving the testator by a stated period as that will result in a period where there is no one able to act.

Number of executors and trustees

22-017 Any number of executors may be appointed but no more than four may take out the grant in respect of the same property. One executor will always suffice. However, two are often appointed in case one predeceases the testator or dies before completing the administration. Moreover, if the executors are also to be trustees, it is desirable to appoint two since two trustees (or a trust corporation) are required to give a good receipt for capital money.

The choice of appointees

Individuals

22-018 A testator may appoint an individual, a firm of solicitors, a bank or trust corporation. The testator must consider the relative merits of such appointees.

Testators frequently appoint friends or relatives to act as executors. Such an appointment has the advantage of ensuring the administration is completed by someone of whom the testator has personal knowledge and who will not charge for the work done. A disadvantage may be that the appointee lacks expertise, but there is nothing to prevent the appointee taking professional advice. However, the need for such advice may mean that the supposed advantage of cheapness is more apparent than real.

The testator has freedom of choice and so can appoint any person to act, including a bankrupt, a criminal, a minor or a person suffering from a mental or physical disability but there are limitations on who can actually take a grant (see para.8-003).

Further points must be considered when choosing individuals. The most important points are the appointees' ability to cope with the burdens of the office and their willingness to act. A commercially inexperienced person may find the problems of dealing with a complicated estate excessively onerous.

It may be appropriate to appoint a beneficiary as an executor. The beneficiary will have a personal interest in ensuring the estate is properly administered. However, the possibility of a conflict of interest may arise. If the only executor is a specific legatee, there may be a danger that the interests of the residuary beneficiary will be disregarded. Appointing several individuals may lead to disputes if they are unable to agree on the appropriate steps to be taken when dealing with the assets. If a beneficiary is appointed, it is usually necessary to include a clause authorising them to act even though they have a beneficial interest.

No matter how suitable the appointee may seem to be, if they are older than the testator, there is the probability of the executor predeceasing the testator. In this circumstance a substitutional appointment should be included in the will.

Professional advisers

The appointment of professional advisers, such as solicitors or accountants, has the advantage of ensuring that the administration is dealt with by experts who, frequently, will have a detailed knowledge of the estate and its assets. Such knowledge, together with their knowledge of estate administration and probate practice, may be invaluable when the estate is complex. The disadvantage of appointing professionals, as compared with individuals, is that the executors will have no personal interest in the estate and will charge for their services. **22-019**

When appointing solicitors or accountants as executors, although the testator may wish to appoint a particular person to act, problems will arise if that person dies, retires or leaves the firm. For this reason it is usual (subject to the testator's wishes) to appoint the firm to act rather than named individuals. Unless the will says otherwise, an appointment of a firm of solicitors is construed as an appointment of the partners in the firm at the date the will is made. Since partners may die, retire or leave the firm, it is advisable to provide expressly that appointment is of the partners in the firm at the date of death. It is possible that the firm may change its name or amalgamate with another firm and the testator may wish to consider making provision to cover this possibility. It is usual to express the wish that only two of the partners should take the grant, but this is not essential.

In the case of a Solicitors' Incorporated Practice (under the Solicitors' Incorporated Practice Rules 2001) care should be taken in drafting to ensure that the individual solicitors who are directors or members of the practice at the time of death are appointed. The practice itself cannot be appointed as it is not a trust corporation.

The appointment is not invalidated if the firm becomes a limited liability partnership. However, it is advisable to make specific provision to include this possibility. An example of a suitable form of appointment is:

> "I APPOINT the partners including salaried partners in the firm of [name] of [address] at the date of my death or of the firm which at that date has succeeded to and carries on their practice to be the executors and trustees of this will [('my Trustees')] and in the event of that firm having been incorporated as a limited company at the date of my death then I APPOINT the directors and shareholders at the date of my death to be the executors and trustees of my will [('my Trustees')] and I express the wish that two and two only of the partners shareholders and directors as the case may be shall act as my executors and trustees."

The words "including salaried partners" are included as otherwise it seems only profit-sharing partners will be included (at least in the case of a limited liability partnership (*Re Rogers (dec'd)* (2006)). In the case of an incorporated practice the probate registry consider the shareholders to be the equivalent of the partners. The inclusion of the words "the directors" allows members of the firm who are not shareholders to be appointed.

When professionals are preparing a will for a client, as a matter of good professional practice, they should make clear to the client that it is not necessary to appoint a professional and that a professional will charge. They should also explain the basis on which charges will be made. There is a Law Society Practice Note "*Appointment of a professional executor*" available on the Law Society website. See also the ethics guidance issued on 6 May 2014 (updated 25 November 2019) by the Solicitors Regulatory Authority: *Drafting and preparation of wills*, discussed at para.13-020.

Trust corporations—banks

22-020 Instead of or in addition to individuals and professional advisers it is possible to appoint corporations sole or trust corporations, such as the trustee department of one of the leading banks.

These institutions generally insist that their own standard appointment clause (which incorporates a charging clause) be inserted in the will otherwise they will refuse to act.

The testator should consider the level of costs such institutions are likely to charge. The appointment of a corporation may prove expensive since if difficulties arise the corporation may instruct solicitors to act on its behalf with the result that there may be an element of double charging. Trust corporations are unlikely to be willing to carry on the business of the deceased except briefly for the purpose of disposal.

The Public Trustee

22-021 The Public Trustee is an officer appointed by the Lord Chancellor under the Public Trustee Act 1906.

The Public Trustee may act as executor when requested to do so, and may also act as administrator of an estate of a deceased person (with or without a will), or as trustee of a trust whether as original or substitute trustee, usually only as a last resort, and in the interests of vulnerable individuals or persons under disability, or where there are differences between executors, trustees, or beneficiaries.

Consent to appointment should be obtained in advance.

4. GUARDIANS

Introduction

22-022 Testators with minor children should consider who will have the care of any minor children who survive them. The relevant law is contained in the Children Act 1989 as amended. The appointment of a guardian may be made by will or by writing signed and dated by the appointor (s.5(5)).

Parental responsibility

22-023 A parent with parental responsibility or an existing guardian may appoint a guardian.

Section 2 of the Children Act 1989 determines who has parental responsibility although the court has power to remove it.

An unmarried mother has parental responsibility for her child (s.2(2)).

Where a child's father and mother were married to each other at the time of his birth, they each have parental responsibility for the child (s.2(1)). A father has parental responsibility if he has been married to the mother at any time later than the date of conception even if he is not married to her at the time of the birth (s.2(3)).

The Human Fertilisation and Embryology Act 2008 (HFEA 2008) introduced the concept of second female parents where children are conceived using donated sperm or eggs. Section 2(1A) of the Children Act 1989 provides that where a child has a second female parent by virtue of HFEA 2008 s.42 the child's mother and the other female parent each have parental responsibility for the child. Under s.42 where the child's mother is in a civil partnership or same sex marriage at the date of the treatment, the spouse or civil partner is the child's parent unless it is shown that she did not consent to the treatment.

Where a child has a second female parent by virtue of HFEA 2008 s.43 the other female parent has parental responsibility if she is married to or the civil partner of the child's mother at the time of the child's birth, or was married to or the civil partner of the child's mother at any time starting with the date of the treatment even if she is not by the date of the birth. Under s.43 a woman is a second female parent if she and the mother agreed this in writing at the time of the treatment.

An unmarried father may acquire parental responsibility by becoming registered as the child's father, by court order or agreement with the child's mother (Children Act 1989 s.4 as amended by Adoption and Children Act 2002 s.111).

A woman who is a second female parent under HFEA 2008 s.43 and who has not been married to or a civil partner of the mother can acquire parental responsibility in the same way (Children Act 1989 s.4ZA, inserted by the Human Fertilisation and Embryology Act 2008).

If a child has two female "parents" the natural father's status is likely to be excluded from 26 April 2009 as a child can only legally have two parents.

In the case of surrogacy arrangements the birth mother (the one carrying the child) is the legal mother of the child and, if she is married, her husband is the legal father. From 6 April 2010 HFEA 2008 s.54 allows the intended parents (who must be married, civil partners or living as partners in "an enduring family relationship" and not within prohibited degrees of relationship) to apply for a "parental order" after the birth to re-designate the intended parents as the actual parents (see HFEA 2008 s.54).

When appointment takes effect

Under s.5(7) and (8) of the Children Act, an appointment by parent or guardian where there is a surviving parent with parental responsibility will not normally take effect until the death of the surviving parent. If the surviving parent also appoints a guardian, the two guardians will act together after the death of the surviving parent. This will often not be a satisfactory arrangement, so it is common for appointments of guardians to be worded to take effect only if there is no surviving parent. **22-024**

There is one case where an appointment would take effect immediately despite the existence of a surviving parent. This is where there is a child arrangement order in force in which the deceased was named as a person with whom the child was to live or the deceased was the child's only (or last surviving) special guardian. For example, H and W have been divorced for five years and there is a child arrangement order in force by which the children live with W; W dies and appoints X as guardian. X will become guardian on W's death and will share parental responsibility with H. In such circumstances H could apply to the court to have the guardianship terminated under s.6(7); the welfare of the child will be the court's paramount concern.

An appropriate form of words for an appointment under the Children Act in normal circumstances is:

> "I APPOINT [AB] of [address] and [CD] of [address] to be the guardians after the death of my [husband/wife] of any of my children who may then be minors."

If a residence order was in force in favour of the deceased parent, the appointment would be "to act jointly with [my husband/wife]".

When a testator is considering appointing guardians, the appointees should be consulted to ensure that they are willing to act. Where guardians are appointed, consideration should be given to the additional expenses that the guardians will incur. If there is a trust fund, the clients may wish to have persons other than the guardians as trustees. Ideally, the parents should leave a record of the circumstances in which they would be happy for funds to be made available to the guardians. It may be appropriate to extend the trustees' powers. For example, power could be given to the trustees to allow the trust's capital to be used to assist the guardians to purchase a larger house. The capital could be lent to the guardians at a low rate of interest; alternatively the money could be used to help fund a purchase of the property in the joint names of the guardians and the trust fund.

5. SPECIFIC GIFTS AND GENERAL LEGACIES

Introduction

22-025 When drafting specific gifts and general legacies, it is important to consider both the nature of the legacy and the status of the beneficiary (for example, particular problems may arise where the beneficiary is a charity or a minor).

Specific gifts

Introduction

22-026 A specific gift is one the wording of which distinguishes the gifted property from all other property belonging to the testator at the date of death.

Section 24 of the Wills Act 1837

22-027 Section 24 provides that, as regards property, the will "speaks from death" unless it expresses a contrary intention. The use of the word "my" coupled with a specific item (for example, "my piano") is often construed as showing such a contrary intention. However, if the word "my" is followed by a description of -property capable of increase or decrease, this is not usually construed as -contrary -intention so that, for example, a gift of "my collection of Dresden china" would be construed as a gift of the whole collection at the date of death.

Drafting specific gifts

22-028 It is important to ascertain the testator's wishes. The testator may wish to give a particular item owned at the date the will is made or may wish to give any item which corresponds to a particular description owned at the date of death.

If the testator wishes to give a particular item owned at the date of the will, the property must be carefully identified. This may be relatively easy where, for example, shares are involved but difficulties can arise where the gift is of personal chattels. Thus, a gift of "my gold ring" may give rise to problems if the testator owned several gold rings. A reference to provenance, a description or an insurance valuation may be helpful in identifying the particular ring given.

When taking instructions, the solicitor should explain to the client that a gift of a particular item owned at the date of the will suffers ademption if the item is sold, destroyed or changed in substance. The result of such ademption is that the beneficiary will get nothing. This may or may not be what the testator wishes.

If the testator wants the beneficiary to receive any item owned at the death corresponding to a particular description, suitable wording should be used. An example of such wording is,

> "I give to [AB] any motor car which I own at the date of my death."

In some cases, the testator may wish to give a particular item with a provision for a substitutional gift if that item is sold, destroyed or changed in substance. A suggested wording is

> "I GIVE to [AB] absolutely my grand piano or any other piano which has replaced it and which I own at the date of my death."

Such wording is not desirable where there may be several changes between the making of the will and the death (for example, where a testator makes a gift of shares) as it may prove difficult to identify the replacement assets accurately. In such a case it may be preferable for the testator to include a pecuniary legacy to be given in substitution of the original property, if that property is not owned at the date of death.

Where a client wants to be sure that certain individuals benefit under the will, a better solution is often to leave them shares of residue. Where some beneficiaries take specific items or pecuniary legacies and others take residue, the result can be an unfair distribution if the estate becomes larger or smaller between execution of the will and death. The residuary beneficiary may take more or less than was intended.

It is usually unwise to draft a gift of "*the house in which I am living at the date of my death*" in case the testator has had to go into care meaning that there is nothing to correspond with the terms of the gift.

Power to select

Specific legacies are often made as a way of passing a "keepsake" to a friend or **22-029**
relative. An outright gift of items of property causes no difficulty but if the testator wishes property to be shared between beneficiaries as they choose then various matters should be considered:

(a) the order of selection if more than one beneficiary has this right;
(b) the insertion of a time limit to avoid the executors' having to wait an unspecified length of time before the beneficiary or beneficiaries make up their minds;
(c) a procedure for resolution of disputes (for example by the exercise of the executors discretion);
(d) a gift over to a substitutional beneficiary in the event of a beneficiary predeceasing or the beneficiaries failing to choose all the items, as the case may be; and

(e) a limit on the value of items selected.

Another possibility is to give the items to a named individual and ask that person to distribute them in accordance with the deceased's wishes. Section 143 of the IHTA 1984 (discussed at para.19-028) provides that if the legatee carries out the deceased's wishes within two years of death, inheritance tax will be charged as if the property had been left in accordance with the wishes. HMRC's view is that the request need not be in writing, but it should be in sufficiently certain terms. If the meanings of the words "bequeathed" and "legatee" in s.143 are taken to be their technical legal meanings, s.143 is confined to gifts of personal property and does not apply to gifts of freehold land or of interests in freehold land.

There is some doubt as to the position if chattels are left to the executors to hold subject to a power to distribute them at their discretion within two years of the testator's death, with a non-binding request to give effect to the testator's wishes, and subject to any exercise of the power to hold the property as part of the residuary estate. Section 143 may not apply to such an arrangement, because the wording only seems to refer to a legatee who takes the property beneficially.

Mortgage, expenses and inheritance tax

22-030 **Mortgage** Where a gift is made of property which was charged during the testator's -lifetime with a mortgage or other debt the Administration of Estates Act 1925 s.35 provides that the property passes to the beneficiary subject to that debt unless the will provides otherwise. The effect of s.35 should, therefore, be explained to the testator so that if he or she wishes the beneficiary to take the property free of the debt, suitable wording can be included.

An example of such wording is

> "I GIVE to [AB] my leasehold property known as [address] free of all taxes and from any mortgage debt or other charge affecting it which I direct shall be paid out of my residuary estate."

In the case of a mortgage, a mortgage protection policy may have been taken out by the testator. The will drafter should, therefore, enquire whether or not such a policy exists so that the testator can give thought to the destination of the estate bearing in mind the existence of the policy (see para.15-010 and following).

22-031 **Expenses** Unless the will provides otherwise, specific beneficiaries bear any costs of insuring, packing and transporting of property left to them in a will. Just as, following an assent, specific legatees become entitled to any accrued profits as from the death by virtue of relation back, so they must bear the costs of upkeep, care and preservation of the relevant assets from the death: see *Re Pearce* [1909]. This should be explained to the testator who may not wish a specific beneficiary to bear the costs. This is especially likely where the nature of the gift or the circumstances of the beneficiary would result in high insurance or transportation costs being incurred, which the beneficiary might have difficulty meeting. Contrary provision in the will may ensure that the costs are borne by residue.

22-032 **"Free of tax"** Whenever the disposition of an estate may give rise to an inheritance tax liability, the testator should consider which beneficiaries should bear the burden. Inheritance tax on UK free estate which vests in the personal representatives is usually a testamentary expense borne by undisposed-of property (if any) or residue unless the will provides otherwise (see para.4-086 and following, for a discussion of the rules on "burden"). The draftsman may consider providing expressly that non-residuary gifts are to be "free of tax" so that the question of burden is brought to the testator's attention. The testator can then consider whether the disposition of the estate is suitable having regard to the burden of inheritance tax.

General legacies

Although a general legacy is usually a pecuniary legacy, it is also a gift of property which is not in any way distinguished from property of the same kind (for example, a gift of "100 shares in ABC Ltd"). If the testator does not own such property at death, the personal representatives will purchase property fulfilling the description. Unless there are special reasons for such a gift, a gift of money is usually more appropriate. **22-033**

6. Gifts of Residue

Introduction

Once the formal parts of the will and any specific or pecuniary legacies have been drafted, it is necessary to consider the drafting of the clause or clauses disposing of residue. The main objective of the will drafter in drafting such clauses is to ensure that the residue of the estate goes to the testator's intended beneficiaries. This will include consideration of whether substitutional beneficiaries should be included in case a primary beneficiary fails to achieve a vested interest and whether a survivorship provision is required. The will drafter should also consider how best to deal with the payment of debts and expenses (which will usually be paid out of residue). **22-034**

Payment of debts

The rules as to payment of debts of the estate were considered in Ch.15 where we saw that, unless there is undisposed of property, unsecured debts are, in most circumstances, payable out of residue. This will usually comply with the testator's wishes but, even so, it is usual to make express provision in a professionally drawn will. One way in which this is commonly done is by making the residuary gift subject to the payment of debts and other expenses. For example: **22-035**

> "I GIVE all the residue of my estate (out of which shall be paid my debts, funeral expenses and testamentary expenses) to [AB] of [address]."

Another way in which payment of debts can be provided for is by creating a trust, the first object of which is the payment of debts.

Where a debt of the estate is charged during the deceased's lifetime on specific property it will be payable out of that property unless the will shows a contrary intention (Administration of Estates Act 1925 s.35). Clauses, such as the one above which deal with the payment of debts generally, are not sufficient to require charged debts to be paid out of residue. If the intention is that charged debts should be paid out of residue then words such as "including any debts charged on specific property" should be added after the word "debts".

Payment of pecuniary legacies

22-036 The rules as to property available for payment of pecuniary legacies are considered at para.16-050 and following. They are complicated and, in order to avoid possible problems, it is desirable to direct that residue be held on trust for sale and proceeds used to pay debts and legacies. It is important to consider whether the residue is likely to be sufficient to cover the payment of debts, liabilities and legacies.

Inclusion of a trust

22-037 In all but the simplest cases a trust of residue should be included. A trust is advisable where the residue is to be divided between two or more beneficiaries or where minors may be entitled to residue. Before the Trusts of Land and Appointment of Trustees Act 1996 (the 1996 Act) an express trust for sale (with power to postpone sale) was generally employed so as to avoid the complication of the Settled Land Act 1925. The trustees of a "trust of land" as defined by the 1996 Act have all the powers of an absolute owner, including sale, so an express trust for sale is no longer necessary. However, if there is no land in the residuary estate, any trust created will fall outside the definition of a "trust of land" with the consequence that the statutory powers will not be available to the trustees. An express trust for sale may, therefore, be considered despite the 1996 Act. If such a trust is included it should include a power to postpone sale. If an express trust for sale is included and the residuary estate does in fact contain land, the trust will be a "trust of land" under the 1996 Act. An alternative approach is to create a trust of residue without a trust for sale but with a power of sale. Again this will be a "trust of land" if there is any land included in the residue. If there is no land, the trustees will be able to exercise their power of sale under the express power of sale in the will.

Personal representatives also have a power to sell the assets of the estate for purposes of administration under the Administration of Estates Act 1925 s.39.

Where a trust is created it will be an express trust "effected by will". So far as the Trust Register is concerned it will, initially, be excluded from the need to register on the Trust Register. However, if the administration of the estate is delayed and is still being administered when the two-year period ends, the personal representatives will have to register it. See paras 13-033 and 13-036 above.

Absolute gift of residue to one person

22-038 Where the residue is to be given to one person absolutely, the drafting of the will is quite straightforward. For example:

> "I GIVE the residue of my estate (out of which shall be paid my funeral and testamentary expenses and my debts) to [AB] of [address]."

The will drafter should consider whether to make a substitutional gift so as to prevent an intestacy if the intended residuary beneficiary predeceases and whether to include a survivorship clause (see para.22-043 and following).

Absolute gift of residue to more than one person

Named beneficiaries

22-039 If the residue is to be divided between two or more persons in equal shares, the following form may be used:

> "I GIVE the residue of my estate (out of which shall be paid my funeral and testamentary expenses and my debts) to [AB] of [address] and [CD] of [address] in equal shares."

If the shares are to be unequal the simplest technique is to divide the residue into a suitable number of equal parts and to say how many parts each beneficiary is to get making sure that the parts add up to the whole. For an example where this was not followed, see *Clarke v Brothwood* (2006).

Where residue is given "equally" or "in equal shares" and any of the residuary beneficiaries predecease, there will be a partial intestacy. It is, therefore, desirable to add words giving the lapsed share to the surviving beneficiaries or words making a substitutional gift of that share (for example, to the children of the deceased beneficiary). If it is intended that the residue is to be divided amongst the surviving beneficiaries, suitable wording of the whole clause would be:

> "I GIVE the residue of my estate (out of which shall be paid my funeral and testamentary expenses and my debts) to such of the following as survive me [by 28 days] and if more than one in equal shares [list names and addresses of beneficiaries]."

Difficulties may arise where some but not all of the beneficiaries are exempt. This is dealt with in para.4-095 and following.

Class gifts

Many gifts of residue to more than one person are gifts to a class of beneficiaries rather than to several named individuals. Most class gifts are gifts to a particular class of relative. The will drafter should explain the class closing rules to the testator and explain that they may artificially exclude certain unborn persons. They should also explain that the exclusion of the class closing rules is possible but may delay final distribution of the estate. **22-040**

A will drafter should consider carefully whether or not it is desirable to include words expressly limiting class gifts to persons *living at the testator's death*. Where there is an immediate gift to a class (for example, "to my grandchildren") the class closing rules apply (unless excluded). Their effect is that the class will close at the date of the testator's death and will include only those class members living or *en ventre sa mere* at that date (if there are no members living or *en ventre sa mere* at that date the class remains open indefinitely). This is likely to accord with the wishes of most testators since, although it will exclude any later born class members, it does allow the benefits of early distribution. Many precedents state expressly that such gifts are to be limited to persons "*living at the testator's death*". These words merely restate the relevant class closing rule but it is desirable to include them to ensure that the testator is aware of the position.

Where a gift to a class is contingent (for example, "to those of my grandchildren who reach 18") or deferred (for example, "to X for life and then to my grandchildren") the class closing rules apply (unless excluded). Their effect is, broadly speaking (and see para.17-025 and following, for a fuller discussion), that such a class will remain open until the first class member fulfils the contingency or until the life tenant dies and will include any persons born after the date of the testator's death and before the date of which the class closes. This is likely to accord with the wishes of most testators. Since any distribution is impossible until one person fulfils the contingency or until any life tenant dies, there is no point in closing the class until distribution is possible. If the words "*living at my death*" are included they limit the gift to persons alive or *en ventre sa mere* at the testator's death and exclude any born thereafter. Unless this is an accurate reflection of the testator's wishes it is desirable not to include the words.

Where a testator wants to keep the class open to include beneficiaries born after the first member has attained a vested interest, it is possible to draft the gift to allow the trustees to distribute the "share" of the first beneficiary and to hold what is left for the remaining class members plus any new additions to the class. A specimen clause is set out below.

> "My trustees shall hold the trust fund on trust absolutely for such of my grandchildren living at my death *or born afterwards* at any time during their parents' lifetime as reach the age of 18 or marry under that age and if more than one in equal shares PROVIDED that the share in the Trust Fund of any grandchild who has attained a vested interest shall not be diminished by the birth or marriage of or the attainment of 18 by any further grandchildren."

Example 4

A testator makes a gift of £600,000 to his grandchildren contingent on reaching 18 in the terms set out above. Three grandchildren, A, B and C are living at the date of death. A reaches 18.

A will take one third of the fund (£200,000) on reaching 18. The class will remain open. If two additional grandchildren, D and E, are born, the trustees will hold the remaining £400,000 on trust for B, C, D and E who will each receive £100,000.

Care should also be taken with the definition of the class so as to avoid any ambiguity and so as to comply with the testator's wishes. If the testator says that they wish to benefit their "cousins", further instructions are needed to establish what degree of relationship is intended. A reference to any class of relative does not include relatives by marriage. Thus, a testator who wishes to benefit "nephews and nieces" should be asked whether the nephews and nieces of their spouse are to be included or only their own nephews and nieces (if the spouse's nephews and nieces are to be included in the gift then suitable words must be inserted in the will). For an example of the problems that ensue when this is not done, see *Wales v Dixon* (2020).

Unless contrary provision is made, a reference to any class of relative is deemed to include adopted relatives of the testator but not, for example, step-children who have not been adopted. The fact that a person's parents were not married to each other at the time of their birth is irrelevant for the purposes of succession to property unless a contrary intention is expressed in the will.

As with gifts to named beneficiaries the will should make it clear what is to happen to the share of a member of the class who predeceases. A class gift (for example, "to my nieces") is normally construed as a gift to those nieces who survive the testator. There will, therefore, be no question of lapse unless all the members of the class predecease the testator. The testator may wish to include a substitutional clause providing that, if any member of the class predeceases the testator leaving issue who survive the testator, the issue will take *per stirpes* the share which their parent would have taken. In the case of a class gift to *children or issue of a testator*, s.33(2) of the Wills Act 1837, as substituted by the Administration of Justice Act 1982 s.19, provides that such a substitution shall take place unless a contrary intention appears by the will. Despite this provision, it is desirable to include express words of substitution so that the matter is brought to the testator's attention and so that there can be no doubt as to his or her wishes. Relying on the section is also unwise as it may be overlooked following the death as happened in *Naylor v Barlow* (2019).

Suitable wording is given in para.22-044.

Successive interests in residue

The testator may wish to create a life or other limited interest in the residue of the estate. In such a case it is best to include an express trust, the first object of which is to pay debts and legacies. The trustees are then directed to pay income to the life tenant and, subject thereto, to hold the balance for the remainderman. For example: **22-041**

> "ON TRUST to pay the income thereof to [name of life tenant] during his lifetime and subject thereto ON TRUST for [name of remainderman] absolutely."

The life tenant will frequently be the testator's spouse or civil partner, in which case the testator is likely to wish to give the trustees power to advance or lend capital to the life tenant.

> "My Trustees may at any time during the Trust Period pay or apply the whole or any part of the Residuary Trust Fund in which my spouse is then entitled to an interest in possession to [him/her] or for [his/her] advancement or benefit in such manner as they shall in their discretion think fit [and in exercising the powers conferred by this sub-clause they shall be entitled to have regard solely to the interests of my wife and to disregard all other interests or potential interests under my Will]."

It is common to give the trustees overriding powers which allow them to appoint capital and income away from the life tenant and the remainder beneficiaries amongst a discretionary class of beneficiaries.

> "MY TRUSTEES shall have power to appoint the whole or any part of the capital and/or income of my Residuary Trust Fund upon trust for or for the benefit of such of the Discretionary Beneficiaries at such ages or times in such shares upon such trusts which may include discretionary or protective powers or trusts and in such manner generally as my Trustees shall in their discretion think fit. Any such appointment may include such powers and provisions for the maintenance education or other benefit of the Discretionary Beneficiaries or for the accumulation of income and such administrative powers and provisions as my Trustees think fit."

If a residence or interest in a residence is included in the life interest trust, the residence nil-rate band will only be available against the trust property if lineal descendants of the life tenant are beneficially entitled to the residence (see IHTA 1984 s.8J(5) and para.22-003 and following). It may, therefore, be appropriate to limit the exercise of the overriding powers to the lifetime of the surviving spouse, at least in relation to any residence included in the settled property.

Contingent interests in residue

A gift of residue, whether to a named beneficiary, a number of named beneficiaries or a class and whether immediate or in remainder, may be contingent on the happening of some event or the satisfaction of some condition. For example: **22-042**

> "To such of my children as survive me and reach 18 or marry under that age."

Wherever the gift is contingent the testator should be asked to decide what is to happen to the residue if the contingency is never satisfied. If the contingency is never satisfied, the capital and any income which has been added to it will pass as on an intestacy unless there is a substitutional gift.

The effect of the rule against perpetuities should be considered whenever a contingent gift is made. A gift which would vest outside the perpetuity period is void. The perpetuity period is fixed at 125 years by the Perpetuities and Accumulations Act 2009—no other period may now be specified. Furthermore, the Act and its predecessor (the Perpetuity and Accumulations Act 1964) introduced various provisions which mitigate the severity of the rule against perpetuities. Thus, a gift which might vest outside the perpetuity period will not fail at the outset as it is possible to "wait and see"; it is possible, where necessary to save a gift, to reduce the age at which a gift will vest and/or to exclude members of a class from benefit where otherwise the whole gift would fail. As a result of these provisions problems of perpetuity rarely lead to failure of benefit.

Section 13 of the Perpetuities and Accumulations Act 2009 removed restrictions on the length of time for which income can be accumulated. The change only affects trusts created on or after 12 November 2009. In the case of trusts created by will, the change does not affect wills executed before that date.

Survivorship clauses

22-043 A beneficiary who survives a testator by a very short time or who is deemed to survive (under s.184 of the Law of Property Act 1925) will obtain a vested interest in any unconditional gift. Often a testator will want to provide that a beneficiary is not to benefit unless he or she survives for a reasonable period. This can be achieved by means of a "survivorship clause" which provides that the beneficiary is only to take if he or she survives the testator for a specified period, if he or she does not so survive, then a substitutional gift takes effect.

The advantage of a survivorship clause in such a case is that the testator retains control of the ultimate destination of the property—without such a clause the property would pass on the death of the beneficiary according to the terms of their will or of the intestacy rules applying to their estate.

It is common to include a general survivorship clause:

> "Any beneficiary who fails to survive me by 28 days is to be deemed to have predeceased me."

It is important to consider whether any gifts should be excluded from the effect of the general clause. There may be inheritance tax reasons for not having a survivorship clause in relation to inter-spousal gifts: see Examples 5 and 6 below. Also a survivorship clause may not be appropriate where two people are leaving their estates to the other with substitutional legacies to the same beneficiaries. Applying the survivorship clause in the gift to the primary beneficiary may result in the legacies being paid twice over if the deaths occur within the survivorship period: see *Jump v Lister* (2016) discussed at para.17-002.

A survivorship clause should not be for more than six months since, if it is for longer, a settlement will be created for inheritance tax purposes and there may as a result be an unnecessary charge to tax. If there is a survivorship clause in a will, distribution of the estate cannot begin until the primary beneficiary dies (when the substitutional gift takes effect) or until the end of the period (when the primary beneficiary achieves a vested interest). Owing to the inconvenience of a long delay, it is usual for survivorship clauses to specify a period of 28 days or one month.

In the case of surviving spouses and civil partners the introduction of the transferable nil-rate band means that there are circumstances in which for inheritance purposes it is preferable not to have a survivorship clause.

Example 5

Halim has £425,000 and his wife, Wahidah has £125,000. They each have a full nil-rate band available and do not own a residence. Halim dies when the nil-rate band is £325,000 and Wahidah dies two weeks later. Each leaves their estate to the other but if the other fails to survive by 28 days to their son, Sadiq. They do not own a residence.

Because of the survivorship clause, Halim's £425,000 passes to Sadiq and tax is payable on £100,000. Wahidah's £125,000 passes to Sadiq but £200,000 of her nil-rate band is wasted.

Without a survivorship clause Halim's estate would have passed to Wahidah. The transfer would be spouse exempt. Wahidah's aggregated estate of £550,000, would pass to Sadiq. It would benefit from an additional nil-rate band transferred from Halim so no inheritance tax would be payable.

If Sadiq is an adult, he can vary the disposition of his father's estate on behalf of his dead mother to remove the survivorship. His father's estate will then pass to him under the substitutional gift.

A survivorship clause is also undesirable from an inheritance tax point of view if spouses or civil partners die in circumstances where it is uncertain which of them died first. The Law of Property Act 1925 s.184 provides that the deaths are deemed to occur in order of seniority so that the older dies first. For inheritance tax purposes a person is deemed to make a transfer on death equal to the value of his estate immediately before death (IHTA 1984 s.4(1) and 4(2) provides that where there is uncertainty as to the order in which two people died, they are to be treated as having died at the same instant). In the case of spouses and civil partners this can lead to a significant tax saving.

Example 6

Harry and Wanda are killed in a car crash and each leaves everything to the other with a substitutional gift to their children. Wanda is older than Harry. They each have an estate of £650,000. They each have one full nil-rate band and do not own a residence. Wanda's estate goes to Harry and is spouse exempt. He has the benefit of her transferred nil-rate band. His estate passes to the children but for inheritance tax purposes does not include her £650,000. Hence his estate is all within his double nil-rate band and no tax is payable. Had Wanda's will included a survivorship clause her estate would have passed to the children and tax would have been payable on £325,000. Similarly tax would have been payable on £325,000 of Harry's estate (the survivorship clause could be removed by way of post-death variation).

As in the previous example, if the children are adults, they can vary Wanda's will to remove the survivorship clause and allow her estate to pass to Harry.

Substitutional gifts

When a specific or general legacy lapses the subject matter "falls into residue" **22-044**
and goes to the residuary beneficiary. When a residuary gift fails, there will be a partial intestacy unless there is a further gift of the residue. The will drafter should ascertain the testator's wishes as to the disposition of property in the event of a

beneficiary predeceasing or failing to survive for a specified period. The testator may prefer to make a substitutional gift rather than have the property pass on intestacy. A suitable clause substituting one beneficiary for another if that other predeceases or fails to survive for a specified period is:

> "I GIVE the residue of my estate to [AB] or if [he/she] shall predecease me or fail to survive for 28 days then to [CD]."

Where the primary beneficiary is the spouse or civil partner of the testator the effect of Wills Act 1837 ss.18A and 18C must be remembered. A divorce or termination of a civil partnership causes a gift to a spouse or civil partner to be treated as if the spouse or civil partner had died on the date of the divorce, annulment or termination. If the will gives residue to the spouse or civil partner, the residue will pass as undisposed of property unless a substitutional gift takes effect.

Often the most appropriate substitutional beneficiaries are the children of the primary beneficiary. If the gift of residue is to the testator's children, the testator may decide that the property be divided amongst the surviving children or that the share of a deceased child should go to that child's children or remoter issue.

If the will is silent, then the Wills Act 1837 s.33 (as substituted) provides that, if a child of the testator predeceases leaving issue who survive the testator, the issue take the share that their parent would have taken. Section 33A provides that a child who forfeits or disclaims an entitlement is to be treated as having predeceased.

Despite these statutory provisions, it is advisable to include an express substitutional gift so that the testator is given an opportunity to consider whether or not the clause accords with their wishes (an express substitutional gift is always required if the original gift is to anyone other than a child or issue of the testator). A suitable clause for a substitution of a child by their own issue on the assumption that there is a trust for sale of residue is:

> "[My Trustees] shall hold [my Residuary Estate] ON TRUST for such of my children as are living at my death and if more than one in equal shares PROVIDED THAT if any child of mine dies before me leaving issue living at my death [or born after it who reach the age of 18] such issue shall take by substitution and if more than one in equal shares per stirpes the share of [my Residuary Estate] as that child of mine would otherwise have taken."

7. PROBLEMS ARISING FROM RECEIPTS FOR LEGACIES

22-045 Particular problems arise where a pecuniary legacy is given to a minor as, in the absence of an express direction, a minor cannot give a good receipt (this problem was discussed at para.18-017).

Problems also arise where a legacy is given to an unincorporated association. Such an association has no legal identity separate from its individual members. Therefore, a legacy to such an association is construed as a gift to all the individual members. In the absence of an express provision in the will the personal representative would have to obtain a receipt from each individual member of the association. This would be an onerous and time-consuming task and, therefore, it is advisable to provide that the receipt of the person appearing to be the treasurer, bursar or other appropriate officer will be sufficient to give the personal representatives a good discharge. An example of such a clause is:

> "I GIVE free of tax to the [name of club or other institution] of [address] the sum of £.

... with freedom to spend it as income. The receipt of the person who appears to [my Trustees] to be the treasurer or other proper officer of [name of club or other institution] shall be a good discharge to [my Trustees]."

When drafting a gift to an unincorporated association, the will drafter, having taken appropriate instructions from the testator, should ensure that:

(a) the association is in existence;
(b) the association is correctly identified; and
(c) should the testator so wish, provision is included to cover a change of name, change of objects, the amalgamation of the association with another similar body or the dissolution of the association prior to the testator's death.

Gifts to incorporated charities also present problems. The charity may go into liquidation after the date of death but before distribution. For example, see *Re ARMS (Multiple Sclerosis Research) Ltd* (1997) and *Berry v IBS-STL Ltd (In Liquidation)* (2012). It is sensible to cover this possibility by giving the executors power to pay the legacy to a similar organisation if insolvency proceedings have commenced. For example:

"If at the date of my death [name of charity] is no longer in existence [or is subject to a winding up order] my Trustees shall pay the legacy to such other charity or charities having the same or similar objects as my Trustees shall select."

Gifts to incorporated associations are beneficial gifts so, in the event of insolvency, legacies will be available to creditors unless the terms of the gift impose a trust. Simply saying "for its charitable purposes" is not enough to create a trust (see *Re ARMS (Multiple Sclerosis Research) Ltd* (1997) and *Re Wedgwood Museum Trust Ltd (In Administration)* (2011). To protect assets from creditors it is necessary to state that the legacy is "on trust for the general charitable purposes" of the charity.

It is helpful to include general words of charitable intent in case the charity ceases to exist during the lifetime of the testator. The gift will not lapse but will be applied cy-près provided the testator showed a general charitable intention. If this is in accordance with the testator's wishes, it may be desirable to include words clearly showing a general charitable intent, for example, "To X association for its general charitable purposes."

Charities Act 2011 s.311 (re-enacting Charities Act 1993 s.75F) makes express provision for merger of charities providing that, subject to contrary intention, any gift to a charity which subsequently merges with another "*takes effect as a gift to the transferee*". It is preferable to make express provision giving the executors a discretion as the merged entity may have different purposes: see *Berry v IBS-STL Ltd (In Liquidation)* (2012). The deceased had left a legacy to an unincorporated charity that had incorporated after the date of the will and gone into insolvent liquidation after the deceased's death but before payment. The personal representatives were given a discretion to pay the legacy to any similar charity if the legatee had ceased to exist at the date of death. The court held that the unincorporated charity had ceased to exist and therefore the executors did not have to pay the legacy to the liquidator.

It is important to check whether any particular institution has charitable status since this will affect the availability of the inheritance tax exemption. See para.4-052.

8. Administrative Powers

Introduction

22-046 As we saw in Ch.11 personal representatives and trustees have various powers conferred on them by statute which can be excluded, restricted or extended by the will. It is also possible for the will to confer additional powers on the personal representatives. We will now list and consider some of the more common extensions and additions. The purpose of including such clauses is to facilitate the administration of the estate and of any trust which may arise under the will.

Common extensions to powers of personal representatives

Power to appropriate assets without consent of beneficiary

22-047 The personal representatives have a power under s.41 of the Administration of Estates Act 1925 to appropriate assets in or towards satisfaction of a legacy bequeathed by the deceased or interest under the intestacy rules but must obtain the consent of the beneficiary (or other specified persons as set out in para.11-009 and following).

It is administratively convenient for personal representatives to be excused from the necessity of obtaining formal consent (even though they would, no doubt, informally consult with the beneficiaries and would be under an obligation to exercise their powers in good faith).

However, excluding the need for consent will prevent the personal representatives claiming inheritance tax loss relief if quoted shares are appropriated to a pecuniary legatee at a time when their value is less than their value at the date of death: see para.12-017.

Since an appropriation is in effect a sale of assets to the beneficiary, any personal representative who is beneficially entitled to a part of the estate and who makes an appropriation in their own favour will be purchasing estate property. There is authority that this is permissible (*Re Richardson* (1896)) but such a purchase might be attacked subsequently as a breach of the equitable rule that a trustee must not profit from their trust (see, for example, *Kane v Radley-Kane* (1999)). Where personal representatives are beneficially entitled it is, therefore, common to authorise such personal representatives to exercise the power to appropriate in their own favour.

Power to appropriate assets at value at date of appropriation

22-048 When personal representatives appropriate assets to a beneficiary in or towards satisfaction of a pecuniary legacy or share of residue, for the purposes of calculating their entitlement assets must be valued at the date of the appropriation not at probate value (*Re Collins* (1975)).

Example 7

Andrew has been left a nil-rate band legacy by his uncle, residue is left to a charity. Included in the estate is a house which was worth £300,000 at the date of death. Andrew would like to take the house in part satisfaction of his legacy. Unfortunately it is now worth £350,000.

If the personal representatives let Andrew have the house at death value, the charity will justifiably complain that he has taken more than he is entitled to.

The will may allow the personal representatives a discretion to appropriate asset at probate value within a stated period following death. This is often two years of death although the second edition of the STEP Standard Provisions allows a period of three years. That provision requires personal representatives who have exercised the power in relation to one appropriation to use the same basis for any other valuation. The third edition does not include the provision on the basis that it should only be included after consideration of its suitability and should be drafted to fit the circumstances of the particular estate.

Power to accept the receipt of parent or guardian on behalf of a minor or of the minor at a specified age

An unmarried minor not in a civil partnership has no statutory power to give a good receipt for capital or income. A married minor or one in a civil partnership can give a good receipt for income only. The minor's parent, guardian, spouse or civil partner has power under the Children Act 1989 to give a good receipt on the minor's behalf (see para.18-017 and following). A testator should consider whether it is appropriate to allow the legacy to pass into the hands of the parent or guardian (or spouse or civil partner). If not, the legacy can be left to trustees to hold until the child reaches a suitable age. It is probably good drafting to include a clause in the will authorising the personal representatives to accept the receipt of parent or guardian so that the testator is aware that this will happen. **22-049**

There is a statutory power under s.42 of the Administration of Estates Act 1925 for the personal representatives to appoint trustees to hold a legacy for a minor who is *absolutely* entitled but this does not apply if the minor has only a contingent interest. There is no reason why the testator should not expressly authorise the personal representatives to appoint trustees in such a case.

The testator may authorise the minor to give a good receipt at a specified age, for example, 16.

Alternatively, the will may direct the personal representatives to purchase a suitable investment (perhaps National Savings certificates) in the name of the minor.

Exclusion of the Apportionment Act 1870 and the common law rules on apportionment

As we saw at para.16-062 and para.18-022 and following, the Apportionment Act 1870 requires that **22-050**

> "rents, annuities, dividends and other periodical payments in the nature of income ... shall, like interest on money lent, be considered as accruing from day to day"

and shall be apportioned accordingly. Interest has to be apportioned under the common law rules. It was usual to exclude the Act and the common law rules as the trouble and expense involved in the calculations was usually thought to outweigh any benefits to the beneficiaries. In the case of trusts made on or after 1 October 2013 it is no longer necessary to exclude the need for apportionments expressly. They are automatically disapplied by the Trusts (Capital and Income) Act 2013 for trusts created or arising on or after that date.

Power to carry on a business of the deceased

As we saw at para.11-013 and following, the powers of personal representatives to run a business carried on by the deceased as a sole trader are limited. It is, **22-051** therefore, usual in cases where a testator is a sole trader to provide that personal representatives may:

(a) continue to run the business for as long as they see fit; and
(b) use such assets of the estate as they see fit.

A specimen clause is set out below.

> "I DIRECT that [my Trustees] shall have power to carry on my business of [nature of business] for so long as they in their absolute discretion think fit and they shall have power to use any assets employed in that business at the date of my death together with any assets in my Residuary Estate I DECLARE that my Trustees shall have the same powers to carry on that business as if they were absolute owners of it without being personally liable for any loss that may arise I FURTHER DECLARE that in the event of my business being carried on at a loss my Trustees shall be reimbursed for any loss they suffer from my Residuary Estate."

It is most desirable that a sole trader should consider and make provision for the running of a business after their death, perhaps by taking in partners or by incorporation of the business during their lifetime. Such matters should certainly be discussed when drafting a will for a sole trader. The question of personal representatives should also be carefully considered. It is usually difficult to find a professional person who is willing to accept the office of personal representative where this would involve the running or supervision of a business. Where the business is to be transferred to a beneficiary it may be helpful to appoint that beneficiary either as a general personal representative or as a special personal representative to deal only with the business.

Where a client is a partner in a business or runs a business through the medium of a limited company it is desirable to discuss with the client what provisions if any have been included in the partnership agreement or articles of association to deal with death. Matters which should be considered are whether persons surviving the deceased should have options to purchase the interest of a deceased partner/shareholder and how the purchase price should be fixed.

Common extensions to powers of trustees

Introduction

22-052 These extensions should be considered where a will creates a trust initially (for example by leaving property to a spouse for life) or where a trust may arise if a beneficiary predeceases the testator (for example, "to my spouse absolutely but if he does not survive me by 28 days for such of our children as may reach the age of 25"; even if all the testator's children are over 25 at the time the will is drafted a trust may still arise if a child predeceases and is replaced by issue).

Power to invest

22-053 As we saw at para.11-023 and following, trustees and personal representatives are now given very wide statutory powers of investment. No express power is needed. In rare cases a testator may wish to restrict the power of investment, for which purpose a clause could be included in the will.

In the case of family businesses the testator may wish to indicate in a letter of wishes that he wishes the business to be retained by the trustees for as long as it is financially viable. The trustees can then take the expression of wishes into account when considering the suitability to the trust of the business and the need for diversification of investments in so far as is appropriate to the circumstances of the trust: see Trustee Act 2000 s.3 and *Gregson v HAE Trustees Ltd* (2008).

Power to purchase a house as a residence for a beneficiary

The Trustee Act 2000 s.8 gives trustees and personal representatives power to buy freehold or leasehold land in the UK including the power to do so "for occupation by a beneficiary" (s.8(1)(b)). An express power would be needed if the personal representatives were to be able to buy a house outside the UK for a beneficiary. **22-054**

Power to apply capital for beneficiaries with a vested or contingent interest in capital

We saw at para.11-019 that trustees have a statutory power under s.32 of the Trustee Act 1925 to apply capital for the advancement and benefit of beneficiaries with a vested or contingent interest in capital, but that it is subject to the following limitations: **22-055**

(a) Any advances must be brought into account when and if the beneficiary becomes absolutely entitled.
(b) Any person with a prior interest (for example, the right to receive income from the trust property) must be in existence, of full age and must consent in writing to the advance.

The Inheritance and Trustees' Powers Act 2014 amended s.32 for trusts created or arising on or after 1 October 2014 to remove the previous restriction which allowed only half of a vested or presumptive share to be applied. It is now possible to apply the whole of a beneficiary's share. Explanatory Note 53 says if a trust is created by will, it is the date of death not the date of execution which is significant.

It has long been common to give the trustees wider powers to apply capital by excluding some or all of the limitations listed above and giving them an absolute discretion. The case of *Henley v Wardell* (1989) illustrates the need for careful drafting. In that case a will enlarged the powers conferred by s.32,

> "so as to permit my trustees in their absolute and uncontrolled discretion to advance … the whole … of any … share …".

The trustees made advances without the consent of the life tenant arguing that as they had an "absolute" and "uncontrolled" discretion such consent was unnecessary. It was held that the only purpose of the enlargement of trustees' powers was to permit the advancement of "the whole" of a share and that the wording was not sufficient to do away with the need for consents. It is important, therefore, in cases where there is a prior interest and reference is made to enlarging the statutory power expressly to exclude the need for consent. For example, in such a case the clause should include the words: "without the need to secure the consent of any person with a prior interest."

A testator may also wish to include an express power authorising trustees to *lend* money to beneficiaries on whatever terms they think fit. This is a very useful power as the funds lent are not lost to the trust and the debt owed to the trust will reduce the estate of the beneficiary for inheritance tax purposes.

Power to apply capital for and make loans to life tenants

22-056 The statutory power to apply capital for the advancement and benefit of beneficiaries is only available where beneficiaries have an interest in capital. There is no statutory power to apply capital for the benefit of a life tenant. Neither is there a statutory power to lend capital to a life tenant. A testator, who is proposing to leave property to a person for life, may wish to give the trustees a power to give or lend capital to the life tenant in case the life tenant finds the income insufficient. This is particularly likely where a testator proposes to leave a life interest to a spouse or civil partner.

Advances and loans to a life tenant with a qualifying interest in possession will have no inheritance tax effect since the life tenant is already treated as the owner of the underlying trust assets. A settlement where the life tenant does not have a qualifying interest in possession is a relevant property settlement and an advance will trigger an exit charge under IHTA 1984 s.68 or s.69.

Power to apply income for maintenance, education or benefit of minor beneficiaries

22-057 We saw in para.11-016 and following that trustees have power under the Trustee Act 1925 s.31 to apply available income to the maintenance, education or benefit of minor beneficiaries and that to the extent that they do not, such income must be accumulated. If the beneficiary reaches the age of 18 and the interest is still contingent the discretion ceases and the trustees must pay the income to the beneficiary until the interest vests or fails. The testator may wish to remove the right so that the discretion continues.

Section 31(1) as originally drafted restricted the trustees' discretion and required them to take certain matters into account. However, the Inheritance and Trustees' Powers Act 2014 has amended s.31 to give trustees of trusts created or arising on or after 1 October 2014 an unfettered discretion. Explanatory Note 53 says if a trust is created by will, it is the date of death not the date of execution which is significant.

It is important to vary Trustee Act 1925 s.31(2) if the intention is to create an immediate post-death interest. To have such an interest, a beneficiary must have a right to income. Where the terms of a trust give a minor a right to income, the effect of s.31(1) is that the trustees have a discretion which allows them to apply income for the minor's benefit if they so wish and to add any unapplied income to the capital. The minor gets the accumulated income under s.31(2) if, and only if, he reaches 18. The effect is that his interest is contingent and he does not have an immediate post-death interest. For examples where failure to vary s.31(2) has caused problems, see: *Fine v Fine* (2012); *Price v Williams-Wynn* (2008); *Bullard v Bullard* (2017). Suitable wording is:

> "During the minority of a Beneficiary Trustee Act 1925 s.31 shall not apply and my Trustees may apply income for his maintenance, education and benefit at their discretion and, to the extent that they do not, shall retain the balance for the Beneficiary absolutely."

Exclusion of the Apportionment Act 1870 and the common law and equitable rules on apportionment

22-058 We have already explained in para.22-050 that it was usual to exclude the need to apportion for the purposes of distribution of the estate on the death of a testator.

It was also usual to exclude the duty to apportion arising in relation to trusts, for example on the death of a life tenant or attainment by a beneficiary of a vested interest. The Trusts (Capital and Income) Act makes this unnecessary for trusts created or arising on or after 1 October 2013.

The Act also makes it unnecessary to exclude the equitable rules as to apportionment which apply where residuary personalty is left to persons in succession: the rules in *Howe v Lord Dartmouth, Earl of Chesterfield's Trusts* and *Allhusen v Whittell* for trusts created or arising on or after 1 October 2013.

Power to charge

The general rule is that personal representatives and trustees may not charge for their services in the absence of express provision to the contrary. However, the Trustee Act 2000 s.29 provides an important exception to this rule. Under this section a trust corporation or a person acting in a professional capacity as a personal representative or trustee is entitled to "reasonable remuneration" for any services that they provide to or on behalf of the trust, provided the other personal representatives or trustees (as the case may be) gives written agreement to this. If the will itself makes "any provision about the personal representative or trustee's entitlement to remuneration" then s.29 does not apply—the terms of the will take priority. **22-059**

Despite the statutory provisions, charging clauses should be included in a will which appoints a professional person to be a personal representative both because the approval of other personal representatives will not then be needed and because it will make the position clear to the beneficiaries. For an example of an executor unsuccessfully seeking to charging without the benefit of a charging clause, see *Shepherd & Co Solicitors v Brealey* (2022).

In *Da Silva v Heselton* (2022) the Court of Appeal considered the effect of a standard charging clause which allowed any trustees:

> "engaged in any profession or business to charge and be paid (in priority to all other dispositions herein) all usual professional and other fees....... for work .... done or time spent by him or his firm in connection with the administration of my estate .... including work done or business outside the ordinary course of his profession and work or business which he could or should have done personally had he not been in any profession or business."

They held unanimously that the power to charge was limited to those professional services provided in the course of the executor's business so, for example, a surveyor could charge for valuing a residence.

The clause authorised an executor to charge not only for "work done" but also for "time spent". Did that mean a professional or person engaged in business could charge their usual hourly rate for time spent?

The Court of Appeal said it did not. Professionals not involved in the administration of estates do not have usual fees for time spent on the administration of estates. They may have usual fees for work done in the course of their profession, but that cannot be applied to work of a different type.

It is possible for beneficiaries to authorise a personal representative to charge but they must be fully informed of the rate of charging and give clear and unequivocal consent. See, for example, *Brudenell-Bruce v Moore* (2014) where the lay trustee thought that he had been authorised to charge following an exchange of emails with a beneficiary, but the court found that the exchange was too inconclusive. For a further example see *Gavriel v Davis* (2019) where the beneficiaries had possibly agreed to the executor making some sort of charge for her services but had clearly not authorised anything like the level claimed (£27,300).

Where provision is made in the will for remuneration to a trust corporation or person acting in a professional capacity, the Trustee Act 2000 s.28 provides that this is not to be regarded as a gift. Consequently, the entitlement to the remuneration will not be void if the professional personal representative witnessed the will nor will it abate if the estate is insufficient to pay legacies. There is now a presumption that provision for payment for services is to include payment in respect of services even if they are services which a lay personal representative could perform personally.

Indemnity

22-060 Personal representatives and trustees have a statutory power to indemnify themselves for expenses incurred in carrying out their powers and duties (Trustee Act 2000 s.31). A testator may wish to extend this to provide that they shall not be liable for any loss resulting from improper investment or from any mistake or omission made in good faith. However, it may be thought inappropriate to include such a clause particularly in the case of professional trustees. In *Armitage v Nurse* (1997) and *Bogg v Raper* (1998) the Court of Appeal stated that clauses limiting liability for negligence were not contrary to public policy nor to the essential nature of a trust. Millett LJ stated that, although many people felt such clauses had gone too far, it would require legislation to change their validity. Subsequently, the Law Commission published a report (No.301) on trustee exemption clauses recommending that professional and regulatory bodies should adopt rules or guidance to the effect that any paid trustee, who causes a settlor to include a trustee exemption clause in a trust instrument which has the effect of excluding or limiting liability for negligence, must before the creation of the trust, take steps to ensure that the settlor is aware of the meaning and effect of the clause.

There is no express reference to this in the SRA Standards and Regulations 2019 replacing the SRA code of Conduct 2011. However, principles 4 and 5 require those regulated to act with honesty and integrity and principle 7 requires them to act in the best interests of the client.

A professional preparing a will or trust instrument for a client which limits liability in negligence, should take reasonable steps before the trust is created to ensure that the client is aware of the meaning and effect of the clause. Extra care is needed if the professional, or anyone in or associated with the firm is a paid trustee of the trust. It is prudent to ensure that there is evidence that the appropriate steps were taken and that the evidence is retained for as long as the trust exists and for a suitable period afterwards.

The same requirements do not apply to lay trustees where it will normally be appropriate to limit liability.

Will drafting implications of the Trusts of Land and Appointment of Trustees Act 1996

22-061 This Act imposes certain terms on trusts of which practitioners should be aware. Section 11 requires trustees of land, so far as is practicable, to consult beneficiaries of full age with an interest in possession when exercising any function in respect of land and so far as it is consistent with the general interest of the trust to give effect to their wishes. The section does not apply if the trust instrument includes a declaration that it should not. It seems desirable in most cases to relieve the trustees from *the obligation* to consult by including such a declaration. It is, however, important to consider the particular facts. Norris J was -critical of the exclusion of the s.11 requirement in a case of a bare trust (see *OH v Craven* (2016)).

Section 12 gives a beneficiary who is beneficially entitled to an interest in possession in land a right to occupy the land if either:

(a) the purposes of the trust include making the land available for their occupation; or
(b) the land is held by the trustees so as to be so available.

"Interest in possession" is not defined in the Act. Land held by trustees "so as to be available" for occupation by the beneficiary includes land which is suitable for this occupation and is not occupied by someone else (such as a tenant under a lease).

Section 13 goes on to provide that where there is more than one beneficiary entitled to occupy land then the trustees may exclude or restrict the entitlement of one or more (but not all) of the beneficiaries. The trustees may impose conditions on the occupying beneficiary (for example, payment of expenses) and may require the occupying beneficiary to make compensation payments to any excluded beneficiaries or forgo benefits to which they would otherwise be entitled.

These provisions seem unduly complex and are to be avoided if at all possible. When drafting a will, it may be desirable to state that "the purposes of the trust do not include making land available for occupation by beneficiaries". The problem is that the testator may wish to give the trustees power to buy land as a residence for a beneficiary. The mere inclusion of such a power might suggest that, despite the declaration, the purposes of the trust did include making land available for occupation (and once the land is purchased it will be "so available" under s.12(1)(b)). There is of course an arguable distinction between a power and a purpose.

A further problem is that if the trustees decide to buy land as an investment for the trust, a beneficiary might be able to insist on occupying it under s.12(1)(b) if the property was vacant. The inclusion of a declaration as to the purposes of the trust would then be of no relevance. However, even though a declaration as to purpose will not *always* be of help in escaping ss.12 and 13, it may help sometimes and it is difficult to see that it can ever do any harm.

Section 19 allows beneficiaries who are of full age and capacity (i.e. sui juris) and between them absolutely entitled to the trust property to require the trustees to retire and to appoint replacements specified by the beneficiaries. This provision will not apply if the trust instrument says that it should not.

While the prospect of beneficiaries arbitrarily removing and replacing trustees may seem alarming, it is important to look at the matter in context. Beneficiaries who are sui juris can in any event always bring a trust to an end and resettle the property with trustees of their choice. The drawback of so doing is that the termination of the trust will give rise to a potential capital gains tax liability. The s.19 power prevents there being a charge to capital gains tax.

It is likely that for most people the tax advantage will outweigh the concern over the arbitrary replacement of trustees so only rarely will it be appropriate to exclude the s.19 power.

Civil partnership and same sex marriages

The Civil Partnership Act 2004 amends statutes so that the status of a civil partner **22-062**
is the same as that of a spouse. However, it contains no provision that terms such

as "spouse", "husband", "wife" or "married" used in a will or other document are to include civil partner or civil partnership. In *Goodrich v AB* (2022) Chief Master Schuman accepted the argument that to make a distinction spouses and civil partners was discriminatory. However, there were insuperable difficulties in reading down the Act in such a way as to make it compliant with the European Convention on Human Rights. Parliament had introduced a new legal relationship. To read down the Act to make it compliant would elide spouses and civil partners and go beyond what the court should do. It would fall the wrong side of the line and become judicial vandalism rather than judicial interpretation. Express provision must therefore be made if, for example, the testator wishes to include civil partners of their children in a gift or trust or if they wish a gift to take effect on civil partnership as well as on marriage.

The extension of civil partnerships to opposite sex couples introduced by Civil Partnerships, Marriages and Deaths (Registration etc) Act 2019 and the Civil Partnership (Opposite-sex Couples) Regulations 2019 (SI 2019/1458) makes this point even more important.

The bulk of the Marriage (Same Sex Couples) Act 2013 came into force on 13 March 2014. Section 11 and Sch.3 amend existing England and Wales legislation so that references to marriage, spouses, etc. in statutory provisions are to be read as including references to marriage of a same sex couple.

Section 11 and Sch.4 provide that references in private legal instruments such as wills and settlements "*made*" before 13 March 2014 will not include same sex marriages unless the instrument says otherwise. However, in *Goodrich v AB* (2022) Chief Master Schuman held that the effect of Sch.4 was discriminatory in that it sought to continue to make a distinction between same-sex couples and opposite-sex spouses in private instruments predating the Act. She directed that the section be read down to be compliant with the European Convention on Human Rights Convention as follows.

Section 11 does not alter the effect of any private legal instrument made before that section comes into force which:

(1) contains a disposition of property, and
(2) the beneficiary of the disposition has done something to avail himself or herself of the property right in question before the coming into force of the Human Rights Act 1998.

References in private legal instruments "*made*" after that date will include same sex marriages unless the instrument says otherwise.

Human Fertilisation and Embryology Act 2008

22-063 Section 48(1) of the HFEA 2008 provides that where a person is treated as a mother, father or parent of a child under ss.33, 35, 36, 42 or 43 (see para.3-006 and following, for details) that person is treated as the mother, father or parent of the child *for all purposes*. Subsection (5) provides that references "to any relationship between two people in any enactment, deed or other instrument or document (whenever passed or made) are to be read accordingly". It follows that gifts in a will to "my grandchildren", "my nephews and nieces", "my brothers and sisters" and similar expressions as well as gifts "to my children" will include persons whose relationship arises as a result of the HFEA 2008. If this is not what the testator wants, careful consideration should be given as to how the will is drafted. It may be that a gift, for example, "to my biological grandchildren" would circumvent s.48(1) but this is far from clear as there is a reference to "a relationship". As with many such problems the safest course is to name the beneficiaries where possible.

9. After the Interview

It is good practice to check the note of the instructions to make sure that it is clear and free of ambiguities. The client should be given an opportunity to check the instructions so either send your note of the instructions immediately after the interview or send the client a copy of the draft will to consider before execution. When sending the draft, also send a covering letter explaining clearly what the will does. It is important not to simply repeat the wording of the will as, if the will is ambiguous, the explanation will be equally ambiguous. **22-064**

Pay particular attention to the effect of substitution clauses. It is helpful to explain how they work with examples.

If the client is anxious to achieve a "fair" distribution between various beneficiaries, point out the effects of ademption and the possibility of the estate increasing or reducing in value. If residue is currently very small, point this out and remind the client that debts and other liabilities will have to be paid from residue together with inheritance tax on UK testamentary gifts (unless the will says otherwise).

If the instructions create a danger which was discussed in the meeting (for example, a risk of a specific gift failing or gaining or losing value, or a risk of a claim under the Inheritance (Provision for Family and Dependants) Act 1975), remind the client. The client may reconsider but if they do not, at least there is evidence that the deceased considered the issue.

10. Execution

If possible, arrange for the client to come into execute the will. Clients are very bad at following instructions and if a disaffected family member wants to challenge a will, they will certainly ask about the exact procedure that was followed. **22-065**

It also gives an opportunity to run through the contents with the client and make sure that there is no confusion. In *Pead v Prostate Cancer UK* (2023), there was an ambiguity in the drafting of the residuary gift (clause 11 of the will). It was unclear whether certain charities were to share the residue with the family members and if so in what proportions. The client did come into the office to execute the will but the fee earner he saw did not go through the will with him despite the fact that his instructions had changed since the initial interview. Master Teverson was critical of the failure to go through the will and said:

> "[32] Had such a discussion and review of clause 11 taken place, there would have been an opportunity to confirm that the deceased did indeed wish the charities to share in his residuary estate. A competent solicitor would have appreciated the need to confirm the deceased understood the effect of clause 11 was to include the charities within the distribution of his residuary estate and the need to ascertain what proportion of his residuary estate the deceased intended each of the charities to receive.
>
> 33. In my view, a vital opportunity was lost on 3 August 2016 to confirm that the deceased did indeed wish the charities to share in his residuary estate. Although the claim to rectify clause 11 of the will so as to refer only to family members failed, the claim was a reasonable one to bring."

APPENDIX A

CHECKLIST FOR TAKING INSTRUCTIONS

1. Details of testator

(a) Testator's full name
(b) Any former name(s) or alias(es)
(c) Address/occupation
(d) Age (for purposes of tax advice)
(e) Previous will? If so, what arrangements for revocation?
(f) Any existing foreign will?

2. Value of estate

(a) Property owned in testator's sole name
    House(s)
    Contents
    Car
    Jewellery
    Collections (e.g. stamps, coins)
    Cash
    Cash accounts (bank, building society, etc.)
    National Savings products
    Quoted shares
    ISAs, bonds, etc.
    Unit trusts, etc.
    Unlisted shares
    Any other assets
(b) Property owned with another as beneficial tenants in common Include all types of property as in (a) above
(c) Property owned with another as beneficial joint tenants Include all types of property as in (a) above
(d) Nominations
(e) Pensions—nominated?
(f) Insurance policies—MWPA,
    written in trust,
    payable to estate
(g) Trust property
(h) Foreign property
(i) Lifetime gifts to date
(j) Property likely to be inherited
(k) Debts charged on property?
(l) Mortgage protection policy

(m) Business and Agricultural property
(n) Digital assets and arrangements for access

3. Intended beneficiaries, etc.

(a) Spouse/civil partner/cohabitee—full name/size of estate of spouse, etc.
(b) Children—names/ages/marital status
(c) Others—names/addresses
(d) are nieces/nephews, cousins limited to the testator's blood relatives or are relatives of a spouse/civil partner to be included?

N.B. Explain family provision legislation particularly if disposition is away from immediate family. Include illegitimate children, children of previous marriage and step-children if any.

4. Disposition of property

(a) Legacies
- (i) specific
- (ii) general
- (iii) free of tax/expenses/mortgage?

N.B. Explain possibility of ademption of specific gifts and fluctuations in value of estate.

(b) Residue
(c) Age at which beneficiaries are to take. N.B. tax consequences.
(d) Directions as to substitutional gift where beneficiary predeceases.
In case of gift to institution directions as to possible change of name, amalgamation, dissolution.
(e) Provision for payment of debts? Secured debts?

5. Extension of statutory powers

(a) No trust created (remember that a trust may arise where minor beneficiaries take by substitution the share of a deceased parent)
- (i) appropriation
- (ii) receipt clause—unincorporated association

(b) Trust created
as above *plus*
- (i) investment
- (ii) power to buy land
- (iii) maintenance
- (iv) advancement
- (v) loans to beneficiaries

N.B. Although powers are implied in "trust of land" consider possibility that land will not be included in estate.

6. Executors/Trustees

(a) Choice—explain merits of individuals, solicitors' firms, banks
(b) Charging clause if appropriate
(c) Special personal representative's to deal with special parts of estate, e.g. literary executors

(d) Name and addresses of intended executors

7. Guardians

(a) Names and addresses
(b) Appointment to have immediate effect?
(c) Willing to act?
(d) Finance?

8. Special problems

(a) Testator suffering from disability—capacity? Special attestation clause?
(b) Testator sole trader—special provisions to deal with business?
(c) Any promises about disposal of property including promises which might lead to promissory estoppel and mutual wills.

9. Directions as to body, funeral, etc.

(a) Organ donation: has testator registered on the NHS Organ Donor Register/informed relatives?
(b) Body to be used for anatomical examination: has testator given required written consent?
(c) Wishes for burial/cremation: has testator communicated wishes to those who are likely to be organising the funeral?
(d) Advance decision: does testator wish to prepare a statement of wishes as to treatment if unable to accept/refuse treatment?

10. Reasons for significant changes from terms of any previous will and reasons for choice of beneficiaries

This may help to prevent challenges to the will. Even if they are not prevented, it will be useful evidence for the court to consider.

11. Comments on capacity/undue influence

(a) Did the client appear to?
(b) Understand the nature and effect of making a will.
(c) Understand the extent of their property.
(d) Be aware of those who might have a claim to their property.
(e) Was there any indication of an insane delusion?
(f) Was there anything to suggest any undue influence?

INDEX

LEGAL TAXONOMY
FROM SWEET & MAXWELL

This index has been prepared using Sweet & Maxwell's Legal Taxonomy. Main index entries conform to keywords provided by the Legal Taxonomy except where references to specific documents or non-standard terms (denoted by quotation marks) have been included. These keywords provide a means of identifying similar concepts in other Sweet & Maxwell publications and online services to which keywords from the Legal Taxonomy have been applied. Readers may find some minor differences between terms used in the text and those which appear in the index. Suggestions to *sweetandmaxwell.taxonomy@tr.com.*

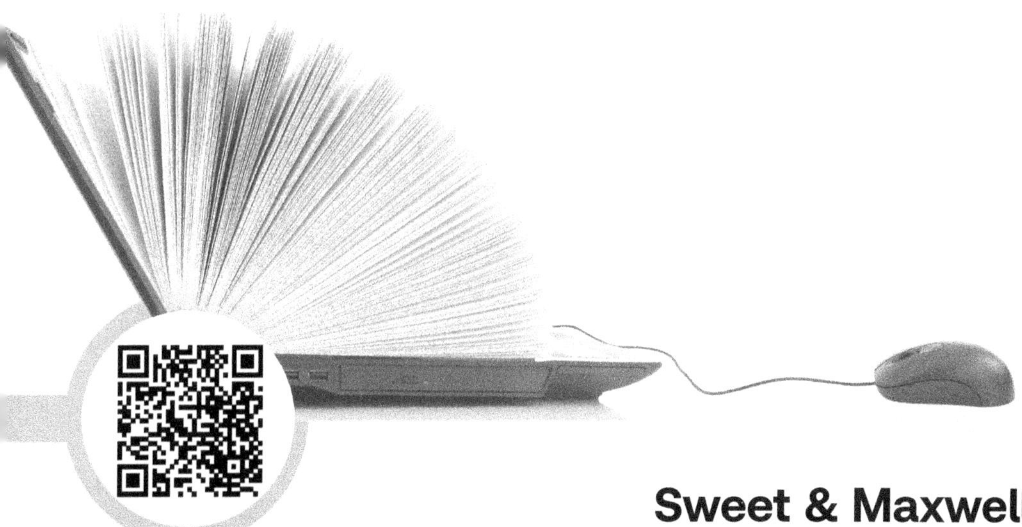